$x - im$	Difference between Exports and Imports	Equation 8.2
π^i	Foreign Inflation Rate	Equation 8.7
ϵ	Real Exchange Rate	Equation 8.9
e^f	One-Year Implicit Forward Exchange Rate	Equation 8.10
R^f	Annual Yield on Foreign Denominated Asset	Equation 8.10
e^s	Spot Exchange Rate	Equation 8.10
A	Assets, in Current Dollars	Equation 9.1
L	Liabilities in Current Dollars	Equation 9.1
NW	Net Worth, in Current Dollars	Equation 9.1
FA	Financial Assets, in Current Dollars	Equation 9.3
NFA	Nonfinancial Assets, in Current Dollars	Equation 9.3
OFA	Other Financial Assets (FA less Money Stock), in Current Dollars	Equation 9.3
c	Real Consumption Spending	Equation 10.3
$u(\cdot)$	Utility Function	Equation 10.4
y^P	Real Permanent Income	Equation 10.5
y^T	Real Transitory Income	Equation 10.5
a	Real Assets, in Constant Dollars	Equation 10.6
g	Government Spending	Equation 10.7
b	Real Value of Government Bonds Outstanding	Equation 10.7
tax	Real Tax Revenues	Equation 10.7
R_{DEP}	Nominal Interest Rate on Bank Deposits	Equation 11.1
R_L	Nominal Interest Rate on Bank Loans	Equation 11.1
Q	Production	Figure 11.1
EQ	Equity, in Dollars	Table 11.4
D	Debt, in Dollars	Table 11.4
q	Tobin's q	Equation 11.4
m	M/P = Real Balances	Equation 12.2
b	Transaction Costs	Equation 12.7
V	Income Velocity of Circulation	Equation 12.13
R^B	Nominal Return on Bonds	Equation 12.15
R^E	Nominal Return on Stocks or Equities	Equation 12.15
W_h	Human Wealth	Equation 12.15
W_n	Nonhuman Wealth	Equation 12.15
R_i^e	Expected Return, Asset i	Table 13.3
pr_s	Probability of Occurence in States of the World	Table 13.3
V_i	Variance of Returns, Asset i	Table 13.3
$\sum_s$	Summation Symbol, over States of the World	Table 13.3
COV_{ij}	Covariance between Returns on Asset i and Asset j	Table 13.4
$CORR_{ij}$	Correlation Coefficient between Returns on Asset i and Asset j	Table 13.4
VaR	Value-at-risk Measure	Figure 13.4
V_p	Variance of a Portfolio	Table 13.5
R_p^e	Portfolio Expected Return	Table 13.5
SD_p	Standard Deviation of Portfolio Returns	Page 242
$E(\cdot\|\cdot)$	Expected Value of a Variable	Equation 14.1
S_t	Stock Price, at Time t	Equation 14.1
ε	Abnormal Return for a Stock	Equation 14.7
d_t	Dividend Payment, at Time t	Equation 14.9
V_S, V_U	Variance of Stock Prices	Equation 14.14
F_T	Futures Contract Price	Equation 15.1

(continues inside back cover)

Money, Banking, and Financial Institutions

CANADA IN THE GLOBAL ENVIRONMENT

FIFTH EDITION

Pierre L. Siklos

Wilfrid Laurier University

Toronto   Montréal   Burr Ridge, IL   Dubuque, IA   Madison, WI   New York   San Francisco
St. Louis   Bangkok   Beijing   Bogotá   Caracas   Kuala Lumpur   Lisbon   London   Madrid
Mexico City   Milan   New Delhi   Santiago   Seoul   Singapore   Sydney   Taipei

Money, Banking, and Financial Institutions
Fifth Edition

ISBN: 0-07-095159-4

1 2 3 4 5 6 7 8 9 10 TCP 0 9 8 7 6

Printed and bound in Canada

Statistics Canada information is used with the permission of the Minister of Industry, as Minister responsible for
Statistics Canada. Information on the availability of the wide range of data from Statistics Canada can be obtained from
Statistics Canada's Regional Offices, its World Wide Web site at <http://www.statcan.ca>, and its toll-free access number
1-800-263-1136.

Care has been taken to trace ownership of copyright material contained in this text; however, the publisher will welcome
any information that enables them to rectify any reference or credit for subsequent editions.

Publisher: Lynn Fisher
Economics Editor: Ron Doleman
Developmental Editor: Daphne Scriabin
Senior Marketing Manager: Kelly Smyth
Supervising Editor: Jaime Smith
Copy Editor: Jim Zimmerman
Production Coordinator: Janie Deneau
Interior Design: Sharon Lucas
Page Layout: Brian Lehen Graphic Design Ltd.
Cover Design: Dianna Little
Printer: Transcontinental Printing Group

Library and Archives Canada Cataloguing in Publication

Siklos, Pierre L. (Pierre Leslie), 1955-
    Money, banking and financial institutions : Canada in the global
environment / Pierre L. Siklos. — 5th ed.

Includes index.
ISBN 0-07-095159-4

    1. Money—Canada—Textbooks. 2. Banks and banking—Canada—
Textbooks. 3. Financial institutions—Canada—Textbooks. 4. Money—
Textbooks. 5. Financial institutions—Textbooks. 6. Securities—Textbooks.
I. Title.

HG655.S55 2006   332.1'0971   C2005-906981-3

To Nagymama, for dignity and courage under fire

ABOUT THE AUTHOR

Pierre Siklos is Professor of Economics at Wilfrid Laurier University, Waterloo, Ontario, Director for its Viessmann Research Centre on Modern Europe, and Associate Editor of the *North American Journal of Economics and Finance*. He is the author of several books, including *The Changing Face of Central Banking: Evolutionary Trends Since World War II* (Cambridge: Cambridge University Press, 2002), Professor Siklos has served as a visiting professor at Oxford University, the University of California, San Diego, an Erskine Fellow at the University of Canterbury, Christchurch, New Zealand, and he has also published numerous articles in eminent economics journals. In 2000–2001, he was Wilfrid Laurier University's University Research Professor.

|B R I E F   C O N T E N T S|

|C O N T E N T S|

$\mathcal{P}$ART THREE   DECISION MAKERS IN THE FINANCIAL SYSTEM 173

*P*ART FIVE   RISK MANAGEMENT 288

| P R E F A C E |

The philosophy of this fifth edition remains the same as in the previous edition: to present a clear, interesting description of the operations, functions, and historical development of the Canadian financial system and, more generally, of the global financial system.

The reception accorded the fourth edition of *Money, Banking, and Financial Institutions,* which has been used at virtually all major Canadian universities, has been heartening and has resulted in many suggestions for change. The text has proven to be very flexible, as demonstrated by the variety of courses for which it has been used. In this fifth edition we have improved on this flexibility by reorganizing some of the material.

The text consists of eight parts, each focused on specific topics. Concepts and models explaining the determination of key financial asset prices (i.e., interest rates and exchange rates) have been grouped together in one part. Similarly, concepts and models dealing with the determination of financial asset prices under uncertainty (e.g., portfolio selection) have also been grouped together.

Since it is not possible to cover the entire text in a one-term course, the following suggestions are made for three alternate sequences through the text:

Sequence #1	Sequence #2	Sequence #3
Basic Money and Banking material	Money and Banking with Finance	Money and Banking with a flavour of Macroeconomics
Parts 1, 2, 3, 6, and 8	Parts 1, 2, 3, 4, 5, and 6	Parts 1, 2, 4, 6, 7, and 8

Following sequence #1 should allow instructors who are interested in purely institutional descriptions to leave out the chapters that are not relevant to their course. Similarly, instructors wanting a more substantive analysis of the economic concepts and models relevant to a study of the financial sector can choose chapters of interest more easily than in previous editions. Instructors who prefer this approach will prefer either sequence # 2 or # 3. The only question is whether an instructor wishes to leave out the role of central banking. If not, then sequence # 3 should be adopted. The largely "microeconomic" flavour of the text, which found favour with most adopters and students, remains.

WHAT'S NEW IN THE FIFTH EDITION?

Several important changes have been made to this edition. The chapter on financial system regulation (Chapter 17 in the fourth edition) has been moved to the end of Part Six, that is, after the Canadian institutional environment has been described. And, given the convergence of financial institutions, it was deemed preferable to combine the chapters on other depository and other financial institutions into a single chapter. The section on Central Banking and Monetary Policy has been moved forward, while the International Banking and Financial Institutions section now appears at the end of the text.

A new pedagogical feature, the Flashback Box, has been introduced. This feature provides students with the opportunity to review important first-year concepts.

Other changes include: A new section on the economics of deflation has been added to **Chapter 2.** A new Focus box dealing with the Balassa-Samuelson effect has been added to **Chapter 8.** The Focus box in **Chapter 11** has been expanded to incorporate new material dealing with the Basel II accords, and is incorporated into a new section. **Chapter 19** examines the market timing phenomenon that has been much in the news lately. In **Chapter 21,** a Focus box has been added which provides the rudiments of the aggregate demand–supply model that appears in most intermediate macro texts. A Focus box dealing with the real-time data issue, a subject of growing academic and policy interest in macroeconomics, is now included in **Chapter 22. Chapter 23** introduces two new Focus boxes: One deals with the issue of why central banks appear to change interest rates infrequently, as well as a Focus box exploring the role of central bank accountability and transparency. **Chapter 24** now includes a Focus box that exploring the way financial crises can spread across the globe; in **Chapter 26,** a Focus box examines the way China sets its exchange rate.

LEARNING AIDS

LEARNING OBJECTIVES AND CHAPTER INTRODUCTIONS

Each chapter begins with an introductory section that outlines what is to be accomplished in the chapter and links the chapter with preceding and following chapters. In this way, students (and instructors) are constantly made aware of the continuity and context of the material being addressed.

> **LEARNING OBJECTIVES**
>
> After reading and studying this chapter, you should be able to
>
> 2.1 identify why monetary economies spread around the world
> 2.2 understand the functions of money and identify the special features of a monetary standard
> 2.3 trace the monetary standards that have existed through history and their evolution
> 2.4 understand the basic features of and definitions used in measuring Canada's money supply
> 2.5 determine why a multiplicity of money supply definitions exists
> 2.6 identify which economic factors affect the purchasing power of money

ECONOMICS FOCUS AND FINANCIAL FOCUS BOXES

Boxes focusing on financial and economic matters appear in most chapters. These boxes serve several functions: They instruct students in certain technical tasks such as reading the financial pages in newspapers. They also stimulate further interest in a particular topic by summarizing existing research or by highlighting commonly held misconceptions about how the financial system operates. Occasionally, the aim of these boxes is to cast doubt on some of the theoretic propositions developed in the text. Many of the issues are illustrated by extensive references to articles in the financial press. Discussion questions are included in the Focus boxes. See, for example, Economics Focus 8.3 on page 160 and Financial Focus 5.1 on page 82. Material available to instructors will provide some guidance about how to answer these discussion questions.

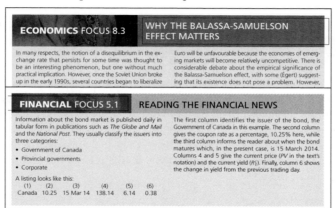

ECONOMICS FOCUS 8.3   WHY THE BALASSA-SAMUELSON EFFECT MATTERS

In many respects, the notion of a disequilibrium in the exchange rate that persists for some time was thought to be an interesting phenomenon, but one without much practical implication. However, once the Soviet Union broke up in the early 1990s, several countries began to liberalize

Euro will be unfavourable because the economies of emerging markets will become relatively uncompetitive. There is considerable debate about the empirical significance of the Balassa-Samuelson effect, with some (Égert) suggesting that its existence does not pose a problem. However,

FINANCIAL FOCUS 5.1   READING THE FINANCIAL NEWS

Information about the bond market is published daily in tabular form in publications such as *The Globe and Mail* and the *National Post*. They usually classify the issuers into three categories:

• Government of Canada
• Provincial governments
• Corporate

A listing looks like this:

(1)	(2)	(3)	(4)	(5)	(6)
Canada	10.25	15 Mar 14	138.14	6.14	0.38

The first column identifies the issuer of the bond, the Government of Canada in this example. The second column gives the coupon rate as a percentage, 10.25% here, while the third column informs the reader about when the bond matures which, in the present case, is 15 March 2014. Columns 4 and 5 give the current price (*PV* in the text's notation) and the current yield (*R$_1^s$*). Finally, column 6 shows the change in yield from the previous trading day.

NEW FLASHBACK BOXES

Students occasionally struggle to remember basic economic concepts learned in their introductory course. To ease the adjustment to more advanced material, new Focus boxes have been created called Flashbacks intended as brief refreshers on a variety of topics.

FLASHBACK 7.1

SHORT- VERSUS LONG-TERM INTEREST RATES AGAIN

In Chapter 5 we introduced a variety of ways to calculate the "interest rate." The data plotted in Figure 7.1 are average yields for instruments that mature in 90 days versus bonds with a maturity of 10 years or more. Those who publish such data, such as the Bank of Canada, average the yields of all outstanding bonds with a maturity of about 90 days as well as those with a maturity of 10 years or more (using an arithmetic average that is slightly more sophisticated than the one we will consider below). As a

result of this averaging there will naturally be a difference between the yields on long-term and short-term bonds. To take a very simple example, if $R_1 = 5\%$ and $R_2 = 5\%$ then, assuming the two-year bond is held until maturity, \$1 invested for two years will result in $(1+.05)(1+.05)= 1.1025$; that is, 10.25 cents of interest, which means that the average annual yield on a two-year bond is 5.125% (10.25% over two years or 10.25%/2 per year). Our calculations below will essentially ignore the compounding feature to make the examples simpler. You also will be told how to make calculations that take compounding into account.

Topics covered include the distinction between nominal and real measures in economics (Chapter 5), how to interpret and work with supply and demand schedules (Chapter 6), the difference between long-and short-run interest rates (Chapter 7), the concept of indifference curve analysis (Chapter 10), what it means to quantify risk and why this is done (Chapter 13), the meaning of the moral hazard and adverse selection concepts in economic analysis (Chapter 16), and the concept of business cycles (Chapter 21). See Flashback 7.1 on page 119.

POINT-COUNTERPOINT BOXES

After a brief introduction to the relevant topic, a Point-Counterpoint box presents both sides of the debate in tabular form. References to the most important articles and books are also included along with Questions for Discussion. For example, see Point–Counterpoint 22.1 on pages 448 and 449.

POINT–COUNTERPOINT 22.1

INFLATION TARGETING: THE HOLY GRAIL OF MONETARY POLICY?

The twentieth century was marked by the adoption of several types of monetary regimes. Ostensibly, the objective was to ensure a combination of stable prices with consistent economic growth. Unfortunately, most of the regimes adopted were eventually abandoned. Dissatisfaction arose for a variety of economic and noneconomic reasons.

Although several adherents continue to use fixed-exchange-rate-type regimes (see Chapter 8) there is, on balance, a slight preference for floating regimes. Together with the growing recognition that central banks are responsible solely for monetary policy and not for economic performance more generally,[1] a need arose for some kind of "anchor" or gauge of monetary policy performance.

CANSIM DATABASE

Most of the tables in this book come from Statistics Canada's CANSIM II (Canadian Socio-Economic Information Management System) database. Since CANSIM is updated daily and is very detailed (with more than 13,000,000 time series), accessing CANSIM directly enables instructors and students to update and extend the knowledge gained from *Money, Banking, and Financial Institutions: Canada in the Global Environment,* Fifth Edition. Access to the CANSIM II database is available at the Siklos Online Learning Centre at **www.mcgrawhill.ca/college/siklos.**

CANSIM II

∑-STAT

∑-STAT is an educational resource designed by Statistics Canada and made available to Canadian educational institutions. Using 450,000 current CANSIM (Canadian Socio-Economic Information Management System) Time Series and the most recent—as well as historical—census data, ∑-STAT lets you bring data to life in colourful graphs and maps.

Access to ∑-STAT and the CANSIM II database is made available to purchasers of this book via the Siklos Online Learning Centre **(www.mcgrawhill.ca/college/siklos)** by special agreement between McGraw-Hill Ryerson and Statistics Canada. The Online Learning Centre provides additional information.

TABLES AND FIGURES

Tables and Figures have been updated and reinforce the chapter content. Figures source the CANSIM II series code.

END-OF-CHAPTER MATERIAL

Summaries

All chapters conclude with a summary of the concepts and theories developed in the chapter.

Important Terms

A list of important terms introduced in the chapter is presented at the end of each chapter, accompanied by the page number on which each term appears.

Problems and Discussion Questions

Each chapter contains problems and discussion questions. No other text in this area has as extensive a list of questions aimed at testing students' understanding of the material in each chapter. In this edition many new questions have been added. Some are meant to help students summarize the main points of the chapter; others are intended to test student's understanding in a more formal, quantitative, or analytical matter.

Online Applications

Students are presented with questions to explore on the Internet that are relevant to the topic discussed in the chapter. On the *Money, Banking, and Financial Institutions,* Fifth Edition Online Learning Centre **www.mcgrawhill.ca/college/siklos** students can find direct links to the Web sites included in these questions.

CANSIM Questions

Questions are included in most chapters that require students to manipulate data available from the CANSIM II database. Each question is identified with a CANSIM II logo, with access to the database available at the Siklos Web site.

References

An extensive list of books and articles can be found on the Siklos Online Learning Centre (**www.mcgawhill.ca/college/siklos**).

■ SUPPLEMENTS AND WEB-BASED RESOURCES

INSTRUCTOR ONLINE LEARNING CENTRE

The Instructor Online Learning Centre at **www.mcgrawhill.ca/college/siklos** includes a password-protected Web site for instructors. This site offers downloadable supplements and access to PageOut, the McGraw-Hill Ryerson course management system.

INSTRUCTOR'S CD-ROM

The CD-ROM contains the Instructor's Manual, PowerPoint® Presentation, and Test Bank.

• Instructor's Manual

The Manual, prepared by the author, includes discussion notes for the Focus Box material and solutions to Problems and Discussion Questions.

- **PowerPoint® Presentation**

The PowerPoint® presentation, also prepared by the author, includes key illustrations from the text.

- **Test Bank**

The Test Bank provided in electronic format contains multiple-choice questions for each chapter.

STUDENT SUPPLEMENTS

Student Online Learning Centre

The Student Online Learning Centre at **www.mcgrawhill.ca/college/siklos** contains Quick Quiz, Internet Application Questions, Key Terms and Glossary, Annotated Web Links, and Learning Objectives for each chapter. In addition, access to Finance Around the World, updated Author Newsletters, updates from the *Globe and Mail* and Statistics Canada, as well as access to ∑-STAT and the CANSIM II database are also included in the site. A new Student Study Section also is available at the OLC and contains the Study Guide with chapters corresponding to the Fifth Edition text. Each chapter includes a chapter focus, section summaries, multiple-choice questions with answers, and problems with answers.

TECHNOLOGY SOLUTIONS

Course Management

Pageout **www.mhhe.com/pageout** is the McGraw-Hill Ryerson hosted course management system and access is free to faculty. It is designed to help faculty easily create a course website, complete with assignments, quizzes, links to relevant Web sites, and more. Contact your *i*Learning Sales Specialist to get set up today.

Content cartridges are available for course management systems such as **WebCT and Blackboard.** These platforms provide instructors with user-friendly, flexible teaching tools. Please contact your local McGraw-Hill Ryerson *i*Learning Sales Specialist for details.

Superior Service

Service takes on a whole new meaning with McGraw-Hill Ryerson. More than just bringing you the textbook, we have consistently raised the bar in terms of innovation and educational research—both in economics and in education in general. These investments in learning and the education community have helped us understand the needs of students and educators across the country and allowed us to foster the growth of truly innovative, integrated learning.

Intregated Learning

Your **Integrated Learning Sales Specialist** is a McGraw-Hill Ryerson representative who has the experience, product knowledge, training, and support to help you assess and integrate any of the above-noted products, technology, and services into your course for optimum teaching and learning performance. Whether it's using our test bank software, helping your students improve their grades, or putting your entire course online, your *i*Learning Sales Specialist is there to help you do it. Contact your local *i*Learning Sales Specialist today to learn how to maximize all of McGraw-Hill Ryerson's resources!

*i*Learning Services Program

McGraw-Hill Ryerson offers a unique *i*Services package designed for Canadian faculty. Our mission is to equip providers of higher education with superior tools and resources required for excellence in teaching. For additional information visit **http://www.mcgrawhill.ca/highereducation/iservices**.

Teaching, Technology and Learning Conference Series

The educational environment has changed tremendously in recent years, and McGraw-Hill Ryerson continues to be committed to helping you acquire the skills you need to succeed in this new milieu. Our innovative Teaching, Technology & Learning Conference Series brings faculty together from across Canada with 3M Teaching Excellence award winners to share teaching and learning best practices in a collaborative and stimulating environment. Preconference workshops on general topics, such as teaching large classes and technology integration, will also be offered. We will also work with you at your own institution to customize workshops that best suit the needs of your faculty.

| A C K N O W L E D G E M E N T S |

I owe a great deal to the many hundreds of students who have used this text and provided me with a great number of useful suggestions for improvements. I am grateful also to the academic reviewers listed below whose criticisms and encouragement assisted me in the task of revision. Eric Kam, of Ryerson University, has been especially helpful with technical feedback and in reviewing the revisions.

Maxym Chaban, *University of Victoria*
George Chuchman, *University of Manitoba*
Joseph DeJuan, *University of Waterloo*
Suzana Janko, *University of Calgary*
Eric Kam, *Ryerson University*
Richard McGaw, *University of New Brunswick*
Marc Prud'Homme, *University of Ottawa*
Gary Riser, *Memorial University*
Duane Rockerbie, *University of Lethbridge*
Amy Sopinka, *Camosun College*
Greg Tkacz, *Carleton University and Bank of Canada*
Mary Ann Vaughan, *Wilfrid Laurier University*

Above all, however, I have my family to thank for putting up with yet another round of revisions and my inevitable absentmindedness as I focused on preparing the best text possible.

Comments and suggestions are welcome. Contacting me at the e-mail address below. Also, please visit my Web site for updates and other relevant material.

Pierre L. Siklos 2006

e-mail address: **psiklos@wlu.ca**
Web site: **www.wlu.ca/~wwwsbe/faculty/psiklos/home.htm**

PART ONE

Overview and Fundamentals of the Canadian Financial System

The Study of Money and Banking

LEARNING OBJECTIVES

After reading and studying this chapter, you should be able to

1.1 identify in broad terms what the study of money and banking is all about

1.2 get a glimpse of some of the many features of the Canadian financial system

1.3 understand the critical role of international influences on the Canadian financial system

1.4 get a good start on enjoying this text!

What is the study of money, banking, and financial markets all about? To answer such a far-reaching question will require this entire book. Chapter 1 seeks to whet your appetite with an overview of the subject and a glimpse of some of the fascinating issues in the field. You will finish the chapter with an idea of the major themes of the book, but you will also be left with more questions than answers; it is the task of the remaining chapters to answer those questions.

1.1 THE ESSENCE OF MONEY AND BANKING

The study of money and banking is essentially the study of the role and function of money in the economy and the study of financial markets—that is, the money, foreign exchange, bond and stock markets, and their interrelationships. The effects of the financial system on the economy are determined by the institutional framework under which the system operates. Thus, the study of money and banking also requires an understanding of the organization, structure, and historical development of the various institutions that constitute the financial sector of the Canadian economy. You must know how government institutions and regulatory bodies influence the behaviour of financial institutions and financial market participants; you must understand the interplay among the financial system, the monetary authorities (that is, the Bank of Canada), and government economic policies, and their effects on economic activity as a whole. These topics are covered in this text.

Clearly, what takes place in the financial system affects the rest of the economy. The same might be said of other key sectors. What distinguishes financial markets from other key markets is the vital role played by confidence or credibility.

Credibility has two meanings here, both of which are essential to the financial system. First, individuals and firms entrust their funds to financial institutions in the confidence that these funds will be managed honestly and efficiently and will be available when promised. The sad truth is that financial systems, worldwide and throughout history, have not always been honest brokers of money. Scandals have plagued institutions in countries such as the United States and

Japan in recent years. In Canada, too, individuals and groups have attempted to rig financial markets to their own advantage or abscond with funds entrusted to them.

The second meaning of credibility is "the extent to which the public believes a shift in policy has taken place when, indeed, such a shift has occurred."[1] Why is this confidence important? Whether the matter at hand concerns inflation, unemployment, or government policies in general, the public acts on the various announcements made by policymakers. If people guess incorrectly about how committed the government is to attaining a particular goal, the lack of synchronization between their actions and those of the government will have widespread consequences for interest rates and for the rest of the financial system. A case in point is the recent debate over deficit cutting, which we will discuss further later.

Thus, all people have ample reason to be interested in the arrangements and operations of their country's financial system.

MONEY

When we say that the behaviour of monetary aggregates is one of our principal topics, we are suggesting the crucial role money plays in the analyses to follow. What is money? This question has no easy answers, as we will see. **Money** is, of course, an asset that embodies purchasing power in terms of goods, services, and other assets. One definition is the currency in circulation plus the deposits of the banking system. (We will discuss a more precise definition in the next chapter.)

Money is important in itself. It is also important because economists have developed explanations linking variations in the amount of money in circulation (caused by the process of monetary policy) to interest rates, stock prices, and economic activity in general. (Interest rate analysis plays a prominent role in the first two parts of this text.) Thus, financial indicators such as interest rate changes, the yield curve, or stock prices may provide clues about future credit conditions—that is, the looseness or tightness of financial borrowing conditions.

For an idea of the central role that money, interest rates, and inflation play in this textbook, consider the various plots shown in Figures 1.1 to 1.3. Figure 1.1 displays the striking way movements in the money supply and the price level have paralleled each other. Visual inspection of the two curves suggests a connection between money or (monetary policy) and price level movements that requires explanation. Oddly enough, it has become fashionable in recent years to downplay the role of money in monetary policy as economists and financial markets have focused their attention almost exclusively on interest rate behaviour. Yet, there is growing recognition that, eventually, the link between money and prices is not so easily broken.[2]

Figure 1.2 shows the similar synchronous movements of the money supply and an aggregate measure of economic activity, real GDP. Again, it appears that a link between the monetary and the real sides of the economy may exist. Despite the importance of the money supply, a major drawback, as we shall see in Chapter 2, is that definitions of the money supply have changed fairly dramatically over the past decade or so. Largely for this reason, it is extremely difficult, unless one performs some possibly questionable calculations, to extend the data past 2000. This does not negate, however, the striking connection between the money supply and important macroeconomic indicators.

A connection between money growth and inflation also follows from the suggested link between money and prices. Figure 1.3 shows that a relationship between interest rates and inflation also exists. Thus, money, since it affects inflation, may also influence interest rates.

---

1 A. Cukierman, "Central Bank Behavior and Credibility: Some Recent Theoretical Developments," *Review of the Federal Reserve Bank of St. Louis* 17 (May 1986): 6.

2 See, for example, A. Fatas, I. Mihov, and A.K. Rose, "Quantitative Goals for Monetary Policy," NBER working paper 10846, October 2004, and Deutsche Bundesbank, "The Relationship Between Money and Prices," *Monthly Report* (January 2005): 13-24.

The apparent centrality of money, both for economic activity in general and for financial markets in particular, suggests that an understanding of the factors that determine its supply and demand must be a leading feature of the analyses to follow.

TRANSMISSION MECHANISMS

Economists have long been interested in how money and monetary policy influence individuals and economies as a whole. As usual, their views on the subject are not unanimous. Figure 1.4, however, illustrates possible transmission mechanisms—that is, the means by which monetary policy affects, or maybe is affected by, other factors in the economy.

Starting from some equilibrium, that is, where none of the variables we are interested in shows any tendency to change, sustained increases in the money supply imply positive money growth, which causes prices to change. Alternatively, a reduction in nominal interest rates, other things being equal, can lead to the same result. But there are other ways that monetary policy can be looser or tighter, as we shall see. For example, the exchange rate, especially in an open economy such as Canada's, can also reflect monetary policy actions, as discussed in Chapter 7. Why? Because, as we shall see in Chapter 6, the market perceives that too much money is chasing too few goods. In an attempt to rid themselves of the "excess" money, prices for goods and services are bid upward. Put differently, lower interest rates, with inflation steady, mean that the real cost of borrowing will fall while the real return on lending will be lower, thereby making saving less attractive. The eventual result is **inflation**, which, by definition, is simply a measure of how quickly prices change over time.

Thus, for example, economists of the "monetarist" persuasion (see Chapter 21) generally believe that inflation must originate with money growth; as Milton Friedman has said, "Inflation

| Figure 1.1 | **Money and Price Level Movements since 1913** |

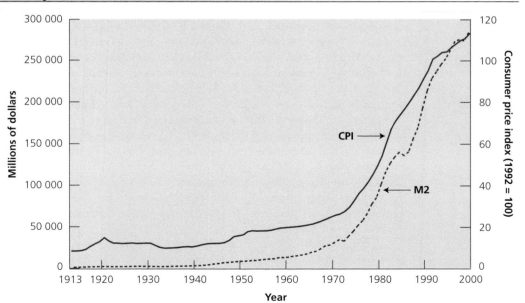

M2 is one of several official measures of the money supply.[a] The consumer price index (CPI) measures the price level (rises show inflation). The two data series appear to have moved in tandem for almost a century.

Source: P.L. Siklos, "Income Velocity and Institutional Change: Time Series Evidence from Five Industrialized Countries, 1870–1986," *Journal of Money, Credit and Banking* 25 (August 1993), with updates from the *Bank of Canada Banking and Financial Statistics,* Tables H8, E1, and A2.

[a]For the definition, see Chapter 2.

Figure 1.2	Money and Real Income since 1913

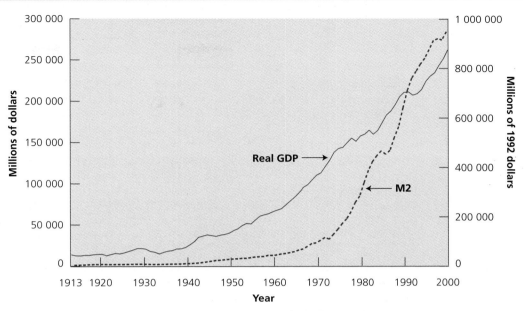

Real income, a measure of economic activity, is nominal national income divided by the price level. A common measure of real income is gross domestic product or GDP. Like the money supply, real income seems to have moved in tandem with inflation for almost a century.

Source: See Figure 1.1. Updates from *Bank of Canada Banking and Financial Statistics,* Tables A2, E1, and H2.

Figure 1.3	Inflation and the Interest Rate since the 1960s

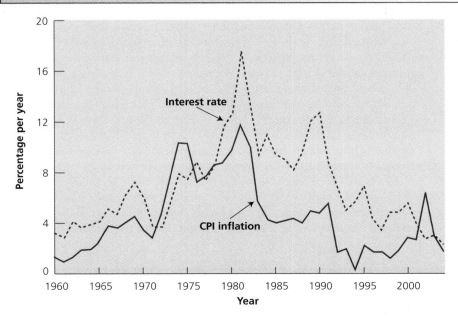

The inflation curve shows the rate of change in the level of prices. It is traced against the interest rate. (The interest rate is measured here by the yield on three-month Government of Canada Treasury bills.)

Source: P.L. Siklos, "Income Velocity and Institutional Change: Time Series Evidence from Five Industrialized Countries, 1870–1986," *Journal of Money, Credit and Banking* 25 (August 1993), with updates from the *Bank of Canada Banking and Financial Statistics,* Table A2.

| **Figure 1.4** | **Transmission Mechanisms for Monetary Policy**

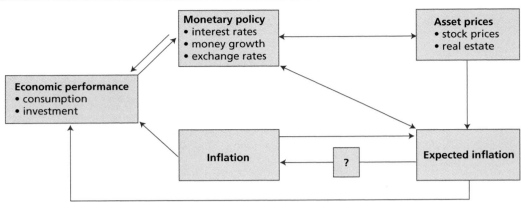

Starting at the top of the diagram, we see that monetary policy leads to changes in expected inflation. It likely also leads to changes in actual inflation (which may itself influence monetary policy—see the text). Expected inflation affects interest rates and thus the level of economic activity.

is always and everywhere a monetary phenomenon."[3] Nevertheless, inflation erodes the purchasing power of money, sometimes very badly as in *hyperinflation*, a situation in which the inflation rate exceeds 50% a month. Governments have been known to respond to sharp inflation by printing increasing quantities of money. Although money growth usually causes inflation, the odd possibility exists that inflation may sometimes cause money growth.

Figure 1.4 also reflects the process by which interest rate change depends crucially on investors' beliefs about the anticipated course of inflation, which are called **expectations of inflation**. The reason, as we see later in greater detail, is that borrowing and lending activities are prompted in part by beliefs about the benefits and costs of purchasing goods and services today relative to purchasing them in the future. In other words, an interest rate exists because individuals enter into contracts either to defer spending or to enjoy more spending today. To postpone spending implies that people are concerned about the purchasing power of financial resources available only in the future, which will be affected by expectations of future inflation.

Finally, because spending is affected, economic activity is influenced by interest rate levels. Economic activity, in turn, may have a bearing on the future course of monetary policy and, therefore on levels of consumption and investment; whether it does or not depends in part on how the central bank and the government react to current economic performance, a topic of considerable interest to economists and to others. Notice also that Figure 1.4 permits a potential role for asset prices. As we shall see in Chapter 14, for example, there is a widely shared view that stock returns affect or are affected by inflation. More recently, policymakers have also voiced concerns over the potential role of housing and land prices, especially in view of the continuing fallout from the real estate "bubble" in Japan, and to lesser extent the tech bubble of 1999–2000 in the U.S.

---

3 This famous quote was repeated most recently in M. Friedman, *Money Mischief: Episodes in Monetary History* (New York: Harcourt, Brace, Jovanovich, 1992), xi. For many years economists presumed inflationary expectations to be influenced solely by the past history of inflation. Recently, however, the profession has been greatly influenced by those who view individuals as forward-looking. In essence, these analysts believe that investors do not wait for inflation to happen before revising their views of the future; instead, they seek to anticipate its course by keeping track of indicators of future inflation, such as the money supply. This view is the reason an arrow is drawn directly from money to expected inflation.

Where is the financial system in all this? The answer, as we begin to see in the next chapter, is that the links from money to economic activity are greatly influenced by the efficiency and innovations of the financial sector of the economy.[4]

WHY STUDY FINANCIAL MARKETS?

We should make clear that many different interest rates exist because financial markets offer a bewildering array of financial assets. To get some idea of this, consider Figure 1.5, which plots two different interest rate measures: One is called a short-term interest rate, because the asset in question matures in the not-too-distant future; the other is called a long-term interest rate, because the asset matures many years ahead. Notice that the two measures move more or less in tandem, but the short-term rate appears to be more volatile. An explanation of this phenomenon can provide clues about the future course of inflation and economic activity.

Another asset market that deserves close scrutiny is the market for stocks. Neither academics nor practitioners agree about explanations of stock price behaviour. Should you really laugh at the idea that the price of an individual stock represents the present discounted value of the future flow of dividends? Why do events such as the stock market crash of 1987 occur and how are they explained? Are stock prices forecastable, or do they simply fluctuate randomly around some value over time?

| Figure 1.5 | **Short-Term and Long-Term Interest Rates since the 1960s** |

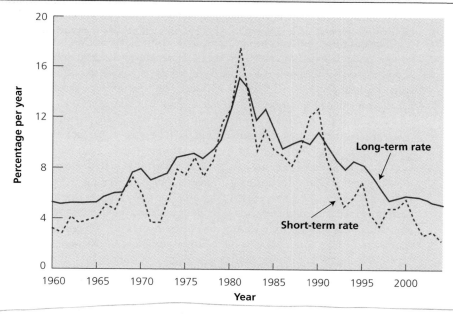

Short-term and long-term interest rates normally differ (the long-term rates are usually higher) but move in tandem.

Source: See Figure 1.3.

Note: The long-term interest rate here is the yield on Government of Canada bonds with a term to maturity of 10 years and more. The short-term rate is the yield on three-month Treasury bills.

---

4 A useful and easy-to-read description of the various channels through which monetary policy is influenced or can possibly influence asset prices and economic activity more generally can be found in F. S. Mishkin, "The Transmission Mechanism and the Role of Asset Prices in Monetary Policy," NBER Working Paper 8617 (December 2001).

The clout of financial markets has increased dramatically in the past decade. A bad word here from a politician or a misstep there by some government official can send bond, stock, and foreign exchange markets into a tailspin. Financial markets trade 24 hours a day and events in Tokyo are no more distant to a trader in Toronto or New York than events in Ottawa or elsewhere.

1.2   THE CANADIAN FINANCIAL SYSTEM

All this discussion about money, interest rates, inflation, and stock prices omits the fact that individuals and institutions are in the middle of all the action in the transmission mechanism. Yet, it is important to study and understand how financial institutions operate, how the economic environment influences decision making in financial institutions, and how the Canadian system compares with other prominent financial systems.

One of the most significant developments in Canada (and in much of the rest of the world) in the past two decades has been the gradual reduction of government involvement in financial systems. Because government intervention has usually taken the form of regulation, the simplification or elimination of regulations is called **deregulation**.

These developments have had a profound impact on the shape of the Canadian financial system. Its institutions used to fit neatly into four categories—chartered banks, trust companies and near-banks, insurance companies, and investment dealers—with government regulations precisely defining the role of each according to its specific functions. Since the 1960s, however, the divisions have been crumbling under the weight of two forces: (1) increased competition in the financial sector and (2) regulatory reform, prompted in large part by financial innovation, the rapid development of computer technology, and the perception of increased volatility in the financial sector.

For example, it is becoming increasingly difficult to distinguish chartered banks from trust companies and credit unions. Nevertheless, all institutional change seems to have a common feature: It comes slowly. Although it is difficult to tell the financial system's players apart, they still retain some distinct characteristics, as we will see. The functions, permitted activities, and customs of Canada's financial institutions do not match those of many other countries (they differ from one another, too) nor those of international organizations, such as the International Monetary Fund (IMF).

Perhaps the most significant change in recent years has been the financing role played by institutions we used to think of in very different terms. Companies such as AT&T, GE, and Canadian Tire perform some of the same functions as traditional financial institutions. This development has implications for the degree of competition in the financial sector, but more important perhaps, it poses serious dilemmas for governments that regulate financial institutions. Combined with the desire expressed by the more traditional banks to branch out into every aspect of finance (e.g., automobile leasing and insurance), the problems that regulators face and their approach to these issues become increasingly complex. We therefore devote a separate chapter to how government regulations can cope with the resulting risks to the financial system.

ARE BANKS SPECIAL?

One of the most valuable aspects of the study of money and banking is gaining a clear understanding of the special role of banks. Although financial innovations and alternatives to traditional banks are eroding their dominant position in the financial sector, banks remain special. Several chapters will outline the details of the unique role of banks, but we can briefly note some of the salient functions of the institutions referred to as **intermediaries**:

- Banks allow individuals to hold otherwise illiquid assets in a more liquid form.
- Banks permit individuals to reallocate consumption. For example, mortgages permit individuals with too little financial capital to purchase a home.

- Banks provide a relatively inexpensive way to complete complex transactions. Given their comparative advantage over other institutions, banks can borrow from or lend to individuals and firms who possess less knowledge of the risks involved. As a result, they provide new financial products and have an incentive to innovate.

- Banks reduce the asymmetric information problem that exists because borrowers tend to know more about their prospects than do lenders.

- Banks offer tools to manage risks more effectively than individuals are able to.

1.3 THE INTERNATIONAL DIMENSION

It is impossible to explore our own financial system in isolation from events outside Canada. One reason is summed up in the catchword "globalization," that is, the growing integration of financial markets worldwide. Another is the nature of the Canadian economy: Small (our gross domestic product—GDP—is only a small fraction of world GDP) and open (exports plus imports reached just over 70% of GDP in 2004).[5]

A third reason is the trend toward the integration of financial transactions and regulations worldwide. This trend has resulted in financial assets growing at a far faster rate than physical assets or the economy's output.

Globalization refers to the ability of investors to access foreign markets easily. For example, a Canadian-based firm can cross-list its stock on the London and New York stock exchanges. An investor in Canada can purchase financial assets from a foreign country.

The benefits of globalization are many. The ability to diversify is enhanced, as is the ability to access more markets. Markets become larger and more liquid, so they can absorb shifts in demand and supply with less impact on prices than can smaller markets. However, some potential risks exist. For example, rules and regulations differ widely from one country to another; an uninformed investor can therefore incur different types of costs when investing abroad.

A bit of historical perspective is useful here, especially since globalization, as we will discover, is neither entirely new nor more prevalent today than it was at the end of the nineteenth or during the early part of the twentieth century. For example, when major economies (including Canada's) were linked to each other via the gold standard, a great deal of capital market integration occurred.[6] Wars, the Great Depression, and the collapse of international cooperation changed all that until the 1980s when, thanks to the freedom of movement of capital, a new wave of globalization took hold.

Nevertheless, measuring the extent of globalization has not been easy. Some have argued that the fall in trade barriers coupled with the fall in transportation costs is reflected in the growth in intensity of trade, especially in commodities. On this basis, the spread of globalization has been "spectacular" since 1913.[7] Others have linked the ebb and flow of globalization to restrictions in the movement of capital. On this score, the "shape" of globalization can be likened to a "U," with the degree of capital mobility reaching a peak in 1914, bottoming out in 1945, and rising ever since.[8] Since the degree of capital mobility has important implications for the theory of interest rate and exchange rate determination across countries, globalization has direct relevance to the Canadian experience.

---

5 *Bank of Canada Banking and Financial Statistics,* Tables H1 and J3.
6 See, for example, M.D. Bordo, B. Eichengreen, and J. Kim, "Was There Really an Earlier Period of International Financial Integration Comparable to Today?" NBER Working Paper 6738 (June 1998); and M.D. Bordo, B. Eichengreen, and D. Irwin, "Is Globalization Today Really Different than Globalization 100 Years Ago?" Wirtschaftspolitisches Blatter, 47(1)(2000): 3–12, 121–29.
7 See K.H. O'Rourke and J.H. Williamson, "When Did Globalization Begin?" NBER Working Paper 7632 (April 2000).
8 See M. Obstfeld and A. Taylor, "Globalization and Capital Markets," NBER Working Paper 8846 (March 2002).

This text explores the phenomenon of globalization in three ways. First, whenever we discuss some important aspect of Canada's financial system or financial history we mention lessons from abroad. Second, an entire chapter is devoted to a survey of the US financial system, the main player in the global economy. Third, we spend some time exploring the role and functions of important international financial organizations such as the IMF.

To see why this international dimension is crucial in a course about money and banking, consider the implications for a small, open economy such as Canada's.

International financial considerations loom large in influencing domestic financial conditions. The flow of funds from abroad, a means of financing both the public and private sectors, is growing rapidly. Thus, such diverse issues as exchange rate systems and the international debt crisis are important topics for Canadian students.

International differences in economic performance further suggest the importance of the international dimension in financial markets. Inflation rates and interest rates vary internationally, even among the leading countries of the industrialized West, such as the G-7 and G-10[9](see Figures 1.6 and 1.7). However, a noticeable convergence of both variables has occurred in recent years. Indeed, France, Germany, and Italy have replaced their separate currencies. Since 1999, most European interest rates have been expressed in terms of the euro, the new currency of the European Monetary Union. Meanwhile, the volatile nature of exchange rates in recent years has rekindled the issue of whether it is better to fix the exchange rate or instead continue to permit it to float. The large gyrations in the value of the Canadian dollar vis-à-vis the U.S. dollar in the aftermath of the fall in commodity prices in 1998 reveal how quickly and strongly financial markets

| **Figure 1.6** | **Inflation Rates in the G-7 Countries** |

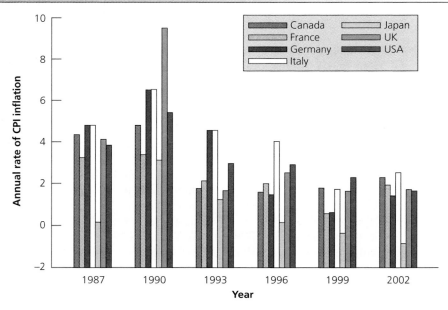

Although inflation rates were similar enough to make it difficult to distinguish one G-7 country's inflation curve from another's here, it is clear that the rate was more volatile (variable) in some countries than in others. Inflation is the annual percentage change in the CPI.

Source: International Financial Statistics CD-ROM (Washington D.C.: International Monetary Fund).

9 The G-7 countries are Canada, France, Germany, Italy, Japan, the United Kingdom, and the United States. The G-10 countries are the G-7 countries plus Belgium, the Netherlands, Sweden, and Switzerland. (Although there are 11 countries, the group is called the G-10 because Belgium and the Netherlands count as one).

| Figure 1.7 | **Interest Rates in the G-7 Countries** |

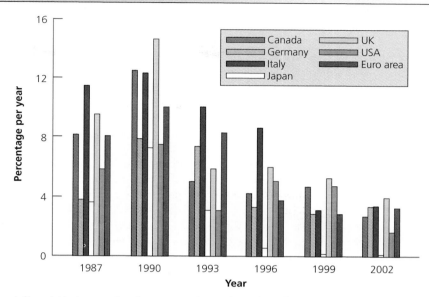

A financial instrument in a Eurocurrency is one denominated in a currency other than that of the country of issue. Here we see the annual yield on a Eurocurrency instrument denominated in each of the G-7 currencies. The interest rate movements are broadly similar, but there are differences in levels and volatility.

Source: See Figure 1.6. For the euro area, France, Germany, Italy, Japan, and the UK, the call money rate is used. For Canada and the U.S., the three-month Treasury bill rate is used. For the UK, the overnight interbank bank rate was used. Since 1999, interest rates in Germany, France, and Italy (as well as in eight other European countries) have also been set by the European Central Bank (ECB). Therefore, interest rates in these countries are the same.

react to "news." Explaining the linkages and some of the reasons for the differences is part of the task of this book.

Although the positive aspects of globalization imply that countries' financial policies are becoming more alike, the potential downside of these same developments is that Canada may not be immune to a crisis in a distant part of the world. As a result, economists have been interested in what is called "contagion" effects; that is, when the impact of a financial crisis in one country spills over to other parts of the world. Such crises have become both more frequent and, possibly, more consequential for the world economy over the past few years. Recent examples include the Mexican crisis of 1994–95, the Asian crisis of 1997–98, the Russian financial crisis, and the financial crisis in Argentina of 2001–02. The extent to which these crises spill over to other parts of the world, or are global in nature is a matter of considerable debate. Nevertheless, it is clear that, however beneficial globalization may be, it must be managed, if only to mitigate the contagion effects. We shall consider both sides of the debate at various times throughout the text.

PUBLIC VERSUS PRIVATE FINANCE

A new trend that is already having an impact on the financial sector is the dramatic reversal of fortunes in public finances. Until recently, governments at virtually all levels were incurring sizable deficits that necessitated vast amounts of borrowing from domestic and international savers, with what some believe were negative consequences in Canada for interest rates, inflation rates, and economic activity as a whole. Today, however, some governments are actually generating surpluses. By contrast, borrowing by the private sector has continued to rise at a fairly rapid rate. These developments, summarized in Figures 1.8 and 1.9, are sure to have an important effect on the evolution of the Canadian financial system.

| Figure 1.8 | Twenty-Year History of Government Financing |

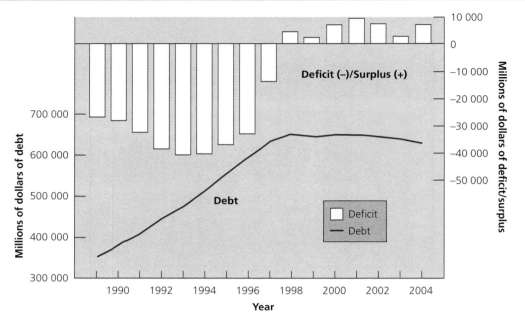

Source: Adapted from *Statistics Canada* CANSIM II database, series V15384 (deficit) and V151537 (debt).

| Figure 1.9 | Growth of Private Sector Borrowing |

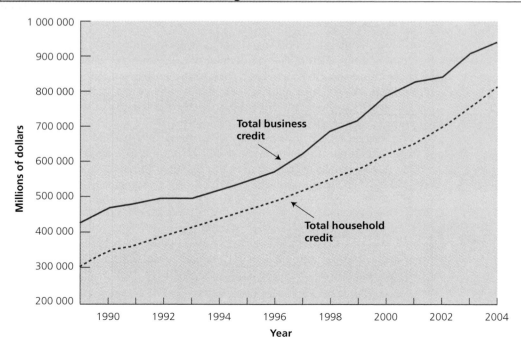

Source: Adapted from Statistics Canada CANSIM II database **http://cansim2.statcan.ca/cgi-win/CNSMCGI.EXE**, series V36415 (household credit) and V122647 (business credit).

1.4   A FINAL WORD

Lest you think that the subject of money and banking is dull, consider the following quote from James Carville, former strategist to the Democrats in the United States: "I used to think, if there was reincarnation, I wanted to come back as the President or Pope or a 0.400 baseball hitter. But now I want to come back as the bond market. You can intimidate everyone."[10]

The idea of studying such diverse and complex material may seem daunting. Take heart. No matter what your background, you have some knowledge of introductory economics. Even if your recall of introductory economics is a bit rusty, there are focus boxes, called "Flashback," that will help refresh some key concepts used throughout this text. The discussions in this book make much use of the material you learned in the study of both microeconomics and macroeconomics (with relatively greater emphasis placed on microeconomic concepts). So, although the discussions in this book are complete in themselves, you may find that your introductory economics textbook is a useful supplementary roadmap.

Enjoy your explorations in this fascinating subject.

SUMMARY

- This chapter attempts to give a flavour of the things to come in this textbook. Specifically, it outlines the aspects of economics involved in studying money and banking.

- Studying money refers to studying monetary policy and how it is linked to the rest of the economy via a transmission mechanism that involves inflation and interest rates.

- Studying the Canadian financial system involves more than learning a description of our own banking institutions. It involves studying the bond market and the stock market as well as international financial institutions.

- Because the Canadian economy is relatively small and open to international influences, discussion of the global dimension of economics is a vital part of the study of money and banking. Exchange rates and other international economic influences are important topics for analysis.

IMPORTANT TERMS

deregulation, 8
expectations of inflation, 6
globalization, 9

inflation, 4
intermediaries, 8
money, 3

PROBLEMS

Although some of these questions can only be fully answered after you have absorbed material from later chapters, try answering these questions using newspaper and magazine articles on the subject of interest rates and exchange rates, or by relying on your own personal experience and knowledge. The purpose of some of the questions below is to get you thinking about some of the key features of the operation of the financial system and the economy that we will be developing throughout the text. You can check later whether you were correct all along!

1. See Figure 1.1. Did the change in the price level accelerate during the 1970s and 1980s relative to earlier periods? (Note: Acceleration refers to how fast prices are rising.)

---

10 As quoted in K. Phillips, "The Tyranny of Traders," *Report on Business Magazine* (November 1994): 65.

2. During a recession there is usually a fall in real income. What events are associated with the dips in real income that occurred in 1929–33, 1973–74, 1981–82, and 1991–92? (Hint: Think of major economic events that are national or international in scope.)

3. Can you speculate about why short-term interest rates tend to be more volatile than long-term interest rates?

4. Notice in Figures 1.6 and 1.7 that interest rates and inflation rates in Germany, Italy, and France tended to converge toward the same value. Was this an accident or a deliberate policy? Explain. (Hint: Think of what happened in European monetary policy during the first couple of years of this century.)

DISCUSSION QUESTIONS

1. Long-term interest rates are generally higher than short-term interest rates (see Figure 1.5). Why would this be the case?

2. Figure 1.7 suggests that the interest rate in Italy is generally higher than the interest rates in the other G-7 countries, at least until mid-1990s. Why would this be the case? (Hint: See Figure 1.6.)

3. Notice from Figures 1.6 and 1.7 that inflation rate and interest rate differences have become much smaller in the 1990s relative to the 1970s. Speculate about why this might be the case. (Hint: Think of the Bank of Canada's current monetary policy.)

4. Globalization has both advantages and disadvantages, according to many analysts. Try to list a few of each.

5. What event prompted the sharp depreciation of the Canadian dollar in the summer of 1998?

6. Why is the change in the pattern of public versus private borrowing in the later 1990s potentially important? Explain.

ONLINE APPLICATIONS

1. Understanding the development of the financial system requires an understanding of monetary and financial history. Go to **www.ex.ac.uk/~RDavies/arian/amser/chrono.html** and examine the major milestones of monetary history. Select a period in history and try to list the events in that period that had potentially major implications for the development of the financial system in Canada or the rest of the industrial world.

2. Go to the Statistics Canada Web site that has collected the *Historical Statistics of Canada* at **www.statcan.ca/english/IPS/Data/11-516-XIE.htm**. Examine the money supply series in particular. Next, go to the Bank of Canada's Web site at **www.bankofcanada.ca** and examine recent developments of the money supply (these are available in several locations, including the regular publication called the *Monetary Policy Report*). Compare the definitions of the monetary aggregate called M2. How has this aggregate changed over time? Is it straightforward to construct a single series such as the one shown in Figure 1.1? Why or why not?

References can be found on **www.mcgrawhill.ca/college/siklos**

CHAPTER 2

What Is Money?

LEARNING OBJECTIVES

After reading and studying this chapter, you should be able to

2.1 identify why monetary economies spread around the world

2.2 understand the functions of money and identify the special features of a monetary standard

2.3 trace the monetary standards that have existed through history and their evolution

2.4 understand the basic features of and definitions used in measuring Canada's money supply

2.5 determine why a multiplicity of money supply definitions exists

2.6 identify which economic factors affect the purchasing power of money

What is money and how do you measure it? These questions are important because a variety of explanations about the behaviour of interest rates and economic activity, to name but two examples, depend crucially on how we define and measure money.

The money supply is at the centre of many economic theories linking the financial sector to the real economy. It is also at the core of central banking policy, another important financial-sector institution. Finally, many economic analyses use the money supply to predict the future course of inflation and to pinpoint the impact of financial innovations, but there has been some controversy about the effectiveness of money supply data in this regard.

In discussing the asset called money, we consider various monetary standards of the past and present. We then turn to a description of the various ways in which the money supply in Canada can be measured.

The chapter ends with a discussion of the economic consequences of inflation. Since inflation affects the value of money, however defined, government policies that influence inflation also influence social welfare. More to the point, inflation performance can have an important impact on the structure and evolution of the financial system.

As noted in the previous chapter, policymakers have been concerned primarily with the effects of inflation. Nevertheless, several countries over the past decade, most notably China and Japan, experienced _deflation,_ that is, falling prices. Indeed, there were serious concerns, at least until 2004, that deflation would stalk Europe and the U.S. Why the concern over deflation? This chapter will provide some basic answers.

2.1   WHY MONEY?

Economists rarely disagree that efficiency, and thus social welfare,[1] is improved by the introduction of an *asset* (something of value) called money. Indeed, as the famous economist the late Sir John Hicks pointed out succinctly: "Money, I consider, is a device which facilitates the working of markets."[2] Notice our use of the phrase "called money." It is important to understand, even before we attempt official definitions, that money is not necessarily the bills people carry in their wallets. Rather, money is whatever people decide it is. In other words, a social agreement exists that some object (or objects) may fulfil the functions of money. Cattle, fish hooks, shells, hunks of stone, and beaver pelts have all been used as money.

BARTER

Some experts believe that the creation of money predates the creation of organized and well-functioning markets where goods and services could be traded.[3] Once conventions were in place, supplemented by enforcement mechanisms that could be guaranteed by government, monetary economies could develop and promote the growth of trade. The more conventional explanation, as will become clear below, presumes that money permitted the improvement in the operation of existing markets.[4]

The reason a money system improves social welfare is that the alternative is **barter**, the direct exchange of goods and services for other goods and services. Barter is probably as old as humanity, and it still persists even in highly industrialized modern economies.[5] You cut your roommate's hair and she drives you to Regina next week.

But what if your roommate has decided to let her hair grow? Or if you're headed for Halifax? The problem here is that barter requires a double coincidence of wants: The transaction the seller desires can take place only if the seller is able to find a purchaser who wants to exchange for what the seller has and if the purchaser has something the seller wants to obtain, or if the seller can arrange a series of transactions ending with possession of the desired good.

Several other problems arise in a barter system. The value of the asset the seller receives in exchange is probably variable. The two parties to each transaction have to negotiate its "price," a time-consuming process involving judgments of intrinsic value. The sheer number of transactions required can be enormous. The problems with barter-type systems are still with us today. Russia and other emerging markets still resort to barter, especially in the industrial sector. As recently as 1998, almost fifty percent of trading in the industrial sector in Russia was in the form of barter.[6] As a result, firms tend to lock into a trading arrangement that reduces the flexibility required to spur efficiency and innovation.

To see the last point, consider a simplified example. Assume an economy has three goods, called 1, 2, and 3. A seller in a simple, barter economy would face the following possible transactions:

See a chronology of the history of money at **www.ex.ac.uk/ ~RDavies/arian/ amser/chrono.html**

---

1 Economists measure welfare in terms of utility, which refers to some quantifiable index of the satisfaction derived by individuals or society from, for example, the consumption of some good. This concept is used extensively in Chapters 10 and 11.

2 John Hicks, *A Market Theory of Money* (Oxford: Clarendon Press, 1989): 2.

3 For example, see J. Melitz, *Primitive and Modern Money: An Interdisciplinary Approach* (Reading, Mass.: Addison-Wesley Co., 1974).

4 An early exposition of this argument can be found in K. Menger, "On the Origin of Money," *Economic Journal* 2 (1892): 238–55. A more recent contribution in this vein is K. Brunner, "The Uses of Money: Money in the Theory of an Exchange Economy," *American Economic Review* 61(5) (1971): 784–805. Modern, technical treatments of this question that are beyond the scope of this text, can be found in N. Kiyotaki and R. Wright, "On Money as a Medium of Exchange," *Journal of Political Economy* 97(4) (1989): 927–54, and "A Search-Theoretic Approach to Monetary Economics," *American Economic Review* 83(1) (1993): 63–77. An easy-to-read account of the nature and role of barter economies can be found in Pierre Siklos, "Barter and Barter Systems," in *Oxford Encyclopedia of Economic History*, Joel Mokyr, ed. (Oxford: Oxford University Press, 2003), 1, 242-44.

5 Indeed, some modern technologies, such as electronic bulletin boards, facilitate and thus encourage barter transactions.

6 According to the International Monetary Fund. See *World Economic Outlook: Focus on Transition* (October 2000): Chapter III, 98–99.

where the arrows indicate the direction of the transaction and the dashes mean no transaction can occur (we assume a good is never exchanged for itself). A total of six transactions are possible.

Now suppose this society elects to call good 1 "money." Any good can be purchased with money and then sold for money to obtain a different good, so there is no longer a need for goods 2 and 3 to be traded with each other. Therefore, a seller now faces only the following transactions:

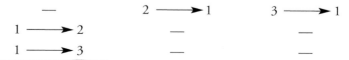

Having a monetary system has reduced the number of potential transactions to four—a more efficient situation. If the economy had more than three goods to exchange, the "savings" would be even greater.

Clearly, a monetary system can reduce transactions costs and simplify trades. Indeed, the bulk of our economy functions only because we use money and thus facilitate exchanges.

THE FUNCTIONS OF MONEY

If a monetary economy is more efficient than a barter economy, money must have special functions that cannot be easily duplicated by anything else. Money is thought to fulfil three basic functions:

1. **Medium of exchange.** Transactions can be settled through the use of the asset called money. This function, probably the most obvious one, eliminates the need for the double coincidence of wants and thereby separates sellers from buyers (you do not have to want to buy a good or service if you want to sell one). Money thus facilitates the division of labour, another aspect of an efficient economy.

2. **Medium (or unit) of account.** The values of goods and services and other assets are denominated in terms of the asset called money. In other words, money provides a standardized way of measuring value in exchange—one that can be recorded for a variety of purposes, not least of which are debts and future payments.[7] The medium of account in Canada is the Canadian dollar.

3. **A store of value and a standard of deferred payment.** The asset called money enables individuals to hold their wealth and postpone purchases or otherwise plan transactions as suits them best. You can store wealth in other assets (think of diamonds and land, as well as bank accounts and bonds), but their usefulness may vary with their **liquidity**, the ease and low cost with which they can be traded for the medium of exchange. If the asset storing wealth is itself the medium of exchange, that asset is said to be perfectly liquid. Since the purchasing power inherent in the value of holding money lasts through time, money permits individuals to rearrange their consumption as they see fit. In other words, money allows payments for goods and services to be deferred.

Unfortunately, it is not always clear which type of financial asset meets the standards of these three functions. For example, some have suggested that money must be designated as legal tender—

7 The medium of account function is sometimes called the unit of account function. The former phrase is more correct, because some physical item, be it gold, silver, or paper, has always served as money. Units of account do not exist, however. For example, the International Monetary Fund expresses the values of some assets in the SDR (special drawing rights) even though no currency bearing the name circulates.

ECONOMICS FOCUS 2.1   LOSING THEIR MONOPOLY?

A distinguishing feature of twentieth-century monetary policy was the development of central banking institutions endowed with a monopoly over the issue of coins and currency as the only items with the status of legal tender. As the twentieth century came to a close, however, financial innovations, driven by technology and deregulation, led to the introduction of transactions media that, while not having the status of legal tender, were virtually the same. Credit cards, of course, come to mind. Credit cards fulfil multiple roles, and their use is influenced to a limited extent by market interest rates and other regulatory policies. The banking system is also used to settle our accounts or to effectively borrow in the form of an outstanding credit card balance. Debit cards come closer to a true transactions medium and have the advantage to the owners of permitting their funds to earn interest right up to the point of making a purchase. Admittedly, there are implicit costs to the user in the form of transactions fees. In addition, the provider of a debit card terminal may also face extra costs, such as charges for installing and operating the terminal. Nevertheless, these costs may be lower than the so-called shoe-leather costs economists use (see Chapter 12) to describe the costs of ensuring that enough cash is on hand for everyday purchases. Not all merchants have debit card terminals, and the debit card is simply a device to allow the transfer of funds between one bank account and another more quickly and more safely than would otherwise be the case. Consequently, there are no immediate implications for the loss of control in the area of monetary policy.

The development of the Internet and the resulting creation of electronic, or e-money, is another matter since it conceivably threatens the use of cash itself and is potentially outside the direct control of the monetary authorities and financial sector regulators. At one of the annual Jackson Hole Conferences held by the Federal Reserve Bank of Kansas City, and attended by the world's most influential central bankers, now-governor of the Bank of England, Mervyn King, said that central bankers' monopoly over the issue of money was under threat. Nothing prevents firms, nonfinancial ones in particular, from offering "credits" or "points" that serve as virtual money and can be exchanged for goods and services. Digital transfers permit the shifting of financial wealth without resorting to the banking system, which is intimately linked to the central bank. Ironically, these developments anticipate the return to the private issue of money, quite common in Canada and elsewhere in previous centuries, which is cheered by advocates for private enterprise in the issue of money.

Questions for Discussion

1. What are some of the main hurdles on the way to a "cashless" economy?
2. Why are central bankers and the banks worried about the development of e-money and can they counter the threat in any way?

Sources

Hal Varian, a noted professor of economics at the University of California, Berkeley, maintains a Web site that keeps tabs on e-commerce developments. Go to **www.sims.berkeley.edu/resources/ infoecon/Commerce.html**.

The Center for Research in Electronic Commerce also maintains a Web site with interesting information about e-commerce and e-money. Go to **cism.bus.utexas.edu**.

The article by the governor of the Bank of England, Mervyn King, is available at **www.kc.frb.org**. Go to *Symposium Proceedings*, where you will find the article entitled "Challenges for Monetary Policy: New and Old."

be specified by the government as something that must be accepted in settlement of transactions—if it is to fulfil the medium of exchange function. This corollary connection is inappropriate for at least two reasons. First, a society seeking efficiency eventually will come up with a medium of exchange—one that everyone can identify easily and use confidently—no matter what the government does. Indeed, a government may not be able to enforce the use of an unsuitable medium. History is full of examples of people resorting to alternatives when their governments have either so debased or devalued the legally defined medium of exchange as to render it virtually useless for transactions or have caused a lack of confidence in it as a store of value.

A second problem with the legal tender view is the issue of **transactions costs**, which are the costs associated with converting one asset into another. People will use financial instruments that are not legal tender if doing so reduces transactions costs. For example, tourists often make purchases with travellers' cheques, which are accepted worldwide. They reduce the potential cost of loss or theft, and may even provide some return when exchanged for other currencies. A traveller's cheque or even a credit card may be a better transaction medium than cash.

Another issue is the relationship between the medium of exchange function and the store of value function. Some economists believe that the first need not imply the second. For example, "smart" credit cards and other computer-based devices could, in theory at least, overcome the need for money as a "temporary abode of purchasing power"[8] arising out of the lack of synchronization between sales and purchases.

A wide range of assets generate interest income but are not generally accepted as a means of payment. Why should people treat cash and chequing accounts as stores of value when they could put their wealth in assets such as government bonds that produce a higher return? We are led once more to view the medium of exchange function as the primary one.

2.2   MONETARY STANDARDS

It is not surprising that all but the most unsophisticated societies have adopted some form of money. A society's monetary standard is the basis of its monetary arrangements. Broadly speaking, history has produced two types of monetary standards:

1. A *commodity standard,* in which the monetary unit is some physical asset in a specified quantity and often quality. For example, the U.S. dollar was once specified as "25.8 grains of gold nine-tenth fine." After 1834, 10 Canadian dollars were valued the same as a US $10 Gold Eagle, with a gold content of 232.2 grams. The *circulating medium*—what people actually use as money in exchanges—may be the physical commodity itself, perhaps marked in some special way. For example, metal may be minted into coins, which are called *specie.*

    In a more sophisticated arrangement, the circulating medium may be paper notes—evidence of a promise to pay—that have no intrinsic value but are backed by and convertible into the commodity. Notes and specie can and often have existed simultaneously.

2. A *fiat-money standard,* in which the circulating medium is notes (and perhaps coins with virtually no nonmonetary uses) that are worth whatever the issuing agent—generally a government—says they are worth. (*Fiat* is the Latin word for "let it be done.") Under such a standard, which is also called a *paper money standard,* the value of the circulating currency is guaranteed not by some precious commodity, but by the taxing and borrowing powers of the government.

Very roughly speaking, societies have moved from a pure commodity standard to fiat money, but the transitions have been neither smooth nor continual. Paper-money standards were introduced in Sweden and China many centuries ago.

No monetary standard is perfect. China may have experienced the world's first hyperinflation when it was using a paper money standard in the eleventh and twelfth centuries. The main issue of the bitter U.S. election of 1896 was whether silver should be part of the country's commodity standard. The issue of how to create a monetary standard has also resurfaced in the case of the republics of the former Soviet Union, many of which were anxious to introduce their own paper money. The same issue also surfaced in the debate about replacing existing European currencies with the euro. Issues such as the design, the size, and the number of denominations for what is, after all, a national symbol can become an emotional one.[9]

Myth is important in understanding how good or bad a monetary standard is. Ultimately, what dictates whether one standard is better than another is public confidence and, in the case

---

8 M. Friedman, "The Quantity Theory: A Restatement," in *Studies in the Quantity Theory of Money,* edited by M. Friedman (Chicago: University of Chicago Press, 1956): 3–21, coined the term.

9 On these questions, see the interesting article by Richard K. Abrams, "The Design and Printing of Bank Notes: Considerations When Introducing a New Currency," International Monetary Fund Working Paper 95/26 (March 1995).

ECONOMICS FOCUS 2.2 — MYTH AND MONEY

The natives of the Pacific Island of Yap in Micronesia are renowned for using as the medium of exchange large, circular stones, which are transported by inserting a tree trunk through a hole in their centre. Some of these stones measure as much as four metres in diameter.

The stones have been used for this purpose for almost 2000 years. Since their denominations are quite large, the stones tend nowadays to be used mostly for large transactions such as the sale of land.

So powerful is the myth surrounding these stones that, for fear of breaking them, they are left largely untouched even though their ownership might change hands. Milton Friedman, in an interesting paper, relates how powerful the myth of stone money is on Yap. When Germany took control of the island from Spain at the end of the nineteenth century, the road network was in terrible shape, but the islanders could not be persuaded, even with threats, to rectify the situation—that is, until the Germans began to paint black crosses on the stones to claim them as payment to finance reconstruction work. This action had the desired effect: The roadways were repaired in short order.

Questions for Discussion

1. Do the size and population of Yap make it easier to operate a monetary system based on stone money?
2. Why does the fact that the stones cannot be transported by the owners not pose a problem for the operation of the monetary system?

Sources

M. Friedman, "The Island of Stone Money," Hoover Institute Discussion Paper E-91-3 (1991).

---

of a commodity standard, the demand for and supply of the asset chosen. Nowhere are these points more clearly illustrated than in the case of monetary economists' favourite example, the stone money of Yap, discussed in **Economics Focus 2.2**.

2.3 THE GOLD STANDARD

Throughout recorded history, gold probably has been the commodity most often used as the basis of monetary systems. Gold is scarce but available, has an intrinsic value (that is, it is valued for use in ornaments and in money), and is readily minted. Thus, many countries have used a **gold standard** in which the market for gold dictates the value of money. Canada was on a gold standard from 1854 to 1914, and then again from 1926 to 1931. The Canadian dollar was fixed in terms of gold at par with the U.S. dollar and with a British Sovereign valued at $4.8666 Canadian.

From the time of the Napoleonic Wars until 1914, much of the Western world, including Canada, was on a stricter version of the gold standard. Each major nation specified the gold content of its currency, and anyone holding notes backed by that currency could redeem them on demand, receiving the face value in gold. In effect, this regime fixed the price of gold and, at least theoretically, held exchange rate fluctuations within narrow limits.[10]

This classical gold standard disappeared amid the chaos of World War I, although weaker versions were attempted afterward. Indeed, many economists long for such a classical standard today. The main attraction is the discipline a gold standard appears to impose on the price level. This rigour stems from the fact that, at least in theory, a pure gold standard—one in which circulating notes are backed 100% by gold—leaves no room for discretionary monetary policy of the kind practised by governments and central banks under an unbacked, paper money standard. No country has enough gold to back all its currency, however, so the crucial question is the degree of backing. That amount can be manipulated by government backing, wherein lies one of the principal weaknesses of the gold standard. In the Canadian context, the quantity of so-called Dominion

---

10 Exchange rates would have been fixed if international payments had actually been made in gold. To avoid shipping and insurance costs, the payments were usually made on paper, and exchange rates fluctuated. But if the premium or discount on exchange was greater than the shipping cost of gold, the metal itself was exported or imported.

notes that could be issued without 100% gold backing increased substantially throughout our adherence to the gold standard. Consequently, there appears to have been a conscious attempt made to practise at least some discretionary monetary policy. Indeed, it is the inflexibility of the strict rules of the gold standard that can exacerbate problems facing an economy when it experiences a recession. Add noncooperation among countries participating in the gold standard, all of whom want to escape the recession at the same time, and the result is a recipe for disaster.[11]

BIMETALLISM

Western nations, including the United States in its earlier years, also have had considerable experience with another commodity standard: **bimetallism**, in which the monetary system is based on not one metal, but on two—usually gold and silver with a fixed exchange rate between the two. Typically, gold is used for coins of larger denominations and silver is used for smaller ones. (Because gold is more valuable than silver, gold coins in small denominations would be too tiny to be practical.)

The problem with bimetallism is that the relative market values of the two metals may vary. The outcome may be an instance of **Gresham's Law**, whose general form is: "Bad money drives out good" (that is, cheap money drives out more valuable money). For example, new discoveries of gold may increase the supply of the metal, thus lowering its market price. It might then be profitable to mint the now relatively cheaper gold, replace the gold-backed currency notes with silver-backed ones, and then melt down some silver and sell it as a metal, thereby removing it from the monetary system. Gresham's law manifests itself in other settings, too. For example, different colonies in Canada rated the metal content of their coins differently. This rating implied the deliberate overvaluing of some coins and the undervaluing of others, given their weight in gold or silver, thereby encouraging or discouraging their use.[12]

CANADA'S EARLY PAPER MONEY

Canada had unhappy early experiences with monetary standards in which the circulating medium was something other than a metal. The persistent shortage of metals from the home countries of Great Britain and France forced local governments to issue various media of exchange ostensibly backed by anticipated shipments of gold or silver. During the French colonial period, for example, playing cards, and later, pieces of cardboard were authorized as temporary media of exchange. Card money was cut in several different sizes to reflect the need for several denominations. Not surprisingly, the authorities in France, for example, were not pleased with this development since it meant a loss of revenues (see the last section of this chapter for an explanation). So long as these devices were fully backed by future redemptions[13] they proved successful. But the advent of the British colonial period and the debasing of card money ushered in an era during which people displayed a distinct preference for some metallic money standard. Although the War of 1812 meant the return to a paper standard, known as Army bills, they were eventually redeemed in full.

The redemption of Army bills did not eliminate the need for some medium of exchange. Prior to Confederation in 1867 it was believed that a private note issue would be the best way to satisfy the need for money. It was understood that the circulating bank notes would be redeemable in gold. It was under these circumstances that well-known banks of today, including the Bank of Nova Scotia and the Bank of Montreal came into existence. Governments were reluctant to issue notes in the then-Provinces of Upper and Lower Canada. Circulating coins made their appearance only in

---

11 For a fascinating and highly readable account of the final years of the gold standard, see Barry Eichengreen, *Golden Fetters* (New York: Oxford University Press, 1992).

12 A fine account of the story of bimetallism is by Angela Redish (2000), *Bimetallism: An Economic and Social History* (Cambridge: Cambridge University Press).

13 Meaning that when the actual currency was shipped in the future, it would replace the temporary currency.

ECONOMICS FOCUS 2.3   BIMETALLISM AND THE WIZARD OF OZ

During much of the nineteenth century, the United States operated on a free coinage basis: that is, gold coins could be exchanged for silver coins and vice versa at a fixed exchange rate. The difficulty was that the price of silver became such that it was profitable to melt down gold and use only part of it to buy silver. The cheap silver dollar thus drove out gold, as Gresham's Law predicts.

Free coinage was suspended in 1873, and a 20-year battle over bimetallism ensued. One bimetallist was L. Frank Baum, whose best-known book, *The Wizard of Oz*, was published in 1900. Rockoff (1990) argues that the children's classic is actually an allegorical account of the battle for silver that reached its height during the Democratic convention of 1896. "Oz," he says, refers to an ounce of gold; the "Wicked Witch of the East" is President Grover Cleveland, a Democrat but an Easterner and an ardent defender of the gold standard; the "yellow brick road" refers to gold and it leads to "Emerald City," which is really Washington, D.C.; and the silver (not ruby as in the movie) slippers that solve Dorothy's problems are an allusion to the silver component of a bimetallic standard.

The 1896 convention was primarily a battle between the pro-gold Easterners and the pro-silver Populists (mostly Westerners) led by William Jennings Bryan. The latter's famous speech, ending "You shall not press down upon the brow of labor this crown of thorns, you shall not crucify mankind upon a cross of gold," won him his party's nomination. Although he carried most of the West and the South, he lost the election to William McKinley, a supporter of the gold standard.

Unlike many contemporaries, who believed the bimetallists were cranks, the Populists actually had good reason to want to see a gold-and-silver standard—though by the time they attained political influence, it was too late.

Questions for Discussion

1. Can you think of other examples of Gresham's Law in action?
2. What was it about the gold standard that led the Populists to favour a bimetallic standard?

Sources

M. Friedman, "The Crime of 1873," *Journal of Political Economy* 98 (December 1990): 1159–94.

H. Rockoff, "*The Wizard of Oz* as a Monetary Allegory," *Journal of Political Economy* 98 (August 1990): 739–60.

1858. The private banks realized, of course, that it could be quite profitable to issue notes that pay zero interest while the resulting deposits created by the note issue could be lent out at a positive interest rate. One way to understand why this development is possible is to recognize that monetary standards in Canada, and elsewhere, tended to be based on some metallic standard, in particular the gold standard. Hence, the notes or certificates issued or backed by the gold held by banks would have value to the holder so long as the notes could be confidently converted into gold. Such monetary systems are referred to as convertible systems and the notes or certificates are called "token money" since they have no *intrinsic* value. It was worthwhile accepting zero interest on the notes so long as the gold was kept secure and the notes were acceptable as a means of payment.

We examine the money creation process in more detail in Chapter 16. By 1866 provincial notes were introduced in order to profit from the foregone seigniorage (the concept is defined in more detail later in this chapter) opportunity. Governments effectively had a monopoly over small denomination notes, while the private banks circulated larger denomination notes.

Following Confederation, dominion notes replaced the provincial notes and the first Bank Act was introduced (see Chapter 17). The arrival of World War I led to the suspension of convertibility of the note issue into gold, and the suspension was made more or less permanent after the collapse of the gold standard in 1929. Dominion notes and private bank notes would eventually be replaced by Bank of Canada notes, beginning in the mid-1930s when Canada created its very own central bank. Although private banks lost the seigniorage opportunity from the private note issue, they had, in any event, begun to rely more heavily on cheques as a means of creating profitable opportunities in banking.[14]

---

14 For pictures and a few additional details about the history of currency in Canada, see "The Currency Museum at the Bank of Canada" at **http://collections.ic.gc.ca/bank/english/**, and J. Powell, "A History of the Canadian Dollar," available at **www.bankofcanada.ca/en/dollar_book/full_tex-et.htm**

FIAT MONEY AND CENTRAL BANKS

The widespread introduction of a fiat-money standard characterized the industrialized world in the twentieth century.[15] The value of the medium of exchange is guaranteed only by the taxing and borrowing power of the government.

The increasing importance of the central banks has paralleled the adoption of the fiat-money standard. A **central bank** is a national bank responsible for the control and management of the country's money supply.[16] Canada's central bank is the **Bank of Canada**. The bills in your wallet are notes that the Bank issues.

Central banks are usually (but not always) owned by the public sector and have a legally defined relationship with the government of the day. Their independence from political interference can be fragile, and is sometimes open to complete subversion. For example, crises such as wars may lead a government to force its central bank to issue ever-larger quantities of money, resulting in hyperinflation.

2.4   MEASURING THE MONEY SUPPLY

How much money is in Canada today? Or, to put the question another way, what is the Canadian money supply? The answer, which is not a simple one, raises many of the issues to be addressed in this text.

The **money supply**, often called the **money stock**,[17] is the amount of money in an economy that is easily available for use in payments (that is, to exchange for other assets, including money itself in some other form). Measuring that amount would be straightforward if only Bank of Canada notes and coins were in circulation. But in Canada, as in almost all countries, considerably more money is "easily available for use in payments." Consider what various financial institutions have in their tills and vaults; individuals' and firms' bank deposits (which are of many different types, some of which are denominated in foreign currency); Canada Savings Bonds; credit card balances; and so on. The problem is knowing where to stop.

After pausing for a few definitions of terms, we list the empirical definitions of the money supply that are in general use. Then we touch briefly on a few theoretical views and objections.

SOME HELPFUL CONCEPTS

Before we launch into a list of definitions of the money supply, it will be helpful to mention a few terms and concepts (most of which are covered in more detail later in the text).

Types of Banks and Deposits

Canadian law used to differentiate between *chartered banks* (institutions such as the Bank of Montreal, the Royal Bank, and the Bank of Nova Scotia) and other financial institutions (trust companies, credit unions, and Quebec's caisses populaires). As we will see, although the distinctions have almost completely disappeared, they still make a difference in arriving at some measures of the money supply.

---

15 In fact, efforts to stay on or be tied to the gold standard lasted well into the twentieth century. The United States held to it until 1971. During much of the immediate post–World War II period, most other Western countries tied their standard largely to the fortunes of the U.S. dollar, as we see in Chapter 3.

16 As we discuss in several later chapters, a central bank may have other responsibilities, specific or implicit. Chapters 22 and 23 deal extensively with central banks, including their independence (or lack of independence) from governments.

17 The term "stock" is useful here because it reminds us that we are dealing with a stock variable—that is, the amount of money outstanding at a particular moment in time, such as 31 December 2005. Recall (from your principles of economics or business courses) that the opposite is a flow variable, which is a quantity measured over a period of time, such as your income last month or the economy's output during 2005. We use many flow variables in this textbook, but the money supply is not one of them.

Both individuals and firms make deposits in banks. In essence, a depositor lends the money to the deposit-taking institution, which is responsible for repaying it in the future with interest. Thus, deposits are assets to the individual and liabilities to the institution. (Similarly, a loan is an asset to the lender and a liability to the borrower.)

The variety of deposit accounts available seems limited only by the imagination of the banks' marketing staffs and by the regulations imposed by law. Nevertheless, all deposits are one of four basic types:

1. **Current accounts** and **personal chequable accounts** must be repaid to the individuals without their having given prior notice (that is, the funds must be returned "on demand"). Such accounts pay little or no interest, but cheques can be written against them.

2. **Savings deposits** may require notice to be accessible, although this is no longer a requirement for personal savings accounts, the most common type in this category. Such accounts pay more interest than current accounts and nowadays generally are chequable.

3. **Term deposits** are made for a fixed term. Early withdrawal may require notice and can mean a loss of the relatively higher interest the deposit would earn if left until maturity. Such accounts typically are not chequable.

4. **Money market mutual funds (MMMFs)** are accounts that pool funds that are then used to purchase large quantities of money market instruments such as Treasury bills. Technically, depositors acquire "shares" from the fund, but they are essentially interest-bearing deposits. The idea for MMMFs originated in the United States as a reaction to restrictive banking regulations in that country.

Although the above deposit types apply to everyone, statistics make a distinction between deposits that are "personal," that is, in the name of an individual or small group of individuals, and those that are nonpersonal, such as current accounts or corporate deposits.

Cheques and Cheque-Clearing

A cheque is simply a written order for a bank to transfer a specific amount of funds from the writer's account to someone else.

If the economy had only a single bank, even one with many branches, sorting out cheques at the end of each day would be simple. Some of the recipients of cheques would have taken their payments in cash; others would have deposited the funds to their accounts, which would mean just bookkeeping entries for the bank. But Canada has many banks and trust companies that use cheques (and similar transfers) against accounts. Suppose your mother writes you a cheque on her account at a branch of the CIBC in St. John's, and you deposit it in your Ottawa branch of the TD-Canada Trust, then immediately write a cheque to your landlord who deposits it later in the day in an account at a Kingston branch of the Royal Bank. Given that these sorts of transfers occur thousands of times every day, how do the financial institutions keep everyone's account straight?

The answer is a clearinghouse, which sorts out net interbank payments. All Canadian banks and trust companies belong to the **Canadian Payments Association**, which operates an automated cheque-clearing system.[18] The CPA was created by an Act of Parliament in 1980 and is mandated to accomplish two primary objectives: (1) to develop and operate the national clearing and settlement system, and (2) to plan the evolution of the national payments system.

The Act was amended in 2001 essentially to add a third mandate for the Association, namely to facilitate the development of new technologies that might impact the payments system. The

---

18 Cheque-clearing is the reason for the string of numerals at the bottom of a cheque. The last few digits identify a particular account. The first few indicate the institution, the branch, and what is called a transit (routing) number.

organization of the CPA consists of a board of 16 members that manages the Association, chaired by a senior Bank of Canada official. Three members of the Board are appointed by the Minister of Finance, with the remaining 12 members elected by the membership of the CPA. Since the CPA is now a separate agency, dues raised from Association members finance operations.

Computer technology has vastly increased the speed of cheque-clearing. Nevertheless, it does take time, and some cheques always are in transit. Thus, a cheque drawn on an account at a branch in one bank and put into an account in a different bank may appear as funds deposited with the recipient bank before those funds actually have been withdrawn from the first bank. When the Bank of Canada tallies the portion of the money supply that is held by financial institutions, it would be easy to double count such amounts. To avoid that situation, an estimated amount called the *private sector float* is used to adjust the demand deposit figures.

The growth of electronically based transactions is reflected in Table 2.1, which shows that the volume of paper-based transactions has fallen by more than half since 1994. During the same period, the volume of electronic transactions has risen more than fourfold. The dollar value of paper versus electronic transactions has also risen quickly.

Visit the CPA on the Internet at **www.cdnpay.ca**

2.5 DEFINITIONS OF THE MONEY SUPPLY

Table 2.2, lists the definitions from narrowest to broadest for August 2004.
The definitions used in Canada are:

1. Currency in circulation. The narrowest possible definition of the money supply is the *currency in circulation*—that is, the currency outside the banking system. These Bank of Canada notes and coins represent, as already explained, a debt of the government accepted by the public. The actual amount is estimated by subtracting bank holdings of notes and coins from amounts reported outstanding by the Bank of Canada and the Royal Canadian Mint.[19]

2. M1. The currency in circulation plus current, demand, and personal chequing accounts (net of the private sector float) is called **M1**. This measure of the money supply was long popular in financial circles and economic studies of the impact of monetary policy because it appears to be the definition that most closely specifies money as it fulfils the medium of exchange function. It is still much used.[20]

3. M2. If we add to M1 personal savings deposits (which are notice deposits but often have a variety of chequable features) and the notice deposits of firms (often called nonpersonal deposits) at chartered banks, we obtain the **M2** measure of the money supply. M2 captures some of the impact of financial innovations in the payment system better than M1 does. Indeed, the component of the Canadian money supply that is notice deposits grew quickly over the years, indicating that innovations permitting a combination of high interest rates and chequing privileges had attracted depositors despite the relatively high inflation of the later 1970s and the 1980s.

4. M2+. The increasing importance of financial institutions other than chartered banks led the Bank of Canada to start reporting a new monetary aggregate, **M2+**, which is M2 plus the deposits held by a variety of other financial institutions. The fact that M2+ is 40% larger than M2 has led the Bank to suggest that it prefers to monitor movement in the broader measure

---

19 From the perspective of the Bank of Canada, it can only control the so-called monetary base or high-powered money, which is the sum of currency in circulation and reserves of the banking system. The latter fell substantially with banking regulation reforms in the early 1990s. In any event, obtaining data for the monetary base is not as straightforward as for the other aggregates discussed here.

20 Actually, the definition the Bank of Canada refers to is called Gross M1. A variety of small adjustments are made to M1 to arrive at the Gross M1 figure. See the notes to Table E1 in Bank of Canada *Banking and Monetary Statistics*.

Table 2.1	Paper versus Electronic Transactions in Canada			
	Paper-Based		Electronic	
	Volume	Dollar Value	Volume	Dollar Value
Year	% of Transactions		% of Transactions	
1994	69.4	98.9	30.6	1.1
1995	61.8	98.3	38.2	1.7
1996	53.7	97.4	46.3	2.6
1997	47.5	97.3	52.5	2.7
1998	43.0	97.6	56.7	3.1
1999	38.6	91.0	61.4	9.0
2000	35.0	85.6	65.0	14.4
2001	31.5	83.1	68.5	16.9
2002	29.3	80.5	70.7	19.5
2003	26.5	73.2	73.5	26.8
2004	25.0	69.8	75	30.2

Source: Canadian Payments Association, **www.cdnpay.ca**.

The figures apply to transactions using the Automated Clearing and Settlement System. Paper items include mostly cheques, travellers' cheques, and money orders. Electronic items include debit card payments and other electronic media used to settle payments. Figures in original source for 1998 do not add to 100 percent. The Figure for 2004 is for June of that year.

when it is carrying out its monetary policy. Indeed, the Bank looked even further; in early 1992, it began to include in M2+ money market mutual funds—funds invested in short-term instruments. M2+ now includes deposits at Alberta Treasury branches, deposits at Province of Ontario Savings offices, and life insurance companies' individual annuities. It is easy to see the growing importance of M2+, which reflects the role of financial institutions other than chartered banks (see Chapter 19).

5. M3. The **M3** monetary aggregate is M2 with two additions: fixed-term deposits and the Canadian dollar value of chartered bank deposits denominated in foreign currencies (mostly U.S. dollars) but owned by Canadian residents. This broader aggregate is useful in understanding monetary policy and general economic activity. At one time, this measure was one of the broadest aggregates available until nonchartered banking institutions became important players in the financial system.

Some Possible Refinements

Still broader measures could be constructed to reflect some highly liquid assets. Some people suggest including Canada Savings Bonds (not included in the narrow money supply measures, such as M1, M2, or M3), which are cashable anytime at little cost and are thus sometimes used in lieu of bank deposits. Others suggest including the unused portion of credit card balances.[21] Still others like to look at consumer or residential mortgage credit. Unlike the monetary aggregates covered in this chapter, however, these are assets to the banking system, not liabilities.

A drawback of all the money supply definitions presented here is that each comprises what people perceive as qualitatively different assets. For example, most people view currency and daily interest accounts as distinct kinds of assets, yet the M2 measure adds them together. Partly as a response to such concerns, analysts have developed *divisia indexes*, which weigh the components

---

21 However, credit cards actually add to the volume of transactions, not to the money supply. Consider that a credit card purchase actually creates two debts: one between the card issuer and the merchant and one between the card issuer and the individual holding the card.

Table 2.2	The Canadian Money Supply, August 2004 (Millions of Dollars)[a]	
Currency outside banks		$ 41 684[c]
Accounts at chartered banks		
Personal chequing accounts		34 865[c]
Current accounts		86 049[c]
Net demand deposits		122 844
M1[b]		**162 368**
Nonpersonal notice deposits		59 551
Personal savings deposits		399 487
M2		**623 318**
Nonpersonal term deposits and foreign currency deposits		250 627
M3		**868 017**
Accounts at other financial institutions		
Trust and mortgage loan companies		10 115[c]
Credit unions and caisses populaires		139 165
Life insurance companies' individual annuities		37 678[c]
Personal deposits at government-owned savings institutions		7 833
Money market mutual funds		53 672
M2+		**872 466[c]**
Other monetary aggregates		
Canada Savings Bonds		21 104
Nonmoney market mutual funds		371 672
M2++		**1 262 935[c]**
Chequable notice deposits at chartered banks		230 754
Chequable deposits at trust companies, mortgage loan companies, credit unions, and caisses populaires		
M1+[d]		**329 422**
Nonchequable deposits at trust companies, mortgage loan companies, credit unions, and caisses populaires		
M1++		**428 307**
Credit measures		
Total consumer credit		259 262[c]
Residential mortgage credit		568 921[c]
Total household credit		**828 183[c]**
Short-term business credit		260 900
Other business credit		693 920
Total business credit		**954 479**
Total household and business credit		**1 779 037**

Sources: Bank of Canada Monetary and Financial Statistics, July 2002, and Weekly Financial Statistics, available at **www.bankofcanada.ca**

Notes:

[a] Not all components are shown. Therefore, items need not add up exactly to money supply figures shown. All figures are seasonally adjusted.
[b] Gross M1, which is M1 less adjustments to M1.
[c] July 2004 figure. Figures are estimates.
[d] M1+ is (Gross) M1 plus all chequable deposits at trust companies, mortgage loan companies, and credit unions and caisses populaires. See notes to Table E1, Bank of Canada *Banking and Monetary Statistics.*

of the various money supply measures according to the degree to which they provide liquidity. Such alternative measures have an obvious attraction, but they too have drawbacks.[22]

---

22 Discussion of these problems would take us too far afield. See D.E.W. Laidler, *The Demand for Money: Theories, Evidence, and Problems* (New York: Harper & Row, 1985): 85. The Bank of Canada ceased publishing divisia monetary aggregates in 1990 because they were expensive to produce and did not outperform the simple-sum aggregates in Table 2.2 as indicators of monetary policy. See David Longworth, and Joseph Atta-Mensah, "The Canadian Experience with Weighted Monetary Aggregates," Bank of Canada Working Paper 95-10 (October 1995).

WHY SO MANY MONETARY AGGREGATES?

In principle, it is difficult to argue that no connection exists between the money supply and inflation or GDP. The Bank of Canada emphasizes this connection repeatedly when it states, for example, that monetary aggregates such as M1 "…provide important information as indicators of near term developments."[23] As noted earlier, the link between the money supply and key macroeconomic aggregates has evolved over time because of financial innovations and deregulation. The sharp rise in interest rates throughout the 1970s led households to switch to higher yielding but relatively liquid assets, such as daily interest accounts and mutual funds. In response to these developments, the Bank of Canada has introduced a series of new monetary aggregates, namely M2++, M1+, and M1++. The details of their construction are in Table 2.2, while Figure 2.1 shows their evolution relative to some of the older, more widely used monetary aggregates of the past.

It has long been known that the construction of a useful monetary aggregate is complicated by the introduction of financial innovations; the problem is not just a Canadian one, but one that has affected almost every industrial country over the past decade. If this is the case then, unless policymakers can immediately observe these innovations, it is difficult to know which aggregate to use. Hence, even if monetary aggregates are a crucial variable in economic analysis, the multiplicity of definitions poses a serious challenge to adherents of the view that monetary policy actions are best viewed through the lens of money growth data.[24]

| Figure 2.1 | **Selected Canadian Money Supply Aggregates** |

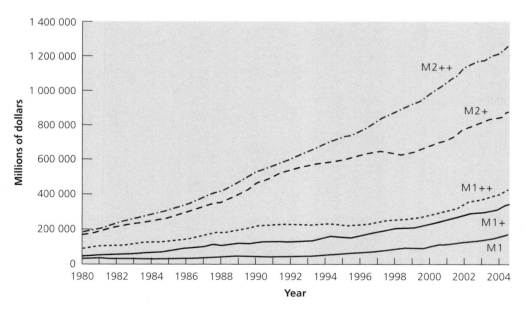

Economists are interested in the relationship of the size of the various components of the money supply over time. During the 1980 to 2002 period shown here, M1 changed relatively little. The explosive growth was in term deposits and the deposits of financial institutions other than the chartered banks.

Source: Adapted from the Statistics Canada CANSIM II database **http://cansim2.statcan.ca/cgi-win/CNSMCGI.EXE**, series V37124 (M1), series V37151 (M1+), series V27152 (M1++), series V37131 (M2+), and series V37150 (M2++).

Note: All data are seasonally adjusted.

23 Bank of Canada, *Monetary Policy Report* (May 1995): 18.

24 For more details on this issue and a return to favour of sorts of monetary aggregates in economic analysis, see P.L. Siklos, and A.G. Barton, "Monetary Aggregates as Indicators of Economic Activity in Canada: Empirical Evidence," *Canadian Journal of Economics* 34 (2001): 1–17.

ECONOMICS FOCUS 2.4   MONEY SUPPLY ANNOUNCEMENTS

The text explains some of the issues in the measurement of the money supply, but there are many others. One is the problem of public announcements about the money supply and subsequent revisions to the data. Every week you can find in the daily press preliminary announcements about the amount of money that is expected to be injected into the economy as well as announcements about the rate of growth in GDP and the unemployment rate. A closer look at some important statistical publications, such as the *Bank of Canada Weekly Financial Statistics*, confirms, however, that many preliminary figures are later revised (they are indicated by an "R" next to the statistics in question). If, as many economists believe, money supply announcements influence investors' and policymakers' decisions and therefore affect interest rates and stock prices, to name two obvious examples, then it is of some interest to consider how the revised and actual figures compare with each other. Although most of the work has been done on U.S. data (see Siklos 1996 and references therein), it is likely that the results apply to the Canadian case as well.

Because data revisions may be thought of as unanticipated or unexpected money supply announcements, economic theory dictates that these should have real effects on the economy—unlike the announced figures, which, if treated as forecasts of the money supply, should be digested or discounted by the public. The difficulty is that the distinction between what the public expects and

what it terms a "surprise" (unexpected monetary policy) is a subject of considerable controversy. The current state of the debate is mixed. There is some evidence that the preliminary announcements, if they are treated as if they were forecasts, could be improved. Therefore, information available to the monetary authorities could be, but is not, exploited by individuals.

Questions for Discussion

1. If money supply data are revised frequently, would investors not be wise to simply ignore this information?
2. Do the size and importance of announcement effects imply that our interpretation of monetary policy actions could be influenced by the vintage of the data being analyzed?

Sources

K.A. Mork, "Forecastable Money Growth Revisions: A Closer Look at the Data," *Canadian Journal of Economics* 23 (August 1990): 593–616. See also the references therein.

P.L. Siklos, "An Empirical Analysis of Revisions in US Macroeconomic Aggregates," *Applied Financial Economics* 6 (February 1996). See also references therein.

P.L. Siklos and J. Anusiewicz, "The Effect of Canadian and US M1 Announcements on Canadian Financial Markets: The Crow Years," *Journal of Economics and Business* 50 (Jan/Feb 1998): 49–66.

Seasonal Adjustment

The public's demand for cash and use of chequing accounts is not evenly distributed over the course of a year. (It is, for example, always high at Christmas time.) Data series are often *seasonally adjusted* to smooth some of the normal variations (see Figure 2.2).

Seasonal adjustment is a useful device for many users of money supply data. It does, however, remove information that is useful to some analysts, such as those trying to make short-term forecasts that depend on the amount of cash or the volume of cheques written in the economy.[25] Luckily, seasonal adjustment becomes less drastic (and less necessary) as we move from narrow to broad definitions of the money supply.

---

25 Some analysts claim that the regular use of seasonally adjusted data has led to omissions of important elements in our understanding of business cycles (fluctuations over time in economic activity). See R.B. Barsky and J.A. Miron, "The Seasonal Cycle and the Business Cycle," *Journal of Political Economy* 97 (June 1989): 53–34. The technique used to filter out seasonal influences is called X-11, a name coined by the U.S. Census Bureau and used worldwide. The Canadian contribution to seasonal modelling is an important one. See Estella Bee Dagum, *The X-11 ARIMA Seasonal Adjustment Method* (Ottawa: Statistics Canada, 1980). Unfortunately, applying X-11 does appear to do undesirable things to time series, but most practitioners are not aware of the problem. See Eric Ghysels, Clive W.J. Granger, and Pierre L. Siklos, "Is Seasonal Adjustment a Linear or Non-Linear Data Filtering Process?" *Journal of Business and Economic Statistics* (July 1996). A new seasonal adjustment technique, called X-12, apparently improves on the X-11 technique, but most of the series used in this text still rely on a version of the X-11 approach.

Figure 2.2   **Currency in Circulation: Seasonally Adjusted and Unadjusted**

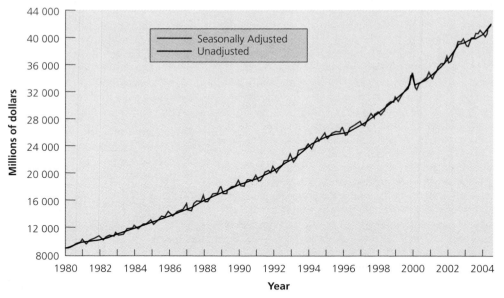

The seasonally adjusted data are smooth; the other series represents the raw data that always peak at Christmas.

Source: Adapted from the Statistics Canada CANSIM II database **http://cansim2.statcan.ca/cgi-win/CNSMCGI.EXE**, series V37148 (adjusted figures) and series V37173 (unadjusted figures).

2.6   INFLATION, DEFLATION, AND SOCIAL WELFARE

We have already mentioned inflation several times in this text, and will do so often again. Since inflation is a monetary phenomenon and influences the financial sector in important ways, it is useful to pause and ask: What is the phenomenon and how does it affect social welfare?

Inflation is an increase in the general level of prices. To put the point another way, inflation reduces the *purchasing power* of money; when the price level rises, a given amount of money buys less than it did before.

There are two types of inflation. Inflation can be fully anticipated, in which case, for example, individuals still may have to make more frequent trips to the bank for cash, assuming they always keep a fixed amount of cash on hand. In Chapter 12 we will introduce a framework that allows us to predict how much cash individuals will choose to hold, given interest rates and the frequency with which interest is paid. In addition, the menu costs described above also are incurred even when inflation is fully anticipated. When individuals make forecast errors, inflation is then unexpected, or unanticipated. It is these costs that policymakers have learned to try to avoid. One way inflation has become more predictable is through a policy of inflation targeting, whereby the central bank, with the tacit support of the government, promises to deliver an inflation rate within a narrow range. We shall study this type of policy in Chapter 23.

Does inflation lessen social welfare? Yes, because it redistributes income, often in unanticipated and socially harmful ways.

1. Inflation can upset the debtor–creditor relationship. As we discuss later in this text, anyone who borrows or lends funds is making a guess about the future course of inflation. The less predictable future prices are, the more likely are negative consequences for lender or borrower.

2. Inflation means that individuals and firms must spend more money to obtain the things they need. So the government must create more money with a consequent increase in **seigniorage**, which is the government's profit from issuing money.[26] Government may spend these extra funds in ways different from the ways the original holders of the money would have spent it.

3. In response to inflation, individuals devote ever more resources to minimizing their cash holdings, which creates a deadweight loss for society (see Chapter 3). One estimate places the social cost of 10% inflation at almost 0.3% of the gross national product.[27] Other estimates are higher.

4. For the most part, our tax system is based on the *nominal* magnitudes of income and expenses, which by definition do not reflect inflation.[28] Although the system has some adjustments for large increases in inflation, tax liabilities tend to rise over time, leading many people to devote valuable resources to minimizing them.

5. As inflation accelerates, firms need to change forms more often, and this process has costs associated with it called "menu costs." The term is derived from the notion that it is expensive to print new menus at restaurants every time prices change (and more so the more frequent are price adjustments!).

6. Inflation poses problems for the accounting profession, which typically records assets and liabilities at "historical costs," not at their current (inflated) value.

7. Higher inflation usually leads to more variable inflation, which exacerbates the difficulties faced by households and firms in forecasting future cash needs.

8. Once inflation is deemed to be unacceptably high, there are potential unemployment or output costs of reducing inflation to a more tolerable level. Others have argued that lowering inflation from very high levels (say 100% to 10%) brings with it net gains in economywide output and productivity.[29] The debate still is unsettled, particularly for economies with moderate-to-low inflation rates.[30]

Surveys of inflation reveal that the public dislikes inflation but is not keen on indexation either because it does not believe that institutions will fully index losses of purchasing power.[31] Those who argue that some inflation is beneficial rest their arguments on the notion of "nominal rigidities," meaning that contracts and other institutional impediments make it difficult to accept lower salaries or wages when prices are falling or are not rising very quickly. However, considerable disagreement remains about how to interpret the existing data, especially about wage settlements. Although the exact size of the social costs of inflation has been hotly debated, there is a consensus that society is clearly better off when inflation is low, even if it is not zero.

It is in large part for this reason that many central banks have opted for inflation targets that range from 1% to 3%. In Chapter 23 we will explore why policymakers in Canada, and elsewhere, opted for inflation targeting.

---

26 The word dates from the days when kings and nobles minted coins. They often imposed a fee for turning individuals' gold or silver into coins; they also got to keep the inevitable shavings, which could add up to a sizable amount.

27 B.T. McCallum, *Monetary Economics: Theory and Policy* (New York: Macmillan, 1989): 128.

28 Suppose you earned $10 an hour last year and paid income taxes on that amount. Suppose, too, that inflation last year was 10%. If you receive a 10% raise, your real income (that is, the amount of goods your income will purchase) does not change at all. But this year you will pay taxes on $11 an hour.

29 See Michael Bruno and William Easterly, "Inflation Crises and Long-Run Growth," *Journal of Monetary Economics* 41 (February 1998): 3–26.

30 For a tolerant view of steady (but low) inflation, see James Tobin, "Stabilization Policy Ten Years After," *Brookings Papers on Economic Activity* I (1990). For an opposite view, see Peter W. Howitt, "Zero Inflation as a Long-Term Target for Monetary Policy," in Richard G. Lipsey (ed.), *Zero Inflation: The Goal of Price Stability*, Policy Study 8 (Toronto: C.D. Howe Institute, 1990).

31 See Robert J. Shiller, "Public Resistance to Indexation: A Puzzle," *Brookings Papers on Economic Activity* (1997): 159–621 and "Why Do People Dislike Inflation?" in *Reducing Inflation: Motivation and Strategy*, C.D. Romer and D.H. Romer (eds.) (Chicago: University of Chicago Press, 1997): 13–65.

Recently concern shifted briefly from worrying about the economic consequences of inflation to the potential dangers of _deflation_. Deflation occurs when there is a general decline in prices. There have not been too many examples of deflation since the 1930s but, by the 1990s, China and Japan, two very large economies, were in the throes of a deflation and fears of deflation were spreading to Europe and the United States. Interestingly, Canada was not on the "hit list" for deflation, possibly because of our policy to aim for a positive inflation rate. Is deflation different from inflation? Academics still debate this issue, and although there is no general consensus there is widespread belief that deflation is worse than inflation.[32] There are at least three reasons why:

1. When prices fall, the real value of outstanding debt rises. Therefore, borrowers are penalized for holding debt, and the effective cost of repaying that debt rises. We shall be able to quantify these effects in Chapters 5 and 6.

2. When prices fall there is the danger that individuals will begin to think that prices in future will continue to fall. If those beliefs become ingrained, then major purchases of durables such as appliances and automobiles will be postponed until absolutely necessary. After all, why buy big-ticket items now when they can be purchased more cheaply later?

3. We have already seen, in Chapter 1, that there is a connection between inflation and nominal interest rates. Therefore, as prices keep falling, so will nominal interest rates. What happens if they fall to zero (as they did in Japan and in the U.S. in the 1930s)? Some economists believe that the central bank will run out of amunition to combat deflation. After all, interest rates can't fall below zero (or can they? See Economics Focus 5.1). In any event, this barrier to interest rates is called the "zero lower bound." Others argue that when interest rates fall to zero the central bank can stem deflationary pressures by increasing the money supply.[33] Open-market operations, as they are called, is the device to accomplish this result. We introduce this concept in Chapter 6.

SUMMARY

- Money exists because it produces benefits relative to those in a barter economy.

- Money is useful because it satisfies three functions: medium of account, medium of exchange, and store of value.

- Monetary standards have evolved over time. The movement essentially has been from a commodity-based monetary system to a paper-based or fiat monetary system. Other systems that have proven to be popular from time to time include bimetallism.

- The gold standard has proven to be an especially popular regime because, in theory, it

provides the least amount of discretion to policymakers.

- In recent years, as the predictive ability to forecast inflation and GDP growth has waned, the Bank of Canada has introduced several new definitions of monetary aggregates.

- There is no unique definition of the money supply. Several definitions coexist. In the remainder of the text we emphasize the narrower definitions such as M1 and M2.

- Existing monetary aggregates, even the recently developed ones, do not include a host

---

32 See Richard C.K. Burdekin and Pierre L. Siklos, _Deflation: Current and Historical Perspectives_ (Cambridge: Cambridge University Press, 2004). Accesible accounts that describe deflation and its consequences also can be found at **www.eh.net**; Pierre L. Siklos, "Is Deflation A Treat? Part I: The Lessons of History"; and Richard C.K. Burdekin, Pierre L. Siklos, and Thomas D. Willett, "Is Deflation A Treat? Part II: Warding off Deflation Today," Claremont Policy Briefs, available at **http://lowe.claremontmckenna.edu/publications/briefs.asp**

33 For a collection of articles dealing with deflation, see Pierre L. Siklos, _The Economics of Deflation_ (Northampton, MA: Edward Elgar, 2005).

of other assets, some more liquid than others, which serve some of the functions of money. Examples include credit card limits and household and business credit.

- Several empirical definitions of money exist. The narrowest is called M1 and consists of currency and demand deposits. One of the broadest is M3, which includes M1, savings deposits, fixed-term, and foreign currency deposits at banks. Another broad measure of the money supply is M2+, which includes deposits at banks other than chartered banks.

- The survival of a monetary standard is partly a function of whether money retains its purchasing power over time. Inflation reduces the purchasing power of money over time and imposes social costs on society.

Consequently, some economists advocate that we aim for low inflation, defined as inflation between 1 and 3 percent in Canada.

- Examples of some of the social costs of inflation include the upset of the debtor–creditor relationship, the government revenue motive for inflation, the added costs of distinguishing nominal from real magnitudes, and the uncertainty associated with higher and more volatile prices.

- In recent years worries over deflation were raised. Deflation takes place when prices fall over time. Deflation raises the real value of outstanding debt, can lead to households postponing major purchases, and may also lead to interest rates hitting the lower bound of zero.

IMPORTANT TERMS

Bank of Canada, 23
barter, 16
bimetallism, 21
Canadian Payments Association, 24
central bank, 23
current accounts, 24
gold standard, 20
Gresham's Law, 21
liquidity, 17
M1, 25
M2, 25
M2+, 25

M3, 26
medium or unit of account, 17
medium of exchange, 17
money market mutual funds (MMMFs), 24
money supply, money stock, 23
personal chequable accounts, 24
savings deposits, 24
seigniorage, 31
store of value, 17
term deposits, 24
transactions costs, 18

PROBLEMS

1. Suppose you are given the following data:

Currency in circulation	$ 1 000
Net Demand deposits at chartered banks	13 000
Nonpersonal notice and personal savings deposits at chartered banks	12 000
Deposits at other financial institutions	6 000
Nonpersonal term and foreign currency deposits	9 000

   What are M1, M2, M2+, and M3? Assume adjustments to the various aggregates are zero.

2. Should a $50 bill stuffed in your mattress be counted as M1? Why?

3. An annual inflation rate of 5% reduces purchasing power by approximately a quarter in six years and by half in 14 years. Explain.

4. Can you generalize the conclusion that the number of transactions in a barter economy is always larger than in a monetary economy?

5. Explain why the new monetary aggregates M1+ and M1++ must be greater than the aggregate M1. Why is M2++ greater than M2+? Explain.

6. How would you calculate seigniorage? Explain.

DISCUSSION QUESTIONS

1. Suppose that all transactions are done by a national computerized network that records purchases and sales and is able to debit and credit the appropriate bank accounts instantly. Individuals need only carry a card to carry out all transactions, and visitors from other countries can purchase credits on a card at the border in exchange for their own currency. All prices continue to be quoted in dollars.

   (a) What is the economy's medium of account?

   (b) What is its unit of account?

   (c) Is this a monetary economy? What unresolved questions or problems would arise from such a system?

2. You read the following statement in the financial press: "Based on data for November, M1 declined by $5 million but M2 rose by $7 million." How could M1 have fallen while M2 rose? Why?

3. Current legislation has eliminated reserve requirements for chartered banks. Will banks bother to keep reserves? Why?

4. Inflation and the pace of financial innovation appear to be related to each other. Is this a coincidence? Why?

5. Would the annual rush to buy RRSPs be reflected in seasonally adjusted or unadjusted data? Which component of the money supply likely would be affected? Explain your answer.

6. Explain how the government can generate revenue from the creation of fiat money. Also, briefly discuss the benefits and costs of inflationary financing. Finally, explain how inflation can be viewed as a tax on money.

7. Give an example of how inflation redistributes income between generations.

8. Of the eight social costs of inflation listed in the section entitled "Inflation and Social Welfare," which do you think are the most important? Why?

9. What are the pros and cons of zero inflation?

10. An article in the London daily the Observer, 4 November 1999, is quoted as follows: "For libertarians, the monopoly of central banks has been a disaster. It simply allows government to cheat their citizens by eroding their savings through bouts of inflation." What does the statement mean? Would the private issue of money necessarily solve the problems?

11. What is the "zero lower bound" for nominal interest rates, and why do policymakers worry about hitting it?

CANSIM QUESTION

Go to the CANSIM Web site and download the following series from 1986: M2++ (series V37150), M1+ (series V37151), and M1++ (series V27152). Calculate the annual growth rates of these series (i.e., $[X_t - X_t - 1]/X_t - 1 \ 3 \ 100$) for the period 1986–90, 1993, 1994, 1995, and 1996–05. Compare the figures up to 1995 with the article by J. Attah-Mensah and L. Nott, "Recent Developments in the Monetary Aggregates and Their Implications," Bank of Canada Review (Spring 1999): 5–19. Are they the same? What has happened to growth rates since? Which aggregate do you think matches most closely inflation in the CPI? (You may wish to download series V737311 and calculate the inflation rate.)

References can be found on www.mcgrawhill.ca/college/siklos

The Role of Financial Intermediaries and Financial Markets

LEARNING OBJECTIVES

After reading and studying this chapter, you should be able to

3.1   explain intermediaries—what financial intermediaries do

3.2   provide a classification of the financial system by type of institution

3.3   name "the four pillars"

3.4   provide a classification of the financial system by type of market

3.5   describe the financial system in the Canadian economy

3.6   discuss the effects of technology and deregulation on banks, and whether banks as we know them will survive

When asked what banks do, most students reply they take in deposits and make loans. That response is partly correct, but it ignores the principal economic role of all financial institutions: their role as **intermediaries.** Indeed, the wave of deregulation and technological innovations sweeping the financial world has greatly reduced the traditional role of deposit-taking and lending in the banking world. Banks, in particular, now underwrite, provide financial advice, manage portfolios, and make available various forms of insurance. More than ever before, financial institutions act as go-betweens. This chapter opens, therefore, by explaining the intermediation function.

However, traditional banks also face dangers that have led some to suggest that their days are numbered. Non-deposit-taking firms are increasingly involved in the provision of credit, and individuals are bypassing banks by holding stocks and funds in nonbanking firms. Despite these changes, traditional banks are fighting back, mainly through consolidation, by exploiting some of the comparative advantage they have over nonbanking firms in the area of client information, and by embracing technological development.

We proceed with a brief description of the principal types of intermediaries in Canada. The structure of Canadian intermediaries is not unique, but it is by no means the only structure possible. Later chapters in this book will consider the intermediaries in other countries, most notably the United States. Next, we outline various ways in which financial markets can be classified. This classification will serve as a starting point for the next chapter, which describes the major financial instruments traded in the Canadian financial system.

Finally, we consider the financial system in the Canadian economy. How vital a role does it play? How important is the financial system? How can we even begin to consider whether the system is an efficient one?

3.1 INTERMEDIATION

What does a firm do? In economic terms, it takes inputs and through a production function turns them into outputs. Thus, General Motors produces cars, The Bay produces retail sales of consumer goods, and your neighbourhood barber produces haircuts. But what does a financial institution produce? Think of a bank. We can view it in several ways. Loans can be seen as its output and deposits as its principal input. Alternatively, we can conceive of a bank as producing deposits, which then represent its output and are the result of making loans. Or, we can see a bank's output as the difference between the return on its assets (for example, its loans) and the cost of its debts (for example, its deposits).[1] Thus, we can speak of the banking firm's output as a set of services. Such a set of services can be termed **intermediation**, which can be thought of as facilitating the transformation of liabilities (that is, deposits) into assets (that is, loans).

An intermediary is a go-between. A financial intermediary is someone (more likely, some institution) that offers financial services to individuals and firms that have excess cash, and individuals and firms that need funds.

This service is enormously useful in a society that uses money. The people who have extra money ("the savers") could, of course, stash it under their mattresses, but they would face problems of safety and convenience. Perhaps worse, their assets wouldn't be doing them any good. Most people want to put their assets to work earning more funds (interest or income).

Without intermediary institutions, the savers themselves would have to find users of their funds ("borrowers"). An individual who wanted to make a car loan would have to find someone who wanted to fund the purchase of a car, ascertain the person's creditworthiness, and work out arrangements for repayment. An individual who wanted to lend to a real estate developer would have to seek one out, and so on. The situation would be almost as complex as barter. Financial intermediaries make life much simpler for savers and borrowers.

Although technology, most notably the Internet, may make certain transactions easier and possibly less costly, this need not be true of all financial transactions. As we will see throughout this text, financial transactions actually have become more, not less, complex, requiring increasingly specialized institutions to take the place of conventional deposit-taking institutions. In particular, an important function of intermediation is the production and, hopefully, efficient use of information that either would be unavailable to ordinary investors or available only at a prohibitive cost.

THE FUNCTIONS OF INTERMEDIATION

Intermediation between borrowers and lenders can improve economic efficiency—that is, channel resources to their most effective use—in at least five ways:

1. It facilitates the acquisition of payment for goods and services. The chequing services provided by the banking system improve economic efficiency. Even though a cheque does not completely settle a transaction, it is a generally accepted form of payment. In later chapters we discuss some of the other financial instruments that facilitate purchases, some as simple as travellers' cheques or debit cards, some as complex as forward contracts for foreign exchange.

2. It facilitates the creation of a **portfolio** (a collection of assets) with all its attendant benefits. The financial system provides what economists call *economies of scale and scope*.[2] Through intermediation individuals can spread their wealth across a variety of assets in a way they could

---

1 Recall from the previous chapter that to the client of a bank, a deposit is an asset and a loan is a debt. But to the bank itself, a deposit is a debt (the client has lent money to the institution) and a loan is an asset. This slippery point will appear repeatedly in this text.
2 Economies of scale are obtained when the unit cost of an operation decreases as more of it is done. Economies of scope are cost savings that stem from engaging in complementary activities.

not accomplish through direct contacts. For example, many investors could not purchase certain types of government bonds directly because the amounts are too large (say, $1 million) to be affordable to individual investors, but the financial system can pool the funds of many investors and purchase the security. As we will see, financial institutions provide such pooling arrangements in a variety of ways.

Cost savings are also possible because a financial institution can offer a large variety of services to its customers at a cost far lower than if they purchased them directly. For example, someone with a chequing account may have access for a relatively small flat fee to services ranging from overdraft privileges to safety deposit boxes to easy purchase of stocks.

3. It eases the liquidity constraint of households and firms, which arises because the liquidity (think cash) required for certain purchases (such as a house or a factory) is grossly at variance with the immediate flow of income available. Recall the classic movie *It's a Wonderful Life*, which pits Banker Potter, who insists that the funds for purchasing a house must be paid up front, against Mr. Bailey, who pools the funds of investors at his savings and loan company and is able to advance the money so that families can buy housing immediately instead of waiting for years. The protagonists represent a long-ago battle that led to the creation of mortgage loan companies and credit unions. The ability to influence the allocation of consumption and investment is perhaps the single most important service that arises from intermediation.

4. It provides a measure of financial security from unexpected or unforeseen events, such as ill health or property damage. The existence of intermediation provides a host of services that reduce or shift risk. We discuss risk in detail in future chapters. Suffice it to say here that *risk* arises essentially because the future cannot be known with complete certainty. Moreover, to deal with uncertainty, all individuals must make informed decisions based on likely future scenarios to insure themselves against undesirable outcomes. Financial institutions influence the riskiness of financial transactions and arrangements in several ways. Lenders and borrowers deal with each other only *indirectly*: Contracting, and thus its costs, are borne by the intermediary. The intermediary specifies all the contingencies required when a contract for, say, a loan is written to spread the costs over all customers in the event of default. Intermediaries also permit insurance, which specifically shifts a potential loss of wealth from individuals to institutions that willingly bear such risks.

5. It provides information. The need for intermediation services arises because information is costly to obtain and to process. In addition, financial transactions are costly to complete. These costs exist because of **asymmetric information**. As a result, two problems emerge. For example, if an individual makes a direct loan to someone, there is a good chance that the lender will have incomplete information about the motives of the borrower. Before the transaction occurs, the borrower has every incentive to put his or her best foot forward and to offer every assurance that interest and principal payments will be made on time and in full. Similarly, after the loan is agreed to and funds are exchanged, the lender can do little to prevent the borrower from using the proceeds of the loan in a manner other than was promised before the loan was made. The first problem is called **adverse selection;** the second **moral hazard**.[3] These types of behaviour are especially evident when deposits of the banking system are insured, as we see in Chapter 16. Banks can, via the process of intermediation, reduce the asymmetric

---

[3] The problems of moral hazard and asymmetric information are commonplace as in, for example, the doctor–patient relationship, the relationship between health insurance providers and those covered by such insurance, or the used-car market. Indeed, examples such as these prompted the now-classic study by economist George Akerlof who shared a Nobel prize for this research. Akerlof's paper dealt with the market for "lemons" where, because of asymmetric information, it is possible to pass off a lemon of a car, for example, as a trouble-free vehicle. See G. Akerlof, "The Market for Lemons," *Quarterly Journal of Economics* 84 (1970): 485–500. The same considerations also are present in the market for deposit insurance. We take up the topic in Chapter 16.

information problem since these institutions have a comparative advantage in offering specialized services (for example, monitoring of borrowers' activities, information about financial markets). However, as agents for the depositors, banks also can exploit the asymmetric information problem by taking on undue risks or through fraudulent behaviour. We will encounter many such examples throughout the text. Consequently, governments have felt the need to regulate the banking sector, perhaps to a greater extent than other industries or sectors of the economy. This reaction also raises some concerns, such as when governments decide to insure depositors against losses when banks fail. Again, we explore the ramifications of government regulations later in the text (in particular, in Chapter 17).

BROKERAGE

The Canadian financial system provides not only intermediation but also brokerage services. The two functions are similar in purpose but differ in the way they operate.

Brokers are agents who bring would-be buyers and sellers together so transactions can be made. Some Canadian financial institutions, such as stock brokers, specifically offer the brokerage function. Other institutions emphasize intermediation but also fulfil a brokerage role to some extent. Consider a bank's chequing services. In a way, they bring buyers and seller "together," and they certainly facilitate transactions. However, unlike intermediaries, brokers simply help "sell" or market the liabilities of an institution that wishes to raise funds. Hence, the issuer of the debt is not anonymous to the holder. By contrast, it is unlikely that the depositor in a bank will be aware of the individuals or institutions that have borrowed from the bank.

EXTERNALITIES

The existence of a financial system creates these wonderful efficiencies, but it also entails some **externalities** (spillover effects whose cost to individuals or society is not compensated by the economic agent that causes them). The reason, as we will see, is that the incentives of the managers of a financial institution may conflict with those of its shareholders, its depositors, or society in general. For example, managers, through some combination of a desire to increase profits, or incompetence or dishonesty, may violate the confidence of depositors and be unable to return their funds to them as promised.

The mere possibility of this kind of externality, which can be socially disastrous, has been used to justify government intervention in the financial system, sometimes via very strict regulations.

3.2   FINANCIAL INSTITUTIONS

What types of financial institutions exist in Canada today? We'll provide only a brief sketch here, leaving details to later chapters. Don't worry if you don't understand all the differences between institutions. These matters will become evident when we describe the history, regulation, and performance of each type of institution.

Nevertheless, one thing is clear: There has been a tremendous amount of consolidation in the financial sector over the past decade or so (also see **Point-Counterpoint 18.1: Consolidation in the Banking Sector: Is It Bad?** in Chapter 18).[4] As a result, there are fewer banks, and the industry is more highly concentrated than before. This is an international phenomenon that does, however, show signs of slowing (except possibly in the United States) as the efficiencies and

---

4 See, for example, Group of Ten (2001), *Report on Consolidation in the Financial Sector,* Basel: Switzerland, OECD (2000); *Mergers in Financial Services,* and European Central Bank (2000); and *Mergers and Acquisitions Involving the EU Banking Industry—Facts and Implications* (Frankfurt, Germany: European Central Bank).

economies that can be gained through such activities begin to dissipate or regulatory hurdles begin to get in the way.[5]

You should be clear about our focus, however. Here we concentrate on **financial intermediaries**—institutions that permit indirect lending, not all of which are deposit-taking institutions.

TYPES OF FINANCIAL INSTITUTIONS

Within the Canadian financial system today, three broad categories of intermediaries exist: (1) deposit-taking institutions, (2) insurance companies and pension funds, and (3) investment dealers and investment funds. See Table 3.1.

Deposit-Taking Institutions

The Canadian Bankers' Association represents the interests of Canadian banks
www.cba.ca

Deposit-taking institutions (also called *depository institutions*) accept and manage deposits and make loans. Because of a combination of historical developments and the regulatory environment (which stems partially from jurisdictional battles between the federal and provincial governments), they are divided into two types: chartered banks and other deposit-taking institutions. *Chartered banks* are large, federally regulated institutions and have a close relationship with the Bank of Canada. Other types of *banks* now resemble chartered banks, and they operate under a combination of federal and provincial regulations. Since the passage of the *Bank Act* of 1992, the significance attached to the term *bank* has been lessened considerably. Nevertheless, it remains convenient to retain a term such as *near-banks* because they still perform slightly different roles in the financial system than do chartered banks. The near-banks comprise:

1. *Trust companies*, which in addition to acting as deposit-taking institutions also operate as fiduciaries (administrators of estates and trusts); in the latter capacity, they do not own the assets, but simply administer them in the interests of the owners.

2. *Mortgage loan companies*, which accept deposits but essentially permit investors to invest in a portfolio of assets primarily invested in real estate. At present most are fully owned subsidiaries of chartered banks.

3. *Credit unions* (called *caisses populaires* in Quebec), which are member-owned; that is, the depositors are shareholders.

Insurance Companies and Pension Funds

The Insurance Bureau of Canada represents insurance companies in Canada
www.ibc.ca

Insurance companies provide a way of channelling savings to provide a cushion against unexpected expenses. By *pooling risks*, such a company can provide clients with protection against a variety of risks without incurring a considerable risk of failure for its owners.

Next are the institutions that cater to the management of pension plans or funds (data not shown in Table 3.1). The various types reflect divisions created in large part by legislation governing how pensions are administered. *Registered retirement savings plans* (RRSPs) are individuals' tax-sheltered funds administered by the individuals themselves or by a deposit-taking institution or an investment dealer on the individuals' behalf. *Registered pension plans* (RPPs) are the pooled retirement savings of a group of employees administered by the employer (or a labour union). Finally, there are *public pension plans*, which are the funds accumulated by the federal government and the government of Quebec through deductions from income and dispersed as pensions through the Canada Pension Plan (CPP) and the Quebec Pension Plan (QPP), respectively.

---

5 An illustration of the latter is the attempt by some Canadian banks (e.g., CIBC, TD-Canada Trust) to open mini-branches in grocery stores or in department stores (such as Wal-Mart) in both Canada and the U.S. Such attempts have met resistance from regulatory bodies in the U.S.

Table 3.1	**Principal Financial Institutions, 2004**
Deposit-taking institutions	
Chartered banks[a]	1 767 665
Other deposit-taking institutions	
Trust companies	11 285[b]
Credit unions and caisses populaires	155 078[c]
Insurance companies[d]	237 083[d]
Other	
Investment funds	450 757
Non-depository credit intermediaries[e]	112 114

Sources: *Bank of Canada Review,* Tables C3, D1, D2, D3, and D5; CANSIM, series V636951.

Note: Data are for the end of the second quarter.

[a] Series V36883.
[b] Series V37035.
[c] Series V122571.
[d] Life insurers, includes segregated funds.
[e] Series V1404811. Includes public and private institutions that lend by raising funds via commercial paper and other debt instruments.

Investment Funds and Other Intermediaries

The list in Table 3.1 is rounded out with a catch-all of intermediaries whose asset size is relatively small but whose services are important in the Canadian economy. Essentially, the many types of *investment funds,* better known as mutual funds, pool funds for investment in a wide range of activities and instruments without fulfilling the other functions of a typical bank. *Sales, finance,* and *consumer loan companies,* also called consumer and business financial intermediaries, make credit available to finance a wide range of purchases, from household goods and services to inventories and capital equipment. *Investment dealers* primarily *underwrite* corporate and government securities; that is, they acquire newly issued securities and resell them to the public.

Government Financial Institutions

The government itself also participates in the financial industry (although its institutions do not appear in Table 3.1). Sometimes it plays a deposit-taking role, as in the Province of Ontario and Alberta savings institutions. Myriad agencies also either channel funds from the public to the private sector, such as the Business Development Bank, or protect private funds in the private financial system, such as the Canada Deposit Insurance Corporation (CDIC).

3.3 THE FOUR PILLARS: SOME HISTORY

If you had been a student during the 1980s, when you were taught the types of Canadian financial institutions, you would have been handed a list of what were called the **four pillars** of the financial system and told that each existed to fulfil one—and only one—financial function. The four pillars and their financial functions were:

1. chartered banks: personal, commercial loans, and deposits

2. trust companies and credit unions: fiduciary responsibilities and personal loans and deposits

3. insurance companies (subdivided into life insurers and property and casualty insurers): underwriting insurance contracts

4. investment dealers: underwriting and brokering securities

Regulations enforced the separation of the four pillars; companies in one category could not engage in the activities of another, and cross-ownership was largely forbidden. The rationale was that specialization made all the institutions less prone to bankruptcy, and thereby protected the public.

The separation of the four pillars was, however, never absolute (for example, credit unions have long offered insurance to their members), and the pillars began to crumble in the late 1960s, when chartered banks were given permission to make mortgage loans and to issue *debentures*.

Since that time, regulatory reform—prompted in large part by innovations in financial instruments, by the rapid development of computer technology, and by a perception of increased volatility in the financial sector—and rising international competition have largely eroded the separation of the four pillars. Federal legislation regulating banks has hastened its demise. Several provincial governments have also relaxed their restrictions on the services that may be provided by near-banks.

Thus, the differences between types of institutions have become increasingly blurred over time. Indeed, economists long ago argued that, in a deregulated environment, the distinction between banks and other types of financial intermediaries would vanish.[6] Nevertheless, institutions probably will continue for a time to specialize in the areas they have served in the past.

REGULATION

As already suggested, Canadian financial institutions are governed by a potpourri of legislation.[7] One reason for the variety is the history of the four-pillars' separation; different laws were written to cover different types of institutions.

Another reason for the variety is the federal–provincial sharing of powers. The federal government has sole jurisdiction over banking. Hence, all chartered banks and other federally regulated financial institutions fall under the federal *Bank Act*, which is revised approximately every 10 years. The most recent revision was passed and proclaimed in 2001.[8]

Other types of financial institutions may be incorporated federally or provincially and are regulated accordingly. Many (not all) insurance companies and trust companies are federally regulated institutions. Most credit unions are supervised by the provinces.

3.4   TYPES OF FINANCIAL MARKETS

Understanding the financial system requires an understanding not only of its institutions, but also of the types of markets they serve. There are many market classifications. It is worth pointing out that some observers speak of "asset," "debt," and "equity" markets. These markets all are included in the classifications described below, but they are, in a sense, less precise definitions than we would like. As we have already seen, one individual's asset is another's debt. As for equities, they come in a wide variety of forms, and where and how they are issued have an important impact on how their prices are set and change over time. The list below will help us better understand the variety of instruments that exist in the financial system today. Market classifications can be described based on:

1.   Type of transaction. We have already encountered this classification. It includes direct transactions, in which lender and borrower deal with each other directly (perhaps with the assistance of a broker or agent) and indirect transactions, which go through a financial intermediary.

2.   Selling and reselling. A **primary market** is one in which assets are sold for the first time; the assets traded in the primary financial market are newly issued securities or shares. A **secondary market** is one in which the same assets are resold (often over and over again).

---

6 Fisher Black, "Banks Fund Management in an Efficient Market," *Journal of Financial Economics* (December 1995): 323–39; Eugene Fama, "Banking in a Theory of Finance," *Journal of Monetary Economics* (January 1980): 39–57; G. Gorton and A. Winton, "Financial Intermediation," in G. Constantinides, M. Harris, and l. Stulz (eds.), *Handbook of the Economics of Finance* (Amsterdam: North-Holland, forthcoming); and F. Allen, "Do Financial Institutions Matter?" *Journal of Finance* 56 (August 2001): 1165–75.

7 The regulation of the various financial institutions is described in more detail in Chapters 17–20.

8 The changes are outlined in Chapter 18. Those pertaining to reserve requirements are described in Chapter 17.

3. Duration (Maturity). Is the asset being lent for a short term or a long term? The problem here is that there are no clear definitions for "short" and "long." Nevertheless, interest rates may vary with the duration of the loan, and we even can perceive separate markets for different types of duration.

    (a) *Term to maturity* (length of time until the loan must be repaid). One set of definitions calls financial instruments that mature in one year or less short term and those that mature in more than one year long term. An alternative set adds another step; maturities of less than one year are short term; maturities of one to five years are medium term; and maturities of more than five years are long term.

    (b) *Markets*. The **money market** is for the trading of short-term instruments, those with maturities of less than a year. The **capital market** is for transactions in long-term instruments, those with maturities of more than a year. The *mortgage market* is also for long-term debt, but maturities are typically more than 10 years.

4. Size. Occasionally, the financial press makes distinctions according to the size of the financial transaction. Thus, transactions of less than, say, $100 000, involve the *retail* side of the market, whereas those greater than $100 000 involve the *wholesale* side. One reason for such a distinction is that financial institutions market to the two sides quite separately. Also, the costs of providing services to them can be significantly different.

5. Style of transaction. Financial transactions carried out in an open market, such as an auction or stock exchange, are said to involve the public market. By contrast, transactions involving face-to-face negotiations between borrowers and lenders, albeit via a financial intermediary, take place in the private market.

6. Sectoral classification. The National Accounts divide the economy roughly into five broad sectors: households and unincorporated businesses, nonfinancial corporations, the financial sector, the government or public sector, and the rest of the world (the foreign sector). Some financial markets involve one sector, some two or more. Driven by the fall in real estate prices, the increase in stock prices, and the growth of investment funds, the financial sector became a larger force in generating assets in the economy as a whole.

7. Complexity. Potentially, several specialists are parties to a transaction. Take, for example, a mortgage loan. For most of us, this involves a trip to the bank and decisions on the size and terms of the mortgage. Formerly, mortgages originated at a bank, which provided the funds, and took in payments until the loan was repaid. Today, one institution might initiate the mortgage (most likely a bank). A separate institution would provide the funds or pool several mortgages into a fund whose income would accrue to holders of marketable securities backed by the pool of mortgages. This phenomenon is known as **securitization** and represents one of the most significant developments in financial transactions in recent years. Finally, a separate agency might collect mortgages because it specializes in data processing.

3.5 THE FINANCIAL SYSTEM IN THE CANADIAN ECONOMY

How important is the financial system in the Canadian economy? Figures 3.1 through 3.3 show three different ways of arriving at an answer. Figure 3.1 tells us that approximately three-fifths of all assets in the Canadian economy are financial in nature. Figure 3.2 shows that almost 60% of all assets in the Canadian economy are held by the financial sector. This ratio has been steadily rising over the years.

Currency and deposits at deposit-taking institutions and mortgages account for almost a quarter of all financial assets. Insurance, bank loans, and corporate claims each account for almost

| Figure 3.1 | The Relative Importance of Financial Assets, 2004 |

(A) Financial and Nonfinancial Assets as Percentages of Total Assets

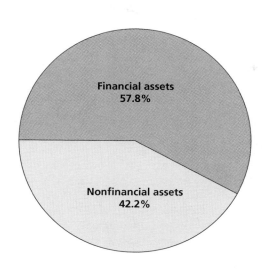

(B) The Most Important Types of Financial Instruments

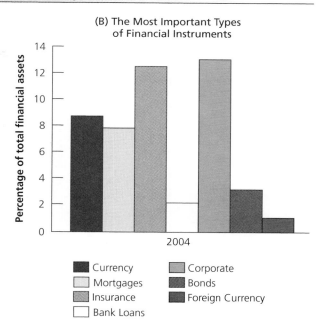

The pie chart in panel (A) shows that financial assets were almost three-fifths of all assets in Canada in 2004. Just over half of those financial assets were in the form of seven major instruments; their relative importance is shown in panel (B).

Source: Adapted from the Statistics Canada CANSIM II database **http://cansim2.statcan.ca/cgi-win/CNSMCGI.EXE**, series V33256, V33211, V34757, V34764, V34770, V34760, V34755, V34765, V34745, V637050, V636951, V636852, V636753, V33472, and V49930. More details are provided in the CANSIM Questions at the end of this chapter.

Note: Currency and deposits include deposits at chartered banks and other deposit-taking institutions. Government bonds include federal bonds only. Corporate debt includes shares issued by corporations.

| Figure 3.2 | The Relative Importance of the Financial Sector, 2004 |

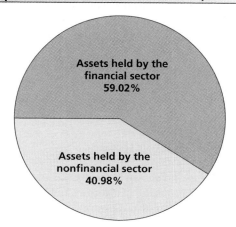

A large proportion of assets in the economy are held by the financial sector, which consists of the Bank of Canada, the chartered banks, the near-banks, insurance companies, pension funds, and various other private and public financial institutions.

Source: Adapted from the Statistics Canada CANSIM II database **http://cansim2.statcan.ca/cgi-win/CNSMCGI.EXE**, series V33256, V33211, V34757, V34764, V34770, V34760, V34755, V34765, V34745, V637050, V636951, V636852, V636753, V33472, V499301. More details are provided in the CANSIM Questions at the end of this chapter.

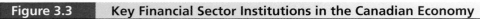

| **Figure 3.3** | **Key Financial Sector Institutions in the Canadian Economy** |

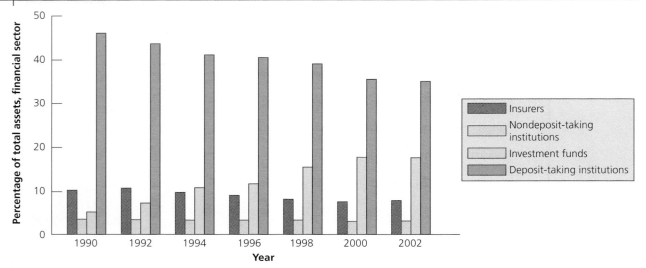

Assets of institutions shown as a percentage of total assets of the financial sector.

Source: Adapted from the Statistics Canada CANSIM II database **http://cansim2.statcan.ca/cgi-win/CNSMCGI.EXE**, series V33256, V33211, V34757, V34764, V34770, V34760, V34755, V34765, V34745, V637050, V636951, V636852, V636753, V33472, V499301. See CANSIM Questions at the end of this chapter for series labels.

6% of financial assets. Trailing behind with about 4% and 3%, respectively, are Government of Canada bonds, and foreign currency and foreign currency deposits. Several other types of financial assets exist, but the ones depicted in Figure 3.1(B) cover many of the most important ones for our purposes.

Figure 3.3 presents some evidence about the size and relative importance over time of key institutions in the Canadian financial sector. Deposit-taking credit intermediaries, non-deposit-taking credit intermediaries, insurers, and investment funds account for roughly three-quarters of the financial sector (the remainder would include the Bank of Canada, government financial institutions, and foreign institutions). Although the size of non-deposit-taking credit intermediaries and insurers has remained stable since 1990, deposit-taking intermediaries have become less important over time, apparently at the expense of investment funds.

Clearly, the short answer to our question is that the financial system plays an enormously important role in the Canadian economy. For more elaboration, let us consider the specific importance of financial intermediaries and the system's overall efficiency.

3.6   WHAT FUTURE FOR BANKING?

Developments of the kind shown in Figure 3.3 are not unique to Canada. Indeed, the shift away from traditional deposit-taking institutions toward other financial institutions as vehicles for facilitating intermediation and the provision of credit has been even more pronounced in the United States and relatively less so in Europe.

Recall that intermediation is all about reducing existing frictions, such as transactions costs and asymmetric information. But what if technology and a reduction in these costs have reduced these frictions to the point that traditional intermediation will wither away? Or are the growth of investment funds and the growing complexity of financial transactions simply reflections of a shift in emphasis toward the management of risks?

The point is that the relative importance of traditional deposit-taking institutions is more a function of a combination of factors already noted, such as the role of regulation and how well these institutions adapt to changing circumstances. There is an ongoing, lively debate on these questions, largely because of evidence suggesting, at least in the United States, that intermediation increasingly is being replaced by market mechanisms to efficiently allocate financial resources. Nonbanks such as AT&T, GMAC, GE, and Canadian Tire, to name but a few examples, have successfully encroached into areas traditionally fulfilled by deposit-taking institutions. Mutual funds and investment dealers can arrange for funds to be deposited into investment and other types of accounts, bypassing the banking system. Finally, the explosive growth of e-commerce could potentially replace conventional types of accounts with chequing privileges. Could it be the case that markets are better at allocating risks from those who want to avoid them to those who want to bear them?

Hence, we are led to ask whether banks or markets are better at spreading risks over time. In Chapters 4, 6, and 7, and again in Chapter 17, we study how this consideration can help us to understand how the myriad financial instruments available to suit various needs as well as how banks can be useful providers of such products, so long as there is not too much competition. Thus, for example, high returns in the stock market until 2000, a reduction in transactions costs of buying or selling shares, together with the ease of access to stock markets, made possible by technological improvements (producing a reduction in so-called participation costs), have no doubt contributed to people opting out of the banking system. Of course, the higher returns come at the cost of greater risk, in a manner to be explored more fully in Chapters 13, 14, and 15. Suffice it to say, however, that the resulting risk management is of a different kind than that historically provided by banks. In part for this reason, banks, in recent years, have attached relatively more importance to fees. They also have downgraded the role played by the spread between borrowing and lending rates, though the latter remains a salient aspect of the intermediation process (we return to these questions in Chapters 11 and 17).

It is certainly a mistake to think that banks will disappear anytime soon or that they have not developed new strategies to deal with technological changes, regulatory changes, and international developments. Indeed, banks in Canada have deliberately sought to expand in both size and scope, believing that this is the only way that they can compete in a global setting. As we shall see, beginning in the next chapter, such developments are viewed by many with considerable skepticism.

The upshot is that although banks will not simply disappear, their roles and functions will evolve in new directions. It should also be noted that the foregoing description of the changing role of banks is neither universally accepted nor uncontroversial. What is clear is that the role of intermediaries, and their place in the financial system, will remain fascinating in the years to come.

SUMMARY

- Intermediation is what the financial system is all about. It represents the process by which the debts of one person or group become the assets of others.

- Intermediation can improve efficiency and therefore add economic welfare in at least five ways: (1) facilitating transactions, (2) facilitating portfolio creation, (3) easing households' liquidity constraints, (4) spreading risks over time, and (5) reducing the problem of asymmetric information.

- In this chapter, we discuss the various types of financial institutions that perform the intermediation function in Canada.

- Banks are particularly adept at intermediation because they can perform the necessary functions more cheaply than most institutions. However, technological change and deregulation have narrowed the comparative advantage of banks.

- Brokers do not intermediate but can facilitate the bringing together of buyers and sellers.

- A crucial characteristic of financial systems, and of intermediaries in particular, is the possibility of externalities. That is, one intermediary's actions can have consequences (usually negative), potentially for the entire system.

- Financial institutions are usually classified into one of four categories: (1) deposit-taking institutions, (2) insurance companies and pensions funds, (3) investment funds and other intermediaries, and (4) government financial institutions.

- Regulation plays a crucial role in the structure of the Canadian financial system. Financial institutions used to be regulated in such a way as to produce four separate "pillars," effectively separating banks, trust companies, credit unions, insurance companies, and securities underwriters.

- The four pillars have crumbled thanks to several years of deregulation.

- The Canadian financial system can be classified according to types of financial markets. For example, markets can be divided according to when the asset or debt in question matures, whether the sums involved are relatively large or small, the size of the transaction, whether the asset is newly issued or resold, when the transaction is conducted, the sector of the economy affected, and the complexity of the transaction.

- To assess how well the financial system is performing, it is important to determine how efficient it is. In this chapter, we looked at two ways of measuring the efficiency of a financial system.

- It is premature to think that banks will disappear. Technology, deregulation, and reductions in transactions and participation costs are forces transforming the financial sector.

- Traditional banks are becoming less important in the financial system, largely because of investment funds. The type of risk management activities demanded today by households and firms is of a fundamentally different kind than even a decade ago.

IMPORTANT TERMS

adverse selection, 37
asymmetric information, 37
brokers, 38
capital market, 42
deposit-taking institutions, 39
externalities, 38
financial intermediaries, 39
four pillars, 40

intermediaries, 35
intermediation, 36
money market, 42
moral hazard, 37
portfolio, 36
primary market, 41
secondary market, 41
securitization, 42

PROBLEMS

1. Can you think of a recent financial innovation that has implications for the efficiency of the financial system? that has influence on economies of scale? on economies of scope?

2. Is an issuer of travellers' cheques a financial intermediary? Why?

3. Give an example of a positive and a negative externality in the financial sector. Explain.

DISCUSSION QUESTIONS

1. Investment funds, such as mutual funds, appear to intermediate just as banks do, or do they? How can two institutions coexist efficiently? How do they differ?

2. Why do issuers of stocks and bonds use an underwriter? (Hint: Explain in terms of efficiency.)

3. What is it about the housing market that makes mortgage lending a problem? Why do you think government intervention in this market has been necessary?

4. For a financial market to be efficient, it is necessary for all participants to be fully informed and up to date. Evaluate this statement.

5. Bankers actually dislike having to deal with cash. Why? In this respect, have automated banking machines made things better or worse for banks?

6. Why do you think deregulation is eliminating the distinction between banks and other financial intermediaries?

7. According to two well-known economic theories, regulation and economic growth can act as spurs to financial innovations. Can you think why this might be the case? Give an example based on Canadian experience.

8. How do lower participation costs favour nonbank institutions? Explain.

9. How can consolidation of the banking sector help preserve the relative importance of banks in the financial sector? Explain.

10. Briefly explain the difference between the brokerage and intermediation functions.

CANSIM QUESTION

1. Go to the CANSIM Web site and download the following series: total assets, financial (V33256) and nonfinancial sectors (V33211), foreign currency and deposits (V34757), mortgages (V34764), insurance (V34760), bank loans (V34760), currency and bank deposits (V34755), Government of Canada bonds (V34765), corporate loans (V34745), investment funds assets (V637050), insurers (V636951), non-deposit-taking institutions (V636852), deposit-taking institutions (V636753), nonfinancial assets (V33472), total assets all sectors (V499301). These series were used to create the pie charts and graphs in Figures 3.1, 3.2, and 3.3. The data are annual and you should download the relevant series since 1990. Now answer the following questions:

   (a) Try to recreate the figures. Remember that you need to calculate the relevant values as a percentage of some total (assets usually).

   (b) Create pie charts for each year since 1990 for all the relevant series mentioned in the figures.

   (c) Are there any forces identified in this chapter that might be responsible for the behaviour of the series since 1990?

References can be found on www.mcgrawhill.ca/college/siklos

CHAPTER 4

Functions and Characteristics of Financial Instruments

LEARNING OBJECTIVES

After reading and studying this chapter, you should be able to

4.1 provide a general classification of the major types of financial instruments in Canada

4.2 explain how money, capital, and derivative market instruments originated, their role in the Canadian financial system, and their relative importance in the marketplace

4.3 explain the market for derivatives

We saw in the previous chapter that among the many ways to classify the financial system, a convenient and easy-to-remember way is by markets: the money market, for transactions in instruments with maturities of less than one year, and the capital market, for transactions in instruments with maturities that exceed one year. We use this division to examine the system's principal instruments.

An understanding of these instruments is important for at least three reasons. First, it provides an overview of how financial markets have developed over time to meet the needs of borrowers and lenders. Second, money market instruments, in particular, serve as a key link in the transmission of monetary policy. Therefore, their operation provides an early glimpse of how the Bank of Canada can influence the financial system to fulfil some of its short-run interest rate and monetary policy objectives. Third, it helps to clarify how market efficiency is enhanced by the development of a vast array of instruments that facilitate the flow of funds from lenders to borrowers.

Before we begin our description of the characteristics and functions of the major financial instruments in the money and capital markets, two points are worth noting:

1. Even this minimum list includes both privately and publicly issued instruments. Private sector borrowing began to outpace public sector borrowing by the end of the 1990s, as government deficits disappeared and the economy expanded rapidly.[1]

2. At this stage we consider only brief descriptions of the most important instruments traded in the Canadian marketplace. In other words, the analysis presented in this chapter is neither exhaustive (if it were, it would be impossibly long) nor detailed (partly because we have yet to discuss how interest rates are determined). Therefore, you should think of what follows as a convenient compendium of financial instruments. More details on some of the key instruments may be found in later chapters.

---

1 See Chart 4 in M. Milville, and A. Bernier, "The Corporate Bond Market in Canada," *Bank of Canada Review* (Autumn 1999): 3–8.

4.1   THE MONEY MARKET

Table 4.1 lists the principal money market instruments and indicates which sectors in the financial system rely on them to obtain funds and whether a significant secondary market exists. You should rely on this list for the essential points of the discussion that follows.

THE OVERNIGHT MARKET

The overnight market represents the shortest available term to maturity. Lenders make available their surplus funds until the following business day. Improvements in technology and cash management techniques facilitated the development of ways to enhance the returns on idle cash balances. A typical day for cash management groups in deposit-taking institutions begins at 7 a.m. as they forecast liquidity needs, that is, projected inflows and outflows of cash by their clients. Once cash needs are forecasted, market participants begin to quote bid and offer rates for overnight funds for their clients. About three-quarters of the activity takes place in the morning although the market closes at 6 p.m. (Eastern time).

Hence, net borrowers in the overnight market quote rates lower than net lenders, and market participants' positions change throughout the day. In mid-1994 the Bank of Canada adopted the operating band for the overnight market that consists of a basis point range for the overnight rate. Therefore, the overnight rate fluctuates within the upper and lower limits of the operating band.

Overnight rate = [Upper limit of the operating band, Lower limit of the operating band]

The overnight rate is also variously called the overnight financing rate, the overnight lending rate, or the overnight money market rate. The Bank of Canada also announces a target for the overnight rate (we study this feature in Chapter 25). The overnight rate is the interest rate the Bank of Canada has the most influence over and the operating band is the Bank's device to inform money market participants of interest rate levels consistent with its desired monetary policy stance. The Bank uses repurchase agreements (covered later in this chapter) to ensure that the overnight rate fluctuates within the band, or to effect shifts in the operating band. We shall explore the behaviour of the overnight rate and its connection to the setting of monetary policy in Chapter 22.

Other parties participate in the overnight rate, such as investment dealers and mutual fund managers. Some use the overnight market to manage unanticipated cash needs; others use the overnight market as a temporary haven for funds until new portfolio decisions are made.

The Bank of Canada
**www.bank
ofcanada.ca**

TREASURY BILLS

A **Treasury bill** (**T-bill**) is a debt incurred by the government. Its issue price is determined in an auction. Until 1997, the auction was held weekly. Since 16 September 1997, the auction has been biweekly. Given the diminished borrowing requirements of the federal government, demand and volume were insufficient to sustain a weekly auction.

This kind of debt has no stated interest rate. Rather, a Treasury bill is sold at a discount (deduction) relative to its **par value** (face value); the difference between the par value and the discounted price indicates the T-bill's return. Maturities range from 91 days to 1 year (the most commonly traded bills are for the 91-day maturity).

On 10 March 1980, the rate on Treasury bills became linked to the **bank rate**, the rate at which the Bank of Canada lends to chartered banks, as follows:[2]

Bank rate = Treasury bill rate + 0.25%

---

2 The kind of link between the T-bill rate and the bank rate also existed between 1 November 1956 and 23 June 1962.

Table 4.1   Selected Money Market Instruments

Instruments	Typical Maturities	Principal Borrowers	Secondary Market
Overnight market	1 day	Deposit-taking institutions	None
Treasury bills	91 to 365 days	Federal government	Yes
Provincial and municipal Treasury bills	91 to 365 days	Provincial governments and municipalities	Yes
Government-backed funds	91 to 365 days	Crown corporations	Yes
Bank of Canada advances	Few days	Chartered banks	None
Special purchase and resale agreements (SPRAs)	1 business day	Money market dealers (jobbers)	None
Purchase and resale agreements (PRAs)	Up to 15 days	Money market dealers (jobbers) and chartered banks	None
Bankers' acceptances	10 to 365 days	Chartered banks and money market dealers	Yes
Day-to-day loans	Callable at any time	Money market dealers	None
Special call loans	Overnight	Money market dealers	None
Certificates of deposit (CDs)	30 days and longer	Chartered banks	None
Bearer deposit notes (BDNs)	30 days to 1 year	Money market dealers	Yes
Interbank deposits	Few days	Chartered banks	None
Eurocurrency instruments	Overnight to 6 months or longer	Chartered banks	Yes
Corporate and finance company paper	30 to 365 days	Business, and finance companies	Small

Some of the instruments on this list are especially important, either because they have wide-ranging effects on the entire financial system or because the volume of trade in these instruments dwarfs that of the others. The highlighted boxes here distinguish the important items in this group.

In the large secondary market for T-bills, banks and investment dealers sell them to the general public in denominations starting at $1000. By the early 1990s, however, the Bank of Canada began to develop a system that permitted same-day settlement of large-value transactions. Accordingly, the Bank of Canada announced on 21 February 1996 that the bank rate would henceforth be set at the *upper limit* of the **overnight rate band** for overnight financing (we deal with this type of transaction later in the chapter). In other words,

$$\text{Bank rate} = upper\ limit \text{ of overnight rate band}$$

The band itself is +/− one-quarter of 1 percent around the target overnight rate, that is, the spread between the upper and lower bands is one-half of 1 percent or 50 **basis points**.

In 1995, the federal government announced a new debt management strategy to shift emphasis toward lower fixed-rate securities. This change occurred because of an apparent permanent shift toward lower and more stable interest rates. As a result, Treasury bills account for less than half of the outstanding stock of money market instruments in Canada.[3]

---

3 Defined as Treasury bills, bankers' acceptances, corporate paper, and securitized debt (see the end of this chapter).

The Treasury Bill Auctions

How is the T-bill rate determined? By the highest bidders in a biweekly auction. Participants are informed a week in advance of the quantities of T-bills to be auctioned.

By 12:30 p.m. (all times are Eastern Standard Time) every other Tuesday,[4] investment dealers and chartered banks electronically place bids for the purchase of T-bills with the Bank of Canada's Ottawa headquarters. Each bid specifies the dollar amount of T-bills the would-be buyer wants to purchase as well as a yield.[5] Meanwhile, the Bank of Canada puts in a reserve bid. For a purchaser, the lower the price, the greater the interest income that can be obtained. The Bank of Canada, on the other hand, seeks the highest possible price since that translates into the lowest debt cost to the federal government, which is borrowing the money. Thus, the game played by the would-be buyers involves guessing the course of interest rates the Bank of Canada expects to pursue in future through other factors, such as interest rates abroad (especially in the United States). The amount of Treasury bills maturing that week versus the quantity of new issues also plays a role in determining the T-bill price.

By 1:30 p.m. the Bank has ranked the bids from highest to lowest and announced the successful ones (in a 2 p.m. press release), which must be delivered by Thursday. In fact, participants can specify both price and quantity combinations (a competitive bid) or simply a quantity (a noncompetitive bid). The Bank of Canada also announces the amounts to be auctioned the next time.[6]

Because of the critical importance of interest rates, it is worth taking a brief detour to consider in broad terms how the Bank of Canada plays a central role in influencing them. Since several chapters (for example, Chapters 6 and 22) delve into the subject in greater detail, here we simply provide the basics. The interaction between the central bank and the financial sector is a recurring theme throughout the text.

The Bank of Canada and Interest Rates

The biweekly T-bill auction provides the Bank of Canada with another lever to influence interest rates. Banks and money market dealers compete for Treasury bills because they are an attractive financial instrument: They are backed by the taxing and money-raising powers of the federal government, they are liquid, and there is a large secondary market for them. Moreover, the Bank of Canada's reserve bid can lead to a T-bill rate that suits its policy at the time.[7]

The Bank of Canada can (and does) influence interest rates in three other ways. First, as the federal government's banker, it can manipulate the government's deposits. This action, in turn, influences the level of reserves.[8] Second, it can conduct **open market operations**, which involve the buying and selling of government securities (including T-bills) in regular markets. Third, the Bank of Canada can manipulate the amount of deposits held by banks as it facilitates the cheque-clearing process and in its role as manager of government deposits in the banking system. This *drawdown and redeposit technique* used to be an important tool of monetary policy before reserve requirements were phased out. Cash management techniques have been refined to such an extent

---

4 Until 24 November 1992, the auction was held on Thursdays. The auction was moved to Tuesdays in part because of the considerable turbulence in world foreign-exchange markets and also to allow auction participants more time to process and distribute each new issue. Another motivation might be the fact that the U.S. Federal Reserve sets its key lending rate also on a Tuesday.

5 When the bidding is done, the successful bidders are allotted their T-bills at a common price (a weighted average of winning bids). Before 11 April 1991, bids were expressed on the basis of a price. The yield (for a $1 million T-bill) is the average, weighted by volume, of all accepted bids.

6 In the 1980s, cash management bills were used—they were introduced in 1968—which were T-bills with maturities ranging from 8 to 50 days (the average is around 35 to 42 days) to finance government cash needs of $500 million or more on short notice (the amount is announced one day prior to the auction).

7 For the most part, the Bank tries to stay neutral because, as we will see shortly, it has other instruments at its disposal.

8 This chapter has many references to reserves or reserve requirements, which are funds that banks hold readily available (in cash or at the Bank of Canada) to meet the demands of the depositors. We deal with the subject in depth later. With deregulation, those requirements were phased out in 1994 (although banks will continue to want to hold reserves to meet their customers' needs).

FINANCIAL FOCUS 4.1   IS THIS ANY WAY TO RUN A MARKET?

Until recently, the U.S. federal government sold its debt through a small group of banks and investment dealers who bid in a weekly auction. Analysts such as Friedman suggested for a long time that this practice could lead to collusion, in which a handful of bidders could corner the market, with anti-competitive results.

The problem is less serious in Canada because all chartered banks may participate in the auction and may hold Treasury bills. Since the Bank of Canada places a reserve bid at every auction and monitors the activities, attempts to monopolize the purchase of newly issued government securities are unlikely (Gravelle 1999).[1]

Canada, the United States, and Japan also have active "when-issued" markets in which dealers commit themselves to future sales and purchases prior to the auction. Because market participants can thus avoid the actual auction, the *Wall Street Journal* has said that attempts to solve problems with Treasury bill auctions are "bogus." Poitras suggests, however, that at least in the Canadian case, buyers and sellers in these advance markets do not predict future T-bill yields very well. As recent U.S. experience attests, however, the current system for auctioning government securities does raise some important questions. Solomon Brothers was caught in 1990 and 1991 violating the U.S. rule that stipulates that dealers can purchase no more than 35% of an issue. By purchasing large blocks of securities, the brokers could dictate the price at which these same securities were resold to other dealers, who often had to promise price and quantity ahead of time to their own customers. The U.S. Treasury solved the immediate problem by allowing all brokers to bid on government securities. But there might be better, more basic solutions.

Why not ask the dealers to specify the quantities they want to buy at various prices and expect all purchasers to pay a single average price at the end of bidding, as in Switzerland? In this fashion the demand curve for the particular security is generated, but since no bidder knows the final price for the issue, there is less chance of collusion. Another option would be to open the market to all interested participants. In Canada, noncompetitive bids (see footnote 5) are awarded in this fashion, whereas competitive bids, awarded after noncompetitive bids, are awarded from highest to lowest price. Typically, participants make competitive bids.

Ironically, just as the United States began to question its marketing practices, other countries, such as France, Belgium, and Italy adopted a version of the U.S. auction system.

In the early 1990s, the Bank of Canada became concerned about how the market for Treasury bills was structured,[2] in part because of developments in the financial system that led to fewer investment dealers (see Chapter

17). Another factor was the drive to reduce government borrowing. The combination of these two factors means fewer buyers are chasing fewer dollars, which can be a recipe for cornering the market. It is possible, under existing rules, for an institution to control the stock of a security and withhold it from the market, thereby artificially inflating its price. Indeed, evidence exists that such occurrences are common in all Treasury bill maturities.

As a result, the Bank of Canada released a discussion paper outlining revisions (proposed at the time, now since adopted) to the operations of Government of Canada bond auctions.[3] The report gives specific examples of bond issues believed to have been "squeezed,"[4] necessitating a re-opening of the auction. Among the many changes to the auction rules, perhaps the most important is the requirement that separate bids be made depending on the ultimate destination of the security. Thus, for example, if a primary distributor is purchasing government securities on its own account and that of a customer, this situation would trigger separate bids. In addition, separate bidding limits were introduced for the primary distributors and their clients. Finally, penalties were instituted for illegal behaviour and market surveillance was intensified, with the Bank of Canada also scrutinizing market behaviour. Because of ever-changing market conditions, not to mention the complications of maintaining market liquidity in a world of recurring government surpluses, the Bank of Canada holds regular consultations to ensure that the market for government bonds operates in the most effective manner possible.

Questions for Discussion
1. Why was there concern over collusion in the U.S. system of auctioning government bonds?
2. Do advances in computing make it easier for everyone to participate in the market for government bonds?

Sources
M. Friedman, "How to Sell Government Securities," *Wall Street Journal*, 28 August 1991.
T. Gravelle, "Liquidity of the Government of Canada Securities Market: Stylized Facts and Some Micro Comparisons to the United States Treasury Market," Bank of Canada Working Paper 99-11 (1999).
N. Harvey, "Recent Initiatives in the Market for Government Securities," *Bank of Canada Review* (Summer 1999): 27–35.
G. Poitras, "The When-Issued Market for Government of Canada Treasury Bills," *Canadian Journal of Economics* 24 (August 1991): 604–23.
P. Thomas, and J. Herman, "Treasury Sets Bidding Rules Aimed at Cleaning up Troubled Auctions," *Wall Street Journal*, 23 October 1992.

1 An outstanding problem is that retail investors can pay a hefty premium for buying bonds from dealers because of the lack of transparency of bond prices. For example, an investor wanting to sell a bond for, say, $100, might only be offered $98 for it. Unlike Canada, the U.S. Securities and Exchange Commission is relatively more concerned with the issue. See Reguly (2004), "It's Time to Change How Bonds Are Traded," *Globe and Mail* 7 August, B2.

2 B. McKenna, "Bank Seeks T-bill Crackdown," *The Globe and Mail*, 20 December 1996.

3 "Proposed Revisions to the Rules Pertaining to Auctions of Government of Canada Securities and the Bank of Canada's Surveillance of the Auction Process," Bank of Canada Discussion Paper 1, 19 December 1996.

4 So called because one seller manages to corner the market and influence prices in a manner that is unfavourable to buyers. See Harvey (1999).

that they permit financial institutions to keep cash on hand at a minimum. Nevertheless, cash needs do arise, and banks, for example, frequently need to borrow very short term to satisfy their liquidity needs, such as when the Bank of Canada shifts government funds deposited in banks to its account at the Bank of Canada. By manipulating the available liquidity in the overnight market, the Bank of Canada can influence the overnight rate and, consequently, send signals to the financial market. Today, the overnight market is the principal focus of monetary policy. By supplying extra cash to the system, the overnight rate will fall as the banking system experiences excess reserves (remember the banks aim for zero reserves). The opposite, of course, is true when the Bank of Canada supplies fewer funds than the banks appear to demand and, consequently, the overnight rate will rise.

With the introduction of the **Large Value Transfer System (LVTS)** (see the following section), the Bank of Canada aimed to maintain net amounts to be settled across the financial system at zero. To accomplish this objective, the Bank must neutralize the net impact of public sector transactions between the Bank and the financial system (i.e., deposit-taking institutions).

Technological developments in recent years have permitted the phasing out of mandatory reserves for the banking system. As we shall see later in the text (e.g., Chapter 16), these proved costly for banks, since they typically earned little or no interest. It should be noted that, in part for political reasons, as well as to insure the existence of a buffer against unexpected drains in the financial system, many other regions of the world, including the United States and the European Union, continue to impose mandatory reserve requirements.

LARGE VALUE TRANSFER SYSTEM (LVTS)

See how the LVTS fares
www.cdnpay.ca

As noted above, the speed with which financial transactions take place means that the Bank of Canada has to focus on the overnight market. Since 1994, the Bank has set a target for the overnight rate and has specified a band around it (50 basis point spread between the highest and lowest rates). By changing the target the Bank sends signals about its monetary policy stance. By the end of 2004, the Bank of Canada had changed the band 75 times. This change is accomplished via the special purchase and resale agreement (SPRA) or the purchase and resale agreement (PRA) instruments described below.

This method of conducting monetary policy is closely tied to the operations of the clearing mechanism, called the Automated Clearing Settlement System (ACSS). Although we look at a more detailed example in Chapter 22, it is sufficient for now to understand that, until recently, cheques were cleared overnight and settled retroactively.

The difficulty is that, under such a system, there is a small chance that a cheque may not clear, creating a transaction to reverse the original one, with the additional possibility of still another transaction when funds are once again available. If such defaults occur on a large scale, confidence in the clearing and settlement system is impeded and the risk of such an outcome is known as **systematic risk**. It is precisely because, under the old system, financial transactions were final that over the course of more than 10 years, an international effort to remove as much of the systematic risk as possible was put in place. Ideally, transactions, such as cheque-clearing, would occur more or less instantaneously so that the duration between the presentation of payment and the receipt of funds to the recipient would drop dramatically. In Canada, the result is known as the Large Value Transfer System (LVTS).[9]

Although not strictly speaking a financial instrument, the operation of LVTS can have repercussions on the holdings of financial instruments, so a basic understanding of this process is useful at this stage. We will revisit the LVTS and its place in the conduct of monetary policy in Chapter 22.

Nevertheless, it is worth considering here some of the institutional details concerning the operation of the LVTS. What follows is a highly simplified account of the system. A majority of the transactions are valued at anywhere from $50 000 to between $100 000 and $1 million. As noted previously, the Bank of Canada aims ideally for settlement balances of zero. This is the surest way to avoid the domino effect of systematic risk leading to a collapse of the payments system when one failure to clear a payment reverberates throughout the financial system. During the course of a trading day, or in unusual circumstances, the Bank may be required to inject or withdraw liquidity to ensure that the target overnight rate is met. Recall that the target overnight rate (ON_t^*) on a particular date t is simply the midpoint of the bank rate (BR_t) and the rate paid on positive settlement balances (R_t^{sb}), or

$$ON_t^* = (BR_t + R_t^{sb})/2$$

Now, suppose for the sake of argument that there are two participants in the LVTS program and that on day t, participant i has a positive settlement balance ($LVTS_i > 0$), while the other participant has settlement balances of $LVTS_j < 0$). Ideally then, the following condition will hold:

$$LVTS_i + LVTS_j = 0$$

However, from time to time, the above summation is either positive or negative. If positive, the Bank of Canada must withdraw the excess supply to return the settlement balances to zero; if the sum is negative (as it often is) the Bank of Canada must then inject an amount sufficient for the system to clear.

The Bank, in addition, faces another problem because the federal government, on a daily basis, injects and withdraws funds from its account at the Bank of Canada. Suppose then that on a particular day the federal government deposits $100 million into its account at the Bank of Canada on account of tax revenues received. To prevent an increase in the money supply, the Bank seeks to neutralize any net inflow (or outflow for that matter). The Bank conducts the necessary transfers twice daily (at 9:15 a.m. and then again at 4:15 p.m.). Now, since it is conceivable that the daily settlement balances in the LVTS stand at –$100 million that same day, the Bank need, in principle, do nothing for the aggregate amount of settlement balances will not have changed (since, obviously, +$100 million – $100 million = 0). Nevertheless, if the Bank wished to end the day with positive settlement balances it could do so by changing the amount of liquidity in the system.

In any event, the Bank of Canada uses repurchase agreements (see later in this chapter) to ensure that the amount of liquidity is consistent with its desired level of settlement balances.[10]

Unlike in most countries, the Bank of Canada neither owns nor operates the LVTS created and owned by the Canadian Payments Association (CPA). In July 1996, the *Clearing and Settlement Act* was enacted into law, giving the Bank of Canada regulatory responsibility over the clearing and settlement system.[11] Supporting this legislation is the 2002 Canadian Payments Act which made clear the objectives and responsibilities of the CPA, including the maintenance

---

9 LVTS participants are connected electronically to one another and to institutions internationally, through SWIFT (Society for Worldwide Interbank Financial Telecommunications).

10 The "market" closes daily at 6 p.m., and LVTS participants have a half hour to carry out additional transactions with one another.

11 This includes the Debt Clearing Service (DCS) operated by the Canadian Depository for Securities (DCS), which handles the clearing and settlement of government of Canada debt and, more recently, private sector debt.

of an effective payments settlement system, and ensuring that new technologies and methods are introduced to keep the system up to date.

Overdrafts are charged at the bank rate, which, as pointed out earlier, has been set at the top of the overnight bands since February 1996. The rate earned on surplus balances is equal to the bottom of the overnight rate band, which means that a spread of 50 basis points exists between the penalty rate and the rate on excess settlement balances.

PROVINCIAL AND MUNICIPAL TREASURY BILLS

Provinces and municipalities also issue Treasury bills. They are similar to the federal government's T-bills, but there are no auctions to determine their rate. Instead, the return is based partly on the return on Government of Canada Treasury bills and partly on other factors such as the creditworthiness of the issuer.

Like the federal government, many provincial governments have sharply curtailed their borrowing requirements in the past few years.

GOVERNMENT-BACKED FINANCIAL INSTRUMENTS

Federal and provincial Crown corporations and agencies also raise funds in the money market (and in the capital market as well). For example, the Canadian Wheat Board sells notes through investment dealers. Like provincial government T-bills, they are sold at a discount and, since they ostensibly are fully backed by the federal or provincial government responsible, there is little risk of default. Unlike the case of the federal government's T-bills, however, the secondary market for government-backed financial instruments is less liquid.

BANK OF CANADA ADVANCES

Central banks fulfil a vital function in today's economies: They are **lenders of last resort**—a source of funds for certain institutions (in Canada, primarily chartered banks, trust companies, and investment dealers)—when other sources of funds essentially have been exhausted.

Bank of Canada advances are one of the mechanisms by which the central bank fulfils this function. It advances funds to members of the Canadian Payments Association, generally for one business day, to meet emergency shortages of funds. The loan rate is equivalent to the bank rate. Like many central banks, the Bank of Canada is reluctant to lend funds to the financial institutions, viewing such action as a distinct sign of weakness in the system. It prefers that the institutions seek funds elsewhere; perhaps even more often in Canadian financial history, it has also encouraged mergers between weaker and stronger institutions.

Figure 4.1 chronicles the dollar amount of advances outstanding at the end of each year since the mid-1980s. Notice their relatively small size. The terms and conditions governing Bank of Canada advances have undergone significant changes over the years. Until the 1960s, the usual term for borrowing from the Bank of Canada was between one week and one month. This term has been substantially reduced. Currently, no specified limits are set on the size of a loan or the number of times a loan can be taken out. However, until 1991, there were strict limits based on a formula involving the amount of reserves a bank had on hand and the dollar amount of deposits, up to some maximum ($10 million at one time). Normally, banks could avail themselves of the line of credit at the Bank of Canada at most once or twice a month.

SPECIAL PURCHASE AND RESALE AGREEMENTS

There are times when the Bank of Canada does not succeed in influencing overnight rates to its satisfaction. When this happens, the Bank can intervene directly in financial markets. A **special**

Figure 4.1   **Bank of Canada Advances**

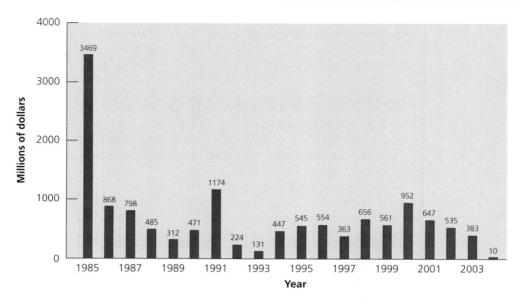

Even over the course of a year, Bank of Canada advances normally do not total huge sums. The overall increase in the mid-1980s is partly explained by changes in the cheque-clearing process following the *Bank Act* of 1980 that increased the number of institutions eligible for financial help from the Bank of Canada. The sharp rise in advances in 1985 resulted largely from the collapse of the Canadian Commercial Bank.

Sources: Adapted in part from the Statistics Canada CANSIM II database **http://cansim2.statcan.ca/cgi-win/CNSMCGI.EXE**, series V36698, and *Bank of Canada Review* (various issues), Table B1. The data are end-of-year figures.

purchase and resale agreement (SPRA) is a two-step transaction between the Bank of Canada and a financial institution, usually an investment dealer. The Bank purchases short-term securities, such as Treasury bills, from the institution, which buys them back the following day. Thus liquidity is injected into the financial system, even if only temporarily. The Bank can also simply reverse the operation—that is, it sells securities one day and repurchases them the next. To distinguish this sort of transaction from an SPRA, it is known as a *reverse PRA* or special sale and repurchase agreement (SRA).

The need for SPRAs arose during the 1980s, when financial institutions were experiencing one-day shortages of liquidity, which drove up interest rates or, at least, made them more volatile. Since the introduction of SPRAs, the Bank of Canada has also used them as a device to ensure that overnight rates stay within the operating band.

An Illustration

Figure 4.2 uses balance sheets to show how an SPRA can be used to avert a temporary liquidity problem in the financial system. Suppose that the Bank of Canada wants to prevent an anticipated rise in the overnight rate. Perhaps this occurs because a bank expects a shortage of liquidity and plans to call in a loan from an investment dealer. If the Bank of Canada wanted to temper the loss of liquidity to the investment dealer, and consequently influence short-term rates, it could offer to purchase an equivalent amount of Treasury bills from the dealer, who uses the proceeds to pay off the loan. The following day, the bank, finding itself with excess reserves, is likely to reverse the transaction and restore the call loan; meanwhile, the SPRA expires and the Bank of Canada is in the same balance sheet position as it was initially. Such transactions can be arranged very quickly, and signals to the money market take literally only minutes to spread throughout the market.

| Figure 4.2 | **Financing through an SPRA** |

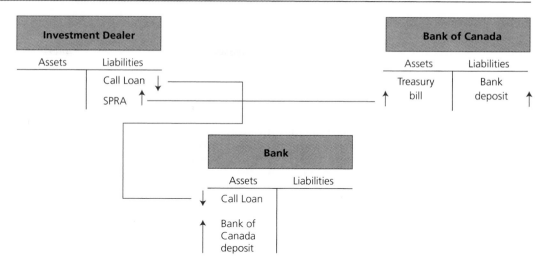

The arrows indicate the direction of changes in assets and liabilities. A bank calls in a loan from an investment dealer and the Bank of Canada offsets the drop in liquidity by offering an SPRA. The transaction is reversed the next day. The SPRA signals an upper limit for overnight interest rates that the Bank of Canada will tolerate.

As noted earlier, SPRAs and SRAs are used in conjunction with the LVTS system. Hence, when the Bank sees that the overnight rate is drifting above the target rate it will intervene via an SPRA to reduce the overnight rate toward its target; obviously, an SRA will be invoked when the Bank witnesses the overnight rate falling below the target rate. We can summarize these two possibilities, using the notation introduced earlier:

$$\text{If } ON_t > ON_t^* \rightarrow \text{ use an SPRA}$$
$$\text{If } ON_t < ON_t^* \rightarrow \text{ use an SRA}$$

The Use of SPRAs and SRAs

The Bank of Canada's most notable use of SPRAs was after the stock market collapse of October 1987. Worried that the tremendous fall in stock prices would lead to a shortage of liquidity and a substantial reduction in the net worth of the money market, the Bank repeatedly made SPRAs available and drove short-term interest rates down by 0.75% in a couple of weeks. When the monetary authorities subsequently viewed the effects of the stock market crash as smaller than anticipated, they reversed the Bank's earlier policy and offered SRAs. By January 1988, overnight money market financing rates had risen to levels higher than they had been before the collapse.

The Bank of Canada used SRAs more frequently than SPRAs in the 1985–94 period, an indication of its policy in those years of generally attempting to keep interest rate levels up. By late 1995 the reverse was true, and the Bank of Canada was putting downward pressure on interest rates.[12]

The situation was reversed for a time from 1997 to early 1999 as overnight rates rose sharply, though not to early 1995 peak levels. SPRA-type transactions dominated the market with no SRAs at all conducted in 1999. The use of SPRAs once again dominated activity in 2001 and 2002

---

12 The data are published in the *Bank of Canada Review,* Table B3.

as interest rates fell sharply. They were used rather infrequently in 2003 and early 2004; there were no SRAs at all in 2003 and 2004.

PURCHASE AND RESALE AGREEMENTS

Purchase and resale agreements (PRAs) operate like SPRAs but are initiated by money market dealers.

PRAs first appeared in Canada in 1953 when the Bank of Canada extended its lender-of-last-resort facility to the emerging money market. Money market dealers can sell the Bank selected assets with an agreement to repurchase them within a 15-day period. (In fact, the repurchase usually takes place the following day). The rate on PRAs has ranged from being equal to the Treasury bill rate minus 0.75% to the T-bill rate plus 0.25%.

PRAs are called "repos" and "reverse repos" in the United States, where they have had a long history as a tool of central bank intervention in the money market.

BANKERS' ACCEPTANCES

A **bankers' acceptance** (BA) is essentially a promise to pay at some future date. As such, a bankers' acceptance can represent a draft drawn by borrowers against their line of credit and are thus "accepted" by the bank. BAs are issued by nonfinancial firms and guaranteed by a bank. The instrument is sold at a discount and is often rediscounted for the sizable secondary market.

The term to maturity can be a few days or up to a year; the most common is the 30- to 90-day range. The denominations can be as much as $1 million; large acceptances are broken into smaller amounts (usually $100 000) for the secondary market.

Illustrating the Mechanics

The need for a financial instrument such as bankers' acceptances originally arose out of the risks inherent in international trade.

A firm selling to another firm on credit may not know enough about the buyer to be comfortable accepting a promise to pay. This scenario is especially likely with a foreign customer. Although the exporter might not be willing to accept an IOU, he or she might be willing to accept the IOU of a customer's bank.

Hence, the attraction of a bankers' acceptance. Figure 4.3 provides a schematic representation of how it works. The importer asks the bank to prepare a **letter of credit**, which is a non-negotiable order from one bank to another, authorizing payment to someone of a particular sum of money up to some maximum. The letter (or *draft*, as it is called), which is in the amount of the goods purchased, is intended for the exporter, which can then discount it, since it effectively implies that the funds exist and are at the exporter's disposal at its own bank. The transaction is completed when the exporter's bank stamps the original letter of credit as accepted, guaranteeing payment. The bank, of course, charges a "stamping" fee, which is equivalent to an interest rate of a fraction of a percent per annum.

Use

Bankers' acceptances have existed for several centuries in the United Kingdom, and they made their appearance in the United States in the early twentieth century. A secondary market emerged in Canada only in 1962, but since then bankers' acceptances have become one of the largest money market instruments in the country.

| Figure 4.3 | **Financing via a Bankers' Acceptance** |

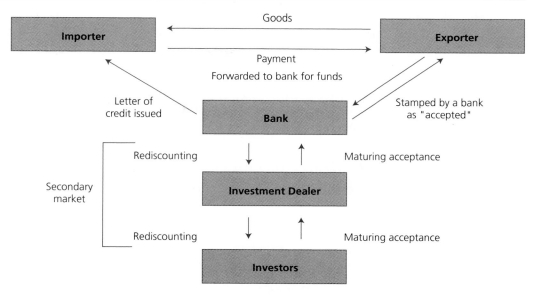

The arrows show the direction of the transactions. The exporter and importer may share the same bank, but it is more likely that each will use his/her bank to obtain a letter of credit and have it accepted.

Indeed, although bankers' acceptances emerged to meet the needs of international trade and to cover the risk of delay between the purchase and subsequent resale of some manufactured good, Canada no longer restricts the type of transaction that can be covered. Since the 1980 *Bank Act*, bankers' acceptances can be issued to virtually any public or private borrower.

Although bankers' acceptances have become relatively less favoured as a money market instrument in recent years, the market for futures in bankers' acceptances has grown exponentially.[13]

DAY-TO-DAY LOANS AND SPECIAL CALL LOANS

Day-to-day loans and special call loans represent the private overnight market. They were introduced in Canada in the 1950s and 1960s to increase liquidity both for the banks and for investment dealers by providing very short-term instruments that could facilitate cash management.

Day-to-day loans (DTDLs) are made, primarily by chartered banks and other financial institutions, to money market dealers that have PRA facilities with the Bank of Canada. For these dealers, DTDLs represent a ready source of liquidity,[14] although the collateral required is of the highest quality: Government of Canada bonds that mature in three years or less, Treasury bills, and bankers' acceptances. The minimum denomination for a DTDL is $100 000.

With the rise of interest rates and their increased volatility, DTDLs, which can be but were not originally overnight loans, are increasingly being replaced by special call loans (SCLs), which are

---

13 In 1990, bankers' acceptances accounted for 21.1% of money market instruments. This percentage fell to 18.3 by 1998. By contrast, bankers' acceptances futures rose threefold in value in the 1995–98 period. See S. Boisvert and N. Harvey, "The Declining Supply of Treasury Bills and the Canadian Money Market," *Bank of Canada Review* (Summer 1998): 53–70.

14 They can also be useful to the lenders. Until reserve requirements were completely phased out, DTDLs could be counted as part of the chartered banks' secondary reserve requirements.

overnight loans made by chartered banks to investment dealers. Unlike DTDLs, SCLs can be secured by commercial and finance company paper as well as by short-term notes issued by the provinces and by financial institutions. Indeed, the overnight market has expanded to include *offstreet lenders*, which include various financial and nonfinancial corporations, as well as government agencies.

No organized market or exchange exists for such loans. Instead, negotiation and trading take place over the telephone. Deals are completed fairly early in the day, when banks receive information about their cash reserve position and European rates on overnight loans are known.

Short-term instruments such as DTDLs and SCLs are useful signals of the stance of monetary policy since the cash requirements of market participants drive the market and, consequently, influence short-term interest rates.

OTHER CHARTERED BANK INSTRUMENTS

So far we have discussed instruments that mainly involve financial institutions of various kinds. In addition, the chartered banks have created a large variety of financial instruments that are used by individuals and other banks, as well as by institutions. The brief list of "other instruments"[15] we consider here concentrates on the wholesale segment of the market (that is, they are issued in amounts of $100 000 or more).

Certificates of Deposit

The bank deposit instruments that enter the money market are called **certificates of deposit (CDs)**, which are issued for fairly sizable time deposits at a fixed interest rate higher than that given for notice deposits. CDs emerged in the United States because legal restrictions on the maximum rate of interest banks could pay did not cover large deposits ($100 000 and up). In Canada, there was a ceiling on the rates banks could charge and thus, by implication, on what they could offer to customers. Deregulation has removed the ceiling, but with the high interest rates of the 1980s, CDs became an important source of funds.

Bearer Deposit Notes

Introduced in 1964, bearer deposit notes (BDNs) are securities not registered in the owner's name (in contrast to CDs, which are). They are sold at a discount and mature at par; maturities range from 30 days to 1 year. BDNs typically are held by money market dealers who then resell them to their clients as buybacks; that is, the dealers arrange to rediscount them and then to repurchase them at a later date.

Interbank Deposits

An **interbank deposit**, as the name implies, is a deposit one bank places in another. The chief advantage of interbank funds has been the opportunity they have provided banks to improve their management of cash reserves as the volume of cheques written on one bank and deposited into another has grown. The need has become particularly great with the increase in the number of foreign banks operating in Canada and the concomitant increase in trading between Canadian and foreign concerns via their respective home banks.

Although banks can deal with each other directly, brokers have emerged to facilitate interbank deposit transactions, particularly between the large institutions.

---

15 Notice that these "other bank instruments" are equivalent to the nonpersonal and notice deposits component of the Canadian money supply.

EUROCURRENCY INSTRUMENTS

The **Eurocurrency** market is the market for financial instruments denominated in a currency other than that of the home country. Eurocurrencies are sometimes called *Eurodollars* because they originated after World War II with U.S.-dollar deposits in European banks.[16] Examples of government instruments under this heading include Canada bills, which are promissory notes issued for a maximum maturity of 270 days, in U.S. dollars, for a minimum denomination of U.S. $1 million. Euro medium-term notes are issued outside the U.S. and Canada, carry either a fixed or a floating interest rate, at either short or long-term maturities, and carry options such as payment of interest in one currency with the principal possibly repaid in another currency. Both these instruments are used to help the government manage its cash reserves in a cost-effective manner. Today, however, they are not limited to Europe or to denomination in U.S. dollars. Japanese banks hold Euromark deposits, Israeli banks issue CDs in Europounds, Germany offers bonds denominated in Swiss francs, and so on.

Not surprisingly, Canada has participated vigorously in the burgeoning Eurocurrency market. The importance of foreign-currency deposits booked by residents at Canadian banks has grown significantly over the past decade. An important reason is, of course, our sizable trading relationship with the United States.

CORPORATE AND FINANCE COMPANY PAPER

Large firms with good credit ratings can borrow funds in the money market directly, rather than indirectly through financial institutions such as banks. So can finance companies.

Corporate paper, called *commercial paper* in the United States, is generally an unsecured promissory note for a specific amount to mature on a specific day. Given the usual short term, the issuers do not necessarily anticipate being able to generate the income required to retire the debt when it matures. Rather, most paper is rolled over; that is, it is simply reissued and sold again (to the same investors or to a new group).

By contrast, finance company paper is a note secured by instalment-debt contracts that have been sold to individuals or commercial concerns for durable consumer or industrial goods.

Both corporate and finance company paper are sold in denominations of $50 000. These instruments are primarily held by institutional investors such as mutual funds, pension funds, and deposit-taking institutions. The corporate bond market has grown, filling the gap left by the reduction in the borrowing needs of the federal government. Indeed, as a result, the Canadian bond market (overall) is ranked sixth in the world, and therefore is comparatively large.[17]

4.2   THE CAPITAL MARKET

The *capital market* is characterized by instruments that generally mature in more than one year.[18] Tables 4.2 and 4.3 describe the principal capital market instruments. You should rely on these lists for the essential points of the discussion that follows.

---

16 See Chapter 24 for more on Eurocurrency instruments, including the history of their development.

17 See Calmès, C. "Regulatory Changes and Financial Structure: The Case of Canada," Bank of Canada working paper 2004 July, 26.

18 All attempts to classify markets, including the one we are using, have drawbacks. It is not always possible to divide financial instruments neatly into mutually exclusive groups of assets that mature in less than one year and those that mature in one year or longer.

| Table 4.2 | Selected Capital Market Instruments | | |

Instruments	Typical Maturities	Principal Borrowers	Secondary Market
Government of Canada bonds	Variable, from 3 years or less to 10 years and longer	Federal government	Yes
Provincial and municipal bonds	Variable, from 3 years or less to 10 years and longer	Provincial governments and municipalities	Yes
Corporate bonds	Variable, from 3 years or less to 10 years and longer	Corporations	Yes
Debentures	2 to 20 years	Private corporations, public utilities	Yes
Stocks	Variable, depending on conditions	Corporations	Yes

As in Table 4.1 the highlighted boxes distinguish the items that are especially important either because they have wide-ranging effects on the entire financial system or because the volume of trade in them is huge. *Source:* M.G. de Vries, *The IMF in a Changing World: 1945–85* (Washington, D.C.: International Monetary Fund, 1986).

| Table 4.3 | Main Types of Financial Derivatives | | |

Instruments	Typical Maturities	Principal Borrowers	Secondary Market
Futures	Contracts can mature in months or over 1 year	Chartered banks and money market dealers	Yes
Options	Exercise at strike price on or before expiration date	Chartered banks, near-banks, and money market dealers	Yes
Swaps	Exchange of interest streams over the lives of the underlying debt issue	Chartered banks, near-banks, and money market dealers	Yes
STRIPS	Can be semiannual to over 10 years	Federal government	Yes
Forward rate agreements (FRAs)	Agreement on an interest rate to prevail in the future	Corporations	Yes
Bankers' acceptances futures (BAX)	Much like FRAs except derived from BAs	Deposit-taking institutions	Yes

As in Table 4.1 the highlighted boxes distinguish the items that are especially important either because they have wide-ranging effects on the entire financial system or because the volume of trade in them is huge.

BONDS

A **bond** is a certificate of long-term debt issued by a public entity or a corporation. Bonds are generally issued at par and return to the investor a *coupon rate* (a rate stated on the bond) one or more times a year. This rate can differ from the effective return because of price fluctuations in the relatively large secondary market for bonds.[19] Federal government bonds are a useful bench-

---

19 Exactly how the return on a bond is measured is the subject of the next chapter.

mark because they are considered default-risk free. The probability that other bond issuers will default is reported by the various services that provide *bond ratings*.

Find out about the Government of Canada securities market **www.fin.gc.ca/ secur/gocsec_e. html** and **www.bankof-canada.ca/en/auct. htm**

Government of Canada Bonds

The federal government issues bonds with an array of maturities and in many denominations. They vary from the Canada Savings Bonds familiar to many individuals to million-dollar bonds purchased by huge investors such as pension funds. Since April 1992, all such bonds have been sold at auction. The auction usually takes place on a Wednesday, but since the *Notice of Call for Tenders* is issued earlier (about a week), the bonds trade on a "when-issued" basis at first. Each bid is for a minimum of $25 000 and a maximum of $3 million. The coupon rate is set to the one-quarter of 1% nearest to the average yield of successful bidders.[20] In contrast, bidding on real-return bonds is based on the principles of a "Dutch auction," that is, all successful bidders are allotted the highest real yield based on tenders.

Government of Canada bonds are held by four groups in society: The Bank of Canada, chartered banks, the general public,[21] and foreigners. Figure 4.4 shows the evolution of the Government of Canada's debt since the late 1980s. The general public holds by far the largest share. The proportion of the total held by foreigners has fallen somewhat from its peak in 1993.

It is also interesting to note the average maturity of the Canadian government's debt. During the 1979–89 period, it peaked at seven years and two months in 1979 and fell to just four years by the end of 1990.[22] Since then the average maturity of Government of Canada debt has risen

| Figure 4.4 | Holders of Canadian Government Debt |

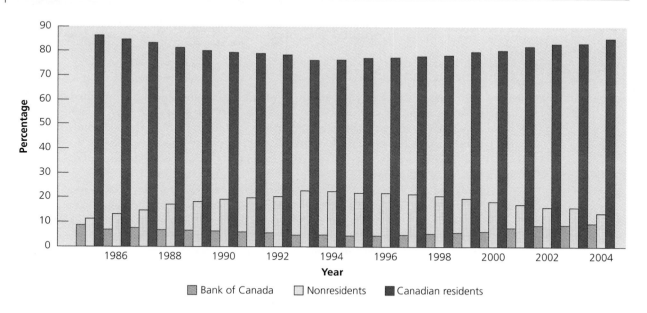

Sources: Adapted from the Statistics Canada CANSIM II database **http://cansim2.statcan.ca/cgi-win/CNSMCGI.EXE**, series V3769 (Bank of Canada), V37336 (residents and nonresidents), V37235 (nonresidents). The figures for Canadian residents include domestic financial institutions.

20 For example, if the average yield is 7.9%, then the coupon rate is set at 6.75%.
21 The general public consists of individuals, nonfinancial firms, near-banks, investment dealers, mutual funds, insurance companies, and provincial and municipal governments.
22 See *Bank of Canada Banking and Financial Statistics,* Table G6. (Series CANSIM II: V37346).

to more than six years, in keeping with the federal finance department's debt strategy. Part of the reason for these developments, as we will see in the next chapter, was changes in the *real* cost of the debt. Both the nominal return and inflation are factors here. In 1979, for example, the return on a Treasury bill was 11.57%, while inflation in consumer prices reached 7.90%. The difference, called the *real interest rate*, was 3.67%, which is quite close to the long-run historical value. By 1994, however, the real interest rate had risen to 5.41%, and it remained relatively high until the beginning of this century, when it fell back to around 3%. High real interest rates make short-term debt more attractive to lenders since they want to earn the high returns while possible (they assume interest rates eventually will fall to their average historical value).

The volatility of interest rates produced so much uncertainty about the real return on long-term bonds that the government of Canada introduced *real return (indexed) bonds* in fall 1991. Patterned after a similar instrument offered in the United Kingdom since 1981, they promise a specific real return—4.25% for the first issue—by adjustment of the semiannual coupon rate as well as the principal according to changes in the consumer price index. If the real cost of borrowing is fixed, the government can better predict its borrowing costs and lenders receive a certain real return.

In 1998, the government of Canada launched a buy-back program for its bonds in the wake of the elimination of federal deficits and the express policy of the government to reduce the public debt. Of course, since government bonds are useful as a signal of interest rates across the term structure, as well as desirable financial assets in most individuals' and institutions' portfolios, there is concern that a rapid reduction in the amount of debt outstanding will reduce liquidity in the financial sector. To prevent such problems, the government can reduce the frequency of new bond issues and buy back less liquid outstanding issues (usually very long-term bonds), replacing them with new issues.[23]

Since there is no national regulator, a variety of groups and institutions oversee the market for bonds. They include the Bank of Canada, the Ministry of Finance, provincial securities commissions, the Canadian Securities Administrators, and the Investment Dealers Association.[24]

Other Bonds

The list of bonds issued is rounded out by provincial, municipal, and corporate bonds. Apart from differences in risk and other characteristics, they are similar to Government of Canada bonds. Such bonds are less likely to be auctioned than Government of Canada bonds. Canada has the distinction of having one of the world's largest corporate bond markets.

Finally, debentures are a special kind of bond in that they are backed by the future sales or earning power of a corporation.

Bonds and debentures generally are sold to the public via an **underwriter** (often a syndicate of underwriters), an investment dealer who helps governments and corporations to raise capital by buying new securities (bonds or stocks) from the issuer at a discount and reselling them to investors. Until recently, commercial banks in Canada and the United States were prohibited from underwriting corporate debt. This regulation was the result of legislation, dating at least from the Great Depression of 1929–33, that separated the underwriting and commercial lending functions. Legislation in both countries has done away with this legal separation in the financial system.

---

23 Bonds can be returned in a number of ways. The government can hold a "reverse auction," which is simply the reverse of the kind of auction conducted for other bonds. Alternatively, the government simply can offer to buy back bonds in a given maturity range (called a coupon pass), or it can convert less liquid bonds into more liquid bonds (called benchmark bonds). See T. Gravelle, "Buying Back Government Bonds: Mechanics and Other Considerations," Bank of Canada Working Paper 98-9 (June 1998).

24 More details can be found in E. Chouinard and Z. Lalini, "The Canadian Fixed-Income Market: Recent Developments and Outlook," Bank of Canada Review (Winter 2001/2002): 15–25.

Figure 4.5	Net New Issues of Bonds and Stocks by the Corporate Sector

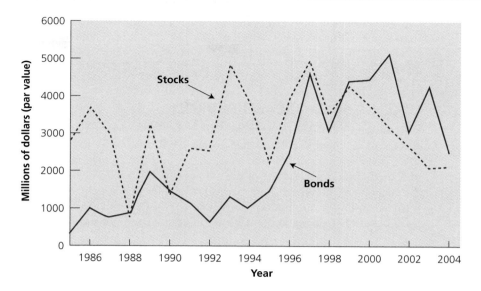

Notice the dramatic drop in new issues of stock in 1988 and again in 2000–2001. This phenomenon reflects the repercussions from the October 1987 stock market crash and the end of the "tech bubble" in 2000. The sharp rise in stock issues in the 1990s reflects the bull market for stocks; while the rise in new bond issues reflects strong economic performance, though this slowed down beginning in 2001.

Sources: Adapted from the Statistics Canada CANSIM II database series V122315 (bonds) and V122358 (stocks).

STOCKS

Private corporations also raise funds in the capital market through the issue of **stocks**, which are shares of ownership. Figure 4.5 reveals that corporations seeking to raise funds rely on both types of capital market instruments in roughly equal proportions, though there is a slight tendency to prefer stocks, especially since 2000.

4.3   THE MARKET FOR DERIVATIVES

As we have already emphasized, the increase in the volatility of interest rates and exchange rates that began in the 1970s has made future rates difficult to predict and increased the likelihood that investors will suffer losses. Consequently the value of products that can mitigate the effects of unpredictable changes in returns has been enhanced. Thus, the last few years have seen the development of many **derivative products**, new financial instruments created from existing ones. We will explore some of the more technical aspects of derivatives in Chapter 15. Some of the most widely used derivatives in Canada are listed in Table 4.3.

FUTURES AND FORWARDS

A *futures contract* is a purchase contract stipulating that a particular asset is to be delivered at a predetermined future date. Because investors use financial futures to hedge against capital losses, delivery generally is not taken. *Forward contracts* also exist, particularly in foreign exchange; these agreements are similar to futures, but the investor actually takes delivery of the financial asset in question.

OPTIONS

An *option* is the right, but not the obligation, to buy or sell an asset on or before a particular date. Investors use financial options as a device to protect themselves from higher- or lower-than-expected future prices. A call option gives the investor the opportunity to purchase a financial instrument at a specified price. A put option is an option to sell a financial instrument at a particular price.

WHEN-ISSUED TREASURY BILLS

When-issued T-bills, introduced in 1978 in the T-bill market, permit the possibility of engaging in forward trading of T-bills. A **when-issued T-bill** is a contract to buy or sell, at an agreed-to price, stated dollar amounts of T-bills to be sold at the next weekly auction. Trading begins when the Bank of Canada announces the size of the following week's auction and ends just before the results of the auction are announced. The market is useful for the participants because it can act as a gauge for determining future interest rates. The Bank of Canada uses the information generated by this market to assess market sentiments about the course of short-term interest rates.

OTHER DERIVATIVE PRODUCTS

More recent derivative products include:

Find out more about derivatives in Canada
www.m-x.ca/ accueil_en.php

1. Interest rate *swaps,* in which investors exchange interest payments.[25] They do so because they have different expectations about the future. For example, suppose a financial officer with a corporation that holds long-term debt with a fixed interest rate believes that short-term interest rates are about to fall. His counterpart officer with a firm that holds short-term debt expects the opposite scenario for interest rates. The two firms have an incentive to exchange interest payments but not the debt.

2. *STRIPS* (Separate Trading of Registered Interest and Principal of Securities), which are zero-coupon instruments created by separating the principal from the coupons or interest payments (which are then sold separately). STRIPS bonds are sold at a discount. The return is paid at maturity so that the discounted price of stripped notes rises until then. The major attraction of STRIPS, which involve no periodic interest payments, is that their yields to maturity are certain (they do not depend on the return from interest payments reinvested over time).

3. *Forward rate agreements* (FRAs), in which an intermediary, typically a bank, agrees to provide funds at a specific interest rate for a specified period of time.

4. *Bankers' acceptances futures (BAX)*, traded on the Montreal Exchange, have become a leading indicator of future money market interest rate conditions. They have existed since the late 1980s, but only recently have become a key money market instrument. The BAX operates on the same general principles as other types of futures contracts.

5. *Securitization:* Some of the financial instruments covered in this chapter, such as bonds, are tradeable, while others, for example, bank loans or mortgages, are not. However, by grouping or packaging outstanding bank loans or mortgages, banks have been able to create a secondary market for such instruments. This process is called securitization (see Chapter 3), which has led to the creation of mortgage-backed securities and asset-backed securities.

---

25 There are also foreign exchange swaps; see Chapter 15.

SUMMARY

- A bewildering variety of financial instruments exists. This chapter defines some of the most important ones.

- A simple classification of financial instruments is into money market instruments, which have a maturity of a year or less, and capital market instruments, which have a maturity that usually exceeds a year.

- Tables 4.1, 4.2, and 4.3 highlight the principal money market and financial market instruments surveyed in this chapter.

- The principal money market instrument is the overnight rate. The Bank of Canada sets an operating band of 50 basis points that it adjusts when it wants the general level of interest rates to rise or fall.

- The Treasury bill market has historically served as the key interest rate indicator. Its influence has waned considerably as governments move into an era of surpluses and declining public debt.

- Treasury bills are sold in an auction setting where buyers bid for new issues. A higher price translates into a lower yield and vice-versa.

- The LVTS is designed to speed up the clearing and settlement process in the payments system and reduce systemic risk. This system allows for almost instantaneous settlement of cheques.

- Bank of Canada advances are loans made to members of the Canadian Payments Association at the bank rate, now related to the overnight rate. The Bank of Canada discourages borrowing, but the lender-of-last-resort function remains an important one for the central bank.

- The Bank of Canada ensures that overnight rates fluctuate within the operating band through special purchase and resale agreements (SPRA) and special sales and repurchase agreements (SRA).

- Bankers' acceptances represent an important private sector money market instrument. They are essentially postdated certified cheques.

- Eurocurrency instruments are important international money market instruments. They represent debt denominated in a currency other that of the home currency.

- Important capital market instruments include Government of Canada bonds and stocks.

- In recent years, many new financial products have been created that are derived from existing financial instruments. Derivatives include futures and options. Such instruments are a promise to buy or sell an instrument at a price to prevail in the near future but which is negotiated today.

IMPORTANT TERMS

Bank of Canada advances, 55
bank rate, 49
bankers' acceptance, 58
basis point, 50
bond, 62
certificates of deposit (CDs), 60
corporate paper, 61
derivative products, 65
Eurocurrency, 61
interbank deposit, 60
Large Value Transfer System (LVTS), 53
lender of last resort, 55

letter of credit, 58
open market operations, 51
overnight rate band, 50
par value, 49
special purchase and resale agreement (SPRA), 55
stocks, 65
systematic risk, 53
Treasury bills (T-bills), 49
underwriter, 64
when-issued T-bill, 66

PROBLEMS

1. Suppose the Bank of Canada feels that the prices being bid at its weekly Treasury bill auction are too low and places a reserve bid. Does this mean that the Bank wants higher or lower interest rates?

2. Why do you think that Bank of Canada advances typically are so small in dollar terms (see Figure 4.1)?

3. What do you think is meant by the real interest rate concept mentioned in the chapter? (Don't cheat by looking at Chapter 5!) Why is the concept an important one in economics?

4. Why do higher real interest rates tend to shorten the average maturity of government bonds?

5. Swaps were created because investors may have opposite expectations about the future course of interest rates. Is this possible? If so, develop a plausible scenario that would produce such a situation.

6. Figure 4.5 shows two ways in which businesses raise funds. Can you think of another source of borrowing that is omitted from this figure?

7. Would you expect the spread of bids for the weekly T-bill auction to be large or small? Why? What are some of the factors determining the spread in bidding prices?

8. Explain how SPRAs or SRAs can be used to influence interest rates. Which one would be used to lower the overnight rate?

9. What are the risks faced by a bank that is involved in the type of bankers' acceptance transaction depicted in Figure 4.3?

DISCUSSION QUESTIONS

1. One of the reasons the federal government has moved away from financing a large part of its expenditures with Canada Savings Bonds is the havoc the sale plays with monetary aggregates. Which monetary aggregates are affected and why is this a cause for concern at the Bank of Canada?

2. In both Canada and the United States, legislators have had an aversion to allowing banks to underwrite corporate debt. The Canadian banks have complained that this puts them at a disadvantage relative to near-banks, which have not faced the same restriction. What is it that legislators worry about?

3. Swaps and FRAs worry central banks because they fear loss of monetary control over the short run. Are their fears unfounded?

4. According to Figure 4.5, corporations have shown a distinct preference for issuing bonds rather than stocks since 2000. Can you explain why?

5. Why might the when-issued T-bill market provide information about future short-term interest rates?

6. The fall in the importance of Canada Savings Bonds might also reflect the changing preferences of investors. Why?

7. How would a reverse auction operate?

ONLINE APPLICATIONS

1. Go to the U.S. Public Debt Web site at **www.publicdebt.treas.gov/**. You can keep track on a daily basis of the size of the U.S. public debt. What is its value today? The U.S. government introduced buy-back rules for U.S. debt in January 2000. Which of the three options to retire Canada's debt considered in this chapter did the United States adopt? Why?

2. Go to the Bank of Canada's Web site at **www.bankofcanada.ca/en/financial_ markets/index.htm** and read about the Bank of Canada's role in managing government debt.

   (a) What is retail debt?

   (b) Why did the government feel the need to create a separate agency for certain types of government debt? (For example, go to the Canada Savings Bonds Web site at **www.cis-pec.gc.ca/eng**.)

   (c) Download the latest *Bank of Canada Annual Report* at the Bank of Canada's Web site **www.bankofcanada.ca/eu/annual/index.htm**. What is the Bank's role in the management of government debt?

   (d) Have there been any notable changes in either the management or structure of government debt noted by the Bank of Canada?

References can be found on **www.mcgrawhill.ca/college/siklos**

Explaining the Behaviour of Financial Asset Prices: Interest Rates and Exchange Rates

Understanding Interest Rates: Definitions and Concepts

LEARNING OBJECTIVES

After reading and studying this chapter, you should be able to

5.1   define the interest rate and the present value concept

5.2   describe the yield to maturity as an interest rate measure and explain why it is important

5.2   list the interest rate calculations associated with different payment schemes

5.2   explain how the yield on simple loans, coupon bonds, zero coupon bonds, STRIPS, and other instruments is evaluated

5.3   explain the real interest rate and why it is an important concept

5.3   identify how strong the connection is between inflation and the nominal interest rate

Having introduced you to the principal institutions and instruments of the financial system, we are now ready to consider models of that system.

Because we are dealing with complex phenomena that involve a number of interrelated factors—interest rates, wealth, savings, inflation, risk, people's expectations, to name but a few—selecting a beginning point is problematic. We're going to start—not quite at random—with interest rates, which are the primary prices of finance.

To see why, consider that financial markets, like all markets, result from the interaction of supply and demand, which sets a price. An individual holding a financial asset forgoes some consumption of goods and services today in the hope of benefiting from more consumption in the future. Similarly, the individual holding the debt forgoes some future consumption to raise current consumption. The same logic applies to firms if we replace "consumption" with "profit." In other words, the individual or firm makes a decision about the extent to which the future is *discounted*. The person lending money today discounts the future to a lesser extent than the one who borrows today. The more an individual discounts the future, the more he or she prefers consumption today. Current and future consumption can, in effect, be traded in a market because individuals differ in the degree to which they discount the future. Alternatively, they may have the same discount rate but expect different future income streams. Someone with surplus current income can seek to trade with someone else whose current income is insufficient to maintain a certain level of consumption.

In other words, individuals (and firms) differ in their *time preference*, which is the degree to which they value immediate consumption over deferred consumption. In effect then, debt is a futures contract for money. The debtor promises to pay the lender stipulated amounts—interest at a certain rate—on specific future dates; eventually, the debt instrument *matures* and the principal becomes due. In Chapter 15, we will explore the many different ways we can contract, which involve future promises of delivery or price of financial products.

Words have to be used carefully here. People sometimes call interest rates the price of money. Such a statement is misleading. The price of money is the amount that money can buy—that is, the *purchasing power* of money. Interest is the price of *renting* money.

Defining the interest rate more exactly is complicated by several factors. First, paying a return on a financial asset can be done in various ways. For example, some debts are to be repaid over time and others in a lump sum.

Because of these complexities, we discuss interest rates in two parts. In this chapter, we consider only definitions and the basic concepts of various interest rate measures. In the next, we examine how financial markets determine interest rate levels and changes.

Then, in later chapters in this part of the text, we turn to discussions of exchange rates and their connection to interest rate developments. By the end of this part, we consider the *structure of interest rates*—that is, how they differ by type of risk, by term to maturity, and across countries.

5.1   THE PRESENT VALUE CONCEPT

Although the activities of borrowing and lending involve a futures contract, the price of that contract must be set at the time the loan is made. To understand how such a price is set requires a clear knowledge of the present value concept.

Suppose an individual borrows $\$PV_t$ at time t, and promises to pay the lender $\$FV$ one year from today. The difference between the amount to be repaid and the amount borrowed is the price of renting money; expressed as a percentage of the debt, it is the **interest rate**. Letting R_t denote the interest rate at time t (today), we write

$$R_t = \text{(dollars to be paid back one year from today} - \text{dollars received today)} \div \text{dollars received today} \tag{5.1}$$

or, in terms of our notation,

$$R_t = (\$FV - \$PV_t)/\$PV_t \tag{5.2}$$

We can also solve equation (5.2) in terms of the amount of the debt, $\$PV_t$, to obtain

$$\$PV_t = \$FV/(1 + R_t) \tag{5.3}$$

The last expression simply states the value today of $\$FV$ to be delivered one year from today. The term $1/(1 + R_t)$ is then the discount factor for a one-year loan at an interest rate of R_t. In other words, we are talking about the **present value** (PV_t) of an amount to be received by the lender at a particular time in the future.

Since R_t is positive (renting money has a positive cost), the denominator in equation (5.3) must be greater than 1, so the $\$FV$ on the right-hand side of the expression must be greater than $\$PV_t$.

Such a result makes sense since a market for debt exists because the debtor is able to consume today but forgoes some consumption tomorrow. Hence, one dollar paid out a year from today is worth less than one dollar today.

Alternatively, we can rewrite equation (5.3) by multiplying both sides by $(1 + R_t)$ to obtain

$$(1 + R_t)\$PV_t = \$PV_t + \$PV_t R_t = \$FV \tag{5.4}$$

$\$PV_t$ is also called the *principal*, or the size, of the debt, and $\$PV_t R_t$ is the *interest cost*.

Note from either equation (5.4) or (5.3) that R_t and $\$PV_t$ are inversely related. Consider a numerical example. Suppose the annual interest rate is 0.10 or 10%. If $\$100$ is to be delivered one year from today, what is the size of the debt today? From equation (5.3),

$$\$PV_t = 100/(1 + 0.10) = 90.91 \text{ or } \$90.91$$

Alternatively, we can ask what the annual rate of interest is on a debt that is valued today at $90.91 and at $100 one year from today. To obtain the answer substitute today's value in equation (5.2):

$$R_t = (100 - 90.91)/90.91$$
$$= 9.09/90.91 = 0.10 \text{ or } 10\%$$

Thus, the present value of $100 at a 10% annual interest rate is $90.91. (Note that in this example $90.91 is the principal and $9.09 is the interest cost of the debt.)

We can easily generalize this one-year example to a case in which an amount borrowed today is to be delivered several years into the future. Since R_t is the annual interest rate—by convention, interest is stated on an *annual* basis—a multiyear debt involves a compounding of interest, that is, the payment of interest on previously reinvested interest payments. Thus, continuing with the previous example, $90.91 will be worth $110 after two years, or equivalently,

$$\$90.91(1 + 0.10)(1 + 0.10)$$
$$= \$90.91(1.1)(1.1)$$
$$= \$90.91 \,(1.1)^2$$

The *term (maturity)* of the loan affects the number of times we multiply the amount of principal. To continue the example, the total amount due on maturity after n years will be

$$100(1 + 0.10)^n \qquad\qquad\qquad \textbf{(5.5)}$$

The present value of $100 received n years in the future is, from equation (5.3),

$$\$PV_t = \$100/(1 + 0.10)^n$$

The higher the value of n, the smaller the value of $\$PV_t$.

To illustrate the effects these relationships create, Figure 5.1 shows the present value in the year 2006 of $100 due between 2007 and 2017 for three interest rate levels. Notice that, for any interest rate, $100 due in 2017 is worth considerably less in 2007 than in, say, 2010.

Higher interest rates have the effect of reducing the present value of $100 regardless of when the loan was taken out. Hence, the general rule that the price of a financial asset is inversely related to the interest rate paid on the asset.

Table 5.1(A) shows that at interest rates of less than 10%, the present value of $100 one year from today is greater than $90.91, and at interest rates of more than 10%, the present value falls to less than $90.91. Table 5.1(B) shows how present value is influenced by the term of a loan for a given interest rate. The longer the term to maturity, the larger the interest cost of the debt.

5.2   YIELD TO MATURITY

In the simple one-year loan we have been considering, the interest rate is the same as the **yield to maturity**, which is the actual rate of return from a stream of payments received when a debt is incurred today. Suppose the amount borrowed today is to be repaid by a single payment at some specified time in the future. By returning to Table 5.1(B), we see that, if the interest rate is 10% and the principal borrowed is $100, the interest cost for a debt repaid in one year's time is

$$\$110 - \$100 = \$10$$

which represents a total yield of

$$\$10/100 = 0.10 \text{ or } 10\%$$

| **Figure 5.1** | **Present Value in the Year 2006 of $100 Due in the Future** |

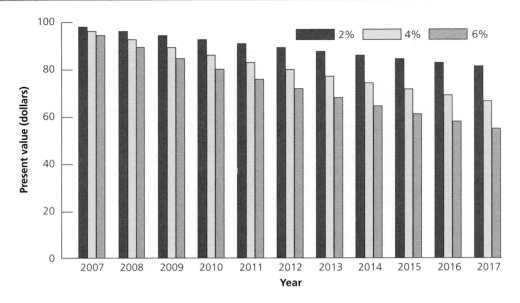

The present values were calculated by applying equation (5.5) for $n = 1$ through $n = 11$ and for interest rates of 2%, 4%, and 6%. For example, $100 to be delivered in the year 2017 represents $80.43 in present value terms at a 2% interest rate. Or $80.43 invested at 2% for 11 years (2007–2017) yields $100.v

For a loan repaid at the end of five years, the interest cost is

$$\$161.05 - \$100 = \$61.05$$

which represents a total return of

$$\$61/\$100 = 0.6105 \text{ or } 61.05\%$$

| **Table 5.1** | **Present Values at Various Interest Rates and Terms** |

(A)

One-Year Term	
Present Value	**Interest Rate(%)**
$100.00	0
95.24	5
90.91	10
86.96	15
83.33	20
80.00	25

(B)

Annual Interest Rate of 10%		
Term (Years)	**Present Value**	$(I + R_t)^n$
1	$100.00	1.1000
2	100.00	1.2100
3	100.00	1.3310
4	100.00	1.4641
5	100.00	1.6105

That amount represents an *average annual rate of return* or *yield* of

$$61.05\%/5 \text{ years} = 12.21\%$$

even though the loan was taken out at an interest rate of 10%. The yield is 12.21% because of the effect of compounding. We now see that there are two ways of thinking about yields. The average annual yield is simply the total return (as a percentage) divided by the number of years until maturity. If the investment is not held until maturity, then we need a different concept, and here we use the yield until maturity. In almost all the examples in the text, we will assume that all investments are held until maturity. However, this is done for simplicity only. Clearly, not all investments need to be held until maturity.

Of course, not all financial instruments mature many years in the future. Indeed, some mature in less than one year, as we shall see below. An annual percentage rate often is stated for such an instrument, but the annual yield will be somewhat higher. The reason again is compounding. For example, if a financial instrument is offered for a term of three months (one-quarter of a year) at 12% per year, the interest rate is equivalent to

$$\frac{12\%}{4} = 3\%$$

for three months. At the end of one year, however, each dollar invested at 3% each quarter (there are four quarters in one year) will be worth

$$\$1 \times (1.03)^4 = 1.126$$

which translates into an annual yield of

$$12.6\%$$

These calculations explain the sometimes confusing bank advertisements that list two annual interest rates for the same financial instrument.

For example, when an advertisement suggests that the annual return on an investment is 20%, you might be tempted to conclude that the monthly return is 1.67%, that is, 20%/12. In fact, the monthly return is only 1.53% per month, which is compounded to yield 20% as follows

$$(1.0153)^{12} - 1 = 0.20 \text{ or } 20\%$$

The *effective* return is 20%, while the annual return is only about 18% (0.015×12). If you are a borrower, then the same advertisement might emphasize the annual return, while a prospectus for some mutual fund might prefer to emphasize the effective return. Either way, it is buyer beware.

Although the foregoing numerical examples are helpful, it is useful to have a formula for calculating the yield to maturity on a simple financial instrument. The yield to maturity is the value for R_t obtained from

$$\$PV_t = \$FV/(1 + R_t/k)^{kn} \tag{5.6}$$

where $\$FV$ is the principal loan and k is the number of times a year interest is compounded. In the typical case considered in this text, k is 1, so the equation (5.6) becomes

$$\$PV_t = \$FV/(1 + R_t)^n$$

If the term of the loan is also one year, $n = 1$ and the expression simply becomes equation (5.3). At the other extreme, if $100 is compounded daily at 10% for a two-year period, then

$$\$PV_t = \$100(1 + 0.10/365)^{365(2)} = \$122.14$$

ECONOMICS FOCUS 5.1   CAN INTEREST RATES BE NEGATIVE?

The obvious answer to the question implied by the title seems to be *no*. After all, it is hard to believe that someone would lend, say, $100 only to receive $99 one year from today. Yet, during 1999 some short-term nominal interest rates in Japan were actually negative! How is this possible? First, the calculations of present value in this chapter assume that holding cash is costless or, rather, that the opportunity cost of holding money is the interest forgone on some interest-earning investment. But when large sums of money are involved, the costs of holding cash are not zero (think of individuals paying a safety deposit box fee because of the possibility of theft or damage to valuables, including large sums of cash). Then there is also the possibility that a government wants banks and other private sector groups to borrow money when economic conditions would lead them not to. A sure way of doing so is to lend them money with a promise of a repayment that is less than the principal. Japan, mired in a serious recession for over a decade, followed this prescription. Moreover, since the Japanese banking system has been largely insolvent for the past few years, or at least financially very weak, investors might actually be willing to receive a "negative" interest rate from a riskless government bond. This is true even if banks offer a small positive interest rate because of public fears that the bank might fail and their cash disappear. Japan is not the only country to have experienced negative interest rates. In the U.S., in late 2003, negative interest rates were recorded on repos (see Chapter 3). Why?

Lenders actually were willing to pay interest to borrowers to obtain the securities that other buyers had placed an order for. This was thought to be cheaper than losing customers (Fleming and Garbade 2003).

Questions for Discussion
1. Go to the Bank of Japan's Web site at **www.boj.or.jp/en/index/htm**. Find out how long short-term interest rates have been negative. Has the Bank of Japan commented on the negative interest rate issue? Discuss.
2. Does a deliberate policy of negative short-term interest rates seem strange? (Although a little difficult, you may find Paul Krugman's discussion of the dilemmas faced by Japanese policymakers rather entertaining. See his "Thinking about the Liquidity Trap" at **www.wws.princeton.edu/~pkrugman/**.

Source
D.L. Thornton, "Nominal Interest Rates: Less Than Zero?" *Monetary Trends*, Federal Reserve Bank of St. Louis (January 1999).
M.J. Fleming and K.D. Garbade "Repurchase Agreements with Negative Interest Rates," *Current Issues in Economics and Finance* 10(5), 2003, available at **www.newyorkfed.org/research/current_issues/ci10-5.html**.

which implies an average annual yield of 11.07%. (In this example we assume that each year consists of 365 days.[1])

In general, the yield on a debt instrument need not be the same as the interest rate stipulated in the contract between the lender and the borrower. (It is the yield to maturity that is typically reported in the financial press.)

MORE COMPLEX REPAYMENT SCHEMES

In the examples we have considered so far, we implicitly assumed that the lender would receive both principal and interest when the debt matured. Most debt contracts, however, specify other repayment schedules. These different schemes can, in a subtle manner, influence how we evaluate the yields on different financial instruments. Below, we consider three common types of debt repayment schemes.

Fixed-Payment Loans

Some debt instruments involve a series of equal, fixed payments throughout the term of the debt so that the principal and the interest are both repaid by the end of the contract, a process called *amortization*. If you have had a course in finance or accounting, you have probably learned to call such

---

1 It is also conceivable that a financial instrument might pay interest only during weekdays, in which case, assuming a year consists of 52 weeks, interest will be paid over 52 × 5 (number of weekdays) = 260 days.

a fixed-payment loan an *annuity*. Some pensions, also called *annuities*, are debts of this type (the individual loans that are repaid by an insurance company or other backer in a stream of constant payments for a specified number of years). Another example is the conventional home mortgage.

Suppose that a mortgage of $100 000 is to be repaid over 20 years at an interest rate of 7%. What are the annual payments? Finding the answer involves solving an equation much like equation (5.7) below. The flow of payments throughout the term of the loan is written as

$$\$Debt = \frac{\$A}{(1+R)} + \frac{\$A}{(1+R)^2} + \ldots + \frac{\$A}{(1+R)^n} \tag{5.7}$$

where $\$Debt$ is the size of the mortgage and $\$A$ is the fixed payment (or annuity as it is sometimes called) throughout the term. In our example, where $\$Debt = \$100\ 000$ and $R = 0.07$ or 7%

$$\$100\ 000 = \frac{\$A}{1.07} + \frac{\$A}{(1.07)^2} + \ldots + \frac{\$A}{(1.07)^{20}}$$

Solving for A yields approximately $9240.

But A is the annual amount, and mortgage payments are typically made monthly. To compute the monthly payment, we need to recognize that 240 payments (12 payments per year for 20 years) will be made over the term of the loan and that a 7% annual interest rate is equivalent to a 0.583% monthly interest rate (7%/12).[2] When we use these figures in equation (5.7), the monthly payment is approximately $770.

In practice, the computation of an equation such as (5.7) often proceeds by assuming a value (or range of values) for the size of the debt, the prevailing interest rate, and the desired term for the loan to arrive at a value (or range of values) for A. The reason is that the size of the debt will be a function of the individual's current and anticipated future income or the firm's expected profit stream.

Tables showing the monthly or annual payment necessary to amortize a loan are widely available. So are computer programs for the calculation. They are based on an expression such as equation (5.7).[3]

Coupon Bonds

A *coupon bond* is a debt instrument in which fixed interest payments are made throughout the life of the contract but the principal is repaid in a lump sum at the end of the term. The interest payment is called the *coupon payment* and the interest rate the **coupon rate**. Coupon interest provides a regular stream of income to lenders, and it is common for bonds to be sold in this fashion.[4]

The formula for the price or present value of such a bond is

$$\$PV = \frac{\$C}{(1+R)} + \frac{\$C}{(1+R)^2} + \ldots + \frac{\$C + \$FV}{(1+R)^n} \tag{5.8}$$

where R has already been defined and

$\$C$ = annual coupon payment
$\$FV$ = face value or par value
n = years to maturity
$\$PV$ = present value or price of the bond

$$\frac{200 + 0}{(1 + 5\%)^{20}}$$

---

2 In Canada, matters are additionally complicated because the number of years over which a mortgage is amortized almost always exceeds the number of years over which the interest rate is fixed. This fact does not affect the principles underlying equation (5.7), however, so we will not pursue the point further.

3 The present value of an annuity of n periods may be stated even more compactly as $PV_t = (A/R)(1 - [1/(1+R)^n])$.

4 Because the price of a financial asset is sometimes referred to as its capital value, the present value of an income stream is called the *capitalization* of the income stream.

Take the example of a $1000 bond that promises to pay interest of $100 per year for five years, so that the coupon rate is 10% ($100/$1000). The present value is the sum of the following payments stream:

$$\$PV = \frac{\$100}{(1 + 0.10)} + \frac{\$100}{(1 + 0.10)^2} + \frac{\$100}{(1 + 0.10)^3} + \frac{\$100}{(1 + 0.10)^4} + \frac{\$100 + \$1000}{(1 + 0.10)^5}$$

$$= \$1000$$

Notice in our example that the present value of the bond is the same as its face value. Therefore, the coupon rate and the yield are identical. When bonds are traded in the marketplace, price and face value often diverge, however. If a particular bond trades at less than its face value, it is trading at a *discount*. One that trades at more than its face value is being traded at a *premium*.

What results in a bond's trading at a premium or a discount? Look carefully at equation (5.8). Since C and FV are given or fixed, a rise in R will reduce PV and a fall in R will raise PV. This relationship is simply the inverse of the one between the price of a debt and its yield noted earlier. Indeed, we can obtain an approximate expression for the prevailing or **current yield**, R_t^C, on a coupon bond by evaluating

$$R_t^C = \frac{\$C}{PV_t} \tag{5.9}$$

where $\$C$ is the amount of the fixed coupon and PV_t is the price of the bond at time t. The inverse relationship between bond price and yield is immediately clear.[5] For example, suppose that coupon payments are $100 while the price of the bond is 1000, that is, $PV_t = 1000$. Then, $R_t^C = \$100/1000 = 0.10$ or 10%. Similarly, if $PV_t = 1050$, and $\$C$ stayed the same, $R_t^C = 0.952$ or 9.52%. Finally, if $PV_t = 950$ while $\$C$ is still $100 then $R_t^C = 0.1053$ or 10.53%. We explore the relationship in (5.9) more fully in the next chapter.

Discounted Bonds or Bills

For more information about real return bonds see www.bylo.org/rrbs. html and www.bankof canada.ca/en/pdf/ real_return_eng. pdf

A **discounted bond** is a debt instrument that is issued at a discount and pays the face value at maturity. In other words, the face value represents the total of principal and interest. An example is the Government of Canada's Treasury bills.

To find the yield on such a debt instrument, we can employ the logic used previously: Find the interest rate on an amount to be received one year from today with a known present value. In algebraic terms,

$$R = \frac{\$FV - \$PD}{\$PD} \tag{5.10}$$

where $\$PD$ is the discounted price.

Consider a discounted bond sold at a price of $975 today with a face value of $1000 to be paid at maturity.

$$\$975 = \frac{\$1000}{(1 + R)}$$

---

[5] Another type of coupon bond, less well known, is the perpetuity or consol bond. As its name implies, such a bond has a fixed coupon, $\$C$, that is paid indefinitely into the future; the principal is never redeemed. Thus, in terms of equation (5.8), since n extends to infinity, $\$PV = \dfrac{\$C}{(1 + R)} + \dfrac{\$C}{(1 + R)^2} + \ldots$ With the help of some simple mathematics, it can be shown that the present value of a consol is $\$PV = \dfrac{\$C}{R}$. Thus, as interest rates rise, the price or present value of perpetuity falls.

Solving for R gives

$$R = \frac{\$1000 - \$975}{\$975} = 0.0256 \text{ or } 2.56\%$$

If the debt instrument in question is a Treasury bill, however, we should keep going. T-bills are typically for three months (approximately 90 days), but yields are conventionally quoted on an annual basis. We can convert the 90-day yield into an annual yield using the following expression:

$$R = \frac{\$FV - \$PD}{\$PD} \times \frac{360}{90} \tag{5.11}$$

where the year is taken to consist of 360 days.[6]

To continue the numerical example, the annual yield on a Treasury bill purchased for $975, with a face value of $1000, 90 days from today is

$$0.0256 \times \frac{360}{90} = 0.1024 \text{ or } 10.24\%$$

STRIPS OR ZERO-COUPON BONDS

STRIPS are a zero-coupon bond created by removing the coupons and trading them separately. The return to the investor from a STRIPS bond comes from increases in price until maturity when the face value is paid.

In general, a zero-coupon bond is one that promises a single payment at some specified date in the future.[7]

The rate of return on a STRIPS can be evaluated by using

$$\$X(1 + R)^n = \$FV \tag{5.12}$$

where $\$X$ is the amount invested today and all other terms have already been defined. For example, if a $5000 STRIPS bought today will return $100 000 in 20 years, equation (5.12) becomes

$$\$5000 (1 + R)^{20} = \$100\ 000$$

or

$$(1 + R)^{20} = \frac{100\ 000}{5000} = 20$$

Therefore,[8]

$$(1 + R) = (20)^{1/20}$$
$$(1 + R) = 1.16$$

so that

$$R = 0.16 \text{ or } 16\%$$

HOLDING PERIOD YIELD

Clearly, the return or yield and the coupon rate or interest rate on a particular debt instrument can differ considerably. Since the price of most forms of debt fluctuates over time, while the

---

6 Actual calculations use 365 in the numerator and 91 in the denominator. In the United States, 360 is used in the numerator.

7 The Treasury bill considered above is, of course, another example of a zero-coupon bond.

8 To find $(1 + R)$ from $(1 + R)^{20}$ we use the fact that $(1 + R)^{n/n} = (1 + R)$. Therefore, $(1 + R)^{20/20}$ implies that, for the right-hand side, we must evaluate $(20)^{1/20}$.

yield to maturity can be evaluated with certainty, an individual may not want to hold a debt until maturity, particularly when a market exists in which it can be traded and when individuals gamble about the future course of interest rates. Therefore, an expression such as equation (5.9) is imprecise because it fails to consider **capital gains** or **losses**—that is, changes in the market value of debt instruments (or any assets) between the time they are purchased and the time they are sold. Yet such changes certainly can affect an investor's return on an asset. Indeed, the **holding period yield**—the return for the period of ownership—may be more relevant than the yield to maturity, either because a financial instrument is not held until maturity or because it was not purchased at par or at the time of issue.

To illustrate, consider the return on a bond held for one year. The total return consists of (1) the current yield on the bond, found from equation (5.9), and (2) the result of any change in the price of the bond—that is, a further gain or loss in return depending on whether the price of the bond has risen or fallen. We can write (dropping the $ for convenience)

$$i = \frac{C}{PV_t} + \frac{\Delta PV_t}{PV_t} \tag{5.13}$$

where

i = return from holding a bond from period t to period $t + 1$
ΔPV_t = change in the price of a bond between period t and $t + 1 = PV_{t+1} - PV_t$

The first part of the right-hand side of the equation is the current yield R_t^C, while the second part is the **capital gain/loss return rate**, which is more compactly denoted as G. Hence, equation (5.13) can be rewritten as

$$i = R_t^C + G \tag{5.14}$$

A simple numerical example will help illustrate equation (5.14). Suppose $\$C=\$100$, $PV_t = 1000$, and $\Delta PV_t = 10$. Then, in terms of equation (5.14), we would obtain $\$100/1000 + 10/1000 = 0.10 + .01 = .11$ or 11%. Similarly, you can work out for yourself that if $\Delta PV_t = -10$, i becomes $0.10 - 0.01 = 0.09$ or 9%. Therefore, a capital gain raises i relative to R_t^C (see equation [5.9]), whereas the opposite is true when an investor suffers a capital loss.

Notice that the return on a bond is a function of the current price (that is, today's price) relative to its future price. Clearly, no investor knows with certainty what that price will be. Therefore, the decision to hold the bond until maturity or to sell it is partly a function of some expectation of future bond prices or, what amounts to the same thing, partly a function of an expectation of future interest rates. We consider the important role of expectations later.

For the moment, let us consider the influence of interest rate changes on bond prices and their return. Suppose that today's interest rate is 10% and that an investor purchases at face value a $1000 bond that matures 20 years from today. The yield to maturity is 10%. Now suppose the interest rate rises to 15% sometime after the first year and remains at that level until the bond matures. What is the effect of the interest rate change on the present value or price of the bond? We can use equation (5.8) to find out. The answer depends on when the change occurs. If the bond has 19 years left to maturity, its price is found by solving

$$\$PV_t = \frac{\$100}{(1.10)} + \frac{\$100}{(1.15)^2} + \dots + \frac{\$100}{(1.15)^{18}} + \frac{\$100}{(1.15)^{19}} + \frac{\$100 + \$1000}{(1.15)^{20}}$$

$$= \$690.99$$

Notice that, beginning in year two, the interest rate in the denominator [i.e., R in the expression $(1+R)$ in the denominator] is now 15% instead of 10%, since this is effectively what competing financial assets return in the marketplace and this now represents the appropriate discount factor. If, however, the bond has only one year left to maturity, its price becomes

$$\$PV_t = \frac{\$100}{(1.10)} + \frac{\$100}{(1.10)^2} + \ldots + \frac{\$100 + \$1000}{(1.15)^{20}}$$

$$= \$912.47$$

Notice that the discount factor only changes when we want to find the present value of payments received in year 20. The preceding two equations illustrate what happens to the price of two hypothetical 20-year bonds when interest rates change at two separate moments in time. On a 20-year bond with 19 years left to maturity, the impact on PV is much larger than on a 20-year bond with only one year left until maturity. An exercise at the end of this chapter considers the equally relevant case of the impact of an interest rate change on a one-year bond versus a 20-year bond.

Table 5.2 presents the results of such calculations for a range of years to maturity. Notice that the longer the time to maturity, the larger the effect on the price of the bond (column 5) and thus on its return (column 7). An interest rate change with 19 years left to maturity produces a price fall of roughly 30%, but a change with only one year to maturity results in a price fall of less than 10%.

Of course, it must be kept in mind that in the example considered above, as well as in the calculations shown in Table 5.2, once the interest rate changes it is assumed that the new rate henceforth will be unchanged. Clearly, this is done for convenience only, since interest rates can and do change more frequently. Therefore, one would expect that the likelihood (called "interest rate risk" in Chapter 13) of an interest rate change will be greater the longer the term left to maturity, and its impact on the price of the bond will also be larger. As a result, bond prices are relatively more volatile at longer terms to maturity than at shorter terms. (**Volatility** refers to some measure of the size of changes—here in the return and price of bonds.)

INTERNAL RATE OF RETURN cont'd

Many business decisions involve both an inflow and an outflow of cash over the anticipated life of a project. The interest rate that equates the present value of outflows and inflows is referred to

Table 5.2   Interest Rates, Bond Prices, and Returns

Example	(1) Years to Maturity When Bond Is Purchased	(2) INTEREST RATE Initial to Maturity	(3) Actual to Maturity	(4) BOND PRICE Initial (FV)	(5) Current (PV_t)	(6) Capital Loss (= $1000 − PV_t)	(7) % Return [= (2) − {(6)/ 1000}100]
1	20	10%	10%	$1000	$1000.00	$ 0.00	10.00
2	19	10%	15%	$1000	690.99	309.01	−20.90
3	15	10%	15%	$1000	730.90	269.10	−16.91
4	10	10%	15%	$1000	799.62	200.38	−10.04
5	5	10%	15%	$1000	862.91	137.09	−3.71
6	1	10%	15%	$1000	912.47	87.53	−1.25

For this 20-year bond, $FV = \$1000$, $C = \$100$, and R is initially 10% but changes to 15% when anywhere from 19 years to 1 year remain to maturity. Therefore, each line is a separate case.

Note: An interest rate change of 5 percentage points in a year may seem extreme. As we will see, however, sharp and rapid changes have been common, especially during the past few years.

FINANCIAL FOCUS 5.1 — READING THE FINANCIAL NEWS

Information about the bond market is published daily in tabular form in publications such as *The Globe and Mail* and the *National Post*. They usually classify the issuers into three categories:

- Government of Canada
- Provincial governments
- Corporate

A listing looks like this:

(1)	(2)	(3)	(4)	(5)	(6)
Canada	10.25	15 Mar 14	138.14	6.14	0.38

The first column identifies the issuer of the bond, the Government of Canada in this example. The second column gives the coupon rate as a percentage, 10.25% here, while the third column informs the reader about when the bond matures which, in the present case, is 15 March 2014. Columns 4 and 5 give the current price (*PV* in the text's notation) and the current yield (R_t^c). Finally, column 6 shows the change in yield from the previous trading day.

as the **internal rate of return (IRR)**. Suppose that some investment involves an initial outlay of $\$NF_0$ at time $t = 0$ and that subsequent net cash flows (that is, the difference between future inflows and outflows) are denoted as $\$NF_t$. The IRR is the interest or discount rate that equates

$$\$NF_0 = \$NF_1/(1 + R) + \$NF_2/(1 + R)^2 + \ldots + \$NF_n/(1 + R)^n \qquad \textbf{(5.15)}$$

The previous equation assumes that the net cash flows can be reinvested at the rate R and that this discount rate stays constant over the lifetime of the project. Although equation (5.15) is similar in many respects to equation (5.7), the difference is that the focus is now on solving for R, given knowledge of the other terms in the equation. As a result, if managers of a project have a goal or threshold value for R, say R^*, then the difference between the left-hand and right-hand sides in (5.15) is usually called the net present value (*NPV*).

As an illustration, suppose an outlay of $10 000 today produces net flows of $4000 per year over a four-year period. In terms of (5.15) we would write

$$\$10\ 000 = \$4000/(1 + R) + \$4000/(1 + R)^2 + \$4000/(1 + R)^3 + \$4000/(1 + R)^4$$

Solving for R, we obtain approximately 21%.[9]

5.3   THE DISTINCTION BETWEEN NOMINAL AND REAL INTEREST RATES

So far we have considered interest rates and yields without any consideration of the effects of inflation or of taxes. Inflation and taxes are realities that everyone must deal with. Moreover, people's expectations about the speed, magnitude, and direction in which they might move have a considerable effect on interest rates.

THE ROLE OF INFLATION EXPECTATIONS

Let us consider then how inflation expectations influence the behaviour of borrowers and lenders. When the consumers or firm managers we encountered at the beginning of this chapter postpone consumption today to consume more tomorrow, it is with the implicit expectation that their purchasing power will increase at some time in the future. Otherwise, there clearly is no incentive to forgo current consumption.

---

9 The solution involves recognizing that the net flows are constant, so that $10 000/$4000 = $[1/(1 + R) + 1/(1 + R)^2 + 1/(1 + R)^3 + 1/(1 + R)^4]$. The right-hand side is basically like an annuity of $1 at R% per year. You can use either the expression in footnote 3 or the many available computer programs and published tables to obtain the result.

FLASHBACK 5.1

FROM NOMINAL TO REAL MEASURES

Nominal interest rates are the ones we encounter in everyday life, i.e., the "price paid per dollar borrowed per year" (Frank et. al. 2003, p. 163). However, as we have seen in Chapter 1, the cost of living changes each year. One way to measure the cost of living is to look at the Consumer Price Index (CPI). During our lifetime, the price level has risen year after year. If we were paid the same salary each year, the purchasing power of our salary would fall continuously over time. Therefore, there is an inverse relationship between cost of living changes and purchasing power when we hold income constant. Although our salary may change, it may not always change at the same rate as changes in the cost of living. In other words, it

helps to know the quantities of goods and services our income is able to buy over time. We refer to the dollars of income we receive from month to month or from year to year as payments in current dollars. Therefore, if we want to compare the value of these current dollars over time in constant dollars, that is, adjusted for changes in prices, we need to divide nominal dollars by the price level. This is because once we deflate current dollars by the price level we obtain a measure that is expressed in real terms. You will learn below to apply this important principle to understanding the difference between nominal and real interest rates.

For more background information see Frank, R., Bernanke, B., Osberg, L., Cross, M., and Maclean, B. *Principles of Macroeconomics,* First Canadian Edition (Toronto: McGraw-Hill Ryerson Ltd., 2003), Chapter 7.

"Consumption" here refers to a real magnitude—to the purchasing power of current income relative to future income. Unfortunately, the price level has tended to rise year after year in a seemingly unrelenting manner. Since price rises represent a measure of purchasing power loss over time, lenders want to protect themselves from such losses when agreeing to a debt contract. How do they do so? They cannot do so perfectly—after all, a debt is a futures contract, and the future cannot be known with certainty—but they can form an *expectation* about the rate of *inflation* and adjust the price of debt accordingly.

Therefore, the **nominal interest rate** stipulated in a debt contract—that is, the amount to be paid in *current* dollars—is in reality the sum of two components:

1. Compensation to the lender for postponing current consumption (equivalently, the loss of future consumption for more current consumption on the part of the borrower). This portion is the **real interest rate**.

2. Compensation for anticipated or expected loss of purchasing power measured or proxied by the inflation rate.

The Fisher Equation

The preceding argument can be translated into what is known as the **Fisher equation**, named after Irving Fisher, one of the great economists of the twentieth century. It states that the nominal interest rate, R, is the sum of the real interest rate, ρ, plus an expected inflation component, or

$$R = \rho + \pi^e \qquad\qquad (5.16)$$

We can see from equation (5.16) that the real interest rate is simply the nominal interest rate less expected inflation,[10] or

---

10 The point can be put more precisely. If an individual sacrifices $1 of consumption today to consume, say, 3% more next year and no inflation is anticipated, that individual receives $(1 + \rho) = \$1.03$ one year from today. If, instead, inflation is expected to average 5% over the year, the nominal interest rate becomes $(1 + \rho)(1 + \pi) = (1.03)(1.05) = 1.0815$, so a lender can preserve the same purchasing power on the $1 loan and the $0.03 interest earned. Thus, $(1 + R) = (1 + \rho)(1 + \pi)$ or $R = \rho + \pi^e + \rho\pi^e$, which differs slightly from equation (5.16). For small values of ρ and π^e, however, the omission of the last term has negligible effect and simplifies calculations.

$$\rho = R - \pi^e \qquad\qquad (5.17)$$

Unfortunately, there is no universally agreed-on measure for π^e.

We can, of course, compute equation (5.17) by replacing expected inflation with a measure of actual inflation, π. Real interest calculations that use π instead of π^e yield the *ex post* real interest rate (from *ex post facto* or "after the fact"), while computations of ρ that use some proxy for π^e result in the *ex ante* real interest rate ("before the fact").[11]

Some Historical Data

Figure 5.2 plots a nominal interest rate, inflation, and an *ex ante* real interest rate measure for Canada over more than a 40-year span. Nominal interest rates and inflation do appear to parallel each other, but there is, nevertheless, considerable variation in real interest rates over time. By the preceding arguments, we might expect real interest rates always to be positive. During the 1970s, however, even *ex ante* real interest rates occasionally were negative, which implies a great incentive to borrow since, in real terms, the debt would be repaid in cheaper dollars.

Ex ante real interest rates are what matter in borrowing and lending decisions, but borrowers would have been much better off had they known that the real interest rates would be negative. Unfortunately, judgments such as these depend on the way the expected inflation component

---

Figure 5.2   **Nominal Real Interest Rates and Inflation in Canada**

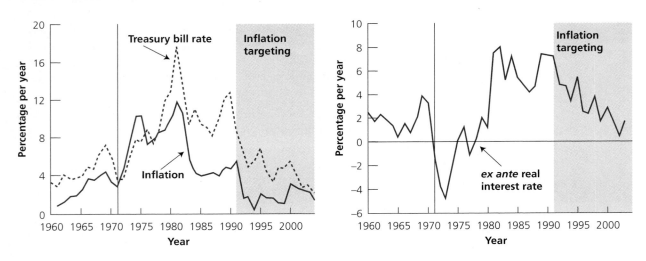

One way of measuring inflation is by calculating the annual percentage change in the CPI ([CPI$_t$ − CPI$_{t-4}$]/CPI$_{t-4}$, where t is time). The *ex ante* real interest rate is $R - \pi^e$, where $\pi^e_t = \pi_{t+1}$, that is, expected inflation is assumed to be equal to next period's actual inflation rate. All data are quarterly. The shaded areas highlight the period since inflation targeting was introduced. The vertical bar identifies the end of the Bretton Woods era of fixed exchange rates.

Source: International Financial Statistics CD-ROM (Washington, D.C.: International Monetary Fund).

---

11 Modern economics assumes that individuals forecast inflation "rationally," which means conditional on a wide variety of macroeconomic information likely to affect inflation in the future. But economists generally treat the information set as consisting of only a few variables. Individuals' formation of expectations of inflation is discussed in Chapter 21.

$R - R_1 - \pi^e$

in equation (5.16) is generated. If the model used to derive expected inflation is correct, investors clearly expected far less inflation than was actually the case during much of the 1970s. One reason could have been that no one knew, until it was too late, about the inflationary consequences of the oil price shocks of the 1970s or those arising from the imposition of inflation targeting in the 1990s. (Alternatively, the model used to derive *ex ante* real interest rates may have omitted some important piece of economic information.)

By the early 1980s, real interest rates reversed sharply and became high relative to the historical average and remained so into the 1990s. Since inflation remained low in 2000 through 2002, combined with fears of a recession in late 2001, nominal and real rates both began to fall sharply. The long-run average for *ex post* real interest rates is approximately 2.73%.

You also will notice roughly three phases in the history of real interest rate behaviour. Real interest rates were stable during the 1960s; that is, when the so-called Bretton Woods era kept exchange rates stable. During the 1970s and 1980s, however, real interest rates were volatile; that is, when the Canadian dollar floated against major currencies. The average real interest rate was, however, almost the same then (2.7%) as in the Bretton Woods era. Finally, real interest rates became stable again during the 1990s, but were considerably higher, averaging 3.84%, following the adoption of inflation targets, but with the Canadian dollar still floating against major currencies. The lesson to be drawn is that there potentially is a connection between the type of monetary regime in place and real interest rates. We will develop this idea throughout the text.

The recent experience with both positive and negative *ex post* real interest rates is nothing new. Real interest rates were quite volatile during the 1914–45 period because of a series of unusual events: the two world wars and the Great Depression. Otherwise, real interest rates have been, on average, quite similar through history. However, they have fluctuated more since the end of World War II than they did before the end of World War I. Some economists believe that this effect is a consequence of abandoning the gold standard, thereby producing more volatile and higher inflation.

The link between inflation and interest rates is not confined to Canada. Figure 5.3 plots average interest rate levels and inflation rates for nine industrialized countries from 1980 through to 1990. According to the Fisher equation, the countries experiencing relatively higher inflation rates also should have higher nominal interest rates. The graph shows clearly that this was the case for the countries in the sample.

It was evidence of this kind that led the Canadian federal government to argue in its 1992 budget that the way to lower interest rates is through lower inflation. In Chapters 22 and 23 we will explore in greater detail the motivation for introducing inflation targeting in Canada and why this policy has spread throughout the world.

Empirical Evidence

The Fisher equation is a convenient device for describing the way expected inflation drives a wedge between nominal and real interest rates. It must be emphasized that other factors, such as the overall productivity of the economy, can also influence real interest rates in the long run. Discussion of these considerations, however, would take us far afield, and so in what follows, we will retain the Fisher equation as the operational device to discuss real and nominal interest rate calculations. Nevertheless, it might be useful to point out that many empirical studies have found a negative relationship between *ex post* real interest rates and inflation.[12] Unfortunately, the exact cause of this relationship is unclear; the view that agents are able to detect permanent shifts in future inflation receives little empirical support.

---

12 M.D. Evans, and K.K. Lewis, "Do Expected Shifts in Inflation Policy Affect Estimates of the Long-Run Fisher Relation?" *Journal of Finance* (March 1995): 225–53.

Figure 5.3 **Inflation and Nominal Interest Rates across Countries: 1980–2003**

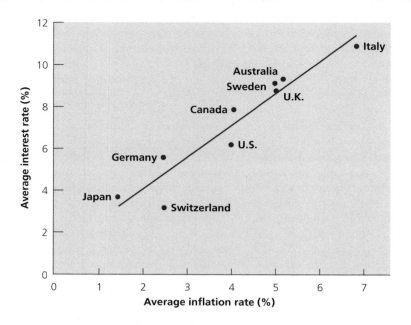

The graph plots inflation–interest rate combinations for major industrialized countries. A best-fit, straight line fits the scatter points well, suggesting that the Fisher equation held true: Higher inflation rates accompanied higher nominal interest rates.

Source: International Financial Statistics CD-ROM (Washington, D.C.: International Monetary Fund).

Note: Annual data are from 1980 to 2003. The interest rate used is the Treasury-bill rate (Canada, United States), the overnight rate (U.K.), the money market rate (Australia, Italy, Switzerland), and the call rate (Japan, Sweden, Germany). Inflation is defined as the percentage change in consumer prices over the previous year. A simple average was used to arrive at the figures plotted.

TAXES

The real interest rate calculations implicit in equation (5.16) are approximate because real interest income in Canada is subject to income tax. The nominal interest rate after taxes, R^* is

$$R^* = R(1 - \tau) \tag{5.18}$$

where τ = income tax rate.

The *ex ante* real interest rate after taxes becomes

$$R(1 - \tau) - \pi^e \tag{5.19}$$

For example, if the nominal interest rate is 5% and inflation is expected to be 2%, the *ex ante* real interest rate, according to equation (5.17), is

$$5\% - 2\% = 3\%$$

Suppose the income tax rate is 30%. The *ex ante* real after-tax rate is then

$$0.05(1 - 0.3) - 0.02 = 0.035 - 0.02 = 0.015 \text{ or } 1.5\%$$

Clearly, borrowing and savings decisions should be affected by after-tax considerations. However, because every individual does not face the same tax rate and because we want to simplify the subsequent discussion, henceforth the term real interest rate will refer to the *ex ante* real interest rate computed from equation (5.17).

FINANCIAL FOCUS 5.2   REAL RETURN BONDS

Most bonds have coupon payments that are fixed, so the purchasing power of their value is subject to erosion by inflation. As mentioned in Chapter 4, the Canadian government sells *indexed* or **real return bonds** in which the coupon and the principal are adjusted for inflation according to changes in the consumer price index (CPI).

To consider how such a bond would work in practice, suppose you purchased a real return bond on 20 January 2006 and the CPI on that date was 126.64194. Now suppose that the same bond is sold 20 July 2006 or six months later. For the purposes of calculating the inflation rate during the time the bond is held, the government uses the CPI on what is called the *reference date*, which is actually the CPI *three months earlier than the selling date*. Moreover, since CPI data are available only on a monthly basis, we need to do some *interpolation* to find a value for the CPI on a particular day. In the present example, this means that to find the CPI for April 20 (three months before July 20), we need the CPI for the end of March, which is, say, 129.9, and April 2003, which is, say, 130.1 (CPI is for end-of-month prices; the data can be found in the *Bank of Canada Review*, Table H8, and represent consumer prices for all items).

CPI 20 July 2006 = (130.1 − 129.9) × (20/31) + 129.9
            = 130.03333

Since July has 31 days, interpolation means that 20/31 of the CPI change between April and May is added to the April CPI to get the CPI for the 20th day of the month.

Since the CPI at purchase was 126.64194, inflation during the holding period was

   (130.03333 − 126.64194)/126.64194 = 2.67794%

Therefore, on a $100 000 real return bond, the investor would receive the following amounts:

   A. $100 000 × 2.67794% = $102 677.94
   B. 2.125% on $102 677.94 = $2181.91
   C. Total = $104 859.83

Part A adjusts the principal for inflation during the holding period; Part B pays interest (the annual rate is 4.25% or 2.125% on a six-month basis) on the inflation-adjusted principal.

In 1993, securities dealers began to issue real return stripped bonds with a variety of maturities of up to 30 years. These bonds combine the features of STRIPS with those of real return bonds. For example, a $1000 real return stripped bond maturing in 10 years with a real return of 3.9% and zero expected inflation over the term of the bond would fetch a price today of $682.09 [$1/(1.039)^{10} × 1000]. If inflation in the CPI is expected to be 5% for each of the next 10 years, the principal repayable at maturity would become $1628.89 [$1000 × (1.05)^{10}], which would compensate the investor for inflation.

The appeal of real return bonds is that the real rate of interest on the bond is held fixed while the nominal interest rate is variable. Typically, for other types of bonds, the opposite is true. Therefore, if we believe in the Fisher equation, then the difference between the nominal rate on real return bonds and the promised real rate should give a rough idea of the market's perceptions of expected inflation.

The table below provides some data about the return on a real return bond, those on a roughly comparable long-term conventional bond, as well as the inflation rate in the CPI, and, finally, an implicit measure of inflation.

Year	(1) Real Return Bond	(2) Nominal Return: 10-Year Government Bond	(3) CPI Inflation Rate	(4) Implicit Inflation Assumed by Real Return Bonds
1995	4.72	7.11	2.2	2.4
1996	4.64	6.37	1.6	1.7
1997	4.14	5.61	1.6	1.5
1998	4.02	4.89	0.9	0.9
1999	4.07	6.18	1.7	2.1
2000	3.74	5.35	2.7	1.6
2001	3.55	5.44	2.6	1.9
2002	3.54	4.88	2.2	1.3
2003	3.09	4.66	2.8	1.6
2004	2.40	4.58	2.4	2.2

Sources: Bank of Canada Review, Table A2, columns 17, 26, CANSIM II series V122553, and application of equation (5.17).

Notice that an inflation rate implicit in the long-term interest rate [column (4), approximated here by applying equation (5.17)], is lower than the actual inflation rate shown in column (3) in 6 of the 10 years shown. Hence, the real return bond can be a fairly good investment. More importantly, perhaps, a comparison of columns (3) and (4) suggests that the real return bonds can be used as a rough guide to expected inflation.

Strictly speaking, you should not take the comparison between columns (2) and (4) literally, because the two bonds considered here do not have the same maturity. For example, even if an investor expected annual inflation to be 2% a year for 10 years, the 4.5% real return bond would yield a real return of 5.37% and 6.15% if expected inflation were 3%, so the real return bond provides comparatively better real returns in this particular case.

Questions for Discussion
1. Do real return bonds guarantee a constant real interest rate? Why? Why not?
2. Would real return bonds be more popular when inflation is rising or falling? When inflation is more or less volatile?

Reference
C. Reid, and F. Dion, "Real Return Bonds: Monetary Policy Credibility and Short-Term Inflation Forecasting," *Bank of Canada Review* (Autumn 2004): 15-26.

ECONOMICS FOCUS 5.2   LIES THE CPI TOLD ME

As we have seen, the calculation of real interest rates involves a measure of inflation. But how well is inflation measured? This question is important for a number of reasons: Canada Pension Plan payments are partially indexed to inflation, the real return bond is also tied to inflation performance, wage claims are often tied to expected inflation, and our personal tax exemption, until recently, only increased if inflation exceeded 3%. Concerns about measuring inflation have resurfaced both because central banks have targeted inflation performance (see Chapter 23) and because governments at all levels are seeking ways to save money.

So what's wrong with the CPI-based measure of inflation? Plenty, it seems. Many economists and government agencies now agree that a positive bias is reported in CPI inflation, which means that inflation is lower than we think. Why? First, if one of the thousands of items surveyed in the construction of the CPI goes on sale, it will leave a mark on the index when it returns to its normal price. Second, the CPI measures the spending habits of a "representative" consumer, whoever he or she is, based on a "basket" of purchases in a particular *base* year (1992 is the latest base year used by Statistics Canada). However, even if we believe in the representative individual, surely our spending habits would have changed since 1992. A recent article in the *Globe and Mail* highlights the dramatic changes in the products and services added or dropped since the 1910s. Moreover, consumers, even the mythical representative one, do substitute items when their price changes. For example, when a frost or a drought drives up the price of a head of lettuce to over $2 a head, most consumers will give up on the leafy vegetable, at least for a time. In addition, the items surveyed in the CPI are based on prices in certain retail stores. This does not consider the impact of discount stores or warehouse-type stores or the effect of "bulk-buying" by families. Also, consumers switch brands if the price is right, and this, too, is not reflected properly in the CPI calculations. Finally, it is difficult to account for quality changes in the products we buy. For ex-

ample, prices for DVDs today are probably lower, on average, than they were in, say, 1999, but the biggest change since then is the increase in the number of features DVDs are equipped with. None of this is directly reflected in CPI calculations. So what is the size of the bias we are talking about? Anywhere from 0.2% a year to 2%. Doesn't sound like much? Over a 10-year period, a 0.2% bias implies, a total overstatement of CPI inflation of approximately 2%, while a 2% annual bias translates into a total overstatement of 21.9%!

Although the bias is not apparently significant for Canada, the same issue has been the subject of considerable debate and controversy in the United States, where the bias is, by some estimates, up to 1%. Since the bias is supposed to have resulted in an overestimate of inflation, politicians were, not surprisingly, wary of instituting reforms that might have reduced the bias and the rate of increase of major entitlement programs, such as Social Security.

Questions for Discussion
1. Is the quality change issue likely to be an important one when prices are compared over a long period?
2. Is there any practical way around the approach of surveying particular stores at particular times for their prices? Would this correct the biases inherent in the construction of the CPI?

Sources
A. Crawford, "Measurement Biases in the Canadian CPI: A Technical Note," *Bank of Canada Review* (Summer 1993), and "Measurement Biases in the Canadian CPI: An Update," *Bank of Canada Review* (Spring 1998): 30–56.

L.M. Ducharme, "Bias in the CPI: Experiences from Five OECD Countries," Statistics Canada 62F0014MIB, no. 10 (September 1997), available at **www.statcan.ca**.

T. Grant "Lard in 1913, Plasma TV now: CPI Tracks Changes," *Globe and Mail* (21 April 2005): B1, B9.

The Statistics Canada Web site contains a wealth of information about the measurement of consumer prices in Canada **www.statcan.ca**

The following Web site is devoted to the measurement of the U.S. CPI. Reports of the commission dealing with biases in the U.S. CPI and other relevant facts about U.S. consumer price calculations are also on the site **www.bls.gov/cpi**

SUMMARY

- Debt is akin to a futures contract between lenders and borrowers.

- The price of debt is the interest rate.

- Present value is the discounted value of a stream of payments made in the future.

- There are many ways of repaying a debt:
  —lump sum in the future
  —fixed payments in the future

- There are many ways of paying interest:
  —fixed at specified intervals
  —compounded

- Interest rates are stated in nominal terms, but borrowers and lenders care about the real interest rate, which is the nominal rate less expected inflation.

- Over time, movements in nominal interest rates are paralleled by movements in inflation.

- Some key expressions related to interest calculations include:

Present value

$$\$PV_t = \$FV/(1 + R)^n$$

Fixed payment loan

$$\$Debt = \frac{\$A}{(1 + R)} + \frac{\$A}{(1 + R)^2} + \cdots + \frac{\$A}{(1 + R)^n}$$

Coupon bond

$$\$PV_t = \frac{\$C}{(1 + R)} + \frac{\$C}{(1 + R)^2} + \cdots + \frac{\$C + \$FV}{(1 + R)^n}$$

Discounted Treasury bill annual yield (90-day Treasury bill)

$$R = \frac{\$FV - \$PD}{\$PD} \times \frac{360}{90}$$

STRIPS

$$\$X (1 + R)^n = FV$$

Current yield

$$R_t^C = \$\frac{C}{PV_t}$$

Fisher equation

$$R = \rho + \pi^e \ (ex\ ante)$$
$$R = \rho + \pi \ (ex\ post)$$
$$R^* = R(1 - \tau) \ \text{after-tax nominal interest rate}$$

IMPORTANT TERMS

capital gain/loss return rate, 80
capital gain or loss, 80
coupon rate, 77
current yield, 78
discounted bond, 78
Fisher equation, 83
holding period yield, 80
interest rate, 72

internal rate of return (IRR), 82
nominal interest rate, 83
present value, 72
real interest rate, 83
real return bonds, 87
volatility, 81
yield to maturity, 73

PROBLEMS

1. Assuming that an interest rate of 8% prevails, calculate the present value for the stream of income produced by the following assets:

   (a) A bond paying $50 in interest per year for two years, to be redeemed for $1000 at the end of two years.

   (b) An asset that earns $75 per year for three years and then $150 per year forever beginning the end of year four.

2. If the interest rate is 10% per annum, what is the present value of a security that pays $1100 next year, $1200 the year after, and $1400 the year after that?

3. If the asset in question 2 is sold for $3000, is the yield to maturity more or less than 10%? Why?

4. A student obtains a government loan of $5000 that requires repayment of $786 per year, which is equivalent to an interest cost of approximately 10%. Payment is to begin after graduation, which is expected four years from today. Is the effective yield to maturity greater or less than 10%? Explain.

5. The real rate of interest is 10% and investors expect 6% inflation in the coming year. What nominal rate of interest will they demand? Will the market necessarily generate it?

6. If the investor in question 5 is in a 30% tax bracket, what is the real after-tax interest rate?

7. Suppose that an investor requires a real after-tax return of 5% and inflation is expected to be 6% in the coming year. If a security with a nominal interest rate of 13% is purchased, what is the effective tax rate on the security based on the investor's expectations? If the after-tax real return is only 3%, what was the *ex post* rate of inflation, assuming a tax rate of 30%?

8. The radio recently carried the following commercial: "Buy an appliance from us and we will give you 50% of the price back 10 years after the purchase. Now there's a deal you can't beat!" If the typical appliance costs $500 and inflation is expected to average 5% per year, how much is the manufacturer's deal worth in current dollars?

9. Which would you prefer to receive:
   (a) $1 million today or
   (b) $1 million in equal instalments of $100 000 over 10 years?
   Explain.

10. The average annual cost of attending a Canadian university in 1991 was $8019. At present rates of growth, the annual cost is expected to rise by 2009 to $127 000 for a four-year program. Compute the discount rate that was used to arrive at this figure.

11. Suppose a Government of Canada STRIPS bond can be purchased for $3816.31 at the end of 2005. At maturity, in seven years, the investor receives $6987.50. What is the annual rate of return on the STRIPS?

12. At 9%, a 48-month loan would result in a monthly payment of $24.89 per $1000. Suppose you borrow $17 192. What is the monthly payment?

13. What do you think the main considerations are in lengthening or shortening the term to maturity of government debt? Explain.

14. Suppose you anticipate 3% inflation in the future. If you want to generate the equivalent of $10 000 in current dollars 10, 20, or 30 years into the future, what amount of future dollars will you require? If you want to accomplish the above objective via annual contributions instead, *rank* the size of each contribution if you have 10, 20, or 30 years until you require the funds. (Note: only a ranking is required for this part of the question, not an actual dollar value.)

15. "I bought a 15-year Government of Canada bond yielding 7.4%. I expect the present inflation rate of 1.7% to continue throughout the 15-year term, yielding me a 5.48% real return. That's well above the 3.5% real rate on a real return bond." How was the 5.48% figure arrived at? Is the investor correct? Why? Why not?

16. Answer the following questions about the table in **Financial Focus 5.2: Real Return Bonds.**

    (a) Verify the calculations in column (4).

    (b) Average the data in each of the columns in the table. You will then obtain averages for interest rates and inflation since 1995. If you could go back in time would you have invested in long-term nominal bonds or real return bonds? Explain.

17. Based on the data in **Financial Focus 5.2: Real Return Bonds** calculate the difference between the nominal long-term interest rate and the interest rate on real return bonds. What does this differential represent? Explain.

18. Suppose you are given the following data about a T-bill: Face value $1,000,000, current price $979,644, days to maturity, 80. What is the effective annualized yield on this T-bill if held until maturity?

19. Figure 5.2 suggests that the *ex ante* real interest rate was negative during the 1970s. How is this possible?

DISCUSSION QUESTIONS

1. Explain why price changes for long-term bonds (term of 10 years or longer) are more volatile than those for short-term bonds (term of 1 year or less).

2. "Current yield is the illusion. Someone will snap up a bond if the broker tells him it yields 9% and reject one for 7% even though it may be the better deal," says one analyst (quoted in the Business Section of the *New York Times,* 10 November 1991). Comment.

3. "Short-term interest rates, in contrast, are less affected by inflation expectations. Investors here tend to have shorter planning horizons and, as a result, tend to be less concerned about the impact of inflation on real returns," says the *Royfund Report* (vol. 1, issue 1, 1991). How does this quote square with the theory and evidence presented in this chapter? Explain.

4. "Short-term interest rates increased sharply during the latter part of 1992. Our investment strategy took advantage of this period by lengthening the term to maturity of the money market section from 91 days to 113 days at year-end." Does this strategy make sense? Why?

5. Examine Figure 5.3. What can you say about real *ex post* interest rates during this period? Which country experienced the highest real ex post interest rate? Which country had the lowest?

6. The break-even inflation rate refers to the difference between yields on long-term Government of Canada bonds and real return bonds. Why is it given this name? Explain. Would this measure represent a good forecast of future inflation? Why? Why not?

7. The federal government regularly holds consultations about its debt management strategy. One report dealt with real return bonds. Go to **www.bankofcanada.ca/en/notices_fmd/market_consult03.htm** and list some of the principal concerns investors have about the market for real return bonds. Why should the government and markets take these concerns seriously?

ONLINE APPLICATIONS

1. Go to **www.royalbank.com/perindex.html**, and click on calculators. Chose the Mortgage calculator and verify what the monthly payment is on a $100 000 mortgage at 7% amortized over 20 years. You will notice that payments are a function of the frequency of payments per year. Does this make sense given the material introduced in section 5.2? Explain.

2. Go to the Web site of any Canadian chartered bank and find out whether they provide a calculator that can be used to calculate present values, future values, or the interest cost of a debt. For example, at **www.royalbank. com/perindex.html**, click on one of the calculators.

3. Go to **www.statcan.ca/english/IPS/Data/ 62-557-XIB.htm** and find "Your Guide to the CPI." Learn what the major components are in the CPI index, the correct way to calculate a real increase in expenditures, and Canada's inflation rate .

References can be found on www.mcgrawhill.ca/college/siklos

Understanding Interest Rates: Determinants and Movements

LEARNING OBJECTIVES

After reading and studying this chapter, you should be able to

6.1 explain how the loanable funds model suggests equilibrium interest rate determination

6.1 list the factors that cause interest rates to change

6.2 identify how individuals determine an equilibrium in their money holdings

6.2 describe how the liquidity preference approach explains equilibrium interest rate determination

6.2 determine how monetary policy affects interest rates

In the previous chapter, we assumed the nominal interest rate to be given. In this chapter, however, we examine how interest rate levels actually are determined through the interaction of borrowers and lenders (generally operating via an intermediary) in a market. Also in this chapter, we consider some of the factors that can cause interest rates to change over time.

We examine two theories of interest rate determination, each of which focuses on a different part of the financial system. The first is the loanable funds theory, which concentrates on developments in the bond market and on the *flow* of funds over a period. The second is the liquidity preference framework, which is concerned with the market for the quantity of money and is thus formulated in terms of demand for a *stock*.[1]

Each of these explanations focuses on a single interest rate, yet the models developed in this chapter suggest what accounts for movements in any interest rate. Clearly, several interest rates do exist in the economy simultaneously. Figure 6.1 plots the yields on three high-quality debt instruments since the 1950s. There have been differences at any given time, and some of the yields have been more volatile than others, yet there is clearly a common trend.[2] Therefore, we need not be specific here about which particular interest rate is being described.

---

1 British economist Dennis Robertson brought forth the loanable funds argument. Keynes is credited with the liquidity preference approach, which at least in theory, is not compatible with the loanable funds approach. However, Keynes used a device somewhat similar to the one we use in this chapter to more or less reconcile the two. For an interesting account of the debate surrounding the two approaches, see R. Skidelsky, *John Maynard Keynes: Fighting for Britain 1937–1946* (London: Macmillan, 2000): 23.

2 In the next chapter we discuss a simple explanation for this phenomenon.

.1   THE LOANABLE FUNDS APPROACH

The loanable funds approach suggests that interest rate levels are determined by the forces of supply and demand for **loanable funds**—new funds available for investment. The interaction between the amount available for investment by lenders (the supply of loanable funds), and the quantity of bonds desired by borrowers (the demand for loanable funds) is assumed to generate a market-clearing price—that is, an **equilibrium interest rate** level.

We analyze separately the determinants of supply and demand for loanable funds before we derive an equilibrium interest rate level. Since loanable funds are generally traded in the form of bonds, we focus on that market.

BOND DEMAND AND SUPPLY

To make the analysis as simple as possible, we assume for now that individuals know with certainty the yield to maturity on bonds. If we further simplify the example by considering a one-year discounted bond (see Chapter 5 for a numerical illustration), then we can write

$$R = \frac{\$FV - \$PD}{\$PD}$$

(6.1)

| **Figure 6.1** | **A Selection of Yields over Time** |

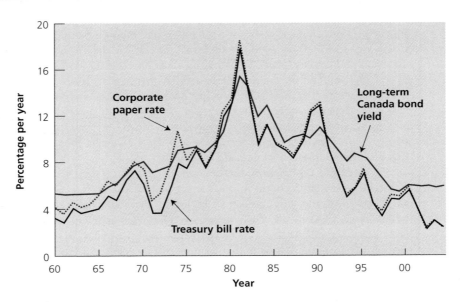

The maturities on the instruments involved were: long-term government bonds, 10 years or more; Treasury bills, 3 months; prime corporate paper, 90 days. Annual averages were used. For the 1960–2004 period, the correlation between yields on Treasury bills and Government of Canada long-term bonds is 92%; on Treasury bills and prime corporate paper, 99%; on prime corporate paper and long-term bonds, 91%. These high correlations indicate the strength of the linear relationships for the time series plotted.

Source: International Monetary Financial Statistics CD-ROM (Washington, D.C.: International Monetary Fund).

FLASHBACK 6.1

SUPPLY AND DEMAND

One of the original characters on the comedy show "Saturday Night Live," Father Guido Sarducci, summarized economics in his "five-minute University" with the words "supply and demand." Indeed, understanding and using the concept of supply and demand is central to many of the theories used throughout this text. However, unlike your principles course, where supply and demand was expressed in terms of goods or services, here it is measured in terms of financial assets such as money and bonds. Does this matter? Not in a fundamental sense (although there is a small twist when using supply-demand analysis to represent the operations of financial markets).

The quantity of money and bonds supplied ultimately will be determined by the price of the asset and, as we have seen in Chapter 5 (see also below for a recap), this is inversely related to the nominal interest rate. Consider the case of government bonds. As the price at which they can be sold increases, the opportunity cost of selling these bonds will rise, since governments will be willing to borrow more the higher the price. Remember that a higher price translates into lower borrowing costs. The argument works in reverse for those who wish to hold bonds, that is, for investors who express a demand for bonds. As the price rises the return on the asset being held falls, making it less attractive, or stated another way, making other assets relatively more attractive.

Finally, recall another crucial concept from your introductory course in economics, namely the *ceteris paribus* device. This means that along any demand or supply curve all other variables are held constant or equal. This allows us to separate movements along the supply and demand curves from the causes of shifts in each one of these curves. One notable feature of the use of supply-demand analysis is that some of the same economic variables affect both supply and demand. Hence, in some of the examples considered below a change in a variable will result in a shift in both the supply and demand curves, usually in the opposite direction.

For more background information see Frank, R., Bernanke, B., Osberg, L., Cross, M., and Maclean, B. *Principles of Microeconomics, First Canadian Edition* (Toronto: McGraw-Hill Ryerson Ltd., 2003), Chapter 4.

where

R = the nominal interest rate[3]
FV = face value of the bond, maturing in one year
PD = discounted purchase price

If $FV = \$1000$, there exist unique combinations of PD and R that satisfy equation (6.1). Note that the relationship between PD and R is inverse. Clearly, the lower price of new bonds—which is to say the greater the return—the more of them lenders will want to hold. By contrast, the higher the price of the bond—which translates into a lower debt cost to the borrower—the larger the quantity prospective debtors will want to issue. Thus, we can draw the bond demand and supply curves depicted in Figure 6.2. For simplicity, the demand and supply curves are straight lines, though, of course, nothing in the foregoing analysis suggests that this need be the case. All we know or need to know is that the curve for bond demand, B^d, is downward sloping, whereas the curve for bond supply, B^s, is upward sloping. A lower price increases the quantity of bonds demanded but decreases the quantity of bonds supplied.

The subject of this chapter, however, is not bond prices, but the determination of interest rate levels. Although there is a known relationship between bond price and return, as embodied in equation (6.1), it seems preferable to specify this relationship in terms of returns. We can do so easily by redrawing the supply–demand diagram with the percentage return measured on the vertical axis, as in Figure 6.3.

---

3 Recall that, unless otherwise stated, the interest rate we refer to in this book is the *nominal* interest rate. The real interest rate concept was introduced in Chapter 5.

| Figure 6.2 | **The Supply of and Demand for Bonds** |

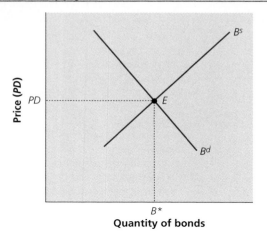

Quantity of bonds

Bond demand is depicted by the curve B^d, which slopes downward to indicate the inverse relationship between the price of bonds and the quantity individuals desire to hold. Similarly, the bond supply curve, B^s, slopes upward since the higher the price of the bond, the lower its cost and, consequently, the greater the desire to borrow.

A demand for new bonds reflects a desire to hold more funds than are being loaned out. Similarly, a supply of new bonds implies that new funds are being loaned out. Consequently, we may call bond demand the supply of loanable funds and bond supply the demand for loanable funds.[4]

If we redraw the diagram as the demand for and supply of loanable funds we obtain Figure 6.3.

MARKET EQUILIBRIUM

Point E is obtained in Figures 6.2 and 6.3 when the quantity of bonds or loanable funds demanded is equal to the quantity of bonds or loanable funds supplied—that is, when

$$B^d = B^s \text{ or } LF^s = LF^d \qquad (6.2)$$

Point E is an equilibrium because it is there that the supply and demand curves intersect, satisfying the conditions for equation (6.2). The point of equilibrium is important since the market gravitates toward it. In this series of figures, R^* is the equilibrium interest rate, the rate that attains this balance of supply and demand. If the interest rate is lower than R^*, there is an excess demand for loanable funds. Thus, in Figure 6.4, when the interest rate is R_0, the quantity of loanable funds demanded is represented by point B, while the quantity of loanable funds supplied is given by point A. As in any market in which prices are allowed to move freely, excess demand pushes up price, which here is the interest rate.

Conversely, if the interest rate is R_1, it is now the quantity of loanable funds supplied (point D in Figure 6.4) that exceeds the quantity of loanable funds demanded (point C). Since an excess supply leads to a rise in price, there is a tendency for the interest rate to fall until point E is reached once again.

Since equilibrium is the point at which an unfettered market eventually will settle, it is convenient to use it as the starting point for our analysis. Accordingly, in what follows, we examine how the equilibrium interest rate changes.

---

4 Notice that the definition of loanable funds being used in the model is narrow—one type of new bond only. This assumption leads to no loss of generality, however. Clearly, the supply of and demand for loanable funds comes from all sectors of the economy (see Chapter 9).

Figure 6.3	The Supply of and Demand for Loanable Bonds

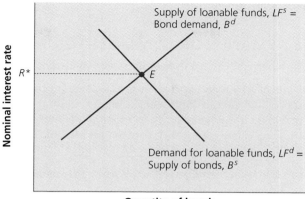

Since the purchasers of bonds provide loanable funds, the demand for bonds curve from Figure 6.2 is replaced by a supply of loanable funds curve. Similarly, since borrowers supply bonds into the market, they are, in effect, demanders of loanable funds. Thus, the supply of bonds curve of Figure 6.2 is replaced by a demand for loanable funds curve. Bond supply is downward sloping because, according to equation (6.1), PD and R are inversely related. Note that R is now measured on the vertical axis instead of PD as in Figure 6.2.

First, however, it is useful to emphasize the distinction between a *movement along* a demand or supply curve and a *shift* in these same curves. Changes in interest rates or in the quantity of bonds produce movements along the curves. Changes in other factors lead to shifts in the demand for or supply of loanable funds.

Consider first Figure 6.5(A), which shows a leftward shift in the demand for loanable funds. The implication is that the demand for loanable funds has decreased at *every* interest rate level (note the left-pointing arrow in the figure). In other words, the demand for loanable funds has fallen. For example, consider an interest rate such as R_1. With a shift to the left in LF_1, the demand for loanable funds falls to LF_2^d from LF_1^d; the desire to borrow funds has decreased at every interest

Figure 6.4	Market Equilibrium

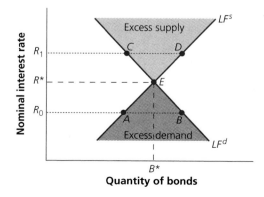

At point E, the quantity of loanable funds demanded equals the quantity of loanable funds supplied. R^* is the equilibrium interest rate. At interest rates of more than R^*, such as R_1, there is excess supply of loanable funds since $LF^s > LF^d$. Conversely, when R is less than R^*, $LF^d > LF^s$.

rate level. To put that point differently, the quantity B_1 will be demanded only if the interest rate falls to R_2 [note the arrow pointing from A to B in Figure 6.5(A)]. If the interest rate remains at R_1, only B_2 will be demanded.

SHIFTS IN THE DEMAND FOR LOANABLE FUNDS

What are the factors that might cause a shift in borrowers' preferences? They include

1. Changes in the rate of return anticipated on investments. Investors (individuals and firms) typically increase or decrease their borrowing as they perceive profitable investment opportunities rising or falling. If they anticipate a recession in the near future, they will want to restrict future borrowing. They reduce their demand for loanable funds, and so the LF_1 curve in Figure 6.5(A) shifts leftward from LF_1^d to LF_2^d.

2. Government policies. Governments typically borrow more during recessions than during boom periods. During a recession, their tax revenue decreases, but their spending on unemployment insurance and other social programs rises; the resulting deficit may have to be financed by borrowing. Conversely, during a boom, general income levels rise and so do government revenues, whereas expenditures may fall, in part because of falling unemployment. A budget deficit means an increase (shift to the right) in the demand for loanable funds, while a budget surplus implies a decrease in such demand.

3. Inflation expectations. Expectations of inflation also influence the desire to borrow and to lend. Thus, for example, if inflation is expected to fall, then, at prevailing nominal interest rates, the real interest rate rises, so borrowing costs, in terms of forgone future consumption, also rise. Therefore, if nominal interest rates are expected to fall in the future, the current demand for loanable funds will fall.

| **Figure 6.5** | **Shifts in the Demand for and Supply of Loanable Funds** |

(A) A Demand Shift   **(B) A Supply Shift**

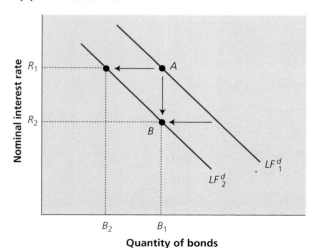
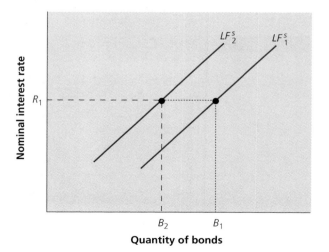

In panel (A), changes in the rate of return on investments, expected inflation, and government policies shift the demand for loanable funds. In panel (B), changes in wealth, relative returns, relative riskiness, and liquidity cause shifts in the supply of loanable funds.

SHIFTS IN THE SUPPLY OF LOANABLE FUNDS

Consider next the factors that can cause a shift in the supply of loanable funds. The desire to lend is influenced by changes in

1. Wealth. An increase in wealth means that there are more funds available for lending. A reduction in wealth—perhaps caused by a recession—has the opposite effect.

2. Relative returns. An increase in bond returns relative to those earned on other assets leads investors to reallocate their asset holdings toward bonds, away from other assets.

3. Relative riskiness. If bonds become more or less risky than they have been, they may become a less or more desirable asset, and wealth holders act accordingly.

4. Liquidity. An increase or decrease in liquidity also means that investors will increase or decrease their supply of loanable funds.

5. Expected inflation. As noted above, expectations of inflation influence the desire to invest.

Any event, such as a recession, that makes bonds a less desirable asset reduces wealth holders' desire to supply loanable funds. In Figure 6.5(B), the loanable funds supply curve shifts from LF_1^s to LF_2^s.

Conversely, any change that makes bonds a more desirable asset to hold increases the supply of loanable funds. Diagrammatically, the result is a rightward shift in the supply curve of loanable funds.

EQUILIBRIUM INTEREST RATE CHANGES

The reason we are interested in shifts in either the demand or the supply curve is that they imply a change in the equilibrium interest rate level. We will consider three applications of shifts in the demand for and supply of loanable funds to illustrate some of the sources of equilibrium interest rate changes.

The Fisher Effect

One of the important concepts introduced in Chapter 5 is the dichotomy between nominal and real interest rates. According to the Fisher equation, the nominal interest rate is the sum of the real interest rate and expected inflation:

$$R = \rho + \pi^e \tag{6.3}$$

which is equation (5.16), reproduced here for convenience. The loanable funds framework lets us analyze how the Fisher effect operates.

Suppose that expected inflation is initially zero, so that $\pi^e = 0$. In that case the nominal and real interest rates are equivalent, or

$$R = \rho \tag{6.4}$$

Let the equilibrium nominal and real interest rates with zero inflation be denoted R_0^* and ρ_0^*, respectively, as in Figure 6.6. Point E then represents the equilibrium interest rates, nominal and real.

Now suppose that the market comes to believe that inflation will rise to 5% in the future. Our discussion of shifts in the demand for and supply of loanable funds suggests that expectations of inflation influence both sides of the market. Borrowers come to believe that the real cost of a bond will fall because, by equation (6.3) and holding the nominal interest rate constant, a rise in π^e must mean a fall in ρ. Since the demand for borrowing is stimulated, the demand curve shifts from LF_0^d to LF_1^d.

As borrowers display an increased desire to borrow because terms appear improved, lenders come to expect a lower real return. Consequently, the supply curve of loanable funds falls from LF_0^s to LF_1^s. The new intersection between LF_1^s and LF_1^d establishes a new equilibrium at point E'.

Clearly, the interest rate has risen, but is it the real or nominal rate that is affected? Since the real interest rate represents the sacrifice made by borrowers or the extra future consumption enjoyed by lenders, and since the only variable to have changed is expected inflation, the real rate must be unaffected. If it is unchanged in equilibrium, the nominal interest rate must have risen by the change in expected inflation, according to equation (6.3). In other words, the difference between the old and the new nominal interest rate is exactly equal to π^e since

$$R_1^* - R_0^* = \rho_0^* + \pi^e - \rho_0^* - 0 = \pi^e$$

which is graphically represented by the distance EE' in Figure 6.6.

Look back at Figure 5.2, which plots inflation as measured by the consumer price index (CPI) as well as the yield on three-month Treasury bills. The preceding discussion corroborates our visual impression of a positive correlation between inflation and the nominal interest rate. Much research has gone into analyzing the significance of this relationship.

Interest Rates and the Business Cycle

Now consider another important issue. We have suggested that factors such as wealth, relative returns, and liquidity may somehow be linked to fluctuations in the overall state of the economy, which economists refer to as the business cycle. Figure 6.7 illustrates the relationship among these factors since the 1960s by plotting the yield on three-month Treasury bills and the average growth rate in real gross domestic product (GDP). It appears that interest rates are roughly procyclical, meaning that they tend to rise and fall with increases and decreases in the average growth of real GDP. This is especially true of the two severe recessions of the early 1980s and 1990s and the sharp slow-down in 2002 in the wake of 9/11 tragedy. The figure also shows how real GDP growth plummeted in the aftermath of the two oil price shocks.

Figure 6.8 uses the loanable funds framework to illustrates the procyclical movements in interest rates. The equilibrium interest rate is initially R_0^*, where the original demand and supply

---

| **Figure 6.6** | **The Fisher Effect** |

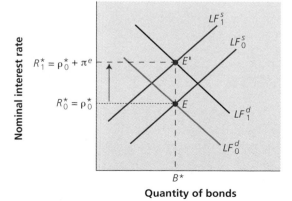

Quantity of bonds

If expected inflation is zero, nominal and real interest rates are the same ($R_0^* = \rho_0^*$). Positive inflation expectations mean the real cost of loans falls for borrowers. Consequently, the demand for loanable funds shifts from LF_0^d to LF_1^d. If the real cost of borrowing falls, the real interest rate from lending is expected to decrease also. Therefore, the supply of loanable funds shifts from LF_0^s to LF_1^s. At the new equilibrium, E', the nominal interest rate rises by exactly the change in inflation expectations, thereby restoring the original real interest rate, ρ_0^*.

ECONOMICS FOCUS 6.1 — THE FISHER EFFECT AND THE NEUTRALITY OF MONEY

Equilibrium relationships are at the heart of economic analysis. For example, "classical" economics considers that monetary policy is neutral in the long run. This means that changes in the money supply are eventually fully reflected in price changes. We saw something of this phenomenon in Chapter 1 and we return to it again in Chapter 12. An additional consequence of this view is that, again in the long run, monetary policy cannot influence output. We analyze this case in greater detail in Chapter 21. A further manifestation of the "neutrality" proposition is in the form of the Fisher equation. Putting aside Keynes famous dictum that "...in the long-run we are all dead..." (Moggridge 1992), there is good reason to believe that, once the public perceives a change in inflation to be permanent, nominal interest rates rise sufficiently to leave real interest rates reasonably constant. Nevertheless, the existing empirical evidence is decidedly mixed on this score (Crowder 1997; King and Watson 1997; Koustas and Serletis 1999). Part of the reason for the considerable uncertainty about whether the Fisher equation holds or not and, as a consequence, whether monetary policy is neutral, is that existing statistical techniques are unable to provide decisive evidence about which portion of changes in inflation is permanent. After all, if a change in expected inflation is temporary or transitory, then it is conceivable that, for example, the shift in LF^s in Figure 6.5 will not take place. For example, consider the figure above. It shows the actual yield on Treasury bills and the yield we would obtain if the real interest rate were assumed to be 1.75% before 1972, 0.5% between 1972 and 1979, 4% between 1980 and 1989, and 2.5% thereafter. It is also assumed that a 1 percent change in inflation leads to a change in the nominal interest rate. The two series parallel each other quite closely, but a couple of questions immediately arise. Why did real interest rates change so much? Could the type of monetary policy in place explain this result? Even though the evidence for the Fisher-type equation is open to question, it is not an unreasonable expression of the link between expected inflation and interest rates. Incidentally, although Fisher is credited with the equation and the first

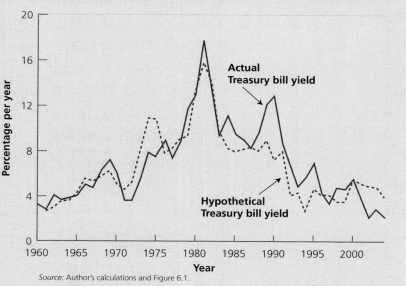

Source: Author's calculations and Figure 6.1.

statistical tests of the kind conducted above, the actual link between these same two variables was known to economists before Fisher's time, as he himself acknowledged (Dimand 1999). In any event, the Fisher equation name has stuck.

Questions for Discussion

1. Would it make much difference to the results in the plot shown in this box if the real interest rate were assumed to be constant throughout the 1960–2001 period?
2. What is the consequence of using actual inflation as a proxy for expected inflation, as the Fisher relation actually requires?

Sources

W.J. Crowder, "The Long-Run Fisher Relation in Canada," *Canadian Journal of Economics* 30 (November 1997): 1124–42.

R.W. Dimand, "Irving Fisher and the Fisher Relation: Setting the Record Straight," *Canadian Journal of Economics* 32 (May 1999): 744–50.

R.G. King, and M.W. Watson, "Testing Long-Run Neutrality," *Economic Quarterly of the Federal Reserve Bank of Richmond* 83 (Summer 1997): 69–101.

Z. Koustas, and A. Serletis, "On the Fisher Effect," *Journal of Monetary Economics* 44 (August 1999): 105–30.

D.E. Moggridge, *Maynard Keynes: An Economist's Biography* (London and New York: Routledge, 1992).

| **Figure 6.7** | **The Nominal Interest Rate and Economic Growth** |

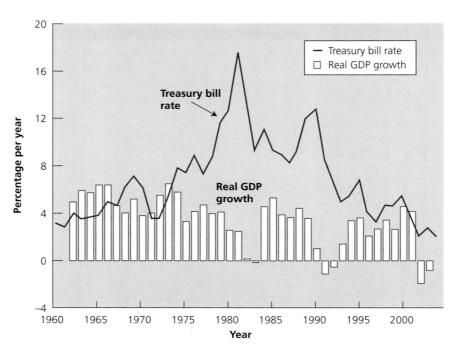

Here the business cycle is proxied by a two-year moving average of annual real GDP growth. (This is by no means the only possible proxy, but it is adequate for exploring the possible links between booms or recessions and interest rate level movements.) Generally, average real GDP growth is positive. Indeed, a recession is often defined as a time when real GDP growth is relatively low, as it was, for example, during the early 1980s and 1990s. Officially, Canada was not in a recession, but, in the aftermath of the 9/11 tragedy, there was a sharp, temporary slowdown in economic growth that is picked up by the methodology used here to proxy economic growth. The picture changes when we allow real GDP growth to be proxied by a three-year moving average of annual real GDP growth. When real GDP growth is consistently positive, interest rates rise. When GDP growth slows down, interest rates tend to fall.

Source: International Financial Statistics CD-ROM (Washington, D.C.: International Monetary Fund).

curves, LF_0^d and LF_0^s, intersect. Then, in anticipation of a recovery, borrowers raise their borrowing plans, so the demand for loanable funds rises to LF_1^d. At the same time, with a recovery expected, income growth is expected to rise. It is reasonable to suppose that the supply of loanable funds also will rise, a phenomenon shown in Figure 6.8 by a shift in the supply curve to LF_1^s.

What is unclear is how large the shifts in the demand and supply curves will be relative to each other. This consideration is an important one, since the relative size of the shifts will dictate whether the resulting equilibrium interest rate level will be higher or lower than the one before the expansion begins. Given the evidence presented in Figure 6.7, we conclude that interest rates rise in an expansion. Thus we have constructed the figure with the new equilibrium interest rate at R_1^*, higher than R_0^*, the interest rate at the original equilibrium point.

An identical argument can, of course, be used to suggest that the equilibrium interest rate will fall when the business cycle is in a recessionary phase. We leave working out the solution to you as an exercise.

A final comment is in order. Recall that the foregoing discussion assumes that inflation is expected to remain constant. In reality, of course, real income and inflation both change over time.

Figure 6.8   **Interest Rates in an Expansion**

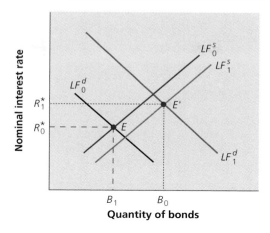

Interest rate level movements appear procyclical, rising and falling with business cycle booms and recessions. During an expansion or in anticipation of one, the demand for loanable funds rises (from LF_0^d to LF_1^d) as the desire to borrow increases. Similarly, since a recovery indicates higher income growth, the supply rises (LF_0^s shifts to LF_1^s). The equilibrium interest rate level is now at point E', which is higher than at point E.

As a result, the downward movement in nominal interest rates, beginning in the 1990s especially, was greatly influenced by lower inflation and expected inflation, but, as anyone who follows Bank of Canada actions knows, the first hint that the economy might be overheating is enough to send interest rates higher.

An astute reader will notice from Figure 6.7 that, whereas previous drops in the growth rate of real GDP signalled fairly sharp drops in the nominal interest rate, the situation appears to be somewhat different in 2001. Real GDP growth rates remain high despite rapidly falling nominal interest rates. Why? As noted elsewhere (see, for example, Chapter 1) central banks have improved the way in which they conduct policy and are, consequently, more "forward looking." Hence, the drop in interest rates, especially in 2001, reflects fears of a looming recession (evident even before the terrorist attacks of September 2001).[5]

6.2   THE LIQUIDITY PREFERENCE APPROACH

Liquidity preference is the desire to hold wealth in the form of money rather than in less liquid forms. It is, in other words, the demand for money.

What does this demand have to do with interest rates? Economists have long believed that interest rate level determination is primarily a *monetary* factor—one depending on the interaction of the demand for and the supply of money. The idea may seem odd at first since, as we saw in Chapter 5, the interest rate is an expression of the price of bonds. Assume that individuals' portfolios consist only of money and bonds. Linking the demand for and supply of money to the interest rate is sensible because, for a given level of wealth, any excess demand for bonds must imply an excess supply of money, and vice versa. If wealth is fixed, the foregoing assumption means

---

5 *The Economist* magazine began tracking the number of times articles (originally in the United Kingdom) in the *New York Times* and the *Washington Post* mention the "R" word (for recession). This index appears to be coincident with the onset of actual recessions in the United States since, by early 2001, the index flashed red. Indeed, in April 2001, the National Bureau of Economic Research (see **www.nber.org/cycles.html** for the statement) declared the U.S. economy to be in a recession. No such declaration was made for Canada.

we can write

$$W = M + B \tag{6.5}$$

where

W = the fixed stock of wealth
M = money stock
B = stock of bonds

If wealth remains constant, we can write

$$\Delta W = 0$$

where Δ refers to a change in a variable. We can, therefore, express equation (6.5) in terms of changes as

$$0 = \Delta M + \Delta B$$

or, finally,

$$-\Delta M = \Delta B \tag{6.6}$$

It is clear from equation (6.6) that any changes in the stock of bonds are exactly offset by changes in the money stock, under the assumption of unchanging wealth.

We can be more specific about this conclusion by considering that equilibrium is determined in both the money and bond markets by the point at which supply and demand are equal to each other. Moreover, if the bond market is in equilibrium, the money market must also be in equilibrium. We can, therefore, write

$$B^d + M^d = B^s + M^s \tag{6.7}$$

where B^d and B^s are bond demand and bond supply, and M^d and M^s are money demand and money supply.

Rearranging equation (6.7) to collect the terms in each market, we obtain

$$M^s - M^d \equiv B^s - B^d \tag{6.8}$$

which simply states that an excess demand ($M^s - M^d < 0$) or excess supply ($M^s - M^d > 0$) of money must be identical (hence the symbol $\equiv$) to an excess supply ($B^s - B^d > 0$) or an excess demand ($B^s - B^d < 0$) for bonds.

As depicted here, the liquidity preference and the loanable funds frameworks are similar. In the liquidity preference framework, however, it is the demand for and supply of liquidity—money—a stock measure, that determines the interest rate.[6]

THE DEMAND FOR MONEY

The desire to hold liquidity is a function of three factors: (1) the interest rate, (2) income, and (3) the price level.

According to the narrow definition of money, it is an asset that earns little or no interest. Thus, holders of liquidity incur the **opportunity cost**—the cost of the forgone action—of not holding an asset that could earn interest income.[7]

Does it make sense then for an individual to hold any money at all? Yes, because holding money is useful for three reasons:

1. **Transactions motive.** Money is useful as a means of settling transactions.

---

6 This explanation reconciling the two approaches is deceptively simple. It took decades of intense debate to recognize how it could be achieved.
7 If we defined money more broadly to include some interest-earning assets, the opportunity cost of money would simply be the difference between the interest on bonds and that on money. For simplicity, we can retain our definition of the interest rate on bonds as the opportunity cost of holding money.

2. **Precautionary motive.** Money is useful as a precaution against unexpected expenditures.

3. **Speculative motive.** Money is held as an asset that can be used to purchase assets when a profitable opportunity arises.

Most economists believe that income level determines the amount of money an individual wants to hold for transactions and precautionary purposes.[8] This relationship is depicted in the top part of Figure 6.9. The vertical axis measures income in current dollars, which is referred to as **nominal income**. Nominal income is affected by changes in its components. If we write

$$Y = Py$$

where Y is nominal income and P is the price level, then

$$y = \frac{Y \ (\text{nominal income})}{P \ (\text{price level})}$$

is **real income**—that is, the purchasing power commanded by nominal income Y. The measurement of income is, therefore, a critical part of understanding what affects money demand and is by no means a trivial exercise, as **Economics Focus 6.2: Measuring Real GDP** explains.

The top part of Figure 6.9 also shows a particular level of transactions and precautionary demand for money, M, associated with a particular level of income. This demand changes with increases or decreases in P, in y, or in both.

The bottom part of Figure 6.9 plots the demand for money as an asset. Since money is assumed not to have any explicit yield, its opportunity cost is measured by the yield on a bond, R. If demand is held constant, the higher the yield on bonds, the greater the opportunity cost of holding money. Therefore, we would expect the quantity of money demanded to fall with higher bond yields. The resulting relationship is the **demand for money** or the demand for liquidity. The curve is marked M^d.

Note that if income rises, the quantity of money held for transactions and precautionary purposes also rises, say from M^* to M^{**}. In terms of the relationship depicted in Figure 6.9, such a change means that the demand for money curve has shifted to the right. A new tradeoff now exists between bond yields and the demand for money. In other words, price changes and real income changes shift the demand for money curve.

THE SUPPLY OF MONEY

It is conventional to assume that the supply of money is entirely under the control of the central bank and that it is unresponsive or unrelated to interest rate levels. This simplistic assumption ignores the behaviour of banks and of the public. Banks, for example, hold reserves[9] against their deposits, and a portion of these reserves return no interest, thereby incurring an opportunity cost.[10]

Banks can manage their reserves (RES). Despite the opportunity costs, they have sound reasons for holding RES periodically (for example, during the Christmas season, when the demand for cash rises). Nevertheless, since banks presumably want to maximize profits, they want to minimize RES. It is also reasonable to suppose that the higher the opportunity cost, the smaller the banks' reserve holdings will be. Money that would otherwise be held in reserves will be loaned out, so deposits in the banking system will rise. Recall that the money supply, by definition, includes some deposits. Therefore, a higher interest rate increases the quantity of money supplied.

---

8 Of course, the precautionary demand for money involves uncertainty and, therefore, more than just income. We return to this issue in Chapter 12. Here, however, it is convenient and correct to make both the transactions and precautionary motives a function of income alone.

9 Legislation has phased out required reserves. Banks will still want, however, to hold some reserves.

10 Many countries, such as Germany and the United States, still impose mandatory reserve requirements on the banking system. Strictly speaking, only the holding of currency incurs an opportunity cost. The reserve management system in Canada (see Chapter 4) does provide for the payment of interest on reserves at the Bank of Canada.

ECONOMICS FOCUS 6.2   MEASURING REAL GDP

In your principles course, you will have gone into some detail concerning the components of real GDP that proxy economywide income. This measure is called current dollar GDP. Because of inflation, however, we need to measure GDP at constant prices called real GDP (or real income as the discussion of money demand in this chapter refers to it). Since real GDP represents the constant dollar value of *all* goods and services in the economy, it does not have some of the problems associated with the CPI (see *Economics Focus 5.2*). However, like the CPI, it is constructed from information collected in the base year. Recently, both the United States and Canada introduced a *chain-weighted* index alongside the usual *fixed-weight* index on which the calculations of real GDP in this chapter are based (the new measure goes back only to 1986). Indeed, dissatisfaction with the manner in which GDP is measured has even led to one proposal to measure GDP according to the weight of raw materials, agricultural products, manufacturing goods, and so on. According to this index, the total weight of GDP, measured since 1977, reached a peak around 1986 before falling, and has remained reasonably stable ever since (see *Wired*). Even if we take this index seriously, what are we to make of technological improvements, such as replacing copper wire with fibre or metals with plastics, which might reduce total GDP measured by weight? Is the *chain-index* better? In a sense the answer is yes, since the new index takes into account the impact of changes in relative prices as well as changes in the composition of output over time. To see how real GDP calculations work under the old and new systems, consider the following extraordinarily simplified example. Suppose the economy produces two goods and services only: haircuts and watches. The table below records the prices and quantities sold in the *base* year.

Base Year

	Expenditure (Price × Quantities)	Quantities Consumed	Price per Unit
Haircuts	$300	30	$10
Watches	$200	10	$20
"GDP"	$500		

Nominal GDP in the base year is $500. The table below gives the figures for the following year.

Next Year

	Expenditure (Price × Quantities)	Quantities Consumed	Price per Unit
Haircuts	$400	20	$20
Watches	$500	20	$25
"GDP"	$900		

Nominal GDP is now $900. Now let's see how real GDP would be calculated under the two weighting schemes. The results are shown below.

Fixed-Weight (Base Year Prices)	Fixed-Weight (Current Year Prices)
[20 × $10 + 20 × $20]/ $500 = $600/$500 = 1.2	$900/[30 × $20 + 10 × $25] = $900/$850 = 1.06
Real GDP rose by 20%	Real GDP rose by 6%

One way of calculating real GDP is to use the current year's quantities and the base year's prices in the numerator and actual expenditure in the denominator. Another method begins by using the actual GDP in the numerator and base year's quantities in the denominator. The difference in the two measures of real GDP growth is striking. One method reports a 20% increase while the other finds only a 6% increase. The chain-weighted index is the *geometric* average of the two evaluated as

$$\sqrt{(1.20)(1.06)} = 1.13$$

That is, the square root of the product of the two growth rates. Therefore, the chain-weighted index uses the weights from adjacent years to construct real GDP.

Are actual differences between the two methods significant for the Canadian economy? The table below shows they are for the years shown (more recent data are unavailable).

Year	GDP Growth (%) Fixed-Weight	GDP Growth (%) Chain-Weighted
1987	4.2	4.2
1988	5.0	4.4
1989	2.4	2.8
1990	−0.2	1.0
1991	−1.8	−1.9
1992	0.8	0.9
1993	2.2	1.2
1994	4.6	3.6

Questions for Discussion

1. Do the significant differences in the growth rates under the old and new indexes suggest something about the overall performance of the Canadian economy since 1987?

2. What do you think motivated the need for a revised index?

Source

"Economic Weighting Game," *Wired* 9 (September 2001): 80.

| **Figure 6.9** | **The Transactions and the Precautionary Demand for Money** |

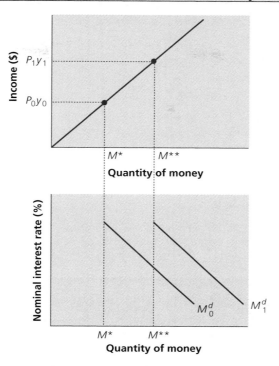

The top portion shows the positive relationship between income (the price level × real income) and the quantity of money demanded for transactions and precautionary purposes. The bottom portion depicts the demand for money as an asset that yields no explicit return. The opportunity cost of holding money thus is approximately the yield on a bond. Price changes and real income changes can shift the demand for money curve.

The public too can influence the quantity of money supplied in the market. The public's holding of currency, another of the constituents of the money supply, also is presumably affected by interest rate levels.[11] Thus, the higher the interest rate, the higher the opportunity cost of holding currency and the more likely that individuals will economize on cash holdings. This translates into a larger money supply.[12]

The size of these effects is not clear. Nevertheless, the foregoing discussion suggests a positive relationship between the interest rate and the quantity of money supplied.

EQUILIBRIUM IN THE MONEY MARKET

Having derived supply and demand in the money market, we can now define the equilibrium. It is shown in Figure 6.10 by point E, which also defines the equilibrium interest rate level, R_0^*.

MONETARY POLICY AND INTEREST RATES

One of the most important uses of the liquidity preference framework is in exploring the influence of **monetary policy** on interest rates—that is, the money supply and credit policies of the Bank of Canada. We introduced some of the institutional devices that link monetary policy and

---

11 And by financial innovations, such as the introduction of automated banking machines.
12 If individuals hold relatively more of their money holdings in the form of bank deposits, their action swells the banks' reserves and the money supply because of the banks' desire to minimize such holdings.

Figure 6.10   **Contractionary Monetary Policy**

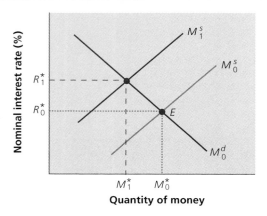

Equilibrium in the money market is at point *E*, the intersection of the demand for money and the supply of money curves. The equilibrium interest rate is R_0^*. A reduction in the money supply shifts the money supply curve to the left, from M_0^s to M_1^s. If the demand for money is held constant at M_0^d, the equilibrium interest rate rises to R_1^*, and equilibrium money holdings fall to M_1^*.

key interest rates in Chapter 4. Below, we discuss the principles linking monetary policy and interest rates in the liquidity preference setting. In Part 7, we discuss how the link actually works in practice. A policy of increasing the money supply is called an **expansionary monetary policy**; a policy of decreasing the money supply is called a **contractionary monetary policy**.

To illustrate the potential impact of monetary policy on interest rate levels, we begin by considering how a reduction in the money supply changes the equilibrium interest rate. The decrease in the level of the money supply causes the money supply curve to shift to the left, from M_0^s to M_1^s, as depicted in Figure 6.10. Assuming that the demand for money is held constant at M_0^d, the new equilibrium interest rate is R_1^*, which is higher than the original equilibrium rate of R_0^*. In other words, a contractionary monetary policy signals higher interest rates.

What is the connection between monetary policy and interest rates? In a dynamic economy, even if the demand for money remains fixed, the money supply rises or falls over time, implying continual shifts in the money supply curve. Most discussions of the link between monetary policy and interest rates are generally expressed in terms of rates of change in the money supply, so it is useful here to emphasize the difference between level changes and rates of changes. Figure 6.11 will help fix some of the ideas.

In Figure 6.11(A), the money supply stays constant at M_0^s until time t_0. Then it rises to M_1^s once and for all. Note that given our assumption, the money supply levels remain constant before and after t_0. Therefore, there cannot be any growth in the money stock. For this reason, the *rate* of change in the money supply, labelled μ in the figure, is zero, except at the instant when the money supply rises from M_0^s to M_1^s.

Figure 6.11(B) displays various growth rates over time. Until time t_0, the growth rate is μ_0. Between t_0 and t_1, the growth rate is negative because the curve describing the evolution of the money supply over time is negatively sloped. By contrast, as the money supply rises between t_1 and t_2, the curve slopes in the other direction, so we know the growth rate in the series is positive again. Finally, after time t_2, the money supply curve becomes flat, indicating zero money supply growth ($\mu_3 = 0$).

It should be clear by now that one way to measure the growth rate in the money supply is to examine the slope of the curve. In algebraic terms, we may compute the rate of change as

$$\frac{M_t^s - M_{t-1}^s}{M_{t-1}^s} \times 100 = \mu \qquad (6.9)$$

| Figure 6.11 | Types of Changes in the Money Supply |

(A) A Level Change in the Money Supply

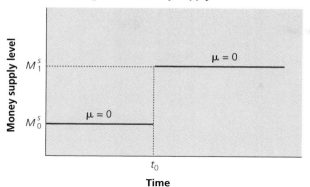

(B) Changes in Money Supply Growth Rates

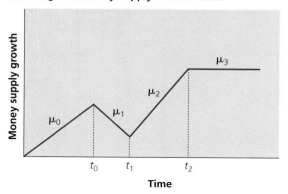

In panel (A), growth is zero ($\mu = 0$), except at time t_0. In other words, the money supply stays constant over time except during its single jump upward, which is a change in level (assumed to be instantaneous). In contrast, panel (B) illustrates several rates of growth in the money supply. The rate depends on the slope of the line describing movements in M_s over time.

where M_t^s, is the current period's value for the money supply, and M_{t-1}^s is last period's value.[13] Equation (6.9) simply evaluates the change in the money supply from one period to the next as a percentage of last period's money supply.

We can now recast our discussion of the link between monetary policy changes and interest rate levels by asking, what is the link between money growth and the interest rate? Figure 6.12 plots average values for money growth along with the yield on three-month Treasury bills since the 1960s. The relationship between money growth and interest rates appears to be inverse. When money growth falls, interest rates tend to rise and vice versa.

The relationship depicted by Figure 6.12 is not of the one-to-one variety; that is, we cannot say that when money supply growth rises by 1% nominal interest rates fall by 1%. Indeed, one can even find periods during which the relationship appears to be positive. One problem with an analysis of the kind resorted to in Figure 6.10 is that changes in one variable, say money growth, will take time to impact interest rates. How long? Milton Friedman once said that lags in monetary policy are long and variable. To understand what this means for the relationship between money growth and interest rates consider our theoretical diagram in Figure 6.13 a little further. Until time t_0, the money supply growth is zero, which is consistent with an equilibrium interest rate level of R_0^*. Now suppose, at time t_0, the Bank of Canada announces a policy that amounts to reducing the money supply growth from μ_0 to μ_2. Doing so requires a temporary negative growth rate, μ_1, during the period t_0 to t_1, until the new money supply growth, μ_2 is reached. According to Figure 6.12, the prediction is that the equilibrium interest rate level, R_1^*, will be higher than R_0^*. And that is exactly what Figure 6.13 shows.

Notice, however, that the figure also shows that the transition need not be smooth. What accounts for the humped response of the interest rate in the bottom part of Figure 6.13?

First, the leftward shift in the money supply curve in Figure 6.10 implies less liquidity in the economy. As long as the original equilibrium interest rate, R_0^*, holds, there is now excess demand for money, which puts upward pressure on the interest rate. Consequently, the interest

---

13 An alternative to using equation (6.9) is to compute 100 times the first difference in the logarithm of M^s—that is, to evaluate $\mu = \Delta \log M_t^s = \log M_t^s - \log M_{t-1}^s$. Economists tend to prefer this form for evaluating μ because there is a natural connection between the use of the logarithms and the computation of an elasticity measure.

Figure 6.12   **Money Growth and Interest Rates**

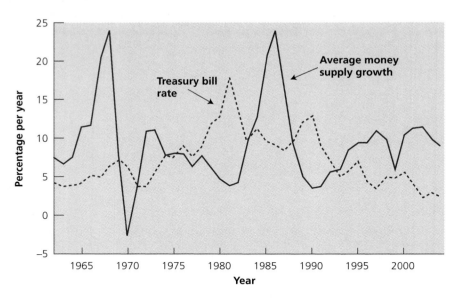

Money growth is measured as an eight-quarter moving average of the growth rate in M1. Generally, when money growth increases, interest rates fall and vice versa.

Sources: Figure 6.1, and *International Financial Statistics CD-ROM* (Washington, D.C.: International Monetary Fund). The series "Money," as defined by the IMF is used.

Figure 6.13   **Money Growth and the Interest Rate: Liquidity versus Income Effects**

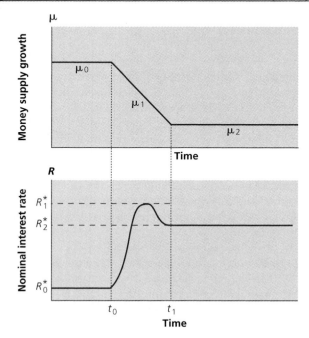

After money supply growth falls from μ_0 to μ_2, the interest rate evolves over time from R_0^* to R_2^*. The equilibrium interest rate rises as long as we assume that the liquidity effect dominates the income effect. This need not always be the case.

rate rises to R_1^*. But the story does not end here. Eventually, the reduction in the money supply affects real income and the price level because, as we saw in Figure 6.9, a lower equilibrium money stock is associated with a lower level of income. As real income and the price level both fall, the demand for money curve also shifts to the left, potentially offsetting the initial increase in the interest rate level. Thus, in Figure 6.13, the equilibrium interest rate ends up at R_2^*, higher than it was originally, but not quite as high as it rose at first. We have, therefore, assumed that the interest rate response to a change in money supply growth is dominated by the liquidity effect. It must be emphasized, however, that it is possible for the real-income and price-level effects to dominate the liquidity effect.[14] In such a case, we eventually would obtain a lower interest rate despite a fall in money supply growth.

The question, of course, is an empirical one. Nevertheless, it is important to realize that any link between money growth and the interest rate depends critically on the central bank's ability to control the money supply, an ability that should not be taken for granted. The difficulty associated with the links between money growth, inflation, and interest rates have led many analysts to focus their attention exclusively on interest rate behaviour.[15] We return to this question in Chapter 23. Hence, higher interest rates are thought of as signalling a contractionary monetary policy, whereas lower interest rates mean a looser policy. However, this can be quite misleading since, as we have seen in Chapter 5 as well as in our discussion of the loanable funds approach, what determines how tight or loose monetary policy will be really is the behaviour of real interest rates. This point is once again underscored by the discussion in **Financial Focus 6.1: Why the Rise in Real Interest Rates?**

THE LIQUIDITY TRAP

We have already mentioned the extraordinarily low nominal interest rates in Japan. As noted in Chapter 1, this is the direct result of very low inflation and deflation that have persisted in Japan for at least a decade. Despite the low interest rates, the Japanese economy was mired in a recession for over decade. So it is appropriate to ask why the usual prescription of lower interest rates (also see Figure 6.7) may not always lead to improvements in economic performance. The resulting problem has been named the **liquidity trap**. The term is associated with the great British economist, John Maynard Keynes, though he was probably ambivalent about its validity.[16] To see what a liquidity trap might entail, consider Figure 6.14, which shows the unusual case of a money supply curve that is perfectly flat at some extremely low interest rate, say 0.25%. For some very large quantity of money, the money supply becomes once again sensitive to the interest rate (i.e., positively sloped). However, a central bank that tries to increase the money supply (from M_0^s to M_1^s) at the current position of the money demand curve (M_0^d) ends up having no impact on the equilibrium interest rate. It remains stubbornly at 0.25% regardless what the central bank does. In other words, in terms of Figure 6.13, if the central bank engineers an increase in μ, there is no decrease in the nominal interest rate, that is, no liquidity effect whatsoever.

---

14 Some economists now believe that the liquidity effect no longer exists. See, for example, Y. Mehra, "Inflationary Expectations, Money Growth, and the Vanishing Liquidity Effect of Money on Interest: A Further Investigation," *Federal Reserve Bank of Richmond, Economic Review* 71 (March/April 1985): 23–35. An article by James D. Hamilton arrives at the opposite conclusion. See "Measuring the Liquidity Effect," *American Economic Review* 87 (March 1997): 80–97.

15 Not all expert observers are content with this situation; they claim that ignoring the potent impact of money on inflation may lead to policy mistakes. See, for example, D.E. W. Laidler, "Taking Money Seriously," *Canadian Journal of Economics,* 21(4) (November 1988): 687–713, and "Monetary Policy without Money: Hamlet without the Ghost," University of Western Ontario, Department of Economics, UWO Department of Economics Working Papers: 20037, 2003.

16 The possibility of a liquidity trap stems from the experience of many economies during the Great Depression of 1929–33 when, despite near-zero nominal interest rates, economic activity continued to slump. For a discussion of Keynes's ambivalence about the liquidity trap see, for example, D. Laidler, *Fabricating the Keynesian Revolution* (Cambridge: Cambridge University Press, 1998), and A. H. Meltzer, *Keynes' Monetary Theory: A Different Interpretation* (Cambridge: Cambridge University Press, 1988).

How could this happen in reality? In Japan, there is deep pessimism about government policies and the future in general. The fact that prices fell for several years, at least until 2005, also means that consumers not only will postpone some purchases (after all they can be bought more cheaply in the future), but that firms too will be reluctant to invest. As one typical Japanese consumer was quoted as saying: "Theoretically, if interest rates are lower, you should use more money." But, he added, "You actually just feel like saving." This "fear factor" means that the central bank's attempts to increase the money supply are like pushing on a string. Nevertheless, some are suggesting that because Japan is caught in a liquidity trap, policymakers should actually consider repaying some of the private sector's debt. Imagine if the Bank of Japan simply deposited a cheque roughly equivalent to 30% of every household's debt? The proposal is not as new or as outlandish as might first appear. Many textbooks have used the device—associated most often with Milton Friedman's work—of the helicopter dropping cash on a grateful population that then goes on to spend the gift, thereby stimulating aggregate demand. Might such a policy actually work? The fact that Japan is experiencing difficulty extricating itself from economic stagnation is leading some to wonder whether drastic action of this type might be the answer to their problems. The decade-old recession in Japan has led several observers to wonder whether the same thing could happen in North America or elsewhere. Most observers think not.[17]

Figure 6.14   **The Liquidity Trap**

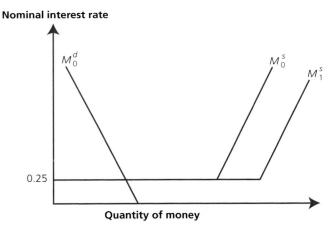

M_0^d is the original money demand curve. An increase in the money supply from M_0^s to M_1^s has no effect on the equilibrium interest rate, which stays at 0.25%. In this case the economy is said to be in a liquidity trap.

---

17 See P. Krugman, "Fear Itself," *New York Times Magazine*, 30 September 2001, P. Krugman, "Its BAAACK: Japan's Slump and the Return of the Liquidity Trap," *Brookings Papers on Economic Activity* 2 (1998); A. Posen and R. Mikitani, *Japan's Financial Crisis and Its Parallels to US Experience* (Washington, D.C.: Institute for International Economics, 2000), and "What a Peculiar Cycle," *The Economist*, 10 March 2001; and P. Krugman, "Thinking about the Liquidity Trap," *Journal of the Japanese and International Economies*, 14 (2000): 221–237.

FINANCIAL FOCUS 6.1   WHY THE RISE IN REAL INTEREST RATES?

High real interest rates were a common occurrence in several countries for several years (see Figure 5.2). What accounts for the rise? The discussion in this chapter suggests many possible influences on real interest rates, including expected inflation, monetary and fiscal policy, and the business cycle. Two other explanations merit special attention. The first relies on the notion that monetary policy can influence real interest rates. The second involves the volatility of energy prices.

In 1991, Canada adopted inflation targets, and the suggestion has been made that one way the central bank was able to generate the required disinflation was through higher real interest rates, with supposedly disastrous effects (Fortin 1996). The evidence, however, about whether real interest rates in Canada were higher than elsewhere in the industrial world, indeed whether inflation-targeting countries deliberately drove up real interest rates, is mixed at best (Siklos 1997). An equally likely scenario is that the fall in inflation during the early 1990s was faster than expected in inflation-targeting countries and that this led to higher real interest rates for a time. It is a bit puzzling, however, that higher real interest rates persisted for as long as they did since, as we saw in Chapter 5, real interest rates had been abnormally high. Nevertheless, we also saw that such an outcome need not be the sign of a restrictive monetary policy alone, but could also be symptomatic of greater returns to investment stemming from improvements in productivity.

Wilcox (1983) makes the case for another explanation of real interest rate changes, focusing on the impact of drastic fluctuations in the price of energy relative to other commodities. During the oil price shocks of 1973–74 and 1979, the price of energy rose sharply. Most other commodities require energy as an input to production, so the relatively higher energy prices would also lead to a lower expected return on investment. The results would be a leftward shift in LF^d with a consequent lower real interest rate. The behaviour of real interest rates during the 1970s appears to lend support to the hypothesis.

Energy prices began to rise sharply beginning the summer of 1999 and again in 2004 but, as the year ended, there was little evidence that the latest oil price "shock" would have the same impact as those that took place in the 1970s.

We would expect the theory to work in reverse so that a falling relative price of energy, as experienced during the early part of the 1990s, would produce a higher real interest rate. Unfortunately, as Tatom (1987) points out, the empirical evidence on this account is weak. It is quite conceivable that, as the public became used to persistent inflation, the reversal of inflation expectations was a slow and difficult process.

The lack of symmetry in the prediction of the theory linking energy prices to real interest rate changes leads us to prefer the monetary policy explanation. Other factors may also have been at work.

Questions for Discussion

1. Why would increased money supply growth translate into higher real interest rates?
2. Do fluctuations in real interest rates outlined in this focus box have any implications for the validity of the Fisher hypothesis?

Sources

P. Fortin, "The Great Canadian Slump," *Canadian Journal of Economics* (November 1996): 761–87.

P.L. Siklos, "Charting a Future for the Bank of Canada: Inflation Targets and the Balance Between Autonomy and Accountability," in *Where We Go from Here: Inflation Targets in Canada's Monetary Policy Regime*, edited by D.E.W. Laidler (C.D. Howe Institute, 1997): 101–84.

J.A. Tatom, "The Macroeconomic Effects of the Recent Fall in Oil Prices," *Review of the Federal Reserve Bank of St. Louis* 69 (June/July 1987): 34–45.

J.A. Wilcox, "Why Real Interest Rates Were So Low in the 1970s," *American Econonmic Review* 73 (March 1983): 44–54.

SUMMARY

- The determination of interest rate levels can be understood in two ways: (1) the loanable funds approach examines the operation of the bond market, (2) the liquidity preference approach views individuals as deciding between holding bonds or money.

In both approaches, it is the interactions of the demand for and supply of financial assets that determine the equilibrium interest rate.

- Some of the important factors that cause interest rates to change over time include liquidity, risk, expectations of future inflation, and government policies.

- Shifts in loanable funds demanded are explained by changes in the anticipated return on investments, in government policies, in inflation expectations, and in risk.

- Shifts in loanable funds supplied are explained by changes in wealth, relative returns, risk, and liquidity.

- Interest rates and inflation tend to move together. The phenomenon is known as the Fisher effect.

- Interest rate movements tend to be procyclical, that is, they rise when the economy is growing and fall when the economy is in a recession.

- Economists discern three reasons for individuals to hold money: the transactions motive, the precautionary motive, and the speculative motive.

- Monetary policy is best understood by examining money growth, that is, the rate of change in the money supply.

- Monetary policy, as practised by the Bank of Canada, influences interest rates. Government actions in the bond market can also cause interest rates to change.

- Typically, falling money growth leads to higher interest rates, while rising money growth means lower interest rates.

- When money growth changes, two opposing forces act on interest rates, a liquidity effect and an income effect, so it is possible for interest rates to rise when money growth is rising.

- A liquidity trap is possible if, for additional increases in the money supply, nominal interest rates no longer fall.

IMPORTANT TERMS

contractionary monetary policy, 108
demand for money, 105
equilibrium interest rate, 94
expansionary monetary policy, 108
liquidity preference, 103
liquidity trap, 111
loanable funds, 94

monetary policy, 107
nominal income, 105
opportunity cost, 104
precautionary motive, 105
real income, 105
speculative motive, 105
transactions motive, 104

PROBLEMS

1. If the demand for loanable funds by the business sector decreases because of a recession but the demand for loanable funds by the government increases by an amount greater than the decreased demand, how is the equilibrium interest rate affected? Show the change on an appropriate diagram.

2. One way the Bank of Canada can affect the money supply is by selling federal government bonds to the public, also known as an open market operation. Use the loanable funds framework to show the effect on the equilibrium interest rate.

3. How does the policy described in question 2 affect the Canadian money supply? Would your answer be the same if you used the loanable funds framework? Use a diagram and explain.

4. Suppose the Bank of Canada succeeds in persuading investors that inflation is expected to fall in the future. Trace the effects such a policy would have, based on the Fisher effect, on the nominal interest rate. Use the loanable funds diagram for your answer.

5. How would accelerating money growth affect the nominal interest rate? (Hint: Use a diagram such as Figure 6.13.)

6. What would be the impact of a sudden and immediate increase in money growth on the nominal interest rate? Would you qualify your answer? If so, how? (Hint: Again, use a diagram such as Figure 6.13.)

7. Using the loanable funds model, show graphically how taxes drive a wedge between nominal and real interest rates.

8. The Bank of Canada believes that slower money growth leads to higher interest rates and that these rates are necessary to fight inflation. Under what conditions will the Bank of Canada's policy work? Use the liquidity preference approach and explain your answer with a diagram.

9. Assume that the economy produces two goods, A and B. The table below provides details of the prices and quantities consumed over a two-year period. Find GDP and real GDP using both the fixed-weight and chain-weighted methods.

Base Year	Quantities	Price
A	20	$40
B	30	$20
Following Year		
A	10	$80
B	25	$35

10. Explain, using the loanable funds and liquidity preference frameworks, how an oil price shock might raise the nominal interest rate.

11. In Figure 6.7, the Treasury bill rate falls sharply after 1990, that is, since the Bank of Canada and the federal government agreed on a set of inflation targets. Is there a connection? Use the loanable funds framework for your answer.

12. In the text, a Japanese consumer is quoted as saying that when interest rates are low, one should "use" more money. Explain what this means in terms of the liquidity preference model and why this notion does not seem to work in the case of Japan.

13. The hypothetical Treasury bill yields plotted in **Economics Focus 6.1: The Fisher Effect and the Neutrality of Money** are drawn based on two assumptions: One, that the real interest rate has changed over time; two, that actual and expected inflation are the same. Does the changing real interest rate say something about the changing stance of monetary policy over time? Explain. Is the assumption that $\pi = \pi^e$ a reasonable one? Explain.

14. During the Great Depression several policymakers equated high nominal interest rates with a contractionary monetary policy, whereas low nominal interest rates were thought to be the result of a loose monetary policy. Why is this incorrect? Explain using the Fisher equation.

15. In Figure 6.14 the money supply function is perfectly elastic at very low interest rates. Explain why this situation might take hold.

16. It has been suggested that one way out of a liquidity trap is to announce a positive inflation target and commit to it. How might this get an economy out of a liquidity trap? Explain using the liquidity preference approach.

DISCUSSION QUESTIONS

1. Under the Bank Act of 1992, required reserve requirements for chartered banks were phased out (see the section entitled "The Supply of Money"). Does this mean that banks will choose to hold no reserves? Why or why not?

2. In Figure 6.1, changes in the long-term government bond yield appear less abrupt than changes in the Treasury bill rate. Can you explain why?

3. "A contractionary policy necessarily involves an increase in interest rates." Evaluate and comment.

4. Comment on the notion that the liquidity effect dominates the income effect of a change in money growth. Can you think of a scenario in which this might not hold?

5. Discuss why the Japanese experience with deflation and a decade-old slump might or might not happen in Canada.

ONLINE APPLICATIONS

1. Go to the Bank of Canada's Web site at **www.bankofcanada.ca/en**. Click on Inflation and then on *Inflation Calculator.* Use the inflation calculator to see what the rate of inflation has been for a period of your choice and compare that with the money growth and interest rate figures shown in the chapter. Are they broadly comparable? Next, go back to the Bank's homepage and click on *Monetary Policy* and then *Monetary Policy Report.* Read the latest *Monetary Policy Report.* Discuss whether the notions of liquidity and income effects, the role of the business cycle, expectations of inflation, and money growth are mentioned as determinants of interest rate actions or monetary policy in general. Which of these factors appears to be the most important in the particular Report you have read? Why? Is the Bank's explanation clear or persuasive?

2. Go to the StatsCan Web site and download the document "The Effect of Rebasing on GDP" at **www.statcan.ca/**
english/concepts/nateco/rebase.pdf. (You will need Acrobat Reader to view the document.) How many times has the base year in real GDP calculations been changed since the data were produced? How would you change price level data from a different base year to the current one while preserving historical estimates of price changes? How many series are used to calculate GDP? How is the price index for each component of GDP calculated, and what is the principal drawback with the methodology used?

3. Go to the Bank of Canada's Web site at **www.bankofcanada.ca/en/.** Click on *Inflation* and then on *Investment Calculator.* Assume a $100 000 investment maturing in 2010 at a nominal interest rate of 3% and inflation at 1%. Find the before- and after-inflation investment values and compare to a situation where inflation is −5%. Which situation would you prefer as an investor and why? Is this scenario likely to happen? Why or why not?

CANSIM QUESTION

Go to the CANSIM Web site and download some of the series used in this chapter. They are the Treasury bill rate (series V122531), the long-term government bond yields (V122544), the 90-day prime corporate paper rate (V122491), real GDP (V1992067), and M1 (V37141). See if you can replicate Figures 6.7 and 6.12. Would your interpretation of the relationship between interest rates and either money growth or real GDP growth change if you used a different moving average calculation? Discuss.

Note: Some of the data are available only quarterly (for example, GDP), while other series are available monthly. All the figures in this chapter were created at an annual rate by averaging the monthly and quarterly figures.

References can be found on **www.mcgrawhill.ca/college/siklos**

Understanding Interest Rates:
The Term Structure of Interest Rates

LEARNING OBJECTIVES

After reading and studying this chapter, you should be able to

7.1 explain why bond yields differ according to the length of time before they mature

7.1 list some of the key properties of the term structure of interest rates

7.1 explain how a yield curve is defined

7.2 describe how the expectations hypothesis is formulated

7.3 identify some of the anomalies in a yield curve's behaviour

7.4 explain how competing theories of the term structure, such as the liquidity premium, segmented markets, and preferred habitat hypotheses are formulated

We have considered various ways in which interest rates can be defined (Chapter 5). Interest rates also differ with an asset's term to maturity. To consider the role of maturity alone, we consider debt instruments that differ solely by term. This gives rise to a yield curve. What determines the term structure of interest rates or the shape and portion of the yield curve? The answer has implications for whether we should believe that interest and inflation rates can be forecast.

7.1 THE TERM STRUCTURE OF INTEREST RATES

Risk is not the only factor that varies among financial instruments. They also vary in their *term to maturity*, a fact that can give rise to the **term structure of interest rates**. Does it exist? Why?

Suppose we consider two securities that essentially differ only because they mature at different dates. Government of Canada bonds are good examples because they are all free from default risk and have the added advantage of being readily marketable (that is, they are *liquid*) since a large secondary market for them exists. Figure 7.1 plots the yield on two Government of Canada securities: short-term (90-day) Treasury bills and long-term (10-year or more) Government of Canada bonds. In general, the yield on the long-term bonds is higher than the yield on short-term bonds.

If instead of simply comparing the yields on two financial instruments, we plot their yields according to how many months or years in the future until maturity, we obtain what is called a **yield curve**, which is how the term structure is usually reported. See **Financial Focus 7.1: The Term Structure in the Press**.

Figure 7.1   Long-Term and Short-Term Government of Canada Bond Yields

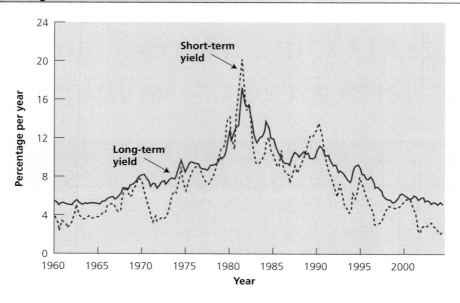

Sources: Adapted from Statistics Canada CANSIM II database **http://cansim.2.statcan.ca/cgi-win/CNSMCGI.EXE**, series V122541 (Treasury bills) and V122487 (long-term rate), reproduced by authority of the Ministry of Industry, 1996.

Note: The long-term interest rate is for Government of Canada bonds with a maturity of 10 years or more. The short-term interest rate is for 90-day Treasury bills. Annual averages were used.

7.2   THE EXPECTATIONS HYPOTHESIS

Why do long-term yields usually differ from short-term yields? The question is worth exploring both because it is an interesting one and because the answer can lead us to the expectations hypothesis, which many people believe to be useful in predicting interest rates, at least in the short term.

Since both long-term and short-term bonds are easily marketable, the choice of whether to hold one over the other does not really hinge on the question of liquidity. Rather, the investor presumably decides based on which bond he or she expects to provide the greatest return. If the investor believes interest rates are peaking, he or she will want to hold a long-term bond because doing so will lock in funds at a high yield. Conversely, if the investor believes interest rates are bottoming out, the investor will want to hold a short-term instrument because buying a long-term one would result in being locked in at a low yield.[1]

In other words, choosing to go long or short hinges on the investor's expectations about future interest rates.[2]

---

1   Note that the yields being discussed are until maturity. What if the holding period differs from the term to maturity? Recall that yields move inversely with price. Although someone selling a long-term bond when interest rates are thought to have peaked out might be able to reinvest on the current wave of higher interest rates, a capital loss is incurred on the sale. Thus, if only for the ease of exposition, we deal strictly with a holding period equal to the term to maturity. It may be useful to go back to Chapter 5, Table 5.2, where a numerical example working out the connection between interest rates and prices is considered.

2   Hedging is, of course, an alternative way of dealing with the question of whether to go long or not (see Chapter 15).

FLASHBACK 7.1

SHORT-VERSUS LONG-TERM INTEREST RATES AGAIN

In Chapter 5 we introduced a variety of ways to calculate the "interest rate." The data plotted in Figure 7.1 are average yields for instruments that mature in 90 days versus bonds with a maturity of 10 years or more. Those who publish such data, such as the Bank of Canada, average the yields of all outstanding bonds with a maturity of about 90 days as well as those with a maturity of 10 years or more (using an arithmetic average that is slightly more sophisticated than the one we will consider below). As a

result of this averaging there will naturally be a difference between the yields on long-term and short-term bonds. To take a very simple example, if $R_1 = 5\%$ and $R_2 = 5\%$ then, assuming the two-year bond is held until maturity, \$1 invested for two years will result in $(1+.05)(1+.05) = 1.1025$; that is, 10.25 cents of interest, which means that the average annual yield on a two-year bond is 5.125% (10.25% over two years or 10.25%/2 per year). Our calculations below will essentially ignore the compounding feature to make the examples simpler. You also will be told how to make calculations that take compounding into account.

Before we examine the implications of this statement, let us introduce some notation to fix ideas. Let

R_1 = yield on a government bond maturing in one year
R_2 = yield on a government bond maturing in two years
E_1^1 = expected or anticipated yield on a one-year government bond one year from today

All yields are on an annual basis and are expressed in nominal terms.

Ignoring considerations other than term to maturity, the investor is presumably indifferent between two one-year bonds and the two-year bond so long as the average yields are the same. In other words, investors are equally likely to go long as to go short if the following condition is satisfied:

$$R_1 + E_1^1 = 2R_2 \tag{7.1}$$

or, to rearrange the terms,

$$R_2 = \frac{R_1 + E_1^1}{2} \tag{7.2}$$

Equation (7.1) is obtained by noting that since the two-year bond earns $\$R_2$ per year, $\$2R_2$ of interest will be earned in a two-year period.[3] By analogy $\$(R_1 + E_1^1)$ is the interest expected to be earned when the investor purchases two one-year bonds. Consequently, an individual will be indifferent between holding the two-year bond and two one-year bonds if the annual return on a two-year bond is equal to the average annual yield on two one-year bonds.[4]

Generalization of equation (7.1) is straightforward. To keep things simple, we restrict the investor to choosing either a bond with a term to maturity of n years or n one-year bonds. Under these conditions, equation (7.1) can be rewritten to express the **expectations hypothesis**, which is the notion that investors are indifferent between long-term and short-term bonds so long as their average yields are the same. That is,

---

3 To be more precise, equation (7.1) should be modified to reflect the fact that the investor who chooses to hold two one-year bonds presumably reinvests the principal and interest after the first year. Indifference will obtain if, for each dollar invested, $(1 + R_1)(1 + E_1^1) = (1 + R_2)^2$, which, after some manipulation, implies that $R_1 + E_1^1 + R_1 E_1^1 = 2R_2 + R_2^2$. However, $R_1 E_1^1$ and R_2^2 are small (for example, if $R_2 = 0.06$, $R_2^2 = 0.0036$; if $R_1 = 0.04$ and $E_1^1 = 0.05$, $R_1 E_1^1 = 0.002$). If we arbitrarily set both terms to zero, we obtain equation (7.2).

4 A possible objection is that although the two-year yield is known with certainty, the average of the two one-year yields is uncertain. We can assume away this problem by stipulating that investors are knowledgable enough so that, on average, the expected one-year yield is the correct forecast of future interest instruments. If you are not prepared to accept this assumption, equation (7.1)—and the entire expectations hypothesis—will not hold.

Table 7.1   The Expectations Hypothesis: A Numerical Example

Choose a Two-Year Bond or Two One-Year Bonds

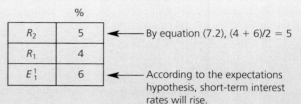

0		R_2		2 years
		Annual yield on a two-year bond		

0	R_1	1 year	E_1^1	2 years
	Yield on a one-year bond		Expected yield on a one-year bond one year from today	

	%	
R_2	5	← By equation (7.2), $(4 + 6)/2 = 5$
R_1	4	
E_1^1	6	← According to the expectations hypothesis, short-term interest rates will rise.

Given an annual interest rate of 5% on a two-year bond, an annual interest rate of 4% on a one-year bond, and an expected annual interest rate of 6% on a one-year bond, application of equation (7.2) yields an average interest rate of 5%.

$$R_n = \frac{R_1 + E_1^1 + E_1^2 + \ldots + E_1^{n-1}}{n} \qquad (7.3)$$

where

R_n = annual yield of n-year government bond
n = years to maturity
E_1^2 = expected yield on a one-year government bond two years from today
E_1^{n-1} = expected yield on a one-year government bond $n-1$ years from today

and all other terms are as previously defined. Equation (7.3) simply states that an investor will be indifferent between going long or short so long as the annual yield on an n-year government bond is equal to the average of n one-year actual and expected yields.[5] Tables 7.1 and 7.2 give numerical examples of the application of equation (7.3).

At low interest rates you can easily verify the fact that the approximation that is equation (7.3) is adequate. The more precise version of the calculation of R_n would involve the following:

$$R_n = \sqrt[n]{[(1 + R_1)(1 + E_1^1) \ldots (1 + E_1^{n-1})]} - 1 \qquad (7.3a)$$

Although equation (7.3a) is not difficult to implement, we will use equation (7.3) throughout.[6]

What are the economic implications of equation (7.3) or (7.3a)? If the expectations hypothesis is correct, the **spread** between the long-term and short-term interest rates should give investors

---

5 Restricting the investor to choosing either an n-year bond or n one-year bonds is done here for simplicity. Clearly, an investor could choose to hold, say, either an n-year bond yielding R_n or an $(n-1)$-year bond with a yield of R_{n-1} plus a one-year bond with expected yield $E^{n-1}{}_1$. In this case, the expectations hypothesis would hold if

$$R_n = \frac{R_{n-1} + E^{n-1}{}_1}{2}$$

Numerous other combinations are also possible, but the central idea of the expectations hypothesis is unaffected.

6 In order to see how equation (7.3a) is found, consider the two-year bond used in footnote 3 above. According to the expectations hypothesis, we need to solve $(1 + R_1)(1 + E_1^1) = (1 + R_2)^2$. First, take the square root of both sides to obtain $\sqrt{(1 + R_1)(1 + E_1^1)} = (1 + R_2)$. Subtracting 1 from both sides of the equality then gives equation (7.3a) where $n=1$.

Table 7.2 The Expectations Hypothesis: Another Numerical Example

Choose a Five-Year Bond or Five One-Year Bonds

	0				R_5			5 years	

Annual yield on a five-year bond

R_1	1	E_1^1	2	E_1^2	3	E_1^3	4	E_1^4	5 years
Yield on a one-year bond		Expected yield on a one-year bond one year from today		Expected yield on a one-year bond two years from today		Expected yield on a one-year bond three years from today		Expected yield on a one-year bond four years from today	

%

R_5	12.6
R_1	14.0
E_1^1	13.0
E_1^2	12.5
E_1^3	12.0
E_1^4	11.5

← by equation (7.3), (14 + 13 + 12.5 + 12 + 11.5)/5 = 12.6

$$R_2 = \frac{14 + 13}{2}$$

$$R_3 = \frac{14 + 13 + 12.5}{3}$$

$$R_4 = \frac{14 + 13 + 12.5 + 12}{4}$$

%

R_1	14.0
E_1^1	13.0
E_1^2	12.5
E_1^3	12.0
E_1^4	11.5

→ By equation (7.3) →

%

R_2	13.5 ✓
R_3	13.2
R_4	12.9
R_5	12.6

← A plot of R_1 through R_5 would produce a yield curve

Summary

Term to Maturity	1	2	3	4	5
Yield to Maturity	14.0	13.5	13.2	12.9	12.6

In this table, equation (7.3) is applied. For example, if we are given annual interest rates on bonds maturing in one to five years (R_1, R_2, R_3, R_4, R_5), the equation allows us to solve for expected interest rates on one-year bonds two to five years into the future.

a forecast of future short-term interest rates. For example, suppose that an investor has to decide between holding a one-year bond or a two-year bond. According to equation (7.2), the expectations hypothesis enables the investor to forecast the interest rate on a one-year bond one year from today. The example in Table 7.2 shows that in the case of a choice between a one-year and a five-year bond, future one-year interest rates are expected to fall one year to four years in the future.

The implicit forecasting is the reason that examining a yield curve provides such a powerful tool for investors who want, at the very least, to find out the direction of change in short-term interest rates. Three possible yield curves are shown in Figure 7.2. Curve (A) is consistent with expectations of higher short-term interest rates because the yield curve is upward sloping. Curve (B) indicates that investors anticipate falling short-term interest rates in the future. Curve (C) suggests that short-term interest rates will remain unchanged.

Figure 7.2	Hypothetical Yield Curves

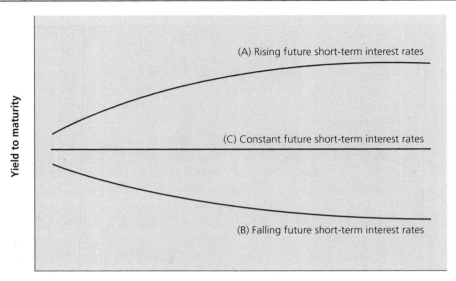

An upward-sloping yield curve (A) means that short-term interest rates are expected to rise, so the long-term interest rate will be higher than the short-term interest rate. The opposite is true for the yield curve (B). Rates are expected to remain unchanged when the yield curve is flat, as in curve (C).

THE ROLE OF THE REAL INTEREST RATE

All the discussion so far has revolved around how nominal interest rates are structured by term to maturity. Yet we know that investors should be primarily influenced by the real interest rate. Does the expectations hypothesis have anything to say in this regard? The answer is a qualified yes. Recall the Fisher effect: The nominal interest rate, R, is the sum of the real interest rate, ρ, and expected inflation, π^e. That is,

$$R = \rho + \pi^e \tag{7.4}$$

which is reproduced here from Chapter 5 for convenience. If we assume that the real interest rate is constant, we can rewrite it as

$$R = \bar{\rho} + \pi^e \tag{7.5}$$

where $\bar{\rho}$ = constant real interest rate. Since a constant, by definition, does not change, equation (7.5) says that any change in the nominal interest rate must be the result of a change in expected inflation. In other words, the change in the nominal interest rate equals the change in expected inflation:

$$\Delta R = \Delta \pi^e \tag{7.6}$$

Now, suppose that, as before, the investor is considering buying a one-year or a two-year bond. In nominal terms, the spread between the two yields is

$$R_2 - R_1$$

In terms of equation (7.5), however, the spread could instead be written

$$(\bar{\rho} + \pi_2^e) - (\bar{\rho} + \pi_1^e) \tag{7.7}$$

FINANCIAL FOCUS 7.1 — THE TERM STRUCTURE IN THE PRESS

The Globe and Mail and the *National Post* regularly publish the financial information necessary to construct a yield curve. Indeed, both newspapers regularly publish a plot of several yield curves. Generally, a yield curve for the most recent data is presented along with yield curves for data a month or a year ago. The *Financial Times of London* publishes yield curves for the major industrial countries.

The figures below illustrate how yield curves are constructed. The vertical axes measure yield to maturity while the horizontal axes measure the number of years to maturity. The points mark several such combinations that prevailed at the time this yield curve was constructed. Connecting the points gives a precise idea of the link between yield and term to maturity. However, to ease interpretation, a straight line (or a curve) is usually fitted to the yield–term combinations, producing the downward-sloping line shown on the graph. Note that the yield curves shown here went from being negatively sloped to displaying a positive slope indicating that expectations of future short-term interest rates had changed.

Although plots of the yield curve can be useful to predict the future course of interest rates, we must be careful not to read too much into the curves shown in most newspapers. Why? As we saw in Chapter 5, Treasury bills are discount or zero-coupon bonds. The remaining bonds plotted on a yield curve pay coupon interest over time. Since the flow of payments differs to the holders of these different types of bonds, they are not really comparable. The holder of a Treasury bill essentially gets the interest portion at the time of purchase, while the holder of a longer-term government bond earns interest over time until maturity. Hence, when analysts look at the yield curve to form predictions about future short-term interest rates, they examine the zero-coupon yield curve; that is, they transform the yields on all bonds as if they were all zero-coupon bonds. Doing so is not straightforward, so we will not explore the issue any further.

You will also notice that many of the published yield curves look smoother than the ones shown below. The problem is that there are not bond yields for every possible maturity structure, so to create a smooth line, analysts need to interpolate the missing yields. Again, several techniques exist to accomplish this objective, but the details are well beyond the scope of this text.

Questions for Discussion

1. Is it likely that yields on government bonds maturing in 20 years or more will be useful in predicting the future course of short-term interest rates?
2. Why is it important in principle to calculate the so-called "zero-coupon" yield when plotting a yield curve?

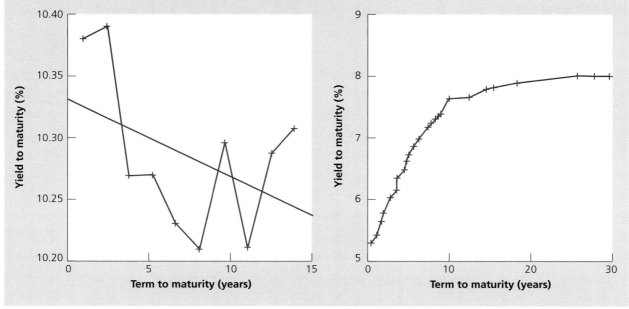

where π_1^e and π_2^e are expected annual inflation rates over one- and two-year horizons, respectively. However, since the constant real interest rates cancel each other, equation (7.7) becomes

$$\pi_2^e - \pi_1^e = \Delta\pi^e \qquad (7.8)$$

Equation (7.8) simply says that the term structure also conveys information about changes in expected future inflation, $\Delta\pi^e$, by term to maturity.[7]

If the term structure provides information about the future course of inflation anticipated by investors, what are the implications? We consider two examples, both of which are illustrated in Figure 7.3.

What happens to the yield curve when there is a sudden and permanent increase in expected inflation? According to the Fisher effect [see also equation (7.4)], the nominal interest rate rises by the increase in expected inflation.[8] Moreover, since the expectations hypothesis links interest rates across the term structure, *all* yields rise by the change in expected inflation. Thus, the spread between long-term and short-term interest rates stays the same, but all nominal interest rates rise by the increase in expected inflation. Figure 7.3(A) illustrates this result with an upward shift in the yield curve from YC^1 to YC^2.

Now consider the scenario illustrated in Figure 7.3(B). Suppose the monetary authorities—here the Bank of Canada—believe that higher inflation is looming in the future (perhaps from world events beyond Canada's control), but investors appear unconvinced, since they expect lower inflation in the future, given the downward-sloping yield curve YC^1. To ensure that investors' future inflation expectations are met, the Bank of Canada drives up short-term interest rates,[9] producing yield curve YC^2, which eventually converges with the original yield curve at some unspecified term to maturity. Since investors' expectations of inflation are unchanged, what must have happened? According to equation (7.4), if π^e remains unchanged, the change in short-run nominal interest rates, ΔR, can be explained only by a change in the real interest rate, $\Delta\rho$. Then, consumption spending might fall, dampening the likelihood that inflation will be higher than future levels currently expected by investors.[10]

Figure 7.3	**The Term Structure and Inflation: Two Examples**

(A) A Shift in the Yield Curve

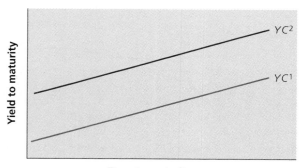

(B) A Rise in Interest Rates Induced by the Bank of Canada Policy

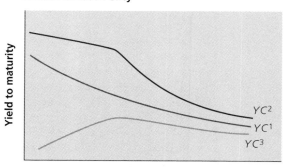

In panel (A), the Fisher effect operates to make all nominal yields rise, with a permanent rise in expected inflation. The yield curve thus shifts from YC^1 to YC^2. In panel (B), short-term inflationary expectations remain unchanged, but the Bank of Canada is determined to dampen the likelihood of higher future inflation. By raising short-term yields, it raises the real interest rate, again via the Fisher effect. The result is yield curve YC^2. The opposite scenario is illustrated by yield curve YC^3.

---

7 Note, however, that this result hinges on the assumption of a constant real interest rate. As we discussed in Chapter 5, this assumption is not uncontroversial.

8 According to the discussion in Chapter 6, there will be a *temporary* change in the real interest rate. We return to this point below. For the moment, however, assume that the change in the nominal interest rate is instantaneous.

9 The most likely reason for the Bank to want to ensure that expectations are met is that it wants to be perceived as credible, trustworthy, and clearly in charge of monetary policy.

A scenario of this kind has often been used to explain the Bank of Canada's drive, particularly during 1990 and again in late 1994 and early 1995, toward attaining its inflation target.[11] Indeed, at times yield curves in the financial press closely resembled the ones shown in Figure 7.3(B).[12] By the summer of 1992, yield curves had become very steep and remained that way for some time,[13] a reflection of the concern about future prospects for inflation in light of ballooning combined deficits at the federal and provincial levels and concerns over Canadian unity. The example considered also works in reverse. That is, if the Bank of Canada is worried that investors expect an economic slowdown and a consequent fall in expected inflation, then it would engineer a fall in short-term interest rates. With unchanged inflation expectations, real rates would fall, stimulating borrowing and raising future economic activity. The resulting yield curve might look like YC^3. As seen in Figure 7.1 (also see the discussion of interest rates and the business cycle in Chapter 6), this is precisely what the Bank of Canada did in 2001. The tragic events of 9/11 simply accelerated the drop in the short-term rates and the consequent rise in the term spread evident from the figure. These examples illustrate the uses and the usefulness of the yield curve as a tool of policy analysis.

7.3   YIELD CURVE PUZZLES

A strong presumption exists that the expectations hypothesis is accurate, at least for a portion of the term structure. Nevertheless, a number of features about the behaviour of the yield curve may not easily be reconciled with the idea that investors can predict the future course of short-term interest rates just by examining the slope of the yield curve. Three such stylized facts are worthy of mention:

- The yield curve is generally upward sloping.
- The yield curve tends to shift over time.
- The slope of the yield curve tends to predict future economic activity.

Let us consider each fact in turn.

The yield curve is generally upward sloping. Table 7.3 shows the spread in the yields between Treasury bills and various Government of Canada bonds, maturing anywhere from one year to more than 10 years in the future. The data are broken down by decade. The remarkable feature of the data is that in every decade since the 1960s, the longer the term to maturity, the higher the spread. This trend persists after 2000 as well. Indeed, if we focus on the difference between the long-term bond yield and the yield on Treasury bills, the spread is positive the vast majority of times. Only during the turbulent decade of the 1980s was the spread smaller than at any other time. Nevertheless, 65% of the time the long bond yield exceeded the Treasury bill yield. During the other decades noted in the table, the same measure is about 90%. Clearly then, yield curves are, for the most part, upward sloping. This fact poses a difficulty for the expectations hypothesis since a more or less permanently upward-sloping yield curve implies that investors nearly always

---

10 In Chapter 23 we shall examine a simple device that many market analysts and economists use to determine whether the Bank of Canada is tightening or loosening monetary policy. As you can imagine from the discussion so far, a tight or loose monetary policy is linked to the behaviour of the real interest rate and, indeed, a version of the real interest rate we have been considering so far plays an important role in this analysis.

11 Success for the Bank's objectives requires meeting a number of other conditions, including (1) that its views are credible—that is, that the public believes in the Bank's objectives and its ability to carry them out, and (2) that its policy is consistent with the federal government's fiscal policy. Clearly, if the federal government pursues an inflationary policy, Bank of Canada attempts to stem inflation in the future by raising real interest rates now are doomed to failure.

12 Alternatively, yield curve YC^2 can be explained by a short-run spurt in anticipated inflation—for example, due to a temporary increase in oil prices—while longer-term inflation rates are expected to fall.

13 In the United States the spread between long-term and short-term rates reached historically high levels. See T.T. Vogel, Jr., "Steepest-Ever Yield Curve May Mean It's Time to Invest," *Wall Street Journal* (20 July 1992): C1. A similar story applies to Canadian spreads.

Table 7.3	Term Yield Spreads in Canada over the Decades				
	(1)	**(2)**	**(3)**	**(4)** 10 Years	**(5)** % of Quarters
Decade	1 to 3 Years	3 to 5 Years	5 to 10 Years	and Longer	Spread Is Positive
1960s	0.513	0.877	1.090	1.255	92.5
1970s	0.442	0.766	1.046	1.531	90.0
1980s	0.044	0.096	0.184	0.455	65.0
1990s	0.544	0.876	1.212	1.606	87.0

Source: CANSIM series V122541 (Treasury bills),V122487 (10 years and over), V122558 (1 to 3 years),V122485 (3 to 5 years), V122486 (5 to 10 years). All data are yields expressed as annual returns. Column (1) is V122558 less V122541, column (2) is V122485 less V122541, column (3) is V122486 less V122541, and column (4) is V122487 less V122541. Column (5) is the number of quarters as a percentage of the total number of quarters in a decade that the spread was found to be positive.

expect higher future interest rates. Yet, Figure 7.1 suggests that this kind of expectation should make no sense. As we show in the next section, a possible explanation, other than the idea that investors are being fooled most of the time, is that investors do not view long-term and short-term bonds as perfect substitutes.

The yield curve tends to shift over time. Figure 7.4 shows five selected yield curves, one from each of the decades considered in Table 7.3. Since only a selection of yields are plotted, the yield curves shown are not as smooth as the ones you might see in the newspaper, but they do illustrate the fact that when inflation changes, the yield curves shifts up or down, much like the case illustrated in Figure 7.3(A). Notice that by early 2002 interest rates were at their lowest since 1961.

Since the expectations hypothesis views long-term and short-term bonds as substitutes, this fact should not be entirely surprising. Consider a scenario whereby the government of Canada decides to aggressively sell long-term bonds. This strategy pushes the price of long-term bonds

Figure 7.4	Shifting Yield Curves

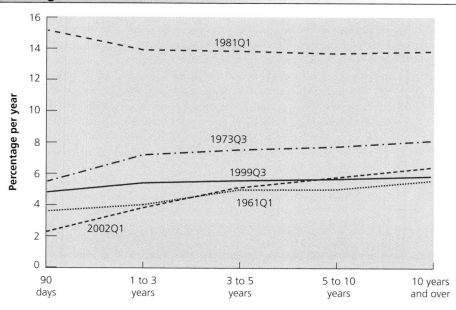

Source: See Table 7.3. Selected yield curves for the dates shown are plotted against the term to maturity. Yield curves tend to shift over time as an event or a shock to one end of the term structure is transmitted to the rest of the term structure.

down, thereby raising their yield. Short-term investors will be induced to sell some of their short-term holdings. The net effect of this action is to push up short-term yields. Hence, the entire yield curve shifts as the effect on yields at one end of the yield curve is transmitted to the rest of the term structure.

Decisions by government or individuals to shift their holdings from long term to short term, or vice versa, are often prompted by expectations of future inflation. It is no surprise, therefore, that the yield curve in 1981 is the highest, since that is around the time inflation peaked. The next yield curve is around the time of the first oil price shock but before the full implications of that shock for inflation were felt by the economy as a whole. Most recent yield curves resemble those of the 1960s, when inflation was low and stable.

The slope of the yield curve tends to predict future economic activity. One of the most intriguing findings in recent years has been that the yield curve has the ability to predict future recessions and is therefore linked to the state of the business cycle. The theory is fairly simple. A positive yield spread has been found to be associated with future expansion in economic activity, while a negative yield spread is a portent of a future economic contraction. Moreover, researchers have found that the size of the spread is linked to the growth rate of future economic activity. How is this possible? Consider the following scenario: Businesses expect economic activity to increase in the future because some development—improved technology, management, or a general feeling of optimism—leads them to believe that now is the time to expand. Consequently, since profitable opportunities in the marketplace are available today, more borrowing is required to finance the necessary expansion. Assuming the type of borrowing in question is of the long-term variety, the demand for loanable funds will rise, which will lead to higher long-term interest rates. Other things being equal, the spread between long-term and short-term rates will rise. Obviously, if future economic prospects are thought to be poorer, the opposite will happen. Businesses will cut long-term borrowing, which will make short-term interest rates higher relative to long-term rates, thereby producing a negative spread.

Figure 7.5 shows the evolution of the spread between long-term and short-term interest rates in Canada and the Organisation for Economic Co-operation and Development's (OECD) assessment of periods when the Canadian economy was in a recession. These periods are highlighted as the shaded areas in the figure. It is quite striking that virtually every recession was preceded by a fall in the spread or a negative spread, wheras expansionary phases in the business cycle were anticipated by a rising or positive spread.

7.4   COMPETING VIEWS OF THE TERM STRUCTURE

Although the expectations hypothesis appears to provide a simple but powerful tool for forecasting future interest rates and inflation and for understanding some central bank policies, it faces several objections from academic studies that have attempted to gauge its empirical validity, as well as from competing theories of the term structure, which are illustrated in Figure 7.6.

The Liquidity Premium Theory

Figure 7.6(A) illustrates the potential effect of a liquidity premium on the yield curve. The market for long-term bonds is "thinner"—that is, long-term bonds are likely to be less marketable—than that for short-term bonds. Therefore, investors who hold long-term bonds may expect a **liquidity premium**—an additional yield for accepting their relatively lower liquidity. If the degree of liquidity or marketability falls with a rise in the term to maturity, as shown by *LP* in Figure 7.6(A), the observed yield curve will provide incorrect information about investors' expectations of future interest rates. For example, the yield curve consistent with the expectations hypothesis may, in fact, be flat, implying that interest rates are expected to be constant in the future.

In terms of equation 7.3 we can write

Figure 7.5   **The Yield Spread and Recessions in Canada**

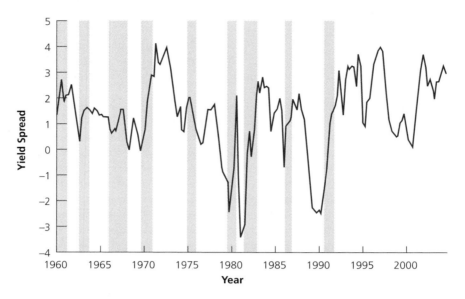

The spread is defined here as the difference between the yield on Government of Canada bonds that mature in 10 years or more and the yield on Treasury bills. The shaded areas represent recessionary periods. The spread is supposed to be falling or negative before a recession and rising or positive before a recovery or expansion.

Sources: See Table 7.3, P.L. Siklos and L. Skoczylas (2002), "Volatility Clustering in Real Interest Rates: International Evidence," *Journal of Macroeconomics* 24 (June 2002): 369–87, and P. Cross "Alternative Measures of Business Cycles in Canada: 1947–1992," *Canadian Economic Observer* (Statistics Canada, Catalogue No. 11-010-XPB, 1996). Data are the same as those that appear in Figure 7.1.

$$R_n = [R_1 + E_1^1 + ... + E_1^{n-1}]/n + LP$$

where LP is the liquidity premium (also called by some the term premium). LP is therefore the difference between the observed yield curve and the yield curve consistent with the expectations hypothesis. The term premium can actually be interpreted as capturing a variety of factors, referred to as "risk," that are important to investors. We can further elaborate on the implications of the liquidity premium theory by recalling a finding first explained in Chapter 5, namely that the price of long-term bonds is more volatile than of short-term bonds (see Table 5.2). Since this is the case, and assuming that investors will only tolerate so much price volatility (we will study the implications of this idea in Chapter 13), it stands to reason that investors will demand a premium for holding a long-term bond over a short-term one. Consequently, regardless of the slope of the yield curve (see Figure 7.2), LP will be positive.

One difficulty with this explanation is that the link between the liquidity premium and the term to maturity may not be as depicted in Figure 7.6(A).

Market Segmentation and Preferred Habitat Views

Another view about the relationship between short-term and long-term interest rates is shown in Figure 7.6(B), which depicts separate loanable funds diagrams for short-term and long-term bonds. In the "pure" **market segmentation** view of interest rate determination, the markets for short-term and long-term bonds are segregated, and there is no substitution between the two kinds of instruments. This separation of the markets may be explained in part by the fact that some investors show a distinct preference for short-term or long-term bonds, perhaps because one type

| Figure 7.6 | Other Views about the Term Structure |

(A) Liquidity Premium

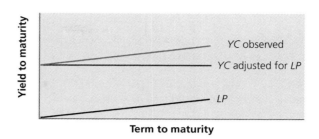

(B) Market Segmentation

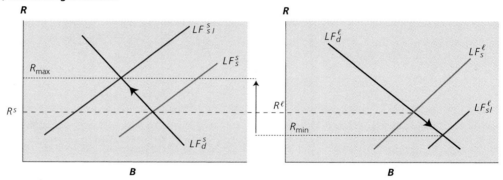

In panel (A), long-term bonds earn a liquidity premium, *LP*, because they are less marketable than short-term bonds. This premium gives rise to the distinction between an observed yield curve, "*YC* observed," and a yield curve that would obtain under the expectations hypothesis, "*YC* expected."

In panel (B), short-term and long-term bonds (labelled with the superscripts *s* and *ℓ*) are viewed as being distinct. In the extreme, there is no substitutability between the two. As the degree of substitutability increases, the spread between the short-term and long-term interest rates begins to reflect the movement of funds (here, from short-term to long-term). Overall, however, the spread has less significance in the market segmentation hypothesis than in the expectations hypothesis.

of risk (for example, inflation risk) is their sole determinant in choosing an asset, whereas another type of risk (for example, income risk) is all that matters to other investors. In other words, shifts in, say, the supply of loanable funds in one market have no impact on shifts in the supply of loanable funds in another market. Therefore, the spread between long-term and short-term interest rates reflects conditions purely local to a particular market.

A potentially important reason to believe the segmented markets view is that how the government manages the debt has a separate impact on the shape of the yield curve. Hence, if the government wants to lower long-term interest rates to foster more investment, and increase short-term interest rates to attract funds from abroad, then the impact of such a policy—this can be illustrated as before via the use of the loanable funds diagram—would be to effectively "twist" the yield curve. Notice that expectations as such are ignored and the shape of the yield curve is driven by the management of the government's debt. However, as shown by Figure 7.7, as interest rates fell throughout the 1980s, the federal government reduced the average maturity of its debt, whereas in the early 1990s, as expectations of lower inflation and interest rates began to take hold, the average maturity of the outstanding debt began to rise. Hence, although in principle the government can twist the yield curve, in practice it has behaved more the way the expectations hypothesis predicts.

POINT–COUNTERPOINT 7.1

HOW USEFUL IS THE YIELD CURVE?

Strictly speaking, most studies find little statistical evidence that yield spreads behave in the way predicted by the expectations hypothesis as developed in this chapter. Yet, the expectations hypothesis remains an attractive theory because it is readily testable with actual data and because some features about the behaviour of the term structure can be reasonably well understood within the expectations hypothesis framework.

First, recall that the discussion in this chapter abstracted from default risk. Yet, even government bonds are plagued by other risks, such as those of liquidity and inflation. It has also been implicit in our discussion that investors form "rational" views about, say, future inflation—that is, they have all economic information available, process it effectively, and use it to form their forecasts of future inflation. Again, the expectations hypothesis may fail if expectations turn out to be less than rational. Finally, there may be "noise" in the relationship between short-term and long-term rates so that the links are not exact in a numerical sense, but rather show a tendency toward the results derived in this chapter.

The scenario depicted in Figure 7.3(B) stems, in part, from Fama's (1990) and Mishkin's (1991) evidence on the expectations hypothesis and the term structure. Mishkin finds that for the United States and several other countries, the term structure provides good forecasts about real interest rates for maturities of roughly six months or less and good forecasts of inflation for maturities of up to five years. These results do not, however, carry over to other countries, except perhaps Canada. Fama also uses U.S. data and finds that for maturities of, say, longer than a year, the term structure provides good forecasts of nominal interest rates. At shorter maturities, the expectations hypothesis provides information about real interest rates but not about nominal interest rates. Thus, attempts at manipulating the yield curve, as in Figure 7.3(B), should

be viewed critically. Nevertheless, at least one study (Estrella and Hardouvelis 1991) suggests that the slope of the yield curve can be a good predictor of future economic activity. Siklos (1998, 2000) provides a review of the evidence about the information content in the term structure. Campbell (1995), again using U.S. data, finds that higher long-term rates are associated with rising short-term interest rates and points out that an understanding of the yield curve is vital to answering such questions as whether governments should borrow long or short. Nevertheless, he points out that, at times, yield curves seem too steep by the standards of the expectations hypothesis.

It is clear that the stance of monetary policy potentially has a separate impact on the shape of the yield curve. When monetary policy is tight, short-term interest rates are pushed up and, other things being equal, the spread is narrowed or is even negative. In contrast, when policy is loose, short-term interest rates fall relative to long-term rates so that the spread rises, producing the usual upward-sloping yield curve.

It should be clear by now that there are potentially several interrelated forces that can influence the spread over time. Nevertheless, it appears, based on the research by Bonser-Neal and Morley (1997) and Estrella and Mishkin (1997), that the connection between inflation and the yield spread and the yield spread's ability to predict future recessions consistently rank as the dominant pieces of information contained in the slope of the yield curve. In part for these reasons, the spread is considered to be one of the elements in so-called leading economic indicators.

Questions for Discussion

1. The expectations hypothesis works in the short run but not the long run. Why?
2. In what sense is the expectations hypothesis a useful tool? What are its principal limitations?

A similar but less rigid view is the **preferred habitat** view of the term structure. Its proponents see some substitutability between the long and short ends of the market but believe particular investors have a preference for certain maturities. The investors' willingness to leave their "preferred habitat" depends on the size of a term premium—an additional yield for accepting a less preferred term. If the term premium is large enough, investors who would otherwise prefer to go short will purchase long-term bonds. The relationship linking short-term and long-term rates is the same as under the expectations hypothesis, except that a term premium is added.

POINT	COUNTERPOINT
• The yield curve is an easy-to-understand concept. • Considerable evidence suggests that, at least in the short run, the yield curve helps predict future inflation, future economic growth, and future short-term interest rates. • The spread is simple to calculate. • The yield curve is useful as a device to understand how the central bank goes about tightening or loosening monetary policy. • The yield curve is useful as a tool to assist in understanding how the government manages the debt.	• Long-term and short-term bonds need not be perfect substitutes. • Transaction costs and liquidity are not the same for long-term and short-term government bonds, so expectations cannot be the sole factor explaining the term spread. • Investors do have preferences for short-term versus long-term bonds if only because this helps them match assets and debts. • The evidence in favour of the expectations hypothesis is mixed: It is weakest for the United States and stronger for other industrial countries; it is sensitive to the exchange rate regime and sample period. • Many forces simultaneously affect the spread and its size; all of these are simultaneously determined and each type of effect is difficult to isolate.

Sources

J. Atta-Mensah, and G. Tkacz, "Predicting Recessions and Booms Using Financial Variables," *Canadian Business Economics* 8(3): 30–36.

C. Bonser-Neal, and T.R. Morley, "Does the Yield Spread Predict Economic Activity? A Multicountry Analysis," *Economic Review, Federal Reserve Bank of Kansas City* 3 (1997): 37–53.

J.Y. Campbell, "Some Lessons from the Yield Curve," *Journal of Economic Perspectives* 9 (Summer 1995): 129–52.

A. Estrella, and G.A. Hardouvelis, "The Term Structure as a Predictor of Real Economic Activity," *Journal of Finance* 46 (June 1991): 555–76.

A. Estrella, and F.S. Mishkin, "The Predictive Power of the Term Structure of Interest Rates in Europe and the US: Implications for the European Central Bank," *European Economic Review* 41 (May 1997): 1375–402.

A. Melino, "The Term Structure of Interest Rates: Evidence and Theory," *Journal of Economic Surveys* 2 (1988): 335–66.

F.S. Mishkin, "A Multi-Country Study of the Information in the Term Structure about Future Inflation," *Journal of International Money and Finance* 10 (1991): 2–22.

———, "What Does the Term Structure Tell Us about Future Inflation?" *Journal of Monetary Economics* 25 (1990): 77–95.

P.L. Siklos, "The Information Content in the Yield Curve: New Zealand in the Reform Era," report prepared for the Reserve Bank of New Zealand, July 1998.

———, "Inflation Targets and the Yield Curve: New Zealand and Australia vs the US," *International Journal of Finance and Economics* 5 (February 2000): 313–92.

The preferred habitat hypothesis might explain why yield curves are sometimes very steeply sloped. At such times, a substantial term premium is required to induce investors to hold long-term bonds even if short-term yields are quite low. Figure 7.6(B) could then be viewed as illustrative of the potential term premium that would be observed if there were perfect substitutability between the two markets. Clearly, however, the objective of the preferred habitat view is to treat the short and long ends of the bond market as being somewhat but not completely distinct from each other.

| Figure 7.7 | **Interest Rates and the Maturity Structure of Government of Canada Debt** |

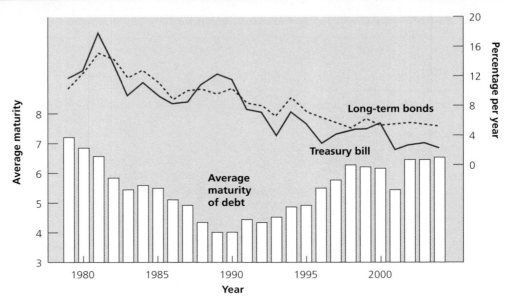

The bars measure the average maturity of outstanding government of Canada debt in years (left axis). When the lower interest rate levels (right axis) appeared to be fairly stable, the government began to increase the average maturity of the debt. Hence, the maturity figures behave more like the expectations hypothesis view than the segmented markets view of the yield curve.

Source: Bank of Canada Banking and Financial Statistics, Tables A1, A2, and F1. Also see Table 7.3 for the definition and source of the long-term and Treasury bill yields.

SUMMARY

- The yield curve describes the relationship between interest rates on government bonds that differ only in their terms to maturity.

- The expectations hypothesis of the term structure says that long-term interest rates are averages of expected short-term interest rates. As a result, interest rates contain predictions about the future levels of interest rates and inflation.

- The yield curve generally slopes upward, shifts over time as inflation rates change, and is related to movements in the business cycle.

- Another view of the term structure says that long-term interest rates contain a liquidity premium, which represents a payment to investors for agreeing to hold debt for a long period.

- The liquidity premium is difficult to measure but, to the extent it exists, its presence makes it more difficult to use the yield curve to predict future short-term inflation.

- The market segmentation hypothesis argues that the long and short ends of the maturity structure of interest rates are separate with little substitution between the two. As a result, interest rates contain no useful information about future interest rates or inflation.

- How the government manages its debt is likely to have an influence on the yield curve. If the government finances its debt mainly through short-term bonds, this puts pressure on short-term interest rates, and vice versa if there is a desire to sell long-term bonds instead.

- The evidence suggests that the expectations hypothesis is a better predictor of the average maturity of the outstanding government debt.

IMPORTANT TERMS

expectations hypothesis, 119
liquidity premium, 127
market segmentation, 128
preferred habitat, 130

term structure of interest rates, 117
yield curve, 117
spread, 120

PROBLEMS

1. The following interest rate structure was observed in two consecutive years.

	Year 1	Year 2
	Yield (%)	
3-month Treasury bill	10.00	12.00
1-year government bond	10.50	11.90
3-year government bond	10.75	12.15
5-year government bond	11.00	11.80
10-year government bond	11.30	11.60

   Plot the yield curves for each of the two years. What does the yield curve say about future interest rates? What might explain the difference between the yield curve in Year 1 and Year 2?

2. Assume that the expectations hypothesis of the term structure is correct. You are given the following data:

Yield	R_1	R_2	R_3	R_4	R_5
%	10	12	13	13.5	13.75

   What are the one-year expected interest rates predicted by the expectations hypothesis?

3. A forecaster of future interest rates provides you with the following data:

Yield	R_1	E_1^1	E_1^2	E_1^3	E_1^4
%	8	12	11	10.5	10

   What yield curve would result from these forecasts, assuming that they are consistent with the expectations hypothesis? Draw this curve.

4. Take the yield curve you have drawn for problem 3. Now suppose that because of short-term inflation risk, investors start to show a distinct preference for long-term bonds. What happens to the yield curve? Use the loanable funds framework to illustrate what happens to the spread between short-term and long-term rates.

5. Suppose that the short-term interest rate is 3% and the long-term interest rate is 7%. Should the government lengthen or shorten the average maturity of its debt? Explain.

6. You are given the following yield information: $R_1=6\%$, $R_2=5\%$, $R_3=3\%$, $R_4=1\%$. If you believe the expectations hypothesis, what general direction is the market predicting short-term interest rates will move in the future? Next, evaluate E_2^1 and E_3^1, using both equations 7.3 and 7.3a. Are the differences in the results large?

7. If short- and long-term bond markets are segmented, use the loanable funds framework to show what would happen to short- and long-term interest rates if investors showed an increased desire to hold short-term bonds.

8. TRUE, FALSE, or UNCERTAIN: The liquidity premium depicted in Figure 7.6 is a function of n. Explain.

DISCUSSION QUESTIONS

1. Suppose a professor asks her research assistant to produce a plot of the spread between the yield on three-month Treasury bills (short) and the yield on government bonds that mature in 10 years (long). The research assistant produces the following plot.

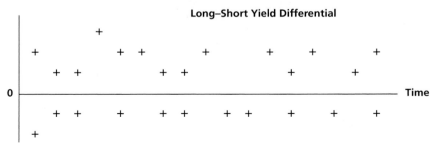

Long–Short Yield Differential

The professor says: "Well, the difference in yields appears to be randomly scattered around a mean of zero. That must mean that the expectations hypothesis holds." True or false? Explain.

2. Explain why government securities are usually graphed on yield curves.

3. Based on Figure 7.1, would you expect the yield curve to be upward sloping most of the time? Explain.

4. Why are yield curves of limited use under the liquidity premium and market segmentation hypotheses? Explain.

5. Compare the two yield curves in Figure 7.4. Could the Bank of Canada's policy of low inflation account for the change? Explain.

6. If you thought that a recession was imminent, would you be better off holding long-term or short-term government bonds? Explain.

7. Suppose that the yield spread increases sharply in the coming months. Does this imply anything about the market's outlook for the economy? Explain.

CANSIM QUESTION

1. Go to **www.nber.org**. This is the Web site of one of the premier research organizations in the United States. They have, over the years, developed recession dates that are widely used and accepted by policymakers. Click on *Data* and choose *Business Cycle Dates*. Canada, unfortunately, has no similar official recession dating scheme. Next, go to the CANSIM Web site and download key U.S. interest rates. They are the Fed Funds Rate (series V122150) and the yield on 10 year "U.S. Treasuries" (series V4429276). Calculate the spread and visually assess whether the yield spread is a good indicator of recessions or expansions.

2. Go to the CANSIM Web site and download the series in Table 7.3. See if you can replicate the results of the table as well as some of the figures in the text. Looking at the decade average, how well is the yield spread related to changes in inflation and changes in real GDP? Discuss.

3. Go to the government of Canada's department of finance Web site at **www.fin.gc.ca**. Search for "*Debt Management Report*." You will find an Annual Report on how the federal government manages the debt. See whether it views interest rate developments along the lines of the expectations hypothesis.

References can be found on **www.mcgrawhill.ca/college/siklos**

Understanding Exchange Rates

LEARNING OBJECTIVES

After reading and studying this chapter, you should be able to

8.1   define an exchange rate and determine how many ways there are to measure exchange rates

8.1   identify the link between the exchange rate and prices in different countries

8.2   describe the types of exchange rate regimes that exist in the world today

8.3   explain how the equilibrium exchange rate is determined

8.4   identify the role of capital flows and the balance of payments in the movement of capital across countries

8.5   determine how interest rates and exchange rates interact

8.6   identify what the purchasing power parity hypothesis predicts

8.6   explain why the real exchange rate concept is important

8.7   analyze why interest rate differentials between countries matter

8.8   explain what the hysteresis hypothesis is

So far we have concentrated on domestic financial instruments—that is, those denominated in Canadian dollars. Canadian investors can, however, purchase securities in other currencies, and foreigners can obtain financial instruments in Canadian dollars. These possibilities provide opportunities. They also pose an additional problem for investors, who must concern themselves with exchange rates, i.e., the prices at which they buy and sell different currencies.

Although exchange rates can be influenced by a number of factors, the principal ones are the flow of goods and services and the flow of funds (capital) across international borders. In this textbook we are interested in the influence of capital flows, which is of particular importance in understanding financial systems.

Government policies aimed a regulating changes in the exchange rate are another important factor covered in our discussion of exchange rate regimes. We consider the role of exchange rates in interest rate determination, as well as how prices in different countries are related to each other through the exchange rate and how exchange rates are influenced by price developments in different countries. Knowing how exchange rates are determined is a vital first step in understanding the interrelationship of interest rates and inflation rates in different countries.

8.1   EXCHANGE RATES

Because the Canadian economy is small and open, most Canadian students are familiar with the idea of currency exchange. The reporting of exchange rate values between currencies is a ubiquitous fact of our daily lives. So much so that, in 2002, a Canadian who robbed a U.S. bank of approximately US$30,000 pleaded for a reduced sentence, arguing that his crime was worth only 62% of what an American would be sentenced with. Unfortunately for the thief, the argument was rejected.[1] Nevertheless, some of the terminology and concepts involved are slippery, so we start our discussion of exchange rates with some definitions. Then we briefly consider how prices are linked internationally by exchange rates.

DEFINITIONS

An **exchange rate** represents the price of one currency in terms of another. Table 8.1 provides the actual exchange rates that prevailed on a particular day in December 2004 between the Canadian dollar and six foreign currencies.

Notice that any exchange rate can be expressed in two ways:

$$1 \text{ unit of country A's currency} = x \text{ units of country B's currency}$$

or

$$1 \text{ unit of country B's currency} = y \text{ units of country A's currency}$$

Let us consider a couple of examples. Looking at the first columns we see that

$$C\$1 = US\$0.8290$$

while examination of the first row reveals that

$$US\$1 = C\$1.2062$$

In other words, one Canadian dollar buys approximately 83 U.S. cents or one U.S. dollar is equivalent to about $1.21 in Canadian currency. As a second example, by reading down the first column of Table 8.1, we find that the exchange rate for the Euro is

$$C\$1 = €0.6086$$

But by reading across the first row, we find

$$€1 = C\$1.6431$$

The point seems obvious (after all, $1.6431 = 1 \div 0.6086$), but it often causes confusion in discussions. To avoid the problem, whenever we speak of the exchange rate in this textbook, we will refer to the price of one unit of a foreign currency in terms of Canadian dollars. In other words, the exchange rate, which is denoted by e, will be interpreted as

$$e = \text{Canadian dollars/1 unit of foreign currency}$$

In Table 8.1, you can read the exchange rate for the Canadian dollar vis-à-vis the Japanese yen as 0.0117, which means that about 1.117 cents buys 1 Japanese yen.

Cross-Rates

The data in the table also allow us to determine the value of any currency listed in relation to any other. For example, US$1 is equivalent to £0.5203 and US$1 yields C$1.2063. So we can calculate:

---

1 As reported by Reuters in 2002.

Table 8.1	A Selection of Exchange Rates					
Currency	C$	US$	£	€	¥	SFr
Canadian dollar, C$	—	1.2062	2.3184	1.6431	0.0117	1.0633
U.S. dollar, US$	.8290	—	1.9221	1.3622	0.0097	0.8815
British pound, £	.4313	.5203	—	.7087	0.0050	0.4586
European Union currency, €	.6086	.7341	1.4110	—	0.0071	0.6471
Japanese yen, ¥	85.4847	103.11	198.19	140.46	—	90.986
Swiss franc, SFr	.9405	1.1344	2.1804	1.5453	0.0110	—

Source: Bank of Canada www.bankofcanada.ca/en/exchform.htm

To find current and historical exchange rates visit www.oanda.com

$$\frac{\text{C\$ per US\$}}{\text{£ per US\$}} = \frac{1.2063}{0.5203}$$

$$= 2.3183$$

$$= \text{C\$ per £}$$

which is called computing the **cross-rate** between the Canadian dollar and the British pound. Our calculation agrees with the published rate shown in Table 8.1.

Knowing how to calculate cross-rates is useful because rates are not published for all currencies (there is insufficient demand for many possible cross-rates). Suppose you want to find the exchange rate of the Australian dollar in terms of the Mexican peso. On 30 December 2004, one Canadian dollar could purchase 9.3023 Mexican pesos (or you needed C$0.1075 to buy one peso); on the same day one Canadian dollar was worth 1.0652 Australian dollars (AUD) (or you needed C$0.9388 to buy one Australian dollar). Therefore, one Mexican peso would buy

$$0.1145 \text{ AUD} = \frac{1.0652}{9.3023}$$

Changes in Rates

Another set of exchange rate definitions involves changes in currency values. When the market brings about changes in an exchange rate (which it does frequently), these changes inform us when a currency has **appreciated** (increased) or **depreciated** (decreased) in value. For example, in 1986 the exchange rate of the Canadian dollar vis-à-vis the U.S. dollar averaged 1.3894. By 30 December 2004, the rate was 1.2062 (see Table 8.1). It cost fewer Canadian dollars to purchase one U.S. dollar. The Canadian dollar had appreciated and the US dollar had depreciated.

In some cases a country's exchange rates are set by government regulation rather than the market (we'll examine how later in this chapter). A government-decreed increase in the value of one currency vis-à-vis another is termed a **revaluation** and a decrease is termed a **devaluation**.

EFFECTIVE OR TRADE-WEIGHTED EXCHANGE RATES

Exchange rates are sometimes averaged over several currencies. A weighted average measure is used since the proportion of the country's trade with one country can be quite different from the proportion of trade with another. For example, in mid-2004, 81.3% of Canadian merchandise exports went to the United States. The next largest major export recipients were the European Economic Community (EEC; 7.0%) and Japan (2.6%). In the case of merchandise imports, we buy mainly from the United States (69.5%), followed again by the EEC (10.0%) and Japan (2.8%).[2] If the remaining trade is with the "rest of the world," then a trade-weighted exchange rate would be calculated as:

$$w_1 e_{US} + w_2 e_{EEC} + w_3 e_J + w_4 e_{ROW}$$

where the w represents the weights, which, of course, add up to one, and e is the exchange rate for the United States, the EEC, Japan, and the rest of the world.[3]

THE LAW OF ONE PRICE

Exchange rates provide a link between the prices prevailing in two countries. For example, suppose a bottle of California wine costs $10 in U.S. currency. What is its price in Canadian dollars? If the exchange rate between two currencies is $1.40, the answer is

$$\$10 \times \$1.40 = \$14.00$$

More generally, the domestic price of an item produced abroad and imported can be written

$$P^f e = P \qquad\qquad (8.1)$$

where

P^f = the foreign price of the commodity
e = the exchange rate
P = the domestic or local price of the same commodity[4]

Thus, prices in Canada are linked to foreign prices via the exchange rate.

One way of understanding the relationship implied in equation (8.1) is to call it the **law of one price**. This law stipulates that the domestic price of a commodity should be equal to the foreign price converted into domestic terms through the exchange rate. That is, the price of a commodity should be the same in Canada as in the United States, Australia, or Japan.

Few economists accept this law literally. Importing commodities creates a variety of costs, such as those for transportation as well as the transactions costs of converting foreign currencies into the domestic currency, to name but two complicating factors. Moreover, the law of one price can apply only to commodities that can be traded.[5]

By contrast, capital can flow from one country to the next at very low cost. Therefore, we would expect a kind of law of one price to apply to financial instruments. The difficulty is that investors who purchase securities denominated in a foreign currency have locked their funds into that currency even if only for a brief time. Hence, they must be concerned not only with today's exchange rate, which is called the **spot rate**, but also with the exchange rate that will prevail when the funds are converted back into the original currency. In other words, investors must make some sort of a guess about future or expected exchange rates (a question we addressed in the previous chapter).

---

2 Data are from the *Bank of Canada Banking and Financial Statistics* (October 2004), Table J3. It should be noted that the fraction of trade vis-à-vis the U.S. rose steadily since the first edition of this text was published in 1994, shortly after the Free Trade Agreement came into force, but fell since the fourth edition appeared in 2004.

3 For the EEC we would use the Euro exchange rate, but for the rest of the world there is no such thing as an exchange rate. These rates could, in principle, be separately calculated as trade-weighted exchange rates. Effective exchange rates are often published in index form. For example, in September 2004, the index for the C$ stood at 93.52 (1992 = 100), meaning that the Canadian dollar fell roughly 6.48% in value against the currencies of the countries it trades with. Bank of Canada *Banking and Financial Statistics,* Table I1. The index is for the so-called C-6 currencies that include the Euro area, the British pound, the Japanese yen, the Swiss franc, and, of course, the U.S. dollar.

4 Ordinarily, this is not the same as the prices discussed in earlier chapters (see note 4, this chapter). The approach followed here has the virtue, however, of avoiding the introduction of a new notation.

5 Labour, for example, is not generally considered a commodity tradable across international boundaries (the costs of commuting and of dealing regularly with customs officials would be prohibitive; moreover, immigration is generally regulated). Many services are also *nontraded commodities*; a taxicab ride in Montreal simply has no value to someone in Vermont.

Nevertheless, for anyone who has doubted the importance of the law of one price, the recent experience of German reunification has illustrated the potentially devastating consequences of side-stepping exchange rate considerations: (see **Financial Focus 8.1: Exchange Rate and Politics: The Case of Germany Reunification.**)

More recently, the Asian financial crisis of 1997–98—we examine this event in greater detail in Chapter 24—put the spotlight back on the question of whether capital flows should be restricted or not. Some economists argue that the current system in which capital can be moved literally at the touch of a button has net costs. The critics make two points. First, they argue that the existing system is not geared toward channelling the funds to their more productive uses, but rather that people tend to channel capital to where the greatest speculative profits are. Second, the evidence suggesting that countries do better when capital is able to move is weak. After all, China and Japan enjoyed very high growth rates even when capital flows were restricted. Note, however, that we must distinguish between capital flows that are long-term investments, which economists refer to as foreign direct investment (FDI), and "hot money," in which holders of capital seek out the country where returns are particularly attractive at the moment and vanish as soon as the returns are less attractive. Almost all economists agree that FDI contributes to economic growth, whereas the latter type of capital flow does not. We ignore the distinction in what follows, though it is surely an important issue.[6]

Before exploring the linkages between interest rates and exchange rates, it is first necessary to understand that different exchange rate regimes exist, with important consequences for the behaviour of both exchange rates and inflation rates in different countries.

8.2   EXCHANGE RATE REGIMES

How are exchange rates determined? The answer depends first on the exchange rate system or regime a country has chosen. Most exchange rate regimes can be classified as belonging to one of three categories:

1. A **fixed exchange rate regime** in which the country's currency is pegged to another currency, such as the U.S. dollar or the French franc. In the past, many currencies were pegged to gold.

2. A **flexible exchange rate regime**, also called a *floating system*, in which market forces are allowed to determine the exchange level independently.

3. A **managed float regime**, sometimes called a **"dirty" float**, in which some central authority, such as a central bank, intervenes in the market for foreign exchange to hold the rate at some desired level (usually a range of levels).

Many countries do not have a pure form of any of the three systems. Table 8.2 gives the exchange rate arrangements of selected countries as classified by the International Monetary Fund (IMF).

The IMF classified Canada's system as the independent floating variety. The Canadian government has not intervened for years in foreign exchange markets, having decided that it is unnecessary to do so (see section 8.3). However, when it chooses to intervene it has committed itself to announce the decision and to publish it on its Web site (announced in July 1998). It has done so only once (in 2000).

In Table 8.2, *exchange rate arrangements with no separate legal tender* means either that another currency circulates (e.g., the U.S. dollar) or the currency is a supra-national one (e.g., the Euro). A *currency board arrangement* means that the exchange rate has been fixed to some currency (e.g., the

---

6 See, for example, J. Bhagwati, "The Capital Myth," *Foreign Affairs* (May–June 1998), and S. Fisher, R. Cooper, et al. "Should the IMF Pursue Capital-Account Convertibility," *Essays in International Finance* No. 207, Princeton University, May 1998.

Table 8.2	Exchange Rate Arrangements

Type of Exchange Rate Regime	Number of Countries	A Sample of Countries Adhering to Each Regime
Exchange rate arrangement with no separate legal tender	41	Euro area (11 countries in Europe including France, Germany, and Italy)
Currency board arrangements	7	Bulgaria
Other fixed peg arrangements	42	Mainland China Malaysia Morocco
Pegged exchange rate within a band	5	Denmark Egypt
Crawling peg	6	Bolivia Costa Rica
Exchange rates within crawling bands	2	Belarus Romania
Managed float	48	Czech Republic Norway Singapore
Independently floating	36	Australia Canada Japan New Zealand Sweden United Kingdom United States

Source: www.imf.org/external/np/mfd/er/2004/eng/0604.htm. As of June 30, 2004.

U.S. dollar) via legislation and that individuals can exchange their own currency for the pegged currency at a fixed exchange rate. *Other fixed peg arrangements* means that the currency is fixed to a group or "basket" of currencies. *Pegged exchange rates within a band* means that the exchange rate is allowed to fluctuate more than ±1% around some central parity but within prescribed limits. Peg changes are usually pre-announced. *Crawling peg* means that the exchange rate is fixed but can be adjusted by some central authority based on a set of indicators. *Exchange rate within crawling bands* is the same as the previous regime, except that the exchange rate is permitted to fluctuate within a prescribed band. Peg changes usually are not announced. *Managed float* indicates active foreign exchange intervention with no prescribed exchange rate for the currency. *Independently floating* means no active intervention except to reduce the volatility of exchange rate fluctuations.

Although Table 8.2 illustrates the richness in the variety of exchange rate regimes, it is useful for now to think in terms of a distinction between fixed versus flexible rates only. Consequently, the first six regime types listed are essentially variations on the fixed rate regime—we will explore some of them in greater detail in Chapter 26—whereas the last two are of the floating variety. In 2004, 103 countries had some type of fixed exchange rate regime, while 74 countries had the floating exchange rate variety.

A word of caution is in order. Although building a theory based on the two polar extremes of fixed versus floating exchange rates makes life easier, many economists, including Nobel laureate Robert Mundell, will point out that the distinction is a bit of an "oxymoron."[7] Why? As we shall see, when a country fixes its exchange rate it must accept developments in interest rates

7 R. Mundell, "Friedman v. Mundell on Exchange Rates," *National Post*, 11 December 2000.

and inflation rates from abroad. So the "anchor" of policy is the monetary policy of the world's most influential economies. On the other hand, when the exchange rate floats, the anchor of domestic monetary policy must be sought elsewhere. In many countries (as we shall see later in this text), central banks have chosen an inflation target as the anchor. As a result, it is preferable to ask what type of monetary policy strategy a country follows and not simply whether it pegs its exchange rate or not. A monetary policy strategy consists of the type of exchange rate regime, the degree of central bank independence, as well as whether the central bank is required to target a certain rate of inflation.[8]

Therefore, a floating exchange rate regime does not tell us the whole picture about a country's monetary policy unless we know what the other aspects of that policy are. Indeed, some have been highly critical of the manner in which the International Monetary Fund (which we study in Chapter 24) has defined exchange rate regimes, arguing, for example, that many countries with floating rates do not really float at all. They have a so-called "fear of floating."[9]

The growing popularity of floating exchange rates has led some observers to argue that intermediate exchange rate regimes are on their way out. This has been termed the "hollowing out" hypothesis.[10] Nevertheless, many other economists argue that this is a dangerous development and draw attention to the need for an intermediate regime between the fixed and floating extremes.[11] The concern also comes from recent evidence that many countries that have moved from a fixed to a floating variety of exchange rate regime have done so in a "disorderly" fashion, meaning that the shift has taken place under crisis-type conditions. At a time when the International Monetary Fund is actively encouraging countries to float their currency, this suggests that improvements ought to be made in the way the transition from fixed to float should be governed.[12] Although it may indeed be desirable to move to a float in an orderly manner, external events beyond most countries' control can thwart any well-thought-out transition. As Harold MacMillan, the former British prime minister, said when asked why his best intentions were being derailed: "Events, dear boy, events!"

8.3   EXCHANGE RATE DETERMINATION AND THE BASICS OF THE BALANCE OF PAYMENTS

Now we are ready to consider the determination of exchange rates. To fix ideas, we consider the two extremes in regimes: purely flexible exchange rates and fixed exchange rates.

We can view the determination of the exchange rates in much the same way as the determination of the price of any commodity—as the result of the interaction of the forces of demand and supply. Just as Canadian dollars are used to facilitate transactions in Canada, trading between countries requires the use of foreign currencies. Therefore, when Canadians express a desire to buy U.S. goods or assets denominated in U.S. dollars, they express a demand for U.S.

8 See K. Kuttner and A. Posen, "Beyond Bipolar: A Three-Dimensional Assessment of Monetary Frameworks," *International Journal of Finance and Economics*, 6: 389-387; P. Siklos, "End Games on the Road to Monetary Union: Between Exchange Rate and Inflation Targeting," working paper, Wilfrid Laurier University, 2005.

9 See G. Calvo and C. Reinhart, "Fear of Floating," *Quarterly Journal of Economics*, 117 (May 2002): 379-408. Also see Levy-Yeyati and F. Sturzenegger, "Exchange Rate Regimes and Economic Performance," *IMF Staff Papers*, 47(Special Issue 2001): 62–98.

10 See S. Fischer, "Exchange Rate Regimes: Is the Bipolar View Correct?" *Journal of Economics Perspective* 15 (Spring): 3–24.

11 See, for example, Willett, T., "Fear of Floating Need Not Imply Fixed Rates: Feasible Options for Intermediate Exchange Rate Regimes," *Open Economics Review* 14 (January 2003): 71-91, and J. Williamson, *Exchange Rate Regimes for Emerging Market Economies: Reviving the Intermediate Option* (Washington, D.C.: Institute for International Economics, 2000).

12 See Monetary and Financial Systems Department, "From Fixed to Float: Operational Aspects of Moving toward Exchange Rate Flexibility," International Monetary Fund, 19 November 2004.

FINANCIAL FOCUS 8.1

EXCHANGE RATES AND POLITICS: THE CASE OF GERMAN REUNIFICATION

When the former East Germany and West Germany were reunited on 30 June 1990, two price and currency systems had to be merged. One of the key economic questions was which exchange rate would be used to convert East German ostmarks into Deutschmarks. East Germans were wary of having to convert essentially worthless currency into a strong currency, fearing that their monetary wealth would be wiped out. Their leaders wanted a one-for-one exchange. By contrast, the German central bank, always mindful of the need to control inflation, proposed a two-ostmark-for-one-Deutschmark exchange. There was an uproar. The then-president of the Bundesbank, Karl Otto Pöhl, resigned in July 1991. He later complained that the German politicians had made "impossibly costly promises" and that the exchange rate between the Deutschmark and the ostmark was too generous for holders of the latter currency. What politicians were missing in this argument is that there are always winners and losers in the game of currency conversion. Clearly, individuals holding assets would be hurt by a two-for-one exchange rate, but debt-holders would be hurt by a one-for-one exchange rate.

Politics interfered and a compromise was reached. Below specific levels—4000 ostmarks in general, but 2000 for those under 14 years of age and 6000 for those over 59 years of age—individuals received one Deutschmark for each ostmark deposited in the bank. Above these limits, the exchange rate was two for one. A total of 191 billion ostmarks were converted, 66 billion at the 1:1 rate and 125 billion at the 2:1 rate. The black market exchange rate at the time was 7:1.

Only nine months later, the president of the Bundesbank declared the monetary union a disaster. Although the actual reasons for the disaster are complex, the law of one price is helpful in explaining an important source of the difficulties with the monetary union of two economically unequal states.

A survey reported in the *Wall Street Journal* shortly before monetary union gave then-current prices for four commodities likely to be comparable in quality.

	Price in DMs	Price in Ostmarks
Loaf of rye bread	3.17	0.52
Potatoes (5 kg)	4.94	0.85
Electricity per kW•h	0.42	0.08
Coffee (1 kg)	17.86	70.00

If the law of one price holds, the exchange rate to equilibrate the two sets of prices would be, according to equation (8.1):

$$e = P/P^f \ (P = \text{ostmark}/P^f = \text{DM})$$
$$0.16$$
$$0.17$$
$$0.19$$
$$3.92$$

Clearly, the ratio of actual prices was not compatible with an exchange rate of one for one. Moreover, all the items on the list except the coffee were highly subsidized by the East German state. With reunification, these subsidies disappeared, and with them any competitive advantage of the kind suggested in the table above. Thus, it is perhaps not surprising that the former East Germany experienced a depression of sorts with a fall in real GNP of at least 15% within months of the monetary union.

Questions for Discussion

1. If the four commodities listed on the data table constituted a sort of "consumer price index," would the law of one price be a good approximation?
2. Can you think of reasons why law of one price calculations might be inappropriate in the case of German reunification?

Sources

G.A. Akerloff, A.K. Rose, J.L. Yellen, and H. Hessenius, "East Germany in from the Cold: The Economic Aftermath of Currency Union," *Brookings Papers on Economic Activity* 1 (1991): 1–106.

A. Fisher, "Pöhl Accuses Bonn of Risking D. Mark," *Financial Times of London*, 15 May 1992, p. 2.

T. Roth, "East German Winners in Election Now Seek Fast Monetary Union," *Wall Street Journal*, 20 March 1990.

dollars. The same goes for U.S. residents who express a desire to buy Canadian goods or assets. Similarly, when the Bank of Canada, for example, decides to sell some of its reserves of U.S. dollars or Canadians decide to reduce their holdings of U.S. dollars, they express a desire to supply U.S. dollars in the market for foreign exchange. It is for these reasons that the demand and supply of foreign exchange is referred to as being derived from the desire to hold or sell assets or

Figure 8.1   Exchange Rate Determination

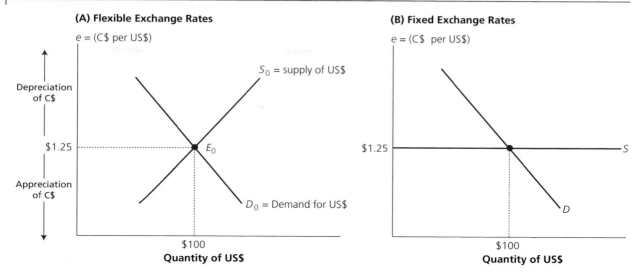

For clarity, we have set up both figures here with an arbitrarily assumed exchange rate of C$1.25 for US$1. The difference between the two diagrams is the way the exchange rate is determined. In panel (A), the driving force is the market. The supply curve for U.S. dollars, labelled S_0, is upward sloping because a depreciation of the Canadian dollar makes it more attractive to supply U.S. dollars to buy cheaper Canadian dollars. Since this also makes U.S. dollars more expensive to buy, the quantity of them demanded falls, making the demand curve for foreign exchange, D_0, downward sloping. Equilibrium is the point at which D_0 intersects S_0.

In panel (B), the exchange rate is fixed by the government at $1.25. To guarantee this rate, the Bank of Canada has to supply sufficient quantities of U.S. dollars to keep the supply curve, S, flat.

commodities denominated in different currencies, as Figure 8.1 illustrates. The horizontal axes measure the quantity of foreign exchange (U.S. dollars) demanded and supplied, while the vertical axes measure the price of U.S. dollars per Canadian dollar, which is the exchange rate.

Consider first the flexible exchange rate regime case depicted in Figure 8.1(A). The demand curve for foreign exchange, D_0, is downward sloping because a lower exchange rate implies that the Canadian dollar appreciates in value against the U.S. dollar. Therefore, it becomes cheaper to buy U.S. dollars. By contrast, a lower exchange rate means that holders of U.S. dollars can now receive fewer Canadian dollars in exchange. These individuals thus supply the market for foreign exchange with smaller quantities of U.S. dollars, so the supply curve, S_0, is upward sloping. Of course, transactions take place only when the market attains an equilibrium, which occurs at point E_0. We'll arbitrarily say the exchange rate it represents is $1.25.

In a floating exchange rate system, demand and supply are allowed to shift freely through time in reaction to other changes. For example, Canadian interest rates might rise, increasing the attractiveness of domestic financial instruments relative to those denominated in U.S. dollars.[13] Both the supply of and the demand for U.S. dollars would change as investors attempt to take advantage of the higher rates in Canada. Similarly, changes in Canadian–U.S. exports and imports of goods and services would shift the demand and supply curves for foreign exchange, respectively. These details are best left for macroeconomic texts so they are not pursued here, though we return to this issue later in the chapter. You could, however, explore the question of interest rate effects as an exercise.

---

13 This assumption is made by abstracting from considerations of differences in risk, which we begin to address in Chapter 13.

Figure 8.1(B) depicts a market in which the exchange rate is pegged (fixed) at $1.25 by government policy. The government guarantees to maintain the exchange rate at the stated figure. The Bank of Canada must, therefore, ensure that the quantity of U.S. dollars supplied in the foreign exchange rate market is sufficient to be equal to the quantity demanded to create a market-clearing price of $1.25 at all times.[14] Should the pegged rate be changed, the supply curve shifts—upward if the Canadian dollar is devalued, downward if it is revalued. An example occurred when countries fixed their exchange rates to the price of gold. There continue to be several adherents to the gold standard, including Canadian Nobel Laureate, Robert Mundell (see **Economics Focus 8.1: Longing for the Gold Standard**).

It is clear then that how a country defines its exchange rate regime has consequences for its trading relationships with the rest of the world. There are less obvious consequences of the choice of exchange rate regimes, as the accompanying Focus Box (**Financial Focus 8.2: Exchange Rates and the Birth of a Monetary Union: The Controversy over Rounding**) discusses.

To appreciate the importance of these flows, however, we need to study a country's balance of payments.[15]

THE BALANCE OF PAYMENTS

A country's **balance of payments** (**BOP**) records its foreign trade in goods, services, and financial instruments. For example, Canada's BOP records all receipts Canadian residents take in from foreigners and all payments they make to foreigners. A positive entry signifies that foreign exchange enters Canada and a negative entry that foreign exchange is lost. If receipts are greater than the payments, the BOP is said to be in surplus; when payments exceed receipts, the BOP is in deficit.

Table 8.3 shows Canada's BOP. Notice that it is divided into two principal categories, the current account and the capital account. The **current account** records trade between Canada and the

Table 8.3	Canada's Balance of Payments, 2004 (Millions of Dollars)

Current Account (Balances)

1. Merchandise trade	80 156
2. Services	–11 696
3. Investment income	–27 244
4. Transfers	452
5. Balance (1 + 2 + 3 + 4)	41 668

Capital Account (Net Flows)

6. Canadian assets net flows	–49 005
7. Canadian liabilities to nonresidents	44 908
8. Net capital flows (6 + 7)*	–2 903
9. Statistical discrepancy	–6 841

Source: Bank of Canada, *Banking and Financial Statistics* (October 2004): Tables J1, J2. Data are for 2004, second quarter, and totals may be rounded.

*Adding lines 6 and 7 does not give –2903. This figure does not account for discrepancies and omitted items (see page 147).

---

14 In other words, the supply curve of foreign exchange is perfectly elastic.

15 We do not, however, develop a full-fledged framework for the analysis of an open economy at the macroeconomic level, a task better suited to a course in international economics or in intermediate macroeconomics. Interested students may see, for example, M. Obstfeld, and K. Rogoff, *Foundation of International Economics* (Cambridge, Mass.: The MIT Press, 1996), or B.T. McCallum, *International Monetary Economics* (New York: Oxford University Press, 1996). It is worth noting that several Canadians, such as Robert Mundell, recipient of the Nobel Prize in economics in 1999, and Harry Johnson, have made prominent contributions in this area. Some excellent references include R. Mundell, *Monetary Theory: Inflation, Interest and Growth in the World Economy* (Pacific Palisades, Calif.: Goodyear, 1971); and J.A. Frenkel, and H.G. Johnson (eds.), *The Monetary Approach to the Balance of Payments* (Toronto: University of Toronto Press, 1976).

ECONOMICS FOCUS 8.1   LONGING FOR THE GOLD STANDARD

During the early 1980s, there was a resurgence of interest in returning to the *gold standard*, a form of fixed exchange rates largely abandoned earlier this century. Some U.S. presidential candidates in 1996 also expressed their admiration for the gold standard and yearned for its return in some form. A country using a gold standard undertakes to fix the price of gold at some value and to ensure that its currency is freely convertible against it.

If most countries are on a gold standard, exchange rates are fixed and exchange rate risk is eliminated.

Another attraction of the gold standard is that it provides the inflationary discipline modern-day governments appear to lack at times. For example, when Canada was on the gold standard (from Confederation until World War I), it generally experienced deflation. Not everyone agrees that this is desirable since deflation in asset prices means that financial wealth is adversely affected although the purchasing power of money is increased.

Given the roaring inflation of the 1970s and early 1980s, it is not surprising that many politicians and others yearned for a return to the gold standard in some form. A further appeal of the gold standard is that it does not require a central bank. All that is required is some central authority to maintain the statutory ratio of the money supply to gold. Yet, historically, the gold standard failed, largely for two reasons: Governments were unwilling to maintain a fixed exchange rate in times of financial crisis or wars; and it prevented the flexibility of conducting policy, both monetary and fiscal, that voters expect politicians to be responsible for. In other words, they did not follow the "rules of the game."

A pure gold standard is akin to a rigidly fixed exchange rate. Since it leaves no room for policymakers to pursue economic policies independent of other countries', any policy to control the money supply has no significance. The loss of monetary control occurs because of what the classical economist David Hume best described as the price–specie–flow mechanism where specie is gold; essentially, a change in price causes inflows or outflows of gold, which, in turn, provide the forces that will equilibrate prices between countries in the manner described in the text.

Unfortunately, it is also costly to maintain and store gold safely. Moreover, so long as the world economy is stable, the gold standard will operate effectively, but if one of the major players is experiencing a recession while another large country is in the expansionary phase of the

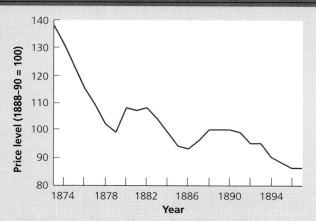

Source: T.J.O. Dick, and J.E. Floyd, *Canada and the Gold Standard: Balance of Payments Adjustment under Fixed Exchange Rates, 1871–1913* (Cambridge: Cambridge University Press, 1992), Table B2.

business cycle, it will be difficult to maintain a fixed exchange rate. Eventually, one currency will become so overvalued and the other so undervalued that the arrangement cannot be sustained. World War I and the Great Depression of the 1930s were shocks so large that they led to the demise of the gold standard.

Questions for Discussion
1. What is the principal appeal of the gold standard?
2. Why is it critical that countries adhering to the gold standard play by the "rules of the game"?

Sources
J.A. Dorn, and A.J. Schwartz, *The Search for Stable Money: Essays on Monetary Reform* (Chicago: University of Chicago Press, 1983).

B. Eichengreen, *Golden Fetters* (Oxford: Oxford University Press, 1992).

G. Rich, *The Cross of Gold: Money and the Canadian Business Cycle, 1867–1913* (Ottawa: Carleton University Press, 1988).

Learn all about the role of gold and the arguments about returning to some form of gold standard
www.gold.org/

rest of the world in merchandise, services, and investment income, as well as transfers (payments made or received in government debt at all levels). Historically, the Canadian balance in merchandise trade typically has been positive, but the balances in services and investment income generally have been negative.

FINANCIAL FOCUS 8.2

EXCHANGE RATES AND THE BIRTH OF A MONETARY UNION: THE CONTROVERSY OVER ROUNDING

When Europe eventually switched from 12 currencies to a single currency in 2002 (we study the process in more detail in Chapter 26), there was outrage over the so-called "rounding phenomenon." This problem arose because prices in French francs, Italian lira, German Deutschmarks, and in eight other currencies had to be converted to prices in euros at an exchange rate that had previously been set. However, as anyone who shops knows, prices are often either in round numbers, or very nearly so (for example, as in gas prices or sale prices that are set a penny or a fraction of a penny below the next highest number, say, $9.99 or $0.649). Therefore, when someone in Vienna goes to a restaurant and is used to paying 300 Austrian shillings for a meal, that would translate to €21.80 (using the exchange rate in Table 26.2). It is tempting then for the restaurant manager to set a price of €22, thereby artificially inflating the price of a meal. There were accusations all around that this phenomenon was widespread, leading politicians and the European Central Bank to promise that such abuses would be monitored and prevented.* Nevertheless, as the flyer handed out to guests at a Viennese restaurant attests, some felt that the rounding was "unavoidable." Subsequent research (Deutsche Budesbank) revealed that one of the consequences of the switch to the euro was a drop in the number of prices ending with a ".99." However, the researchers could find no systematic price gouging, blaming instead the combination of bad weather, the "mad cow" scare, and higher taxes for the sudden rise in prices following the introduction of the new currency.

Questions for Discussion

1. Is rounding unavoidable under the circumstances described in this Focus Box?
2. Is rounding more likely for some products than others?

HOTEL BRISTOL

A WESTIN HOTEL
Vienna

Sehr geehrte Damen und Herren! Liebe Gäste!

In diesem Jahr vollziehen 12 europäische Staaten die Umstellung ihrer Wdhrung auf EURO.

Unser Haus bemüht sich, die dafür erforderlichen Schritte rasch und gästeorientiert durchzüfiihren.

Die Ihnen vorliegende Rechnung ist bereits in Euro ausgestellt. Wir müchten Sie darauf hinweisen, dass es bei der entsprechenden Schilling-Summe zu Rundungsdifferenzen kommen kann.

Sollten Sie dazu noch Fragen haben — unsere Mitarbeiter informieren Sie gerne!

Ladies and Gentlemen, Dear Guests!

Throughout this year twelve European countries will complete the conversion of their national currency unit to EURO. For our guests we will try to make this change over as fluent and comfortable as possible.

Your present bill is already issued in EURO. The equivalent total in national currency (ATS) might result in unavoidable differences caused by rounding the total amount.

Our employees are willing to help you in case of any questions.

Thank you.

---

*J. Schmid, "Despite Price Data, Germans Smell a Rat," *International Herald Tribune*, 25–26 (May 2002): 11.
Deutsche Budesbank "Consumer Prices and the Changeover from the Deutsche Mark to the Euro," *Monthly Report* (July 2002): 15-24.

The **capital account** reflects flows of money for investment and government grants and loans. For simplicity, items are classified according to whether Canadians have claims on nonresidents or whether they have liabilities toward nonresidents. These amounts arise because Canadians invest directly abroad or hold foreign securities. Similarly, claims on Canadians arise because, for example, nonresidents may invest in Canada or hold Canadian stocks or bonds. Figure 8.2(A) records Canada's current and capital accounts since the late 1970s. A current account that is in deficit needs to be financed. Thus, a deficit in the current account implies a surplus in the capital account.

■ 8.4   EXPLAINING THE BALANCE OF PAYMENTS

In principle, we would expect the deficit in the current account to be financed by a surplus in the capital account so that the BOP should be zero. Yet, the two do not offset each other exactly for two reasons. One is the difficulty of recording international transactions (stemming only in part from tax evasion and other illegal activities). The resulting statistical discrepancy is often very large, as can be seen in Figure 8.2(A). Thus, although the current account in 2004 had a surplus of $41 668 million, there were $2983 million in net capital *outflows*. Notice also that the difference between lines 6 and 7 in Table 8.3, that is, $-49 005 + $44 908 = $-4097, not $2903. The resulting difference is referred to as the "statistical discrepancy." A second reason has to do with errors made in recording transactions and the differences in efficiency with which statistical agencies in different countries operate. As a result, although the sum of external surpluses across countries should be equal to the sum of external deficits, the statistical discrepancies have turned out to be quite large, prompting questions about the usefulness of these data.[16]

Over the past 20 years, Canada experienced net inflows every year until 1999 (except for 1996), as shown in Figure 8.2(A). Canadian interest rates lower than those in the United States and a depreciating Canadian dollar were two of the culprits. As the dollar began to appreciate after 2002, net flows also began to reverse their course.

FOREIGN EXCHANGE INTERVENTION

The Bank of Canada occasionally used to intervene in the market for foreign exchange, either to moderate fluctuations in the exchange rate or in its capacity as the manager of the country's for-

| Figure 8.2 | The Canadian Balance of Payments and Related Measures |

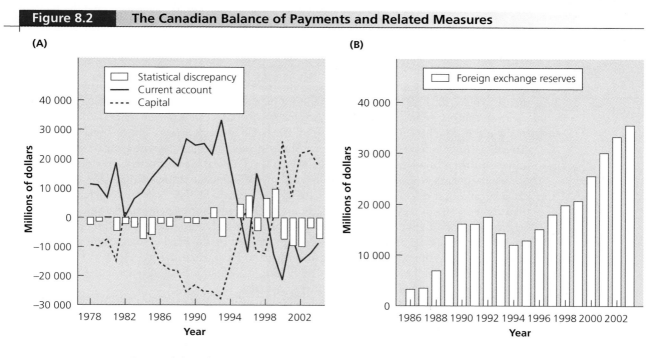

Source: Bank of Canada, *Banking and Financial Statistics* (various issues): Tables I2, J1, and I2. International reserves include U.S. dollars and other currencies, gold, and Special Drawing Rights (see Chapter 26).

16 See J. Marquez and L. Workman, "Modeling the IMF's Statistical Discrepancy in the Global Current Account," *IMF Staff Papers* 48(3)(2001): 499-521.

eign exchange reserves. As shown in Figure 8.2(B), these reserves have changed considerably through the years.

If the exchange rate floats freely, then the market for foreign exchange will clear. However, a country's exchange rate can be either overvalued or undervalued for some time. This discrepancy could occur because the central bank has deliberately intervened in the foreign exchange market to artificially influence the exchange rate. The notion of over- or undervaluation in the exchange rate presumes that we know what the equilibrium exchange rate is. We have already seen that exchange rates change frequently and by large amounts (see Chapter 1). This makes it difficult to estimate whether a currency is over- or undervalued. As a consequence, it is difficult to know when a central bank ought to intervene in foreign exchange markets. More commonly, central banks intervene to eliminate what is considered to be excessive day-to-day volatility in the exchange rate. Excessive exchange rate volatility is deemed undesirable because it is thought to interfere with the efficiency of foreign exchange markets; the international flow of goods, services, and investment capital; and ultimately to disrupt domestic financial markets and the conduct of monetary policy.

Foreign market intervention is common in many countries; Canada is among the least interventionist countries in this regard. Since changes in the foreign exchange reserves have been important through the years, it is worth illustrating the connection between the exchange rate and change in foreign exchange reserves.

Consider Figure 8.3. In the absence of any intervention by the Bank of Canada, suppose the market for foreign exchange would clear at an exchange rate of $1.20 per U.S. dollar. At this price, the quantity of U.S. dollars demanded would be exactly Q^*, equal to the quantity supplied, and the BOP should be zero. Suppose, however, that the current exchange rate should be $1.15. This figure implies that the Canadian dollar is undervalued. The price of the undervaluation, however, is an excess demand for U.S. dollars. To maintain the exchange rate, the Bank of Canada must sell U.S. dollars and thus reduce its foreign reserves.

As we shall see later in this chapter, theory tells us that the Canadian dollar has been undervalued in recent years. Foreign exchange reserves thus should have risen, other things being equal, which is exactly what Figure 8.2(B) shows.

In recent years, Canada's current account has moved from a deficit to a surplus. Can any theory explain the link between the balance of payments and the evolution of foreign exchange reserves? A theory known as the *monetary approach to the balance of payments* claims to do just that.[17] In a world in which exchange rates are fixed, we would expect a balance of payments deficit to be cancelled through flows of money. The act of buying and selling foreign exchange reserves has an impact on the Canadian money supply. When the Bank of Canada sells U.S. dollars, it buys Canadian dollars. Normally, the result is a fall in the Canadian money supply, but the Bank of Canada can offset this tendency by **sterilizing** (offsetting) the flow of foreign exchange: Rather than allowing the money supply to fall, it purchases bonds in the open market. Since *open market purchases* increase the Canadian money supply (see Chapter 6), use of this sterilization device can offset the pressure of a falling money supply caused by the fixed exchange rate set at a disequilibrium level. But a central bank can only go so far in draining its reserves of foreign exchange. Eventually, it will be unable or unwilling to defend a particular exchange, a situation that will force a devaluation of the country's currency.

Figure 8.2(B) shows what happened to foreign exchange reserves in Canada during the period when the dollar floated against all major currencies. Under flexible exchange rates, the monetary approach suggests that the exchange rate itself is the device that produces the necessary adjustments in the balance of trade, instead of the domestic money supply, by ensuring that the exchange rate is in equilibrium. Thus a country can control the domestic money supply

---

17 This is an old idea, first explained brilliantly in D. Hume's classic work "Of the Balance of Trade," in *Essays, Literary, Moral, and Political*, vol. I (London: Longmans Green, 1898). Hume's basic ideas have since been rejuvenated and extended in, for example, J.A. Frenkel and H.G. Johnson's work cited in footnote 15.

Figure 8.3	**Exchange Rate Intervention**

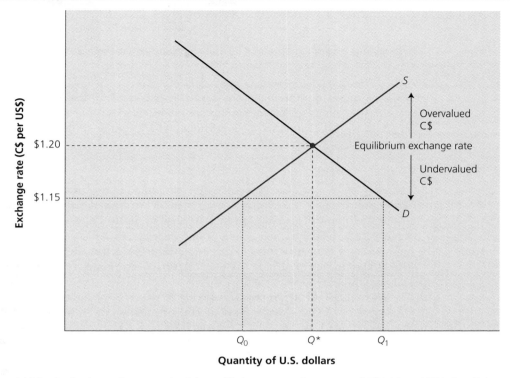

Initially, the foreign exchange market is in equilibrium at an exchange rate of C$1.20 per US$1. But, if the exchange rate should be $1.15 instead, the Canadian dollar is undervalued. The resulting disequilibrium in the market for foreign exchange leads the Bank of Canada to sell U.S. dollars, reducing its reserves of foreign exchange. In a purely floating exchange rate, the exchange rate's value would tend to be the equilibrium value. Nevertheless, actual exchange rates can be over- or undervalued for a time. Foreign exchange intervention by the Bank of Canada can be used either to change the exchange rate or to reduce its volatility.

independently. Therefore, the current account surplus has been translated partly into an increase in foreign exchange reserves, as shown in Figure 8.2(B).

An alternative view of the balance of payments, called the *absorption approach*, views surpluses or deficits in the balance of trade as resulting from the difference between what an economy produces and what it consumes domestically (that is, what it absorbs).

THE TWIN DEFICITS/SURPLUSES

Until the early 1990s, Canadian governments ran deficits. Figure 8.2(A) suggests that Canada had also, until the early 1990s, been running another kind of deficit, namely a current account deficit. Canada's position is rather unusual, since many advanced economies currently are experiencing a renewed bout of deficits in their national governments' budgets and current accounts. This situation gave rise to the concept of **twin deficits** (or, more aptly for Canada, twin surpluses). Is there a connection between these two deficits (surpluses)?

Recall from your principles of economics course that an economy's output can be divided into consumption (c), investment (i), government expenditures (g), and the difference between exports and imports ($x - im$). Algebraically, we can write

$$y = c + i + g + (x - im) \tag{8.2}$$

But output is also a country's income or GDP, which can be divided into the portion consumed, saved (s), and the amounts paid to government in taxes (t). Again, algebraically we can write

$$y = c + s + t \tag{8.3}$$

Subtracting c from equations (8.2) and (8.3) and equating them both, we obtain

$$i + g + (x - im) = s + t \tag{8.4}$$

Now, we know from the analysis in this text (see Chapter 3) that there is a connection between i and s. After all, the principal function of intermediaries is to channel savings into investment. Similarly, we can summarize the government's budget as the difference between g and t. So, re-arranging (8.4), we get

$$s + (t - g) = i + (x - im) \tag{8.5}$$

Therefore, if $(x - im)$ is negative, then the current account deficit takes away from investment. Similarly, if $(t - g)$ is also negative, government deficits take away from s. Financing these deficits requires an inflow of loanable funds, as we shall see in the following section, with potential consequences for the interest rate. Thus, raising interest rates will attract capital inflows. Higher savings (raising s) is an alternative to offset a government deficit. In the past few years, government deficits have turned to surpluses. These forces have contributed to the fact that we now have current account surpluses.

We can see more clearly the connection between $(t - g)$ and $(x - im)$ by assuming that i and s are constant. Taking changes on both sides of equation (8.5), we get (since $\Delta i = \Delta s = 0$)

$$\Delta(t - g) = \Delta(x - im)$$

In other words, the two "deficits" (when both sides of the equation are negative) or "surpluses" (both sides are positive) move together. Of course, s and i are not likely to be constant over long periods, so current account deficits are also due in part to changes in investment. Empirical evidence on the connection between the "twin deficits" is mixed.[18]

8.5   THE EXCHANGE RATE AND INTEREST RATE DETERMINATION

When we used the loanable funds framework to explain the determination of the equilibrium interest rate in Chapter 6, we implicitly assumed that all borrowing and lending occurred in a domestic market. What happens if the model reflects capital flows across international boundaries?[19] Consider Figure 8.4(A), which depicts the impact of international lending and borrowing on the Canadian economy. The curve labelled LF^s is the supply of loanable funds ignoring international considerations. It is, in other words, the same as the supply curve we examined in Chapter 6. Now let us drop the assumption of restriction to the domestic economy and draw a new curve that reflects the supply of loanable funds from both Canadians and foreigners. We can label it $LF^s + LF^{sf}$.

Where will we put the new curve? We can assume that foreigners will be attracted to Canadian investments if, other things being equal, the rate on Canadian securities is relatively higher than that prevailing in other countries.[20] Suppose that the latter rate is 6%. At this rate, Canadian and foreign interest rates are equally attractive, so the total quantity of loanable funds supplied will

---

18 See, for example, J.M. Rock (ed.), *Debt and the Twin Deficits Debate* (Mountain View, Calif.: Mayfield and Bristlecone Books, 1991); and K. Kasa, "Finite Horizons and Twin Deficits," *Federal Reserve Bank of San Francisco, Economic Review* 1994 (3): 19–28.

19 We could also use the liquidity preference framework to address the same question, but nothing of substance would be gained for the following discussion.

20 The rate for comparison need not be that of the United States alone, although it often is. We could view the comparison between Canadian interest rates and some average of interest rates in, say, all industrialized countries.

be the same as if international considerations were ignored. In panel (A) that consideration gives us our first quantity, B_0, along the loanable funds supply curve $LF^s + LF^{sf}$. Now suppose that the interest rate on Canadian securities rises from 6% to 8%.[21] They become relatively more attractive, prompting an inflow of capital, which means an increase in the total quantity of funds supplied. The result is quantity B_1. Not surprisingly, when Canadian interest rates are lower than elsewhere, the opposite takes place: Capital flows out of Canada, reducing the quantity supplied to B_2.

Notice the difference between slopes LF^s and $LF^s + LF^{sf}$. The supply of loanable funds is more responsive to interest rate changes when foreign and domestic funds are considered.[22] This difference is present because, when interest rates in Canada increase relative to those in the rest of the world, loanable funds supplied are increased by foreign lending, whereas Canadian interest rates that are low relative to those of the rest of the world turn foreigners into borrowers.

The effects of international borrowing and lending on the equilibrium interest rate are shown in Figure 8.4(B). When only domestic considerations matter, that rate is R_0, which is obtained at the intersection of LF_0^d and LF^s. Introducing international borrowing and lending initially makes no difference since the demand for loanable funds, LF_0^d, intersects $LF^s + LF^{sf}$ also at R_0. But if the demand for loanable funds shifts to LF_1^d, then with international borrowing and lending the equilibrium interest rate is R_1. Note that this interest rate is lower than R_2, which is where the new equilibrium would be if international considerations were ignored. Of course, the opposite conclusion would hold if the demand curve for loanable funds shifted lower than LF_0^d. We leave the solution to this problem to you as an exercise.

Figure 8.4	Loanable Funds with International Borrowing and Lending

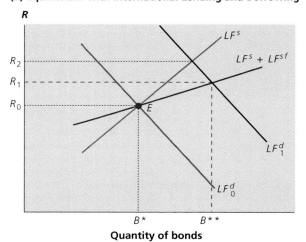

(A) Total Supply of Loanable Funds

(B) Equilibrium with International Lending and Borrowing

In panel (A), the domestic supply of loanable funds, LF^s, is supplemented by foreign funds, LF^{sf}, so long as the interest rate exceeds a certain rate (here assumed to be 6%). Below that rate, funds are invested abroad.
In panel (B), international lending and borrowing affect the equilibrium interest rate depending on the location of the demand for loanable funds. On LF_0^d, the effect is nil. But on LF_1^d, the equilibrium interest rate is R_1, which is lower than R_2, the equilibrium rate if international considerations are ignored.

---

21 Canadian interest rates might become higher for a variety of reasons. One is that the risk involved in Canadian investments might be perceived as becoming higher. We deal with perceptions of risk in Chapter 13. Another reason is that the Bank of Canada has chosen to tighten monetary policy, as we saw in Chapter 6.

22 That is, with international lending and borrowing, the supply of loanable funds becomes more elastic.

In brief, the principles used to find the equilibrium interest rate are the same whether international considerations are ignored or not, but international considerations are likely to affect the actual level of the equilibrium interest rate because they make the quantity of loanable funds relatively more sensitive to interest rate changes. It is partly for this reason that Canadian policy-makers, such as the Bank of Canada, must always consider domestic interest rates relative to those prevailing abroad.

8.6   PURCHASING POWER PARITY

We can summarize the relationship between exchange rates and prices by deriving an important proposition in economics. The purchasing power parity theory relates the domestic price level to the price level of another country, suggesting that the relationship between the two is uniquely explained by the exchange rate.

Purchasing power is the amount of goods and services that one dollar or euro or unit of any currency will buy. Hence, the **purchasing power parity** (**PPP**) hypothesis is that the exchange rate between two currencies is at equilibrium when their domestic purchasing powers are equivalent at that rate of exchange.

The PPP condition is reminiscent of the law of one price. More formally, the PPP hypothesis is that

$$e = \frac{P}{P_f} \tag{8.6}$$

All the terms are as defined previously, but P, domestic prices, and P^f, foreign prices, are measured in terms of an index of overall prices, such as the consumer price index (CPI), not just the prices of traded goods as in the law of one price. Thus, equation (8.6), which is often called the *absolute form of PPP*, simply states that the exchange rate is a reflection of relative prices in two countries.

We can rewrite equation (8.6) in terms of rates of change in the variables:[23]

$$\Delta e = \pi - \pi^f \tag{8.7}$$

where

Δe = rate of change in the exchange rate
π = domestic rate of inflation
π^f = foreign rate of inflation

Equation (8.7), which is called the *relative form of PPP*, states that exchange rate changes reflect differences in inflation rates between two countries.

Suppose, for example, that Canada's inflation rate is 1% while the U.S. rate of inflation is 3%. According to equation (8.7),

$$\Delta e = 1\% - 3\% = -2\%$$

Remembering that a fall in the exchange rate means an appreciation of the Canadian dollar relative to other currencies, we see that this use of the relative form of PPP predicts that the Canadian dollar will rise in value over time.

Note that nothing has been said about whether the difference in inflation rates or the change in the exchange rate comes first. The direction of causality between the two sides of the equation makes no difference to the PPP hypothesis (though the issue of causality is an important one in

---

23 From equation (8.6) with $\log e_t = \log P_t - \log P_t^f$, where log is the logarithm of a variable and a time subscript (t) has been added. Then $\log e_t - \log e_{t-1} = (\log P_t - \log P_{t-1}) - (\log P_t^f - \log P_{t-1}^f)$. Using previously introduced notation (see Chapter 6), this last equation becomes (dropping the time subscripts): $\Delta e = \pi - \pi^f$.

practice).[24] Also, neither equation (8.6) nor (8.7) is specific about how long the adjustment process to a new equilibrium will be. Rather, these equations should be viewed as equilibrium conditions that hold in the long run.

So far our calculations have assumed a flexible exchange rate regime. What happens if the exchange rate is fixed? The relative form of the PPP equation (8.7) becomes

$$\Delta e = 0 = \pi - \pi^f \tag{8.8}$$

which implies

$$\pi = \pi^f$$

In other words, if the Canadian–U.S. exchange rate were fixed (as it was for most years between 1945 and 1970), U.S. and Canadian inflation rates would be the same. If two or more countries set up a fixed exchange rate system at a time when their inflation rates differ from each other, they could be expected to converge over time. (Arguments such as these have prompted many European countries to join the European Monetary System. In particular, by pegging their exchange rate to the deutschmark, they implicitly committed themselves to eventual adoption of the German rate of inflation, traditionally one of the lowest among the industrialized countries).[25]

WHAT'S THE EVIDENCE ON PPP?

Are there empirical data in favour of the absolute and relative forms of PPP? Comparisons of the Canadian and U.S. inflation rates yield mixed evidence, but careful analysis suggests that equations (8.6) and (8.7) are valid expressions of the equilibrium relationship.

Panel (A) of Figure 8.5 on page 156 plots the consumer price index for Canada and the United States since 1960. Panel (A) also plots the exchange rate between the two currencies as defined at the beginning of the chapter. Panel (B) implements a version of equation (8.6) to ascertain how well the absolute PPP hypothesis holds.

Recall from (8.1) that foreign prices expressed in domestic currency units should equal the domestic price level under the absolute PPP theory. Deviations from this equality are shown in panel (B) of Figure 8.5.[26]

If the absolute form of PPP holds, differences between the exchange rate and relative prices are plotted in Figure 8.5(C), which shows that deviations from absolute PPP have persisted. We return to this question later in the chapter. Also see **Economics Focus 8.2: Big Mac Parity**.

Finally, panel (C) also separately plots the left- and right-hand side terms of equation (8.7) for a shorter period, namely since the 1980s. If the equilibrium condition implicit in that equation always holds, then whenever Canadian inflation is higher than U.S. inflation, the Canadian dollar should depreciate, and vice versa when the Canadian inflation rate is lower than the U.S. inflation rate. Figure 8.5(C) reveals that, until the early 1990s, the Canadian inflation rate was higher than the rate in the United States. Consistent with that outcome, the Canadian dollar fell in value and then rose again as Canadian and U.S. inflation rates began converging. By the

---

24 If causality goes from inflation to exchange rates, countries with high inflation need to reduce the value of their currencies to remain competitive. Alternatively, countries may try to remain competitive by attempting to reduce the value of their currency. But this course eventually has the effect of producing more inflation. These questions have important policy implications, but they are beyond the scope of this text.

25 There is some evidence that this happened. See Pierre L. Siklos, and Mark E. Wohar, "Convergence in Interest Rates and Inflation Rates across Countries and over Time," *Review of International Economics* 5 (1997): 124–41.

26 For those with a statistics background, (8.6) in logarithms is written $\log (P^f e) = \log P$. To generate the values shown in panel (C), you have to estimate the regression $\log (P^f e) = \beta_0 + \beta_1 \log (P) + u_t$, where β_0 is the intercept and β_1 is the slope coefficient. Under absolute PPP, β_0 should be zero and the slope coefficient should be one, while u represents deviations from PPP. Estimates for the data shown in Figure 8.5 yielded the following results: $\log (P^f e) = -0.266 + 1.122 \log (P)$. The intercept was found to be statistically significant but the slope was statistically different from one rejecting the approximate validity of PPP as a *long-run* proposition. For more on related issues in this context, see W. Enders, *Applied Economic Time Series* (New York: John Wiley, 1995), Chapters 5 and 6.

ECONOMICS FOCUS 8.2   BIC MAC PARITY

The *Economist* magazine has developed an ingenious way to illustrate the application of the purchasing power parity concept. From time to time it publishes a list of the price of a McDonald's Big Mac in various countries around the world. For example,

Year	Canada (1)	U.S. (2)	Japan (3)	U.S. (4)	Japan (5)	U.S. (6)	Japan (7)	U.S. (8)	Japan (9)
		P			*P/P*^{f}		*e*		Over- or Undervalued
1986	1.89	1.60	370	1.18	.005	1.39	0.0080	Under	Under
1990	2.19	2.20	370	1.00	.006	1.16	0.0070	Under	Under
1995	2.77	2.32	391	1.19	.007	1.39	0.0170	Under	Under
1999	2.99	2.43	294	1.23	.010	1.51	0.0130	Under	Under
2001	3.33	2.54	294	1.31	.013	1.56	0.0126	Under	Over
2004	3.19	2.90	2.57	1.10	.012	1.37	0.0117	Under	Over

Sources: Calculations adapted from "Big Mac Currencies," *Economist*, 18 April 1992 and 3 April 1999; "On the Hamburger Standard," *Economist*, 6 September 1986, 5 May 1990, 15 April 1995, 21 April 2001, and 16 December 2004.

Columns 1 through 3 give the price for a Big Mac in the local currency. Columns 4 through 5 are found by applying equation (8.6); that is, the exchange rate that would equate the relative prices shown. Columns 6 and 7 give the actual values for the exchange rate at approximately the same time as the prices for Big Macs were sampled. In 1995, for example, the actual Canadian–U.S. exchange rate was $1.39, so the actual price of a Big Mac in the United States was C$3.22 (2.32 × 1.39). In other words, Big Macs were relatively cheaper in Canada or relatively more expensive in the United States in 1995 when the U.S. price is converted into its Canadian dollar equivalent. Thus, the Canadian dollar was undervalued in 1995 against the U.S. dollar since it cost more Canadian dollars to buy a unit of a foreign currency than predicted by PPP. According to the Big Mac index, the situation has not changed since 1986.

It is easy to see why the persistent undervaluation of the Canadian dollar against major currencies has contributed to complaints about the floating exchange rate regime in Canada. It is interesting to note that the publicity surrounding the Big Mac index has spawned a literature among academic economists. Some have sought to determine whether the Big Mac index is statistically consistent with PPP. The results are mixed [Click (1996) finds for PPP, Pakko and Pollard (1996) find against] in part because, as the *Economist* magazine is careful to point out, factors

such as the cost of the inputs used to make the Big Mac and sales taxes, to name but two such factors, are not controlled for in the above calculations. Some (Cumby 1996) have asked how good the index is at forecasting future exchange rates and have found the Big Mac index reasonably good in this respect.

Questions for Discussion

1. Can you think of two significant limitations of the Big Mac index as a measure of PPP?
2. According to PPP, is it possible for a currency to be undervalued for as many years as the Canadian dollar appears to have been, at least according to the Big Mac index?

Questions for Discussion

Sources

R.W. Click, "Contrarian MacParity," *Economics Letters* 53 (November 1996): 209–12.

R. Cumby, "Forecasting Exchange Rates and Relative Prices under the Hamburger Standard: Is What You Want What You Get with McParity?"NBER Working Paper 5675 (July 1996).

M.R. Pakko, and P.S. Pollard, "Purchasing Power Parity and the Big Mac," *Review of the Federal Reserve Bank of St. Louis* 78 (January–February 1996): 3–21.

early 1990s, Canada's inflation rate was consistently below the U.S. rate, but, on the whole, the Canadian dollar still fell in value throughout the decade. Notice, however, that in 2003 a sharp reversal in the fortunes of the Canadian dollar took place. Indeed, the dollar appreciated over 30% between the end of 2002 and 2004. As a result, the deviation from the predictions of PPP narrowed, as is seen in Figure 8.5(B). Indeed, since the 1980s, the exchange rate has tended to overreact to inflation differentials. Clearly then, relative PPP does not hold except over long periods, and even then there is a discrepancy between the left- and right-hand sides of equation (8.7). Indeed, persistent departures from PPP have given rise to the idea called the "peso problem," which refers to the possibility that an expected change in the exchange rate may take many years to materialize. See **Financial Focus 8.3: Peso Problems and the Pitfalls of Exchange Rate Management**. As we will see below, this discrepancy is reflected in an important measure used by economists to determine how competitive our goods are in relation to goods produced abroad.

REAL EXCHANGE RATES AND PPP

Suppose we want to find the purchasing power of money in Canada relative to the purchasing power of money in another country. In other words, we are interested in how many goods and services C$1 can buy in, say the United States, at current exchange rates. For example, if US$1 buys C$1.25, and the ratio of domestic to foreign prices is 1:1, so that price levels are the same in both countries, then the purchasing power of C$1 is simply

$$e \cdot (P/P^{US}) = 1.25$$

which is nothing more than another application of equation (8.6). Of course, it is highly unlikely that price levels in both countries will be the same, so we need to generalize the type of calculation performed above. Continuing with the same example, say inflation in Canada over a one-year period is 1%, while the U.S. inflation rate is 3%. If the two price levels were the same initially, then, after one year, the U.S. price level will become 103(100 × 1.03), while the Canadian price level will have risen to 101(100 × 1.01). Since the inflation rate is higher in the United States than in Canada, we would expect the exchange rate to appreciate, at least according to equation (8.7). Say the exchange rate falls to C$1.23 per U.S. dollar. Repeating the above calculation yields the following:

$$1.23 \cdot (101/103) = 1.206$$

The exchange rate adjusted for price differences has now fallen to 1.206 from 1.25, which represents a change of 3.52% [(1.206 − 1.25)/1.25]. Notice, however, that the price adjusted exchange rate has appreciated by more than the appreciation of the nominal exchange rate [1.6% = (1.23 − 1.25)/1.25)]. Normally, we would expect higher U.S. prices to translate into an improvement in the competitiveness of Canadian products. An appreciation means the opposite since Canadian goods become more expensive for U.S. importers to purchase.[27] Hence, in net terms, Canadian goods are more competitively priced, since the currency appreciation has not been entirely offset by the rise in U.S. prices relative to Canadian prices. It should be clear by now that calculations such as those made above can be used as indicators of competitiveness. Consequently, we can write

$$\varepsilon = \left(\frac{1}{e} \frac{P}{P^{US}} \right) \tag{8.9}$$

where ε = the **real exchange rate**—that is, the price of domestic goods relative to foreign goods. Equation (8.9) says ε is the product of the nominal exchange rate, e, and domestic prices divided by foreign prices. The real exchange rate concept has often been used as an indicator of competitiveness. Thus, an appreciation of the real exchange rate means ε *rises* or that domestic prices rise relative to foreign prices (P/P^{US} rises), and so the country has become less competitive.[28]

---

27 The flip-side is that it is cheaper for Canadians to shop in the United States or to spend their holidays there.

28 From the previous equation, set the right hand side equal to 1. Then we have $P/P^{US}=1/e$. The real exchange rate definition shown in equation (8.9) is derived from this equality. Unfortunately, some publications refer to the real exchange rate using essentially the reciprocal of this equation (as in previous editions of this textbook!), but the definition used here is the one used later (for example, in Figure 8.6). If we wish to measure competitiveness between countries, then the price index used should be for tradable goods only. Indeed, some analysts use a measure called the *terms of trade*, which measures the (real) relationship between the prices of a country's imports and exports. Other analysts prefer to look at labour costs in one country versus another as a gauge of competitiveness.

Figure 8.5   **Absolute and Relative PPP between Canada and the United States**

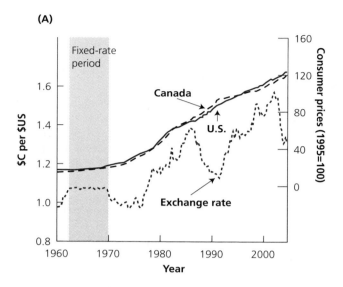

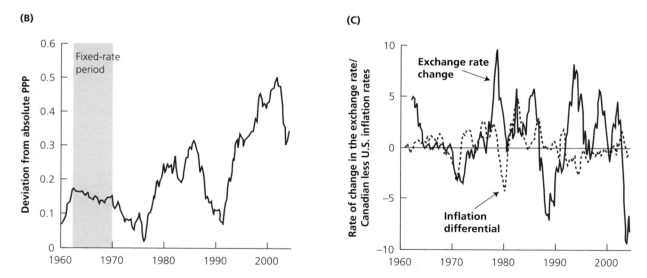

Panel (A) plots the price level for the United States and Canada since 1960, and the Canadian–U.S. exchange rate. Panel (B) plots deviations from the PPP rule (see equation [8.1]). Panel (C) reveals that deviations between the rate of change in the exchange rate and inflation have tended to fluctuate around zero over time.

Sources: *Bank of Canada Review,* Tables H1 and H8, *Survey of Current Business* (Washington, D.C.: U.S. Dept. of Commerce), and *International Financial Statistics* (Washington, D.C.: International Monetary Fund).

Note: In panel (A), the consumer price index was used to proxy P, P^f. The vertical lines in panels (A) and (B) separate the periods of fixed and flexible exchange rates between Canada and the United States. Panel (C) was created as explained in footnote 26.

FINANCIAL FOCUS 8.3

PESO PROBLEMS AND THE PIFTALLS OF EXCHANGE RATE MANAGEMENT

Milton Friedman is credited with coining the term "**peso problem**" in his analysis of the behaviour of the Mexican peso during the 1970s. This problem arises because, as we have seen, economic theory predicts that an exchange rate should be devalued if the domestic inflation rate exceeds inflation in other countries. However, in some instances, the decision to devalue may take many years more than most would expect, and the Mexican peso is a case in point. Between April 1954 and August 1976, the exchange rate of the peso was fixed at 0.08 U.S. dollars per peso. During this time, consumer prices in Mexico more than tripled while the CPI only doubled in value in the United States, Mexico's largest trading partner. It clearly took an inordinate amount of time for the peso to be devalued.

A similar event appears to have taken place in late 1994 when the Mexican government decided to allow the peso to float following a devaluation of 15% announced on 20 December 1994. The result was disastrous for the Mexican economy, whose output fell by more than 20% in 1995. The world's capital markets were shaken by the decision. For Mexico, the decision to float was supposed to be the crowning achievement of a struggle to relieve itself of previously acquired large foreign debts and the culmination of a drive to modernize its political and economic system. But the devaluation and subsequent sharp depreciation of the peso reflected the markets' view that not all was well with the Mexican economy. Much of the capital inflow during the 1990–93 period was for short-term portfolio investment ("hot money") and was not destined to finance infrastructure development or plant and equipment construction. Moreover, the Mexican banking system, largely state-owned, was financially weak. Finally, the rebellion in the Chiapas region of the country, the assassination of a presidential candidate, and political intrigue, meant that the government of President Ernesto Zedillo, elected in August 1994, inspired little confidence inside or outside Mexico. The events in Mexico, on the heels of the passage of the North American Free Trade Agreement (NAFTA), produced a crisis in the United States where politicians became concerned that, almost overnight, the U.S. economy would become flooded with now suddenly cheap Mexican goods. The U.S. government proposed a rescue package, but the newly elected Republican Congress refused to go along with the plan and President Clinton was forced to use the country's Exchange Stabilization Fund to bail out Mexico to the tune of $20 billion. Canada, Germany, and other countries and financial institutions also were somewhat reluctant participants in a deal that saw a total of $50 billion lent to Mexico. The events that transpired in major capitals around the world in late 1994 and early 1995 were the stuff of suspense novels.

Other analysts of the Mexican crisis attributed the devaluation and subsequent crisis to balance-of-payments problems, a subject we will cover in Chapter 26.

Questions for Discussion

1. What does the Mexican experience tell us about the operations of a fixed exchange rate regime?
2. What did the Mexican policymakers do wrong? Why would they have made these mistakes?

Sources

G. Graham, P. Norman, S. Fiddler, T. Bardacke, "Bitter Legacy of Battle to Bail-Out Mexico," *The Financial Times of London*, 16 February 1995.

International Capital Markets: Developments, Prospects, and Policy Issues, World Economic and Financial Surveys (Washington, D.C.: International Monetary Fund, 1995).

Martin D.D. Evans, "Peso Problems: Their Theoretical and Empirical Implications," *Handbook of Statistics*, edited by G.S. Maddala and C.R. Rao (Elsevier: North Holland, 1995).

G.A. Calvo, and E.G. Mendoza, "Reflections on Mexico's Balance-of-Payments Crisis: A Chronicle of a Death Foretold?" *Journal of International Economics* 41 (November 1996): 235–64.

Although equation (8.9) suggests that ϵ should always be one, we know that this is an equilibrium condition only. In the short run, there will be deviations away from equilibrium. If prices in Canada rise above those in other countries, so that P/P^{US} rises, the nominal exchange rate, e, will rise ($\frac{1}{e}$ will fall). Higher prices in Canada have signalled a lower purchasing power; if a dollar is worth less, it should buy smaller quantities of foreign currencies. One implication of equation (8.9) then is that any inflationary monetary policy—that is, one that leads to higher domestic prices—will create a depreciation in the Canadian dollar.

The exchange rate may take some time to find its market-clearing value, and it may overshoot its target for a while. The phenomenon of *overshooting*[29] is one of the ingredients contributing to the volatile exchange rates experienced since the Western industrialized nations returned to flexible exchange rates.[30] Therefore, the real exchange rate variable can be interpreted as a measure of departure from purchasing power parity.

Figure 8.5 (B) provides some evidence. The plot reveals that there have been some pronounced deviations from the absolute PPP condition. By the mid-1990s our competitive position had improved dramatically, although a sharp reversal began after 2002 in line with the sharp appreciation of the Canadian dollar.

UNDERSTANDING REAL EXCHANGE MOVEMENTS

The fact that the real exchange rate can deviate from its equilibrium, as understood by the theory of purchasing power parity, has led to considerable research in this area in an attempt to pro-

| **Figure 8.6** | **Canada's Real Exchange Rate and the Bank of Canada Equation, 1981–2004** |

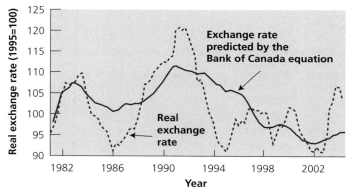

Real exchange rate movements can be used as a gauge of competitiveness. When the rate rises, domestic goods become less competitive; our competitive position improves when the real exchange rate falls. There have been large swings in the exchange rate over time and only occasionally is the behaviour of the real exchange rate consistent with equation (8.9). The line labelled *predicted by the Bank of Canada equation* represents a forecast of the real exchange rate from the estimation (using a statistical technique known as "least squares") of the following relationship written in equation form: $\Delta\boldsymbol{\epsilon}_t = constant + \alpha_0\,\boldsymbol{\epsilon}_{t-1} + \alpha_1 COM_{t-1} + \alpha_2 ENE_{t-1} + \alpha_2\,(R - R^f)_{t-1} + v_t$, where t is a time subscript, $\boldsymbol{\epsilon}$ is the real exchange rate as defined in the text, Δ indicates a change in the variable from the previous period, the α are coefficients that are estimated from the data, COM is the Bank of Canada's commodity price index (CANSIM V36382) divided by the U.S. consumer price index, ENE is the energy price index (CANSIM V735608) again divided by U.S. consumer prices, and $R - R^f$ is the differential between Canadian and U.S. short-term interest rates (measured by the yield on commercial paper; CANSIM V122491 for Canada and V122141 for the U.S.), and v is a "residual" that captures all other factors not accounted for by the other variables in the equation.

Source: International Financial Statistics (Washington, D.C.: International Monetary Fund and CANSIM). The real exchange rate measure shown here is based on relative labour costs.

---

29 The process and pattern of overshooting are similar to what we saw in Chapter 6 when we analyzed the effect on interest rates of a monetary policy aimed at reducing the growth rate of the money supply. The idea of overshooting was introduced by R. Dornbusch, "Expectations and Exchange Rate Dynamics," *Journal of Political Economy* 84 (December 1976): 1161–76.

30 From 1945 to 1971, most of the industrialized countries were on a quasi-fixed exchange rate system called the Bretton Woods System, which is explained in Chapter 25.

vide some answers. It appears that there are several explanations for the type of persistent deviations in € from its equilibrium value (of 1 or 100 in price index terms). First, goods prices do not change as quickly as exchange rates. Contractual obligations and loyalty to the consumer or buyer mean that businesses are reluctant to change their prices on a daily basis (not to mention the fact that such behaviour is costly). Second, transactions tend to be concentrated within borders or regions. Hence, additional costs from trading are not reflected in the simple PPP criterion. Third, the structure of the Canadian economy is rather different from the United States's because we are still an economy driven relatively more by commodities than by services. Therefore, large changes in commodity prices or the prices of raw materials, as happened during the summer of 1998, will have a significant impact on the Canadian dollar. Indeed, when it comes to explaining the behaviour of the real exchange rate in Canada, researchers at the Bank of Canada have found that a relatively simple relationship can predict movements in the real exchange rate reasonably well.[31] In what has come to be called the Bank of Canada equation, the real exchange rate can be explained over time by a few key factors that seem to support the contention of some that movements in the Canadian dollar are those that one would expect from a "commodity-based" economy. Essentially, the equation says that commodity prices, energy prices, the past history of the real exchange rate, as well as differences between Canadian and U.S. interest rates (we study the role of this variable next) do a fairly good job of predicting movements in the real exchange rate.[32] A version of this equation is implemented and the results are shown in Figure 8.6, where it is seen that these few variables appear to capture the main determinants of real exchange rate movements in Canada.[33]

There is also the issue of productivity. Some analysts have pointed out that the productivity of the Canadian economy is lower than that of the United States, though there are likely to be considerable differences across sectors in productivity performance.[34] Not surprisingly, large variations in the exchange rate (sometimes referred to as excess exchange rate volatility), and the role played by Bank of Canada policy in this context, have led to suggestions that Canada should consider a monetary union with the United States, a topic we take up in more detail in Chapter 24.

The notion that real exchange rate fluctuations reflect productivity differences is known as the Balassa-Samuelson hypothesis.[35] A rise in productivity usually is accompanied by a rise in wages as labour's output becomes relatively more valuable. This eventually has the effect of raising P in equation (8.9), thereby contributing to a rise in the real exchange rate, other things being equal. Unfortunately, the evidence for this hypothesis is quite mixed. Of course, a depreciation of the nominal exchange rate also makes it more expensive to invest in new technologies, especially if they come from abroad. As a consequence, firms may prefer to "invest" in labour rather than capital, causing a further deterioration in labour productivity, with negative consequences for the real exchange rate.

Alternatively, if a depreciation of the Canadian dollar occurs but PPP fails to hold, in the short-run at least (see equation (8.1)), then this has the same effect as if Canadian prices fell relative to

31 See R. Amano and S. van Norden, "A Forecasting Equation for the Canada-U.S. Dollar Exchange Rate," in *The Exchange Rate and the Economy*, Proceedings of a Conference Held at the Bank of Canada. June 1992 (Ottawa: Bank of Canada, 1992): 207–65.

32 See D. Laidler and S. Aba, "The Canadian Dollar: Still a Commodity Currency," *Backgrounder* (Toronto: C.D. Howe Institute), 11 January 2001, "Productivity and the Dollar," *Commentary* No. 158 (Toronto: C.D. Howe Institute), February 2002, and R. Lafrance and L. Schembri, "The Exchange Rate, Productivity, and the Standard of Living," *Bank of Canada Review* (Winter 1999–2000): 17–28.

33 The Bank of Canada equation easily outperforms some competing models such as the random walk approach (we will see this model repeatedly throughout the text) in which the best forecast for next year's real exchange rate is this year's value.

34 Some readers will note that changes in the exchange rate (see Figure 8.5) appear to fluctuate around zero over long periods. For this reason, the exchange rate seems to follow a "random walk," a phenomenon that is common to many time series as we shall see (e.g., stock prices and consumption). A growing literature documents how changes in technology— and, hence, productivity—or in tastes, give rise to this type of random walk behaviour. As the issues go beyond the scope of this paper, readers might find the following Web site (**http://www.geocities.com/brian_m_doyle/open.html**) a useful resource for recent research in open economy macroeconomics.

35 B. Balassa, "The Purchasing Power Parity Doctrine: A Reappraisal," *Journal of Political Economy*, 72 (December 1964): 584–96, and P. Samuelson, "Theoretical Notes on Trade Problems," *Review of Economics and Statistics* 46: 145–54.

ECONOMICS FOCUS 8.3

WHY THE BALASSA-SAMUELSON EFFECT MATTERS

In many respects, the notion of a disequilibrium in the exchange rate that persists for some time was thought to be an interesting phenomenon, but one without much practical implication. However, once the Soviet Union broke up in the early 1990s, several countries began to liberalize their economies. This meant that those industries that competed on the world market had to become as productive and efficient as their foreign rivals, or their output would not sell. In contrast, the portion of the economy that does not trade internationally might take much longer to achieve a level of efficiency comparable to that found in competing economies. The problem is that workers in industries that lag in productivity want their wages to rise as fast as those in the industries that have become much more productive, and this will have implications for the overall behaviour of the price level. This phenomenon, generally called the Balassa-Samuelson effect (though another British economist, Roy Harrod, deserves some credit here too), has proven to be a major policy issue, especially among the emerging market economies that have just joined the European Union (such as Poland, the Czech Republic, and Hungary), since these same countries aspire to adopt the Euro, the common European currency, which requires that a fixed exchange rate be established at the time the domestic currency is exchanged for the common currency. If the Balassa-Samuelson effect is large, it is likely that the chosen exchange rate at the time of the conversion to the

Euro will be unfavourable because the economies of emerging markets will become relatively uncompetitive. There is considerable debate about the empirical significance of the Balassa-Samuelson effect, with some (Égert) suggesting that its existence does not pose a problem. However, others (Breuss and Hochreiter) are concerned about the problem, and officials of the European Central Bank, among others, have recognized the challenges posed by the Balassa-Samuelson effect (Padoa-Schioppa).

Sources

F. Breuss, E. Hochreiter (Eds), *Challenges for Central Banks in an Enlarged EMU* (Vienna and New York: Springer, 2005).

B. Égert, "Estimating the Impact of the Balassa-Samuelson Effect on Inflation and the Real Exchange Rate During the Transition," *Economic Systems* 26 (2002): 1-16.

T. Padoa-Schioppa, "Trajectories toward the Euro and the Role of ERM II," *International Finance* 6 (1) 2003: 129-144.

Questions for Discussion

1. Explain how an emerging market can become less competitive if the Balassa-Samuelson effect is large.
2. What does the existence of the Balassa-Samuelson effect imply for EU newcomers who desire to join the Euro area?

the U.S. Since Canadian prices are now relatively lower, Canadian firms have no incentive to invest in labour or capital improvements because the exchange rate has done the job for them. The "lazy" Canadian hypothesis, as it might be called, goes against the notion that firms are profit maximizers. Moreover, if unused productivity improvements could be exploited by someone else, why have such firms not been prime candidates for a takeover? Finally, is the Canadian market so uncompetitive that there are no domestic entrepreneurs to exploit a profitable opportunity? Although the hypothesis has some political appeal, even those who support such views find the evidence inconclusive.[36]

Beyond the forecasting question raised above, if models such as the Bank of Canada equation perform reasonably well, this suggests that the Bank of Canada considers whether it should respond to exchange rate movements. Moreover, since the exchange rate is an asset price, as are stock prices, bond prices, and even housing prices, the more general policy question arises whether the central bank ought to respond to asset price movements more generally.

---

36 See, for example, T. Courchene and R. Harris, "From Fixing to Monetary Union: Options for North American Currency Integration," Commentary (Toronto: C.D. Howe Institute), No. 127, 1999, and R. Harris, "The NAMU Debate," *Canadian Public Policy* 25 (1999). A complication in the debate is the role the tax system plays in promoting or discouraging productivity improvements in Canada. Obviously, this question is beyond the scope of this text.

8.7 INTERNATIONAL LINKAGES IN INTEREST RATES

BASIC CONCEPTS

Canada's is a small, open economy in a world of increasing *globalization*. Capital funds can cross borders freely, a phenomenon called **capital mobility**, which can influence and be influenced by international differences in exchange rates.

When investors purchase bonds and other financial instruments denominated in foreign currencies, they open themselves to *foreign exchange* risk.

Consider an investor who has to choose between investing in a one-year Government of Canada bond or a one-year U.S. Treasury bill. The yield on the Canadian bond is 10%, while the yield on the U.S. security is 8%. Is the Canadian investment, with its higher interest rate, automatically the better one? The answer depends on the difference between the Canadian–U.S. dollar exchange rate today versus the one that will prevail one year from today.[37] Alternatively, the answer depends on the difference between the Canadian–U.S. dollar yield today and the foreign exchange rate brought forward one year (including any adjustments for transactions costs). Let us consider each strategy in turn.

If the investor buys either asset today and plans to wait until it matures and then put the proceeds into Canadian dollars, the investor must make a calculation about the implicit **forward exchange rate**, which is the future exchange rate that would make him or her indifferent between holding Canadian and U.S. securities for that amount of time.[38]

Each dollar invested in Canada will yield $1.10 one year from today since

$$\$1 \times (1 + R) = \$1 \times (1.10) = \$1.10$$

If the investor chooses the U.S.-dollar-denominated investment, each dollar will yield $1.08 one year later since

$$\$1 \times (1 + R) = \$1 \times (1.08) = \$1.08$$

But that return is still in U.S. dollars. To compare the two returns, the investor has to apply exchange rates. The purchase will be at today's spot exchange rate. Suppose it stands at $1.38. One Canadian dollar will buy roughly US$0.72 (= C$1.00/$1.38). But the spot exchange rate for a year from

today is not known, so the investor must calculate the implicit forward rate. The solution is obtained as follows:

| Return per Canadian Dollar after One Year | = | Return per Canadian Dollar after One Year Invested in the United States | × | Implicit Forward Exchange Rate |

$$\$1 \times (1.10) = \left(\frac{\$1}{\$1.38}\right)(1.08)(e^{f})$$

The left-hand side of the equation is simply the Canadian-dollar return after one year invested at 10% in the Government of Canada bond. The first term on the right-hand side shows the amount of U.S. dollars that can be purchased for each Canadian dollar at a spot exchange rate of $1.38, and the second is simply the U.S. return after one year. The only unknown is e^{f}, which represents the one-year implicit forward exchange rate necessary to equate the yields on the Canadian and U.S. investments.

Solving our equation for e^{f}, we obtain $1.41, since

---

37 Throughout the following discussion, we will suppose that a system of perfectly flexible exchange rates prevails. Although this assumption is not entirely realistic, it allows us to focus on the link between exchange rates and interest rates.

38 In what follows, we abstract from transaction costs.

$$\left(\frac{\$1}{\$1.38}\right)(1.08) \times \$1.41 = \$1.10$$

Notice that if the Canadian dollar is expected to depreciate, what is lost in terms of the yield difference between the U.S. and Canadian investments (10% − 8% = 2%) is recovered because more Canadian dollars will be obtained in the future for each U.S. dollar held today. We can write this result more generally as

$$\frac{(1 + R)}{(1 + R^f)} = \frac{e^f}{e^s} \tag{8.10}$$

where

R = annual yield on a Canadian-dollar-denominated asset
R^f = annual yield on a foreign-denominated asset
e^f = one-year implicit forward exchange rate
e^s = spot exchange rate

Equation (8.10) allows us to compute any implicit forward exchange rate, one that makes the investor indifferent between holding an asset denominated in Canadian dollars and one de-nominated in any foreign currency. We can also rearrange equation (8.10) to solve for the implicit forward rate to obtain

$$e^f = \left[\frac{(1 + R)}{(1 + R^f)}\right] e^s \tag{8.11}$$

We will see (Chapter 15) that a forward transaction can be used to hedge against foreign ex-change risk. By hedging foreign exchange risk and investing in a foreign currency, an investor is engaging in what is known as *covered interest arbitrage*. Quotes for forward exchange rates for a variety of maturities are readily available in the financial press. To continue our example, say the one-year forward rate is $1.39. What is the significance of the difference between this rate and the implicit forward exchange rate of $1.41? It means that the 2% interest rate differential is not entirely covered by the differential between the spot and forward exchange rates since, by equa-tion (8.10), we obtain

$$\frac{1.39}{1.38} < \frac{1.10}{1.08}$$

or

$$1.01 < 1.02$$

Therefore, *if the market is correct*, our U.S. investment will yield less than the Canadian investment.

Conversely, if the actual implicit forward rate were, say, $1.42, there would be added profit in the U.S. investment since, again according to equation (8.10),

$$\frac{1.42}{1.38} > \frac{1.10}{1.08}$$

or

$$1.03 > 1.02$$

Presumably, the market will quickly notice any such profit opportunities and act on them until the differential is eliminated. But for those lucky investors who are able to benefit from such in-vestment strategies, this is the essence of **covered interest arbitrage**, which means the purchase and sale of assets denominated in different currencies to generate a profit on potential changes in exchange rates.

The implication, however, is that the covered interest arbitrage is only a temporary phe-nomenon. Real-world data confirm the point. Ideally, the covered interest differential should be about zero or, at least, average close to zero over a period. Indeed, statistically speaking, the average has been close to zero since 1970, although there were persistent departures after 1978.[39]

If we regard the case in which arbitrage opportunities are no longer present as an equilibrium condition, this implies what is known as the **interest rate parity** condition. If the actual and implicit forward exchange rates provide the investor with information about what the market expects exchange rates to be in the future, and if this information is correct on average, the interest rate parity condition is simply

Canadian Dollar Interest Rate	=	Foreign Interest Rate	+	Expected Percentage Change in the Expected Rate

or, using the notation introduced earlier,

$$R = R^f + \left(\frac{e^{exp} - e^s}{e^s} \right) \tag{8.12}$$

where $e^f = e^{exp}$. That is, the forward exchange rate, e^f, proxies the expected exchange rate, e^{exp}, at maturity.

Equation (8.12) follows from equations (8.10) and (8.11). We can verify the point by using our hypothesized numerical values:

$$10\% = 8\% + \left(\frac{1.41 - 1.38}{1.38} \right)$$

$$10\% = 8\% + 2\%$$

Thus, in our numerical example, investors are indifferent between the U.S. and Canadian investments so long as the Canadian dollar is expected to depreciate relative to the U.S. dollar. Although such an equality holds as an equilibrium condition, arbitrage is possible as the markets seek equilibrium. Empirical research suggests that equation (8.12) is a good approximation for Canadian and U.S. data.[40]

A CASE STUDY

Table 8.4 also suggests that interest rate parity is a reasonable approximation of reality in many instances. The annual yields on three-month Eurodeposit rates denominated in four different currencies, selected at random, are listed along with the relevant spot and three-month forward exchange rates and the differential with the Canadian yield. In every case, the expected rate of change in the U.S. dollar is approximately the same as the yield differential. Changes in interest rates quickly show up in the market for foreign exchange as an expected depreciation or appreciation of a particular currency. Therefore, foreign interest rates need have no lasting influence on Canadian interest rates so long as (1) exchange rates float freely, and (2) there is considerable capital mobility—which is also known as the condition of internationally integrated markets.

Clearly, both conditions are violated occasionally, but apparently not in a systematic fashion. The illustrations in Table 8.4 suggest that the foreign exchange market is fairly efficient. It may

---

39 Roughly speaking, after the Bank of Canada expressed public concern over exchange rate fluctuations and apparently began to try to manage them. See, for example, P. Howitt, *Monetary Policy in Transition: A Study of Bank of Canada Policy, 1982–85* (Montreal: C.D. Howe Institute, 1986), Chapter 6.

40 See A.W. Gregory, "Testing Interest Rate Parity and Rational Expectations for Canada and the United States," *Canadian Journal of Economics* 20 (May 1987): 289–305; P. Boothe, "Interest Parity, Cointegration, and the Term Structure in Canada and the United States," *Canadian Journal of Economics* 24 (August 1991): 595–603; P.L. Siklos, and M.E. Wohor, "Convergence in Interest Rates and Inflation Rates across Countries and over Time," *Review of International Economics* 5 (1997): 124–41.

Table 8.4	**A Case Study of Interest Rate Parity: Eurodeposits**				
	(1)	**(2)**	**(3)**	**(4)**	**(5)**
	Three-Month Eurodeposit Rate	**Spot Exchange Rate**	**Three-Month Forward Exchange Rate**	**Interest Rate Differential**	**Expected Percentage Change in the Exchange Rate**
U.S. dollar	6.08	1.4755	1.4718	−1.15	−1.00
Canadian dollar	4.93	—	—	—	—
Euro	3.37	1.5134	1.5198	+1.56	+1.69
Japanese yen	0.18	69.3800	68.5500	+4.75	+4.86
British pound	5.87	2.3993	2.3945	−0.94	−0.80

Note: The exchange rates are in columns (2) and (3). Column (4) is the difference between the Canadian yield and that in other currencies. Column (5) is the percentage difference between columns (3) and (2) converted to an annual basis. Exchange rates are C$ per unit of the foreign currency, except for the ¥, which is expressed as ¥ per C$. Calculations are rounded. For example, the expected change in the U.S. dollar Eurodeposit is calculated as

$$\left[\frac{(1.4718 - 1.4755)}{1.4755} \right] \times 400 = -1.00$$

also be helpful, by way of a summary, to graphically illustrate the connection between exchange rates and returns expressed in different currencies.

INTEREST RATES AND EXCHANGE RATES: A DIAGRAMMATIC EXPOSITION

Figure 8.7(A) shows the relationship between relative returns and the exchange rate. For a given domestic interest rate (R), the foreign interest rate is inversely related to the exchange rate. Why? Because, according to equation (8.12), if we hold constant the left-hand side, (R), then the two right-hand-side terms must be inversely related. When no exchange rate appreciation or depreciation is expected, then interest rates in two countries should be the same (R 5 Rf in terms of equation 8.12). This occurs at the intersection of the R and Rf curves. If the Canadian dollar is expected to to depreciate vis-à-vis the U.S. dollar ($e^{exp} > e^s$) then the U.S. interest rates can be lower than Canadian rates and still satisfy the interest rate parity equation (8.12). This occurs to the right of the intersection of the R and Rf curves.

Conversely, an expected appreciation ($e^{exp} > e^s$) will mean higher U.S. interest rates relative to Canada. This framework is also useful because it can help us to understand the impact of, say, an increase in expected inflation or the real interest rate. These cases are illustrated in Figure 8.7(B). Starting from the initial equilibrium position at point A, suppose that the real interest rate rises in Canada. This means, according to the Fisher equation (recall from Chapter 5: $R = \rho + \pi^e$, where ρ is the real interest rate and π^e is the expected inflation rate), that domestic nominal interest rates will rise. This expectation is illustrated by the upward shift in the R curve to R_1 from R_0. The result is an appreciation of the Canadian dollar as shown by point B. This result should not be surprising since a higher Canadian real interest rate means that Canadian returns are more attractive than those on U.S. investments. If, on the other hand, the rise in the Canadian nominal interest rate were due to higher expectations of inflation in Canada then, again according to the Fisher equation, this would translate into a *lower* real interest rate, which would mean that capital would flow out of Canada into the United States, raising the foreign interest rate curve to R_1^f from R_0^f. The new equilibrium, at point C, would imply a depreciation of the currency, again as predicted by equation (8.12).

Also note that, ignoring transactions costs, we have shown that there will always be the appearance of some arbitrage opportunities, even though few will actually exist. Arbitrage is an expression of the profitable opportunities that can arise in foreign exchange transactions (see **Economics Focus 8.4: What Is Arbitrage?**) It may be that if there are strong preferences for domestic financial instruments over foreign ones or if the risk of default differs across countries, what appear to be arbitrage opportunities are, in fact, a risk premium of the kind that we explored in this chapter and that we will explore in Chapter 14.

Notice, finally, that Figure 8.7(B) can also be used to see how a central bank might use higher domestic interest rates to offset an expected depreciation (i.e., higher e^{exp}). We leave this as a problem. Indeed, this was the prescription followed by many countries during the Asian crisis as well as crises that affected some European countries in 1992 (see Chapter 24). The basic idea, of course, as mentioned earlier, is that higher interest rates make domestic financial assets relatively more attractive. But there is a potential catch not obvious from Figure 8.7: When interest rates are higher there is also a greater probability that, because debts are more expensive to carry, default rates will rise. We shall study this possibility in Chapter 13.[41]

8.8   HYSTERESIS

An earlier section on "Real Exchange Rates and PPP" revealed that, at least in terms of PPP, an overvalued or undervalued Canadian dollar can persist for some time. Recently, some econo-

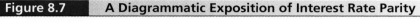

Figure 8.7   A Diagrammatic Exposition of Interest Rate Parity

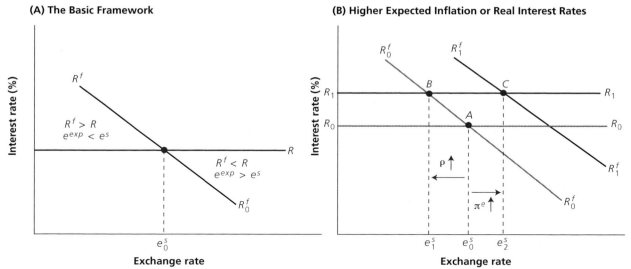

Panel (A) illustrates equation (8.12) in a diagrammatic fashion. For a given domestic interest rate, R, the foreign interest rate, R^f, is inversely related to the exchange rate. A depreciated exchange rate means that Canadian rates have to rise for foreign holders of Canadian dollars to hold onto them or to prevent outflows of Canadian investments to the United States. Panel (B) illustrates what happens to the exchange rate when the Canadian real interest rate rises or when the Canadian expected inflation rate rises. In both cases, the Canadian nominal interest rate rises, but with quite different implications for the exchange rate. A higher real interest rate leads to an appreciation of the Canadian dollar because Canadian investments are relatively more attractive, whereas a rise in Canadian expected inflation has the opposite effect, which leads, therefore, to a depreciation of the Canadian dollar.

---

41 Nobel laureate Joseph Stiglitz, for one, believes that it is precisely this type of thinking that led to the Asian financial crisis in the first place. Although one can question whether the scenario depicted above applies to the Canadian situation, it should be noted that Canada's public debt (and some of its private debt too) was downgraded for several years during the 1990s for a variety of reasons we study throughout this text. See J. Stiglitz, "Financial Market Stability and Monetary Policy," *Pacific Economic Review* 7(February 2002): 3–12.

ECONOMICS FOCUS 8.4 — WHAT IS ARBITRAGE?

Arbitrage comes from the French word "arbitre" (referee) and refers to the fact that markets act as a referee of sorts in influencing prices. Indeed, as explained in this chapter, market participants, by their actions, will quickly exploit profitable opportunities, whether they are available in one location or in different locations. In the examples considered in this chapter, arbitrage profits can arise from the sale and purchase of assets that match (in terms to maturity and risk characteristics) but are denominated in different currencies to obtain a profit until the interest rate parity condition takes hold.

Typically, arbitrage opportunities in the market for foreign exchange arise when the values of two currencies in relation to a third are inconsistent. For example, if the Canadian dollar is quoted at $1.38 in terms of the U.S. dollar and $0.0128 per Japanese yen, we would expect that a U.S. dollar could be purchased for ¥107.27, ignoring transaction costs. If this is not the case, profitable opportunities exist to sell one currency for another to buy a third currency.

The market for foreign exchange adjusts so quickly to any such discrepancies, however, that they are very difficult to detect, and they disappear quickly. This fact does not prevent the search for new ways to seek profit in foreign exchange markets. Recent forecasting techniques rely on mathematical models of "chaos." These models try to find patterns in data that appear to behave in a chaotic fashion. But even if such models provide new arbitrage opportunities, they are far from perfect. Occasionally there is no substitute for a trader's experience in currency markets. Moreover, as we have seen, exchange rates are prone to "overshooting"; that is, they change sharply when there is a change in the interest rate differential but return to the equilibrium fairly slowly. Various other inefficiencies have also been reported.

Questions for Discussion

1. Would improvements in computing and communications decrease arbitrage opportunities? Why or why not?
2. Could false news reports or some kind of overreaction to some news reports affect arbitrage opportunities in different markets?

Sources

R.L. Hudson, "Currency Traders' Computers Improve," *Wall Street Journal* (25 September 1992): A5.

"In Search of Inefficiency," *Economist* (5 September 1992): 81.

H. Riehl, and R. Rodriguez, *Foreign Exchange and Money Markets: Managing Foreign and Domestic Currency Operations* (New York: McGraw-Hill, 1977), Chapter 8.

mists[42] have found that the slow response of some economic variables appears to be a fairly pervasive phenomenon. In the present context, the problem, called *hysteresis*,[43] refers to an effect that does not disappear when the causes of the over- or undervaluation themselves fade away. One of the implications of the result is that it makes exchange rate forecasting that much more difficult. Hysteresis does *not* mean that deviations from PPP will never be corrected. Figure 8.6, for example, makes it clear that this is not so. What it does mean is that the length of time before equilibrium is restored is itself uncertain.

What forces might prompt the hysteresis phenomenon? As noted earlier, there is some inflexibility in wages and prices in most countries, certainly relative to the behaviour of the exchange rate under the floating regime. In addition, there may be other institutional barriers to the adjustment in prices when exchange rate changes originate in either the labour market or in the costs of trading between different countries. For example, it may not make much sense for many firms to change prices as frequently as the exchange rate changes. Not only is this costly, but it is also likely that consumers will be put off by too much price volatility. Alternatively, firms may find it preferable to maintain prices, even if the exchange rate has changed permanently, to maintain market share or because they are able to adjust some other costs of production. In any event, the rapid appreciation in the Canadian dollar in 2003 and 2004 took place even though inflation remained fairly stable, suggesting that hysteresis is a real phenomenon.

---

42 A nice statement of the issues covered in this section is in P.R. Krugman, *Exchange Rate Instability* (Cambridge, Mass.: The MIT Press, 1989).

43 The term was originally used in physics to describe the effect of the previous history of some phenomenon on its subsequent development.

SUMMARY

- An exchange rate expresses the relative price of two currencies.

- In the absence of transactions costs or other market positions, the prices of commodities should be the same in two countries. This relationship is known as the law of one price.

- Two principal exchange rate systems exist: fixed exchange rates, which are set by government regulation, and flexible exchange rates, which are set by the demand for and supply of foreign exchange.

- Exchange rate determination can be explained by the focus of demand and supply for foreign exchange.

- Canada typically has experienced current account deficits and capital account surpluses.

- Trade is dependent in part on the exchange rate. Central banks typically intervene in foreign exchange markets to reduce volatility in the exchange rate.

- Central banks can intervene through open market operations. To prevent any impact from foreign exchange operations on the domestic money supply, the Bank of Canada can sterilize the flow of foreign exchange.

- Trade permits countries to expand consumption at the expense of foreign debt, but a danger exists that the current account deficit can reach crisis proportions.

- Current account deficits have been linked to government deficits, the so-called twin deficits.

- The consequences of international trading in goods and money become clear in a nation's balance of payments, which consists of a current account and capital account. Both accounts record the value of movements of goods, services, and money between that country and the rest of the world.

- The loanable funds model extended to an open economy implies that the supply of loanable funds is more elastic than in a closed economy.

- Purchasing power parity (PPP) comes in two forms. Absolute PPP says that the exchange rate is simply the relative price of domestic versus foreign goods. Relative PPP says that exchange rate changes reflect differences in inflation rates between two countries.

- The real exchange rate expresses relative prices between two countries in purchasing power terms.

- Interest rates can differ because of the currency in which the debt is denominated. The relationship between interest rates in different countries is explained by the interest rate parity condition: Interest rates will differ between countries by the expected change in the exchange rate.

- Hysteresis refers to forces that prevent an equilibrium relationship from being restored for a long time even though the fundamentals of the relationship suggest that equilibrium conditions exist. This is one hypothesis that has been advanced to explain persistent departures from PPP. Institutional factors may be one reason for the hysteresis phenomenon.

IMPORTANT TERMS

appreciation, 137
balance of payments (BOP), 144
capital account, 146
capital mobility, 161
covered interest arbitrage, 162
cross-rate, 137
current account, 144
depreciation, 137
devaluation, 137

exchange rate, 136
fixed exchange rate regime, 139
flexible exchange rate regime, 139
forward exchange rate, 161
interest rate parity, 163
law of one price, 138
managed ("dirty") float regime, 139
peso problem, 157
purchasing power, 152

PROBLEMS

1. Assume the following exchange rates:

Currency	Exchange Rate (C$ per unit of the foreign currency)
United States	1.1368
United Kingdom	2.0268
France	0.2076
Germany	0.7096
Japan	0.0080

   Calculate cross-rates for

   (a) yen per Deutschmark

   (b) pounds per French franc

   (c) Deutschmark per U.S. dollar

2. As noted in the **Economics Focus 8.2: Big Mac Parity**, the *Economist* publishes prices for a Big Mac in a variety of countries. In the 1990 survey a Big Mac that cost C$2.19 cost 3900 lire in Italy. The exchange rate between the lira and the Canadian dollar was 0.00098 (or 1023.86 lire per Canadian dollar). What was the price of a Big Mac in Canada in terms of lire? The Canadian price of a Big Mac in Italy? For absolute PPP to hold, should the dollar have appreciated or depreciated relative to the lira? Explain.

3. Below are some hypothetical exchange rate data for three countries' currencies in U.S. dollars. (US$ per unit of the foreign currency)

	1998	1999	2000
Canada	0.813	0.845	0.857
Denmark	0.149	0.137	0.159
Spain	0.009	0.008	0.010

   If relative PPP holds, which country had relatively higher inflation than the United States in 1999 and 2000? Explain your answer.

4. The Canadian consumer price index (using a base year of 1992 = 100) stood at 55.9 in 1978 and 119.5 in 1990. The U.S. price index stood at 61.5 in 1978 and 122.0 in 1990, again at 1986 prices. The exchange rate against the U.S. dollar similarly went from 1.1402 in 1978 to 1.1668 in 1990. If absolute PPP holds, was the Canadian dollar overvalued or undervalued relative to the U.S. dollar in 1990? (Since the data cover a period of 12 years, you will find it easier to make the calculations on an annual basis; that is, dividing by the number of years.) Had you known this would happen, would you have bought or sold Canadian dollars in the foreign exchange market? Explain your answer.

5. Suppose that the Bank of Canada and the U.S. Federal Reserve peg their currencies against each other such that the Canadian dollar is undervalued relative to the U.S. dollar. Which central bank will gain foreign exchange reserves? Which bank will lose reserves? Explain your answer.

6. Suppose the Bank of Canada intervenes in the foreign exchange market and sells Canadian dollars. How does this action affect Canada's monetary base? Use T-accounts for your answer.

7. Suppose that in the situation illustrated in Figure 8.3 the Bank of Canada pegged the exchange rate at $1.25. Would the currency be undervalued or overvalued? Why? Explain.

8. Suppose that in Figure 8.3, Canadian trading shifted toward the purchase of more U.S.-made goods. Would the Canadian dollar appreciate or depreciate? If the Bank of Canada pegged the exchange rate at $1.20, would the resulting exchange rate be over- or undervalued?

9. Show what would happen to the exchange rate if interest rates in Canada rose above U.S. interest rates. Use a diagram like the one in Figure 8.1 to explain your answer.

10. In the May 2004 issue of *The Economist*'s Big Mac index, the following data were reported for a selection of countries:

Country	Big Mac price in CAD dollars	Implied PPP of the CAD dollar	Under (-)/over (+) valuation against the dollar (%)
Britain	4.61	1.45	-42
U.S.	3.97	1.24	-15
Euro area	4.49	1.41	-9

Based on the above figures can you estimate the actual exchange rate levels in the three countries when the index was computed? Where would you buy a Big Mac if you ignored travel and transactions costs? Explain.

11. Suppose that foreigners suddenly felt that it had become much riskier to invest in Canada. What would happen to the $LF^s + LF^{sf}$ curve depicted in Figure 8.4? to the equilibrium interest rate? Explain.

12. The 1993 version of the *Economist* Big Mac parity survey showed the following price and exchange rate data. Find the PPP exchange rate. Is the Canadian dollar over- or undervalued? (The prices shown are in domestic currency units; the exchange rate shown is against the Canadian dollar.)

Country	Domestic Price	Actual e
Canada	2.76	
U.S.	2.28	1.260
France	18.50	0.190
Japan	391.00	0.009
Germany	4.60	0.630

13. Calculate the percentage *over-* or *under*valuation of the exchange rates in **Economics Focus 8.2** and in the question above.

14. According to the OECD, the following are the purchasing power parities for Canada vis-à-vis the United States for the years given in parentheses: 1.28 (1985), 1.30 (1990), 1.26 (1992), and 1.25 (1993). The following are the closing exchange rates for the same years, respectively: 1.40, 1.16, 1.27, 1.32. Was the Candian dollar overvalued or undervalued for each of these years? Explain.

15. Use the exchange rate determination framework (Figure 8.1) to explain the consequences for Mexico's reserves of an overvalued exchange rate.

16. Use the loanable funds framework (Figure 8.4) to illustrate the consequences of Mexico's attempt to keep interest rates artificially high (given the fixed exchange rate) as well as the implications of the devaluation/depreciation for the demand for Mexican bonds. Explain.

17. The exchange rate is ¥120 per Canadian dollar (or 0.0083 Canadian dollars per yen). The one-year interest rate is 10% in Canada and 6% in Japan. What is the implicit one-year forward exchange rate?

18. Suppose you are given the following data:

Country	Currency	Yield on Two-Year Government Bonds
Canada	$	11.0%
United States	$	7.0%
Switzerland	SFr	6.5%
United Kingdom	£	12.0%

What is the annual expected appreciation or depreciation of the Canadian dollar relative to the other currencies in the table?

19. Suppose that the implicit forward rate is $2.00 per £, but the actual forward rate is $2.05 per £. Is there any profit to be made? If so, how?

20. Trace out the effect of the following using the framework developed to illustrate diagrammatically the interest parity concept (Figure 8.7):

    (a) a fall in the Canadian real interest rate

    (b) a rise in the Canadian money supply (Hint: go back to Chapter 6 and review the liquidity preference model)

    (c) a rise in U.S. interest rates

    (d) a rise in the expected exchange rate

    Use diagrams for your answer.

21. The following table was reported in an article from *The Globe and Mail*.

    Answer the following questions based on the table.

    (a) Which countries' exchange rates appreciated or depreciated in 1995?

    (b) Canada's return in local currency is the highest among this group of countries. Can risk considerations explain this result?

Country	1995 Percentage Return in Local Currency	In Terms of U.S. dollars
Canada	20.4	23.3
Spain	20.0	30.7
Australia	19.4	15.0
The Netherlands	18.5	28.5
Italy	18.0	21.4
Belgium	17.5	27.4
Britain	17.0	17.0
United States	16.9	16.9
Germany	16.9	26.6
France	16.8	27.7
Japan	13.9	10.5

Reprinted with permission from *The Globe and Mail*.

Source: M. Stimson, "Foreigners Love Canadian Dollar Bonds," *The Globe and Mail,* 24 February 1996.

22. Suppose that Canada decides to adopt the gold standard at an exchange rate of $1.15. What would happen to Canada's gold reserves? Use Figure 8.3 to provide an answer and an explanation.

23. If savings are persistently below investment explain the implications for the "twin deficits." Use equation (8.5) for your answer.

24. Suppose that the nominal exchange rate against the U.S. dollar is $1.30, and inflation is 4% in Canada and 2% in the U.S. Assuming that the price levels in the U.S. and Canada are the same in year 0, and that the nominal exchange rate one year later is $1.33, what is the real exchange rate? Show calculations and explain your answer.

25. Verify the calculations in Table 8.4.

DISCUSSION QUESTIONS

1. Say a country's inflation rate is higher than the U.S. inflation rate by 2%, but its exchange rate has depreciated over the same period by only 1% against the U.S. dollar. Has the country's competitive position improved? Explain. Does it matter over how many years such calculations are made? Why?

2. Discuss various reasons why actual exchange rates might deviate from their equilibrium values for long periods.

3. Why do profitable opportunities in foreign exchange markets disappear so quickly?

4. What are some of the arguments for and against the liberalization of capital flows? Discuss.

5. Write out and explain the equilibrium condition for covered interest arbitrage.

6. Assume that inflation is 3% in the UK, 2% in Japan, 4% in the United States, and 1% in Canada. What would you expect would happen to the exchange rate of the Canadian dollar against the currencies of these countries?

7. Suppose that the real return on investments in Canada is lower than in the United States. What impact would this have on the exchange rate?

8. Explain the connection between interest rate parity and purchasing power parity theories.

9. If a country has a current account deficit, is it a net lender or borrower to the rest of the world? Should a country be concerned if it runs such a deficit? Explain your answer.

10. Explain how a balance-of-payments disequilibrium can be self-correcting.

11. Explain why speculative attacks on a currency—this occurs when foreign exchange market participants bet that a currency will have to devalue or revalue in the near future—are more prevalent under a fixed exchange rate system than under a managed float.

12. How can a current account surplus contribute to generating inflation? Explain your answer.

13. Under flexible exchange rates, foreign exchange transactions have no direct effects on the domestic money supply. Explain why or why not.

14. Under flexible exchange rates, countries are able to pursue more independent monetary policies. Comment.

15. What is sterilization?

16. What is the twin deficit and why is it a policy concern?

17. How do an appreciating Canadian dollar and lower Canadian interest rates than those of the United States contribute to creating a net capital outflow?

18. Why is excessive exchange rate volatility considered economically undesirable?

19. A country with a current account deficit can maintain a capital account surplus by raising domestic interest rates. Explain.

20. Explain the principles behind the Balassa-Samuelson effect.

21. Assess how well the Bank of Canada equation explains real exchange rate movements. Are there any other variables you might consider adding to this equation? Why?

22. Is there a connection between the hysteresis concept and the finding that there are large and persistent departures from PPP, at least according to Figure 8.5?

ONLINE APPLICATIONS

1. Go to the Bank of Canada's Web site at **www.bankofcanada.ca/en/exchange_ org_pdf.html**. (Note: You will need the Adobe Reader, which is available free from **www.adobe.com**.) Compare the average annual exchange rate for the U.S. dollar, the Yen, and the euro in terms of the Canadian dollar. Which currencies appreciated against the Canadian dollar? Which ones depreciated? Go back to the Exchange rates page of the Bank of Canada's Web site and click on *Currency Converter*. See how many exchange rates the Canadian dollar can be expressed in and examine the current exchange rate for some countries.

2. Go to the *Economist* magazine's Web site at **www.economist.com** (Note: You may need to pay a fee to register.) Find previous articles on the Big Mac. Are most currencies over- or undervalued against the Canadian dollar? How is the commentary about PPP related to the material covered in the chapter? What does the magazine think of the Big Mac index?

CANSIM QUESTIONS

1. Go to the CANSIM Web site and download the 3-month forward premium (+) or discount (–) on U.S. dollars in Canada (series V122505). It is defined as the annual interest rate equivalent of the spread between the spot and forward exchange rates for U.S. dollars in Canada. Relate this series in terms of equation (8.12). How would you expect this series to behave? Why? Plotting the series against time will help.

2. Replicate Figure 8.2 by downloading the following series from the CANSIM Web site: V114423 (merchandise trade balance), V114425 (nonmerchandise trade balance), V114405 (investment income), V114441 (transfers), V114421 (current account balance), V114558 (Canadian assets net flows), V114575 (Canadian liabilities to nonresidents), V11458 (statistical discrepancy), and V112396 (total official international reserves in U.S. dollars).

3. Is there a connection between over- or undervaluation of the exchange rate discussed in this chapter and the behaviour of international reserves?

4. Is the balance of payments always zero?

5. Has the statistical discrepancy become larger or smaller as a percentage of the current account balance in the period considered in Figure 8.2? Comment on the evidence and its implications for measuring trade flows.

References can be found on **www.mcgrawhill.ca/college/siklos**

Decision Makers in the Financial System

Decision Makers: Introduction

LEARNING OBJECTIVES

After reading and studying this chapter, you should be able to

9.1 identify the main sectors in the Canadian economy

9.2 determine how the flow of funds is evaluated and what it measures

9.3 identify some of the limitations of the way in which data from the national balance sheet are presented

This chapter is the first of several examining the economic behaviour of the principal participants in the Canadian financial system: the household, business, financial, government, and international sectors. The collective decisions of each sector—the sum of millions of decisions made by its economic agents, be they individuals, managers of firms, or bureaucrats—shape an economy. In a macroeconomics course, the focus would be on this economywide behaviour. Here, however, we are more interested in the behaviour of the major participants in the operation of the financial system.

Before we can describe theories of consumer, firm, and bank behaviour however, we need a device to organize the financial system in a manner that highlights the roles played by the major participants. Accordingly, this chapter opens with a brief review of some principles and conventions of the **System of National Accounts**, which is Statistics Canada's accounting system for the entire economy. You are probably familiar with its short-term statements of economic activity, such as gross domestic product (GDP) and its components, which are analogous to a firm's income statements. However, we are more interested here in examining the **national balance sheet accounts**, which are the set of balance sheets prepared for each group in the economy and for the economy as a whole, and the **financial flow accounts**, which report how funds are used in borrowing and lending activities. Such an analysis will allow us to determine, for example, which sectors of the economy tend to be borrowers or lenders over time, as well as the financial relationship between sectors of the economy. In other words, financial flows inform us about capital movements between lending and borrowing sectors of the economy. Our approach is a very general one and merely serves as a device to illustrate the net financial contribution of the major sectors of the economy.

9.1 SOME BASIC NATIONAL INCOME ACCOUNTING PRINCIPLES

The economy is divided into four major **economic sectors** (divisions that can be studied by themselves):

1. Households, formally called the persons and unincorporated business sector.

2. Businesses, which are divided into nonfinancial private corporations and financial corporations. The latter are subdivided into (i) banks and near-banks, (ii) insurance companies and pension funds, and (iii) other private financial institutions.

3. Governments, of which the federal government is only one segment.

4. The foreign sector, often called the rest of the world.

Each sector generates revenues and incurs expenditures during a given period, say a year. The difference between the two determines whether the relevant sector experiences a surplus or is in a deficit position. A financial surplus implies net lending to the financial sector, whereas a deficit requires borrowing from financial markets. Thus, for each sector, we can write

$$\text{Current Receipts} - \text{Current Expenditures} = \text{Surplus } (> 0) \text{ or Deficit } (< 0)$$

Notice that the difference between expenditures and receipts is for the current period—the year in this case. An expression such as this one is an **income statement** (if it were for a firm it might be called an earnings statement), but it is a form that can be integrated with a sector's **balance sheet**, which is a statement summarizing its **net worth**—that is, it is the value of assets and liabilities at a particular moment in time.[1] In the case of government operations, net worth is essentially the accumulated deficit or outstanding debt of the nation.

Figure 9.1 shows how information from a sector's income statement feeds into its balance sheet. A surplus represents an addition to the sector's net worth; a deficit represents a reduction. For an illustration, consider the government of Canada.

In the 2003-04 fiscal year, which runs from April 1 to March 31, current receipts totalled $198 547 million. Current expenditures were $189 464 million. The difference of $9083 million ($198 547 − 189 464) represents the budget surplus for that fiscal year. It is useful to point out, at this stage, that although the national income accounts say that the deficit is a certain amount, that is *not* the same as saying that the government needs to *borrow* an amount equivalent to the published deficit figure. Similarly, it is not the case that the entire surplus goes to pay down the debt.

The reason is that there is an item referred to as *nonbudgetary transactions*[2] which, at least in the 2003–2004 budget year, meant that the federal government actually paid down the debt by over 8 billion dollars. Second, beginning with the 1996–97 budget year announced at the end of February 1996, the federal government has routinely added a "contingency reserve" in the event its assumptions about the future prospects for the economy turn out to be overly optimistic. Obviously, this too will affect the actual size of the deficit and borrowing requirements.

Unlike other sectors of the economy, the federal government only records financial assets and liabilities. Other balance sheets usually divide assets and liabilities into two components. **Nonfinancial assets** are essentially physical assets, such as equipment, machinery, and land; they are also called *real assets*. **Financial assets**, for the most part, consist of cash, the value of foreign exchange accounts, and financial loans and investments. Roughly half of the financial assets are classified as cash. Liabilities consist primarily of interest-bearing debt (i.e., unmatured debt and pension obligations). Notice that the net worth of the government is negative. Net worth essentially represents the net accumulated debt of the government, and it rises or falls with every additional deficit or surplus incurred. (In later chapters we examine the balance sheets of other sectors of the economy as well.) Does it appear odd that the federal government has negative net worth? After all, the land, resources, and infrastructure built, maintained, and owned by the

---

1 Following the usual accounting practice, these values reflect those at the time of purchase less some adjustment for depreciation (dictated by tax considerations). In general, balance sheets are not evaluated at current market values but at *historical cost*, which is the cost at the time of purchase.

2 For example, when a government announces an infrastructure project, the funds will be spent over several years even though they may be *budgeted* in a single fiscal year.

| **Figure 9.1** | **A Sectoral Income Statement and Balance Sheet for the Government of Canada** |

Income Statement

(millions of current dollars)

| Current expenditures | = | Current net revenues |
| $189 464 | | $198 547 |

+

Surplus

$9083

Balance Sheet

| Assets | | Liabilities | $701 093 |

+

| | | Net worth | −$501 493 |

| Total | $199 600 | | $199 600 |

Look at the government's fiscal monitor at www.fin.gc.ca/pur/fiscmon-e.html

Source: Canada Customs and Revenue Agency. Reproduced with permission of the Minister of Public Works and Government Canada, 2005. Condensed Financial Statements of the Government of Canada. The figures are for the financial year 2003/2004. The figure for surplus is shown as a negative number, since it is necessary to balance the income statement.

government (that is, the public) must have some value as assets. Although national income accounting generally eschews these items as assets in the National Balance Sheet, at least one government does not, as explained in **Financial Focus 9.1: A Novel Way of Accounting for Government Operations: The New Zealand Model.**

Now, recall the definition of net worth (sometimes called net wealth) as expressed in the basic accounting identity:

$$A - L = NW \qquad (9.1)$$

where

A = assets, in dollars
L = liabilities, in dollars
NW = net worth or net wealth, in dollars

That identity is the compact statement of any balance sheet.

The generic terms "surplus" and "deficit" accurately describe additions or subtractions to net worth, but they are usually applied to the government sector; different terms are used for each sector of the economy. For example, surplus funds in the household sector are known as *savings*. In the business or firm sector they are often referred to as *retained earnings*.

The accounting identity makes it quite clear that changes in net worth will influence asset holdings, which can be nonfinancial assets (a house or a factory) or financial assets (money or bonds), as well as liabilities. It is also clear that one sector's activities cannot be analyzed in isolation from the others' activities. For example, tax payments are an important component of current expenditures for households and of current receipts for various levels of government.

Since the magnitudes in equation (9.1) are measured at a particular moment in time—say, December 31 of a particular year—they are known as **stock measures**. Since we are primarily interested in financial trends over time, we have to convert these stock measures into **flow measures**, which are measures of activity over time. By comparing successive balance sheets—say, between one year and the next—we can determine the change in the balance sheet position of a particular sector. All we need to do to convert stocks into flows is to determine the changes in equation (9.1) during the period of question:

$$\Delta A - \Delta L = \Delta NW \qquad (9.2)$$

where Δ indicates the change during the period—say, from one year to the next. In other words,

$$\Delta A_t = A_t - A_{t-1}$$
$$\Delta L_t = L_t - L_{t-1}$$
$$\Delta NW_t = NW_t - NW_{t-1}$$

So the change in asset holdings, ΔA_t, is simply the difference between the balance sheet value of assets at time t, which could be 31 December 2005, less their value at time $t-1$, which could be 31 December 2004. The calculation of ΔL and ΔNW are interpreted in a similar fashion.

We can simplify the notion by agreeing that the Δ symbol refers to a year-over-year change. Then we can drop the time subscripts in the subsequent discussion.

9.2   THE FINANCIAL SYSTEM IN THE FLOW OF FUNDS

What is the role of the financial system in the **flow of funds**? Finding the answer requires that we further analyze equation (9.2). We have already noted that liabilities tend to be mostly financial in nature, but assets may be financial or nonfinancial. We shall denote them as FA and NFA, respectively. We can rewrite equation (9.2) as

$$\Delta NW = (\Delta FA + \Delta NFA) - \Delta L$$

It will be convenient for our analysis to further subdivide financial assets into money, M, which, as we have seen, plays a central role in economic analysis, and other financial assets, OFA, such as bonds.

Thus, changes in financial assets, ΔFA, represent the sum of changes in money holdings, ΔM, and changes in other financial assets, ΔOFA. Keeping the distinction between types of financial assets, we can further rewrite equation (9.2) as

$$\Delta NW = [(\Delta M + \Delta OFA) + \Delta NFA] - \Delta L \qquad (9.3)$$

where

$$\Delta FA = \Delta M + \Delta OFA$$

Now consider that additions to other financial assets, OFA, stem from the particular sector's contribution to the financial system. They represent sources of funds or the amount of *lending* that takes place.[3] By contrast, changes in liabilities are an indication of the amount of additional *borrowing* by a particular sector—that is, the uses of funds.

We are now able to describe the flow of funds, which describes the interlocking nature of the economic relationship among the principal sectors of the economy. Figure 9.2 shows the evolution

---

3 Changes in money holdings are often called a *hoarding* activity because these funds are not made available for use by the financial system.

FINANCIAL FOCUS 9.1

A NOVEL WAY OF ACCOUNTING FOR GOVERNMENT OPERATIONS: THE NEW ZEALAND MODEL

In 1994 the Parliament of New Zealand passed the *Fiscal Responsibilities Act*, which is intended to ensure that governments practise prudent financial management. It forces the government not only to publish its fiscal forecasts but to explain why they might miss them, as well as how to get back on track. It also requires that the minister of finance issue a "Statement of Responsibility" in which he or she must accept "overall responsibility for the integrity of the disclosures" to the report required to be tabled in Parliament by the government. But equally important, it requires that the government publish a balance sheet according to generally accepted accounting principles (GAAP). Public roads, bridges, and national parks are to be given a dollar value and henceforth appear in the national balance sheet as assets. The Act also means that expenditures and receipts are recorded on an accrual basis, which recognizes the fact that obligations voted on by the Parliament in one year bind fiscal policy throughout the expected stream of spending. For example, if the New Zealand government passes an infrastructure program costing, say $6 billion

over five years, then rather than assuming that the money is all spent in the current year, as is the current practice in countries such as Canada, each budget over the next five years will have to account for the portion spent on the program each year the funds are spent. Therefore, in fiscal matters at least, "bygones are no longer bygones."

What are the implications of this approach to national income accounting? Well, for the first time, government sector net worth became positive in 1995–96, and it has remained positive since. The table below gives a summary of the New Zealand government's balance sheet for fiscal 2004 (July 1 to June 30).

Questions for Discussion
1. Discuss whether the Canadian government's balance sheet would show a positive "net worth" if it adopted the New Zealand standards. In the absence of actual data, speculate on the results.
2. Would a fiscal responsibility act be a good idea for Canada?

Assets (millions) NZ$	Fiscal 2004	Liabilities	Fiscal 2004
Market securities and cash	28 086	Payables and provisions	12 486
Advances[1]	20 028	Currency	3 009
Physical assets[2]	62 558	Borrowings	36 825
Total	110 672	Pension liabilities	22 889
		Total	75 209
		Crown balance[3]	35 463

Source: Financial Statements of the Government of New Zeland (Wellington: Department of the Treasury).

[1] Includes receivables and inventories, other investments, and intangible assets.
[2] Property, plant and equipment, commercial forests
[3] Roughly equivalent to net worth; includes taxpayers' funds and revaluation reserve

of the flow of funds for three key sectors of the economy: households, nonfinancial corporations, and the federal government.

Notice the impact of the turn from deficits to surpluses on the flow of funds from the federal government. The negative sign after around 1996 is symptomatic of the federal government's policy of beginning to pay down the national debt. The figure also makes clear that flows, in sheer dollar terms, originating from the household sector are larger and more volatile than those of the nonfinancial sector. Households especially respond to changes in income (a flow), interest rates, and taxes, among other considerations, in assessing their borrowing and lending requirements.

Since changes in financial assets have to equal changes in financial liabilities, according to the accounting principles outlined above, the financial sector is the one that makes possible the required capital movements between the various sectors of the economy. The resulting transactions are at the centre of the equality between savings and investment that is at the core of the principles of national income accounting.[4]

Figure 9.3 illustrates in a simplified form the workings of the flow of funds. The Bank of Canada, government (principally the federal government), and the financial sector stand between the sectors that supply funds to the financial system and those that are the main users of funds. Included in the former group are households, government, and the foreign sector (or rest of the world), while the corporate (or nonfinancial) sector, along with governments and the rest of the world, round out the sectors that use funds.

9.3 LIMITATIONS OF THE DATA

Changes in the holdings of other financial assets, which include stocks and bonds of various kinds, are primarily accounted for by the private sector of the economy—that is, the household, business, financial, and foreign sectors. Periods of recession usually see the smallest overall annual change in holdings of other financial assets.

Most changes in liabilities are incurred by the business and financial sectors. Note, however, one important difference between real assets and financial assets. A real asset appears only on the balance sheet of its owner.[5] In contrast, a financial asset, such as a government bond, is an asset to the individual holding the bond *and* a liability to the issuer, who undertakes to make regular interest payments and return the principal on maturity of the financial instrument. Thus, when a business acquires a debt or a liability at an interest cost, it usually does so to gain funds to purchase an

| Figure 9.2 | Flows of Funds in the Canadian Economy by Major Sector |

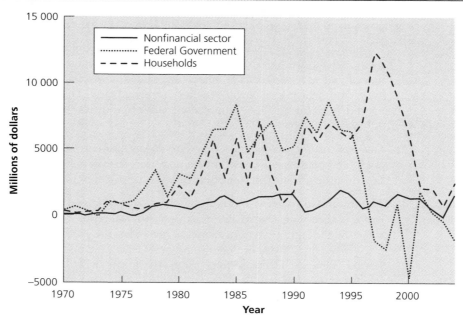

Source: Adapted from the Statistics Canada CANSIM II database **http://cansim2.statcan.ca/cgi-win/CNSMCGI.EXE**, series V33403 (nonfinancial sector), V33402 (households), and V33425 (federal government).

---

4 See, for example, C.R. McConnell, S.L. Brue, and T.P. Barbiero, *Macroeconomics,* 10th Cdn ed. (Toronto: McGraw-Hill Ryerson Ltd, 2005).

5 Of course, the asset may have been purchased via a loan, but the item itself does not appear on any other balance sheet.

Figure 9.3   **A Diagrammatic Version of the Flow of Funds**

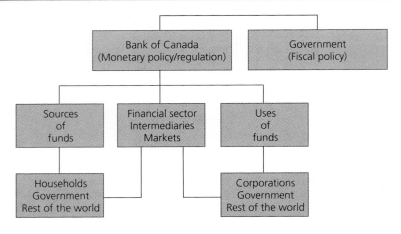

asset that also yields interest income. This practice of investing borrowed funds is known as *leverage*. We address this concept in greater detail in Chapter 11. Household debt, on the other hand, is financed through current and future labour income.

Finally, it is quite clear that households accumulate much of the economy's net worth and are thus the principal lenders in the economy. At the other end of the spectrum is the federal government, whose changes in net worth were, until recently, consistently negative—a result of its policy of incurring substantial deficits over time.

In considering the kind of information in the national balance sheet accounts, we should remain aware of several problems inherent in the way the data are kept and reported.

1. Government budget statistics, unlike those from households, businesses, and the financial sector, do not distinguish between spending on assets and current spending. Thus, government funds spent on roads or schools are treated as current spending, although these are assets from which society will benefit over many years.[6] This approach distorts government deficits (or surpluses), especially relative to those of the other sectors, but we cannot say by how much.

2. Financial institutions and most businesses report historical values, not market values, for their assets. This practice can lead to, for example, the overreporting of net worth if the assets in question drop significantly in value over time (as happened in the late eighties in real estate).

3. All measures introduced in this chapter have been expressed in nominal terms ("current dollars"). In theory they could also be expressed in real terms if we simply deflated the nominal values by the appropriate price index. Therein lies the problem: The relevant price index is often either unavailable or does not properly reflect the purchasing power of the goods and services of interest. Hence, sectoral income statements and balance sheets are generally reported in current, not constant, dollars.

4. The data can only inform us about the historical experience, and this may or may not be a good guide to the future. As we have seen already, however, the financial sector has undergone tremendous changes over the past three decades, and these changes have affected all

---

6 The United States publishes national accounts that properly distinguish current from capital expenditures. See K.M. Carlson, "The U.S. Balance Sheet: What Is It and What Does It Tell Us?" *Review of the Federal Reserve Bank of St. Louis* 73 (September/October 1991): 3–18.

sectors of the economy. Also, until 1996, the federal government was always a net borrower in the financial system. Now its flows have turned negative, and the consequences may not become apparent for years to come.

SUMMARY

- This chapter explains the way the national economy is subdivided by major sector groupings and how the size of each is measured.

- The major sectors are households, businesses, governments, and the foreign sector.

- The key balance sheet relations are:

A (assets) $- L$ (liabilities) $= NW$ (net worth)

$$\Delta NW = [(\Delta M \text{ (money)} \\ + \Delta OFA \text{ (other financial assets)} \\ + \Delta NFA \text{ (nonfinancial assets)}] - \Delta L$$

$$\Delta M = \Delta M + \Delta OFA$$

- The flow of funds shows, for the entire economy, changes in the holdings of assets and liabilities by sector and asset type.

- Limitations of flow of funds analysis include reliance on historical costs and the accounting framework used by governments.

IMPORTANT TERMS

balance sheet, 175
economic sectors, 174
financial assets, 175
financial flow accounts, 174
flow measures, 177
flow of funds, 177

income statement, 175
national balance sheet accounts, 174
net worth (net wealth), 175
nonfinancial assets, 175
stock measures, 177
System of National Accounts, 174

PROBLEMS

1. Recall that a definition of the money supply is the sum of currency and demand deposits. If we were to list currency separately in the flow of funds and add the flow of funds from the Bank of Canada, what would be the change in net wealth for the economy as a whole? Explain. Does this result contradict the discussion in Chapter 2?

2. Why do all financial assets appear on two balance sheets but physical assets on only one?

3. Suppose you are provided with the following flow of funds data for the household sector:

Year	1998	1999	2000	2001	2002	2003	2004	2005	2006
ΔFA	64 462	58 548	33 764	63 874	67 819	67 663	57 261	74 844	88 828
ΔL	17 464	8 914	2 569	13 411	9 641	23 918	28 076	38 900	42 690
ΔNW	112 195	104 421	61 595	82 679	88 321	84 525	92 725	109 611	124 932

Find the change in the holdings of nonfinancial assets.

DISCUSSION QUESTIONS

1. Why are liability changes considered a source of funds? Explain your answer.

2. Explain the difference between stocks and flows.

3. What are the advantages and drawbacks of the New Zealand system of balance sheet accounting?

4. Do you think government net worth is positive or negative? Why or why not? Explain.

5. Name a few inaccuracies that exist in the National Account and briefly explain each.

6. In analyzing the financial needs of the government, do you prefer to look at the surplus/deficits on a National Account's basis or the actual borrowing requirements of the government? Briefly explain.

ONLINE APPLICATIONS

1. Go to the finance department's Web site at **www.fin.gc.ca/fin-eng.html**. Click on *Economic and Fiscal Info*. Next, find *Annual Financial Report of the Government of Canada*. Select the report for the most recent year. Are Canada Savings Bonds an asset or a liability? Why? What about the Canada Pension Plan? Is foreign exchange (e.g., U.S. dollars) an asset or a liability? Why?

2. Go to the New Zealand's Treasury Web site at **www.treasury.govt.nz**. Click on *Budgets and Forecasts*, scroll down the page, and click on *Economic and Fiscal Updates*. Find information about how the New Zealand government values roads and commercial forests and, in general, about the differences between their government accounting standards and ours. To do so, scroll down the page and click on "Putting It Together: An Explanatory Guide to the New Zealand Public Sector Financial Management System."

References can be found on www.mcgrawhill.ca/college/siklos

Decision Makers:
The Household Sector

LEARNING OBJECTIVES

After reading and studying this chapter, you should be able to

10.1 define savings

10.1 determine the principal elements of the consumption–savings decision

10.2 identify the main features of an intertemporal model of consumption behaviour

10.2 analyze the impact of interest rates, income, and other institutional constraints on consumption behaviour

10.3 distinguish between short-run and long-run consumption behaviour and describe the importance of the difference between the two

10.3 determine why consumption spending is not volatile

10.3 describe both the permanent income hypothesis and the lifecycle hypothesis and what they tell us about consumers' lifetime spending–saving habits

10.4 understand the potential connection between government spending, taxes, and consumption or savings behaviour

Households provide a major portion of the savings flow into the economy. The purpose of this chapter is to explore how a household determines its *savings rate* (the proportion of *disposable income*—after-tax income—devoted to saving rather than to consumption). The topic is clearly important to households themselves. It is also a matter of concern to governments and firms, which need to ensure a steady flow of funds to finance their borrowing. Moreover, since the flow of savings provides the raw material necessary for the continued existence of financial intermediaries, it is important to understand some of the key elements of a theory of savings behaviour.[1]

Since savings represent a household's residual income—what is left after it pays for consumption spending and taxes—a theory of savings is also a theory of consumption. This approach is the one traditionally taken in economic analysis, and we follow it here. This chapter is not, however, a survey of existing models of consumption or savings behaviour. Instead, we first build on the idea, introduced in Chapter 5, that savings is nothing more than consumption postponed and conversely, borrowing represents savings postponed. We also know that lenders and borrowers exchange funds at the equilibrium real interest rate. Now we explore how an individual's discount rate (the rate at which the individual values the future versus the present) interacts with existing interest rates to determine the amount of savings or borrowing for a given level of income.

---

1 Scholars in the United States have recently focused much attention on household savings because that country's savings rates have been low in recent years. In Canada, savings rates have also been falling.

We then consider how consumption and savings are determined economywide. Complicating factors include differences in the behaviour of consumption between the short run and the long run and the age of the consumer.

We conclude the chapter by examining briefly more sophisticated models of savings behaviour: those that consider that consumption and thus savings are a function of age and the type of income earned.

10.1 INTERTEMPORAL SAVINGS BEHAVIOUR

We begin by assuming that an individual earns a level of real income, denoted y, in each of two periods.[2] To avoid any element of uncertainty, we simplify by assuming that the flow of income over the individual's lifetime is known with certainty. In addition, we assume that this person or household has no wealth (from inheritance or from previous savings) and does not wish to bequeath anything to the next generation at the end of the second period. We also initially assume that the interest rate does not change.

To begin, we know from the discussion of Chapter 5 that the terms of trade or the discount factor between the present and the future are measured by the real interest rate. Thus, if the real interest rate is ρ, a \$1 investment will, after one year, yield

$$1 + (1 \cdot \rho) \tag{10.1}$$

where $1 \cdot \rho$ represents the interest earned on \$1 one year later. Equation (10.1) can be rewritten as

$$1 + (1 \cdot \rho) = 1 + [1 \cdot (R - \pi^e)] \tag{10.2}$$

since the Fisher equation (again, see Chapter 5) equates the real interest rate with the nominal interest rate less expected inflation.

We now have at our disposal the two basic facts that determine consumption opportunities. We can combine them to define the budget constraint of the individual,[3] who can make one of several choices:

1. To keep each period's consumption spending even with income.

2. To save at least part of the income in period 1 and then consume it in period 2 (along with the period 2 income).

3. To consume more than the income in period 1, financing the extra consumption by borrowing. The loan must, of course, be repaid from period 2 income.

Which course will the individual choose? As always in economic analysis, we assume it will be the one that provides **utility maximization**—that is, the one that provides the greatest satisfaction, which economists interpret as the most consumption.

To build our model, let c_t represent real consumption spending in period t and let y measure the real income level again for period t. First we evaluate the present value of consumption spending and of income over the two periods (go back to Chapter 5 to see how this was done):

$$c_1 + \frac{c_2}{1 + \rho}$$

---

2 A period can be a year, a month, a week, or a decade. The length of the period is not crucial for the discussion that follows. For the moment, income is the only constraint facing the individual. The model presented below is a version of the so-called "overlapping generations model" that was introduced by Nobel laureate Paul Samuelson in 1958. In this model, individuals can be thought of either as living indefinitely into the future or living finite lives in generations that overlap. Regardless, the discussion focuses on two periods, however one wishes to define their length.

3 Following the usual convention in microeconomics, all individuals are assumed to be alike.

$$y_1 + \frac{y_2}{1 + \rho}$$

Therefore, if we restrict individuals to spending no more than the present value of their lifetime (two-period) income, the budget constraint facing each of them can be written

$$c_1 + \frac{c_2}{1 + \rho} = y_1 + \frac{y_2}{1 + \rho} \tag{10.3}$$

The term "constraint" comes from the fact that, according to (10.3) the consumer cannot spend more than his or her income in present value terms. Therefore, there is an upper limit to spending that is assumed to hold. Consider the following numerical illustration. If an individual earns \$40 000 in the current year and \$60 000 a year later and the real interest rate is 3%, the present value of income will be

$$\$40\ 000 + \$60\ 000/(1.03) = \$98\ 252.43$$

Therefore, if this individual chose to consume \$20 000 in the current year, that would leave savings of \$20 000, which could earn 3% interest. Together with the following year's income, total consumption in year 2, such that total consumption over the two years does not exceed income, is

$$\$20\ 000 + \$78\ 252.43 = \$98\ 252.43$$

where \$78 252.43 = \$80 600/(1.03). If, instead, the same consumer chose to consume \$60 000 in the first year, thereby borrowing \$20 000, then the same principles as the ones used above could be used to show that consumption in period 2, such that total consumption does not exceed \$98 252.43, would be \$38 252.43.

We can now illustrate the situation in an intertemporal choice diagram often called a Fisher diagram (after the great economist Irving Fisher on whose analysis much of ours depends). Figure 10.1 provides the basic elements. Suppose that the individual chooses neither to save nor to borrow but simply to consume in each period exactly the income received in that period. In that case, $c_1 = y_1$ and $c_2 = y_2$.

Since the individual knows with certainty that income of y_1 and y_2 will be forthcoming in the two periods, selecting a consumption–income combination represented by the equalities above amounts to choosing to consume at point E in Figure 10.1(A). It is called the *endowment point* because it reflects the income with which the individual is endowed.

The other two possibilities are, of course, saving in period 1 or borrowing in period 1. Given the endowment point, E, saving in period 1 occurs whenever $c_1 < y_1$ and borrowing takes place whenever $c_1 > y_1$. Notice, however, that the total consumption possibilities are limited by the interest income earned from savings in period 1 or the interest cost of a debt, which must be repaid in period 2. The consumption choices available to the consumer—called the set of **consumption possibilities**—are given by the triangle formed by the two axes in Figure 10.1 up to the limit imposed by the income available in the two periods, which is called the consumer's **budget constraint** (the downward-sloping line AB).

The trade-off is between current and future consumption. The slope of the trade-off must, therefore, be determined by the real interest rate since that is what expresses the extent to which future consumption can be increased or decreased when a portion of current income is saved or sacrificed. Thus, the slope of the budget constraint is

$$-(1 + \rho)$$

Figure 10.1(A) also illustrates how different interest rates change the slope of the budget constraint. Recall that we have assumed that the income combination y_1 and y_2 is always available, no matter what the prevailing real interest rate. Therefore, all consumption possibilities or budget constraints must pass through the endowment point, E. The higher the real interest rate, the greater the future consumption possibilities for every dollar of real income saved in period 1.

Figure 10.1   Fisher Diagrams

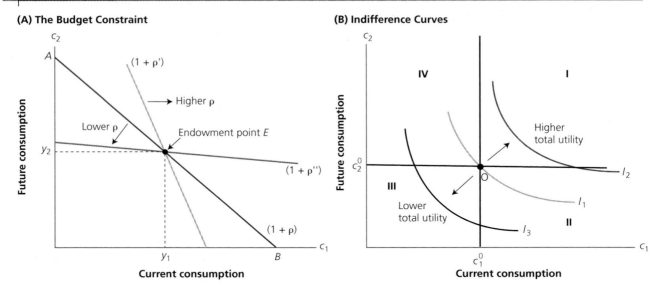

(A) The Budget Constraint

(B) Indifference Curves

Panel (A) illustrates the endowment point, E, and the way in which the real interest rate determines the slope of the budget constraint. Since the endowment (here y_1, y_2) is given, all consumption possibilities must pass through point E. A higher real interest rate signifies a steeper budget constraint.

Panel (B) illustrates an individual's preferences using indifference curves. They depict combinations of consumption in the two periods such that total utility is constant. Total utility along I_2, is higher than for I_1, which is lowest along I_3.

Hence, as shown in the figure, a higher real interest rate ($\rho' > \rho$) means a steeper budget constraint slope. Conversely, a lower real interest rate ($\rho'' < \rho$) signifies a flatter slope.

Next, we must incorporate the preferences of individuals. The utility an individual derives from consumption in this two-period case can be written

$$u = u(c_1, c_2) \qquad\qquad (10.4)$$

where u is the subjective utility that is a function of consumption spending in the two periods. Individuals are assumed to maximize equation (10.4) subject to the constraint of equation (10.3).

The combinations of consumption (in both periods) that yield constant total utility are depicted by an *indifference* curve. Three such curves are shown in Figure 10.1(B). The slope of an indifference curve at a particular point is a measure of the rate of *time preference*—that is, of the relative preference for current over future consumption.[4] Recall that indifference curves cannot intersect. The reason, of course, is that we assume that the individual not only has an ordered set of preferences (i.e., the consumer is able to rank alternatives from best to worst) but also that he or she chooses the preferred combination of consumption today and consumption tomorrow. Therefore, of necessity, an intersecting set of indifference must violate these assumptions. Consequently, in terms of Figure 10.1(B), consumption combinations in quadrant III are less preferred than combination c_1^0, c_2^0. Of course, the opposite is true for any consumption choice in quadrant I. Indifference curves can, however, shift if tastes change. As shown in Figure 10.1(B), a rightward shift signifies higher total utility since large combinations of consumption in both periods become possible. Therefore, utility is increasing or decreasing in the direction of the arrows shown in Figure 10.1(B).

---

4 Technically, the slope of an indifference curve is called the *marginal rate of substitution, MRS*. Algebraically, the MRS is the ratio of the marginal utilities of current and future consumption. The *marginal utility of consumption, MUC*, is simply an expression of the value of a change in consumption spending in utility terms.

FLASHBACK 10.1

INDIFFERENCE CURVES

An indifference curve is a graphical representation of the preferences of an individual. The first thing to remember is that, as far as any consumer is concerned, "more is better." This means that more of c_1 and c_2, that is, consumption in both periods raises, total utility (or u in equation 10.4). We are then in a position to ask: What combinations of c_1 and c_2 would leave total utility unchanged? Plotting all such hypothetical combinations of consumption in the two periods such that there is no change in utility gives us an indifference curve such as the one depicted in Figure 10.1(B).

We are now in a position to find the individual's optimal consumption pattern for the two periods, which is accomplished in Figure 10.2. Utility is maximized when the slope of an indifference curve is equated to the terms of trade between current and future consumption. Graphically, this equality occurs at the tangency between the indifference curve and the budget constraint. Such a tangency is depicted as point O (which stands for optimal) in Figure 10.2. The optimal consumption allocation for each period is given by c_1^* and c_2^*, respectively.

In Figure 10.2(A), the individual is a saver. Optimal consumption in period 1 is less than income in that period, so savings equal $y_1 - c_1^*$. Thus, consumption in period 2 is

$$(1 + \rho)(y_1 - c_1^*) + y_2 = c_2^*$$

Since the real interest rate, ρ, is positive, clearly $c_2^* > y_2$. In other words, consumption in period 2 exceeds income in the same period.

A borrower, in contrast, will select the optimal consumption pattern illustrated in Figure 10.2(B). The individual chooses an optimum to the right of the endowment point, an indication of relatively greater consumption in period 1.

Figure 10.2   The Optimal Consumption Choice

(A) Savings Equilibrium

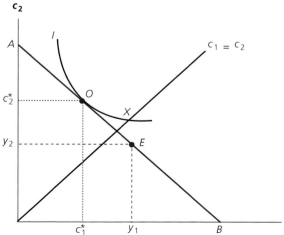

(B) Borrowing Equilibrium

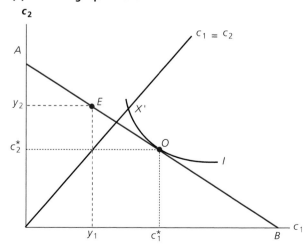

Point O is optimal because it represents the tangency between indifference curve I and the budget constraint AB. The optimal consumption allocation is c_1^* and c_2^* in periods 1 and 2, respectively. Since income in period 1 exceeds consumption in panel (A), a saver is depicted; consumption in period 2 can exceed income earned in period 1. The optimal consumption combination for a borrower is shown in panel (B). Point X and X' represent the intersection of the 45-degree line and the indifference curve. The slopes at these points reveal why an individual lends (lower rate of time preference) or borrows (relatively high rate of time preference).

In using these Fisher diagrams to understand consumer behaviour, it is helpful to draw a 45-degree line emanating from the origin. All along this line, the consumption combinations in the two periods are equal to each other ($c_1 = c_2$). One way of expressing the time preference of an individual is to evaluate the slope of an indifference curve along the 45-degree line from the origin. The indifference curve for the saver [point X in Figure 10.2(A)] is flatter than that for the borrower [point X' in Figure 10.2(B)].

In other words, the saver finds consumption in period 1 relatively less valuable than consumption in period 2, and the opposite is true for the borrower.[5] Thus, the two are said to have different *discount rates*—to place different values on the present versus the future. Since the saver prefers future consumption over current consumption, such an individual tends to discount the future relatively less heavily than a borrower. The discount rate concept suggests, therefore, that individuals have a rate of time preference. This measures the rate at which an increase in consumption today increases an individual's utility or satisfaction relative to an increase of the same amount in future consumption. It is in large part for this reason that a 45-degree line is drawn in Figure 10.2 to clarify the concept that the degree of preference for current over future consumption will be determined by the slope of the indifference curve at that point.[6] The importance of the concept also lies in the fact that the extent to which individuals prefer current over future consumption affects not only the rate at which consumption grows, but also explains why some countries grow faster than others and even why children of poorer parents might not stay in school as long as the children of wealthier parents. We shall consider some examples in the sections that follow.

10.2 THE DETERMINANTS OF INTERTEMPORAL SAVINGS BEHAVIOUR

The basic framework we have just established can be used to illustrate a number of interesting factors that influence savings behaviour. We will consider three examples.

EFFECT OF AN INTEREST RATE CHANGE

If the real interest rate increases, what is the effect on the optimal consumption pattern chosen by a saver [Figure 10.3(A)] or a borrower [Figure 10.3(B)]? Since the endowment point, E, in both diagrams is fixed (income in the two periods is given), any real interest rate change must cause the budget constraint to rotate about that point.

With an interest rate increase, $1 saved today means greater future consumption opportunities than before; $1 borrowed also has a higher interest cost, thereby reducing future consumption opportunities. Hence, the budget constraint rotates clockwise when the real interest rate rises, whether the individual's choice is to borrow or to save.

For the saver [Figure 10.3(A)], the initial optimal consumption pattern is c_1^*, c_2^*, since the tangency of the individual's indifference curve, I_1, and budget constraint, AB, occurs at point O_1. Thus, savings of $y_1 - c_1^*$ permit consumption c_2^* in period 2, which exceeds that period's income by $c_2^* - y_2$. The difference, of course, is accounted for by period savings plus interest:

$$(y_1 - c_1^*)(1 + \rho) + y_2 = c_2^*$$

---

5 The mathematically inclined can suppose that equation (10.4) is written as

$$u(c_1, c_2) = u(c_1) + \frac{u(c_2)}{(1 + \rho)}$$

This expression assumes that total utility is time separable so that we can determine consumption choice in period 1 given consumption in period 2. At the point where $c_1 = c_2$, it can be shown that the ratio of marginal utilities for the saver is such that the discount rate or rate of time preference is lower than ρ. The opposite holds for the borrower.

6 Again, for the mathematically inclined, $-$slope $= MU_2/MU_1$ where MU is the marginal utility of consumption in periods 1 or 2. The slope is >1 as $MU_1 < MU_2$, and vice versa.

The opposite occurs in the case of a borrower [Figure 10.3(B)], whose initial optimal consumption pattern is given by c'_1, c'_2.

Evaluating the effect of an interest rate change on individual behaviour involves considering two factors. First, the rise in the real interest rate means that the price of current consumption rises relative to that of future consumption. The reason is that each dollar saved before the interest rate change now yields more future dollars and thus more future consumption than before. It is apparent from Figure 10.3(A) that if an individual decides to continue to consume c^*_1 in period 1, consumption opportunities in period 2 can now exceed c^*_2, the level of period 2 consumption chosen initially. This logic applies no matter what level of consumption is chosen for period 1, provided that the individual saves some portion of income in that period.

The same description applies to the borrower in reverse. Thus, a rise in the real interest rate means that the initial cost of the outstanding debt becomes higher than it was initially, prompting smaller period 2 consumption possibilities. Thus, for example, we see that consumption of c'_1 during period 1 is no longer possible for the borrower in Figure 10.3(B).

The upshot is that with the change in the terms of trade between present and future consumption, both a saver and a borrower will opt to reduce current consumption in favour of higher future consumption.[7]

The utility-maximizing individual must also contend with the fact that a change in the real interest rate affects total income over the two periods and consequently total consumption.[8] As already noted, if saving or borrowing are unchanged, the total available consumption will be higher or lower, respectively, after the rise in the real interest rate.

| **Figure 10.3** | **Effect of a Higher Real Interest Rate on Optimal Consumption** |

(A) Savings Equilibrium

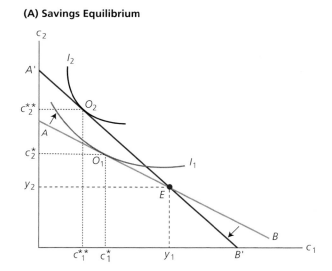

(B) Borrowing Equilibrium

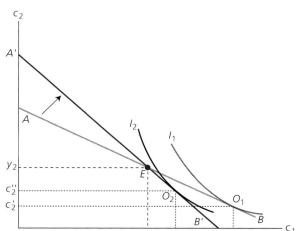

In panel (A), current income, y_1, exceeds current optimal consumption, c^*_1, so a saver is depicted. A rise in the real interest rate results here in the selection of the optimal consumption pattern c^{**}_1, c^{**}_2. Preferences (the shape of the indifference curve) dictate whether current consumtion rises or falls when the real interest rate rises.

In panel (B), current consumption, c'_1, exceeds current income, y_1, so a borrower is depicted. A rise in the real interest rate means lower current consumption since future consumption becomes relatively more expensive. The net effect on future consumption is ambiguous since it depends on the individual's preferences. Usually, however, one would expect lower current consumption and higher future consumption.

---

7 Technically, this is known as the *substitution effect* of a higher interest rate.
8 This is known as the *income effect*.

Continuing with our earlier numerical example, if the individual with the $98 252.43 in income over the two years suddenly faced a 5% interest rate instead of the original 3%, then the present value would become

$$\$40\ 000 + \$60\ 000/(1.05) = \$97\ 142.86$$

that is, $1110.57 lower than previously. The reason, of course, is that it has become more expensive to consume today relative to the future. However, if the same person chose to save $20 000 in the first period, then the same amount translates into $21 000 (= $20 000[1.05]) instead of $20 600 (= $20 000[1.03]) because every dollar saved now earns 5% instead of 3%. On balance, as shown in Figure 10.3, most individuals will respond to the net fall in available funds ($710.57 or –$1110.57 + $400.00) by reducing their consumption in the first period.

What will the final response be? Some individuals will choose less current consumption and more future consumption, but the opposite is also possible. The answer depends on the preferences of the individual. Figure 10.3 reflects an individual who is relatively patient and sees a higher real interest rate primarily as a means of increasing future consumption at the expense of current consumption. However, someone who greatly discounts the future (that is, has a relatively higher marginal rate of time preference) will favour more current consumption over future consumption. The net effect, therefore, is uncertain although the results depicted in Figure 10.3 are the ones generally expected.

EFFECT OF AN INCOME CHANGE

So far we have maintained the assumption of a fixed endowment, here, an equal amount of income in the two periods ($y_1 = y_2$). But suppose the individual has a windfall—for example, lottery winnings or a salary bonus—in one period. Figure 10.4 illustrates the effect of an increase in income during period 1. (Income in period 2 is assumed to be constant and remains, therefore at y_2.) Clearly, if y_1 is increased, the original endowment point, E, is no longer the relevant starting point for the budget constraint. The new endowment point is E', with the distance of EE' representing the magnitude of the increase in income (that is, $y_1' - y_1$). The increase in period 1

Figure 10.4   **Effect of an Income Change**

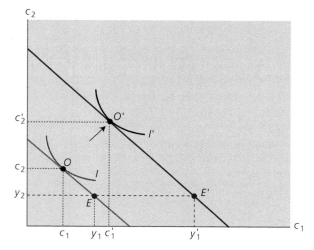

An increase in period 1 income (y_1' instead of y_1) moves the endowment point from E to E'. Since consumption is believed to be positively related to income, optimal consumption is expected to rise in both periods, here from O to O'.

income implies a parallel rightward shift in the budget constraint since the endowment point also moves to the right. (The shift is a parallel one since the real interest rate is unchanged.)

What is the effect on the optimal consumption pattern? An increase in period 1 income is usually believed to lead to more consumption in both the present and the future. The individual depicted in Figure 10.4 initially chose the optimal consumption pattern at point O; then, following the increase in income, point O' was chosen, which implies more consumption in both periods.[9]

EFFECT OF A LIQUIDITY CONSTRAINT

So far we have assumed that preferences—technically, the marginal rate of time preference—dictate the choice between borrowing and saving as well as the amounts of debt incurred or assets accumulated. The only constraint is the budget constraint. But suppose the individual also faces a *liquidity constraint*. That is, the individual does not have sufficient liquidity to consume as much as desired in period 1 and cannot borrow (or cannot borrow enough) to finance consumption that is greater than that period's income even though the next period's income is expected to be larger.

Figure 10.5 illustrates this situation. An individual is endowed with y_1 in period 1. It is sufficient to meet basic consumption needs, but no more. A considerable increase is expected for period 2 income ($y_2 > y_1$), but there is a liquidity constraint in period 1. Consequently, the individual is likely to spend all of his or her meagre income in period 1 and not save anything. Although the individual would like to consume at point O' along indifference curve I', the constraint is binding, so point E is selected along a lower indifference curve, I. The kink in the opportunity set is the point likely to be chosen by the liquidity-constrained individual.

Figure 10.5	**Effect of a Liquidity Constraint**

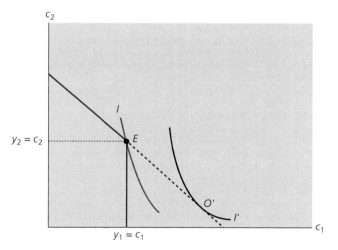

An individual with a liquidity constraint has a low period 1 income, so all of it is likely to be consumed in that period ($y_1 = c_1$). Such an individual is constrained to consume at point E. But there is relatively high period 2 consumption. In the absence of a liquidity constraint, the individual might have consumed at O'.

---

9 Such an outcome is consistent with the notion that the *income elasticity of demand* is positive (that is, percentage changes in demand increase and decrease with percentage changes in income). We could, of course, depict a case in which period 1 consumption falls following an increase in period 1 income, but such an outcome would generally not accord with our everyday experience. Thus, consumption in both periods is presumably a *normal good* (the quantity demanded rises with increases in income).

This situation is not an unusual one. Consider the position of many students. Their income level is low, and the financial marketplace thinks the likelihood of default too high to grant them loans, even though they expect their education to yield them much higher incomes in the future.[10] Figure 10.5 illustrates their liquidity constraint in the consumption–savings decision. This situation is the primary reason governments have found it necessary to intervene by providing loan guarantees, by directly subsidizing students through loans, and by providing subsidies to educational establishments.

The example considered here, albeit simplistic, does at least vividly illustrate how a constraint that strictly binds the consumption opportunities of students in period 1 has persuaded governments to offer loans on relatively favourable terms that can be repaid after graduation. Of course, in a world of certainty, this kind of policy makes sense. But what if y_2 is not certain or, put differently, what if y_2 for some ends up being higher than for others despite roughly the same education costs? An alternative that is being considered in Canada, and that is in place in countries such as Australia and the U.K., is to make loans more strongly contingent on future income.[11]

A final comment is in order. There has been no explicit mention of "money," a concept we have already discussed and one that obviously permeates the entire text. The approach adopted here effectively assumes that money is like any other asset that can be used to facilitate the reallocation of consumption (and, therefore, as suggested in Chapter 2, improves society's welfare relative to a barter system). It has the virtue of simplicity, but more astute readers may wonder how economists deal with the question of the "demand for money" (a topic we consider separately in Chapter 12). An alternative, for example, would be to explicitly include money in the utility function equation (10.4). Another approach, which we shall consider in Chapter 12, is to view the holding of money as creating transactions costs. In other words, holding money instead of other assets is a costly activity. Finally, one might require individuals to actually hold money in advance of the purchase of goods. In other words, consumers face an additional constraint beyond the income constraint developed in this chapter. The so-called "cash-in-advance" models have proved popular in economics in analyzing several problems such as finding the optimal rate of inflation.

10.3 LIFECYCLE EXPLANATIONS OF CONSUMPTION BEHAVIOUR

THE LONG-RUN AND SHORT-RUN BEHAVIOUR OF CONSUMPTION SPENDING

The simple consumption–savings model we have developed can be useful in understanding the determinants of savings behaviour. Real interest rate changes, temporary changes in income, liquidity constraints, and the extent to which an individual discounts the future are all factors influencing optimal consumption choice.

The difficulty with the two-period model is that an individual's optimum consumption choice is likely to be influenced primarily by the individual's age and by the nature of income changes over a lifetime (that is, are they short term—transitory—as modelled in Figure 10.4, or long term?). You are probably acquainted with economists' explanations about how consumption and savings behaviour are likely to be affected by what is known as the lifecycle. Such a discussion appears particularly important in light of Canada's aging population. The age distribution in an economy may influence the flow of savings.

---

10 Economists call education and skill *human capital*. A liquidity constraint arises in part because we can borrow against physical capital (such as a house or a car) but normally not against human capital.

11 See **http://www11.hrdc-drhc.gc.ca/pls/edd/CSL.html** which summarizes issues and considers policy proposals relative to the Canada Student Loans program. Also, see the so-called Rae Report requested by the Ontario government, in which an income-based loan repayment scheme was advocated. **http://www.raereview.on.ca/en/default.asp?loc1=**

The great British economist John Maynard Keynes introduced the idea of the consumption function in the 1930s. According to his theory, consumption is largely determined by *disposable income*. The **consumption function** is the relationship between total consumer spending and total disposable income when all other determinants of that spending are held constant. A related concept is the **marginal propensity to consume (MPC)**, which is the ratio of a change in consumption to the change in disposable income that produces it, or $\Delta c / \Delta y$. The MPC measures the slope of the consumption function.

Several difficulties arise with the Keynesian theory because it neglects a variety of empirical facts that have come to light during research into the consumption function over the past 30 years. Figure 10.6 shows two scatter plots of consumption expenditure and personal disposable income, with both series expressed in real terms on a per capita basis.[12] Panel (A) shows the relationship between levels of consumption and income since 1970. Added is the straight line that most closely fits the scatter points.[13] Panel (B) plots changes in consumption and income.

Notice that the correlation between levels of income and levels of consumption is high [Figure 10.6(A)], whereas changes in consumption are not so closely related to changes in income [Figure 10.6(B)].

We can call Figure 10.6(A) a model of a *long-run* consumption function because it shows the relationship between levels of consumption and income for the past 20 years or so of data, and Figure 10.6(B) a *short-run* consumption function because it shows how changes in consumption are influenced by changes in income. Then we can state that the long-run marginal propensity to consume is larger than the short-run marginal propensity to consume. The source of the

---

| Figure 10.6 | Consumption Spending versus Disposable Income |

(A)

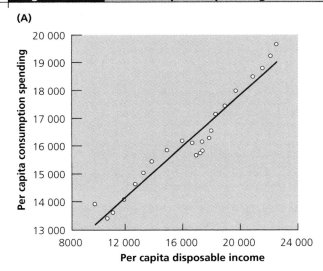

(B)

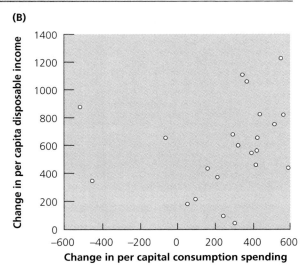

In panel (A) of these scatter plots, the long-run marginal propensity is given by the upward-sloping straight line. In panel (B) the short-run marginal propensity would be a relatively flatter straight line. Thus, a $1 increase in disposable income raises consumption spending by more in the long run than in the short run.

Source: Adapted from the Statistics Canada CANSIM II database **http://cansim2.statcan.ca/cgi-win/CNSMCGI.EXE**, series V691782 (Disposable income), V1992115 (Consumption).

Note: Consumption spending represents total consumption expenditures, seasonally adjusted, on an annual basis. Income is personal disposable income, also seasonally adjusted on an annual basis.

---

12 That is, nominal consumption spending and income are deflated by an appropriate price index and by population. Thus, if the series X is to be deflated by P for price and N for population, the real per capita value of $X = X/PN$.

13 This line is called the least squares fitted line. See any introductory statistics textbook for details.

difference lies in the fact that consumption spending evolves more smoothly over time than income (see Figure 10.7). As a result, temporary changes in income appear to have a relatively small influence on consumption, whereas over long periods of time changes in income and consumption seem to move more or less together.

THE LIFECYCLE PATTERN OF CONSUMPTION: A STYLIZED SKETCH

The relative smoothness of consumption over time suggests either that individuals are influenced in their consumption behaviour by whether they expect an income change to be temporary or not or that individuals attempt to smooth their consumption spending over a lifetime even though their income varies considerably during that period. Figure 10.8(A) shows, in highly stylized form, how labour income evolves relative to consumption during an individual's lifetime. The individual depicted here is assumed to have a life expectancy of 85 years and to earn labour income from age 25 onward.[14] Labour income is assumed to grow with experience and seniority and to cease abruptly on retirement at age 65. We could make a number of other assumptions to increase the realism of the example but the essential conclusions of the analysis would be unaffected: Individuals *dissave* (spend savings or take on debt) during the early and the latter stages of their lifecycle and accumulate wealth during much of their working lives. Figure 10.8(B), which is derived from Figure 10.8(A), shows lifetime accumulation of financial wealth.

| **Figure 10.7** | **Consumption Spending and Income over Time** |

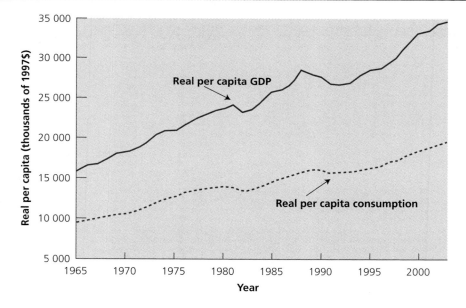

Real per capita GDP and total consumption spending appear to move in tandem over the long term, but the former is more volatile than the latter in the short term.

Source: Adapted from the Statistics Canada CANSIM II database **http://cansim2.statcan.ca/cgi-win/CNSMCGI.EXE**, series V1992115 (Consumption), V1992067 (real GDP), VI (Population).

Note: Consumption spending represents total consumption expenditures, seasonally adjusted, on an annual basis. Income is GDP, also seasonally adjusted annually. Both series were deflated by population and prices (consumer prices for consumption expenditures and the implicit price deflator for GDP, both 1997 = 100).

---

14 Of course, the individual may also have acquired and accumulated assets in earlier years or plan lifetime consumption on the assumption that a bequest to the next generation will be made. These complications are ignored in the analysis.

What if income does not exhibit the regular pattern depicted in Figure 10.8? This is one of the premises of Friedman's permanent income hypothesis. Alternatively, what if the situation described above is a reasonable approximation of lifetime income and consumption patterns? This leads to the lifecycle hypothesis of consumption.

Both hypotheses draw on Fisher's view that an individual's lifetime income is the ultimate determinant of consumption and savings behaviours. Both embody the notion that individuals are forward looking in deciding their consumption spending levels. Both emerged at approximately the same time and are related to the notion that income varies over individuals' lifetimes.

THE PERMANENT INCOME HYPOTHESIS

Milton Friedman, a Nobel laureate in economics, proposed the **permanent income hypothesis**, a theory that an individual consumes an amount equivalent to a stable income stream that would produce the same lifetime wealth as the one shown in Figure 10.8(B) if we had used actual labour income. Friedman calls this income measure permanent income. Since it is stable, consumption spending is also stable. Thus, in the long run, consumption is determined by permanent income. As Figure 10.9 shows, however, if we think of permanent income as proxied by the relatively smooth permanent income line, actual disposable income deviates from permanent income as shown in the bottom portion of the figure. If permanent income captures the long-run feature of consumption, the difference between actual and permanent values, called transitory income, captures its short-run aspects. Thus we can write

$$y = y^P + y^T \qquad\qquad (10.5)$$

Figure 10.8	Lifetime Income, Consumption Spending, and Wealth: A Stylized View

(A) Income and Consumption Spending (Saving and Dissaving)

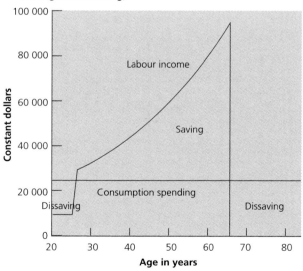

(B) The Accumulation of Wealth

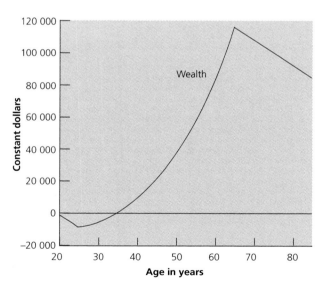

In this typical lifecycle, the individual has a very low income in young adulthood (presumably, student days). He or she enters the full-time labour force at age 25 and earns a steadily increasing income until retirement at age 65. Death occurs at age 85. The consumption level remains the same throughout the lifecycle. Thus, panel (A) shows that income exceeds consumption spending ($y > c$) from ages 25 to 65; the opposite is true before and after that period. Panel (B) shows the same lifetime pattern for the accumulation of wealth.

Source: Author's assumptions and calculations.

Note that the dollar amounts are stated in real terms: Individuals care about purchasing power, not the nominal dollars earned or spent.

where

y = actual real income
y^P = permanent income
y^T = transitory income

Friedman hypothesized that the marginal propensity to consume permanent income (that is, the long-term MPC) is high, so that it captures the long-term behaviour of consumption, whereas the marginal propensity to consume transitory income is low.

The latter point corresponds to the empirical facts pertaining to short-run consumption behaviour described earlier. In Figure 10.9, notice that transitory income turned sharply negative during the 1982–83 recession, and again in 1991 when another recession was hitting the economy. By the end of the 1990s, the Canadian economy was growing strongly again and transitory income experienced a positive shock.

Notice that the time horizon over which permanent income is defined is not made precise. Although the proxy shown in Figure 10.9 is one that many have used in theory, permanent income can be defined as the discounted present value of income into the indefinite future. Friedman also recognized demographic variables and risk, factors already discussed in the text, but these are not explicitly included in (10.5).[15] All of these considerations make it difficult to test whether the permanent income hypothesis is consistent with the data. Nevertheless, on balance, the data seem favourable toward the hypothesis.[16] If this is the case, note that transitory income seemingly

| Figure 10.9 | Permanent and Transitory Income |

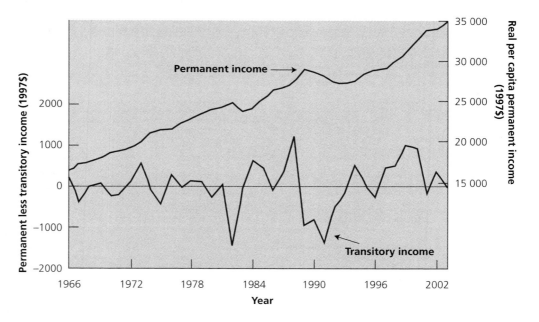

The upper curve is a proxy for permanent income; notice that it is relatively smooth. By contrast, transitory income (the bottom curve) fluctuates considerably. If the graph included actual income (permanent income plus transitory income), its curve would closely parallel that of permanent income.

Source: Adapted from the Statistics Canada CANSIM II database **http://cansim2.statcan.ca/cgi-win/CNSMCGI.EXE**. Permanent income is proxied by a first-order autoregression fitted to the data on per capita real GDP. See Figure 10.7 for series labels.

---

15 For a more thorough and succinct discussion of Friedman's permanent income hypothesis, see C. Meghir, "A Retrospective in Friedman's Theory of Permanent Income," *Economic Journal* 114 (June 2004): F293-307.

fluctuates randomly over time. As discussed in **Economics Focus 10.1 – The Behaviour of Consumption Spending**, there is a parallel behaviour in changes in consumption spending as well.

THE LIFECYCLE THEORY OF CONSUMPTION

The **lifecycle hypothesis**, proposed by Franco Modigliani, another Nobel laureate in economics, focuses on the relationship between consumption spending and how wealth is accumulated over an individual's lifetime. Consumption is determined by labour income as well as by the return on assets accumulated during the lifetime, so we can write

$$c = k_0 y + k_1 a \qquad\qquad (10.6)$$

where

$\quad y \quad$ = real disposable income over a lifetime
$\quad a \quad$ = real assets
$\quad k_0 \quad$ = marginal propensity to consume out of disposable income
$\quad k_1 \quad$ = marginal propensity to consume out of assets

The distinction between the short-run and long-run consumption functions is explained here by the higher value of k_0 relative to that of k_1. Since wealth is accumulated over a long period, a transitory change in its value (perhaps because of a temporary change in the value of one of the assets in the individual's portfolio, such as stocks), is unlikely to have more than a temporary effect on consumption. By contrast, a change in y is likely to have a much larger impact on consumption, for the reasons already elaborated.

This distinction can also be seen by thinking of k_0 and k_1 as being influenced by the age of the individual or his or her expected time horizon. For example, if we examine the choices facing the hypothetical individual in Figure 10.8 at age 25 with a life expectancy of another 60 years (85 less 25), then a rough measure of the percentage of current income that will be consumed might be 60/85 or 71%. This figure would represent an estimate of k_0. An estimate of k_1 could be 1/85 or 1.1% which means that this individual spends, on average 1.1% of his or her wealth for every year of life expectancy.

Note that assets influence consumption in this model. Thus, a connection between interest rates and consumption is possible, although, as already noted, the net effect is an ambiguous one. The notion that consumption is relatively unaffected by wealth lay dormant for many years until the 1990s when the tremendous performance of the stock market as well as the rise in property prices combined to give the impression to many observers that the "wealth effect" may in fact be much more important than previously anticipated. Indeed, there are some who believe that Canada avoided a "mini-recession" of the kind that hit the U.S. economy in 2001 in part because a sufficient number in the population felt wealthier and, consequently, were able to maintain their consumption spending. Great Britain is another country that apparently avoided recession at the same time for much the same reason.[17] However, there are others who argue that dangers lurk in the belief that growing financial and property wealth will forever protect us from a future downturn. It is quite possible, for example, that if a stock market downturn lasts, the future fall in consumption predicted by equation (10.6) will be much larger than the rise from the recent run-up in wealth. Others believe that the impact of wealth on consumption is based on the overly optimistic views of many about the value of their stocks and especially of their

---

16 See, for example, J. P. DeJuan, J. J. Seater, and T. S. Wirjanto, "A Direct Test of the Permanent Income Hypothesis with an Application to the U.S. States," *Journal of Money, Credit and Banking* 36 (December 2004): 1091-1103.
17 See, for example, T. Raphael, "Britons are Irrepressibly House Bound," *Wall Street Journal Europe* (14 November 2001): 11.

ECONOMICS FOCUS 10.1 — THE BEHAVIOUR OF CONSUMPTION SPENDING

How can we most accurately forecast levels of consumption spending? The graph below uses growth rates since 1962 computed from the consumption series in Figure 10.7. What is particularly striking is the way the plot fluctuates more or less randomly near or around the zero line. Also note the sharp drop in consumption growth in the 1982 and 1991–92 recessions, and the sharp rise since then. What does such a plot say about the behaviour of consumption?

A convenient way to calculate growth rates is to evaluate the first difference in the logarithm of a series. Thus, we write

$$c_t^\star = \log c_t - \log c_{t-1}$$

where c_t = level of real per capita consumption spending. Now let us define randomness as a situation whereby the transformation of c_t produces a series with a mean of zero.

In other words,

$$c_t^\star = v_t$$

where v is random in the sense just described. Now note that we can summarize the above equations as

$$\log c_t = \log c_{t-1} + v_t$$

If this equation is used to forecast consumption, the striking result is that the best forecast for consumption spending next year is this year's value since the random element v_t cannot, by definition, be forecast. This idea, first suggested by Robert Hall of Stanford, has stimulated much research into what is called the *random walk hypothesis of consumption*.

In what way does such an assumption make sense? According to the permanent income hypothesis, consumers look to the future, by estimating the present discounted value of their income, when deciding how much to consume today. Therefore, all the information one needs to predict next year's consumption (c_{t+1}) is contained in c_t. By definition then, all that is left is unpredictable.

Of course, not everyone agrees that consumption can be modelled merely as a random walk. Some researchers have suggested that wealth and interest rates, for example, also help us forecast consumption spending levels. Nevertheless, there is considerable empirical evidence that the random walk hypothesis of consumption is a reasonable empirical approximation.

Questions for Discussion

1. Does the random walk hypothesis imply that we cannot improve on forecasts of consumption spending other than by looking at last year's consumption levels?
2. What are the policy implications, if any, of the random walk hypothesis?

Sources

J.Y. Campbell, and N.G. Mankiw, "Consumption, Income, and Interest Rates: Reinterpreting the Time Series Evidence," *NBER Macroeconomics Annual* (1989): 155–216.

R.E. Hall, "Consumption," in *Modern Business Cycle Theory*, edited by R.J. Barro (Cambridge, Mass.: Harvard University Press, 1989): 153–77.

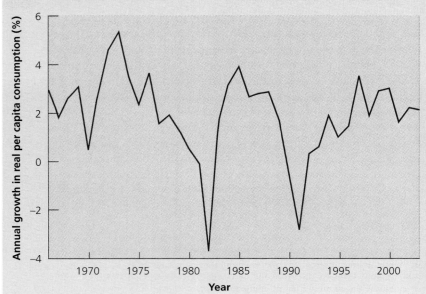

property. After all, although it is fairly easy to sell stocks, it is considerably harder to sell or properly value private property. We may have a tendency, therefore, to believe that a rising tide lifts all boats and perhaps mistakenly believe that the value of our property has risen by the same amount as those that have recently sold.[18]

10.4 THE ROLE OF GOVERNMENT AND TAXES

While we have been focusing on the connection between income and consumption, we seem to have left government out of the equation. After all, much of the discussion above was in terms of *disposable* income, that is, income after taxes. But what about the impact of fiscal policy? How do government spending and taxes affect consumption? Governments have long used tax cuts or spending increases to indirectly boost consumption. Indeed, this was the original Keynesian policy prescription, which has since fallen out of favour. Why? In part, because of the hypothesis called the **Ricardian equivalence theorem** coined by Harvard economist Robert Barro to describe the connection between deficits and economic activity. The general thrust of the Ricardian equivalence idea can be illustrated fairly easily.

Just as we can write a budget constraint for the representative consumer considered at the beginning of this chapter, so we can write a government budget constraint as follows:

$$g_t + \rho \, b_{t-1} = \text{tax}_t + \Delta b_t \tag{10.7}$$

where g represents government spending at time t, ρ is the real interest rate as before, b represents the (real) value of government bonds outstanding, tax represents real tax revenues, again at time t, and Δb represents the change in government bonds outstanding between t and $t-1$ (i.e., $\Delta b_t = b_t - b_{t-1}$). Assume also, as we did for the consumer analyzed earlier, a two-period case.

Equation (10.7) says simply that government spending is made up of what it spends on goods and services as well as the interest cost of the debt outstanding. On the revenue side, the government earns income from taxes and from what it can raise in the bond market. The equality in (10.7) says that, in present value terms, the government must meet its budget constraint.[19]

Suppose now that we consider an example where, initially at least, $b_0 = 0$. Now let us suppose that in period 1 the government decides to finance a tax cut of $1 (or $1 billion if you prefer) by raising the funds in the market so that $b_1 = 1$. If equation (10.7) is to hold (and the government neither rolls over the debt nor incurs more deficit spending)[20] then the government must pay back the $1 in principal as well as the interest cost on the debt which is $\rho \cdot \$1$ for a total of $\$(1 + \rho)$ in period 2. But, in present value terms, this last amount translates into

$$(1 + \rho)/(1 + \rho) = \$1$$

Therefore, the decrease in period 1 taxes of $1 is completely neutralized in present value terms by a $1 increase in taxes in period 2 to finance the retirement of the debt. More realistically, as the permanent income hypothesis would have predicted, a temporary tax decrease (or increase in disposable income) should have little or no effect on current consumption. Part of the debate then revolves around questions such as whether current generations selfishly consume their tax cut, leaving future generations to incur the costs (See **Financial Focus 10.1**).

---

18 These ideas are discussed in, for example, J. Poterba, "Stock Market Wealth and Consumption," *Journal of Economic Perspectives* (Spring 2000), M. Lettau and S. Ludvigson, "Aggregate Wealth and Expected Stock Returns," *Journal of Finance* (2000), and R. Herring and S. Wachter, "Real Estate Booms and Banking Busts," Group of Thirty, Summer 1999.

19 Another way governments can raise revenues, as we have seen in Chapter 3, is via the printing of money. We return to this issue in Chapter 12.

20 All these complications can be accommodated by the theory without changing the flavour of the conclusions.

FINANCIAL FOCUS 10.1   IS THE BEQUEST MOTIVE IMPORTANT?

Do individuals have future generations in mind when they plan lifetime consumption decisions according to the intertemporal utility maximization discussed in this chapter? Evidence suggests that parents act as a "safety net" of sorts when their children fall on hard times, and that consumption during recessions does not fall very much, as the lifecycle hypothesis might predict, because of parental transfers to children. The question has attracted considerable attention in economics lately because the answer affects our view of whether interest rates and government deficits are linked to each other.

The Keynesian approach suggests that a deficit financed by a tax cut raises disposable income and consumption through a change in the real interest rate. Future generations do not play an important role. If, however, we examine the deficit question in the light of a model much like the one considered in this chapter, one in which the individual's utility is determined not only by lifetime consumption and savings, but also by the utility to be derived by future generations from decisions made now and passed on via bequests, then a deficit today is merely a tax increase postponed. Hence, current consumption should be unaffected by a current deficit. Instead, savings will increase to finance future generations' higher tax liability. This theory has, perhaps inappropriately, been named the Ricardian equivalence theorem (after the great economist of the nineteenth century, David Ricardo).

The most prominent economist to advance the idea of Ricardian equivalence is Robert Barro of Harvard University. Bernheim (and others), however, have attacked the theorem, which assumes that individuals behave altruistically. This assumption and others, they say, appear to be unrealistic or falsified through empirical observation. Some have argued that parents leave bequests as a way of controlling their children's lives (one study found that children of wealthy parents visit them more often than children of poorer parents).

Nevertheless, Barro, Evans, and Siklos have produced a significant body of empirical evidence suggesting that deficits and interest rates are independent of each other in a variety of countries. It is unclear, however, whether such a result arises strictly from Ricardian equivalence effects or from other, more complex considerations. This area is one of fairly intense disagreement among economists.

The above-mentioned research suggests a tension between economists who believe in altruism and those who favour the so-called "behavioural economics" approach

whereby individuals, for good reasons, appear to act irrationally. For example, it is well known that, in Canada and the U.S., the favourable tax status accorded certain forms of retirement savings, such as RRSPs in Canada, are not fully used up by taxpayers. However, in some U.S. studies it was found that if saving for retirement purposes could be increased by "hiding" the increased contributions by taking away a portion of future wage or salary increases, then most individuals would find this more palatable. In other words, rather than acting "rationally," individuals need to be fooled or "forced" into choosing the correct optimizing solution. Needless to say, this approach has sparked considerable controversy in the economics profession.

Questions for Discussion

1. Use the loanable funds framework to illustrate the Keynesian and Ricardian equivalence hypotheses. What are the implications for interest rates?
2. Would the utility function of an altruistic individual be different from the one depicted in equation (10.4)? Why or why not?

Sources

R.J. Barro, "The Ricardian Approach to Budget Deficits," *Journal of Economic Perspectives* 3 (Spring 1989): 37–54.

B.D. Bernheim, "Ricardian Equivalence: An Evaluation of Theory and Evidence," in *NBER Macroeconomics Annual* 1987, edited by S. Fischer (Cambridge, Mass.: The MIT Press, 1987): 263–303.

B.D. Bernheim, A. Schleifer, and L.H. Summers, "The Strategic Bequest Motive," *Journal of Political Economy* 93 (1985): 1045–76.

P. Evans, "Do Budget Deficits Raise Nominal Interest Rates? Evidence from Six Industrialized Countries," *Journal of Monetary Economics* 20 (September 1987): 281–300.

G.P. O'Driscoll, "The Ricardian Non-Equivalence Theorem," *Journal of Political Economy* 85 (1977): 207–10.

M. Rabin and R. Thaler, "Anomalies: Risk Aversion," *Journal of Economic Perspectives*, 15 (Winter 2001): 219–32.

P.L. Siklos, "The Deficit–Interest Rate Link: Empirical Evidence for Canada," *Applied Economics* 20 (December 1988): 1563–78.

G.P. Zachary, "Parents' Gifts to Adult Children Studied," *Wall Street Journal* (9 February 1995): A2.

SUMMARY

- Consumption spending by individuals can be thought of as being spread out over a lifetime.

- Individuals must make intertemporal choices between current and future consumption, given the interest rate and the present value of their lifetime income.

- A simple model assumes that consumption choices are confined to two periods, with the interest rate and income being the factors that determine whether borrowing or savings take place.

- It is generally believed that when the real interest rate rises, both savers and borrowers will reduce current period consumption to maintain or increase future consumption.

- Some individuals face a liquidity constraint that can severely limit their current consumption opportunities.

- In the short-run, economywide consumption is not as closely related to income as is long-run consumption. This puzzle can be resolved by looking at consumption in relation to lifetime income.

- More elaborate and elegant explanations of lifetime consumption behaviour are the permanent income and lifecycle theories of consumption.

- The permanent income hypothesis says that consumption is more stable than income because individuals prefer to keep their consumption spending more or less a constant percentage of their expected lifetime income (permanent income).

- The lifecycle hypothesis says that in the face of variable income, individuals keep consumption spending stable by adding or subtracting from their wealth over their lifetime.

- Whether fiscal policy, implemented either through a tax cut or via higher government spending, can effectively influence consumption depends on how it is financed. If it is financed via government debt, then Ricardian equivalence argues that consumers will react by consuming less to save the funds necessary to repay the principal and interest on the debt.

IMPORTANT TERMS

budget constraint, 185
consumption function, 193
consumption possibilities, 185
lifecycle hypothesis, 197

marginal propensity to consume (MPC), 193
permanent income hypothesis, 195
Ricardian equivalence theory, 199
utility maximization, 184

PROBLEMS

1. Using a two-period income–consumption diagram, show the impact on current savings of a fall in the interest rate. Assume that the individual saved part of her income in period 1.

2. Using a two-period income–consumption diagram, show the impact on current savings of a transitory fall in income. Assume the individual borrowed part of his income in period 1.

3. Using a two-period income–consumption diagram, show the impact on current savings of a permanent rise in income. If the individual is a saver in period 1, what is the effect on savings? (Hint: What does the permanent income hypothesis predict?)

4. Using a two-period income–consumption diagram, show the impact of a rise in the interest rate assuming the household borrows in period 1.

5. Suppose the liquidity constraint in Figure 10.5 could be eased but only by permitting loans at a premium over market interest rates. Show a possible optimum in such a case. How does time preference matter?

6. Explain how k_0 and k_1 are both a function of age in the lifecycle hypothesis.

7. TRUE, FALSE, or UNCERTAIN: Transitory income should be unrelated to permanent income. Explain.

8. TRUE, FALSE, or UNCERTAIN: Demographic factors affect the (average) propensity to consume, according to the permanent income hypothesis.

DISCUSSION QUESTIONS

1. Can the lifecycle concept of consumption explain why middle-aged individuals spend a smaller fraction of their income than do the young or the elderly? (Hint: Examine Figure 10.8.)

2. What does the permanent income hypothesis say about the role of income in influencing consumption spending?

3. In terms of the permanent income hypothesis, contrast the effect on consumption of a temporary versus a permanent tax cut.

4. Why is it difficult to borrow against human capital in financial markets?

5. An alternative way of explaining the idea of the random walk hypothesis of consumption is to say that differences between consumption and income are transitory. Explain.

6. What does the permanent income hypothesis predict would happen to consumption if someone wins a lottery? if someone is temporarily laid off? Explain.

7. Explain how uncertainty would affect the (average) propensity to consume, according to the permanent income hypothesis.

ONLINE APPLICATION

Based on the CANSIM question, calculate real per capita consumption spending on semi-durables and nondurables (V1992046 + V1992047). Also obtain the data on total household credit (V36415) and deflate it by the consumer price index (V18702611) and by population (V1). Next, go to the OECD's Web site at **www.oecd.org**. Search for "revenue statistics" and look for a table showing the tax revenues as a percent of GDP. The table shows the total government tax revenue as a percentage of GDP. Compare the experience of Canada with those of other OECD countries. Have Canadian governments taken an increasing share of GDP in the form of taxes over, say, the last decade? Could this explain, in part, the strong growth in total household debt in real terms? Does the overall burden of taxation possibly play a role in explaining consumption spending data?

CANSIM QUESTION

Go to the CANSIM Web site and download the following series: constant 1997 $ GDP (V1992067), constant 1997 $ consumption spending on nondurables (V1992047), population (V1), consumer prices (1992 = 100, V18702611), and personal disposable income (CANSIM II Table 3840013). Retrieve the series at the annual frequency. Calculate per capita measures of consumption, GDP, and real per capita personal disposable income. Note that the disposable income series is in 1997 dollars while some of the other series are in 1992 dollars. How would you transform the series so that they are all based on 1997 dollars?

References can be found on **www.mcgrawhill.ca/college/siklos**

Decision Makers: The Financial and the Nonfinancial Sectors

In this chapter, we continue to develop models of the participants in financial markets by considering the case of business firms, which, as we saw in Chapter 9, may be either financial or nonfinancial. Firms exist, for the most part, because they borrow to invest or create assets that they hope will earn more than their borrowing costs. What differentiates firms from households is the *production process*. That is, firms use inputs to produce outputs, which are often physical in nature but can be nonphysical commodities such as those produced by the service sector of the economy.

When households borrow and lend, the amount of utility they derive is determined primarily by their income, which the previous chapter took largely as given. By contrast, firms, financial and nonfinancial, derive income from the sale of the commodities they produce. Financial firms, in particular, derive income primarily from the spread between borrowing and lending rates,[1] a phenomenon ignored in the analysis of the previous chapter. This concept of leverage is basic to the financial firms with which we are primarily interested. We add it, therefore, to our analysis of consumption decisions. (The framework can also be used to explain the behaviour of nonfinancial firms.)

This chapter also considers other interesting questions related to firms' behaviour, such as whether they should borrow by issuing bonds or by selling shares. Surprisingly perhaps, the choice does not matter under some very special (and probably unrealistic) circumstances.

Finally, in this chapter we look at the association of stock prices with future economic performance. Observers often make this connection in the media. Is such a view warranted? As we will see, it has some validity.

---

1 Financial firms also derive income from various fees, but for the sake of simplicity we focus only on the spread in this chapter.

11.1 LEVERAGE

Leverage refers to the practice of making investments or buying assets with borrowed funds with the object of profiting from the difference between the yield or return on the investments or assets and the cost of borrowed funds. One of the important ways in which a bank borrows is by taking deposits from clients. If a bank is able to borrow at an average rate of R_{DEP} while simultaneously lending at a rate of R_L, we would expect

$$R_L > R_{DEP} \tag{11.1}$$

to hold. In other words, the **spread** (difference) between the borrowing and lending rates must be positive for the financial institution to make a profit.

To see why the spread is so important to a financial institution and its owners, the shareholders, consider the balance sheets in Table 11.1. The opening balance sheet in Table 11.1(A) is typical for a bank. Its assets consist of bonds and its liabilities of deposits and equity. Presumably, the bank uses the deposits to invest in the bonds. What is not typical, and is done to emphasize the risks of insolvency, is that the assets are perpetuities (see Chapter 5), the liabilities are variable rate. Clearly, these are mismatched. We shall see in Chapter 13 how this problem can be avoided, at least in theory. Although the numerical example is a hypothetical one, the presumed severe mismatch between assets and liabilities is one that many banks have experienced, either because of regulatory constraints or poor risk management. Hence, the example has some useful implications.

Suppose that the assets are valued at market value (not at book value, which is the normal accounting practice). Now suppose that interest rates rise by 3%. Since bond prices are inversely related to interest rates, the market value of these bonds falls.[2] Although we know that the maturity structure of the assets will influence the size of the fall, assume for simplicity that a 3% rise in the interest rate results in a 3% fall in the market value of the assets. Now look at the balance sheet in Table 11.1(B). The impact of a seemingly small change in interest rates is to practically wipe out equity!

One way of ascertaining the impact of an interest rate change is to examine the **leverage ratio**, which is defined as

$$\frac{\text{Debt}}{\text{Equity}} = \text{Leverage ratio} \tag{11.2}$$

Table 11.1	**Leverage and the Influence of Interest Rate Volatility**

(A) Opening Balance Sheet

	Assets (Millions)		Liabilities (Millions)
Bonds	$52.00	Deposits	$50.00
		Equity	2.00
Total	$52.00		$52.00
Leverage ratio = $50/2 = 25			

(B) Balance Sheet after a Three Percent Rise in Interest Rates

	Assets (Millions)		Liabilities (Millions)
Bonds	$50.49	Deposits	$50.00
(52/1.03 = 50.49)		Equity	0.49
Total	$50.49		$50.49
Leverage ratio = $50/0.49 = 102			

---

2 See the discussion in Chapter 5.

ECONOMICS FOCUS 11.1 THE SPREAD

The model in this chapter, like most economic models, assumes that the spread between borrowing and lending rates is positive. But is it always so in the real world? The answer is usually, but not always, yes.

The rather volatile nature of interest rates has caused the spread between borrowing and lending rates to become volatile too. The figure below illustrates by plotting the chartered banks' prime rate—the rate at which they lend to their most creditworthy clients—and the interest rate on nonchequable or savings deposits. The spread is usually positive, indicating that equation (11.1) is satisfied, whereas a negative number, of course, points to the opposite result.

Given the data used in the figure, the assumption of a positive spread is a reasonable one. Indeed, notice that beginning in the mid-1980s, the spread increased considerably compared to that of earlier years.

The spread then narrowed in the early 1990s, only to widen again until the year 2000, when it began to narrow once more.

Questions for Discussion

1. Is the spread shown in the figure below appropriate? Can you think of other spreads you might want to look at?
2. Are spreads linked to competition or technological developments?

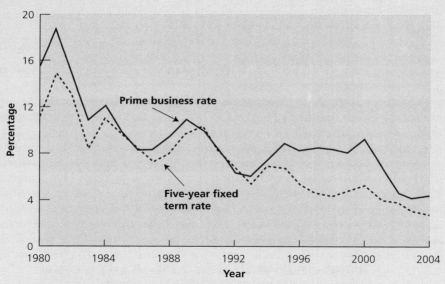

Source: Statistics Canada, *The Spread*, from CANSIM database, reproduced by authority of the Ministry of Industry, 1996; *Bank of Canada Review*, Table F1. Adapted in part from the Statistics Canada CANSIM II database **http://cansim2.statcan.ca/cgi-win/CNSMCGI.EXE**, series V122148, (prime business rate) and V122515 (five-year personal fixed-term rate). Data are averages of monthly data.

Since deposits represent the bank's debt in Table 11.1, the leverage ratio on the date of the opening balance sheet is

$$\frac{\$50 \text{ million}}{\$2 \text{ million}} = 25$$

After the interest rate rise, the leverage ratio has more than quadrupled to

$$\frac{\$50 \text{ million}}{\$0.49 \text{ million}} = 102$$

Notice that the greater proportion of assets financed through debt, the higher the leverage ratio. In the opening balance sheet, some 96% ($50 million/$52 million) of assets are financed through deposits or debt. After the interest rate rises, the figure is more than 99%. Thus, a rise in the leverage ratio signals a greater reliance on debt to finance asset purchases.

Some analysts prefer to evaluate the ratio of assets to equity (or capital) as an indicator of leverage. The **capital ratio** is defined as [3]

$$\frac{\text{Equity}}{\text{Assets}} = \text{Capital ratio} \qquad (11.3)$$

For the balance sheets in Table 11.1, they are

Opening

$$\frac{\text{Equity}}{\text{Assets}} = \frac{\$2.00 \text{ million}}{\$52.00 \text{ million}} = 0.04$$

After the Interest Rate Rise

$$\frac{\text{Equity}}{\text{Assets}} = \frac{\$0.49 \text{ million}}{\$50.49 \text{ million}} = 0.01$$

After the interest rate rises, assets are more than 100 times larger than equity, roughly a fourfold rise from the level before the interest rate changed!

Notice that the lower the capital ratio, the more leveraged the firm. A fall in the capital-asset ratio gives the same signal as a rise in the leverage ratio: a bank that is less sound following the rise in interest rates.

How realistic are the capital ratios of Table 11.1?

Table 11.2 provides some recent data on leverage or capital ratios for some Canadian chartered banks. The figures suggest little variation among banks. One reason for this is the capital convergence requirements we will examine shortly. The historical record suggests that these ratios have been fairly stable over time.

Of course, capital ratios are not the sole indicators of bank soundness or performance, as we will see. Moreover, the figures given in Table 11.2 are based on book values, not the market values assumed in Table 11.1.

As we will see in Chapter 13, not all items in a firm's balance sheet are equally risky. Holding some assets, such as corporate bonds, entails greater risk of an unfavourable price change than does the holding of cash or government bonds.

Unfortunately, some banks, in their pursuit of profit and market share, put their shareholders at great risk of insolvency. Among these were the Herstatt Bank in Germany in 1974 and the Franklin National Bank in 1977. Canadian banks are no exception, as we will see (Chapter 17). An international effort to give regulators worldwide a better idea of the risks that their banks were facing led to the formulation of risk-based capital standards, which have had mixed success at limiting banking crises. We review some of their key features below.

Table 11.2	Selected Capital or Leverage Ratios for Canadian Banks
Banks	**Capital or Leverage Ratios (December 2004)**
CIBC	22.2
Royal Bank	20.1
TD Canada Trust	21.3
Laurentian Bank	22.6
National Bank	19.1
Bank of Nova Scotia	20.1
Bank of Montreal	21.3

The debt–equity ratio is short-term and long-term interest-bearing debt divided by shareholders' equity. The higher the debt–equity ratio, the greater risk of insolvency. This definition is the same as in equation (11.2)

Source: The Globe and Mail, Report on Business, "The Top 1000," July 2005. Reprinted with permission from The Globe and Mail.

---

3 The actual definition is somewhat more complicated, as we shall see, since potentially there is a different capital ratio for different kinds of equity.

11.2 THE BIS CAPITAL CONVERGENCE REQUIREMENTS

The difficulties that faced banks worldwide during the 1980s have resulted in considerable attention being paid to the financial health of banks. One development was the 1987 adoption of regulations relative to capital standards by the Bank for International Settlements (BIS), an international central bank for central banks. (Its work is discussed in Chapter 24.) In June 2004, a new capital accord was reached that introduced more flexible rules following complaints by member countries that "one size does not fit all" when it comes to capital adequacy or risk standards. Central banks and the agencies responsible for supervising the banks agreed that there was a need for the methods used by authorities to assess risks of all kinds to converge with those used in the private sector. The sheer speed of financial innovations—you have already been given a taste of this in this text, but there is more to come!—meant that regulators were behind the curve in ascertaining the strengths and weaknesses of their respective countries' banking systems.

The original BIS capital standards, called the *capital convergence requirements*, were phased in during the early 1990s and were developed to prevent one country from taking advantage of lower capital–asset ratio requirements in another. The new capital accord is to be phased in, with completion by the end of 2006 or 2007.

In 1999, the Basel Committee on Banking Supervision introduced revisions to its capital adequacy framework.[4] After consultations, the revised plan was implemented in 2000.[5]

The capital adequacy standards consist of three "pillars":

1. minimum capital requirements

2. supervision review process

3. disclosure of risk information

The target for the capital–asset ratio is 8%.[6] By and large, banks met this goal. Equally important, the assets are risk-weighted, that is, the riskiness of an asset affects its value for the purposes of calculating the ratio.

What about derivative products, often referred to as off-balance-sheet items? (See Chapter 4 for a definition.) For these increasingly important sources of business to many intermediaries, the BIS adopted conversion factors. Banks multiply the currency equivalent amount of such an item by the conversion factor to obtain an amount equivalent to the cost of capital should the instrument fall in value. Table B provides a selective list. The lower the conversion factor, the smaller the drain on capital should a loss occur.

The essence of the new standards is contained in what is known as the "internal-ratings based approach," or IRB for short. The standards are meant to be flexible enough so that they can be adapted to individual banking systems' standards. In particular, the new standards consist of four elements that are thought to contribute to excessive risk in financial institutions. They are:

- probability of default;

- the financial loss arising out of a default;

- the exposure of the financial institution at the time of default;

- the term to maturity of the transaction at the time of default.

Depending on the particulars of the country's supervisory system, different methodologies may be used to assess these magnitudes, and these can be fairly complex. The relevant material is long

---

4 "A New Capital Adequacy Framework," Basel Committee on Banking Supervision (June 1999); "Basel Committee on Banking Supervision," *Core Principles Methodology* (October 1999).

5 "Basel Committee on Banking Supervision," Consultative Document: The Internal Ratings-Based Approach," July 2002 (Basel: Bank for International Settlements).

6 This requirement remains in place under Basel II. However, depending on the methodology used to risk-weight balance sheet items, some institutions will have to increase their capital holdings, while others may see a reduction.

and not for the faint-hearted.[7] Suffice it to say that the concept of "value-at-risk," introduced in Chapter 13, plays an important role in the new standards. Perhaps the only easy way to understand the potential impact of the Basel II standards is that, in the simplest possible scenario, it provides banks with the ability to risk-weight their claims according to some rating (such as the bond- and credit-rating schemes we shall encounter in Chapter 13). The better the quality of the claim in question, the smaller the risk-weight, which is equivalent to saying the smaller the inherent risk of a loss if the holder of the asset in question defaults.

Although the standards rely on the book value of assets, not their market value, they are significantly higher than the standards previously allowed in many countries. The rules are still somewhat open to interpretation, especially in defining capital.

The improvements recommended in 1999, and agreed to in 2004, were aimed at dealing with the growing complexity of banking and financial transactions more generally. Thus, for example, although the original standards applied to market risks, the new proposals were also meant to deal with credit risk. This application is thought to be feasible thanks to the development of increasingly sophisticated credit rating and portfolio models. In addition, the Basel Committee wanted to give supervisory agencies in member countries the ability to require banks to hold capital in excess of the minimum standards, in case this was deemed necessary. Finally, the Basel Committee wanted to put into place improved disclosure requirements on banking activities and financial performance to improve the transparency of banking operations. It was felt that such a requirement would lead to more disciplined banking since markets would be able to more easily assess banks' exposure to risk.

To illustrate a hypothetical example of how these standards ought to work, consider the simple balance sheet in Table 11.3.

The actual values are organized according to whether the assets are balance sheet or off-balance-sheet (OBS) items, as shown in part (A) of Table 11.3.[8] Next, we have to multiply the asset values by a conversion factor to obtain what is called a risk-adjusted value, as shown in part (B) of the table. We see that since there is no perceived risk to holding cash or government bonds, these assets receive a zero weighting. The impact of the BIS standards has been to *reduce the risk-adjusted* total assets and total OBS items relative to their originally recorded balance sheet values. If the capital ratio was assumed to be 0.21 in the absence of risk-weighting, application of the BIS standards increases the capital ratio to 0.56. Therefore, banks that engage in risky activities relative to other banks are more easily identified using the risk-weighted method. In the present case, because the hypothetical bank has almost half of its assets zero-weighted, its risk-weighted capital ratio means that it is "safer" than it is by the standards of the traditional capital ratio measure.

The BIS
www.bis.org

11.3 THE PRODUCTION–INVESTMENT DECISION AND THE SPREAD BETWEEN BORROWING AND LENDING RATES

Clearly, firms do engage in leverage. We consider in this section why the process of intermediation creates a divergence between borrowing and lending rates, why leverage increases the welfare of financial institutions,[9] and what the optimal amount of leverage may be. We use a framework reminiscent of that described in Chapter 10. Recall that, in that chapter, we described the consumption decision of the consumer who is endowed with a certain income. For the firm, it is a

---

7 See **http://www.bis.org/publ/bcbs107.htm** "New Capital Requirements for Credit Institutions (Basel II)," *Monthly Report* of the Deutsche Bundesbank, September 2004, pp. 73-94, and "The New Minimum Requirements for the Credit Business of Credit Institutions and Basel II," *Monthly Report* of the Deutsche Bundesbank (January 2003): 45-58.

8 These OBS items typically are derivative products you were introduced to in Chapter 4. We explore them in more detail in Chapter 15.

9 Although our focus is on the behaviour of financial institutions, our discussion also applies to nonfinancial firms since they too borrow funds to invest in assets.

| **Table 11.3** | **Hypothetical Assets of a Bank: The Effect of Risk-Weighting** |

(A) Basic Financial Information

Balance Sheet Assets	Dollars
Cash	1 000
Government bonds	10 000
Loans to corporations	5 000
Mortgage loans	8 000
Total	24 000

Off-Balance-Sheet Items (OBS)	
Standby letter of credit	2 000
Commercial letter of credit	4 000
Total	6 000

Equity: 5 000   Capital ratio: $5000/$24 000 = 0.21

(B) Risk-Adjusted Assets and OBS

Category	Actual (1) (Dollars)	Conversion Factor (2)	Risk-Adjusted (1) × (2)
Cash	1 000	0	0
Government bonds	10 000	0	0
Loans to corporations	5 000	1	5 000
Mortgage loans	8 000	0.5	4 000
Total	24 000		9 000
OBS			
Standby letter of credit	2 000	1	2 000
Commercial letter of credit	4 000	0.2	800
Total	6 000		2 800

Risk-adjusted capital ratio $5000/$9000 = 0.56

little more complicated since its owners must also decide how much to produce as well as how much to consume. To keep matters simple, we begin by describing the production decision a firm faces. By necessity, this material, like the consumer's choice problem considered in Chapter 10, is somewhat abstract. As usual, this is done to simplify the discussion as much as possible and to permit a focus on the main points.

THE PRODUCTION POSSIBILITIES FRONTIER

Consider a firm that produces some output over time. If the firm is a financial institution, we label this output intermediation. (If the firm is a nonfinancial one, the output is a physical product or a service.) Suppose this idealized firm has no borrowing or lending opportunities and can decide only how much output to produce this period (the current period or period 1) and the next one (the future period or period 2).

We graph its choice in Figure 11.1, where Q stands for the amount of production (which might be the volume of financial transactions generated or the number of units produced).

We assume that the firm can shift production between the two periods.[10] It can decide on any combination of Q_1, Q_2. It can even produce all its output during the current period, at Q_1' or all during the future period, at Q_2'. The **production possibilities** frontier, the curve describing the set of trade-offs between production in the current period and production in the next, is thus $Q_1'Q_2'$.

---

10 We include here the assumption that technology does not change during the two periods.

Figure 11.1   **The Production Possibilities Curve and Optimal Production**

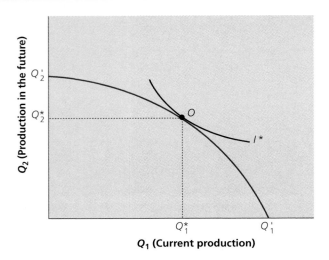

$Q'_1 Q'_2$ is the production possibilities curve. I^* is an indifference curve. Utility is maximized at point O, where the production possibilities curve is tangent to the indifference curve.

Note the concave (bowed outward) shape at the curve. The reason is the presence of **diminishing marginal returns** in production. If the firm decides to produce at Q'_1, it will be accomplishing two periods' worth of production within the time of one period—a considerable amount of effort. The inputs into the production process, such as labour and machinery, might be used more efficiently if the production were spread out over two periods instead of one. In other words, sacrificing one unit of output in the current period can actually increase output in the next period by more than one unit. The same may be true of two or three or even a hundred units. But as production is shifted more and more away from the current to the future period, problems of congestion and overuse of the factors of production arise again. Thus, although postponing some production now produces some efficiencies, the rate at which these efficiencies raise production diminishes as too much production is relegated to the future. In other words, the returns "diminish."

To the production possibilities curve in place in Figure 11.1, we now add an indifference curve, labelled I^*. Its essential meaning and properties are the same as in the case considered in the previous chapter. The only difference is that, in Figure 11.1, it is used by the firm to select the optimum combination of production over two periods. We obtain an optimum at, say, point O, at which the production possibilities curve and the indifference curve are tangent to each other. Here output is Q^*_1 in the current period and Q^*_2 in the future period. Just as with the consumer, a firm's (its owners' really) rate of time preference will dictate whether it will prefer relatively more production today versus future production.

THE PRODUCTION–INVESTMENT DECISION

So far our firm can only make intertemporal shifts of production. It cannot borrow or lend. What happens if we relax that assumption and allow it to invest with borrowed funds, that is, engage in leverage? Its opportunities are enhanced, as illustrated in Figure 11.2.

For convenience, we reproduce the findings of Figure 11.1. Notice that both production (Q) and consumption are evaluated on the horizontal and vertical axes because the firm must make the joint decision about production and consumption. In the absence of any borrowing or lending opportunities, the firm is limited to consume what it produces. It selects the highest indifference curve tangent to the production possibilities curve $FQ'G$. Utility is maximized at the optimum point O on indifference curve I^*.

Suppose, however, that the firm can invest current savings or borrow at the real rate of interest, ρ. What are the implications of engaging in such leverage? Can the firm increase its consumption possibilities? Line AB in Figure 11.2 is the consumption possibilities constraint derived in Chapter 9 when the real interest rate is ρ in periods 1 and 2.[11] Recall that the slope of the line AB is given by the real interest rate, we assume that ρ is given, meaning that there is enough competition to ensure that the firm depicted in Figure 11.2 is unable to dictate its value. Given a borrowing rate of ρ, the firm will wish to produce at Q', the point at which the production possibilities curve $FQ'G$ is tangent to the consumption possibilities curve AB. Why? Because the firm is bound to produce no more than its production possibilities and the decision about how much to produce in the current period (Q_1) versus the future period (Q_2) is dependent on market opportunities to save or invest at the prevailing real interest rate (ρ). Notice that a firm facing a real interest rate of ρ chooses to produce less in period 1 than in the case in which no borrowing or investing was permitted, which was the case depicted in Figure 11.1 (that is, Q_1' is less than Q_1^* in Figure 11.2). Now that consumption possibilities have expanded beyond $FQ'G$ (the no-leverage case) to AB, the next decision is choosing the optimum level of consumption in the two periods. The firm maximizes utility at O', where indifference curve I^{**} is tangent to the consumption possibilities constraint.

Notice that optimum O' is along indifference curve I^{**}, which is higher than I^*, the indifference curve when borrowing and lending opportunities did not exist. The firm chooses to consume Q_1^{**} worth of output but produce only Q_1'. The difference is borrowed and reinvested, thereby permitting production of Q_2' in the second period. Of course, since borrowing is costly, the firm (its owners actually) can only consume Q_2^{**} of the output in the second period, as principal and interest must be repaid by the end of period 2. Therefore, leverage improves welfare by expanding the opportunity set available to the firm and, as a result, improves total utility.

Let us now pause to consider what is happening to the economy as a whole, rather than what is happening to just a single firm, The fact that not all investment is financed through savings implies that some people in society must be saving more than their investment. In the aggregate, however, savings must equal investment.[12] How is this the case if the interest rate is ρ for everyone? The answer is that everyone does not obtain the same return on investment (that is, the lending rate) or face the same borrowing rate. Risk characteristics differ and so does the desired term to maturity for both borrowers and lenders. In addition, banks provide intermediation services by matching prospective savers with interested borrowers. Consequently, as shown by equation (11.1), borrowing rates (from banks or lending rates by banks) will be higher than deposit rates.

More generally, as we have seen, all economic decisions are governed by considerations of present value. A particular investment or loan will yield its return in the form of a stream of income generated over time. Similarly, borrowing will entail interest costs over time. If we assume, for simplicity, that the borrowing and lending rates are fixed, the firm will invest and borrow funds—engage in leverage—so long as the yield on an additional dollar invested (that is, the marginal return) exceeds the borrowing rate. Presumably, the number of such profitable investments will be limited.

---

11 Again, recall that firms in this setup are thought of as producing as well as consuming. Think of the firm's owners (that is, its shareholders) as the ones consuming. Also recall that, as in Chapter 10, borrowing and lending rates are the same. Again, this is done to simplify the exposition.

12 See Chapter 9, where we derive essentially the same condition in terms of the sources and uses of funds.

Figure 11.2   **Leverage**

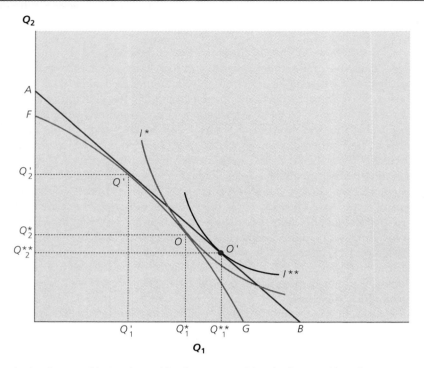

In the absence of borrowing and lending opportunities, the firm would reach an optimum of O along the indifference curve I^*. By borrowing, the firm can end up at the optimum O', which is along the higher indifference curve I^{**}. Thus, leverage opportunities increase total utility by expanding the available opportunity set. Instead of producing and consuming $Q_1^* Q_2^*$, as in the case where no leverage is permitted, the firm can produce $Q_1' Q_2'$, consume $Q_1^{**} Q_2^{**}$, and enjoy higher total utility.

Of course, the fact that leverage improves welfare might, at first glance, appear to lead to the prediction that higher leverage generates a greater welfare gain than lower leverage. This, of course, strictly speaking is not true since there are risks, which we have essentially ignored, that come into play; the most obvious one being the risk of default for a firm whose debt load becomes excessive. Indeed, empirical evidence suggests that capital structures are remarkably similar across countries. In Canada, for example, approximately 35–39% of capital is financed through debt.[13] The point here is simply that leverage increases the flexibility of the firm in managing its production (and consumption) over time.

Since this section of the chapter has demonstrated that firms can be made better off through leverage, this is presumably reflected in the profits of the firm or bank. Is there a connection between bank profitability in particular and leverage? This question is tricky because profitability is a function of many factors. Although we will return to this issue in Chapters 17 and 18, it is worth noting that profits represent the difference between revenues (primarily from interest charged to borrowers) less expenses, which include taxes and operating expenses. By this standard Canadian banks are highly profitable, but larger banks elsewhere in the industrial world are not necessarily profitable. Unfortunately, however, there appears to be little connection between the size of banks, as measured by equity, and the return on equity, partly driven by leverage. The

13 See R.G. Rajan and L. Zingales, "What Do We Know About Capital Structure? Some Evidence from International Data," *Journal of Finance* 50 (December 1995): 1421–460.

issue continues to be hotly debated, however, and the existing evidence is conflicting. To a great extent, the importance of the debate lies in the fact that the large Canadian banks continue to argue that size and profitability are linked to each other, although a number of studies dispute this contention.[14]

11.4 THE IRRELEVANCE PROPOSITION

The previous section focused on the choice of optimal proportion of leverage, not on what the firm uses for leverage. Does it make any difference whether a firm (financial or nonfinancial) opts to raise funds by selling shares, by obtaining loans, or by turning to the myriad other sources of funds?

The point here is not the relative merits of the variety of financial instruments in today's financial markets. It is rather the choice between financing with the sale of stock and financing with bonds (or any kind of loan). An influential theory in economics suggests that, under particular conditions, the choice between bond and stock financing is irrelevant. This theory is known as **Modigliani–Miller** (**MM**) theorem (named after two economists who were awarded the Nobel Prize in economics), or as the irrelevance proposition. The essence of the MM theorem is that the value of a firm, defined as the anticipated stream of income generated by the firm, is independent of the debt–equity mix. What matters ultimately is the net return on the firm's investment, not how the investment is financed.

Let us consider an example, keeping in mind the accounting identity

$$\text{Assets} = \text{Debt} + \text{Equity}$$

Recall that the reason the right-hand side of the equation provides a proxy for the value of a firm is that the value of debt (for example, bonds) is presumably determined by the discounted value of the future income stream that the firm will generate to pay off the debt. Similarly, the value of equity also reflects anticipated future income that, in turn, will generate the dividends the shareholders expect.[15] Consider the example given in Table 11.4, which contrasts two firms. Firm A has no debt and has raised all its funds in the form of equity, in the amount EQ_1. Firm B, by contrast, has financed part of its asset purchases via equities in an amount of EQ_2 and the rest via debt valued at D_2. The firm's value is thus $EQ_2 + D_2$. In all other respects, however, we assume the two firms are alike. They can borrow and lend at the same rate, ρ, and both are expected to generate the same future income streams. All the income earned by A accrues to its shareholders, whereas income generated by firm B is shared by its shareholders and its debtholders.

Now consider two scenarios:

1. Suppose an individual can purchase k% of firm A's shares. The cost is kEQ_1. Alternatively, the same individual can buy k% of firm B's shares and debt at the cost of $kEQ_2 + kD_2$. Then

Table 11.4	An Illustration of the Modigliani–Miller Theorem	
	Firm A (No Leverage)	Firm B (Leverage)
Equity	EQ_1	EQ_2
Debt	$0	D_2
Value	EQ_1	$EQ_2 + D_2$

---

14 See, for example, R. Todd Smith, "Money in the Bank: Comparing Bank Profits in Canada and Abroad," C.D. Howe Institute (May 1999), and A.N. Berger, R. DeYoung, H. Genay, and G.F. Udell, "Globalization of Financial Institutions: Evidence from Cross-Border Banking Performance," *Brookings-Wharton Papers on Financial Services* 3 (2000).

15 See Chapter 13 for more about this issue.

$kEQ_1 = \$kEQ_2 + kD_2$. That is, the values of the two firms are the same. Why? Since investors know the true value of both firms, they will only permit both firms to survive if they are valued exactly the same. Otherwise, no rational investor would buy into the firm that is relatively less valuable. Hence, the fact that firm A raised funds in the equity market, while firm B raised funds in both the equities and bond markets, is irrelevant.

2. Suppose the owners of firm B borrow kD_2 in the bond market and use the proceeds to purchase kEQ_1 of shares in firm A. The net cost of this transaction is $kEQ_1 - \$kD_2$. Again, since all investors know the true value of both firms, holding kEQ_1 of firm A must have the same value as $kEQ_2 + \$kD_2$, that is, $kEQ_1 = \$kEQ_2 + kD_2$, which was the result obtained under the first scenario. Hence, whether investors are debt or equity holders, both firms must be worth the same under the assumptions made.

The conclusions are unmistakable: The leveraged firm's value is no higher than that of the unleveraged firm.

The following analogy may also be helpful in fixing ideas. "The economic intuition is simple, equivalent to asserting that in a perfect market...the value of a pizza does not depend on how it is sliced."[16] But the same analogy also implies that "...the values of pizzas *do* depend on how they are sliced. Consumers are willing to pay more for the several slices than for the equivalent whole."[17]

But, you may say, surely firms are not indifferent between holding either stocks or bonds at any given moment. Consider some of the crucial assumptions behind the MM proposition. It assumes that dividends (the earnings of shareholders) and interest payments (the earnings of debtholders) are the same. This clearly is not the case. Tax treatments of debt and equity, for example, have tended to favour the former form of financing.[18] Moreover, the managers of firm A must answer only to the shareholders of that firm. By contrast, managers in firm B must deal with the preferences of shareholders and bondholders, which, of course, need not be the same. Also, the transactions costs of bond financing need not be the same. It may, at times, be cheaper to raise money in the stock market than in the bond market. Firms clearly weigh all these factors in making decisions about financing. Finally, there is the presumption that shareholders and bondholders are equally knowledgable about the firm's activities. However, as we saw in Chapter 3, there is asymmetric information in financial markets.

Despite all the indications that the MM theory is wrong in reality, it endures in economics, in part because of the controversies Modigliani and Miller's arguments engendered.

11.5 TOBIN'S *q*

Value Line (a U.S. firm) provides calculations of Tobin's *q* (at a cost) in its investment survey
www.valueline.com

In the previous section, we considered the problem firms have about whether to incur debts in the form of stocks or bonds. Many choose to issue stocks, and the daily gyrations in stock prices, for individual firms as well as for groups of them, often are viewed as a portent of the future for each company and for the economy as a whole. Some justification for this view exists: The purchase of assets with borrowed funds is, of course, a form of investment. Nevertheless, and despite the downturn in the stock market in the late 1990s (also see Chapter 14), there is an ongoing debate about the extent to which current stock prices can predict future economic activity. The

---

16 As quoted (page 85) in S.C. Myers, "Capital Structure," *Journal of Economic Perspectives* 15 (Spring 2001): 81–102. The analogy apparently is one that Merton Miller also used to make clear the point of the MM theorem. See O. Hart, "Financial Contracting," *Journal of Economic Literature* 39 (December 2001): 1079–1100.

17 Ibid., page 85.

18 Mainly because interest payments are tax deductible for firms, whereas dividend payments are not. (For the individuals providing the financing, interest income is taxable, but equity holdings offer the possibility of capital gains, which receive favourable tax treatments.)

developing consensus is that although stock prices certainly are an indictor of future economic performance, using stock prices to forecast future GDP growth is fraught with problems.[19]

James Tobin, a Nobel laureate in economics, proposed an investment decision rule based on the performance of a company's shares in the stock market. Presumably, a higher share price reflects the market's belief that the firm offers profitable investment opportunities. In other words, share prices reflect incentives to invest in the stock of a particular company. Tobin suggested a measure of these incentives, since called **Tobin's *q***.

The measure *q* is simply the ratio of the value of a firm's assets, as perceived in the stock market, to the current cost of replacing the same capital. In other words,

$$q = \frac{\text{Market Value of a Firm}}{\text{Replacement Cost of a Firm's Assets}} \qquad (11.4)$$

When *q* is one, this means that the stock market values $1 worth of assets at exactly $1. Market value reflects investors' view of the present (discounted) value of the current and future profits of the firm. Thus, if investors value the firm more than the sum of the cost of its assets, they must be anticipating relative profitability, a *q* > 1. As long as that condition holds, the firm's managers have an incentive to try to raise the market value of the firm's shares by purchasing more capital, which, of course, involves more borrowing. The opposite argument holds if *q* < 1. The firm has no incentive to replace capital because the market apparently believes that such investment will not generate a larger stream of income in the future.

For firms eyeing other firms, a low *q* means that a firm can be purchased more cheaply than its replacement cost. So a merger and acquisitions boom is to be expected. A low *q* means that stock prices should rise, since an investor in effect purchases a portion of a company at less than the replacement cost of the assets of that company.

Thus, lower anticipated income signals lower investment and eventually lower output, and higher anticipated income signals the reverse. For this reason, investment and business cycles are related to each other, and the stock market is watched closely as an indicator of future economic activity.

To illustrate the way in which Tobin's *q* can be useful, suppose you are head of mergers and acquisitions for your company and are considering taking over a company whose assets are estimated to have a replacement cost of $20 million. You also expect the company to generate an annual profit of $2 million indefinitely (that is, a 10% return, or 2/20 = 0.10). If interest rates on risky types of investments are 5%, then, as we saw in Chapter 5,[20] the present value of the cash flow is expected to be

$$\$2 \text{ million}/0.05 = \$40 \text{ million}$$

Consequently, the firm's market value should be $40 million, which is twice the replacement cost, yielding a *q* of

$$\$40 \text{ million}/\$20 \text{ million} = 2$$

Tobin's *q* is greater than one because the 10% profit rate is greater than the 5% investors expect from this type of investment.

19 See J.H. Stock and M.W. Watson, "Forecasting Output and Inflation: The Role of Asset Prices," *Journal of Economic Literature* 41 (September 2003): 788–829.

20 Notice that we are assuming no growth in cash flows, which of course, is unrealistic. Modifying our calculations to allow for growth is straightforward, as we will see in Chapter 14.

SUMMARY

- The simultaneous existence of borrowing and lending gives rise to an interest spread.

- Firms borrow to invest. This is the process of leverage.

- Measures such as the leverage ratio and the capital ratio tell us about the firm's level of indebtedness and the likelihood of failure or insolvency.

- The leverage ratio is debt over equity; the capital ratio is equity over assets.

- The Bank for International Settlements is an institution that has, over the past decade or so, developed capital adequacy standards to ensure the safety and stability of financial institutions worldwide.

- Using utility maximization principles, we can show that leverage can increase society's welfare.

- By separating the production and consumption decisions, firms can borrow or invest today to reallocate current and future consumption in a manner that is more desirable than when leverage is not permitted.

- There are many ways of incurring debt. Typically, a firm sells bonds or issues stock. Does it matter which form of debt is incurred? According to the Modigliani–Miller theorem, the choice is irrelevant. But the MM theorem holds only under very special circumstances.

- Many firms issue stock and many watch stock prices. Do stock prices tell us about the future state of the economy? The answer is, to some extent, yes, since the decision to incur some debt is an indication of a firm's future earning potential. A measurement based on this idea is known as Tobin's q.

IMPORTANT TERMS

capital ratio, 206
diminishing marginal returns, 210
leverage, 204
leverage ratio, 204

Modigliani–Miller (MM) theorem, 213
production possibilities, 209
spread, 204
Tobin's q, 215

PROBLEMS

1. Redo Table 11.1 assuming that interest rates *fall* by 3%. What are the leverage and capital ratios for the opening and eventual balance sheets?

2. What would happen to the production possibilities curve in Figure 11.1 if a technological improvement were introduced? Explain your answer.

3. What kind of preferences would lead the firm depicted in Figure 11.2 to become a lender instead of a borrower? (Hint: Look at Chapter 10 again.)

4. Using a diagram, explain why a financial institution benefits in utility terms from engaging in leverage.

5. Explain why the Modigliani–Miller proposition fails when transaction costs, asymmetric information, or conflicts arise between the preferences of bondholders and shareholders.

6. Explain whether the risk-adjusted capital ratio in the following situations would be higher or lower than the unadjusted ratio (Hint: Examine Table 11.3 again):
   (a) 80% of assets are other than cash or government bonds
   (b) OBS activities amount to 100% of total assets
   (c) 90% of assets are in the form of residential mortgages
   (d) 90% of assets are in the form of cash or government bonds

7. In the numerical example illustrating Tobin's q, suppose that the interest rate on risky investments is 10% instead of 5%. What is Tobin's q? What if profits are $1 million annually and the return on risky investments is 5%? 10%?

8. In Table 11.3, suppose that mortgage loans are $15 000 and government bonds are now $3000. All other balance sheet values are the same. What is the risk-adjusted capital ratio? What if cash were $5000 and government bonds were $6000, and all other values are as in Table 11.3?

DISCUSSION QUESTIONS

1. In explaining the spread, suppose we had used the rate on government bonds with a five-year term to maturity instead of the rate on five-year fixed-term deposits. Would the spread have been larger or smaller? Why? (Assume the prime rate is still used as a measure of the borrowing rate.)

2. Would the Modigliani–Miller theorem hold if borrowing and lending rates differed? Explain your answer.

3. "Debt financing is cheaper than equity financing, because investors take on less risk when purchasing debt, and thus require a lower return" said an analyst in the *Economist*, 8 December 1990, p. 81.

Explain why this might be the case. If the statement is true, how does it affect a firm's leverage ratio?

4. Why do you think the spread pictured in **Economics Focus 11.1** changed as it did during the 1980s and 1990s?

5. Why is Tobin's q likely to be an imperfect predictor of future stock prices?

6. Explain how a low q might lead to an increase in mergers and acquisitions.

7. Why is risk-weighting of assets a good idea?

8. Do capital adequacy standards make the world financial system safer?

ONLINE APPLICATIONS

Go to the BIS's Web site at **www.bis.org.** Click on *Basel Committee*, then on *Publications* and then on *Working Papers* on the right hand side of the page. Next, download working paper no. 2 "Supervisory Lessons to be Drawn from the Asian Crisis" (toward the bottom of the page). Read pages 23–29. Assess the role and usefulness of the BIS standards in light of the events in Asia, and assess the report's recommendations.

CANSIM QUESTIONS

1. Download the data series from CANSIM listed in **Economics Focus 11.1** (series labels are provided in the caption to the figure). Also download V122520 (one-year conventional mortgage rate), V122493 (nonchequable savings deposits), V122528 (daily interest savings account rate), and V122524 (one-year GIC rate).

(a) Calculate appropriate spreads from a bank's perspective.

(b) Are there differences across the various spreads?

(c) Can competition, technology, or other economic factors help explain change in a spread?

References can be found on **www.mcgrawhill.ca/college/siklos**

Explaining the Behaviour of Financial Asset Prices: Money, Risk, and Uncertainty

The Demand for Money

After reading and studying this chapter, you should be able to

12.1 explain the important role of money demand analysis in economics

12.1 identify how consumption, income, and the nominal interest rates affect the demand for money

12.1 describe what the demand for money represents

12.2 identify how we manage cash, in theory

12.2 determine optimal cash holdings in the presence of transactions costs and inflation

12.3 explain how the theory of the demand for money has evolved over time

12.4 examine some estimates of actual money demand in Canada

12.5 describe why the velocity of circulation is an important concept in understanding movements in the demand for money and the evolution of the financial system

It should be apparent by now that money plays a central role in any economic analysis of the financial system. We saw earlier in the text that money is one of several financial assets that individuals and firms hold in their portfolios. In this chapter, we specifically explore the demand for money as a separate asset.

We begin by sketching what governs the demand for money, a relatively straightforward task since previous chapters have laid the foundation. Next we explore two different ways of understanding the demand for money: One treats money much like an inventory of commodities that are costly to hold and must be managed efficiently, and the other treats money as it fits into a model in which individuals hold a variety of different assets.

Our approach is not historical, that is, we do not trace the history of thought dealing with money demand. Instead, we begin with some foundations that will be useful throughout the rest of this text and then ask whether there are other ways of thinking about demand for money, and why. After these theoretical discussions, we briefly outline what the demand for money might look like for the Canadian economy.

The chapter concludes with an explanation of the velocity of circulation. Such a discussion can be viewed as nothing more than another analysis of the demand for money, but, as we will see, there are valuable insights to be gained from exploring the subject separately.

How do we define the money supply in these discussions? In Chapter 2, we discussed various measures and concluded that although there is no widespread agreement on which is "best," the narrow definition of money—M1, which consists of currency and coins in circulation and demand deposits in the chartered banks—will do for our purposes. We therefore depend on it throughout this chapter, except when the data available require the use of M2.

Much of the modern thinking about money demand is not new but has been formalized and popularized only during the past three or four decades. The writings of Sir William Petty in the 1660s made clear his understanding of the connection between velocity and income. By the early nineteenth century such notable economists as Henry Thornton, Jean-Baptiste Say, and Nassau Senior understood that money demand was also influenced by the opportunity cost of money and expectations of inflation. Therefore, theories of the demand for money have a long and venerable history.[1]

Money is the central financial asset in economic analysis. Consequently, building an understanding of what determines the behaviour of financial asset prices more generally requires beginning with a discussion of views about what drives the demand for money.

12.1 THE MICROFOUNDATIONS OF THE DEMAND FOR MONEY: A SKETCH

Let us review a few principles, developed in earlier chapters, that will allow us to derive relationships explaining the quantity of money demanded.

First, the foremost reason for holding money is the transaction motive. Money has convenience in use and, therefore, permits an individual to economize on time spent shopping. Presumably, the time saved making trips to the bank and, more generally, protecting the value of their financial assets translates into the benefit of more leisure time. However, since the return on M1 barely exceeds 0% (most of its components are noninterest-bearing) the more money an individual holds, the more interest is forgone. The **opportunity cost** limits the quantity of money that an individual will hold.[2] It is clear, therefore, that the definition of money alluded to in the discussion above is M1, that is, currency and demand deposits, or possibly M2, which is M1 plus personal savings deposits.[3] Arguably, the proliferation of bank machines might lead one to think that transactions costs in accessing cash have been reduced dramatically. However, this is not necessarily true. First, consider that banks have increasingly outsourced bank machine locations to private firms. Naturally, they charge a service fee for cash withdrawals which is a transactions cost. Next, in spite of the fact that banks have agreed on developing common networks to permit depositors access to their funds, withdrawals from machines that do not belong to the institution where the individual banks are also subject to a transactions cost. Even debit cards, which offer immediate access to one's chequing or savings account, can be effectively subjected to transactions fees or minimum purchase requirements. Lastly, to the extent that there is a (hopefully small) possibility that the debit or ABM network is down, this too effectively imposes a cost of sorts if this happens when an individual is attempting to complete a transaction and does not have sufficient cash on hand.

We also know from our analysis of the household sector that the optimal consumption choice is an intertemporal decision problem. In deciding how much to save today, individuals must weigh how much they want to consume now relative to the future. Moreover, since part of savings is normally in the form of money, the allocation of consumption over time significantly influences the demand for money.

---

1 See T.M. Humphrey, "The Origins of Velocity Functions," *Economic Quarterly of the Federal Reserve Bank of Richmond* 79 (Fall 1993): 1–17.

2 This concept was developed in greater detail in Chapter 6. We also discussed there the precautionary and speculative motives. These motives will find their way into our sketch of money demand later in the chapter when we discuss the role of transaction costs, inflation, and the interest rate.

3 Go back to Chapter 3 for details about the various money supply definitions used in Canada. Interest rates paid on most personal savings deposits are so low, as this is written, that there is little to be lost in essentially treating the return on M2 as being very close to zero.

Finally, individuals making decisions about consumption and savings are interested in the *real* values of that consumption or savings. To put the point differently, what matters to individuals is the **purchasing power** of money held. The purchasing power of money—what money can buy—can be given as

$$\text{purchasing power of money} = \frac{1}{P} \tag{12.1}$$

where P represents the price level.

Prices are usually expressed in index form. For example, the consumer price index (CPI) may be arbitrarily set at 100 in 1992, so that prices in the past and in the future can be compared with those prevailing in 1992. Equation (12.1) makes it clear that if the CPI rises, the purchasing power of money falls. Therefore, discussions of the demand for money refer to a demand for the purchasing power of money, or what economists call **real balances**:

$$\text{demand for money} = \text{demand for } \frac{M}{P} = \text{real balances}^4$$

where M = the (nominal) money stock.

We now have all the necessary information at our disposal to sketch a behavioural relationship that describes the demand for money.

Individuals face an income constraint on the total of what is to be consumed and saved. Preferences for consumption now versus the future, also known as a person's *discount rate*, dictate how consumption will be allocated over time. Once that choice is made, the individual must also decide whether to hold the savings in money, in bonds, or in other assets, financial or non-financial. Therefore, the demand for money during any particular period is influenced primarily by consumption and interest rates. For the moment let us assume only one interest rate is relevant to the consumer. In other words, a demand for money emerges from the principles of individual utility-maximizing behaviour. More formally, we can write a **demand for money function**, $f(c_t, R_t)$—the relationship of the relevant variables—as

$$\left(\frac{M}{P}\right)^d_t = m^d_t = f(c_t, R_t) \tag{12.2}$$

$$c \uparrow \rightarrow m^d \uparrow; \; R \uparrow \rightarrow m^d \downarrow$$

where m_t is the shorthand for real balances, M/P, and, as defined previously, c denotes real consumption spending and R the nominal interest rate.[5] The flowchart below equation (12.2) shows how changes in each of the determinants of the demand for money change the quantity of money demand. Thus, a rise in consumption spending increases the desire to hold money, while a higher opportunity cost leads to a fall in the quantity of money demanded.

Although equation (12.2) appears to describe the demand for money adequately, it looks somewhat different from the one alluded to in Chapter 6. The reason is that it uses consumption instead of income as a determinant of the demand for money. The discrepancy is readily reconciled, however. We saw in Chapter 10 that a fairly stable relationship exists between consumption planned over a lifetime and permanent income. Thus, we can rewrite equation (12.2), substituting real permanent income, y^P, for c and obtain

$$m^d_t = f(y^P_t, R_t) \tag{12.3}$$

---

4 If the monetary authorities supply enough money to satisfy the quantity of money demanded, this expression is an equilibrium one.

5 Recall that although individuals make consumption–savings decisions based on what they believe the real interest is or will be, financial markets transact on the basis of nominal interest rates; it thus is this measure that should influence the demand for money.

6 Various proxies for permanent income have also been devised. See Chapter 10.

The substitution of y^P is straightforward, but there is the question of how to do it. It is common to use a measure of actual real income, y_t.[6] Then equation (12.3) can be rewritten as

$$m_t^d = f(y_t, R_t) \tag{12.3a}$$

Equations (12.2) through (12.3a) have some interesting features. Recall that R, the nominal interest rate, can be defined as the sum of the real interest rate and expected inflation:

$$R = \rho + \pi^e$$

A rise in either expected inflation or the real interest rate means that individuals will reduce their holdings of money. If inflation soars, individuals reduce their holdings of cash and seek out assets that will yield sufficient return to cover the expected rise in the nominal price level.[7]

These costs are usually referred to as the "shoe-leather costs" of money because they refer to the wear and tear on shoes from frequent trips to the bank or the ABM.

Since inflation has such negative consequences, what would be an ideal solution? According to Friedman's rule, named after the Nobel laureate Milton Friedman, if we set $\pi^e = -\rho$ then $R = 0$. In other words, a zero nominal interest rate requires negative inflation, that is, deflation. Why? According to equation (12.1), if prices fall then the purchasing power of money will rise. Therefore, eliminating any opportunity cost from holding cash requires either that cash pay interest or that the monetary authorities engineer a deflation, which effectively amounts to the same thing. While Friedman did not advocate deflation, his theoretical analysis suggests that society is better off with low to negligible inflation, a controversial suggestion, as we shall see in Chapters 21 and 23. How important are these "welfare" costs? These costs are, of course, difficult to measure since they involve guesswork about the nature of the functional form in equations such as (12.3a), as well as other assumptions about the operations of the financial system. A 10% inflation rate is thought to cost anywhere from 0.3% to about 1.5% of GDP. Put differently, reducing inflation to 0% results in approximately an extra 1% in GDP. This change may seem small, but note that the savings are permanent. Moreover, as we saw in Chapter 2, inflation imposes a number of other costs to society.[8]

Another feature of the demand for money equation is that when P increases, the quantity of money demanded should not change. In other words, the *price elasticity of money demand*—which measures the responsiveness of demand to changes in price, or $\%\Delta M / \%\Delta P$—is 1 in this theory. A rise in the price level simply means that more money is required to buy the same quantity of goods. Therefore, the quantity of real balances will remain unchanged. One can see this result more clearly by rewriting equation (12.3a) as

$$M_t^d = M_t = P_t \cdot f(y_t, R_t) \tag{12.4}$$

Notice that equation (12.4) is a demand for money function in *nominal* terms. In theory, it should translate easily into real terms. But what if people suffer from what is called **money illusion**—the belief that nominal values are not the same as real values—and hence do not understand that if prices rise by 10%, then 10% more cash is required to purchase the same quantity of goods? They simply do not think effectively about consumption or income or the demand for money in real terms. Thus, the actual price elasticity of money is an empirical question.

A final important question about any functional relationships such as the ones considered here is whether they are *stable*. How reliable is the relationship as a tool for analysis or forecasting? Nobel laureate Robert Lucas of the University of Chicago warned in 1976 of the dangers inherent in re-

---

7 Alternatively, in what is known as the phenomenon of currency substitution, people may seek assets, financial or nonfinancial, denominated in a foreign currency that are more stable in value. For example, prices in some countries are as likely to be quoted in U.S. dollars as in the home currency.

8 Recent theoretical developments are beginning to generate more precise estimates of these welfare costs. For example, one recent estimate has inflation reducing consumption by about 1%. However, the estimate is highly sensitive to the assumed economic environment (e.g., how competitive it is, or whether prices are "posted" in advance before individuals are permitted to search across prices). See G. Rocheteau, R. Wright, "Inflation and Welfare in Models with Trading Frictions," working paper, University of Pennsylvania, 2003.

lying on a particular estimate of the relationship between a set of economic variables when changes in the economic environment could dictate different estimates for the same relationship over time. Economists had long believed that equations such as (12.3) and (12.3a) were invariant in the face of changes in the economic environment caused by crises such as oil price shocks, but as the 1980s progressed, doubts began to surface about the predictability of the demand for money based on variables such as real income and an interest rate.[9]

12.2 THE BAUMOL–TOBIN MODEL: OPTIMAL CASH MANAGEMENT

The arguments just used to derive expressions describing the demand for money are fundamentally based on the notion that money's most important function is as a medium of exchange. There remains the problem of deciding how much money to hold since holding it incurs significant costs. One approach, called optimal cash management, provides a useful, if incomplete, way of thinking about the transactions demand for money.

The **optimal cash management approach**, also called the Baumol–Tobin inventory theory, applies a framework to the demand for money that firms have found useful in considering inventory control.

William Baumol, formerly of Princeton, and Nobel laureate James Tobin of Yale saw that firms and individuals face similar problems of income–expenditure gaps.[10] Because firms cannot synchronize their production and sales perfectly (a car must be made—and its components paid for—weeks or months before it is sold), they carry inventories of parts and finished goods. Similarly, individuals cannot synchronize their income and expenditure streams perfectly (the paycheque comes every other Friday, but the rent is due on the first of the month, the phone bill on the tenth, and grocery shopping is most convenient on Wednesdays), so they hold cash and chequing accounts.

FUNDAMENTAL CONCEPTS

To see the basic concepts of inventory control as applied to the demand for money, consider Figure 12.1(A). Money is measured by M1, so it can be held in either notes and coins or in a chequing account. An individual is assumed to receive a paycheque monthly and to spend all of the income on a constant basis throughout the month.[11] The price level is initially assumed to be constant, so that changes in nominal money demanded are equivalent to changes in real balances.

The assumption of a constant rate of spending—as evidenced by the straight lines in Figure 12.1(A)—implies that average cash holdings during a particular month will be the simple average of the beginning cash balance (say $2000) and the end-of-the-month cash balance ($0). If the individual's monthly (nominal) income is $2000, the *average* amount of dollars held during any particular month is

$$M^d = \frac{\$2000 + \$0}{2} = \$1000$$

This kind of cash management gives rise to a sawtooth income–expenditure pattern.

You probably can think of a number of practical problems with the results so far. First, many individuals are paid twice each month or even more frequently. This difficulty is easily handled, as also shown in Figure 12.1(A). If the biweekly income is $1000 (it still totals $2000 during the month), the average monthly cash holding is

---

9 See D. Laidler, *The Demand for Money: Theories, Evidence and Problems*, 4th ed. (New York: HarperCollins, 1993).

10 Baumol first made the point in 1952, and Tobin extended it in 1956. The two pointed out that Maurice Allais, a French economist and Nobel laureate, may have written about the same idea earlier.

11 The assumption that all income is spent is a simplification that does not affect the conclusions of the analysis.

$$M^d = \frac{\$1000 + \$0}{2} = \$500$$

which is simply one-half of the demand for cash of the individual who is paid monthly. This procedure can easily be extended when the frequency of payments is increased.

Second, many individuals often buy items using devices such as credit cards, thereby delaying the actual payment for purchases for several days or weeks. This situation is also easily handled in the model. Suppose that the individual who is paid monthly makes half of his or her expenditures with a credit card whose payments are due the first of each month. Since we have assumed that all of the $2000 is spent, the credit card bill is $1000. Figure 12.1(B) shows what happens. When the $2000 paycheque is received on the first of the month, $1000 is quickly paid to the credit card company, leaving the individual $1000 in cash or a chequing account. The average monthly demand for cash becomes

$$M^d = \frac{\$1000 + \$0}{2} = \$500$$

Figure 12.1 **Optimal Cash Management: An Inventory Approach**

(A) Constant Expenditures through a Monthly and a Bimonthly Pay Period

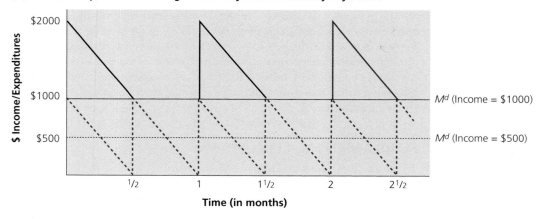

(B) Variable Expenditures through a Monthly Pay Period

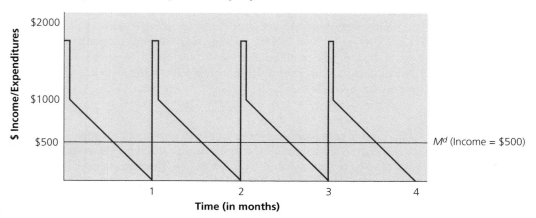

In panel (A), an individual who is paid $1000 once a month spends this income at a constant rate, giving rise to a sawtooth pattern of money holding (solid line). If the same individual is paid twice a month, the pattern is the same (dashed line), but the peaks (and average holdings) are half as high and occur twice as often.

In panel (B), the individual must pay off a number of debts after receiving each $500 monthly paycheque; expenditures then proceed at a constant rate throughout the rest of the month.

which is half the amount demanded in the no-credit case. Thus, credit cards effectively permit individuals to economize on their cash and chequing account holdings. (The same result occurs if the individual transfers a sum of money from a savings to a chequing account at the beginning of the month. We leave the modelling of this solution to the reader as an exercise.)

Optimal Cash Balance Holding

With the help of a little bit of algebra, we can derive the optimal amount of cash for the individual to hold. What is meant by "optimal" here? It refers to the level of holdings that will minimize the opportunity costs of holding cash. Why is it important to know the optimal cash holdings? For one thing, that information will enable us to examine how the demand for money is affected by inflation. We already touched on this question earlier—see equation (12.3a)—in suggesting that a 1% increase in the price level increases the quantity of (nominal) cash held by 1%.

We will find it helpful to have some notation. Let

Y = nominal income = Py = real income × price level
b = transactions cost (cost each time a transfer is made in or out of cash)
R = nominal interest rate, which is the opportunity cost of money
n = number of transactions per period

The individual must decide how many transactions are optimal to minimize the costs of holding money. Since each transaction costs $\$b$, the number of transactions should increase until one additional $\$b$ is greater than the amount that could have been earned had the funds been left in some interest-bearing account or asset.

Although $\$b$ is a fee, it can be interpreted more generally as incorporating all the various types of costs incurred in managing financial wealth and facilitating payments, including the cost of time.

To measure this opportunity cost, we need to know how much cash the individual would hold on average. By our previous calculations, the answer is

$$\left(M^d = \frac{Y}{2n} \right) \tag{12.5}$$

Y is the amount of funds available at the beginning of the month, so $(Y/2)$ is the average amount of cash held during the month. Since there are n transactions (or withdrawals) during the month, $(Y/2)/n$ or $(Y/2n)$ is the average amount of cash held by the individual adjusted for the number of transactions in a month.[12] The interest lost on $\$(Y/2n)$ held in cash is

$$\left(R\left(\frac{Y}{2n}\right) \right)$$

since each dollar could have earned R interest monthly.[13] Consider now what would happen if the individual contemplated $(n + 1)$ transactions instead of n. What are the consequences of this marginal transaction? The interest forgone in making $(n + 1)$ transactions instead of n transactions is simply

$$\left(\frac{RY}{2n} - \frac{RY}{2(n + 1)} = \frac{RY}{[n(n + 1)]} \right) \tag{12.6}$$

Since we assumed that the fee is $\$b$ per transaction, regardless of its size (no more than a simplifying assumption), then setting $n=1$ in (12.6) allows us to illustrate a simple rule that will tell us when it is sensible to hold cash versus leaving it in our account. In particular, when

---

12 Recall that, in Figure 12.1(A), the first example has $n=1$, $Y=\$2000$, so $M^d = \$2000/2X1 = \$1000$; in the second case $n=2$, so $M^d = \$2000/2X2= \$500$.

13 The interest rate here is defined on a monthly basis to render the analysis compatible with the numerical example considered.

$$b > \frac{RY}{2} \tag{12.7}$$

the transactions costs exceed the interest that could have been earned had the cash been invested in an interest-earning asset. The optimal number of transactions is thus the value of n that equates the marginal cost of holding money to the marginal revenue of holding money. This condition can be written

$$b = \frac{RY}{2n^2} \tag{12.8}$$

where $RY/2n^2$ is the additional interest earned.[14] Solving equation (12.8) for n, we find

$$n^2 = \frac{RY}{2b}$$

$$n = \sqrt{\frac{RY}{2b}} \tag{12.9}$$

Figure 12.2(B) shows the relationship between real balances and real GDP. Once again, as the theory would predict, and as summarized by the straight line, the relationship is a positive one. Finally, Figure 12.2(C) shows plots of real balances against the nominal interest rate (here proxied by the yield on long-term government bonds). The relationship depicted here is negative. Finally, by substituting equation (12.9) into (12.5), we can find the optimal demand for money.

$$M^d = \frac{Y}{2n} = \frac{Y}{2\sqrt{RY/2b}}$$

which can be simplified considerably[15] to

$$M^d = \left(\frac{b}{2}\right)^{0.5} \cdot Y^{0.5} \cdot R^{-0.5} \tag{12.10}$$

(Note that the exponent 0.5 denotes square root.)

Finally, since $Y = Py$, we can rewrite the demand for money[16] as

$$M^d = P \cdot \left(\frac{b}{2P}\right)^{0.5} \cdot y^{0.5} \cdot R^{-0.5} \tag{12.11}$$

Equation (12.11) can be interpreted as indicating that a 1% increase in real income increases the demand for money in nominal terms by the square root of 1%. By contrast, a 1% increase in the opportunity cost of money reduces the demand for cash by the square root of 1%. Notice also that a 1% rise in prices, all else the same, raises the demand for nominal balances by less than 1%. Hence, we can express the demand for money in terms of real balances as follows:

$$M^d/P = \left(\frac{b}{2P}\right)^{0.5} \cdot y^{0.5} \cdot R^{-0.5} \tag{12.12}$$

---

14 Recall again that b is the cost of making an additional transaction and it stays constant regardless of the size of n. The opportunity cost over the month totals $(RY/2n)$. For the technically inclined, the marginal revenue or benefit of keeping more money in the bank by reducing the number of transactions by one (i.e., of reducing the average amount of cash held during the month) is $\partial(RY/2n)/\partial n$, that is, the partial derivative of $(RY/2n)$ with respect to n, since this measures the change in $(RY/2n)$ for a given change in n. $\partial(RY/2n)/\partial n = (2RY)/4n^2$, which is equation (12.8).

15 As follows:
$$\begin{aligned} M^d &= (Y/2)/[R^{0.5} \cdot Y^{0.5} \cdot (2b)^{-0.5}] \\ &= (b/2)^{0.5} \cdot YY^{-0.5} \cdot R^{-0.5} \\ &= (b/2)^{0.5} \cdot Y^{0.5} \cdot R^{-0.5} \end{aligned}$$

16 Using equation (12.5) we can write $M^d = Py/2n$, or $M^d = P \cdot y/2n$. The demand for real balances is then expressed as $M^d/P = y/2n$.

Figure 12.2 The Determinants of Money Demand, 1960–2004

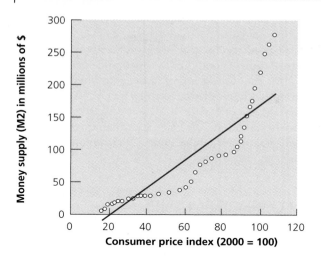

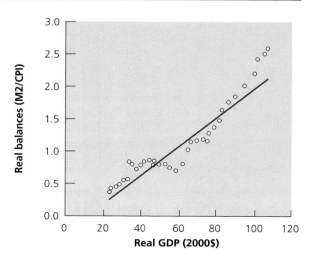

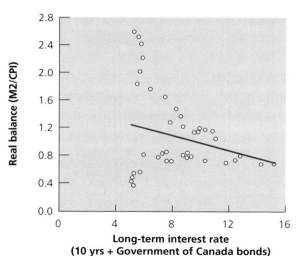

Over four decades of data suggest the existence of a fairly strong link between M2 and the price level and real M2 and real income. The relationship between real balances and the nominal interest rates, though negative, is weak. The reason is financial innovation.

Source: International Monetary Fund, *International Financial Statistics* CD-ROM (Washington, D.C.: International Monetary Fund). The CPI is series 64, M2 is proxied by the IMF's definition of money (series 34), the long-term interest rate is series 61, and real GDP is series 99BVRZF.

THE ROLE OF INFLATION

Using the optimal cash management model, we have just concluded that inflation—a sustained rise in the price level—does affect the demand for money. But earlier, when we discussed the demand for money function in nominal terms [equations (12.3) and (12.4)], we said that a rising price level should not change the quantity of money demanded. Have we managed to contradict ourselves?

The answer is no. In deriving the earlier equations, we assumed that the opportunity cost of holding money remained constant. The optimal cash management model uses no such assumption.

Indeed, it treats money like an inventory of commodities, and inflation will clearly increase the cost of keeping it idle. The frequency of payment increases, so as we saw in Figure 12.1(A), average cash holdings will fall. The individual must make more trips to the bank, which means greater transactions costs [a look at equation (12.7) will make this point clear].

The conclusion that real balances will fall as inflation accelerates is borne out by the experience of economies that have suffered **hyperinflation**, a condition in which price rises accelerate very quickly and very sharply (usually by 50% a month or more), money becomes worthless, and the financial system collapses. For example, when inflation skyrocketed in Hungary after World War II, real balances fell to almost zero in just one year.

What about more normal experiences with inflation? We will see in the next section that the predictions contained in equation (12.11) are not entirely accurate. The inventory approach does not tell us the whole story about the demand for money.

12.3 A MORE COMPLETE MODEL OF MONEY DEMAND

Another approach to estimating the demand for money rests on the fact that since money is a medium of exchange, some money changes hands whenever a transaction occurs. Variables of interest include the quantity of money in circulation—that is, the size of the money supply—and the **velocity of circulation**, which is the number of times a given quantity of money turns over to produce a given level of spending.

QUANTITY THEORY

The **quantity theory** is very old. In its simplest form, it links the real and monetary sides of an economy in the following relationship:

$$M^s V = Py \tag{12.13}$$

where

M^s = the quantity of money in circulation
V = the velocity of circulation
P = the price level (for example, as expressed by a consumer price index)
y = the economy's *real* income (that is, real GDP or GNP)[17]

The equation is actually an identity. A given stock of money circulating in the economy changes hands a number of times, as measured by velocity. The dollar value of the stock of money multiplied by its rate of turnover, V, should equal the value of the goods and services purchased during a given period. For example, if the stock of money was $100 billion in 2000 and changed hands four times during the year, then $4 \times 100 = \$400$ billion worth of purchases were generated.

If we assume that the market for money is in equilibrium so that $M^s = M^d$, equation (12.13) then becomes

$$M^d V = Py$$

or, by rearranging the terms,

$$M^d = \left(\frac{1}{V}\right) Py \tag{12.14}$$

Thus, the quantity theory becomes a theory of the demand for money.

---

17 Early versions of the quantity theory related the quantity of money to the volume of transactions. Problems of measurement led analysts to proxy transactions with aggregate output or income.

ECONOMICS FOCUS 12.1 — WHEN PRICES GO WILD

Economists have long been fascinated with episodes of hyperinflation since these are viewed as near laboratory-type situations in which to study money demand. Hungary has the distinction not only of having the highest inflation rate on record but of experiencing hyperinflation twice in one century (1920s and 1940s), each time after the end of a major war (Siklos).

Under conditions of hyperinflation, prices rise so quickly that the impact of income changes on money demand are trivial (hyperinflation also tends to last for a short time). In Germany and in Hungary, workers often were paid more than once a day and even then arranged for children to run to the store to buy foodstuffs before the prices were raised again. In the later stages of the Hungarian hyperinflation, wages were set in terms of calories because the price increases for food after wages were paid wiped out a considerable amount of purchasing power in a matter of hours. Moreover, the real interest rate is so small relative to inflation that it too can be ignored. What dominates money demand then are expectations of inflation. This led Philip Cagan, in a now-classic article, to suggest that a money demand function under hyperinflation conditions can be written as $m^d = f(\pi^e)$, which is a highly simplified version of equation (12.3a). Cagan used a version of the above equation to study money demand for a number of episodes of European hyperinflation. Hyperinflation was defined as occurring whenever the inflation rate ex-

ceeded 50% per month. Equally fascinating is the study of policies needed to end hyperinflation. The end of hyperinflation tends to occur rather abruptly. The study of hyperinflations proved to be especially useful to policy-makers in Latin and South America during the 1970s and 1980s when they too had to grapple with high or hyper-inflation. Hyperinflations are not a thing of the past. Most recently, the former Yugoslavia, Russia, and the Ukraine, have experienced runaway inflation.

Questions for Discussion
1. Inflation and the size of the financial sector are positively related to each other. Why is this the case, and why is this exacerbated during episodes of hyperinflation?
2. What are the welfare costs of inflation? Are these costs higher the higher the inflation rate?

Sources
P. Cagan, "The Monetary Dynamics of Hyperinflation," in *Studies in the Quantity Theory of Money*, edited by Milton Friedman (Chicago: University of Chicago Press, 1956): 25–117.

P.L. Siklos, *War Finance, Reconstruction, Hyperinflation, and Stabilization in Hungary* (London, Macmillan, 1991).

P.L. Siklos, *Great Inflations of the Twentieth Century* (Aldershot: Edward Elgar, 1995).

Early quantity theorists treated the reciprocal of velocity, $1/V$, as a constant. Some wanted to focus on the direct and predictable relationship between money and income. Some felt that features of the financial system that could influence velocity, such as the payments system and technology, changed slowly or infrequently.

In the 1930s, John Maynard Keynes noted that the nominal interest rate could affect velocity. But the point was little emphasized in his exposition and that of his followers. They focused on a stable consumption function, relegating the role of money in the economy to the sidelines.

FRIEDMAN'S MONETARY THEORY

The Keynesians reigned in academic economics until the mid-twentieth century when Nobel laureate Milton Friedman, then of the University of Chicago, offered a model of the demand for money that incorporated a restatement of the quantity theory. The work of Friedman and his followers led to a revival of the view that money is the central macroeconomic variable.[18]

Friedman began with his **permanent income hypothesis** in which money is an asset in a portfolio of many assets and thus the desire to hold money is a function of the rate of return on

---

18 For more on this view, see Chapter 21.

a variety of alternative assets (see Chapter 10). Specifically, Friedman's version of the demand for money function is a generalized version of (12.3a) that can be expressed as[19]

$$\frac{M^d}{P} = f(R^B, R^E, \pi, W_h/W_n, y, u)$$

$$\quad\quad\quad - \quad - \quad - \quad + \quad\quad + \quad ?$$

(12.15)

where

M^d = desired demand for money
P = nominal price level
R^B = nominal return on bonds
R^E = nominal return on stocks or equities
π = return on money as measured by the rate of inflation
W_h = human wealth
W_n = nonhuman wealth
y = real income
u = other factors omitted in the functional relationship that can influence the demand for money

The signs below each variable in equation (12.15) denote how a change in a particular term of the function changes the quantity of real balances demanded.

Note that equation (12.15) is like equation (12.3a) in the sense that it specifies the demand for money as a demand for real balances. The first three terms in the functional relationship are various measures of the opportunity cost of holding money. Increases in the nominal return on bonds, on stocks or equities, or on goods (measured as the inflation rate) produce a fall in the quantity of real balances demanded.

One of the novelties of Friedman's approach to the demand for money is that it allows for the influence of *all* forms of wealth, as represented by the variable W_h/W_n. Thus, in contrast to the definition given earlier, wealth here includes both nonhuman wealth—physical and financial assets, which we earlier called *net wealth*—as well as human wealth—essentially the present discounted value of earnings, which will be influenced by, for example, an individual's level of education. Because the human component of wealth is not easily marketable, its "return" does not directly enter the formulation in equation (12.15). (However, individuals who accumulate relatively more human wealth also tend to acquire more nonhuman wealth in the future, assuming income and human wealth are positively related to each other.)

The term y represents real income, which influences the demand for money in the manner already described.

Finally, the residual, u, reflects various factors, such as an individual's tastes and preferences, that may influence the demand for money but that are not easily captured by the other variables in the equation. The relationship between u and the demand for money is unclear, however, so a question mark appears below the variable in equation (12.15).

Since, as we saw in Chapter 10, permanent income is related to individuals' wealth constraint, it is influenced indirectly by alternative returns on assets, which affect the amount of wealth accumulated over a lifetime. Like the liquidity preference framework, Friedman's model shows that a rising interest rate reduces the quantity of money demanded, *other things being equal*. But, Friedman argued, other things are *not* equal. In particular, when bond yields increase, the return on money (proxied by the inflation rate) does not remain constant. Why? Say the yields on bonds rise. With bonds becoming a relatively more attractive asset and people considering the transfer of an increasing share of their wealth to bonds from money, the banks, eager to protect the aggregate size of their deposits (a major component of the money supply) are likely to raise the return paid on money (that is, deposits). Thus, the quantity of money demanded may not change after all.

---

19 The differences between equation (12.3a) and the one derived by Friedman are inconsequential for our purposes.

These insights enabled Friedman to suggest that equation (12.15) can be greatly simplified as

$$\frac{M^d}{P} = g(y^P) \tag{12.16}$$

where y^P = permanent income and all other terms are as already defined. This equation simply says that the demand for money is a function of $g(y^P)$, permanent income. It contains no interest rate variable. Friedman believed some early empirical evidence that the demand for money is insensitive to interest rate changes. The overwhelming bulk of modern empirical evidence from several countries suggests, however, that interest rates do influence the demand for money. With correction for that fact, Friedman's framework becomes equation (12.3a).

12.4 DEMAND FOR MONEY FUNCTIONS: EMPIRICAL ESTIMATES

The demand for money that most economists rely on is a demand for real balances, which assumes that the price elasticity is 1.[20] How accurate is such a view? Figure 12.2(A) shows the money supply M2 plotted against the consumer price index for annual Canadian data since 1960. The relationship is positive, as expected, but is not equal to 1. Nevertheless, the relationship appears weak. Does this mean that the interest rate is not an important component in the story of money demand? The next section points out that we have neglected to incorporate a role for financial innovations, a critical force, especially since the mid-1980s. The next section fills this gap.

12.5 VELOCITY OF CIRCULATION

So far we have largely ignored the behaviour of the velocity of circulation, treating this variable essentially as a constant. Is this assumption too strong?

Recall that the quantity theory is central to the understanding of the demand for money (see equation 12.13). Thus, the demand for money, $\underline{M^d}$, is a function of (real) income multiplied by the reciprocal of the velocity of circulation, or, as earlier denoted in equation (12.14),

$$M^d = \left(\frac{1}{V}\right)Py$$

Suppose now that velocity is a constant. Then, the demand for money is a function of real income alone, which is, in essence, Friedman's theory of the demand for money.

But how realistic is the assumption of a constant velocity? Figure 12.3 plots velocity for Canada for more than a century of data. We see that velocity is far from being a constant. It seems then that, at least for long periods, it is not appropriate to treat velocity as a constant in the demand for money function.

Notice that the curve in Figure 12.3 is a rough U-shape as shown by the smooth line. Why? Some analysts suggest that the shape reflects the timing of **monetization** and financial innovation. During the early twentieth century the use of cash and cheques was becoming increasingly common. As a consequence, the growth of money exceeded that of income during the prewar period. The 1930s and 1940s saw a change in the direction of velocity. The Great Depression and World War II produced forces that promoted financial innovation and sophistication. Two obvious examples come immediately to mind: credit cards and automatic banking machines. Both innovations permit individuals to keep some of their financial wealth in interest-earning assets longer than would

---

20 In other words, a 1% rise in prices leads individuals to hold 1% more money.

ECONOMICS FOCUS 12.2   THE DECLINE AND FALL OF MONEY DEMAND?

In the 1960s, many economists thought they had settled on an approach to the demand for money function. A decade later, however, some of them, especially in the United States, were questioning its adequacy. The conventional demand for money function was regularly overpredicting actual money demand by the mid-1970s (Goldfeld called the difference between actual and predicted values "the missing money"), and underpredictions appeared just as regularly in the early 1980s. Various researchers (for example, Judd and Scadding, and Cooley and LeRoy) pointed out a number of flaws in the way analysts had estimated demand. But it was becoming apparent that the demand for money had an endemic lack of stability.

The most promising solution to the problem of finding a stable demand for money function may lie in explicitly incorporating the influence of financial innovation. On a more practical level, watching movements in velocity can be very useful. For example, during the recession of 1991–92, money growth was sluggish, providing evidence of the importance of money in influencing economic activity. Of course, sluggish money growth and recessions need not go hand in hand (for example, velocity may rise to offset slow growth, as it does in the simple quantity theory equation analyzed in this chapter).

The difficulty with using some measure of financial innovation to make the demand for money stable again is that there are no obvious candidates to proxy such developments. Consequently, if one looks at the monthly publication of the Bank of Canada, *Bank of Canada Banking and Financial Statistics* (Table E1), one finds at least six definitions for the money supply, each one adapted to capture some change that has occurred in the financial system over time. Moreover, even though money growth can still be useful in forecasting inflation (Siklos and Barton),

economists have lost interest in recent years in estimating money demand functions despite valiant attempts by some (Laidler) to warn the profession that it ignores "money" at its peril.

Questions for Discussion

1. What do economists mean when they say that the demand for money may be unstable?
2. What are the traditional and institutional determinants of velocity? Could some or all of the institutional determinants of velocity themselves be related somehow to some of the traditional determinants?

Sources

T.F. Cooley, and S.F. LeRoy, "Identification and Estimation of Money Demand," *American Economic Review* 71 (December 1981): 825–44.

S. Goldfeld, "The Case of the Missing Money," *Brookings Papers on Economic Activity* 3 (1976): 683–730.

J.P. Judd, and J.L. Scadding, "The Search for a Stable Money Demand Function," *Journal of Economic Literature* 20 (September 1982): 993–1023.

D. Laidler, "The Quantity of Money and Monetary Policy," Bank of Canada Working Paper 99-5, April 1999.

P.L. Siklos, "Income Velocity and Institutional Change: Some New Time Series Evidence, 1870–1986," *Journal of Money, Credit and Banking* 25 (August 1993): 377–92.

P.L. Siklos and A. Barton, "Monetary Aggregates as Indicators of Economic Activity in Canada: Empirical Evidence," *Canadian Journal of Economics* 34 (February 2001): 1–17.

---

otherwise be the case. Over time, these events shifted the economy away from reliance on money for transaction purposes. This phenomenon, combined with the worldwide postwar boom in economic growth, resulted in a situation in which income grew faster than money, which explains the postwar tendency for velocity to rise over time. The theory that links velocity or money demand to financial development and innovation is known as the institutionalist hypothesis.[21] The Canadian evidence is not unique; most other industrialized countries have had the same experience.[22]

---

21 A detailed description of these ideas can be found in M.D. Bordo, and L. Jonung, *The Long-Run Behavior of the Velocity of Circulation* (New York: Cambridge University Press, 1987).

22 See M.D. Bordo, L. Jonung, and P.L. Siklos, "Institutional Change and the Velocity of Money: A Century of Evidence," *Economic Inquiry* (October 1997): 710–24.

Figure 12.3	Velocity of Circulation in Canada since 1872

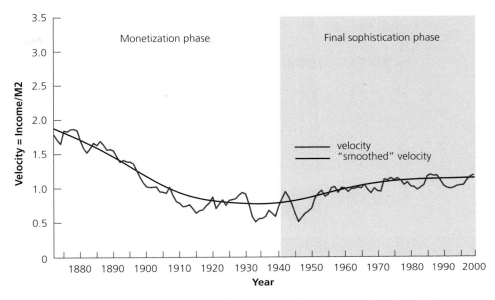

Note: Velocity is derived from equation (12.14) by rearranging its terms to produce $V = Y/M$.
Since $y = Y/P$, and $m = M/P$, $V = (Y/P)/(M/P) = Y/M$, where Y is nominal GNP and M is the stock of money, measured here as M2. Note too that M^d was replaced with M—that is, with actual values for the money supply. The implicit assumption is that the money market is in equilibrium.

Source: M.D. Bordo, and L. Jonung, *The Long-Run Behavior of the Velocity of Circulation* (New York: Cambridge University Press, 1987), updated from data in *Federal Reserve Bulletin* and the *Bank of Canada Review*. Figures after 1986 are comparable with figures for earlier years but not identical due to definitional changes.

SUMMARY

- The demand for money represents a way of explaining how much cash (and bank deposits) individuals choose to hold.

- Income, interest rates, and prices are the principal determinants of the demand for money.

- Money illusion refers to the possibility that individuals do not realize that when prices increase, more cash has to be held to purchase the same quantity of goods.

- One way to think of the demand for money is as an inventory control problem. Individuals attempt to synchronize income with expenditures as well as possible and to minimize the opportunity costs of holding money. This is called the optimal cash management approach to the demand for money.

- Under the cash management approach, the demand for money function is of the form $M^d = P(b/2P)^{0.5} \cdot y^{0.5} \cdot R^{-0.5}$ where 0.5 or −0.5 represent the elasticities of the various determinants of money demand. These are: transaction costs (b), the price level (P), income (y), and the nominal interest rate (R).

- The quantity theory expresses a relationship between the money supply and total spending. Interest rates play no direct role but can play an indirect role in this version of the demand for money.

- Friedman suggests a theory of the demand for money that essentially comes down to a restatement of the quantity theory. Money is but one asset in a portfolio of assets, some financial, some nonfinancial.

- Empirical evidence suggests that the interest rate, prices, and income all play important roles in explaining the demand for money over long periods.

- Over long periods the velocity of circulation is important for understanding the demand for money because it can reflect the influence of financial innovations.

IMPORTANT TERMS

demand for money function, 221
hyperinflation, 228
monetization, 231
money illusion, 222
opportunity cost, 220
optimal cash management approach, 223

permanent income hypothesis, 229
purchasing power, 221
quantity theory, 228
real balances, 221
velocity of circulation, 228

PROBLEMS

1. Describe the effect of the following on the velocity of circulation:
   (a) Credit cards or debt cards become increasingly common in use.
   (b) All types of chequing accounts pay market interest rates.
   (c) Automatic banking machines become available in so many places that individuals can, at very little cost, obtain cash or transfer funds from one type of account to another.

2. Suppose that the total spending in an economy is $200 billion and the money supply is $5 billion. What is the value of velocity?

3. An economy has a money supply of $50 billion. The average price of goods and services being exchanged is $50. A billion transactions take place each week. On average, how long is a dollar held between transactions?

4. Suppose that Bank of Canada implements a policy of 3% annual growth in M2 to achieve zero inflation. Under what circumstances might zero inflation be attained? (Hint: Look at the quantity theory equation.)

5. Suppose that the demand for money is given in equation (12.11). Assuming $b = 4$, answer the following:
   (a) If $P = 100$, $y = 20$, and $R = 0.10$, what is the demand for money?
   (b) If $b = 2$ and Py and R are as in (a) above, what is the demand for money?

6. Would the case depicted in Figure 12.1(B) be the same if the bills were paid by a transfer of funds from a savings account? Explain.

7. Suppose that transactions costs in the Baumol–Tobin framework were (b/n), so that average transactions costs fall as the number of transactions increase. What would be the marginal cost of an additional transaction? Would money demand be affected?

DISCUSSION QUESTIONS

1. According to the model of optimal cash management, would rich individuals differ from poor ones in their demand for money? Explain your answer.

2. Explain how we can associate strong growth in the money supply with either strong economic growth or weak economic growth. (Hint: Think about what must happen to velocity.)

3. The interest elasticity of demand for M1 appears to have risen since the end of World War II. What role might financial innovations have played in this trend?

4. The income elasticity of the demand for money has been low since 1960. Can you explain why this might be the case?

5. Why is it that, under hyperinflation, we can ignore the effect of income and the real interest rate on money demand? Explain.

6. Could the interest elasticity for the monetary aggregate M3, for example, be positive? Explain.

7. What is the institutionalist hypothesis of velocity? What does it explain that the quantity theory cannot? Explain.

8. According to the empirical estimates presented in the chapter, is there much evidence of money illusion? Do the results surprise you? Why or why not?

9. How would credit cards affect M1 and M2 velocity? automatic banking machines? Explain.

10. The growing acceptance of credit cards for all sorts of transactions is having the effect of reducing the demand for money. Comment.

ONLINE APPLICATIONS

Studies of money demand continue to be popular. Go to **www.ssrn.com**. Click on *Search & Download Papers* then *Search* for an abstract using the keywords "money demand" or "demand for money." Select a title of your choice and download a paper that interests you. Are the results reported broadly in line with the material presented in this chapter?

CANSIM QUESTIONS

Go to the CANSIM Web site. Download the following money stock series (since the 1980s only at the annual frequency): M1 (V37124), M2+ (V37128), M2++ (V37150), M1+ (V37151), and M1++ (V37152). Next, download nominal GDP (V1992067), also at the annual frequency. Compute the velocity of circulation. Compare the various measures of velocity. Could the institutionalist explanation of velocity's behaviour partly explain the differences in velocity? Next, download the CPI (V18702611) and compute the inflation rate, and download the three-month Treasury bill rate (V122531). Plot the different measures of velocity against inflation and the interest rate. Is a relationship between these series apparent? Are any apparent relationships consistent with the standard money demand function?

References can be found on www.mcgrawhill.ca/college/siklos

Asset Demand and Supply under Uncertainty: The Risk–Return Relationship

LEARNING OBJECTIVES

After reading and studying this chapter, you should be able to

13.1 define risk and uncertainty and explain the difference between them

13.1 list some of the most common forms of risk

13.1 describe how to measure and evaluate the return and risk of an asset portfolio

13.2 determine how attitudes toward risk and risk aversion can be expressed

13.2 identify how to select a portfolio and the implications of mixing risky and riskless assets

13.2 describe what the capital–asset pricing model tells us about stock selection and portfolio risk

13.3 analyze how the value-at-risk approach assists in business decision making

13.4 understand why the capital asset pricing model (CAPM) is a useful tool in finance

13.5 determine how the matching principle aids in managing assets and debts and the role of risk

In analyzing the consumption, saving, and borrowing choices faced by the private sector, we omitted incorporating an important feature, namely the role risk plays in these decisions. Can we measure risk as it pertains to the demand for assets or the supply of debt?

Since the answer seems to be yes, the individual's attitude toward risk is an important element in the portfolio balance decision.

Accordingly, we begin this chapter by defining risk, listing its sources, and exploring the implications of different attitudes toward it. Next, we investigate the portfolio balance decision by examining the choices facing an individual who must allocate his or her wealth among risky assets. In Chapter 15, we consider how some people attempt to mitigate risk through what is known as *hedging* behaviour.

13.1 RISK AND ATTITUDES TOWARD IT: DEFINITIONS

Generally, **risk** is the possibility of potential loss against which insurance is provided. In this chapter, however, we are more specific and identify risk as the kind of potential loss on investments against which borrowers provide a higher return than they would otherwise.

When risk is present, the number of possible future events exceeds the number of actual events that will occur, and some measure of probability can be attached to those possibilities.

Notice that risk does not mean uncertainty. Uncertainty reflects an ignorance about the future. Risk, on the other hand, is a fact of life. People can make informed decisions even in the face of risk because they can assess and rank the chances of experiencing a particular eventuality in the future.

SOURCES OF RISK

Risk originates from a variety of sources and is often named according to them.

1. Default. **Default risk** represents the likelihood that a borrower will evade his or her financial obligations with respect to interest, principal, or both. Various services exist to evaluate the degree of default risk. For example, **bond rating** schemes, such as those displayed in Table 13.1, attempt to rank the chances that the issuer of a particular bond will or will not default. **Financial Focus 13.1–Junk Bonds** considers the history of one particular group of bonds much in the news the last few years.

2. Liquidity. Lenders face the possibility that they will require funds earlier than planned. If there is a large market in which the investor can sell a particular financial asset quickly, its liquidity is enhanced. By contrast, if the instrument is not easily convertible, the prospect of being short of funds at some time in the future is increased and so is **liquidity risk**. (This notion is sometimes referred to as the "marketability" of an asset.)

3. Market Risk. Unless an asset is held until maturity, its price may fluctuate over time.[1] Since the timing of the sale of an asset is not always known in advance, there is an inherent **market risk**: the possibility of a future change in price with a consequent loss of return.

4. Systematic Risk. Some risk is systemwide—that is, it is caused by a factor or factors common to all or most assets in the financial system. Price fluctuations can result from external factors arising out of political, legal, or aggregate domestic or international changes in economic conditions, each of which can influence **systematic risk**. Prices and asset returns vary systematically with such events. For example, when banks were becoming insolvent in Japan during the 1980s a common factor was the bursting of the asset price bubble in that country, which affected the whole financial system. Another example is the impact of the collapse of the tech bubble in the U.S. in 1999-2000, with reverberations throughout the economy.

5. Foreign Exchange Risk. Investors dealing in assets denominated in a foreign currency face an additional market risk—that the exchange rate between that currency and the domestic currency may fluctuate in an unanticipated direction or to an unanticipated degree. Such risk is called **foreign exchange risk**.

6. Income Risk. Since borrowing is, to some extent, a function of the anticipated future earning power of an individual or a firm, any change in the stream of income or profits will influence the ability to pay the interest and principal on a loan. The possibility of unexpected fluctuations in income, therefore, produces **income risk**.

7. Inflation Risk. Lenders and borrowers have an incentive to accurately predict inflation, especially in the case of a debt instrument whose nominal interest rate is fixed.[2] An underestimate of future inflation benefits the borrower and penalizes the lender, and an overestimate has the opposite effect. Consequently, investors face **inflation risk**.

8. Tax Risk. Changes in the tax treatment of interest income, registered retirement savings plans, and capital gains influence the after-tax returns of investors (see Chapter 5 for a numerical

---

1 Of course, the asset need not be a bond. The price of many fixed assets, such as housing, also fluctuate over time.
2 Even bonds or pensions indexed to inflation are subject to some inflation risk to the extent that inflation usually cannot be forecast precisely. Even the Canadian tax system is not fully indexed.

Table 13.1	Canadian Bond Rating Schemes

Dominion Bond Rating	
AAA	Highest quality
AA	Superior quality
A	Satisfactory grade
BBB	Adequate
BB	Speculative
B	Highly speculative
C	Very highly speculative
D	In arrears

The two Canadian bond rating services consider Government of Canada bonds to be of the highest quality (possess the least risk) simply because the federal government is always able either to print money to pay interest and principal or borrow from abroad, if necessary, to meet its financial obligations. Next in line are other levels of government, usually beginning with the provincial governments. Corporate bonds are ranked according to the issuer's size, profitability, expectations about future success, and so on.

Of course, any country's ability to borrow is hampered by expectations of its future growth. Accordingly, Moody's and Standard and Poor's, both of which also publish bond rating schemes, evaluate credit ratings across countries. Notice that the above list is only suggestive of the types of credit ratings available. A variety of credit ratings lists have been constructed that use different terminology or are more formally stratified than the list in the above table.

example). This type of risk is called **tax risk**. As governments in the 1990s dealt with the impact of mounting deficits, changes in tax rates and coverage occurred more frequently, with important consequences for investors. By the end of the 1990s, both provincial and federal governments began trying to ease the tax burden, but the tax changes were complicated by the introduction of surtaxes and the shifting of the tax burden to local levels of government.

We have already seen that risk shifts the supply of loanable funds to the left (see Chapter 6). Consequently, risk drives a wedge between the return on a risk-free asset and one that is risky.

THE MEASUREMENT AND CONSEQUENCE OF RISK

By definition, risk can be quantified. To do so, we borrow from statistical methods.

Variations in an Asset's Return

Risk stems from variation in returns over time, which is associated with "boom" and "bust" cycles in the economy. These variations are influenced by any or a combination of default, liquidity, market, income, and inflation risk. To keep the discussion simple, let us focus on only one set of future prospects or "states of the world"—namely the business cycle, whose swings can be assigned the subjective probabilities listed in Table 13.2. We assume that the world has three assets, whose rates of return vary with the business cycle, as shown in the table. For now, we also ignore term to maturity considerations, a topic examined in Chapter 7, and one we return to at the end of this chapter. Although these assumptions simplify actual choices facing investors, they do not affect the key principles of portfolio selection we want to highlight in this chapter.

The diagrams at the bottom of Table 13.2 display the presumed relationship between probabilities and returns for the three available assets; this relationship is known as the *probability distribution of returns*.

Finally, let us assume that individuals choose to hold no more than two assets simultaneously. In other words, they may hold any one of the following six portfolios:

1. Asset I only.

2. Assets I and II.

3. Assets I and III.

4. Asset II only.

FINANCIAL FOCUS 13.1   JUNK BONDS

One of the spectacular financial markets of the 1980s was the junk bonds market, whose growth and eventual disintegration was associated with the name of Michael Milken.

Junk bonds are not an innovation. They are simply low-rated bonds. Those that are graded are rated by a variety of services, and the so-called junk bonds are rated lower than BBB. The same bonds used to be called *deep discount bonds* because their price is significantly lower than for higher grade bonds; consequently, their yields are significantly higher.

What set Milken apart was his exploitation of an anomaly in the pricing of bonds. Using previous academic research, Milken exploited the apparent excessive yield on junk bonds in relation to their risk. To put the point differently, the market may have set the default rate on such bonds too high, giving rise to profitable opportunities. In other words, since the market believed the default rate to be higher than it actually was, the return on such bonds overcompensated the investor for the risks taken. Hence, Milken was able to profit from this anomaly. This apparent fact led to an explosion in the amount of debt during the 1980s, especially as a source of funds previously unavailable to many firms was now made possible.

More recent evidence about the behaviour of junk bonds also suggests that default rates do not stay constant over time. Rather, default rates peak in approximately three to four years for the lowest rated bonds (CCC according to Table 13.1) and then decline thereafter. If a junk bond does not default after 10 years or so, the default rate in the United States for B-rated bonds is about half of that for C-rated bonds. The result has been called the "ticking time bomb" theory because it suggests that sometime in the future the market will be flooded with bond issues that have defaulted. It is clear that opportunities to profit from anomalies in bond ratings come from the man-

ner in which the ratings are set. There are only four firms in North America that offer this type of service, and it has long been suggested that there is a conflict of interest between the ratings agencies and the companies whose bonds they rate. After all, these ratings agencies charge fees to the companies they rate, so those who pay for the service also are the ones whose debt is being assessed for quality. Markets apparently realize this too, since a recently formed debt rating company, though not officially approved by the main regulatory agency in the U.S.(the Securities and Exchange Commission), has more impact on the stock prices of companies whose debt rating is changed than have the remaining debt rating agencies (Beaver, Shakespeare, and Soliman, 2004).

Questions for Discussion

1. Could there be a problem with the bond ratings as opposed to the return on the bonds themselves?
2. If you were a borrower or a lender, what lessons would you have drawn from Milken's analysis?

Sources

Beaver, W.H., C. Shakespeare, and M.T. Soliman, "Differential Properties in the Ratings of Certified vs. Non-Certified Bond Ratings Agencies," working paper, Stanford University Graduate School of Business, September 2004.

C. Bruck, *The Predator's Ball: The Junk Bond Raiders and The Man Who Staked Them* (New York: Simon and Shuster, 1988).

D.B. Henriques, "Debunking the Junk 'Bomb' Theory," *New York Times*, 22 March 1992, Money section: 15.

G. Morgenson, "Wanted: Credit Ratings. Objectives Ones, Please," *New York Times* 6 February 2005, section 3: 1, 3.

---

5.   Assets II and III.

6.   Asset III only.

Notice that because asset III displays no variation, it is *risk-free* or *riskless* in relation to the state of the market. By contrast, asset II generally displays lower returns than asset I, and the distribution of its returns is narrower.[3]

A common way of measuring risk, borrowed from the science of statistics, is to evaluate two statistics (or *moments*, as they are called) that can be used to characterize a probability distribution: (1) the average of mean returns, and (2) a measure of the spread of variability of returns called the variance of returns. Table 13.3 provides the general formula for each of these two measures, as well

---

3 Think of the risk-free asset as the return on a Government of Canada bond or Treasury bill.

FLASHBACK 13.1

QUANTIFYING RISK

The future is not known with certainty. Nevertheless, individuals need to plan ahead and make conscious decisions about the chances that various events will or will not take place. Consider the following example: You would like to take a trip six months from today but are unsure whether it's better to buy your airfare now or nearer the time of your departure. You find a fare for your destination, say $500, but you also realize that there is a chance that the fare might rise or fall for a variety of reasons as the departure date nears. Suppose further that there is an equal chance that the fare to your preferred destination will either be $400 or $600, based on searching for airfares for same destination. The range of fares, here $400 to $600, says nothing about whether you will end up paying $400, $500, or $600. What you really need to know is a measure of the dispersion of prices you might encounter as you survey airfares. In this simple example, the average, or mean fare, based on a sample of three airfares, is $500 ([$600+$500+$400]/3), so one measure of dispersion or variation is to ask how each airfare compares to an average. If we simply added up the difference between the sampled airfares and the average, that is, [$500-$400] and [$500-$600], then the result is $0. This is true no matter how many airfares you sample (add a couple of other sample airfares, recalculate the average, and verify that this is true). Obviously, this measure of dispersion or variation is not useful in large part because there are always above average and below average airfares. However, we can avoid the problem by squaring the differences from the mean to obtain [$500-$400]^2 and [$500-$600]^2, or 20,000. If we then take the average of these two numbers we obtain 10,000. Squaring gets rid of the problem of adding positive and negative values. But there is another very important advantage, namely that the further you are from the mean the larger is this value of dispersion, also called the variance. For example, had you sample airfares of $350 and $650 instead of $400 and $600, the variance would be 22,500/2=11,250. Since the dispersion of prices in this second example is greater, so is the "risk" that your airfare will be farther away from the average. This is the insight that led Harry Markowitz to suggest the square root of the variance (the text explains why) as another measure of risk.

as sample calculations for asset I. The *mean return* is simply the return weighted by the probability of occurrence of each state of the world. Because the probabilities measure potential variation in future returns, mean return is often called the **expected return**. The **variance of returns** is simply the weighted average of the squared deviations from the expected returns. (Some prefer to express risk as the **standard deviation of returns**, which is the square root of the variance of returns. Using the standard deviation enables interpretation of risk in percentage terms, whereas variance is an absolute measure of risk.)[4]

The results in Table 13.3 confirm what we suspected all along: Asset I has the highest average return and it is a riskier proposition than asset II, which has a smaller expected return. Asset III has by far the lowest expected return, but it is also riskless since its variance is zero.[5]

Correlation of Returns

Once we start to examine the risk inherent in a portfolio of assets, we must consider the possibility of an additional complication: Fluctuations in the returns of one asset may be influenced by fluctuations in the returns of alternative assets. There is a degree to which assets fluctuate *systematically* with each other; that is, some components of the returns of several assets may fluctuate with each other. Concomitantly, the return of an asset has components specific to it (or to the

---

4 Variance is not the only possible measure of risk but simply one that is in common usage. You could, for example, measure risk in terms of market size (i.e., its liquidity), which, as noted earlier, is often an important consideration for investors. Another measure of risk could be the absolute value of deviations in mean returns.

5 Strictly speaking, no asset is riskless. Money, for example, is riskless in the sense that it can always be used to purchase commodities. In some countries, however, high inflation produces a risk of a currency becoming essentially worthless! In addition, there is the risk that governments, normally assumed to be default-risk free, will renege on their debts.

Table 13.2   States of the World and Returns

State of the World	Probability of Occurence	Asset Returns		
		I	II	III
Severe Recession ("bust")	.10	6	11	4
Mild Recession	.20	9	9	4
Normal	.40	12	8	4
Mild Expansion	.20	14	7	4
Strong Expansion ("boom")	.10	15	5	4

Probability Distribution of Returns

We assume that a business cycle has five stages, ranging from a severe recession ("bust") to a strong expansion ("boom"), and that a subjective probability can be associated with each. For example, the normal state of the world (the economy is operating at, say, its historical growth rate) is assumed to occur 40% of the time. The diagrams plot how the returns for each of the assets vary according to the probability of the economy being in a particular stage of the business cycle. The information in such probability distributions helps us define risk.

particular firm, industry, or market) that vary over time or states of the world *unsystematically*.

Once again, statistics are available to quantify the extent to which fluctuation in asset returns is common. The covariance and the correlation express the degree of linear association between asset returns across states of the world. The **covariance** measure provides an absolute value for the degree to which asset returns move together or in opposite directions; the **correlation statistic** provides a relative measure of association. Table 13.4 provides the relevant formulae, as well as calculations for two of the assets we have been considering.

Table 13.4 also shows a plot of returns across states of the world with the appropriate adjacent points connected to each other. What is clear is that returns of assets I and II move in opposite directions. Therefore, the returns for these two assets are negatively correlated (inversely related), which explains the negative values for the covariance and correlation between assets I and II found at the bottom of Table 13.4. The calculations for the other two pairs of assets—I and III, and II and III—are not made because the returns of asset III display no variance whatsoever. Hence, the covariance between these pairs is zero.

Correlation has no particular advantage over covariance except that the former provides a measure that is easily interpretable. In the case of assets I and II for example, the correlation is –0.95, which signifies that a 1% rise in the return on asset I implies a 0.95% fall in the return on asset II. In other words, the correlation statistic is a quickly interpreted measure of the degree to which two returns vary systematically with each other.

Table 13.3	Expected Returns and Variances	

Asset	Expected Return	Variance
I	11.5	6.85
II	8.0	2.20
III	4.0	0.00

Formulae

- Expected Return $= R_i^e = \sum_s pr_s R_i^s$
- Variance of Returns $= V_i = \sum_s pr_s (R_i^s - R_i^e)^2$

where R_i^e = expected return, asset i

s = state of the world

pr_s = probability of occurrence for each state

R_i^s = return in state s, asset i

$pr_s R_i^s$ = product, for each state, of the probability of occurrence and return for asset i

V_i = variance of returns, asset i

$\sum_s$ = summation symbol over states of the world

Example of Calculation for Asset I

$R_i^e = 0.1(6) + 0.2(9) + 0.4(12) + 0.2(14) + 0.1(15) = 11.5\%$

$V_i = 0.1(6 - 11.5)^2 + 0.2(9 - 11.5)^2 + 0.4(12 - 11.5)^2 + 0.2(14 - 11.5)^2 + 0.1(15 - 11.5)^2$

$= 6.85$

Note: Data on probability and asset returns are from Table 13.2.

Risk in a Portfolio

We are now in a position to determine the overall risk of a portfolio of assets. For our example, we'll continue with the three assets we've been using, as evaluated in Tables 13.3 and 13.4, and maintain the simplifying assumption that a portfolio can contain one or two but not all three of them.

Table 13.5 lists 15 of the many possible portfolios and evaluates the variance for each, which is influenced by the covariance or correlation of any pairs of assets in it,[6] and the portfolio return, which is influenced by the proportion invested in each asset. The investor selecting a portfolio faces trade-offs, of course. The table shows that investing a greater proportion of wealth in asset III— a riskless asset—reduces portfolio risk, but at the expense of a lower return. Similarly, for a portfolio comprising assets I and II, investing a greater proportion in asset II reduces portfolio risk (since the riskiness of asset II is lower than that of asset I), but the investor is clearly worse off investing only in asset II since the riskiness of such a portfolio is greater and the return is lower than if, say, half the available funds were invested in asset I and the other half in asset II.

Plotting the 15 combinations, as in Figure 13.1, gives the *feasible set*, which is like the opportunity set facing the consumer or firm. Some combinations are superior in the sense that they produce the highest return for any given level of portfolio risk. These combinations are de-

---

6 The expression for portfolio variance is derived from the expression below, the variance of a sum of two assets:

$$V_p = [k_i \sum_s (R_i - R_i^e) + k_j \sum_s (R_j - R_j^e)]^2$$

If we expand that expression, we obtain the expression that appears at the bottom of Table 13.5:

$$V_p = k_i^2 \sum_s (R_i - R_i^e)^2 + k_j^2 \sum_s (R_j - R_j^e)^2 + 2k_i k_j \sum_s (R_i - R_i^e)(R_j - R_j^e)$$

$$V_p = k_i^2 V_i + k_j^2 V_j + 2k_i k_j COV_{ij}$$

Table 13.4	Covariances and Correlations	
Pairs of Assets	**Covariance**	**Correlation**
I and II	–3.70	–0.95
I and III	0.00	0.00
II and III	0.00	0.00

Formulae

- Covariance: $COV_{ij} = \sum pr_s(R_i^s - R_i^e)(R_j^s - R_j^e)$

- Correlation: $CORR_{ij} = \dfrac{COV_{ij}}{\sqrt{v_i}\,\sqrt{v_j}}$

where i and j are two different assets and $\sqrt{v_i}$ and $\sqrt{v_j}$ are the square root of their respective variances, that is, the standard deviations of asset returns.

Example of Calculation for Asset I and II

$COV_{I,II} = 0.1(6 - 11.5)(11 - 8) + 0.2(9 - 11.5)(9 - 8) + 0.4(12 - 11.5)(8 - 8) + 0.2(14 - 11.5)(7 - 8)$
$\qquad + 0.1(15 - 11.5)(5 - 8) = -3.70$

$CORR_{I,II} = \dfrac{-3.70}{(2.62)(1.48)} = -0.95$

The diagram shows the variation in asset returns as a function of the state of the world. The returns on assets I and II are inversely related and so are negatively correlated (see the chart above). Asset III returns are constant and unrelated to the returns of either asset I or asset II; the result is a zero correlation between the returns of assets I and II and assets II and III.

fined by the line _ABCD_, which describes the **efficient frontier**.[7] As we will see, under fairly general conditions, individuals will always select a portfolio on the efficient frontier.

---

7 The envelope of efficient portfolios—that is, the portfolios that lie on the efficient frontier—is also called the _Markowitz frontier_. Harry Markowitz did the pioneering work in establishing and evaluating such frontiers and shared the Nobel Prize in economics in 1990 for his work. You can see the original efficient frontier that Markowitz created in 1959 at **http://viking.som.yale.edu/will/finman540/classnotes/class2.html**.

Table 13.5   Portfolio Return and Risk

Assets I and II				
	Proportion (%) Invested in		Expected Return (%)	Variance or Risk
Portfolio No.	I	II		
1	100	0	11.50	6.85
2	75	25	10.63	2.60
3	50	50	9.75	0.41
4	25	75	8.88	0.28
5	0	100	8.00	2.20

Assets I and III				
Portfolio No.	I	III		
6	100	0	11.50	6.85
7	75	25	9.63	3.84
8	50	50	7.75	1.71
9	25	75	5.88	0.41
10	0	100	4.00	0.00

Assets II and III				
Portfolio No.	II	III		
11	100	0	8.00	2.20
12	75	25	7.00	1.23
13	50	50	6.00	0.55
14	25	75	5.00	0.13
15	0	100	4.00	0.00

Formulae

- Portfolio Expected Return = $R_p^e = k_i R_i^e + k_j R_j^e$
- Portfolio Variance or Risk = $V_p = k_i^2 V_i + k_j^2 V_j + 2k_i k_j COV_{ij}$

where R_p^e = portfolio expected return
V_p = variance or risk of portfolio
V_i, V_j = variance or risk of assets i, j, and $i \neq j$
COV_{ij} = covariance between assets i and j
k_i, k_j = proportion invested in asset i or j

Example of Calculation: Portfolio No. 2

$R_p^e = 0.75(11.5) + 0.25(8) = 10.63$
$V_p = (0.75)^2(6.85) + (0.25)^2(2.20) + 2(0.75)(0.25)(-3.70) = 2.60$

Note that the efficient frontier in Figure 13.1 results from portfolios made up of assets I and II. What drives this result is the negative correlation or covariance between the two assets. Thus, diversification reduces portfolio risk so long as the assets within the portfolio are negatively correlated (this is demonstrated in an Appendix available on the text's Web site at

| Figure 13.1 | Deriving the Efficient Frontier |

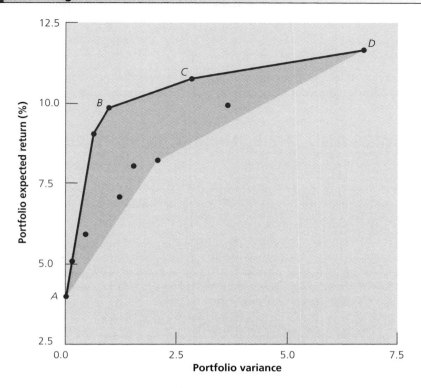

This figure continues the model set up in Table 13.5. The feasible set (the entire triangular area) includes all the combinations of risk and return available to the investor. *ABCD* is the efficient frontier; it marks the highest return for every level of risk. Point *A* is equivalent to portfolios 10 or 15 in Table 13.5; point *B* is portfolio 3; point *C* is portfolio 2; and point *D* is equivalent to portfolios 1 or 6.

Source: Table 13.5.

www.mcgrawhill.ca/siklos).[8] Indeed, we have now arrived at a precise definition of the term **diversification**: this activity implies constructing a portfolio that reduces total portfolio risk.

Unfortunately, many people think diversification means increasing the number of assets in a portfolio. But that meaning applies only in a special and generally unrealistic case. Suppose, for simplicity that the individual invests in equal proportions in a variety of assets:

$$k = 1/n$$

where k represents the portfolio share, which is assumed to be the same for each of the n assets in the portfolio. Moreover, suppose that these assets are uncorrelated with each other so that $COV_{ij} = CORR_{ij} = 0$.[9] We have now imposed a sufficient number of conditions that the variance of such a portfolio is simply the sum of the individual asset risks, or

---

8 It must be added, however, that this conclusion is the result of combining two assets to construct a portfolio. Indeed, if we combine risky assets with riskless assets—in effect creating a portfolio of three assets—we can reduce portfolio risk even if some of the asset returns are positively correlated. A more advanced treatment of this topic would consider the details and ramifications of this case.

9 Lack of correlation is imposed here primarily to simplify the calculations. The assumption is relaxed in an Appendix available on the text's Web site at **www.mcgrawhill.ca/siklos**.

$$V_p = k_1^2 V_1 + k_2^2 V_2 + \ldots + k_n^2 V_n$$
$$= \sum k_1^2 V_i$$
$$= \sum (1/n)^2 V_i$$
$$= n(1/n)^2 V_i = (1/n) V_i$$

Thus, unless we believe that all the assets in a portfolio are uncorrelated—an unlikely event,[10] diversification does not work the way some people think it does.

13.2 PREFERENCES AND THE EQUILIBRIUM PORTFOLIO

How does an individual select from among the portfolios on his or her efficient frontier? Before we can answer the question, we need to develop an understanding of preferences in the face of risk. Attitudes toward risk are generally explained as ranging among three alternatives:

1. Risk Aversion. The **risk-averse** individual is one who is willing to sacrifice either return or wealth to reduce risk. Such an individual is, for example, willing to accept a lower expected return if the probability distribution of returns is narrowed as a result. The extent of the sacrifice the individual is willing to make depends on the degree of risk aversion. One extreme example would be preferring a portfolio consisting only of asset III; although it yields the lowest return, it is also risk-free.

2. Risk Neutrality. An intermediate case is **risk neutrality**. As the term implies, an individual with this attitude is neutral with respect to the riskiness of a portfolio and instead focuses on maximizing return. Such an individual will select the portfolio with the highest return irrespective of portfolio risk.

3. Risk Seeking. A final possibility is **risk seeking**. The risk seeker is an individual who prefers risk over return. Although we think we encounter few such individuals, many people seem to have at least an element of risk loving—consider, for example, the purchase of lottery tickets.

Despite the gamblers we all know, most people tend to be cautious about wealth-building portfolios, both in the types of assets included and in the riskiness of the individual assets. Indeed, as **Economics Focus 13.1** points out, it is useful to think of gambling as an activity consisting of a large dose of entertainment instead of as a type of a risk-seeking activity.

Is risk aversion constant? Some economists argue that risk aversion is time-varying, rising when the economy is in a slump and falling when the economy is expanding.[11] The reason is that investors may make decisions in relation to their current economic situation; if times are good, they feel less threatened by an investment with greater risks than they do when their standard of living is lower. There is, therefore, a type of "habit formation" element to investment behaviour.

Another intriguing possibility is that investors may be risk averse when faced with a potential investment gain, but risk seeking when faced with a loss.[12] Consequently, investors are readier to gamble when the memory of, say, a stock market crash has faded than in the immediate aftermath of a sharp downturn in financial asset prices. The study of behavioural finance challenges the rationality assumption implicit in the efficient markets approach, and researchers in this field use experimental methods to demonstrate their results.

---

10 To see why this case is unlikely, see Figure 6.1, which plots yields on assets that individuals are likely to hold. The returns have a high positive correlation.

11 See G. Constantinides, "Habit Formation: A Resolution of the Equity Premium Puzzle," *Journal of Political Economy* 98 (1990): 519–43, and J.Y. Campbell, and J.H. Cochrane, "By Force of Habit: A Consumption-Based Explanation of Aggregate Stock Market Behavior," NBER Working Paper 4995 (1995).

12 See K.L. Fisher, and M. Statman, "A Behavioural Framework for Time Diversification," *Financial Analysts Journal* (May/June 1999).

In what follows, we ignore these complications, but the approach developed below can, in principle, handle the case of changing risk aversion over the business cycle. Consequently, we restrict ourselves to the risk-aversion case only.

CHOOSING AMONG RISKY ASSETS

Figure 13.2 illustrates the essentials of optimal portfolio choice under risk aversion. The arguments rely on the kind of indifference curve analysis we already used to describe the optimal consumption stream for an individual in a two-period setting. Here we amend the utility introduced in Chapter 10 so that

$$U = U(c, V_p) \tag{13.1}$$

where U is total utility, c is consumption, and V_p is portfolio risk.

Since combinations of expected portfolio return and portfolio risk determine total utility, we can rewrite equation (13.1) as

$$U = U(R_p^e, V_p) \tag{13.2}$$

The individual is now assumed to maximize equation (13.2), subject to the constraint imposed by the efficient frontier. Note that the marginal utility of a higher portfolio return is positive, but the marginal utility of an increase in portfolio variance is negative since the risk-averse individual wants, by definition, to reduce portfolio risk.

The point is made graphically in Figure 13.2, where the vertical axis plots expected portfolio return and the horizontal axis plots portfolio risk. Indifference curves for the risk-averse individual recognize the explicit tradeoff between expected return and risk. Combinations of expected return and risk that leave total utility unchanged represent an individual's indifference

---

| **Figure 13.2** | **Optimal Portfolio Choice under Risk Aversion** |

(A) Indifference Curves

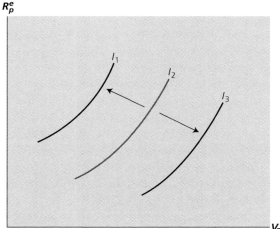

(B) The Optimal Portfolio

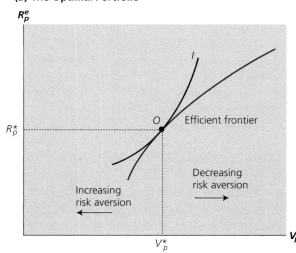

Because the risk-averse individual dislikes risk, total utility can be held constant when portfolio risk rises only if expected portfolio return also rises. For this reason, the indifference curve slopes upward in panel (A). In panel (B), the optimal portfolio is at O, the tangency of the efficient frontier and the risk-averse individual's indifference curve, I. Individuals who are relatively more risk averse than the individual depicted will select an optimal portfolio to the left of O, whereas those who are relatively less averse to risk will pick a point of tangency to the right of O.

ECONOMICS FOCUS 13.1 — UTILITY, THE DEMAND FOR INSURANCE, AND GAMBLING

One way to understand the concept of risk aversion is to first understand that individuals prefer certainty over uncertainty. They are willing, therefore, to forgo some part of their wealth to increase certainty. The amount an individual will forgo depends on the degree of the individual's aversion to risk.

In a classic work on game theory, John von Neumann and Oskar Morgenstern worked out what has become known as the Von Neumann–Morgenstern utility theory. It states that we can construct a utility function such that a level of utility is associated with each level of wealth. Total utility is assumed to rise with wealth, but at a diminishing rate, which is indicated by the fact that the utility of wealth curve becomes flatter as wealth rises. (This is the result of the standard assumption of *diminishing marginal utility* in microeconomic analysis.) Consider then the situation depicted in the figure below where utility, a subjective measure of satisfaction or enjoyment, is measured on the vertical axis, while different levels of wealth are measured on the horizontal axis.

The straight line AB describes the expected utility of wealth for levels of wealth. If there were no uncertainty, we could simply evaluate the total utility associated with each level of wealth. Unfortunately, uncertainty is a fact of life. Wealth may be either $900 or $100 depending on whether events, such as illness or a fire, occur. The expected level of utility depends on the probabilities of occurrence of the events that lead to a wealth level of $100 or $900. In general, expected utility is evaluated according to

$$U^e = \sum pr_i U_j$$

where U^e represents expected utility, pr is the probability associated with event i, and U_j is the utility associated with wealth level j.

The expected utility function is a linear combination or weighted average of different levels of wealth where the weights are the respective probabilities of various events. Thus, in the present example, there are probabilities such that

$$pr(W = \$100)\$100 + [1 - pr(W = \$100)]\$900 = U^e(500)$$

where $pr(W = \$100)$ is the probability that $W = \$100$. Since probabilities must sum to 1, the probability of $W = \$900$ is simply $1 - pr(W = \$100)$.

Notice in the model that the utility associated with $500 with certainty, $U(500)$, is greater than the expected utility of $500, $U^e(500)$. The latter is a combination of the utility of $100 and $900 weighted by the probabilities associated with each level of wealth. The

$$U(500) - U^e(500)$$

difference measures the loss of utility resulting from the existence of uncertainty. The utility function depicted here is obviously that of someone who dislikes uncertainty, a risk-averse individual. We can express the extent of this person's dislike of uncertainty by noting that he or she is indifferent between an expected utility level associated with $500 in wealth with uncertainty and, say, $340 in wealth with certainty. In other words,

$$U^e(500) = U(340)$$

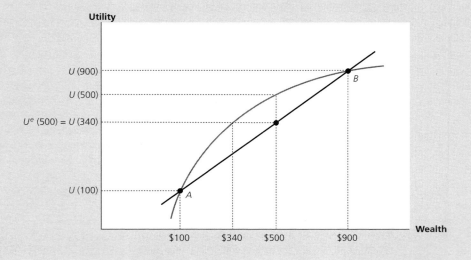

Presumably this risk-averse individual would be willing to forgo up to $160 in wealth to obtain $U(340)$ with certainty. (This explains why markets for various forms of insurance arise.) You can think of the $160 as a "risk premium." The larger it is the more an individual is willing to pay to avoid uncertainty. An alternative way of assessing this result is to express it in terms of the individual's expected wealth. Say the pr(W=$100)=pr(W=$900)=0.50. Expected wealth is then $500. Although the premium is expressed in dollar terms here it can also be evaluated in percentages. Continuing with the previous example, $160/$500=0.32 or 32%. Two questions naturally arise. First, what if the $900 and $100 events were doubled instead, to $1800 and $200, respectively, but the risk premium was unchanged at $160? This case implies that the risk premium stays constant in absolute terms and, hence, is referred to as a case of constant, absolute risk aversion. In relative terms, however, the premium has fallen. For example, if the probabilities remain unchanged, then $160/$1000=0.16 or 16%, where $1000 is now the expected level of wealth, when wealth for either event is doubled. Therefore, the premium would have to double, that is, reach a level of $320, in order for the relative premium to remain at 32% (=$320/$1000). In other words, one can also ask what the risk premium is if relative risk aversion remains the same. We leave it as an exercise to discuss how the shape of the utility curve AB affects the size of the risk premium. The important point is that models must take a stand on what happens to absolute or relative risk aversion, say, as incomes change. Some assume the degree of either form of risk aversion stays constant. Others hypothesize that investors display decreasing absolute risk aversion, but increasing relative risk aversion. In recent years, economists have resorted to experiments to determine investors' attitudes toward risk. For example,

Levy (1994) reports that investors display decreasing absolute risk aversion, but he rejects the hypothesis of increasing relative risk aversion.

Although the preceding analysis seems convincing, it has serious deficiencies. It does not explain why most people will accept very risky propositions under certain circumstances. For example, many will purchase lottery tickets, which involves gambling a small portion of wealth for a very slight probability of obtaining a large return. They will derive considerable enjoyment from the prospect of winning a large sum of money. In these circumstances the individual appears to behave like a risk seeker, not the risk averter depicted in the figure. Friedman and Savage suggested that the utility of wealth may not be a smooth line but a function with an initial segment displaying the characteristics of risk aversion and another segment consistent with risk taking.

Questions for Discussion

1. Does gambling conflict with the utility function described in this box?
2. What would a risk seeker's utility function look like? Explain.

Sources

R. Brenner, and G.A. Brenner, *Gambling and Speculation: A Theory, A History, and a Future of Some Human Decisions* (Cambridge: Cambridge University Press, 1990).

M. Friedman, and L.J. Savage, "The Utility Analysis of Choices Involving Risk," *Journal of Political Economy* 56 (1948): 279–304.

Levy, H., "Absolute and Relative Risk Aversion: An Experimental Study," *Journal of Risk and Uncertainty* 8 (May 1994): 287-307.

curve; it is upward sloping, as shown in Figure 13.2(A). For any given level of risk, a risk-averse individual will choose a portfolio yielding the highest expected return, so the indifference curves yield higher total utility as they shift leftward. Thus, I_1 produces the highest total utility and I_3 the lowest.

Figure 13.2(B) displays the optimal portfolio choice in the present framework. As in the optimal consumption model considered in Chapter 10, the point of tangency between the individual's indifference curve and the efficient frontier produces the optimal portfolio. Given detailed knowledge of the various return–risk combinations that produced the results of Table 13.5, we could evaluate the proportions of assets I and II that would be selected by the individual depicted.

It is useful to consider how risk aversion will affect the location of the optimal point, O. As shown by the arrows in Figure 13.2(B), individuals whose aversion to risk is less than that of the individual who selected the portfolio (R_p^*, V_p^*) will choose portfolios yielding higher expected returns *and* higher risk. By contrast, individuals with even more aversion to risk will opt for portfolios that have lower risk and consequently lower returns.

THE CASE OF A RISK-FREE ASSET

Another interesting case is the one in which the portfolio is made up of two assets, one of which is risk free. For convenience, assume the two are money (the archetype riskless asset), which earns a zero nominal return, and corporate bonds, whose return is the opportunity cost of holding money. Technically, holding money *does* involve inflation risk, a point we ignore here for the sake of simplicity.

The expected return on such a portfolio is

$$R_p^e = k_m R_m + k_b R_b = k_b R_b$$

where R_m is the yield on money, assumed here to be zero, R_b is the return on the risky bond, and k_m and k_b are the portfolio shares. Portfolio variance is, therefore (see footnote 7)

$$V_p = k_m^2 V_m + k_b^2 V_b + 2k_m k_b COV_{mb} = k_b^2 V_b$$

where V_m is the risk associated with money, and V_b is bond risk. Since, by assumption, $V_m = 0$, $COV_{mb} = 0$ also. Hence, portfolio variance is a function of bond risk alone. If we now take the square root of the portfolio variance equation, we obtain

$$SD_p = k_b SD_b$$

where $SD (= \sqrt{V})$ represents the standard deviation, which, as we have seen, is an alternative measure of risk. It is convenient here to use the standard deviation measure because it makes portfolio risk a linear function of bond risk. In other words, the efficient frontier becomes a straight line.

Figure 13.3 illustrates the risk–return combination in this example. It also illustrates how uncertainty about the future combined with money's role as a liquid asset can produce a demand for money.[13] Given moderate risk aversion, an equilibrium will be somewhere along the efficient

| Figure 13.3 | **Liquidity Preference and Risk** |

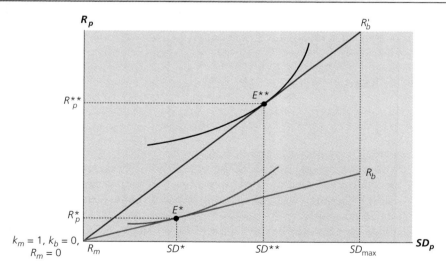

The figure shows the risk–return combinations of a portfolio consisting of a risk-free asset (money) and a risky asset (bonds). Because such a portfolio's risk is a function of bond risk alone, the efficient frontier is a straight line such as $R_m R_b$. The initial equilibrium is E^{**}. A lower interest rate reduces the opportunity costs of money and raises the quantity of money held in the portfolio. As in Chapter 6, the quantity of money is negatively related to the interest rate.

---

13 This model was introduced by Nobel laureate James Tobin of Yale University.

frontier $R_m R_b$. The risk-averse individual will always choose to hold some money; at the equilibrium E^{**}, say, $k_b^{**} = 1 - k_m^{**}$ is held in the form of bonds. Now suppose the return on bonds falls from R_b' to R_b. The implications are a flatter efficient frontier and, since the opportunity cost of holding money has fallen, a greater desire to hold money. Consequently, equilibrium is attained in a new position, such as point E^*, whereby the portfolio shares become $k_m^*(>k_m^{**})$ and $k_b^*(<k_b^*)$. If we continue along these lines, we can trace out the quantity of money held for each level of bond return. We can conclude that even though bonds are a risky asset, the quantity of money demanded is negatively related to interest rate changes, just as we concluded in Chapter 6 when we first encountered the demand for money concept.

Figure 13.3 also makes clear that money, despite being a riskless asset with a relatively lower expected return, is nevertheless held in a portfolio that includes risky assets.

13.3 VALUE-AT-RISK

One of the drawbacks of the preceding analysis is that none of the techniques provides an assessment of the dollar cost to investors or management in the event that an investment decision in a "bad" state of the world actually transpired. Consider again, for example, the information in Table 13.2. Although it is perfectly sensible for investors to evaluate the expected return and risk, it would be equally useful to know what the loss of interest income would be from, say, holding asset I in a severe recession when the economy was expected instead to deliver a strong expansion. In other words, suppose we concentrated our analysis on the worst-case scenario and translated such an outcome in dollar terms? Why? If, as an investor, you stand to lose your investment if the worst-case scenario comes true, you may wish to protect yourself against this event taking place. Unfortunately, knowing the expected return and the variance or standard deviation of returns will not provide you with sufficient information about the costs associated with the worst scenario, or outcome. This is precisely the idea behind the **value-at-risk** or **VaR** approach.

The principle behind VaR is to estimate the dollar cost of a decision made under the condition of the worst possible outcome. Of course, in doing so, we must associate a probability with the worst-case scenario. For example, suppose we expect to lose $100 000 over a month with a 5% probability. We then say that the VaR at the 5% level is $100 000. Clearly, we can estimate a VaR at any probability level but, as is also clear from the information in Table 13.2, the dollar cost at different probability values will differ. Table 13.6 illustrates hypothetical VaRs for different probability values.

According to the above figures, there is a 10% chance that losses on a particular project or investment will amount to anywhere from $50 000 to $100 000, but there is also a 75% chance (20% + 20% + 20% + 15%) that the same project will yield a net inflow of somewhere between $0 and

Table 13.6	Illustrating the VaR Concept	
VaR **(Estimated Loss/Gain in $)**	**Probability of Occurrence**	**Cumulative Probability**
–$100 000 to –$50 000	.10	.10
–$49 999 to $0	.15	.25
$0 to $25 000	.20	.45
$25 001 to $49 999	.20	.65
$50 000 to $74 999	.20	.85
$75 000 to $100 000	.15	1.00

The table shows the gains or losses in dollars according to the probability of occurrence. Hence, there is a 10% chance that losses will range from $50 000 to $100 000. By contrast, we can add up the probabilities of incurring losses and instead say that there is a 25% chance that losses will range from $0 to $100 000.

Figure 13.4 Probability Distribution of Returns

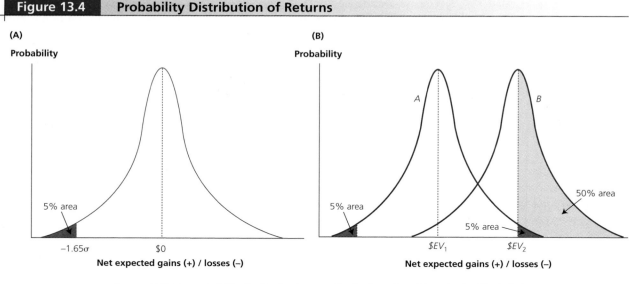

In panel (A), the probability distribution is normally distributed, so it has the familiar bell shape. Because it is centred around $0, 5% of the area is 1.65 standard deviations (σ) away from the centre. In panel (B), two normal distributions are drawn with centres at different dollar amount ($\$EV_2 > \$EV_1$). As a result, a 5% VaR in the left-hand area of distribution A is not a possibility if it is believed that distribution B is appropriate. Moreover, if we are interested in a 5% VaR in the right-hand side of distribution A, then there is a 50% probability of such an outcome if distribution B is appropriate.

$100 000. As is plain from the information in Table 13.6, gains or losses depend on a particular probabilistic scenario and this, in turn, depends on the underlying probability distribution in question. Figure 13.4 illustrates the critical role played by beliefs about the underlying shape of the probability distribution.

Panel (A) of Figure 13.4 shows a very commonly encountered probability distribution, namely the normal, or bell-shaped probability distribution. Suppose that the distribution is centred around $0, which represents the expected net inflow of dollars from the particular project under consideration. It is conceivable that the managers responsible for the project want to know the expected gain or loss under different best-case or worst-case scenarios. For example, it is well known that 5% of the area under the curve is plus or minus 1.65 standard deviations from the expected return.[14] Panel (B) illustrates what happens when there are two sets of scenarios or probability distributions for a project. If probability distribution B is thought to be valid, then the worst-case scenario under distribution A is irrelevant since it has no chance (i.e., a zero probability) of happening when distribution B prevails. In other words, there is no overlap of the two distributions in the worst-case scenario for distribution A. Similarly, if we look at the best 5% VaR for probability distribution A, then the probability of this scenario becoming a reality is far higher if we apply distribution B to the question. It should also be clear that the shape of the distribution also matters in determining the VaR for a particular project, even if the expected dollar returns are believed to be the same. We leave this question to you as an exercise.

ESTIMATING VaR

One relatively simple way of estimating VaR is suggested by our earlier discussion of portfolio selection. For example, suppose we have a portfolio of $50M to invest in two assets. The relevant

14 Actually, this applies to what is called a standard normal distribution, that is, where the distribution is centred around zero. However, none of the arguments in the text is affected by this consideration since we can simply "standardize" any mean so that its expected value becomes zero.

Table 13.7	Hypothetical Returns and Risk from a Portfolio Investment: Estimating VaR	
Size of Investment	$50	
Correlation	0.45	
Share	**Expected Return**	**Standard Deviation**
40%	0.10	0.14
60%	0.06	0.09

An investor has $50M to invest in a 40–60 split between two assets whose return and risk are as shown in the above table. The correlation between the returns of the two assets is 0.45. All figures are in annual terms.

information about each one's expected return and risk is provided in Table 13.7. It is assumed that 40% is invested in *A*, while the remaining dollars are invested in *B*.

Portfolio expected return and risk are then calculated as follows:

$$R_p^e = 0.4(0.10) + 0.6(0.06) = 0.076 \text{ or } 7.6\%$$

$$V_p = 0.4^2(0.14)^2 + 0.6^2(0.09)^2 + 2(0.4)(0.6)(0.14)(0.09)(0.45) = 0.0088$$

$$SD_p = (0.0088)^{1/2} = 0.094$$

Suppose now that the investor is interested in the VaR over the following month. The above calculations must be converted to a monthly basis. Ignoring compounding, this simply involves dividing portfolio expected return and risk by 12 and the square root of 12, respectively, since there are 12 months in a year. This implies

$$R_p^e - \text{monthly basis} = 0.076/12 = 0.0063$$

$$SD_p - \text{monthly basis} = 0.094/(12)^{1/2} = 0.0271$$

If the underlying probability distribution is normal, then we know that a 5% VaR for the worst-case scenario (recall that 5% of the area under a normal curve is 1.65 standard deviations from the expected return) is

$$0.0063 - 1.65(0.0271) = -0.0384$$

Since VaR is expressed in dollars, this implies that an investment of $50M will have a 5% VaR of

$$\$50M(-0.0384) = -\$1.92M$$

which means that the portfolio under consideration will incur a loss of 3.84 percent 5% of the time. This result translates into an expected loss in a month of $1.92M 5% of the time.

Other techniques can be used to estimate VaR. For example, we could use historical evidence of mean returns and risk—much in the same way this information is used in the estimation of the beta of an asset—to estimate the mean and risks of various portfolios. Alternatively, we could experiment extensively with scenarios for either the shape or the location of some probability distribution. This experimentation might enable us to estimate the loss of different projects for the expected size of the area under a selected probability distribution, in much the same way as is done in panel (B) of Figure 13.4. These topics are, however, best left for a more advanced treatment of the VaR subject.

A wealth of information about the VaR approach can be found at **www.contingency analysis.com** or **www.gloria mundi.org/**

13.4 THE CAPITAL ASSET PRICING MODEL (CAPM)

For an investor holding a large diversified portfolio, the evaluation of the efficient frontier according to the mean-variance analysis developed in this chapter is not especially practical. If the

For detailed descriptions of the origins and currrent uses of CAPM, visit **www.ibbotson.com/default.asp?Try=yes**

portfolio consists of 1000 assets, for example, it would be necessary to compute almost 500 000 covariances! Nevertheless, our analysis has taught us some useful rules. For example, if asset returns are positively correlated, portfolio variance is raised, whereas asset returns that are negatively correlated reduce portfolio risk.

In other words, total portfolio risk can be thought of as the sum of systematic and unsystematic risks—the return on an asset is partly a function of the return on other assets and partly determined by factors related to the asset in question. Therefore, an investor's portfolio management decision-making problem must consist of the following principles:

- diversification can reduce risk

- there are limits to diversification since some risks, conceivably, can affect all potential assets, such as a global economic slowdown

- return and risk should be positively correlated since the former represents a reward for undertaking the latter

- asset returns vary systematically with the market and are therefore influenced by the latter

We can formalize these ideas in a simple equation analyzed by William Sharpe, who shared a Nobel Prize in economics for his research in this area. Let

$$R_i = \alpha_i + \beta_i R_m + e_i \tag{13.3}$$

where R_i = return on asset i, R_m = return on all assets in the market or the asset return on a market portfolio, α_i and β_i are constants, and e_i is a catch-all term to capture influences other than the market's return on the return on asset i.

The central idea behind equation (13.3), usually called the *characteristic equation* or *Sharpe's model*, is that since interest rates tend to move together and stocks tend to be affected by common influences, we can predict asset i's return on the basis of how strongly it is related to average returns in the rest of the market, R_m. The strength of the relationship is measured by β_i, which is called the beta of an asset. Thus, if $\beta_i = 0$, the asset's return is uncorrelated with the market return, whereas if $\beta_i > 0$, asset i's return will move in the same direction as the market, and if $\beta_i < 0$, the correlation is negative. The error term e_i covers other factors that may influence asset i's return independently (that is, uncorrelated with the influence of the market portfolio); they could be firm-specific factors, such as technological change, strikes, and so on.

Since an investor chooses a portfolio of assets, it is perhaps preferable to replace R_i with R_p for portfolio return. But notice that, as the number of assets used to compute R_p increases, the value of R_p approaches that of R_m. By contrast, as the number of assets in a portfolio approaches the market portfolio, the influence of the unpredictable component, e_i, would be expected to become smaller. Investors, of course, also have the option of investing in a risk-free asset such as a Treasury bill. If investors choose such an asset then, given the third principle outlined above, we would expect that risky assets would deliver a return over and above the risk-free return. Denote the risk-free return R_F. These considerations allow us to explain the *premium* associated with the holding of an asset (or a portfolio of assets) and the risk-free return. Using the argument summarized in (13.3), we can then write

$$R_i - R_F = \beta_i (R_m - R_F) + v_i \tag{13.4}$$

where β_i is the "beta" of asset i, $R_m - R_F$ is the difference between the market return and the risk-free return, and v_i represents other factors that can influence the risk premium.[15] According to the **capital asset pricing model** or **CAPM**, on average, factors other than the "beta" of an asset should have no effect on the risk premium so that

$$(R_i - R_F) = \beta_i (R_m - R_F) \tag{13.5}$$

---

15 We could add an intercept, let's call it alpha, which would represent the excess return on stock i when excess market return is zero. It is not added here because, in theory, alpha is expected to be zero.

| Figure 13.5 | Illustrating the CAPM Model |

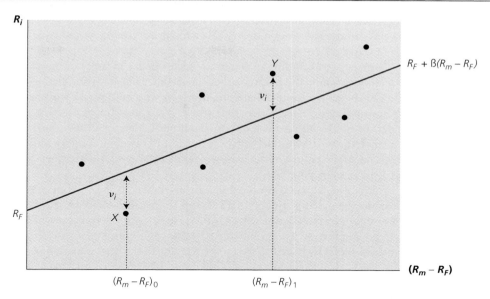

The horizontal line measures the difference or premium return of the market portfolio over the risk-free asset. The vertical axis measures the return on a particular stock or portfolio of stocks. The upward-sloping straight line is equation (13.4) and describes expected returns, while the scatter points represent actual combinations of returns. The v_i represent the unsystematic component of a portfolio's return while points on the line represent the return predicted according to systematic factors. Hence, at point X, the unsystematic variation in the portfolio reduces R_i relative to what is predicted by systematic variation in the market's return, whereas the opposite is true of the portfolio at point Y.

where $(R_i - R_F)$ is the premium on the return of asset i over the risk return. Therefore, if $\beta_i = 0$, the risk premium is also expected to be zero. There is then no systematic risk. If $\beta_i = 1.0$, then asset i has the same systematic risk as the market portfolio and, consequently, the same risk premium. It is helpful at this stage to summarize the relationship in equation (13.4) with the help of Figure 13.5.

The horizontal axis measures the differential between the market return and the risk-free rate, while the vertical axis measures the return on a particular asset or portfolio of assets. The risk-free rate is the intercept term, while the straight line shows the linear relationship between R_i and the premium return. Any point along the line represents the expected return on asset i given the difference between the market return and the risk-free return. The points are hypothetical combinations of $(R_m - R_F)$ and R_i actually produced by the market. Therefore, some assets will produce returns greater than expected, while others will produce lower returns than expected. In the former case, v_i is positive, while in the latter case, v_i is negative. Although the securities market line has been drawn to be upward sloping, there is no requirement that this be so. The implications of the ideas contained in (13.4) for portfolio risk can also be easily summarized as in Figure 13.6.

The vertical axis measures total portfolio risk, V_p, while the horizontal axis measures the number of assets in a portfolio, n. As n increases, approaching the market portfolio, the diversifiable component of V_p, whose source is e, falls. The part that is nondiversified rises because some part of the portfolio risk varies systematically with that of the market portfolio and is constant (because β_i is assumed to be constant).

In terms of portfolio risk, it can be shown that

$$\beta_i = \frac{COV_{im}}{V_m} \tag{13.6}$$

where COV_{im} is the covariance between the return on asset i and the return on the market portfolio. This is the conclusion of the capital asset pricing model (CAPM), which, despite its rather strong assumptions, has proven to be extremely useful for managers of large diversified portfolios, especially in the securities industry. (Any finance textbook will provide students with all the details of CAPM.)

Notice that, according to equation (13.6), β_i is a measure of the sensitivity of the return on asset i to variation in the return on the market (m). That is, β_i summarizes the dependence on portfolio risk. Not surprisingly, therefore, investors who hold stocks with betas greater than 1 are referred to as "aggressive," since their stock "overreacts" to changes in market returns, whereas holders of stocks with betas less than 1 are called "defensive" investors.[16]

Since the CAPM model says that the cost of capital is a linear function of the risk-free rate and the beta of a project, it is not surprising that this model has been extensively used by corporate managers in managing risk.[17]

It is fair to ask whether all risk can be diversified as shown above. An alternative view, called the **arbitrage pricing theory** (**APT**), suggests that other factors [summarized in v_i in equation (13.5) but essentially ignored by CAPM], such as the overall state of the economy, can influence the "beta" of an asset. One way of dealing with other factors is simply to include other relevant variables which are believed to be relevant to the determination of the risk premium on the right-hand side of equation (13.4). Still others have pointed out that CAPM is flawed because of expected return changes over time, a feature also ignored in the above description of CAPM. Furthermore, how should we define R_m? Should we use U.S. data only or, in keeping with the globalization of markets, should we also include stocks in major industrialized countries? One study found that diversifiable risk is greater when investors buy equities across countries as opposed to a single country. This too seems to matter in how well CAPM works.

Finally, we would expect that beta would be helpful in predicting stock returns. Unfortunately, the empirical evidence on this score is mixed. In fact, some researchers have reported that a measure similar to Tobin's q (see Chapter 11), but using the book value of assets instead of the replacement costs of assets, predicts stock returns better. The problem then, as we noted earlier, is that there is no unique way of measuring risk. If risks are not measured as the CAPM hypothesizes, then the beta concept is not very helpful. The debate centres in part around the question of whether or not investors rationally process information in making investment decisions (see **Point–Counterpoint 13.1: Is CAPM Dead or Alive?**).

13.5 MATCHING ASSETS AND DEBTS

Neither individuals nor businesses can borrow risk-free since both groups choose a type of debt that suits their anticipated income or sales flows as well as their interest rate expectations. The question arises then as to whether they manage assets and debt separately or jointly.

Economic agents with income that is steady (at least when averaged over some period, such as a lifetime) presumably try to match return on assets with debt costs. Not doing so would affect the return of their wealth, which, as you recall, is the difference between assets and debts. If asset yields are perfectly correlated with debt costs, the spread between them will be constant, thereby ensuring a constant return on wealth. This happy state is unlikely, but a positive corre-

---

16 We might also refer to holders of stocks with negative betas as "contrarian" investors.

17 An influential paper found, however, that CAPM was useless. The technical details as well as the criticisms raised against Fama and French are beyond the scope of this text. However, Jagannathan and McGrattan (1995) have concluded that CAPM is alive and well. See R. Jagannathan and E.R. McGrattan, "The CAPM Debate," *Quarterly Review of the Federal Reserve Bank of Minneapolis* (Fall 1995): 2–17.

| Figure 13.6 | Diversifiable and Nondiversifiable Risks |

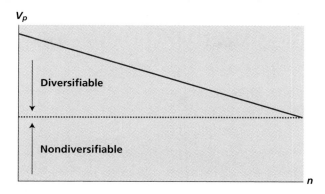

The vertical axis measures portfolio risk while the horizontal axis measures the hypothetical number of assets in a portfolio. As the number of assets in a portfolio grows, investors benefit from a reduction in portfolio risk due to the benefits of diversification. At some point, however, once the portfolio consists of all assets in the market, the benefits of diversification are completely dissipated.

lation between asset yields and debt costs ensures a positive net return on wealth. And clearly, the smoother the pattern of net returns, the smoother the anticipated pattern of future consumption for the households or dividends for the firm.

Unless households or firms are so risk averse that they want to minimize the variability of net returns, however, they will act on the understanding that a tradeoff exists between the expected return on wealth and the variance of consumption or equity. A positive correlation between asset returns and debt costs reduces the variance of consumption or equity because net returns become less variable.

SUMMARY

- This chapter explains how return and risk can be quantified. Doing so is necessary because economic agents have to make informed decisions about the future, which is unknown.

- Average return on an asset is measured by its expected return, which is a weighted average of the various possible returns expected in the future.

- Risk of an asset is measured as the variance of expected returns and is related to the concept of the probability distribution of returns.

- A portfolio of assets is the various assets that an economic agent combines in allocating wealth. Portfolio risk is akin to the risk of an individual asset except that the former is

also influenced by correlation of returns, the common fluctuations in the returns to the assets in the portfolio.

- Diversification does not necessarily mean buying more assets. It means, in the case where investors choose to own two assets, including in the portfolio assets whose returns are either uncorrelated or negatively correlated with each other.

- The optimal portfolio is the one that gives the highest expected portfolio return for a given level of portfolio risk. Utility is maximized at this point, which is found on the efficient frontier.

- The efficient frontier describes the highest returns available in the market for each level of risk.

POINT–COUNTERPOINT 13.1

IS CAPM DEAD OR ALIVE?

The table below gives some data on the return on selected stocks and bonds since 1960.

Years	Stocks		Bonds	
	TSE300	Paper and Wood Products Stock Index	Ten-Years and over Government of Canada Bonds	Three-Month Treasury Bill
	Annual Return in %		**Annual Yield in %**	
1960–69	9.32	8.62	5.62	3.94
1970–79	9.73	12.88	8.42	6.88
1980–89	15.05	25.98	11.75	11.30
1990–99	8.78	7.01	8.07	6.47
	Risk (%)		**Risk (%)**	
1960–69	22.67	36.10	0.76	2.07
1970–79	31.13	49.40	0.97	2.29
1980–89	36.42	67.68	1.99	3.03
1990–99	23.97	37.11	1.70	2.94

There are two notable features in the data. First, return and risk are positively related, as the discussion on portfolio management points out. Therefore, the efficient frontier is positively sloped. Second, a plot of the return on long-term government bonds and the return on stocks in the paper industry against the return on the TSE300 across the four decades considered here suggests a positive relationship: As the average returns on the TSE300 stock rose, so did the returns on long-term government bonds and on paper industry stocks. However, if we look at the data over the entire period since 1960, an entirely different picture emerges. The table below shows the various estimates of beta based on the above data, found by estimating equation (13.3), although equation (13.6) can also be used to obtain the results provided below.

	Data by Decade	Quarterly Data since 1960
Beta for government bonds	0.750	–0.025
Beta for paper stocks	2.910	11.550

- When a portfolio is made of a risk-free asset as well as risky assets, the basic principles of portfolio management are unaffected. Moreover, the negative relationship between interest rates and money demand (a riskless asset) remains unchanged.

- Portfolio risk can be thought of as the sum of systematic and unsystematic risks. The CAPM approach exploits this idea to show how the return on stocks, over and above the return on a risk-free asset, is a function of the return on a portfolio made up of a large number of stocks, as measured by the return in a stock index like the TSE300.

- Value-at-risk (VaR) is the maximum dollar amount that can be lost over a specified period with a known probability.

- Economic agents typically have assets as well as liabilities. To minimize the risk to their net wealth, they try to match the asset returns with liability costs so that the two are positively correlated with each other.

The table illustrates that it does not take much to change estimates of the beta of even the simplest portfolio. It remains to be seen how the downturn in global stock markets that began in 2000 will affect beta values and, indeed, the relative return of stocks versus bonds. Unfortunately, it is too early yet to reach any definitive conclusions about these questions.

POINT	COUNTERPOINT
• The CAPM is a simple and useful device that correctly predicts that a positive correlation between risk and return exists. • The CAPM is helpful in that it explicitly recognizes that asset returns are to some extent correlated so that the return performance of an asset is partly influenced by the return performance of the entire market. • It is sensible to assume that investors make investment choices on the basis of available information and, as such, behave rationally. • A fairly large body of evidence exists that supports the implications of beta for a cross-section of international stocks.	• Investors are not always rational. There is some evidence of herding behaviour in the buying of stocks. • The CAPM is overly simplistic in that it argues that unsystematic risk deserves no risk premium. • Other factors such as firm size, sample period, business cycle, and international considerations are relatively more important predictors of return on investments. • The empirical evidence in favour of beta is simply weak. In addition to the problems above, several data-related issues stem from the impact of estimating returns on a monthly, quarterly, or annual basis: The role of "survivor bias" in the data, short-run versus long-run measurement of returns, and firm size all weaken the usefulness of beta as an investment strategy tool.

Questions for Discussion

1. Can you find evidence to support the criticisms levelled against CAPM based on the data presented above? Explain.
2. Should investors use CAPM if indeed they are rational?

Sources

E. Fama, and K.F. French, "The CAPM is Wanted, Dead or Alive," *Journal of Finance* 51 (December 1996): 1947–58.

K. Grundy, and B.G. Malkiel, "Reports of Beta's Death Have Been Greatly Exaggerated," *Journal of Portfolio Management* 22 (Spring 1996): 36–44.

R. Jagannathan, and E.R. McGrattan, "The CAPM Debate," *Quarterly Review of the Federal Reserve Bank of Minneapolis* (Fall 1995): 2–17.

G.B. Malkiel, and Y. Xu, "Risk and Return Revisited," *Journal of Portfolio Management*, 23 (Spring 1997): 9–14.

J. Stein, "Rational Capital Budgeting in an Irrational World," *Journal of Business* (October 1996).

IMPORTANT TERMS

arbitrage pricing theory (APT), 256
bond rating, 237
capital asset pricing model (CAPM), 254
correlation statistic, 241
covariance, 241
default risk, 237
diversification, 245
efficient frontier, 243
expected return, 240
foreign exchange risk, 237
income risk, 237
inflation or deflation risk, 237

liquidity risk, 237
market risk, 237
risk, 236
risk averse, 246
risk neutrality, 246
risk seeking, 246
standard deviation of returns, 240
systematic risk, 237
tax risk, 238
value-at-risk (VaR), 251
variance of returns, 240

PROBLEMS

1. Consider investments A and B, given the following information:

State of the World	Probability of Occurrence	Rates of Return (%) A	B
1	0.15	3.00	10.00
2	0.20	7.00	7.00
3	0.35	8.00	8.50
4	0.20	13.00	12.25
5	0.10	17.00	4.75

(a) Calculate the following:
   (i) Expected returns
   (ii) Variances and standard deviations of returns
   (iii) Covariance and correlation between A and B
(b) Compute the risk–return combinations achieved by combining assets A and B in the proportions given below.

Proportion in A	Proportion in B
100%	0%
75	25
50	50
25	75
0	100

2. Suppose an investor can choose among three assets and that the entire portfolio may be invested in any one of them or split equally between any two. Also suppose that the states of the world are all equally likely (that is, probability of each state is 25%).

State of the World	Rate of Return (%) A	B	C
1	10	90	5
2	30	70	25
3	70	30	85
4	90	10	105

Which portfolio would be selected by the highly risk-averse investor? (Hint: Look at the pattern of rates of return.)

3. Using the liquidity preference under risk framework (see Figure 13.3) trace the effect of an increase in bond risk. All other factors should be held constant. Does the allocation of wealth between money and bonds change?

4. Using liquidity preference theory, show graphically what happens to money demand when bond yields rise. Explain.

5. Show graphically why a rise-averse individual is willing to pay insurance to avoid risk.

6. Why is the efficient frontier the only relevant part of the feasible set? Explain.

7. Define the concepts of diversifiable and nondiversifiable risks. Illustrate them graphically.

8. Suppose you observe the following rates of return on an asset traded in the stock market and on an index of the performance of the entire market. Each return is equally likely.

Year	2001	2002	2003	2004	2005	2006	2007
Asset (%)	15	30	5	−10	8	−22	10
Market (%)	7	9	3	−7	15	−5	10

(a) Compute the beta for this asset. Explain your result.
(b) Given the value for beta, is the rate of return, on the asset in question in 2007 above or below the one predicted by the CAPM? Explain.

9. Consider investments, given the following information:

State of the World		1	2	3	4	5
Probability		0.1	0.2	0.4	0.2	0.1
Rates of Return	–A	0.0	5.0	8.0	10.0	15.0
	–B	–12.0	5.0	9.0	12.0	24.0

(a) Compute the expected return, variance, and standard deviation for the returns of each of the two investments. Compute the correlation coefficient and covariance for the two investments.

(b) Plot the risk–return combination achieved by combining the two assets in the following proportions: 0:100%, 25:75%, 50:50%, 75:25%, 100:0%.

10. Using the liquidity preference model, illustrate graphically the effect of an increase in the return on the safe or risk-free asset. Explain.

11. The CAPM model suggests that diversifiable risk can be eliminated by buying the entire market portfolio. Do you think this is, strictly speaking, necessary? Why or why not?

12. If a stock's return falls by 6% but the return on a market portfolio rises by 12%, what is the "beta" for this stock?

13. Using the portfolio choice model, explain whether you would buy more or less of Nortel (a well-known Canadian-based technology stock) under the following scenarios:

(a) there is a surge in trading volume of the stock

(b) stock analysts expect stock market prices to fall

(c) fees for buying stocks fall

(d) the Bank of Canada is expected to raise interest rates

14. Assume that two projects have the same expected dollar return but that the underlying probability distribution of these returns differs in such a way that one such distribution is skewed to the "right" more than the other. How do these considerations influence VaR-type calculations? Explain.

15. You are asked to explain the concept of VaR to managers who have not taken a course in money and banking. Explain the following statements in easy-to-understand terms:

(a) VaR of –$20M in one month with a probability of 5%

(b) VaR of +$5M in one week with a probability of 5%

16. Suppose you invest $25M in a portfolio made up of $15M invested in the TSE300 and $10M invested in government of Canada Treasury bills. The TSE300 has an expected return of 11% and a standard deviation of 20%, while the return on T-bills is 4% with a standard deviation of 2%. The correlation in the two assets' returns is 0.25. All figures are annualized. What is the VaR for one year at the 5% probability level? What would the VaR be for one quarter of a year?

17. What would you expect to happen to the spread between a risky asset and a riskless asset if the bond rating on the risky asset were downgraded? Illustrate by using a diagram of the loanable funds framework.

18. Suppose your newspaper gives the following hypothetical bond yields:

Province of	Yield (%)
Quebec	10.50
Ontario	10.25
Newfoundland	11.25

Name two risk characteristics that could explain the yield differences. Which one is likely to be more important?

19. Consider a figure such as the one in **Economics Focus 13.1: Utility, the Demand for Insurance, and Gambling**. Now answer the following questions:

    (a) graphically show that the risk premium is greater the more curvature there is in the utility of wealth line

    (b) explain in economic terms what more curvature in the utility of wealth line means

20. Suppose you are buying a house, and monthly payments are as follows, with interest rates in parenthesis: $850 (8%), $715 (6%), and $650 (4%). There is a 25% probability that interest rates will either be 8% or 4%, and a 50% probability that the interest rate will be 6%. You also have the option of locking into a fixed interest rate of 6% and you cannot afford to pay more than $720 per month. What is the VaR for the worst case scenario? Explain.

DISCUSSION QUESTIONS

1. An investor must allocate her wealth between cash, which earns no interest, and a corporate bond, which earns a positive rate of return. Soon after her choice is made, inflation suddenly rises. How is the investor's portfolio likely to be affected?

2. List and briefly define as many types of risk as you can.

3. Is each of the following statements true or false? Explain your answer.

    (a) When constructing a portfolio of assets, it is useful, in terms of total portfolio risk, for the assets to be highly correlated with each other.

    (b) Systematic risk between asset returns and debt costs increases equity risk (or risk of net worth).

    (c) No one who is risk averse will ever buy a security that has a lower expected yield, has more risk, or is less liquid than another security.

4. "Portfolio diversification always reduces risk." Comment.

5. Explain the advantages and problems with the CAPM model.

6. Is buying stocks in different sports organizations likely to produce results consistent with the notion of diversification? Explain.

7. Does a risk-neutral investor care about the variance of returns? Explain.

8. What is the difference between risk and uncertainty? Explain.

9. Explain the logic behind references to "aggressive," "defensive," and "contrarian" investors, and to the value of beta in the CAPM model.

10. Explain the difference between CAPM and the arbitrage pricing theory.

11. Explain the connection between risk aversion and the slope of the efficiency frontier of the chosen portfolio.

ONLINE APPLICATIONS

1. Go to **www.globefund.com**. Follow the instructions required to construct your own portfolio of mutual funds. Once you have obtained a login name and a password, you can go back periodically and check how your portfolio is faring.

2. Go either to **www.dbrs.com** or **www2.standardandpoors.com/**. If you choose the former click on *ratings scale*. Examine the various ratings categories for different types of instruments. Do rating scales appear to be roughly comparable across ratings agencies?

3. If you subscribe to the *Economist* magazine at **www.economist.com**, then you can follow the magazine's quarterly poll of investment managers to see how they allocate their funds' assets among cash, bonds, and equities. Tracing these developments over time can give you some idea of how risk averse these portfolio managers are.

 CANSIM QUESTIONS

The series used to construct the tables in **Point–Counterpoint 13.1** are as follows: V122620 (TSE300), V122624 (stock index for paper and forest products), V122531 (three-month Treasury bill yield), V122487 (yield on Government of Canada bonds 10 years and over), V18702611 (CPI for Canada). Download these series for the sample 1960–99 using the quarterly sample frequency and see if you can replicate the results. Note that series V122624 is not updated past June 2003.

Note: Appendix 13a, "The Algebra of Portfolio Selection," is available on the text's Web site at **www.mcgrawhill.ca/siklos.**

References can be found on **www.mcgrawhill.ca/college/siklos**

CHAPTER 14

The Stock Market and Stock Prices

LEARNING OBJECTIVES

After reading and studying this chapter, you should be able to

14.1 describe how over-the-counter markets or stock exchanges function

14.2 explain how stock indexes are evaluated

14.2 determine how the efficient markets hypothesis and the fundamentalist approach explain stock prices

14.2 identify why the amount of information investors possess is crucial to how well they can forecast stock price movements

14.2 describe what a random walk is and describe what it looks like

14.3 explain why excessive volatility, calendar effects, and bubbles are puzzles

14.4 identify what home-bias is and why it happens and other anomalies in stock price behaviour

14.5 explain international linkages in stock prices

Like bonds and money, stocks are a fascinating financial asset to analyze. Everyone seems to have an opinion about the stock market and the future behaviour of stock prices. The proliferation of approaches—from that of chartists, who graph the past behaviour of stock prices in every conceivable fashion; technical analysts, who claim to make sense of the past and anticipated future performance of the stock market; contrarians, who deliberately go against the judgment of others—could make you think that stock prices can be predicted with some degree of accuracy.

Economists, in contrast, believe that the past is not a good guide to the future when it comes to stock prices. Yet their explanations face some considerable difficulties, particularly when it comes to attempting to understand large fluctuations in stock prices, such as those of 1987 or 2000.

We take the same approach in this chapter as in previous chapters, beginning by exploring how stock prices should be determined at the level of the firm and then assuming that this model applies to all firms. We consider two approaches: (1) the efficient markets hypothesis, which views investors as rational forward-thinking individuals who process information quickly and efficiently, and (2) an alternative way of determining individual stock prices called the fundamentalist approach.

Each of these approaches can tell us only about how the level of stock prices is determined, not about volatility. On the latter subject, economists have considerably more diversity of opinion, and a satisfactory explanation seems to elude the profession. Nevertheless, it is interesting to consider some anomalies in stock price behaviour that seem consistent with the economists' basic model.

14.1 THE MARKETS FOR STOCK

Some stocks are traded in brokers' informed **over-the-counter** (**OTC**) markets ("over the phone," "over the fax," or "over the Internet" would be more accurate names today). In Canada, the TSX Venture Exchange quotes more than 1000 OTC stocks worth several billions of dollars. In the United States, the network that performs the same function is called the National Association of Securities Dealers Automated Quotations (NASDAQ). There is a Canadian version also, called Nasdaq Canada. There has been some consolidation in the stock exchanges (see below).

The Ontario Securities Commission regulates the over-the-counter market in Ontario. Alberta, British Columbia, Newfoundland and Labrador, PEI, and Quebec have their own securities commissions. Although there have been attempts to coordinate the activities of the various securities commissions and, indeed, to create a national agency, these efforts have so far been unsuccessful.[1] However, there are now more direct links among the existing securities commissions than in the past.

Trading in the TSX Venture Exchange (**TSX**) is driven by electronic quotations of bid–ask spreads. Buyers and sellers are not directly brought together. Instead, trading is carried out through securities dealers who hold an "inventory" of stocks. But many more stocks are traded on **stock exchanges**, which are organized markets, each of which sets its own rules for which corporations can list shares and how they are traded.[2]

In such markets, investors exchange shares with one another, again either electronically through a broker or, as in New York, on the open floor, where bids and offers (asking prices) are shouted by members of the Exchange acting as agents for investors. As a result, such auction markets are "order driven."

In May 2001, the Toronto Stock Exchange (see below) purchased the predecesor of the TSX. The combined institution is now known as the TSX and the TSX Venture Exchange. This is the result of a consolidation that sees equities being traded in Toronto while derivative products (see Chapter 15) are traded on the Montreal Exchange.

Canada had four stock exchanges: the Montreal Stock Exchange, the Toronto Stock Exchange (TSE), the Alberta Stock Exchange, and the Vancouver Stock Exchange. In November 1999, the TSE became the sole market for "senior" stocks, that is, for stocks traded on current exchanges, while junior stock issues were consolidated with the merger of the Alberta and Vancouver stock exchanges into what became the TSX. In April 2000, the TSE, now renamed the TSX, became "demutualized" (i.e., ceased to be owned by its members) and became a for-profit institution. Many Canadian corporations also have their shares listed on one of the large U.S. exchanges.

The TSE began to operate in 1852, and trading occurred on the floor of the exchange. The trading floor was closed on 23 April 1997, and since then all trading has been done electronically.

Modern technology is changing the way stock exchange prices operate. Canadian investors can easily use brokers who have seats on exchanges in Tokyo, London, or Paris. Computer technology is also modifying stock exchanges internally. Increasingly, buyers and sellers transmit their orders to a computer. The advent of Internet trading via Instinet, for example, is threatening the established exchanges.

Prices of individual stocks are published daily for the major Canadian, U.S., and overseas exchanges. Investors are also interested in the performance of the stock market as a whole, and a variety of **stock price indexes** are available. The best known Canadian index is the Standard and Poor's TSX Composite, which is an average of over 200 stocks (of fewer companies, however,

Anatomy of a trade:
www.nyse.com/ pdfs/NYSE_activities_Mech.pdf

Visit the homepages of some major exchanges
www.tsx.com
www.nyse.com
www.nasdaq.com
www.nasdaq-canada.com

The world's largest agency brokerage firm can be found at **www.instinet. com**

---

1 However, regulators continue to press for the establishment of a single regulator. We return to this issue in Chapter 20. One of the latest in a series of reports or drafts on the subject can be found at the Web site of the Ontario Securities Commission at **www.osc.gov.on.ca/index.html** under "Uniform Securities Legislation Project."

2 It is worth noting that this centralized-market approach, which relies heavily on the intermediation of brokers through a computerized network, is used in many industrialized countries besides Canada and the United States, but not in all.

FINANCIAL FOCUS 14.1
STOCK PRICES IN THE FINANCIAL PRESS AND THE BID–ASK SPREAD

The financial press and many daily papers regularly present stock prices. In April 1996 Canadian stock exchanges fell in line with European and Asian exchanges by switching to the decimal system of reporting stock prices. A major advantage of the move is that stock prices are not constrained by ⅛ of a cent changes in prices.

A typical line for an individual company reads as the table below. BBD is Bombardier. During the first half of 2004, the price of a share of its stock fluctuated between a high of $2.33 and a low of $2.20 a share. The difference between high and low prices during the day is sometimes referred to as the bid–ask spread. Typically, stock market charts report the high, low, and close as in the accompanying chart, which shows the high, low, and close for the TSX in 2004. Because the index changes frequently it is difficult to come up with a figure that is directly comparable over long periods of time. As a result, what is termed a "synthetic" index exists. This gives a reasonably good idea of the evolution of stock prices over time. In a competitive market the spread should be small. However, in an article that created quite a stir in U.S. financial markets, Christie and Schultz found that collusion in the NASDAQ market meant that spreads were higher (and therefore dealer profits were higher) than necessary. A subsequent study concluded that spreads began to narrow right after the publication of the article!

On 2 June 1997, in part because of the furor, the NASDAQ formally reduced its quotation increments from ⅛ to 1/16. The result was a significant drop in the bid–ask spread (of 20.5%, according to the NASDAQ's estimates).

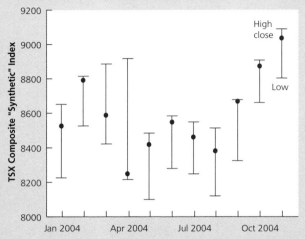

The chart shows the highest (top line), lowest (bottom line), and closing (small circle) values for the TSE300 index on a monthly basis for the 2004 calendar year. Data are adapted from the Statistics Canada CANSIM II database, series V122618, V122619, V122620, and V122620.

| 365-Day | | Stock | Div | | | | Cls or | | Vol | Yield | P/E |
High	Low	Symbol	Rate	High	Low	Latest	Change	100s	%	Ratio
7.13	1.87	BBD.SV.B	0.09	2.33	2.20	2.21	–0.12	87705	4.16	NA

since some firms have more than one type or class of securities listed on the exchange). Like most indexes, it is based on the market value of the shares being traded (since the volume of shares traded is not the same for every company). Stock indexes are frequently adjusted to reflect changes in trading patterns, preferences for certain stocks, their relative importance in the stock market, as well as other more technical factors.[3] Thus, for example, the venerable Dow Jones Industrial Average (DJIA) in the United States was revised three times in 1990s, and 11 of the Dow's 30 stocks are new to the index since 1990. In 1999, for example, Intel, Microsoft, Home Depot, and SBC Communications were added to the DJIA. These companies did not even exist before 1968. In addition, had these companies been included earlier in the Dow, the value for this index would have far exceeded its current reported value.

---

3 In the case of the S&P/TSX composite there is a committee that maintains the index and follows specific rules about which stocks to include or exclude from the index. See "S&P/TSX Composite Index" available at **www.tsx.com/en/pdf/0000Maintenance.pdf.**

According to at least one study, the NASDAQ has indeed become more efficient in the sense that bid–ask spreads have narrowed considerably. Several Canadian studies have also looked at the TSX's performance since decimalization and have reported an apparently puzzling result. Although small traders have clearly benefited from the reduction in the spread, large institutional traders (who typically buy and sell thousands of shares at a time) have since broken up large orders into several smaller orders, and this has had the effect of increasing trading costs, or what are called execution costs. These studies point out that market efficiency may need to be evaluated not only along the bid–ask dimension, but also taking into account the total costs of transacting in the marketplace.

Div rate is the size of the dividend payment, which may be quarterly or semiannually (an "r" next to the stock in question would signify that dividends are in arrears).

The *High* and *Low* columns show the ranges of price the previous day; *Cls* is the price at the close of trading. *Net change* indicates the absolute change in the price of the stock between closing on the previous day and closing the day before that. *Vol 100s* shows the number of shares traded in hundreds. *Yield* and *P/E* ratio are measures of the stock's and the company's performance; yield is simply the dividend to stock price ratio at close converted into a percentage, and the P/E ratio, when it is published, is the price of the stock divided by the company's earnings per share over a period (usually 12 months).

Questions for Discussion

1. Is the quotation increment issue an important one? Try to list points on both sides of the debate.
2. Would the growth of Internet-based trading have any significant impact on the bid–ask spread in stocks?

Sources

H-J. Ahn, C.Q. Cao, and H. Choe, "Decimalization and Competition Among Exchanges: Evidence from the Toronto Stock Exchange Cross-Listed Securities," *Journal of Financial Markets* (January 1998): 51–87.

J.C. Bacidore, "The Impact of Market Quality: An Empirical Investigation of the Toronto Stock Exchange," *Journal of Financial Intermediation* 6 (1997): 92–120.

M. Barclay, W.G. Christie, J.H. Harris, E. Kandel, and P.H. Schultz, "Effect of Market Reform on the Trading Costs and Depths of NASDAQ Stocks," *Journal of Finance* (February 1999): 1–34.

W. Christie, and P.H. Schultz, "Why Do NASDAQ Market Makers Avoid Odd-Eighth Quotes?" *Journal of Finance* 50 (May 1995).

P. Harverson, "Study Makes New Claims of NASDAQ Collusion," *Financial Times* (13 October 1996): 22.

C.M. Jones, and M.L. Lipson, "Sixteenth: Direct Evidence on Institutional Execution Costs," Graduate School of Business, Columbia University (February 2000).

14.2 STOCK PRICE DETERMINATION

Analysts have conceived two quite different approaches to understanding price determination in the stock market: the efficient markets hypothesis and the fundamentalist approach. On the surface they seem at variance with each other, but, as we will see, they are not necessarily contradictory.

THE EFFICIENT MARKETS HYPOTHESIS

The **efficient markets hypothesis**, which economists favour, is that market participants use all available information efficiently in anticipating future prices; hence no one can earn abnormal economic profit.

Put differently, the prevailing stock price should fully reflect the available information. Moreover, market efficiency can be tested since existing information in the marketplace should have no influence on stock prices.

What is "information" and how does it make markets efficient?

Economic efficiency includes the way in which individuals are assumed to obtain, use, and process relevant information in the determination of the price of any asset. The presence of efficiency in the stock market implies that the price of a stock reflects its inherent riskiness. No stock return can be excessive because it must reflect all information that might influence its price up to the time of trading.

In Oliver Stone's 1987 movie *Wall Street*, unscrupulous financier Gordon Gekko craved information, and its pursuit sowed the seeds of his eventual ruin. As he told one of his colleagues: "I know of no more valuable commodity than information."

Note that the proponents of this view do not say that the stock market offers no profitable opportunities. Rather, they imply that foreseeable events offer no special opportunities. For example, construction activity in Canada is at its lowest during the winter months and toy sales peak in December. Yet, stocks traded in these industries show no obvious seasonal patterns. Why not? Because these events are well known or fully anticipated. By contrast, events that are unanticipated can influence prices in an unexpected fashion, opening opportunities for profitable trades.

What are the implications of these principles? Answering that question requires distinguishing between three different versions of the efficient markets hypothesis.

Weak Form

The weak form of the efficient markets hypothesis says that past stock prices contain no information useful in predicting the future course of prices. It is referred to as a weak because it makes fairly minimal demands on what investors based their decisions on when making predictions about future stock prices. Subsequent forms of the expectations hypothesis make increasingly strong demands on what investors are thought to know or base their decisions on. Let

E = expected or anticipated value
S = price of a stock
t = time

Then we can write formally,

$$E(S_{t+1} \mid S_t, S_{t-1}, S_{t-2}, \ldots) \qquad (14.1)$$

to mean the expected or anticipated value[4] of a stock at a time $t + 1$, which is tomorrow, based only or conditionally, on (the symbol $\mid$), the past performance of that stock $(S_{t-1}, S_{t-2}, \ldots)$.[5]

The weak form of the efficient markets hypothesis then says that the anticipated *change* in the price between today and tomorrow cannot be predicted by anything that influenced that price in the past. Since the price of stock today, S_t, is known and presumably reflects all information contained in the price previously, the best forecast of tomorrow's price is today's price, or

$$E(S_{t+1} \mid S_t, S_{t-1}, S_{t-2}, \ldots) = S_t \qquad (14.2)$$

In the absence of new information, an investor would conclude that tomorrow's price is expected to be equal to today's price.

Of course, all sorts of *unpredictable* economics events, company-specific or economywide, can affect tomorrow's stock price. This fact would imply that the best forecast of tomorrow's stock price (S_{t+1}) is today's price (S_t) plus an unpredictable component (U_t). In other words, we can write

$$S_{t+1} = S_t + U_t \qquad (14.3)$$

where U_t represents the unpredictable component that explains stock price changes. Alternatively, note that (14.3) can be rewritten

$$S_{t+1} - S_t = \Delta S_{t+1} = U_t \qquad (14.4)$$

which restates what has already been argued: Changes in stock prices are unpredictable. If we assume that, on average, the unpredictable component is zero, then from equation (14.3) we obtain[6]

---

4 There is a way of calculating such an expected value, otherwise known as a mathematical expectation. See the Appendix to this chapter on the text's Web site at **www.mcgrawhill.ca/siklos**.

5 It is not necessary to specify how far in the past we need to go. The essentials of the story are unaffected whether we look back 10 days or a year.

6 Taking expectations of both sides of equation (14.3) we get $E(S_{t+1}) = E(S_t + U_t) = E(S_t) + E(U_t) = S_t$ because S_t is known at the time a forecast is made and U_t is expected to average zero. As we shall see in Chapter 21, this type of expectations formulation is known as rational expectations.

$$E(S_{t+1}) = S_t + E(U_t) \qquad (14.5)$$
$$= S_t$$

This prediction is known as the **random walk**. If it is correct, we might as well pick stocks by throwing darts at a dartboard. Indeed, the *Wall Street Journal* for several years ran a contest between a group of expert stock pickers (who change from time to time) against a selection of common stocks picked by throwing darts at a list of stocks on the New York, American, and NASDAQ exchanges. Research shows that the experts did not consistently outperform the "dartboard portfolio."[7] In March 2002, just in time for the market meltdown of that summer, the *Wall Street Journal* decided to retire the competition. The "darts," however, got their revenge when they won the last contest in April 2002. Nevertheless, in 142 contests, the darts were outperformed on average by both the investors and the Dow Jones Industrial Average (the pros won 87 times, while the darts were victorious 55 times; interestingly, the DJIA outperformed the pros 86 to 76). The pros even outperformed WSJ readers who participated in the contests since 1999.

Can such a possibility really be entertained? Consider Figure 14.1(A), which shows the performance of the TSE300 since 1976. Despite several noticeable downturns, such as those in 1982, 1987, and 1998, the general price trend has been upward.[8] Does not such a clear trend imply that stock prices should be predictable? In Figure 14.1(B), which shows stock returns (i.e., percentage changes in stock prices), notice that the values hover around zero, leaving it in a seemingly random fashion (hence the term "random walk"). But also notice the sharp spikes in the curve. They indicate that a buy-and-hold strategy cannot produce excess returns over the long run and that losses are possible in the short run.[9] Canada's *Globe and Mail* has also been running a stock-picking contest for the last few years, with one analyst winning three years running. Notice that the competition is for the highest return alone. This means that risk considerations are ignored. As a result, the strategy involved in winning such a contest is quite different from the one used to build a portfolio.[10]

The prevalence of the random walk hypothesis has not prevented individuals from developing techniques to try and beat the market. For example, the so-called Beardstown Ladies—named after the small Illinois town they live in—tried, with embarrassing consequences. This group of stock-picking grandmothers rose to popularity after claiming that their stocks earned 23.4% annually in the 10 years ending in 1993. This announcement led to the formation of a mini-publishing and public speaking empire, along with considerable media exposure. Unfortunately, first a magazine, then an audit by Price Waterhouse later confirmed that their stocks actually returned only 9.1%, which was considerably less than the 14.9% return for the S&P500 or the 12.7% return on U.S. Treasury bonds over the same period. Although the Beardstown Ladies' error was apparently unintentional, it is further evidence of the difficulty, but not the impossibility, of beating the market.[11]

Keep track of the investment dartboard at
online.wsj. com/home/us

---

7 See G.E. Metcalf, and B.G. Malkiel, "The *Wall Street Journal* Contest: The Experts, the Darts and the Efficient Markets Hypothesis," *Applied Financial Economics* 4 (October 1994): 371–74. It is not even clear whether the "pros" outperform the "amateurs" in such contests as these. The investment dartboard was discontinued. See G. Jasen, "Journal's Dartboard Retires After 14 Years of Stock Picks," *Wall Street Journal Online* 18 April, 2002. In late 2004 it was revived, with the first contest scheduled for 2005 between six subscribers to the *Wall Street Journal* and darts thrown by six *Wall Street* staffers.

8 The same trend is apparent in stock prices on stock exchanges in several industrialized countries. Moreover, the downturn in stock prices that began in 2000, although interrupted several times, is perhaps the most significant episode of falling stock prices in a couple of decades. Nevertheless, there is an unmistakable upward trend generally in stock prices.

9 Not everyone agrees with the conclusion. For example, one study found that information from the distant past can indeed be used for forecasting stock prices. See Z. Ding, C.W.J. Granger, and R.F. Engle, "A Long Memory Property of Stock Market Return and a New Model," *Journal of Empirical Finance* 1 (1994).

10 A point made by the three-time winner. See M. Milevsky and T. Salisbury, "How to Win the Globe and Mail's One-And-Only Contest," *Globe and Mail* (6 January 2005): B13.

11 See D. Kadlec, "Jail the Beardstown Ladies," *Time* 151, 30 March 1998, and T. Petruno "Beardstown Ladies Could Have Done Worse," *Los Angeles Times* (19 March 1998): D1, D7.

| Figure 14.1 | The Random Walk of Stock Prices |

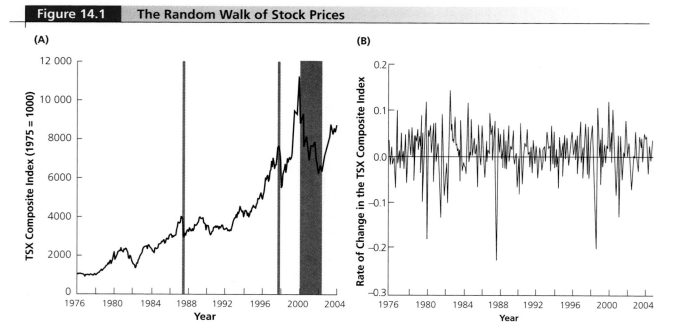

A graph of the level of the TSX stock price index in panel (A) shows a more-or-less steady rise since the mid-1970s. Noticeable downturns are in green. But a graph of the month-by-month percentage change in those price levels in panel (B) reveals no discernible pattern. The latter phenomenon is referred to as a random walk. The green areas in Figure 14.1 (A) highlight large drops in the TSE300, which occurred in 1987, 1998, and between 2000 and 2003.

Sources: Adapted in part from the Statistics Canada CANSIM II database, series V122620, reproduced by authority of the Ministry of Industry and *Bank of Canada Review*.

The above illustration reveals an oft-noted tendency of individuals or groups to exaggerate their returns. The author of an investment newsletter was quoted as saying "I know of no brother-in-law in the entire world who has ever lost money in the stock market."[12]

Semistrong Form

The semistrong version of the efficient markets hypothesis suggests that relevant information contained in the past behaviour of interest rates, inflation, and even company performance is as irrelevant as past prices in forecasting future prices. Figure 14.2 shows, for example, that although there is no obvious link between interest rates and stock prices, there appears to be a weak negative relationship between these two variables. We shall see later how the loanable funds framework can be used to explain such an outcome. For the time being, however, we will treat the link between stock prices and any past macroeconomic information (this would include variables such as inflation and money supply growth) as not being useful in improving forecasts of future stock prices. Indeed, research suggests that sharp changes in individual stock prices are triggered by unexpected events and are very temporary. (Nevertheless, there are differences in

---

12 As quoted in J. Clements "How to Deflate Your Boastful Relatives," *Wall Street Journal*, 26 January 2000. The article points out that just because an investor has a "hot" stock does not imply that his or her portfolio is either well constructed or is outperforming the market. It goes on to suggest that you ask your boastful friend or relative four questions to find out how well he or she is really doing. They are: "How much do you have in the stock?" "How are your other stocks faring?" "What did you pay?" and "How much of your portfolio is in stocks?"

| Figure 14.2 | **The TSX and the Treasury Bill Rate, 1976–2004** |

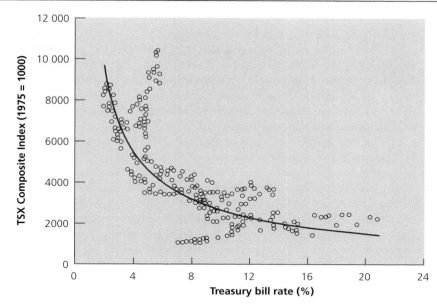

The TSX index is the same one used in Figure 14.1(A). The horizontal axis is the annualized yield on government of Canada Treasury bills. Monthly data from CANSIM were used, so each point represents a combination of returns on the TSX relative to the annualized yield on Treasury bills. The straight line represents a line of best fits.

Source: Adapted from the Statistics Canada CANSIM II database **http://cansim2.statcan.ca/cgi-win/CNSMCGI.EXE**, series V122620, and V122531.

opinions about what are sometimes referred to as large "corrections" in stock prices—sharp swings up or down.)

In going from the weak to the semistrong form of the efficient markets hypothesis, the idea is to expand the information set that might determine stock prices so that it includes other macroeconomic variables. Equation (14.1) could now be written

$$E(S_{t+1} \mid S_t, S_{t-1}, S_{t-2}, ..., R_t, R_{t-1}, R_{t-2}, ..., \pi_t, \pi_{t-1}, \pi_{t-2}, ...) \qquad \textbf{(14.6)}$$

where R_t is the interest rate and π is the rate of inflation. Other relevant macroeconomic information could also be included. The remainder of the analysis is unaffected, however, so we still conclude that

$$\Delta S_{t+1} = U_t$$

The only difference is that the possibility of forecasting errors is even more restricted because even less information can be profitably exploited.[13]

Strong Form

There remains a final possibility: that there is no information whatsoever, public or private, that can be profitably exploited by an investor. This alternative is known as the strong form of the ef-

---

13 The accumulated body of evidence favours the weak or semistrong forms of the efficient markets hypothesis. A review of the literature is B.N. Lehmann, "Asset Pricing and Intrinsic Values: A Review Essay," *Journal of Monetary Economics* 28 (1991): 485–500.

ficient markets hypothesis. Few economists believe in it literally because there are well-documented cases of profit from *insider* information (information available to a corporate officer, director, or major shareholder but not to all shareholders or the public at large).[14] Certainly, some causal evidence exists that insider information does contribute to stock price movements in the TSE. For example, in 1999, it was suggested that some corporate executives, and other insiders,[15] may have profited or avoided losses in stocks they owned thanks to privileged information that the rest of the market could not have had before some official announcement (of a merger or acquisition or some other major deal). A case in point is that of Corel Corp., makers of software, whose CEO was alleged to have sold nearly one-quarter of his holdings in advance of a highly unfavourable earnings report.

How can we tell whether there is anything unusual in stock price movements? One method is the investigative reporting route such as the one regularly conducted by major newspapers or magazines. An alternative is the event study approach. The idea is simple and builds on the efficient markets hypothesis. If new information is available, then it should be quickly reflected in stock prices. Researchers then look for "abnormal" returns. These returns are defined as the actual return less the expected return on a particular stock over some arbitrarily chosen period, prior to some known announcement that is suspected of prompting the insiders to act before the actual date of the announcement. Normal means that no new information was released that would have influenced stock prices. Using some notation, we would write

$$\varepsilon_{it} = R_{it}^a - E(R_{it}) \tag{14.7}$$

where ε_{it} is the "abnormal" return for stock i at time t, R_{it}^a is the actual return, and $E(R_{it})$ is the expected stock return. Returns are defined as before so that

$$R_{it} = [(S_{it} - S_{it-w})/S_{it-w}] \times 100 \tag{14.8}$$

is the percentage change in stock price S over the period $t - w$ to t. The period w is referred to as the event window, and is usually a few days or weeks long. Statistical criteria are then used to decide whether ε_{it} is "abnormally" high. It should be noted, however, that there is a difference between insider information, which cannot be acted on legally, and a rumour or gossip based on knowledge of a collection of events and information available publicly or privately. The distinction is not always clear.

THE FUNDAMENTALIST APPROACH

Although the efficient markets approach admits that company-specific information may have impinged on the past performance of a firm's stock, it does not emphasize the connection. By contrast, the **fundamentalist approach** suggests that how well a firm performs over time determines the value of its earnings and thus the price of its stock.

Suppose, for simplicity, that a firm pays out all its profits in the form of dividends,[16] that it is expected to operate indefinitely into the future, and that suspension of dividends is not expected at any time.[17] Since dividends reflect the flow of profits to be generated now and into the future, they presumably should dictate the value of the firm and its stock as perceived by the market. It is for this reason that this approach to explaining stock price behaviour is known as the

---

14 Some years ago, Ivan Boesky of New York made (and subsequently lost) a fortune based on insider information. Similar instances occurred during the 1920s. And, during the spate of corporate takeovers and buyouts in the 1980s and 1990s, the volume of trading in shares of the companies involved sometimes rose during the few days preceding the official announcement.

15 An insider is any stockholder who has at least 10% of the voting stock.

16 We assume here that dividends are paid annually, even though they typically are paid quarterly, or semiannually.

17 These assumptions are certainly strong, but relaxing them would complicate only the final expression linking dividends and stock prices; it would not break the essence of the link between these two variables.

fundamentalist approach. As we have said repeatedly, a dollar paid today is not valued the same as a dollar paid in the future. Therefore, we must first discount the value of future dividend payments. Thus, we write

$$S = \frac{d_1}{(1 + R)} + \frac{d_2}{(1 + R)^2} + \cdots \tag{14.9}$$

where d_1, d_2, ... represents the dividend payments paid out in years 1, 2, and so on, and $1/(1 + R)$, $1/(1 + R)^2$, ... represents the discount factors.

So far nothing has been said about whether these dividend payments are fixed or not. Let us assume that as a firm grows, so do its dividends—say, at a rate of g percent per year. In other words, if d_1 is the dividend paid in year 1, d_2, the dividend paid in year 2, is $d_1(1 + g)$. In this fashion, we can relate the dividends in any year to the dividends paid in the first year; that is,

$$d_n = d_1(1 + g)^{n-1} \tag{14.10}$$

where d_n is the dividend paid out in the nth year, and $(1 + g)^{n-1}$ is the factor by which these dividends have grown over the n years relative to the dividends in year 1. The net effect is that we can rewrite equation (14.9) as

$$S = \frac{d_1}{(1 + R)} + \frac{d_1(1 + g)}{(1 + R)^2} + \cdots \tag{14.11}$$

This equation has a fairly simple solution:[18]

$$S = \frac{d_1}{R - g} \tag{14.12}$$

Thus, the price of a stock, given a particular dividend, d_1, is determined by the interest rate in relation to the rate at which dividends grow. For a given interest rate, R, the faster dividends grow (that is, the higher is g) the higher is the price of a stock. Since dividends are presumably a function of a firm's performance, the better a company performs, the higher the price of its stock. See **Financial Focus 14.2: Explaining Stock Market Crashes** for a practical implementation of equation (14.12) together with some obvious limitations of the analysis.

Since equation (14.9) emphasizes the role of future dividends affecting current stock prices, these likely will be related to the overall state of the economy. Therefore, if future economic activity is expected to fall, as in a recession (see Chapter 6), then current stock prices also will likely fall. This reduces the value of the company and the collateral a firm can use to back up a loan. Banks then might add a risk premium to existing loans, further depressing the outlook for some firms in the economy. The so-called credit channel then creates a link between GDP growth, interest rates, and stock returns. Notice also from equation (14.12) that an inverse relationship exists between stock returns and the interest rate. This establishes a link between the bond market, discussed earlier, and the stock market. Figure 14.3 illustrates the link in terms of the loanable funds framework introduced in Chapter 6. The left-hand figure shows the usual loanable funds diagram. The interest rate fluctuates between R_1 and R_2 depending on the position of the loanable funds demanded curve. According to equation (14.12) a rise in R, other things held constant, would reduce stock prices. This is illustrated in the right-hand diagram, which clearly shows the negative relationship

---

18 The proof is as follows: Multiply equation (14.11) by $(1 + R)/(1 + g)$ to obtain

$$\left(\frac{1 + R}{1 + g}\right) S = \frac{d_1}{(1 + g)} + \frac{d_1}{(1 + R)} + \frac{d_1(1 + g)}{(1 + R)^2} + \cdots$$

From this equation, subtract equation (14.11) to get

$$\left(\frac{1 + R}{1 + g}\right) S - S = \frac{d_1}{(1 + g)}$$

which, when solved for S, yields equation (14.12). Since the price of a stock can never be negative, equation (14.12) holds so long as $R > g$.

between R and S. Figure 14.2 shows a broadly similar relationship between the TSX index and the yield on Treasury bills. American economist Fred Yardeni, who frequently comments in the media, came up with a relationship between the long-term bond yield and earnings per share, which he called the "Fed Model," after interpreting some commentary from the U.S. Federal Reserve which seemed to suggest that the Fed believed that such a link exists.[19] Why? We have already seen that equation (14.12) predicts a relationship between dividends in the near and distant future and current share prices. Therefore, an investor might well compare the return on a long-term bond and expectations of the return on yields over, say, the next ten years. Indeed, there seems to be some evidence that there may be a statistical link between proxies for these two variables.[20]

Although equation (14.12) is simple to implement and a powerful alternative to the hypothesis developed earlier in this chapter, it does rely on some rather strong assumptions. In addition, implementing equation (14.12) faces the difficulty that, in recent years, corporations whose stocks trade on stock markets, have shown a growing taste for getting rid of dividends altogether. Recently, Fama and French[21] have argued that the dramatic drop in the number of firms paying dividends—down from 66.5% in 1878 to just over 20% by 1999, at least in U.S. markets—reflects not only the fact that "new economy" firms have joined the stock market and are less profitable, but also that characteristics of these firms (smaller, riskier ventures with low profitability but strong growth potential) have led to fewer of them offering dividends. Should this trend continue, then the value of d_1 in equation (14.12) would effectively disappear, although one could presumably find a proxy for this variable based on an estimate of how much of a dividend might be paid out if the company in question followed such a policy (perhaps based on some measure of profitability). More recent research reveals that, although the trend spotted by Fama and French is correct, the disappearance of dividends occurs predominantly among smaller firms. Larger firms still persist in paying dividends, and there are no signs this feature of the marketplace is going away.[22]

| Figure 14.3 | Interest Rates and Stock Prices |

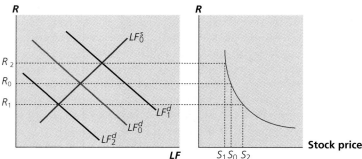

The diagram on the left shows the equilibrium interest rate as determined by the loanable funds model. The diagram on the right shows the connection between the interest rate and stock prices when dividends and dividend growth are constant in equation (14.12).

19 This view has not been endorsed by the U.S. Fed, though something resembling the "Fed Model" appears in the testimony of the so-called Humphrey-Hawkins report on monetary policy delivered to the U.S. Congress in July 1997.

20 See D. Jansen and Z. Wang, "Evaluating the Fed Model of Stock Price Valuation: An Out-of-Sample Forecasting Perspective," working paper, Texas A&M University, October 2004.

21 See E. Fama and K. French, "Disappearing Dividends: Firm Characteristics or Lower Propensity to Pay?" *Journal of Financial Economics* 60(1) (April 2001): 3–43.

22 See Harry DeAngelo, Linda DeAngelo, and Douglas J. Skinner (2004), "Are dividends disappearing? Dividend concentration and the consolidation of earnings," *Journal of Financial Economics* 72 (June 2004): 425-456.

CAN THE TWO APPROACHES BE RECONCILED?

We appear to have two separate explanations for the behaviour of stock prices; but a reconciliation begins with the observation that a future stream of dividends, like any future event, cannot be known with certainty. It can only be forecast, and if we exclude the use of insider information, that forecast must be based on existing information known to all investors. The only information that could possibly alter the price of the stock is information on any alteration of the projected flow of future dividends. By definition, that information cannot be anticipated. But this is just another way of saying that stock price exchanges are unpredictable. Thus, the fundamentalist and efficient markets approaches need not conflict.

14.3 STOCK MARKET VOLATILITY

The *volatility* of the stock market can be defined in several ways. We examine a particular definition shortly; for the moment, just think of it as representing some measure of the size of changes in stock prices.

Figure 14.1(B) shows this volatility. Contributing to this volatility has been the tremendous growth in the volume of trading, as shown in Figure 14.4. Notice the sharp rise in the volume of trading beginning in 2000, around the time of the bursting stock market tech bubble.

Although economists have not reached a broad consensus on this question of volatility, some do suggest explanations. One is based on the notion that the stock market has two types of participants:[23] "informed traders," who behave much as the efficient market hypothesis suggests, and "noisy traders," who follow fads and trends, jumping on or off particular bandwagons. Suppose that individuals attempt to forecast stock prices as in equation (14.12), but investors cannot evaluate the equation with certainty because information about the future behaviour of dividends is incomplete. Let S^* represent the price of a stock evaluated with some imprecision and S the price we would obtain if the indefinite future stream of dividends were completely known. We can write a relationship between these two prices as

$$S = S^* + U \tag{14.13}$$

where U is the measure of the imprecision with which investors can evaluate equation (14.12).

Equation (14.13) is, however, only an expression of the *level* of stock prices. A statement about their volatility is more useful. If we measure volatility of stock prices as their variance, we can, under certain conditions,[24] rewrite equation (14.13) as

$$V_S = V_{S*} + V_U \tag{14.14}$$

where V_S, V_{S*}, and V_U represent the volatilities of S, S^*, and U, respectively.[25]

The noisy investors can be viewed as raising V_U for a given V_S. Because they are likely to react to information that is irrelevant to the fundamental value of a stock, the volatility of prices as measured by V_S will become relatively less important in explaining actual volatility. In other words, if all stock market participants were informed traders, V_S would largely be explained by V_{S*} since they all presumably would calculate the prices of stock on the basis of equation (14.12). By contrast, the uniformed investors who do not follow equation (14.12) are the ones who create noise, or V_U, and thus weaken the success of the efficient markets approach to explaining the behaviour of stock prices.

---

23 A recent reference that stimulated much of this research is R.J. Shiller, *Market Volatility* (Cambridge, Mass.: The MIT Press, 1989), Chapter 4.

24 In Chapter 13, we explored these conditions and other aspects of this measure.

25 Equation (14.14) is valid so long as the variances of S^* and U are independent of each other—that is, as long as they are uncorrelated. Correlation was defined more formally in the previous chapter.

| Figure 14.4 | Volume of Shares Traded in Toronto |

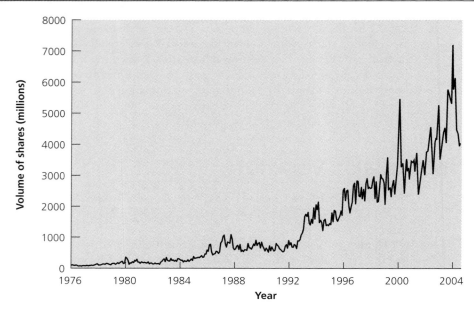

Source: The data are the monthly volumes of shares, in millions, traded on Toronto stock exchanges. The data are monthly averages of daily data adapted from the Statistics Canada CANSIM II database, series V37413.

One of the factors thought to contribute to "noise" in the marketplace is the prevalence of "news." It should come as no surprise, for example, that the words of key figures in the world of finance, such as Alan Greenspan, the chair of the U.S. Federal Reserve Board, can move markets, and that investors may overreact to such pronouncements.[26]

Although this explanation may sound reasonable, it is not accepted by all economists. Indeed, many economists believe that the level and volatility of stock returns are linked to each other and have developed a number of statistical tools to explain this phenomenon.[27]

14.4 OTHER ANOMALIES?

The volatility of prices is but one of many "anomalies" in stock price behaviour that economists have difficulty explaining.[28] Another is the market's failure to act on the well-documented evidence that stocks of companies with low price–equity (P/E) ratios outperform those of companies with high P/E ratios. Presumably, the former are underpriced in the sense described in equation (14.12) and the latter overpriced. If so, stock market participants should be able to make regular profits by following a simple strategy based on information available to everyone. That they do not implies that something is wrong with the efficient markets hypothesis.

---

26 A point emphasized in, for example, D.B. Sicilia, and J.L. Cruikshank, *Words that Move the World's Markets: The Greenspan Effect* (New York: McGraw-Hill, 2000), and R.J. Shiller, *Irrational Exuberance* (Princeton, N.J.: Princeton University Press, 2000).

27 One of the Nobel Prize recipients in 2003, Robert Engle, was rewarded for developing just such models. See **http://nobelprize.org/economics/laureates/2003/**.

28 The term anomalies is in quotation marks because what seems like an anomaly one year sometimes turns out not to be one, at least based on subsequent research. Hence, although the anomalies below are thought to exist by many, not all financial economists are yet prepared to deviate from the efficient markets hypothesis.

FINANCIAL FOCUS 14.2

EXPLAINING STOCK MARKET CRASHES: AN APPLICATION OF THE FUNDAMENTALIST APPROACH

Stock market crashes appear to contradict the efficient markets hypothesis because the fall in prices seems out of proportion to any influence new information could possibly have on stock prices. We know that all markets have some inefficiency (without it there would be no incentive to search for information and exploit profitable opportunities at the expense of other investors). We also know the fundamentalist and efficient markets approaches can be viewed not as competing arguments but rather as different explanations of the information content used by investors to price stocks. Can any of these arguments be reconciled with the sharp fall in prices in the aftermath of Black Monday, 1987?

The figure below shows what happened to stock prices and the Treasury bill rate during that year. Stock prices and interest rates rose sharply until October when both fell dramatically—but temporarily.

From the end of April to the end of September, the Treasury bill rate rose from 8.08% to 9.35%. The TSE300 fell during October from 3902.37 to 2978.34, a drop of approximately 23.7%. Suppose that a typical firm's stock also fell by 23.7%. Moreover, suppose that this firm paid out annual dividends of $10 and that these dividends were expected to grow at an annual rate of 4%. At the end of April, according to equation (14.12), the present discounted value of the dividends and, therefore, the price of the stock were

$$S = \$245.10 = \frac{\$10.00}{8.08\% - 4.00\%}$$

The same calculation for the end of September gives

$$S = \$186.92 = \frac{\$10.00}{9.35\% - 4.00\%}$$

a drop of nearly 23.7%! Thus, relatively small changes in interest rates over a short time span can produce very large stock price changes.

Clearly, however, the foregoing calculations leave several unanswered questions. First, would the dividend rate and its growth stay the same after the crash? Second, why did stock prices not fall earlier? After all, it is clear that interest rates had risen sharply over several months and yet stock prices kept climbing. In other words, why did investors allow stock prices to be overvalued for so long?

How valid are these calculations for other "crashes"? The question is difficult to answer since large falls in stock prices since 1987 usually have been confined to particular regions of the world (such as Asia in 1998) or particular indexes. For example, although the Dow Jones Industrial Average peaked around December 1999 only to fall approximately 12% by the end of February 2000 (that is from 11497.1 to 10128.3), the TSE300 rose by more than 8% during the same period. Meanwhile, interest rates in both the United States and Canada rose, with the Canadian three-month Treasury bill rate rising from 4.93% at the end of December 1999 to 5.05% at the end of February 2000. A key short-term U.S. interest rate, the Fed funds rate (see Chapter 23), rose from 5.01% to 5.72%. If we use the same numerical values for dividends and dividend growth as in the 1987 stock market crash example but substitute current interest rate values, S shows a decline of 41%! In this case, the present discounted value approach is not as accurate as before.

Some of the foregoing limitations of the fundamentalist approach come into play even more forcefully if we look at the drop in the stock market since early 2000. The reason? There has been a dramatic drop in both stock prices and interest rates.

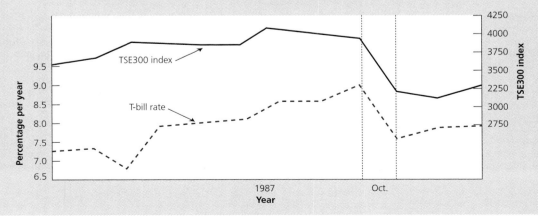

Indeed, our numerical example described earlier cannot work with a dividend growth assumption of 4% (why not?), and not even if we drastically cut the size (in $) of annual dividends. We leave examples such as these as exercises.

Questions for Discussion
1. Is a stock market crash necessarily a sign of "inefficiency" in the stock market?
2. The interest rate change explanation of the crash seems persuasive, but can you think of problems with this explanation?

Another anomaly is called the "January effect." Stock returns are regularly higher in January than in December of the previous year. December and September are regularly the best and worst months, respectively, for the Dow Jones Industrial Average (DJIA). But such regularities should be fully anticipated by market participants and consequently disappear. Again, the efficient markets hypothesis stands contradicted.

Two other anomalies that have raised considerable interest in the study of stock prices are the behaviour of futures prices and the possible role of mass psychology on price behaviour. A good example of anomalies in futures prices is the case of the price of oranges in Florida. We would expect that adverse weather conditions, such as winter freezes, would affect the future size of the crop of oranges in Florida and that this information would be fully incorporated in futures prices. Yet empirical evidence suggests that futures prices for oranges are hardly influenced by variables such as weather.

Mention of the role of mass psychology conjures up famous episodes of explosive stock price behaviour, which economists call *bubbles*. The most famous is the South Sea Bubble. In 1720 the South Sea Company took over the British government's debt in exchange for exclusive trading privileges with Spain's American colonies. As individuals rushed to join this and similar ventures, the price of the South Sea stock rose phenomenally. During the five months from 28 January to 22 June 1720, the stock soared at an annual rate of approximately 5000%. Then the South Sea bubble burst, and even the eminent Sir Isaac Newton was not spared from large losses. About a century earlier, Holland had seen several years of wild speculation in tulip bulbs (1634–37). At the height of this "tulip mania," some bulbs sold for as much as US$50 000.[29] Given that a tulip bulb is intrinsically worthless, the bubble eventually burst and many people lost fortunes. The extraordinary high prices were for tulips with unusual colours that were truly rare. Yet, there seems nothing outlandish about tulips, highly prized in Holland, compared to some of the stock prices for Internet-based companies seen in 1999.

Another famous example of a speculative bubble occurred closer to home during the early nineteenth century. The Mississippi Bubble arose when France attempted to implement the economic ideas of John Law, a Scotsman who had become a financier in France. Law suggested that the government issue securities and use the proceeds to finance productive investments. The Regent of France, whose country's economy was depressed at the time, was attracted to Law's ideas and awarded him the monopoly right to develop Louisiana. Law refinanced France's entire national debt through the issue of stock in his company, the Compagnie des Indes formed in 1719. As he acquired more assets, by issuing ever-greater quantities of stocks, France's central bank, the Banque Royale, issued more currency to make loans to enable individuals to purchase that stock. The growing supply of shares eventually reduced the price of the stock. In March 1720, Law forced the Banque to exchange currency for shares at a fixed price (which he set). Since individuals expected the share price to fall because of the overissue, there was a rush to exchange the shares for currency. The result was a tremendous rise in the price level. The bubble burst when Law, realizing the consequences of his actions, ceased converting shares into currency. The price of the Compagnie's shares collapsed to one-fifth of its peak value within a few months.

---

29 The calculation is based on gold valued at US$450 an ounce.

Law fled France soon after.

The stock market crash of 1929, which may have precipitated the Great Depression, is yet another example of how asset prices can plunge at a prodigious rate. On 24 October 1929 and again on 29 October 1929, panic selling in New York gripped the market, and shares that might have been worth $40 or more at the beginning of the month could be had for about $1 after "Black Tuesday," as the 29th came to be called. A similar outcome afflicted markets in Canada.

A recent addition to the list of anomalies is the finding that the stock of a company traded on different exchanges performs differently. For example, if Nortel were simultaneously traded on the TSX, the NYSE, and the Frankfurt DAX, we would expect the stock's performance not to be influenced by geographical location. However, this does not appear to be the case, at least according to one recent study, which found that the stock price of a company traded on exchanges in different geographical locations was also influenced by the performance of the exchange where the shares are traded.[30] In principle then, investors could have purchased shares of the same company traded in different geographical locations and profited from such trades. This result hardly squares with the predictions of the efficient markets approach.

Traditional explanations of such erratic ups and downs emphasize the "madness of crowds" or "speculative frenzy." More recent explanations, such as those of the 1987 stock market crash, emphasize that very large price changes can be justified by relatively small changes in fundamentals that govern stock price behaviour. For reasons that are beyond the scope of this text, however, economists have difficulty empirically distinguishing between a process that indicates explosive behaviour and one that has a more "rational" explanation.

A couple of examples will help to illustrate the point that what seem like anomalies may instead reflect institutional or demographic considerations. For example, research reveals that investors should avoid buying stocks on the last day of each quarter and, especially, on the last day of the year because of the type of trading that mutual funds engage in (we address the mutual find performance issue in Chapter 19).[31]

Another seemingly anomalous aspect of stock market behaviour is the pronounced fall in stock prices that began in 2000 with the bursting of the tech bubble. The correction, clearly noticeable in Figure 14.1(A), seems to have been reversed beginning in 2003. However, new research predicts that stocks are in for a pronounced and predictable slump. Why? Simply because of demographics. Apparently, as the baby boom generation ages they are more likely to sell stock, and their numbers are likely to dwarf the proportion of investors who are younger and tend to buy stocks.[32]

14.5 INTERNATIONAL LINKAGES IN STOCK PRICES

The globalization of financial markets has meant that investors have opportunities to purchase equities in many countries. Canadians, of course, have long been interested in U.S. stocks, and several Canadian companies have their stocks traded on both the Canadian and U.S. stock exchanges. Indeed, anyone doing research comparing U.S. and Canadian stock prices has to be

---

30 K.A. Froot, and E.M. Dabora, "How Are Stock Prices Affected by the Location of Trade?" *Journal of Financial Economics* (August 1999). This author's personal experience also appears to vindicate the hypothesis. On March 16, 2001 I purchased a few Nortel shares foolishly thinking that the stock had hit bottom. Because the computer trading system in use at the time by the TSX broke down—it has since been replaced, as we discussed earlier—I purchased the stock at the New York Stock Exchange. That day Nortel in Toronto closed at $26.92, down $0.78, while the same share in New York rose to US$16.88, up US$0.98.

31 See Mark M. Carhart, Ron Kaniel, David K. Musto, and Adam V. Reed, "Learning for the Tape: Evidence of Gaming Behaviour in Equity Mutual Funds," *Journal of Finance* 57(2)(2002): 661-693. Also see M. Hulbert, "Why Dec. 31 Is a Good Day to Stay Out of the Market," *New York Times* (6 October 2002): BU6.

32 See J. Geanakopolos, M. Magill, and M. Quinzii, "Demography and the Long-Run Predictability of Stock Returns," *Brookings Papers on Economic Activity* 1 (2004): 241-325, and M. Hulbert, "A 16 Year Slump? If So, Blame It on the Boomers," *New York Times* (1 December 2002): BU7.

ECONOMICS FOCUS 14.1   THE EQUITY PREMIUM PUZZLE

Stocks and bonds compete with each other in thousands of portfolios. Yet, if we look at the annual return of common stocks versus the annual return of, say, long-term bonds, stocks usually seem like the better bet in terms of return.

Although the return on the DJIA has clearly been more volatile, the mean return is almost double that of the long-term bond. This feature of the data has been present for more than 200 years and has been termed the **equity premium puzzle**. But then, is it not the case that the higher return is at the expense of more risk? The answer is a tentative yes, but many studies have argued that even if we adjust for the higher risk of holding equities, stock returns appear to be "excessively" high. Can the puzzle be explained in any way? There are no definitive answers yet, but some argue that stocks command a premium because they are held by individuals who have very short-term horizons and who demand extra compensation for holding stocks. An interesting explanation comes from the fact that, with the exception of the New York and London stock exchanges, all other stock exchanges are recent phenomena. Precisely because these are the only two markets to have survived for so long, they are not typical of all stock markets or of all stock market returns.

To underscore this point, Siegel and Thaler point out that a prescient individual investing US$1000 in 1925 in the U.S. stock market would end up with US$842 000 at the end of 1995, while the same $1000 would have yielded only $1270 if invested in U.S. Treasury bills. The amounts would be a little less impressive if stock market developments since the late 1990s were taken into account.

The puzzle only deepens when we realize that the real returns on bonds have been particularly poor over long periods, while the same is not true of equities. In other words, the equity premium is larger still than originally thought!

Recently, Fama and French have suggested that the equity premium is really a feature of the last 50 years or so of higher than (long-run) average economic growth, and that U.S. investors simply were fortunate to invest in an age of rapidly rising share prices. Indeed, their results would imply that, sooner or later, equity returns would fall back to their long-run average, and it is quite possible that the behaviour of the stock market since early 2000 is a reflection of this feature of the data. Yet another interpretation of the equity premium puzzle also suggests that it is not a puzzle at all. Gabaix and Laibson take the view that, since it is costly for individuals to constantly change their consumption behaviour for every large gyration in stock markets, the puzzle is in part due to the fact that statistical studies implicitly assume otherwise. Indeed, surveys reported by the authors suggest that the average investor either does not realize what the return on his or her portfolio actually is or, worse still, tends to greatly underestimate

the size of equity returns. Finally, it was argued in Chapter 10 that consumption and, therefore, savings go through a life cycle; it is equally likely that the young display a greater taste for equities than do the middle aged (or the old). The reason, of course, is that the risk inherent in investing in equities is relatively greater and the young are more willing to bear such risks (and enjoy the potentially higher returns too). But there is a problem. Recall Figure 10.5, which points out that the young are "liquidity constrained." This means that their ability to invest in equities is impaired. Hence, to make stocks more attractive there has to be an equity premium. This is the essence of the recent contribution of Constantinides, Donaldson, and Mehra.

Part of the reason academics have been baffled by the behaviour of equities involves the subtle concept we first encountered in Chapter 5, namely the difference between ex ante and ex post measures. Ex ante investors may not have expected equity returns to be as high as they have been, but, ex post, that is exactly what seems to have happened (at least until the stock market meltdown that began in 2000 and showed signs of ending in 2003). All of this suggests that we must be careful in concluding that stocks necessarily outperform other financial instruments.

Questions for Discussion

1. Why is the relationship between equity and bond returns referred to as a puzzle?
2. Why can risk differences between stocks and bonds not adequately explain the equity premium?

Sources

Arnott, R. and P. Bernstein, "What Risk Premium is Normal?" *Financial Analysts Journal* 58 (March/April 2002): 64-85.

S. Brown, W. Goetzmann, and S. Ross, "Survival," *Journal of Finance* (July 1995).

G.M. Constantinides, J.B. Donaldson, and R. Mehra, "Junior Can't Borrow: A New Perspective on the Equity Premium Puzzle," *Quarterly Journal of Economics* 117 (February 2002): 269–96.

E. Fama and K. French, "The Equity Premium," *Journal of Finance* 57 (April 2002): 637–59.

X. Gabaix and D. Laibson, "The 6D Bias and the Equity Premium Puzzle," *NBER Macroeconomics Annual 2001* (Cambridge: MIT Press, 2002): 257–312.

J. Siegel, *Stocks for the Long-Run* (Burr Ridge, Ill.: Irwin Professional Press, 1994).

J. Siegel, and R.H. Thaler, "Anomalies: The Equity Premium Puzzle," *Journal of Economic Perspective* 11 (Winter 1997): 191–200.

R. Thaler, "Myopic Loss and the Equity Premium Puzzle," *Quarterly Journal of Economics* 110 (February 1995): 73–92.

FINANCIAL FOCUS 14.3   DAY TRADING

The tremendous growth in the speed of communication, combined with the falling costs of using such technologies, has created an apparently new breed of investor who spends his or her day sitting in front of a terminal watching the second-by-second gyrations of markets and uses the computer mouse to execute trades. But this development is not as new as it may first appear. In the era of the Great Depression of the 1920s, "bucket shops" traded simply on the prices on the stock ticker—the 1920s era equivalent of today's stream of price information appearing on computer screens. Traders, or speculators as they came to be known, did not actually exchange the stocks, they merely traded on the price, as in current over-the-counter markets. Hence, they did not face annoying, potentially costly delays. Waiting for the order to be executed or confirmed is time consuming, and a trader also has to deal with the inevitable uncertainty about the actual price at which the trade will go through. Demand–supply conditions are rarely the same at the time the trade is made relative to when the decision to trade is made.

The modern-day "bucket-shops" are the day traders, and they either operate in groups or as individuals. They seemingly watch every movement of a stock, most likely several stocks simultaneously, and buy and sell large quantities of these to profit, they hope, from a rise in price (or a fall when short-selling, as we shall see in Chapter 15). The ability to execute orders quickly and cheaply through the Internet has created a whole new breed of investor. The chart on the next page shows movements in the price of HP Computers at five-minute intervals. These and other charts are available at **www.stockcharts.com**. The vertical bars in the middle part of the chart are referred to as "candlesticks" and indicate the range of prices traded over the time interval in question, that is the high and low prices. The horizontal line indicates the price at which trades were executed. The smooth lines are moving averages, that is, averages of stock price movements over either a 50-day or a 200-day interval. The longer the interval over which the stocks are averaged, the smoother the moving average. Technical analysts use such figures to determine whether there is any "momentum" in the price of a stock. The bottom part of the chart shows the volume of shares being traded. Notice that price changes are relatively larger when the volume is larger, whereas price changes are very small, as is the bid–ask spread, when there is little volume.

Various other indicators of stock performance including CMA and PPO are shown. CMA (Chaikin Money Flow) and PPO (Percentage Price Oscillator) are indicators of whether there is rising demand or price in the stock. Notice that the stock price is higher when CMA rises. The PPO can be used to indicate when the volume of trading in the stock is rising or falling on average.

Considerable debate arises about the merits and implications of day trading in the stock market. Do day traders increase stock price volatility? Do they care about the economic fortunes of the stock they are trading? Do they care about the economic fundamentals that drive the stock market more generally? The media and some recent books on the subject certainly give the impression that day traders are individuals who do not research the companies they trade in, caring only about the direction of change in the price of the stock. Yet, many other day traders rely on the Internet and its various news and information retrieval services (such as **www.money.cnn.com**, and **www.money-central.msn.com/investor/home.asp**, and many others) to gauge market "sentiment."

Although it is a bit too early to tell, there is some empirical evidence that day traders, also known as "bandits," who use the NASDAQ's small order execution system (SOES) actually trade profitably even though they have less information than the market-makers. One reason is that they have a stronger incentive to make profits since their livelihoods depend on this kind of activity.

Questions for Discussion

1. Discuss whether you think day traders do or do not worry about the underlying "fundamentals" in making stock trading decisions.
2. An individual who runs a day trading course has suggested that the first rule of day trading is to "forget everything you ever knew about investing." What do you think is meant by this statement?

Sources

S. Bodow, "Short-Term Prophets," *Wired* 7 (January 1999).

J.H. Harris, and P.H. Shultz, "The Day-Trading Profits of SOES Bandits," *Journal of Financial Economics* 50(1), October 1998: 39–52.

M. Klam, "The Solitary Obsession of a Day Trader," *The New York Times Magazine* (21 November 1999).

G.J. Millman, *The Day Traders* (New York: Time Business Random House, 1999).

careful to make corrections for the **inter-listing of stocks** in U.S. and Canadian exchanges. However, unlike bond markets, where cross-border trading developed quickly as exchange controls and other regulations affecting international capital flows were gradually removed, the same has not occurred in the market for stocks. Figure 14.5 shows industrial stock price indexes for the U.S., Japan, Germany, and Canada. Since the indexes are based on the 2000 base year, they are comparable. Notice, in particular, that stock price changes after 1990 are vastly different between the United States and Canada, on the one hand, and Japan, for example, on the other. Clearly, investors looking for positive stock returns would have been well advised to stay away from Japanese (and German) stock markets beginning in 1990. Yet, a look at portfolios of domestic investors suggests that they hold too few foreign stocks relative to what would be optimal in terms of the gains from diversification explained in the previous chapter. Unfortunately, research has not yet pinpointed exactly why the internationalization of stock markets has not proceeded with the speed that might have been expected. One explanation might be that the transactions costs of monitoring foreign stocks are high because it is relatively more difficult to keep track of what foreign companies do than what domestic companies do. Of course, as computer technology facilitates such monitoring (for example, via the World Wide Web) these costs should fall. Another possibility is that a lingering effect from past capital controls still persists.[33] Another reason is the complex mix of tax treatments that might deter investors from taking advantage of apparently higher returns in other countries. Is it possible that this "home-bias" in investments is irrational or are there good economic or institutional explanations for this result? For example, it could be that investors are relatively better informed about their own markets than about markets abroad. Moreover, when investors do venture abroad, it is toward internationally known companies

---

33 Papers on the subject include the one by Karen Lewis, "Consumption, Stock Returns and the Gains from International Risk Sharing," NBER Working Paper no. 5410 (January 1996) and "What Can Explain the Apparent Lack of International Risk Sharing?" *Journal of Political Economy* (April 1996).

| Figure 14.5 | International Stock Price Behaviour |

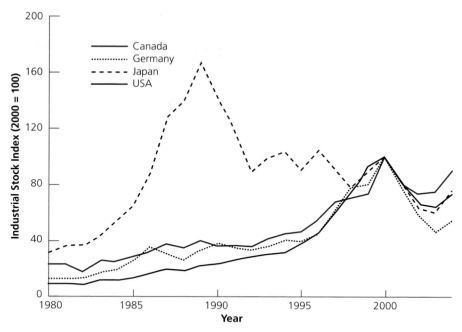

Source: *International Financial Statistics CD-ROM* (Washington, D.C.: International Monetary Fund).

www.adr.com, for example, provides daily quotes for ADRs issued by J.P. Morgan

based in other countries.[34] In Canada, regulatory considerations dealing with the foreign content in registered retirement savings plans (RRSPs—see Chapter 19) imply some government involvement in fostering a home-bias in investment. Lastly, given the financial scandals that have plagued financial markets in recent years, investors naturally will gravitate toward markets that provide standardized and credible information about company performance. Arguably, this makes the U.S. market, in particular, very attractive.[35]

Never underestimate the ingenuity of the financial sector for creating opportunities to facilitate the cross-border ownership of stocks. In 1927, when U.S. investors were interested in purchasing shares in the U.K., the law required such investors to use a British intermediary. In response, American Depository Receipts (ADRs) were created whereby a U.S. bank would take ownership of a share and then resell it to U.S. investors who would, in turn, receive a "receipt" for their investment. Like the underlying shares they represent, ADRs are traded on the NYSE. They have the advantage that dividends are paid in U.S. dollars. However, the value of the shares will fluctuate with changes in the exchange rate. For companies needing to raise capital, ADRs offer the opportunity to raise funds in the U.S., while U.S. investors gain the opportunity to diversify their investments internationally. Investments in ADRs are in the hundreds of billions of dollars.

---

34 See J-K. Kang, and R.M. Stulz, "Why Is There a Home Bias? An Analysis of Foreign Portfolio Equity Ownership in Japan," *Journal of Financial Economics* 46 (October 1997): 3–28, and K. Lewis, "Trying to Explain the Home Bias in Equities and Consumption," *Journal of Economic Literature*, 37 (June 1999): 571–608.

35 See A. Ahearne, W.L. Griever, and F. E. Warnock, "Information Costs and Home Bias: An Analysis of U.S. Holdings of Foreign Equities," *Journal of International Economics* 62 (March 2004): 313-36.

SUMMARY

- Stock markets are where stock prices are determined. Some of these markets are organized in exchanges and are order driven; others are quote driven and are referred to as over-the-counter markets.

- Stock market performance can be gauged by examining one of many stock market indexes.

- There are two main views about stock price determination. The efficient markets hypothesis argues that stock prices behave like a random walk—that changes in them display no predictable pattern over time. The alternative fundamentalist view is that future company fortunes, as represented by dividends, should explain the current price of a stock.

- The information set influences how well investors can form predictions of future stock prices. If only the past history of stock prices is used, this gives rise to the weak form of the expectations hypothesis. If the information set includes other publicly available information, then it is the so-called semistrong form of the efficient markets hypothesis. If insider information is part of the information set, the strong form of this efficient markets hypothesis applies.

- The fundamentalist approach predicts that stock prices will be inversely related to interest rates, as summarized by the following equation:

$$S = d/(R - g)$$

  Where S is the stock price, R is the interest rate, d is the dividend, and g is the growth rate of dividends.

- The two approaches to stock price determination may appear to contradict each other, but they can be reconciled since it is conceivable that firm-specific or business cycle data are part of the investor's information set.

- Despite the popularity of the random walk hypothesis, it cannot explain a number of anomalies in the behaviour of stock prices. To name but two: Stock prices are too volatile, and they can reach incredible highs and lows, called bubbles.

- Despite vastly different returns across major stock markets, investors have failed to take advantage of profitable opportunities outside their own country. The so-called "home-bias" in stock markets remains a puzzle.

IMPORTANT TERMS

efficient markets hypothesis, **267**
equity premium puzzle, **280**
fundamentalist approach, **272**
inter-listing of stocks, **282**
over-the-counter (OTC), **265**

random walk, **269**
stock exchanges, **265**
stock price indexes, **265**
TSX, **265**

PROBLEMS

1. You feel so enlightened by your courses in economics that on becoming a very wealthy business person, you decide to endow your alma mater with a chair (in economics, of course). If the university's financial officer tells you that your money can earn 10% a year, how large must your donation be to generate $150 000 a year forever? To avoid problems with inflation, you want your endowment to rise by 6% a year. (Hint: Look at the equation determining stock prices according to the fundamentalist approach.)

2. Suppose a particular stock is expected to generate dividends of $5 a share annually. Assume that stock prices are determined as in equation (14.12). What is the price of the stock if

(a) Dividends are constant and the opportunity cost is 10%?

(b) Dividends are expected to grow by 3% annually and the opportunity cost is 8%?

(c) The dividend growth rate is 3% and the opportunity cost is 12%?

3. An investment advisor says: "Since we know stocks are going to fall as well as rise, we might as well get a little traffic out of them. A man who buys stock at 10 and sells it at 20 makes 100 percent. But a man who buys stock at 10, sells it at 14½, buys it back at 12 and sells it at 18, buys it back at 15, and sells it at 20 makes 188 percent." How would you evaluate this advice?

4. The *Wall Street Journal* used to regularly hold a stock-picking contest. In its November 1999 issue, it summarized the following results:

	% Change in Stock Prices: 1 June – 30 Nov 1999
Experts as a group (Pros)	+58.45%
Dartboard portfolio (4 stocks)	−0.88%
"Amateurs"	+54.55%

Are the above results evidence in favour of the random walk hypothesis? Explain.

5. The following table shows the return on the S&P500 in January as well as over a 12-month period. Is there a January effect? Charting the relationship between the two sets of returns will help.

Year	January Return	12-Month Return
1965	3.3	9.1
1967	7.8	20.1
1969	−0.8	−11.4
1971	4.0	10.8
1973	−1.7	−17.4
1975	12.3	31.5
1977	−5.1	−11.5
1979	4.0	12.3
1981	−4.6	−9.7
1983	3.3	17.3
1985	7.4	26.3
1987	13.2	2.0
1989	7.1	27.3
1991	4.2	26.3

Source: Louis Rukeyser's Wall Street, February 1993.

6. Suppose a firm has earnings of $10 million that it pays out in the form of dividends to its five million stockholders. Assuming an interest rate of 5%

(a) what is the price of the stock?

(b) what is the dividend yield?

(c) if earnings grow 1% per year, what is the price of the stock?

7. Use Figure 14.3 to explain what would happen to the relationship between R (the nominal interest rate) and S (stock price) if there were an increase in loanable funds supplied. Explain.

8. Using the values provided in **Financial Focus 14.2** verify that S declines by 41% in 2000. Next use a dividend growth rate of 2%. Does the fundamentalist approach work better now? What if dividend growth is 2% and d=$6? Explain your answer.

DISCUSSION QUESTIONS

1. Comment on the statements below, indicating whether they invalidate the weak form of the efficient markets hypothesis.

    (a) Money placed in a mutual fund that invests in stocks only consistently earns a positive return.

    (b) When the stock market goes down in January, it usually goes down during the following 11 months.

    (c) Whenever a New Democratic Party government is elected, the stock market goes down.

2. Can you detect any relationship between the average return in the portfolios listed below (ranked by size) and their P/E ratios? If so, does this result represent an anomaly in stock price behaviour?

Portfolio Size	Mean Return	Mean P/E
Smallest	1.79	0.84
2nd	1.53	0.90
5th	1.25	0.85
9th	1.03	0.63
Largest	0.99	0.63

3. Does the random walk hypothesis of stock prices imply that an investor could just as well pick stocks by throwing darts at a dartboard? Explain.

4. In 1993, the Royal Bank of Canada issued preferred shares in Canadian dollars yielding 7.1% in dividends per year. The same bank also issued preferred shares in U.S. dollars, yielding 6.3%. Ignoring transactions costs and taxes, why would an investor buy the lower-yielding U.S.-dollar-denominated shares?

5. If the stock market were truly efficient, the probability that the darts portfolio would beat the experts would be .5. Is this true? Explain.

6. Because of the prominence given the *Wall Street Journal* stock-picking contest, we might expect the prices of selected stocks to rise on the day of publication. Is this possible? Explain.

7. Would anyone purchase a stock that gave out no dividends? Explain.

8. Can you think of reasons why geographical location might matter in the trading of a stock for the same company listed on different exchanges? Explain.

9. List four reasons why ex ante equity returns might be expected to be lower than ex post equity returns. Explain.

ONLINE APPLICATIONS

1. Go to **online.wsj.com** (note: access requires a paid subscription but temporary free subscriptions are possible). Next, search for *Investment Dartboard*. Check out current and past competitions. Pick a stock or a group of stocks and see how you stack up against the dartboard, the amateurs, and the pros. Better still, why not select stocks by creating your own dartboard portfolio and see how its performance compares with the one selected by the *Wall Street Journal*?

2. Most stock market Web sites allow you to construct a portfolio and track its performance over time. For example, if you go to **www.tsx.com**, choose *My Stock List* and follow the directions to create your own stock portfolio. Note: First-time users will have to register in order to use this service.

3. Wilfrid Laurier University runs a stock market competition. Go to **invest.wlu.ca** and follow the instructions to join.

CANSIM QUESTIONS

Go to the CANSIM Web site and download the data used to create the figure in **Financial Focus 14.1** as well as Figure 14.1. The series are: V122618 (TSX high), V122619 (TSX low), V122620 (TSX close). Plot the indexes for a year other than the one shown in the Financial Focus. Does it appear that the spread between high and low values has changed over time? Calculate the average return on the TSX Composite Index for a variety of samples. Are the returns close to zero, on average? Relate this result to the efficient markets hypothesis.

Note: Appendix 14a, "Mathematical Expectations: Some Basics," is available on the text's Web site at **www.mcgrawhill.ca/siklos**.

References can be found on **www.mcgrawhill.ca/college/siklos**

Risk Management

CHAPTER 15

Hedging Instruments: Futures, Forwards, Options, and Swaps

LEARNING OBJECTIVES

After reading and studying this chapter, you should be able to

15.1 identify how derivatives are created

15.1 describe the roles that uncertainty and the desire to reduce risk play in derivative products

15.1 explain the crucial difference between a hedger and a speculator

15.1 determine how investors can buy or sell a financial asset in the future at a price negotiated today

15.2 identify the differences between futures and forward contracts

15.3 describe how the values of options are determined and their role in financial markets

15.3 explain how swaps function

The world is a risky place. Since most economic agents are risk averse, they naturally attempt to eliminate risk or at least to shift it to other agents. This chapter explores some *derivative products* that attempt to shift the risk of holding various assets. The term derivative products, or derivatives for short, originates from the notion that their value depends on the value of some "underlying asset."

To understand the popularity of these hedging devices, recall the tradeoff between risk and return. They rise and fall together. Thus, if someone introduces a financial innovation that reduces risk to one party in a transaction, it will not be long before a market for that innovation begins to thrive.

The past quarter century has seen a large number of such innovations. One driving force has been the tremendous fall in the cost of computing and the concomitant rise in the volume of calculations that computers can handle. This technological revolution has made possible some new financial instruments and greatly widened the use of others. It has also increased the volume of available information about financial markets and the economy as a whole—increased it so much that diverse but widely held views about the future are common. These differences in expectations are also a stimulus for the development of financial instruments that enable the shifting of risk. Other factors include the globalization of financial markets and competition among bonds and securities dealers who have responded by creating new financial products. Finally, the recent volatility of interest rates has made current decisions riskier than in the past—and the parties to a transaction have yet another incentive to shift some risk elsewhere.

In this chapter, we examine several types of increasingly important financial instruments: financial futures, forward markets, options, and swaps of interest payments or of foreign exchange.

A word of caution is in order. What follows is only an introduction to an enormous subject. The literature on futures and options has grown tremendously over the past decade. Entire texts are devoted to their bewildering diversity and complexity. Indeed, it is the mystery of derivatives and the peculiar jargon used by market participants that has made politicians and the public occasionally suspicious of these financial instruments.

15.1 DEFINITIONS

Our discussion can be made clearer with some definitions.

Hedging is a process of protecting oneself against future price changes by shifting some or all of the risk to someone else. The individual who wants to shift risk away from him- or herself is often called a *hedger,* while the one who accepts greater risks is referred to as a **speculator**.

Hedgers typically have a *position* to protect: They either already own the commodity or financial instrument in question or they expect to do so sometime in the future. By contrast, speculators take no position; rather, they bet on price changes in the hope of making a profit.

Hedging has been in the news often lately because of the intense debate surrounding so-called **hedge funds**. This debate is the result of the near collapse of Long-Term Capital Management,[1] which led to large scale intervention by the U.S. Federal Reserve in particular to prevent an international financial meltdown. Hedge funds are a private investment vehicle for institutional and wealthy investors. The idea is to combine two operations that are central to the discussion of this chapter, (1) borrowing a security and selling it with the hope of buying it back more cheaply later (called short-selling as we will see below) and (2) leverage, a concept developed in Chapter 11. Leverage allows hedge funds to take advantage of anticipated increases in the price of a financial asset (such as a stock) via borrowing, while short-selling protects investors against a fall in prices. In theory, such funds can protect investors whichever way markets move but that is not always so, as we will see.[2]

Not to be forgotten in all this is the perennial role of intermediation in the process. As we will see, this feature brings together buyers and sellers of derivatives to "make" markets. And as in all other financial endeavours, there are underlying risks to be considered. We will examine some of the ways that investors respond to such risks.

Does the existence of speculators mean that some market participants are risk seekers, not risk averters? Not necessarily. The speculator foresees a very high return from a relatively small investment made by *purchasing on margin.*

Margin, which is the amount of cash put up by the investor, is a fraction of the value of the asset. The remainder is a loan from the broker handling the sale, and it must be backed by collateral. Buying on margin is regulated, and the amount of the loan cannot exceed a set percentage of the value of the instrument. Hence, if the price falls, the broker must make a *margin call* and obtain more funds from the investor.[3]

---

1 Among the principal figures in this hedge fund was Myron Scholes, a Nobel Prize winner in economics whose theory of options pricing transformed financial markets. Options are one of the derivatives we study in this chapter. For an entertaining account of this episode see C.R. Morris, *Money, Greed, and Risk: Why Financial Crises and Crashes Happen* (New York: Random House, 1999).

2 In part for this reason, some of the largest existing hedge funds issued a report calling for better management practices, not more regulation. See M. Pacell, "Five Hedge Funds' Report on Industry Stops Short of Call for New Regulation," *Wall Street Journal*, 8 February 2000 at **interactive.wsj.com/archive/retrieve.cgi?id=SB949959461972389456.djm**.

3 Alternatively, the investor can sell the asset and take the loss.

15.2 FINANCIAL FUTURES AND FORWARDS

Future markets trade **futures contracts**, which are agreements to accept or make delivery of an asset on a particular future date at a price struck today.[4] In contrast, an exchange of assets that occurs at the same time the price is agreed upon is said to be a trade in the **spot market**, sometimes called the *cash market*.

A futures contract may be for a commodity (such as pork bellies or wheat) or for a financial asset (such as foreign exchange or an instrument linked to specified stock prices). Here we concentrate on financial futures, but it is worth knowing that commodity futures are much older. As early as the twelfth century, trading fairs in Europe gave producers of agricultural commodities an opportunity to make contracts for the future delivery of their products. Modern futures markets probably originated in the nineteenth-century United States. The Chicago Board of Trade began organizing a futures market in 1848 as a means of correcting some inefficiencies in the market for grain. Technological changes during the same period, such as the invention of the telegraph and improvements in rail transportation, doubtless improved the chances of establishing viable futures markets, since instabilities and uncertainties were inherent in producing agricultural commodities today to be sold and delivered sometime in the future. The principal form of uncertainty, of course, lay in the future price of the crop.[5]

Financial futures markets are a phenomenon of recent decades. When the postwar system of fixed exchange rates ended in 1971, the variability of exchange rates became a problem in financial circles. Soon after, many countries began what has become a worldwide movement toward deregulation of financial systems. One result was increased volatility in the prices of all financial assets. It was not long before financial futures appeared on the scene. Futures markets have now spread around the world.

Most market transactions are conducted electronically, although a few exchanges continue to do business the old-fashioned "open outcry" way. Indeed, in 2000, the CBOT decided to split into two exchanges, one using the open outcry method, the other relying exclusively on electronic trading.

FORWARD MARKETS

Before proceeding with a description of how participants can hedge with futures contracts, it is important to be clear about **forward contracts**.

Forward and Futures Markets Compared

Forward and futures markets are alike in many ways. Both deal in durable, storable products;[6] both can be used for hedging; both require estimates of the future from participants.

There are also differences. The most obvious is that the buyer in a forward market transaction generally intends to take future delivery of the asset or commodity in question. By contrast, futures market participants rarely plan to take or make delivery. Typically, they intend **offset transactions**—that is, a purchase is to be offset by a subsequent sale.

Another difference is in the relationship between buyer and seller. In a forward transaction, the two are usually directly responsible to each other for ensuring that the terms of the agreement

The major exchanges that trade in derivatives include the Chicago Board of Trade (CBOT at **www.cbot.com**), the Chicago Mercantile Exchange (CME at **www.cme.com**), Eurex in Frankfurt, Germany, (**www.eurexchange.com**), and in Europe, Amsterdam, Brussels, Lisbon, London, and Paris have combined their markets to create a pan-European derivatives exchange market: **www.euronext.com**
In Canada, an agreement in late 1999 saw the Montreal Exchange (**www.m-x.ca**) become the exclusive marketplace for derivatives in Canada.

---

4 Thus, one requirement for the existence of a futures market is that the commodity in question be durable and able to be stored.

5 For additional historical details, see W.W. Libeck, "The Origins of Futures Markets," in *The Handbook of Financial Futures*, edited by N.H. Rothstein (New York: McGraw-Hill, 1984): 9–22.

6 Although this generally is the case there are exceptions. For example, electricity is a commodity that is neither durable nor storable, yet trades on the New York Mercantile exchange (NYMEX): **www.nymex.com**.

are fulfilled. In a futures market transaction, however, an intermediary, which can be a bank but is often an organized exchange, ensures that payment (or, less often, delivery) is made. The bilateral nature of trading in forward markets makes it difficult for participants to change positions; there is considerably more flexibility in futures market trading as evidenced by the ability to offset transactions.[7]

In addition, futures markets operate in an auction setting; forward transactions are generally concluded over the phone. Items traded in futures markets are standardized so that the only decision variable of interest to investors is price.[8] Finally, as will become clear later in the chapter, expectations of future prices are better reflected in forward markets than in futures markets.

Financial Focus 15.1: Forward Prices in the Financial Press on page 293 shows how forward and spot rates are reported in the financial press; Table 15.1 summarizes some of the major differences between futures and forward markets.

The Forward Market in Operation

Perhaps the best way to explain the operation of the forward market is to use an example. Because forward transactions in foreign exchange are common, we base our example on this type of transaction.

Table 15.2 sets out the highlights. A Canadian importer expects delivery three months hence of widgets valued at €2 000 000. Today's spot exchange rate is C$1.50 = €1, so the current Canadian value of the shipment is C$3 000 000 (€2 000 000 × $1.50).

Now assume the importer believes that the Canadian dollar will depreciate in the coming months. That means he anticipates that his cost for the imports will rise. If, for example, the exchange falls (i.e., depreciates) to €1 = C$1.60, the Canadian dollar cost of the imports will rise by

$$(\$2\ 000\ 000 \times 1.60) - (\$2\ 000\ 000 \times 1.50) = \$200\ 000$$

Table 15.1	Forward versus Futures Markets

Differences	
Forward	**Futures**
1. Delivery likely.	1. Offset likely.
2. Product may or may not be standardized.	2. Standardized product; price is the only variable of interest.
3. Transaction is bilateral in nature.	3. Intermediary involved.
4. Trading generally by phone.	4. Trading in an auction setting.
5. Self-regulated.	5. Even if conditions 1 to 4 are not met, will exist if forward markets break down.
	6. Regulated by agencies.

Similarities
1. Can be used for hedging or speculating.
2. Products are generally durable and storable.
3. Product price variations are large.
4. Have large numbers of suppliers and demanders and are competitive.

---

[7] Indeed, the number of steps required to complete a futures or an options transaction is surprisingly large. See, for example, P.S. Rose, *Money and Capital Markets*, 4th ed. (Homewood Ill.: Irwin, 1992): 861, Exhibit 12-11.

[8] For example, in the case of commodities such as oil, a futures contract would operate for a specific grade only, such as light sweet crude oil. In the case of financial futures, standardization is less problematic.

FINANCIAL FOCUS 15.1	FORWARD PRICES IN THE FINANCIAL PRESS

Forward market prices for foreign exchange are regularly reported in the financial press. The listings are easy to read.

The first column gives the name of the foreign currency as well as the horizon over which forward transactions can be made. Only in the case of the U.S. dollar can one actually buy up to five years ahead of time. Generally, the longest horizon for forward transactions is 12 months, and only for a few currencies between countries where a considerable amount of trade takes place. The next two columns give the exchange rate at which forward transactions can be made either in terms of Canadian dollar or in terms of the foreign currency.

Late afternoon wholesale, rates in Toronto, 18 January 2005.

	US$1 in C$ =	C$1 in US$ =
US/Canada spot	1.2241	.8170
1 month forward	1.2242	.8169
3 months forward	1.2239	.8170
6 months forward	1.2227	.8179
12 months forward	1.2190	.8204
3 years forward	1.2119	.8252
5 years forward	1.2131	.8244

Country/Currency	C$ per unit	US$ per unit
British/Pound spot	2.2850	1.8668
1 month forward	2.2805	1.8629
3 months forward	2.2729	1.8571
6 months forward	2.2613	1.8495
12 months forward	2.2408	1.8383
Europe/Euro spot	1.5944	1.3026
1 month forward	1.5951	1.3030
3 months forward	1.5964	1.3043
6 months forward	1.5984	1.3073
12 months forward	1.6027	1.3148
Japan/Yen spot*	83.58	102.30
1 month forward	83.38	102.07
3 months forward	83.03	101.63
6 months forward	82.48	100.85
12 months forward	81.29	99.09

Note: *Yen per C$ and US$ shown.

Source

National Post (19 January 2005): IN9.

Questions for Discussion

1. Suppose you export to the United States, thereby generating revenues in U.S. dollars. However, all your costs are in Canadian dollars. How does uncertainty about your U.S.-dollar receipts turn a forward contract into a speculative position?
2. Would the fact that the forward and futures spot prices consistently differ influence your interpretation of the usefulness of forward markets as a predictor of future spot rates?

To avoid this foreign exchange risk, the importer can fix the Canadian dollar price of products to be delivered in the future. He does so by arranging with a bank to deliver in 90 days €2 000 000 at today's prevailing three-month forward rate—say, €$1 = C$1.55. Upon acceptance of the forward contract, the cost of the imports is fixed at C$3 100 000 (€2 000 000 × $1.55), and decisions about profit margins, among other things, can also be made today with certainty. Delivery is fully anticipated by both parties to the transaction. Note also that this example ignores several considerations. First, it does not take account of discounting, since we know that $1 today is not the same as $1 in the future (even 90 days in the future). Second, the importer has the option of purchasing euros today and buying a 90-day financial instrument denominated in euros. The choice will depend primarily on the difference between euro-denominated and Canadian yields (a consideration discussed in Chapter 8). Alternatively, the importer may have to borrow €2 million and sell it on the foreign exchange market today at an exchange rate of $1.50, costing $3 000 000 plus the interest cost on the loan. Borrowing in euros may or may not be easy for the importer. Finally, we have ignored transactions costs, which may or may not be reflected in the forward rate being offered.

Table 15.2 — A Transaction in the Forward Market

	Spot Exchange Rate: $1.50		Forward Exchange Rate: $1.55
Current costs of imports	€2 000 000 × 1.50	=	€3 000 000
Anticipated future cost of imports in the spot market	€2 000 000 × 1.60	=	€3 200 000
Cost of imports at forward rate foreign exchange delivered in the future	€2 000 000 × 1.55	=	€3 100 000
Savings relative to future anticipated spot exchange rate	€3 200 000 − $3 100 000	=	€100 000

The current spot exchange rate is C$1.50 = €1. The exchange rate is expected to depreciate in value to C$1.60 = €1. The importer, however, can arrange to have €2 000 000 delivered three months hence at a rate of C$1.55 = €1 today. If the importer's exchange rate prediction is correct, the savings will amount to C$100 000.

THE WORKINGS OF FUTURES MARKETS

To understand how the market for financial futures operates, it is necessary to understand how participating in it enables investors to hedge against risk.

An individual who expects that prices for some asset will *rise* is said to take a **long position**. By contrast, someone who expects asset prices to *fall* is said to take a **short position**.[9] Clearly, a buyer has the intention of selling the asset at a higher price in the future and therefore takes the long position. By contrast, the seller would like to sell the asset at a higher price than he or she anticipates will prevail in the future and, for this reason, takes a short position.

Hedging takes place through the purchase of a futures contract, which specifies today both the delivery date and the price at which the asset will be acquired. Trading also requires, of course, that there be someone who takes a long position and another who takes a short position. Therefore, it can involve taking one position in the cash market and an *opposite* one in the futures market. This positioning is known as the "current spot position" method. There are other methods that may or may not be more suitable depending on the investor's circumstances. For example, an investor may assume that futures and their spot prices move together and then consider how to hedge depending on whether spot prices will move up or down in the future. This method is sometimes called the "worst case scenario." Another possibility is that the investor is more concerned with the type of transaction when the hedge is terminated, that is, in the future. To keep things as simple as possible, we only consider the second strategy.

A relationship exists between spot and future prices. The differential between the spot price and the futures price is known as the **basis**.[10]

At time t then we have

$$F_\tau(t) - S(t) = \text{basis} \tag{15.1}$$

where $F_\tau(t)$ = futures contract price purchased at time t for delivery date τ and $S(t)$ = spot price at time t.

Futures contracts are **marked-to-market**, which means that gains and losses are settled at the close of trading each day, *not* at the end of the contract. If the price falls below the currently prescribed minimum margin, the buyer must deposit an amount equivalent to the change in price

---

9 An often heard expression is *short-selling* (or *selling short*). An investor sells an asset at one price with the intention of buying it back at a lower price. The investor usually does not own the asset. Rather, he or she borrows it, usually from a broker's inventory of assets.

10 Not to be confused with the "basis point" that means 1/100th of a percentage point. Depending on the commodity or asset in question, one might further refine the concept of basis. For example, there is a location basis because there can be transportation and/or storage costs involved (e.g., in the case of electricity). In this case location basis is the difference between the spot price at the local market and the spot price at the delivery location. Similarly, one can measure time basis, that is, the difference between the spot and futures price which will be equal to zero at the end of contract maturity when the spot and futures prices are one and the same (see the discussion below). For ease of exposition we refer simply to the basis.

into the seller's account to maintain the margin. Thus, a change in the price of the futures contract affects the position of the buyer and seller in opposite ways.[11]

Financial Focus 15.2: Futures Prices in the Financial Press on page 296 shows how futures prices are quoted in the financial press. It is important to understand that the reporting of financial futures differs from that of the spot market. Consider the $1 000 000 bankers' acceptance in the example. The prices listed are not percentages of face value. Rather, they are points of 100 percent. Thus, the settlement (closing price) of 92.94 means an implied discount yield of

$$100.00 - 92.94 = 7.06\% \text{ per year}$$

This is equivalent to a delivery price of

$$100\left(1 - \frac{90(0.0706)}{360}\right) = 98.235$$

per $100 of face value. This translates into a settlement price of $98 235. Notice the term in parentheses, which is the adjustment factor required because the discount is expressed in annual terms. For a 90-day maturity period, an annual discount of 7.06% represents

$$7.06 \times \left(\frac{90}{360}\right) = 1.765\%$$

The brisk trade in futures means that their market price changes almost constantly. However, there are limits on how much the price of an instrument can vary during any one day, to ensure that margin accounts do not get wiped out by large price changes, and that brokers (who must make up losses on defaulting customers) have time to make margin calls.

Stock index futures are sold in multiples of the prevailing index. In the example in **Financial Focus 15.2**, an investor can purchase $200 times the index of the S&P TSX 60 Index. Thus, if the 60-stock index is 500, you could purchase $200 \times 500 = $100 000 worth of the portfolio.

Finally, the "open interest" column reports the number of futures contracts not yet delivered or offset. This information is a measure of the size of the futures market on any particular day. It can also be used to evaluate the future direction of prices.

A Long Hedge

We are now in a position to illustrate how interest rate risk can be hedged through the use of financial futures. Will the investor hedge long or short? It depends on circumstances and the individual's expectations about the future.

Suppose interest rates are currently high but the investor expects them to fall. Suppose too that this investor expects to obtain $100 000 three months hence. If interest rates do fall, the yield on the $100 000 asset the investor purchases will be less than the same asset would produce today. Some potential interest income will be lost. Preferably then, the investor wants to lock into current interest rates by purchasing a futures contract today and selling it three months from today.

Table 15.3(A) describes the position facing the investor considering a long hedge. Believing that on March 1 interest rates have peaked, the investor purchases a futures contract for a $100 000 bond to mature June 1. Today in the spot market a 9% government bond currently yielding 10.51% is available at 87.35; the futures price is 89. If the investor's expectations are correct, spot prices and futures prices in the bond market will rise as interest rates fall. Thus, on June 1, as the futures contract purchased March 1 matures, the investor sells the futures contract at 90. Meanwhile, in the spot market, bond prices have risen to 89. The investor purchases a bond. Had the investor had the cash on March 1, the bond could have been purchased at 87.35. In

---

11 By contrast, in forward markets, gains and losses are not settled daily. Moreover, marked-to-market contracts and margins are negotiable.

FINANCIAL FOCUS 15.2   FUTURES PRICES IN THE FINANCIAL PRESS

Most financial newspapers publish futures prices. Two examples are shown here: one for bankers' acceptances with a face value of $100 000 and one for an index called the S&P TSX 60 Index.*

ME is the Montreal Exchange. The listing gives the month of delivery, the lifetime and the trading day's opening, high, and the low prices for a contract, the settlement price ("Settle") at the close of the trading day, and the previous opening interest ("Prev Op Int"), which is the number of contracts outstanding for trading. These represent contracts that have not yet been offset by opposite futures transactions.

The prices listed are not dollars but points of 100 percent of face value. Thus, the bankers' acceptance's closing (settlement) price of 92.94 means an implied yield of 100.00% − 92.94% = 7.06% per year. (See text for more information.)

The notation "0.05 = $10 per contract" is the margin requirement; for the $1 000 000 bankers' acceptance, it

is 0.05 × $1 000 000 = $50 000. Alternatively, it is referred to as the price of a tick or, for example, 0.0001 × $100 000 = $10 where 0.0001 is 1/100 of 1%.

*The S&P/TSX index is a capitalization-weighted index of the 60 largest and most liquid stocks in Canada.

Questions for Discussion

Assume you open an account with an initial margin requirement of $2000. On August 1 you sell one bankers' acceptance at 93.50 and you hold your position until August 4. On August 2, the settlement price is 93.45, on August 3 it is 93.51, and on the 4th it is 93.49. On the 5th you buy back the contract at 95.00. Now answer the following questions:
1. What is the settlement price in dollars?
2. What is the marked-to-market?
3. What are the daily settlement prices?
4. What is the account balance on a daily basis?

Three-Month Bankers' Acceptances (ME) $1 000 000 (points of 100%; 0.01 = $25 per contract)

| Lifetime | | | | | Daily | | Net | Prev |
High	Low	Month	Open	High	Low	Settle	Chge	Opt Int
93.42	92.95	Jun 02	92.95	92.95	92.95	92.94	−0.03	1 675

S&P/TSX 60 (ME) 200 × index (0.05 pt = $10 per contract)

511.60	451.20	Mar 00	511.00	511.60	506.10	507.60	+1.60	49 590

Source: *Financial Post* (1 January 2000): C17.

other words, the investor has a loss of 89 − 87.35 = 1.65 or $1650. This loss, however, is largely offset by the profit of 90 − 89 = 1 or $1000 earned in the futures market from rising prices.[12] Put differently, the investor on June 1 buys the bond not at 89 (or $89 000) but effectively at $89 000 − $1000 = $88 000 thanks to the profits made in the futures transaction. Hence, hedging has made the investor better off than remaining in an unhedged position.

A Short Hedge

Now consider an alternative scenario in which the investor anticipates a rise in interest rates. In this case, the investor will want to engage in a short hedge.

Table 15.3(B) illustrates the features of a short hedge. Our investor owns a $100 000, 9% Government of Canada bond due on 1 March 2011; it currently sells in the spot market at 87.35 and yields 10.51%. At the same time, a futures contract is sold at a cash price of 95. If the investor's expectations are correct, bond prices in the cash market will fall by June 1, say to 86.8, thus leading to a loss of $550 on the sale of the $100 000 bond by that date. By contrast, since the futures

---

12 Notice that this numerical example and the next are idealized. They omit transactions costs and brokerage costs and assume the investor knows with certainty what bond prices will be three months in the future. Of course, as we saw in Chapter 7, investors can look to the yield curve to estimate a forward interest rate.

Table 15.3	Hedging with Interest Rate Futures

(A) Long Hedge

Cash Market — Unhedged Position		Futures Market — Hedged Position	
March 1:	Interest rates are believed to have peaked. Lock into current high rate. 9% Government of Canada bonds, currently yielding 10.51% and due 1 March 2011, are priced at 87.35 or $87 350.	March 1:	Buy the equivalent of a $100 000 bond in futures at a cash price of 89 worth $89 000.
June 1:	With the cash received today, buy a $100 000 Government of Canada 9% bond at 89, yielding 9%.	June 1:	Sell the futures contract at 90, worth $90 000.
Loss:	$89 000 – $87 350 = $1650	Gain:	$90 000 – $89 000 = $1000
	NET DIFFERENCE = $1650 – $1000 = $650		

(B) Short Hedge

Cash Market — Unhedged Position		Futures Market — Hedged Position	
March 1:	Investor owns a $100 000, 9% Government of Canada bond, due 1 March 2011, currently yielding 10.51% and priced at 87.35. Investor expects rates to rise.	March 1:	Sell the equivalent of a $100 000 bond in futures at a cash price of 95 for $95 000.
June 1:	Sell $100 000 bond at 86.8.	June 1:	Buy a futures contract at a cash price of 94.50 for $94 500.
Loss:	$87 350 – $86 800 = $550	Gain:	$95 000 – $94 500 = $500
	NET DIFFERENCE = $550 – $500 = $50		

The above examples are idealized since they ignore time costs and transactions costs and assume that the investor knows with certainty what the future will hold. However, at the end of the period depicted in the examples above, either the long or short investor will turn out to be correct, but not both. Essentially, the unsuccessful investor will see gains in the spot market turn into losses, but the losses in the futures market will turn into gains, or vice versa. But this only serves to further illustrate the point that hedging is a device to minimize variability in expected returns, regardless of whether expectations are correct or not.

price will also have fallen to 94.50, from 95 on March 1, the investor gains $500. In this example, a net loss of $50 on the hedge is made instead of the $550 loss in the unhedged position.

Put differently, instead of selling the bond at 86.8 (or $86 800) the bond is effectively sold at $86 800 + $500 = $87 300 thanks to the transaction in the futures market.

Notice, of course, that both investors cannot be correct in the above illustration. However, if the long hedge is incorrect in Table 15.3(A), so that futures prices *fall*, this will be offset by a rise in the spot price. Similarly, in Table 15.3(B), the gain in the futures market might turn into a loss if rates *fall*, but this will be offset by an unexpected *rise* in bond prices in the spot market.

The Difficulty of Perfect Hedges

If a sequence of transactions in the futures market produces a gain exactly equal to the loss, the investor has what is called a *perfect hedge*. Such an outcome is unlikely for several reasons.

First, it is not always possible for an investor to buy and sell the same asset in the futures market. He or she may have to settle for a *cross-hedge*, which means buying futures for one asset—say, Government of Canada bonds—and selling them for another—say, bankers' acceptances. Such transactions involve so many variables that they are unlikely to balance exactly.

Second, spot and futures prices do not necessarily move in concert.

Finally, futures prices in both the spot and futures markets are uncertain. Indeed, any error in the wrong direction can have disastrous consequences for the net gain or loss from hedging. Therefore, hedging cannot eliminate risk entirely.

Future Prices and Spot Prices

As the delivery month approaches, the spot price for an asset converges to the future price so that the basis essentially becomes zero. In the intervening period, however, the basis clearly differs from zero, which is what imparts some risk to hedging.

Why? As delivery approaches, investors have less uncertainty about what spot prices will be. Indeed, at expiration there is no uncertainty whatsoever about spot prices. Therefore, we expect the basis to disappear as the futures contracts approach the maturity date.

We can illustrate the connection between the futures price and the spot price with a simple expression. As before, let $F_\tau(t)$ denote the price in the futures market with delivery date and $S(t)$, the spot market price, both at time t. Then,

$$F_\tau(t) = S(t) + (R^S - R^L) \frac{\tau - t}{360} \cdot S(t) \tag{15.2}$$

Equation (15.2) states that the futures price, $F_\tau(t)$, is the spot price, $S(t)$, plus the **cost-of-carry**, which is the opportunity cost of carrying the contract until delivery as a proportion of the spot price.

The cost-of-carry can be measured, for example, as the difference between the yield on a short-term instrument, R^S, and a long-term instrument, R^L, adjusted for the term of the contract (the carryover period). Since τ is the date of the delivery, and t is today's date, $\tau - t$ is simply the number of days the contract is carried while $(\tau - t)/360$ is the carryover period in a fraction of a year defined as 360 days in length. The reason for including the term $(R^S - R^L)$ in equation (15.1) is that differences between short-run and long-run interest rates provide a measure of the direction interest rates will take during the carryover period.[13]

Note that, as the delivery date approaches, $\tau - t$ approaches zero and so $F_\tau(t)$ approaches $S(t)$; the cost-of-carry becomes more and more irrelevant.[14]

15.3 FINANCIAL OPTIONS AND SWAPS

Like futures, options have a long history. Indeed, early forms of options trading apparently existed in ancient Rome and Greece. The Netherlands' tulipmania described in Chapter 14 involved extensive trade in options.[15]

An *option* is the right to buy or sell a given amount of a particular security in the cash or futures market at a particular price before a specified expiration date.[16] The right need not be exercised if the holder thinks it unprofitable to do so. The buyer of an option pays the seller for the *right* to exercise it; payment is not made until the exercise occurs. If the option is allowed to expire, the writer (seller) of the option realizes the original price, which is called the *premium*. The writer provides the insurance to the holder for taking on the risk against which the buyer wants to protect himself or herself. The premium is, therefore, the writer's compensation. Hence, although

---

13 An explanation of this result is the subject of Chapter 7, where the topic of the term structure of interest rates is explored.

14 In the case of stock index futures, equation (15.2) would be written

$$F_\tau(t) = S(t) + (R - Div) \frac{\tau - t}{360} \cdot S(t) \tag{15.2a}$$

where R represents the interest cost of carrying the index portfolio, and Div is the dividend income earned by carrying the index portfolio. Equation (15.2a) is interpreted in the same manner as equation (15.2). Dividends are paid discontinuously, however, so $F_\tau(t)$ does not approach $S(t)$ as smoothly as in the case of interest rate futures.

15 One of the difficulties of that episode was that because there was no enforcement mechanism to ensure that contractual obligations would be met, many options writers simply refused to honour their obligations when the extraordinarily high prices for tulip bulbs collapsed in the spot market.

16 Such a device is called an "American option." A "European option" permits the investor to exercise it only on the contract's expiration date.

ECONOMICS FOCUS 15.1 — BEWARE OF THOSE DERIVATIVES

The public exposure of derivatives and of their implications for the financial system was heightened by a series of spectacular financial losses incurred over the last few years by well-known institutions. Included in the "hall of shame" were losses experienced by Procter and Gamble (US$137 million), and Orange County, California (US$1.7 billion). One of the best known of these was the collapse of the Barings Investment Bank, which took place after a trader, Nick Leeson, had built up profitable positions in the Japanese futures and options market (the Nikkei) until the Kobe earthquake in 1995 and concern over a recession in Japan turned them to sharp losses, so much so that the margin calls exceeded the bank's entire capital! The reason? Instead of trading the normal 1000 contracts or so, Leeson arranged to trade between 18 000 and 20 000 contracts to try to recoup earlier losses, only to increase his losses when he made the wrong bet about the direction the market was taking. A Dutch bank (ING) was persuaded to purchase Barings and take on its losses for the grand sum of £1 (approximately C$2.12). Go to **www.numa.com**, click *Reference Index*. Scroll down to the *Collapse of Barings Bank* for a list of references.

Another notable incident was the huge loss incurred by the German firm Metalgesellshaft AG (MG), which lost more than US$1 billion in 1993 on what appeared to be a safe bet. The company sold gasoline, diesel, and heating fuel at a fixed price to its customers for up to 10 years ahead of time (in effect arranging forward contracts with clients). To protect itself, the company hedged the full amount. If prices rose, for example, the company's costs would potentially rise above the receipts from the sale of fuels. So the company resorted to futures and swaps to hedge against the risk it faced. But oil prices fell and this led to large losses being sustained on MG's futures contracts. As we have seen, prices in futures can move in the opposite direction of spot prices and are made for relatively short-terms, unlike the long-term contracts with its customers. MG had fallen into the trap of mismatching its assets against its liabilities (see Chapter 13). Eventually, a group of German banks stepped in to rescue MG in 1994.

In the ensuing debate over the dangers posed by derivatives, some blamed these huge losses on a combination of bad luck and incompetence, while others assumed that speculative-type behaviour was the culprit. In any event, central banks around the world have since tightened their supervision over such markets.

Morris offers an entertaining account of the events covered in this box and more.

In 2001 and 2002 the sorry list of scandals and failures surrounding the use of derivatives grew longer with the announcement of the bankruptcy of Enron, the U.S. energy giant. As this is written the story is still unfolding (see the *Wall Street Journal*'s "A Chronology of Enron's Recent Woes" at **http://online.wsj.com/article/0,,SB10174245 26944009440,00.html**.[1] At the centre of the controversy, in addition to questionable accounting and ethical practices at the company, lies the unravelling of bad debts in the market for energy derivatives based on the transaction known as securitization. We will encounter securitization when we discuss interest rates on credit cards in Chapter 18 (see **Economics Focus 18.1**).

Questions for Discussion

1. What is the connection between the mismatch of assets and liabilities and the use of derivative financial instruments?
2. What lessons can be drawn from the Barings and Metalgesellschaft cases?

Sources

J. Harding, and C. Middelmann, "The Signs that Spell Danger," *Financial Times* (Derivatives) (16 November 1995): 2.

International Capital Markets: Development, Prospects, and Policy Issues (Washington, D.C., International Monetary Fund, 1995).

R. Lapper, "Complex Jigsaw of Trade Emerging," *Financial Times* (27 February 1995): 2.

R. Lowenstein, "Is Corporate Hedging Really Speculative?" *Wall Street Journal* (20 July 1995): C1.

C.R. Morris, *Money, Greed, and Risk: Why Financial Crises and Crashes Happen* (New York: Random House, 1999).

A. Steinherr, "Taming the Wild Beast of Derivatives," *Financial Times* (16 December 1994): 14.

[1] A subscription is required to access this article.

---

similar to futures, the option holder is not required to exercise it. Given the one-sided nature of the insurance provided, there is, of course, a price to be paid for this peace of mind.

The right to buy a financial asset is a **call option**. The specified price, known as the *call price*, includes the interest to maturity and hence is more than face value. For example, the right to buy a $1000 bond paying 12% that matures one year from today will at least incorporate one year's interest. Hence, the call price for such a bond might be $1000 + (0.12 \times 1000) = $1120.[17]

---

17 For simplicity, we ignore default risk in this example.

FINANCIAL FOCUS 15.3 — OPTIONS PRICES IN THE FINANCIAL PRESS

The financial press gives considerable information about option prices. For example,

BOMBARDIER B	$2.32		Opt vol 1482	
Strike price	**Bid**	**Ask**	**Vol**	**Op Int**
July $2.50C	0.30	0.40	25	5279

The months indicate the date of expiration of calls (c; right to buy) or puts (p; right to sell). The strike price for a share of Bombardier is $2.50. The stock closed at $2.32 per share. The prices shown are for call options; prices bid and asked ranged from $0.30 to $0.40. Each option is for 100 shares so an investor would pay $250 for each contract. The contract expires in July.

In the case of Bombardier, the current price of the stock is $2.32, while the exercise price is $2.50. The intrinsic value of a call, for example, would be $2.50 − $2.32 = $0.18. If a call sells for $0.16 it would not be worthwhile to exercise the right to buy it at $2.22. The reason is that $2.32 + $0.16 = $2.48 is less than the exercise price of $2.50.

Questions for Discussion
1. Suppose that the data in the table refer to a call. Construct a hypothetical situation under which an investor would find it profitable to exercise the option.
2. Using *The Globe and Mail* or *Financial Post* (a section of the *National Post*), select a stock that has a put option and evaluate conditions under which the put will be exercised.

Source
Financial Post (19 January 2005): N8.

By contrast, the right to sell a financial asset is known as a **put option**.

The price at which options are set is known as the **exercise** or **strike price**.

Financial Focus 15.3: Options Prices in the Financial Press above illustrates how options prices are presented in the financial press.

If the asset itself trades at a strike price that is below the market price, it is said to be "in the money"—the strike price is favourable because the investor has the option of acquiring the asset below its current market value. Conversely, an option whose strike price is above the market price is said to be "out of the money"—the option is unfavourably priced for purchase. Lastly, an option whose price is at the strike price is said to be "at-the-money." For put options, the arguments operate in reverse.

Consider another simple numerical example to illustrate the workings of options. Suppose that in December 2005 shares of Iwish.com close at $202 and that January 2006 calls at $210 cost $1.75 while January 2006 puts at $210 cost $7.50. An investor will find the call worthwhile if the price of Iwish.com shares rises sufficiently above $210 to cover the cost of the option (and trading costs, which we ignore). For example, if Iwish.com trades at $215 then the investor's profit is $215 − $210 − $1.75 = $3.25. A similar logic applies to the put. Hence, if Iwish.com trades at say $200, the put permits the investor to sell at $210, which results in a net profit of $210 − $200 − $7.50 = $2.50.

A buyer of a call option is thus protected against unexpected price increases, while buyers of put options are guarded against unanticipated price falls. In this way, options can be used to hedge against interest rate risk. For example, should interest rates rise significantly (implying a fall in bond prices), the lender can put the debt instrument and protect against opportunity cost. Similarly, if interest rates are expected to fall significantly, a borrower can call the bond and finance anew at a reduced interest cost. Of course, the change in the interest rate must be of a sufficient magnitude to offset the fact that options have transactions costs as well as the fact that the price of a call is above the face value of the financial asset.

THE MECHANICS OF AN OPTION: TWO ILLUSTRATIONS

Let us consider two illustrations of how options represent a form of insurance against risk. Suppose a Canadian company exporting to the United States expects to earn U.S. dollars in the

| Figure 15.1 | The Value of a Put or a Call |

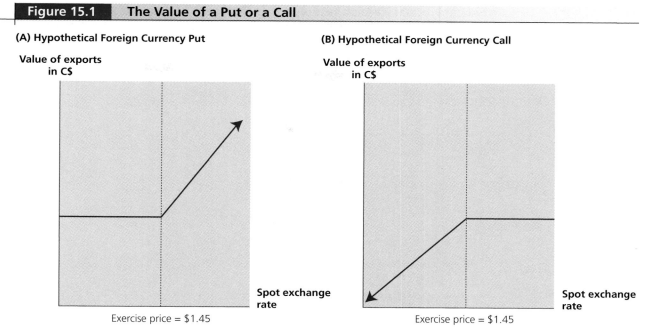

(A) Hypothetical Foreign Currency Put

(B) Hypothetical Foreign Currency Call

Value of exports in C$

Value of exports in C$

Spot exchange rate

Spot exchange rate

Exercise price = $1.45

Exercise price = $1.45

In panel (A), the put places a minimum value on U.S. income in Canadian terms; in panel (B) a call option places a maximum cost on the purchase of U.S. dollars, again in Canadian dollar terms.

future. There is, of course, uncertainty about the value of these future U.S. dollars in terms of Canadian dollars. Figure 15.1(A) shows that, for a hypothetical exercise price of $1.45, the holder of a put option is protected against exchange rates falling below $1.45, which would reduce the value of the U.S. dollar income in Canadian terms. Why? If the exchange rate were to fall to, say, $1.40, the U.S. dollars earned would fall in Canadian terms, whereas, by exercising the option, revenues would not fall below $1.45 for each U.S. dollar earned. The opposite, of course, is true of call options, as shown in Figure 15.1(B). In this case the option provides protection against having to buy U.S. dollars for an exchange rate greater than the hypothetical exchange rate of $1.45.

An alternative way of illustrating the insurance benefits of options is to examine how options can affect the probability distribution of returns an investor may face. We will consider a highly simplified view of such a probability distribution to highlight the key implication of options. Figure 15.2 presents a hypothetical case for an option in stocks.

With no options, the probability distribution of returns for a particular stock is as portrayed by the probability distribution *OABC*. If a call option exists, the holder will exercise it whenever the spot price exceeds the strike, or exercise price, *z*; thus, the probability distribution of returns becomes *OGHz*. Similarly, a put option will be exercised wherever the spot price falls below the exercise, or strike price, *x*; thus, the probability distribution becomes *xIFC*. The probabilities at strike prices consistent with prices of *x* to *z* become higher than they were when no options existed. Consequently, call and put options have the effect, among other things, of raising the likelihood of a price in the vicinity of the strike price. Note too, that if an investor purchases both a put and a call option simultaneously, the probability distribution becomes *xDEz*, guaranteeing a price of between *x* and *z*.[18] Recall that the area under a probability distribution must always sum to one. Therefore, any form of insurance that removes one segment of the probability distribution, by eliminating the relevant risks, must shift it to the remainder of the same probability distribution.

---

18 This strategy is known as using collars or *range forwards*. It effectively permits investors to limit their gains and losses to some range.

Figure 15.2 **Hypothetical Probability Distributions in the Presence of Options**

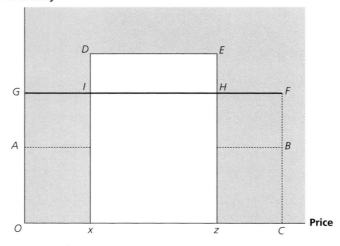

An option narrows an asset's distribution of returns and hence reduces interest rate risk. *OABC* is the probability distribution of a stock with no call or put features. If a call feature is present, any segment of the probability distribution above the strike price of *z* disappears. A similar effect obtains for the probability distribution of a stock with a put feature; anything below the strike price of *x* disappears. For a call, the probability distribution becomes *OGHz*, and for a put, *xIFC*.

Note: For simplicity of exposition, the probability distribution of returns is assumed to be uniform (equal probability for every price). This clearly is not the case in reality, but is done for the sake of simplicity.

THE VALUE OF OPTIONS

Since options represent a form of insurance, how should the "premium" be valued? The value of call and put options can essentially be expressed in fairly simple terms. The value of a call at expiration can be written

$$Call = MAX\{0, S - E\} \tag{15.3}$$

where

$Call$ = value of the call at expiration
MAX = maximum of the quantities in brackets
S = spot price
E = exercise price

The value of a call is simply the larger of the two numbers in the brackets. If the option is not exercised, its value is zero. Alternatively, if the difference between the spot and exercise prices is positive, then the option is exercised. In terms of Figure 15.2, if the spot price is greater than *z* at expiration, the call will be exercised; otherwise, it will be allowed to expire.

The value of a put option can be expressed in a similar manner:

$$Put = MAX\{0, E - S\} \tag{15.4}$$

As described in Figure 15.2, whenever an asset's price falls below *x* (that is, *S* is less than *x*), *E* − *S* has a positive value and the put should be exercised. Alternatively, when *E* − *S* is negative the investor is better off letting the put option expire since a zero value is preferred to a negative value.

Note that equations (15.3) and (15.4) give no indication that the value of an option is a function of the particular financial health of the firm whose stock is being traded. Indeed, according to the options pricing technique known as the Black–Scholes options pricing model, three other factors also help determine the value of options. They are the anticipated volatility of the underlying asset's price, the interest rate on a riskless asset, and the time until the exercise date. All of these factors are known with certainty, except the volatility of the underlying asset price.[19] As a result, options prices are often quoted in terms of the (implied) volatility of an asset to which the option writer and purchaser agree.[20]

A NUMERICAL EXAMPLE

It is also relatively straightforward to illustrate the use of an option numerically. Consider a currency option. Suppose that a British company will require C$2 000 000, 90 days from today to pay for a shipment of goods, and that in the spot market for foreign exchange a Canadian dollar can be purchased for £0.465. Suppose too that the exercise price on a call 90 days from today is £0.50. Each option is for the purchase of C$100 000, so the company must purchase 20 options. As we have seen, the call option will be purchased at a premium—say, £0.01 per Canadian dollar or £0.01 × 2 000 000 = £20 000. Thus, for £20 000 the importer in the United Kingdom can obtain C$2 000 000, 90 days from today at a cost of £1 000 000 if the option is exercised.

Clearly, the importer must be expecting the Canadian dollar to appreciate against the British pound since at the spot rate $2 000 000 would cost only £930 000 ($2 000 000 × £0.465).[21] Indeed, so long as the spot rate 90 days from today exceeds £0.51, the option will not be exercised. At a £0.50 exchange rate, C$2 000 000 will cost

$$£0.50 \times \$2\ 000\ 000 = £1\ 000\ 000$$

Since the option costs £20 000, the total cost of a wait-and-see position is £1 020 000, which is what it would cost to exercise the option ($2 000 000 × £0.50 = £1 000 000 + £20 000 = £1 020 000).[22]

If the spot rate 90 days from today has risen to £0.55, the option will be exercised. We leave it as an exercise to complete the calculations to show why.

HEDGING WITH OPTIONS

It may be useful to summarize our discussion of options with a table similar to Table 15.3 used for the case of financial futures. Table 15.4 shows four cases, namely writing a call or a put, or buying a call or a put.[23] A separate line makes clear the obligation of the holder in each case. Hence, for example, an individual writing a call implies that the buyer will sell shares (or foreign exchange) if the option is exercised. The opposite, of course, is true in the event of a put. As noted above, there is a fee or a premium for each transaction that is either received from the buyer or paid to the writer of the option. The crucial point that drives the choice of a call or a put is the expectations of investors. For example, if shares are expected to fall in the near term then the investor will want to write a call, whereas writing a put will be called for when prices are expected to rise in the short run. These

---

19 It is, therefore, of considerable importance to determine the change in the value of an option when there is a small change in the value of the underlying asset in question. The resulting measure is known as the delta of an option, or the hedge ratio.

20 How these factors influence equations (15.3) and (15.4) is beyond the scope of this text. However, the Black-Scholes options pricing model consists of the following determinants: the price of the underlying asset, the riskless interest rate, the expected volatility of the underlying asset price, and the time until the exercise date. For the exact formula, see, for example, Kolb (2002, chapter 13).

21 In addition, of course, there is the opportunity cost of money, which we are ignoring for simplicity. Thus, if the interest rate is, say, 12%, then £20 000(0.12/4) = £20 000(0.03) = £600 is the interest cost of purchasing a 90-day option.

22 Another possibility would be to buy Canadian dollars today and invest in, say, Government of Canada T-bills. However, if U.K. interest rates are sufficiently high, the British company might do better investing in U.K. funds.

23 I am grateful to Lawrence Lynch from Fanshawe College for providing me with a version of this table, which I have adapted for the purposes of this text.

Table 15.4	Hedging with Options			
Action	**Write Call**	**Buy Call**	**Write Put**	**Buy Put**
Obligation	SELL if exercised	BUY if exercised	BUY if exercised	SELL if exercised
Fee/Premium	From buyer	To writer	From buyer	To writer
Expectation	Lower in short term	Higher in short term	Higher in short term	Lower in short term
Strategy	Wait or buy until near expiration	Exercise (BUY) if profitable or allow expiration if not	Wait or buy until near expiration	Exercise (SELL) if profitable or allow expiration if not
Potential Gain or Loss/Adjustment for Cost of option	(Market *less* Exercise) *less* fee	Market > Exercise = profit from selling call *less* fee	(Exercise *less* Market) *less* fee	Market > Exercise = profit from selling put *less* fee

Note: The table summarizes the information used in both graphical and numerical examples considered in the section on options. Investors can either write or buy calls or puts that imply certain obligations on their part. The choice of a call or a put also implies that the investor has certain expectations and requires particular strategies depending upon whether those expectations are correct or not. Finally, at expiration of the call or put, there will be gains or losses depending on the actual behaviour of the prices of the financial asset in question (e.g., shares or foreign exchange).

expectations will also, of course, drive the strategy of the investor as the expiration date of the call or put approaches [also see equation (15.2)]. Finally, gains or losses from the choice of options will depend on the fee/premium and the differential between the market and exercise prices.

SWAPS

As we have already seen on several occasions, considerable interest rate variability exists. Borrowers like to have some stability in interest rate costs unless, of course, they expect interest rates to fall. Lenders, on the other hand, prefer not to be locked into an interest rate if they expect interest rates to rise.

Uncertainty about future interest rate levels signals an opportunity to insulate borrowers and lenders against unfavourable future interest rate outcomes. Similar arguments can, of course, be made concerning the uncertainty about future exchange rates. Interest rate and foreign exchange swaps are derivatives designed to reduce these types of uncertainties.

A **swap** is an agreement to swap or exchange, for a pre-agreed period into the future, a series of interest payments or foreign exchange at fixed rates for a series of variable interest payments or foreign currency at a variable exchange rate.

Take the example of a bank that offers a fixed-rate mortgage at 7%. Since mortgages represent an asset, a bank must match them with fixed deposit rates. However, this is difficult to do nowadays since depositors expect floating deposit rates. The risk then to the bank is that, if deposit rates should rise to 7% or more, it will lose money. The bank cannot leave deposit rates unchanged, of course, for fear of losing deposits. To offset this perceived risk, the bank could swap interest payments by paying a fixed interest payment to someone in the swap market who is willing to borrow at a fixed rate, say 6%. The bank, therefore, lends at 7% and pays 6% for the funds it raises during the term of the swap. Figure 15.3 illustrates how a floating-rate debt is turned into a fixed-rate debt.

The classic illustration of the need for swaps emerged in the United States when the student loan marketing association (Sallie Mae as it is better known), an agency of the U.S. government for student loans, faced a severe mismatch between its assets and liabilities. Because Sallie Mae is akin to a Canadian Crown corporation, it could borrow cheaply in the fixed-rate market. However, student loans are long-term floating rate loans. To clear the mismatch of assets and debts, Sallie Mae needed to swap its fixed-rate interest payments for floating-rate payments.

| **Figure 15.3** | **Illustrating an Interest Rate Swap** |

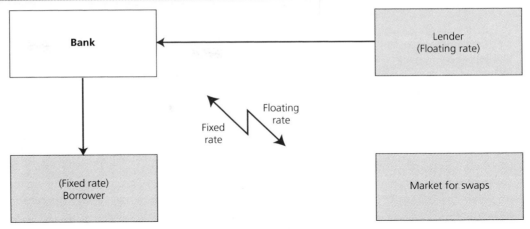

A bank is at the centre of a swap transaction by bringing together a lender, who wants to have a floating interest rate, with a borrower, who prefers a fixed rate instead. The parties to the transaction exchange only interest payments.

15.4 THE IMPORTANCE OF HEDGING IN THE FINANCIAL SYSTEM

How important are hedging instruments to our financial system? It is a little difficult to measure the dollar value of futures and options since they appear, for example, as off-balance-sheet items in chartered banks' financial statements.

Banks are not the only entities that have become enamoured of derivatives. Large corporations and small businesses also use derivatives to hedge against adverse movements in interest rates and exchange rates. Globally, the spread of hedging instruments also has been rapid.

The value of derivatives contracts are of almost unimaginable size. For example, at the Chicago Mercantile Exchange, $211.7 million contracts valued at US$127 trillion were traded in 2003. At Euronext, more than 695 million contracts were traded in 2003, valued at 252 billion euros (or approximately C$403 billion).

How dangerous are derivative products such as swaps to the financial system? Economists speak of "systemic risk," that is, of the risk that the credit markets and the payments system will break down if some of the parties to derivatives transactions default. One U.S. study[24] suggests that there is relatively little systemic risk in the case of existing swaps because banks hedge their positions. In other words, banks avoid the risk of having to pay a fixed rate when rates are falling or a floating rate when rates are rising by arranging offsetting swaps to hedge against the possibility of an adverse change in interest rates. A more recent study[25] indicates that hedge funds differ substantially from, say, mutual funds. Unlike mutual funds, hedge funds appear to have low systemic risk, although hedge fund returns are more volatile.

Nevertheless, systemic risk potentially could remain a problem for other types of derivatives products. A difficulty with such products arises because the party entering into a derivatives transaction ordinarily is an agent managing money for outside principals who cannot fully monitor the agent's behaviour, leaving open the possibility of speculative behaviour. This type of behaviour, a reflection of the perennial problem of asymmetric information in financial markets, is especially evident in recent losses reported widely in the press (e.g., Metalgesellschaft, Orange Co., California).

24 G. Gorton, and R. Rosen "Banks and Derivatives," *NBER Macroeconomics Annual* 1995 (Cambridge, Mass.: The MIT Press, 1995).
25 B. Liang, "On the performance of hedge funds," *Financial Analysts Journal* 55 (July/August 1999): 11–18.

FINANCIAL FOCUS 15.4   PROGRAM TRADING

The stock market crash of October 1987 has largely been associated with what is known as *program trading*, an electronic device by which investors can buy and sell blocks of stocks. Trading is based purely on a stock's price in relation to others on a predetermined basis. Trading is not based on a company's earnings, dividends, or growth prospects, nor even on any overall economic factor such as interest rate movements, currency fluctuations, or other fundamentals.

For example, a program might automatically signal a buy if the futures price on, say, the TSE300 exceeds the actual TSE300 by some predetermined threshold. Similarly, when the same spread falls below a certain threshold, the program orders a sell.

In this fashion investors can build their own version of an index of stocks much like the one sold on most Futures Exchanges. In the case of the 1987 episode, computers allowed investors to trade stock index futures and the stocks whose prices were incorporated into the index (for example, the TSE100). One strategy was to sell index futures and buy the stocks in the TSE100 when the price of the TSE index futures was sufficiently above the prices of the underlying stocks in the index.

One wonders whether this program trading really had that much influence. If stock prices reflect the market's assessment of the value of the stock, the same should be true of stock index futures. Although "noisy" traders theoretically can cause large price variations to take advantage of arbitrage opportunities, the reality seems doubtful since traders in futures tend to be well-informed market participants. Nevertheless, the 1987 collapse of stock prices was large enough to prompt the introduction of some restrictions in trading.

Questions for Discussion
1. Is it a good idea to impose restrictions on program trading?
2. How might program trading protect investors?

SUMMARY

- Investors who are risk averse want to avoid risk. In recent decades many derivative products have been introduced to allow them to try either to shift risk or to avoid it entirely.

- A hedger is someone who wants to reduce risk. A speculator is willing to accept greater risks in the hopes of earning a relatively large return.

- Forward markets and futures markets trade financial instruments that are delivered at an agreed on price at an agreed on date in the future.

- The major difference between futures contracts and forward contracts is that investors in the former have little or no interest in taking delivery of the asset. By contrast, investors in forwards typically do wish to take delivery of the financial asset.

- Forward contracts are customized; futures contracts are standardized. Otherwise, the two instruments are similar.

- A long hedge involves an attempt to reduce the risk of lower future interest rates. By contrast, a short hedge is a device to reduce the risk of a future rise in interest rates.

- Futures and spot prices tend to move together but, since the futures contract eventually expires, futures and spot prices converge.

- Options also are a financial device for taking delivery of an asset in the future at a price determined today. The costs and benefits of holding options differ from those in either futures or forward markets.

- An option is a form of insurance against unfavourable changes in interest rates, stock prices, or exchange rates.

- The "premium" for this form of insurance is costly and depends, in part, on the difference between the price at which an option can be exercised and the spot price of the underlying asset.

- Swaps represent an exchange of interest payments or foreign currencies. The ownership of the underlying asset does not change.

- Typically, an investor or an institution facing a severe mismatch between its assets and liabilities would engage in a swap.

IMPORTANT TERMS

basis, 294
call option, 299
cost-of-carry, 298
exercise or strike price, 300
forward contract, 291
futures contracts, 291
hedge funds, 290
hedging, 290
long position, 294

margin, 290
marked-to-market, 294
offset transactions, 291
put option, 300
short position, 294
speculator, 290
spot market, 291
swaps, 304

PROBLEMS

1. A Canadian asset holder can purchase a U.S. security for $950 and sell it for $1050 one year later.

    (a) What is the yield on the U.S. security?

    (b) If the spot exchange rate is $1 today and $1.10 one year later, what will the effective yield be to the Canadian investor?

    (c) If the spot exchange rate is $1 today and $0.90 one year later, what will the effective yield be to the Canadian investor?

2. If you plan to take out a short-term loan a year from today and you expect interest rates to rise, how can you use financial futures to reduce interest rate risk?

3. Suppose that an investor will require US$1 million one year from today. The current spot exchange rate is $1.15 and the one-year forward exchange rate is $1.20. Is the Canadian dollar expected to appreciate or depreciate relative to the U.S. dollar? Under what circumstances would it be advantageous for the investor to purchase $1 million today to be delivered one year from today?

4. In constructing Table 15.2, we ignored the role of discounting. How would interest rate considerations affect the calculation of the savings generated by buying currency in the forward market? Assume there is an interest rate of 10%.

5. An investor believes that interest rates have peaked but does not have the cash required to purchase a financial instrument today. Assuming that this investor is able to enter the futures market, would she engage in a long hedge or a short hedge?

6. Suppose the investor in question 5 is interested in a bond that sells for 71 today and for 79 two months from today in the cash market. In the futures market, a contract maturing in two months can be had for 72 today and sells for 78 in two months. If the investor buys this futures contract, what will be the gains and losses? What considerations have you ignored in making your calculations?

7. Show numerically why the currency option described on page 303 of this chapter will be exercised when the exchange rate is £0.55 for each Canadian dollar. Ignore the problem of discounting.

8. Suppose that the yield on a 90-day security is currently 10%, but you believe that it will fall to 7% in one year. Do you want to buy a call or a put option? Assume that one $1 million Treasury bill option costs $10 000 and ignore other discounting factors. Would you exercise the option if the actual yield one year from today is 8%?

9. Consider the following scenario: Current exchange rate C$1.40 = US$1, current forward exchange rate C$1.45 = US$1, and exchange rate forecast for spot rate one year ahead C$1.43 = US$1. Now assume, that US$100 000 must be purchased by one year from today. What is the hedged cost of US$100 000? Fill in the table below.

After-the-fact spot exchange rate scenarios	Cost of purchasing U.S. in the spot market	Gain or loss on forward contract
$1.30		
$1.40		
$1.45		
$1.50		

10. In the example considered in Table 15.2, if interest rates on funds were 8% in Canada and 6% in the United States, would buying forward still make sense? Explain.

11. Suppose that silver sold for $8/oz in the spot market. Futures can be bought for $5.90/oz and sold for $8.45/oz. What would be the net cost 90 day of financing 10 000 oz? Explain.

12. Suppose that the settlement price for a 90-day Treasury bill option is 89. What is the implied yield and dollar delivery price for this instrument?

13. Explain Figure 15.2 assuming that bond return instead of stock price is measured on the horizontal axis.

14. The second edition of this text reported spot and forward prices for the Canadian dollar on 17 August 1996. The forward rate against U.S. dollars to be delivered 17 August 1999 was 1.3608, the actual exchange rate was 1.4925. In hindsight, should investors have bought U.S. dollars in August 1996? Explain.

15. The following table gives call and put prices for some asset whose spot price is given in bold numbers.

Spot	85	90	95	100	105	110	115
Calls	14.05	9.35	5.50	2.70	1.15	0.45	0.20
Puts	0.10	0.45	1.55	3.70	7.10	11.35	16.10

Suppose we believe the spot price will be 108 by expiration. What is the profit or loss for a call priced at 2.70 against the various spot prices given in the above table? Is the profit/loss the same if the investor is long or short? Explain.

DISCUSSION QUESTIONS

1. Explain how the fact that margins on derivatives are called in daily can lead to large losses.

2. Explain the logic behind equations (15.3) and (15.4).

3. What is the link between credibility of monetary policy and derivatives? Explain.

4. Explain, in broad terms, how the Barings and MG strategy in derivatives could have led to such large losses.

5. Why is the marked-to-market requirement a sensible one? Explain.

6. What are the advantages and drawbacks of open outcry versus electronic trading in derivatives markets?

ONLINE APPLICATIONS

1. Go to the Chicago Board of Trade's Web site at **www.cbot.com**. Click on *Education*, and then *Tutorials*. Follow the instructions for the Dow Tutorial. (Another site offering real-time simulation with the possibility of actually winning some money can be found at Investment Challenge at **www.ichallenge.net**.)

2. Go to the Montreal Exchange's Web site at **www.m-x.ca**. Choose *English*. Next, in the top right-hand side you will see *Main Navigation*. Click on it and choose *Monthly Reports*. Select some month to analyze. Document the increase in the number of transactions in the BAX derivative instrument in recent years (go back to Chapter 4 to see the relationship between the BAX and bankers' acceptances).

3. Euronext has an online trading simulation game that takes you through the process of trading in options. Go to **www.liffe.optioneasy.com**. Next, you need to register (it's free) before you can play (read the rules first!).

4. Return to the Montreal Exchange's Web site (see question 2), follow the same instructions as in question 2, but instead, choose *Rules* (under the *Publications* heading) and look for *Minimum Margin Requirements*.

    (a) Why are margin requirements different for hedgers and speculators?

    (b) Why are margin requirements higher for speculators?

5. Go to **www.numa.com**. Click on the Numa options calculator to find out the price of any option, real or hypothetical. The calculations are based on the Black–Scholes options pricing model referred to in the text.

References can be found on www.mcgrawhill.ca/college/siklos

Managing Risk: Deposit Insurance

LEARNING OBJECTIVES

After reading and studying this chapter, you should be able to

16.1 describe why deposit insurance is necessary

16.1 list some common problems with insurance and describe the importance of moral hazard and adverse selection

16.2 explain how the Canada Deposit Insurance Corporation is structured, how it functions, how it interacts with other regulatory institutions, and how it deals with insolvent banks

16.2 determine how deposit insurance works in other countries and whether the Canadian plan is relatively generous

16.3 list some of the public policy issues surrounding deposit insurance, analyze whether the present scheme can be improved, and describe any political factors that impede reforms

Insurance against losses from holding deposits, commonly referred to as deposit insurance, was introduced in Canada in 1967. But with the savings and loan fiasco in the United States and the Canadian federal and provincial governments' inconsistent attitudes and practices toward depositor protection, the subject has been receiving considerable public attention.

In this chapter, we examine the operation of deposit insurance in Canada and, briefly, in some other countries. First, however, we consider why deposit insurance is thought to be necessary. This requires that we examine moral hazard and adverse selection, two problems that arise in all types of insurance, but that are especially important to understand in the context of deposit insurance. We also discuss why government intervention in providing deposit insurance is controversial. The chapter concludes by asking whether Canada's existing deposit insurance scheme is in need of reform.

16.1 RATIONALE FOR DEPOSIT INSURANCE

The need for deposit insurance arises because the consequences of a bank failure differ from those of the failure of firms in other industries. The failure of a single bank can lead to fears of failure in other banks and thus create the potential for a run on the banks, or a banking panic.[1]

---

1 Some have argued that the introduction of deposit insurance in Canada was motivated by the need to increase competition between the chartered banks and near-banks.

FLASHBACK 16.1

MORAL HAZARD AND ADVERSE SELECTION

We saw in Chapter 3 that intermediaries exist because of the problem of asymmetric information. Recall that asymmetric information describes a situation in which the parties to a transaction are not fully aware of each other's motives or the extent of their knowledge about a particular problem or service. Therefore, markets create devices to protect consumers; for example, through the provision of warranties or guarantees in the case of failure, or the government may impose additional requirements to protect consumers in case of defective products. Alternatively, individuals or institutions will attempt to "signal" that their product or service is exceptional and, if such signals are credible and verifiable, then this too can mitigate the moral hazard and adverse selection problems.

Despite the potential to reduce asymmetric information, it is doubtful that it can be eliminated entirely. Hence, moral hazard and adverse selection are problems that are at the core of understanding how the market for insurance operates.

If a banking system is fully insured, banks have good reason to search for the highest yield among investments as well as give their officials incentives to lend as much as possible regardless of the quality of the borrower. Why? Because in both cases the bank's business will grow, and insurance, at least in the hypothetical case considered here, will cover any potential losses. There is, therefore, no reason to weigh risk and return as was done in Chapter 13. This type of phenomenon is known as moral hazard and stems from the risk that, once the contract has been concluded, one party to a contract may change its behaviour to the detriment of the other party.

Although the moral hazard problem focuses on the behaviour of banks, when insurance protects depositors against losses, there is another side to this coin, namely that when depositors are offered full protection against losses in the banking system, their behaviour too is affected. This is the main reason why insurance companies practise a form of price discrimination; for example, when they charge higher premiums for young drivers. The reason ostensibly is that younger drivers are more likely to file a claim. The difficulty is that it is impractical for insurance companies to assess the risks of each indivdual insured. Instead, the insured are grouped into categories according to age or some other indentifiable characteristic. It is highly likely that within each group, some individuals will exhibit a relatively greater risk of filing a claim, while others within the same group will be less likely to file a claim than the average for the group. Therefore, those with higher-than-average risks within the group will find buying some insurance more attractive than those with lower-than-average risks in the same category. When this happens, the likelihood that claims will be made will rise, prompting further increases in premiums or more focused attempts at screening potential applicants for insurance. This is referred to as the adverse selection problem.

It is useful to end this flashback with a brief definition of each of the two problems associated with markets due to the presence of asymmetric information.

Moral hazard: The risk that, once a contract is entered into, its existence will change the behaviour of one or both parties to the contract.

Adverse selection: A situation in which one party to a transaction has relevant information that the other party lacks about some aspect of a good or service.

This contagion of fear has caused regulators and legislators to suggest deposit insurance as a means of preventing widespread banking crises.[2] They want to avoid the social costs of widespread banking failures. (If a country's financial system is disrupted, its firms in all other industries will be severely hampered in trying to complete financial transactions.)

Nevertheless, there is still considerable debate about whether deposit insurance does more harm than good for the safety and stability of the financial system. Indeed, it is interesting to note that the concerns over deposit insurance now transcend our borders, so much so that in 2002 the International Association of Deposit Insurers was launched with the president and CEO being the Canadian representative from the CDIC.

Visit the IADI at
www.iadi.org

---

2 In Canada, legislators were prompted by the recommendations of the Royal Commission on Banking and Finance (the Porter Commission) released in 1964 and some failures among near-banks. Although there is general agreement that banking crises can be averted via deposit insurance, there is some evidence of a positive correlation between the generosity of a deposit insurance system and banking crises. See E.J. Kane and A. Demirgüç-Kunt, "Deposit Insurance Around the Globe: Where Does it Work?" *Journal of Economic Perspectives* 16 (Spring 2002): 175–96.

MORAL HAZARD AND ADVERSE SELECTION

The need for insurance arises because uncertainty exists about future prospects, whether for our lives or our wealth. But the kind of risk-avoidance that is insurance always raises difficulties of moral hazard and risk avoidance. Sometimes they seem especially problematic in the forms of deposit insurance used today in North America. The concern here is about how banks and depositors react to the existence of deposit insurance.

Moral Hazard

At the root of all problems with insurance is the fact of asymmetric information: One group, the insurers, has relatively less relevant information than do those who are being insured.[3] One consequence of this problem is called moral hazard.

Moral hazard refers to the tendency of insured institutions to take on, perhaps unwittingly, more risks than they would in its absence. For example, knowing that depositors are protected, financial institutions can undertake riskier investments to improve their bottom lines. In so doing, the risks of insolvency are exacerbated. This type of activity already is not in the interests of the depositors because, even if their deposits are fully protected, costs of various kinds will be incurred when a financial institution fails.

We can illustrate the moral hazard problem with the help of a simple diagram. Figure 16.1(A) illustrates what happens to the banking industry when a moral hazard problem exists. Without deposit insurance, we assume that there are an equal number of banks with a high risk of insolvency (H) as ones with a very low risk (L). Once deposit insurance is provided, moral hazard provides an incentive for some banks to increase their exposure to risk. Conceivably then, the number of high-risk banks increases, while the number of low-risk banks decreases.[4] Therefore, the moral hazard problem arises after a transaction is completed.

There are ways to mitigate the moral hazard problem. One is **co-insurance**, whereby the injured party pays a fraction of any loss. More common is the device of a **deductible**: The insured party is covered (up to some maximum) for any loss *beyond* some fixed sum. But despite a variety of proposals and reforms,[5] policymakers have not, as yet, entirely eliminated the moral hazard problem for deposit insurance.

Adverse Selection

Is the probability of the event insured against affected by the availability of insurance? Although few would argue that individuals will deliberately become seriously ill because they have health insurance, there is definitely room to believe that their vigilance against minor accidents might be adversely affected. For example, the more heavily deposits are insured, the less likely people are to worry about the safety of the bank that holds these deposits. If individuals act in this fashion, there will be a tendency to bank not where it is safest to hold deposits, but where interest rates are highest or where the other perks of banking are most generous. Would-be depositors will turn to banks offering free DVDs or TVs, instead of those offering the best return in relation to risk. Most forms of insurance are affected by this problem, which is known as the problem of **adverse selection**: The mere existence of insurance increases the probability that the particular event will take place.

---

3 The information relevant here is the degree of risk aversion on the part of the depositors, as well as the abilities (and honesty) of the banks that manage the depositors' funds.

4 One study reveals that in the 1920s in the state of Kansas, institutions that voluntarily joined an existing deposit insurance scheme were more likely to fail than uninsured banks. This illustrates the practical importance of the moral hazard problem. See D.C. Wheelock, "Deposit Insurance and Bank Failures: New Evidence from the 1920s," *Economic Inquiry* 30 (July 1992): 530–43.

5 See, for example, J.L. Carr, G.F. Mathewson, and N.C. Quigley, *Ensuring Failure: Financial System Stability and Deposit Insurance in Canada* (Toronto: C.D. Howe Institute, 1994), and Canada Deposit Insurance Corporation, *Annual Report 1998–99*, Ottawa, Ontario. Also see the last section of this chapter.

| Figure 16.1 | Moral Hazard and Adverse Selection |

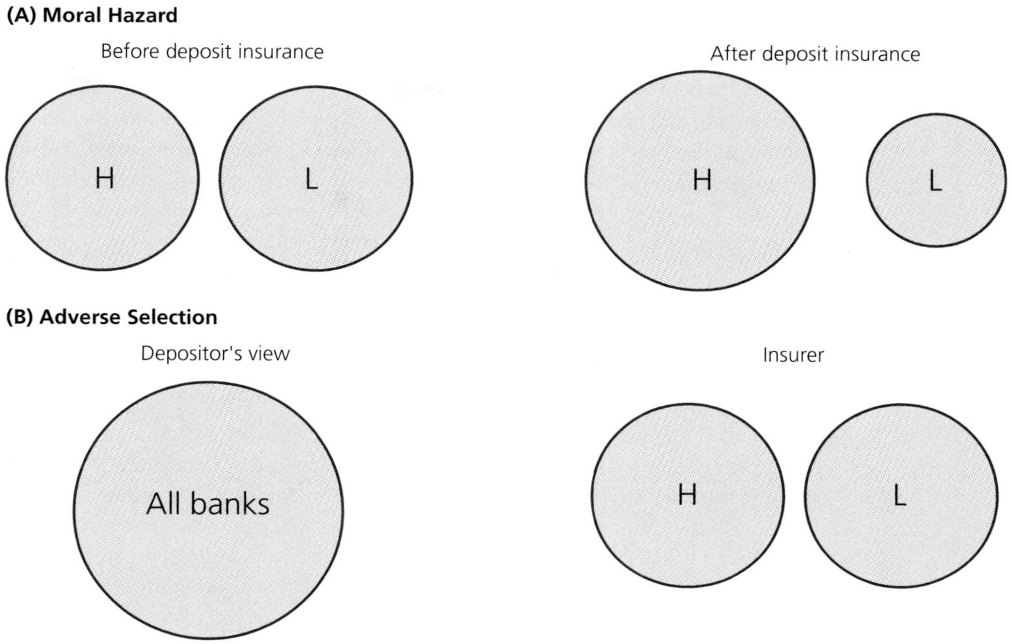

(A) Moral Hazard

Before deposit insurance   After deposit insurance

(B) Adverse Selection

Depositor's view   Insurer

In panel (A) there are an equal number of high-risk and low-risk banks. Once deposit insurance is in place, moral hazard makes it relatively attractive for banks to take on more risks, resulting in a higher proportion of high-risk banks than before. In panel (B), depositors make no distinction between high- and low-risk banks since they do not pay the premiums directly. Insurers, however, can distinguish between banks and charge premiums accordingly. As a result, depositors seek out the best returns or service rather than monitoring the financial activities of the banks. This situation is the adverse selection problem.

In the case of bank deposits the existence of adverse selection implies less concern over the riskiness of particular investments on the part of depositors since some information about banking activities becomes effectively hidden in the presence of insurance.

Why do depositors react in this fashion? Consider panel (B) of Figure 16.1. Even if the insurer assesses risk-based premiums by identifying the high-risk (H) and the low-risk banks (L), the public views all deposit-taking institutions in the same manner, since their deposit insurance is not based on a particular bank's chances of becoming insolvent. Recall that, although the CDIC assesses risk-based premiums (see Section 16.2), its risk scores for member institutions are hidden from the public. Depositors, therefore, have little incentive to care about the prospects for insolvency of a particular bank. We could also argue that it is difficult for small depositors to monitor the behaviour of financial institutions, and still more difficult to assess the chances that a bank will become insolvent.[6] The bottom line, therefore, is that adverse selection exists because banks know their financial state better than do depositors, and this problem arises before a transaction is completed. As a result, if there are a sufficiently large number of "bad" banks, then depositors may not be willing to deposit any money in any bank, since asymmetric information

---

6 The same problem arises when consumers purchase used cars. It is difficult to tell whether a car will be a "lemon" unless the car is subject to extensive testing, which can be costly. See G. Akerlof, "The Market for 'Lemons': Quality, Uncertainty, and the Market Mechanism," *Quarterly Journal of Economics* 84 (1970): 488–500. Extensions to the lemons' principle in the area of finance include S. Myers, and N.S. Majluf, "Corporate Financing and Investment Decisions When Firms Have Information that Investors Do Not Have," *Journal of Financial Economics* 13 (1984): 187–221.

leads them to believe that all banks are of the "bad" variety.[7] Solutions to these problems include the release of financial information by private firms or government, and outright government regulation. However, as we will see in the final section of this chapter, each of these solutions can raise additional public policy problems.

A final word is in order. Figure 16.1 does not explicitly deal with the "social" costs of moral hazard and adverse selection. Although it is possible that more banks will enter into the marketplace as "high-risk banks" [see especially panel (B)], or previously conservative banks will become more financially reckless, this assumes that regulators ignore developments in the financial sector.[8] This may or may not happen. Indeed, this is one reason why, in Chapter 20, we consider in broader detail, the role of financial sector regulation.

THE ROLE OF GOVERNMENT IN DEPOSIT INSURANCE: IS THERE A POLITICAL MOTIVE?

Is it appropriate for governments to offer deposit insurance? The government's involvement is often justified on the grounds of the presence market failure—that is, there are externalities that may prevent private markets from offering certain forms of insurance. Nevertheless, it is appropriate to question whether state intervention will result in a better allocation of resources than private markets will. As we shall see, deposit insurance in other countries is not always state run, and it is unclear, based on the historical record, whether private deposit insurance performs more poorly than the public variety. The political motive for deposit insurance appears to be an important one. Thus, deposit insurance is created because it is a popular entitlement program, much like unemployment insurance or health insurance. Like other entitlement programs, membership is compulsory, risk considerations are secondary, and the regulators are appointed by the government.

16.2 DEPOSIT INSURANCE IN CANADA

If a deposit-taking institution fails, what happens to the funds that have been deposited with it? The short answer is that they disappear,[9] leaving the depositors out of luck. The only existing protection against this risk is **deposit insurance**, which compensates depositors for at least some of their loss if an institution fails.

THE MECHANICS

Canada provides deposit insurance through a Crown corporation called the **Canada Deposit Insurance Corporation** (**CDIC**). "The primary objective, of course, is to ensure the safety of small investors who are usually not in the position to judge for themselves the financial soundness of the institution to which they entrust their savings."[10] Federally chartered banks, trust compa-

---

7 Based on the experiences in Mexico, Argentina, and Chile, at least one study found that depositors "vote with their feet" and withdraw their funds when they perceive banks to be weak. See M. S. Marinez Peria, and S.L. Schmukler, "Do Depositors Punish Banks for Bad Behaviour? Market Discipline, Deposit Insurance, and Banking Crises," in L. Hernando and K. Schmidt-Hebbel (Eds.), *Banking, Financial Integration and International Crises* (Washington, D.C.: World Bank): 2001.

8 At the same time, some depositors, especially if they are risk averse, will seek out insured deposits instead of holding other financial assets. This type of activity may also have economywide implications, since individual portfolios and the money supply will be affected. We do not consider these extensions.

9 When the failed institution's affairs are wound up, there may be some funds to be divided among depositors and other creditors. But there will not be enough to cover everything (recall that *insolvency*, by definition, means that assets are less than liabilities). In some cases, depositors will be lucky to get back a few cents on the dollar.

10 *Final Report of the Working Committee on the Canada Deposit Insurance Corporation* (Ottawa: Minister of Supply and Services (24 April 1985): 3.

nies, and mortgage loan companies must be members; provincially chartered institutions may also belong, and many do.[11]

As of 2005, the CDIC had over 80 members. The membership is distributed among domestic banks, domestic trusts and loan companies, and foreign bank subsidiaries. Each used to pay a flat premium of one-tenth of 1% of insurable deposits.[12] On 1 May 1993, premiums were raised by 25% (from $1 per $1000 of insurable deposits to $1.25) and were raised again by a further 33.6% (to $1.67 per $1000 insurable deposits) on 1 May 1994. Put a different way, the premiums represented one-sixth of 1% of insurable deposits.

In 1999, a type of risk-based premium, called a differential premium, was implemented following 1996 legislation permitting the CDIC to levy different premiums based on the risk profile of the member institution. Four premium categories exist,[13] and the actual premium an institution pays depends on the score earned in a test based on the CDIC's Standards of Sound Business and Financial Practices.[14]

Links to other deposit insurance agencies can be found at **www.cdic.ca**

In return, all eligible deposits—Canadian-denominated savings and chequing accounts; term deposits (including GICs maturing in fewer than five years); money orders, drafts, and travellers' cheques issued by members; trust deposits; and deposits held in registered retirement savings plans (RRSPs) and registered retirement income funds (RRIFs)[15]—are insured to a maximum of $60 000 per deposit. Following approval of the 2005 budget (bill C-43), the limits were increased to $100 000.[16] The changes became retroactive to February 23, 2005.[17]

This limit can, however, be rendered inconsequential in a number of ways. First, since it applies to deposits held with a single member, an individual or firm can enjoy protection of $60 000 multiplied by the number of members it has deposits with. Second, since joint deposits, RRSPs, RRIFs, and deposits held in trust are insured separately, investments in these instruments can multiply coverage many times over. Moreover, public perception of what is and what is not insured is confused by several factors. First, some financial institutions are organized in such a way that a separate entity manages RRSPs and RRIFs; thus, investment in some of these plans may not be insured at all. Second, the depositor-protection agencies that some provinces operate (mainly for the benefit of all credit union members) have rules that differ from the CDIC's; Alberta, for example, guarantees 100% of credit union deposits, and British Columbia covers deposits denominated in U.S. dollars. The public often fails to understand distinctions between types of deposits, institutions, and deposit-protection agencies.

Third, the federal and provincial governments *sometimes* go well beyond the coverage of the relevant deposit-protection agency. When the Canadian Commercial Bank failed in 1985, for example, the federal government covered some $720 million of *uninsured* deposits (the CDIC paid out $352 million for insured deposits). Yet no such bailout occurred in some other instances.[18]

---

11 In fact, all the provinces except Quebec now require their trusts and mortgage loan companies to join the CDIC. These provinces insure their own credit unions' deposits, however, and some also provide insurance for deposits with trusts that is more extensive than that of the CDIC. Quebec has its own deposit insurance agency, the *Régie de l'assurance-dépôts du Québec (RADQ)*. Largely modelled on the CDIC, it covers all deposit-taking institutions in the province except the chartered banks.

12 A "member" includes all the branches of an institution. Thus, the multibranch Canadian Imperial Bank of Commerce is one member; so is a single-branch trust company in New Brunswick.

13 There is a $5000 minimum.

14 They are 1/24th of 1% of insurable deposits, 1/12th of 1% of these same deposits, 1/6th of 1%, or 1/3rd of 1% of insurable deposits. Needless to say, the sounder the institution, the lower the premium category.

15 The score consists of measures of capital adequacy (20% of the score); profitability, efficiency (in terms of operating costs); asset quality (i.e., loans in default); and asset concentration (i.e., degree of asset diversification) represent the next group of criteria (60% of the score). The remaining 240% of the score is based on "qualitative" characteristics, such as the examiner's opinion and adherence to CDIC standards.

16 The CDIC provides no protection against losses in, for example, foreign-currency deposits, term deposits that mature in more than five years, debentures, Treasury bills, or funds invested in mortgages, stocks, and mutual funds.

17 The link **http://www.parl.gc.ca/LEGISINFO** provides a chronology of the proposal.

18 L. White, *The S&L Debacle* (New York: Oxford University Press, 1991): 211. White points out that some uses of the term "bailout" are misleading because the word suggests financial relief to an undeserving group. This characterization is inappropriate since deposit insurance is an obligation the government has committed itself to. To the extent that uninsured deposits are redeemed, however, the relief is a form of subsidization.

For example, when the Calgary-based Tower Mortgage failed, uninsured depositors incurred sizable losses. The discrepancy arises because governments have viewed some institutions as too big to fail. Depositor's in large banks are treated as covered, whether they are or not, because regulators view such institutions as too costly or difficult to liquidate. By contrast, losses incurred by uninsured depositors at smaller banks are viewed as tolerable.

Table 16.1 summarizes some of the salient features of the Canadian depositor protection scheme.

THE CDIC

The CDIC is run by a board of directors whose members, significantly, include the governor of the Bank of Canada, the deputy minister of finance, and the superintendent of financial institutions.[19] The chair is appointed for a five-year term. Four of the board members, including the chair, are representatives from the private sector.

The Corporation's powers to intervene in the affairs of its members are quite broad, however. It can acquire assets from a member institution, make loans or deposits with members without any collateral if it wants, borrow from the Canadian government or issue debt instruments to raise funds, act as a liquidator, and assume the costs of winding-up operations.

As we will see below, although the Canadian financial system has been among the most stable in the world, an extensive amount of financial turbulence in the 1980s led to considerable re-examination of the role and functions of the CDIC. Beginning with the Wyman Committee in 1985, followed by the Estey Inquiry of 1986, and culminating with the Dodge Committee in 1993, the CDIC's mandate was significantly revised. Although it is mistakenly believed that deposit insurance can be a vehicle to enhance competition between banking institutions by removing the need to worry about depositor protection, it could instead be a device to encourage reckless investment behaviour. However, the CDIC's mandate was changed to focus on its role as a means of promoting the stability of the financial system, more likely the paramount concern of small depositors.

In the event of a failure, the CDIC has one or more of the following options:

1. Pay off the depositors and close the bank.

Table 16.1	Key Facts about CIDC Coverage of Depositors in Canada

Insurable Deposits at Member Institutions	Some Noninsurable Deposits at Member Institutions
Savings and chequing accounts	Foreign currency deposits
Term deposits (up to five years)	Debentures issued by banks
Money orders	Government and corporate bonds
Drafts	Treasury bills
Certified cheques and drafts	Mutual funds
Travellers' cheques	Stocks

How much is insured?*

$100 000 per member institution
$100 000 per joint account
$100 000 per RRSP (Registered Retirement Savings Plan)
$100 000 per RRIF (Registered Retirement Income Fund)
$100 000 per deposit held in trust in member institution

Source: CDIC.

* Amounts apply only to "insurable" deposits. See text.

---

19 This office was created in 1987 by merging the Office of the Inspector General of Banks and the Department of Insurance. The latter office had been responsible for supervising trust, mortgage loan, and insurance companies.

2. Merge with a solvent bank (sometimes referred to as purchase and assumption).

3. Transfer of the deposits to another institution, which receives funds necessary to assume the liabilities. The insolvent bank is then wound up.

4. Bailout to permit the insolvent institution to continue operations.

Although these powers appear fairly wide, critics complain that the Bank of Canada's role in the process is unclear and that the CDIC cannot formally order the merger of weak banks with strong ones.[20]

In 1993 and 1994, the CDIC's functions were extensively re-examined in a government White Paper entitled "Enhancing the Safety and Soundness of the Canadian Financial System." This review culminated in a clarification of the respective functions of the CDIC and the OSFI (Office of the Superintendent of Financial Institutions), as well as an outline of the circumstances under which both institutions would have to coordinate their activities.[21] Essentially, the Corporation can force action only after a member institution effectively has become insolvent. Since it has extensive powers of inspection, the agency might be able to prevent some problems if it could step in *before* it is too late and an institution has to be wound up in some fashion.

Rules have been further clarified recently, since the CDIC and the OFSI are in the process of developing a formal guide to interventions, to deal with circumstances under which both institutions can intervene to avert the outright failure of a member.

Canadian financial history has been one of avoiding bank failures. Only 22 banks failed between 1867 and 1923, and none whatsoever from 1923, the date of the failure of the Home Bank, until 1966. From 1967 through 1989, the CDIC was called on to act in 23 instances. From 1984 on, there was a string of failures, and the agency paid out considerably more than it was expected to recover.

The two largest failures occurred in 1991 and 1992. Standard Trust, the ninth-largest trust company in Canada, filed for bankruptcy in April 1991, when the holders of more than $100 million in debt contended that the institution was essentially insolvent. The following year Central Guaranty Trust Co. failed and the size of the rescue was the largest in the CDIC's history. The resulting losses, due to bad commercial real estate loans, might have been larger had the Toronto-Dominion Bank not agreed to take over Central Guaranty's branches and operations. One of the most celebrated cases may have been the failure of the Bank of Credit and Commerce International (BCCI). Among the charges were that the offices operated a Ponzi (pyramid) scheme[22] in which money from new depositors was used to finance the needs of others, including illegal activities of all kinds. When the number of new investors was insufficient to cover the cash needs of earlier ones, the scheme collapsed.

Since the 1990s, however, the financial position of the CDIC has improved considerably. The fraction of "impaired" loans, that is, ones likely to default, has dropped dramatically at all institutions.[23] It should also be noted that low interest rates since the end of the 1990s, combined with the development of close substitutes for insured deposits, have led to a sharp drop in the percentage of insurable deposits.[24]

An important development in the banking industry over the past 20 years or so has been the growth of off-balance sheet items. In Chapter 15, we studied some of the most important elements

---

20 It must seek permission from the minister responsible (federal institutions minister). Historically, however, this has often been the outcome in the Canadian banking industry. See "Central Bank Role Urged in CDIC Act," *Financial Post* (11 March 1992): 15.

21 See CDIC, *Annual Report 1994–1995* (Toronto: CDIC, 1995): Appendix 2.

22 Named after Charles Ponzi, of Boston, Massachusetts, who operated such a scheme in the 1920s. It was not the first attempt at this kind of fraud. The South Sea Bubble (see Chapter 14) was an earlier version of a Ponzi scheme.

23 In 1994, 2.2% of loans at domestic banks were impaired, while at domestic trusts the same percentage stood at 4.7%. By 2000, the fraction of loans impaired was 0.7% and 0.5% respectively, at the same institutions. See CDIC, *Annual Report 2000/2001*.

24 In 1996, 47.8% of deposits at domestic banks and 88.3% of deposits at domestic trusts were insurable. By 2000, the same ratios were 36.1% and 87.1%, respectively. See CDIC, *Annual Report 2000/2001*.

of how such instruments work in practice. It is worth pointing out that the CDIC, for example, is well aware of the potential for instability and failure in the financial system if there is abuse of derivative products or if these are utilized to hide or obfuscate the true financial picture of a bank. Indeed, the CDIC has published a document called "Standards of Sound Business and Financial Practices"[25] in which it outlines the various risks facing financial institutions (we studied these in Chapter 13) and emphasizes that its practices apply equally to on and off-balance sheet items. The recent publicity over whether to treat stock options as an expense is an example of how important these off-balance sheet items can be to properly ascertaining the true financial health of any firm.

16.3 DEPOSIT INSURANCE IN OTHER COUNTRIES

Visit the FDIC's homepage at **www.fdic.gov**

Canada is not the only nation that offers deposit insurance. Indeed, it was far from being the first in this area of financial regulation (see Table 16.2). The first country to provide deposit insurance was the United States.

State-sponsored schemes can be traced back to the 1820s in New York. National deposit insurance was introduced in the 1930s when the country's banking legislation was overhauled, following the financial excesses of the 1920s, which had been replete with fraudulent and imprudent banking practices.[26] The agency that handles deposit insurance is the Federal Deposit Insurance Corporation (FDIC for short), which maintains two separate funds, one for the country's commercial and savings banks and one for its savings and loan (S&L) institutions.[27] Like the CDIC, the FDIC is a government agency. Insurance is provided on deposits to a current maximum of $100 000,[28] but, as in Canada, there are ways to raise effective coverage many times over. The scheme is so popular that recent U.S. banking reforms did not touch it, despite experts' widespread dissatisfaction with its current structure.[29]

Other industrialized countries also have deposit insurance schemes; their generosity varies widely. What is interesting is that many programs, except those of Great Britain, the United States, and Canada, are financed privately by the institutions themselves and administered by an association of members without the help of an officially sanctioned agency.

16.4 HOW COULD DEPOSIT INSURANCE BE IMPROVED?

As we have seen, Canada's deposit insurance scheme is fairly generous. Although the country has not faced the same problems that led to the S&L fiasco in the United States, it is nevertheless proper to ask whether Canada's current deposit insurance scheme is too generous, particularly since some bank failures in the 1980s and early 1990s severely strained the CDIC's reserves for a time. More broadly, what kinds of reforms would best serve the nation?

In a financial world in which the distinctions between financial institutions are blurring, it is relevant to ask why banks and trusts are insured against losses but other institutions, such as insurance companies, have a separate investor protection program.

The 1998 Task Force on the Future of the Canadian Financial Sector tackled this issue and recommended that the CDIC be amalgamated with the Canadian Health Life and Health

---

25 Available at **www.cdic.ca/bin/ENG_Stand_Report.pdf**

26 For an excellent account of this period in U.S. financial history, see C. Calomiris, "Is Deposit Insurance Necessary?" *Journal of Economic History* 50 (June 1990): 283–96. Remember, however, that there is still much controversy about whether the many bank failures of that time were the consequence of bad monetary policy or of reckless behaviour by the private sector.

27 Until the S&L scandal, two separate agencies handled deposit insurance for the two types of institutions.

28 Originally, the maximum insured deposit was set at $5000. Maximum insured amounts have been raised five times since 1949.

29 Indeed, one view is that U.S. legislators consider deposit insurance to be a kind of social or entitlement program. See "Won't Banking Be Splendid When Risk Is Whisked Away," *Los Angeles Times* (3 April 1991): B9.

| Table 16.2 | Deposit Insurance in Selected Countries |

Country	Intro-duced	Maximum Insured[a]	Type of Deposits Covered	Premium	Membership	Administration
Canada	1967	$100 000	C$ only	risk-based	Compulsory[b]	Government
France	1980	FF400 000 ($100 000)	FF only	on demand but limited	Compulsory	Industry
Germany	1966	100% up to a limit of 30% of liable capital of bank, per depositor	all	0.03% of all deposits but can be doubled	Voluntary	Industry
Italy	1987	($165 000 CAD)	Savings accounts, CDs	risk-adjusted	Compulsory	Industry
Japan	1971	($115 000)	¥ only		Compulsory	Government & Industry
The Netherlands	1979	€ 20 000($32 000)	all	contributions based on individual and industry pooled funds	Compulsory	Government
Norway	1923	Over ($390 000)	Most	0.005% of total assets and 0.01% of deposits	Compulsory	Industry
Switzerland	1984	SF300 000 ($30 000)	SF only	on demand	Voluntary	Industry
United Kingdom	1979	90% of protected deposits up to £31 700 ($73 000 CAD)	£ and EU currencies	on demand	Compulsory	Government & Industry
United States	1933	$100 000 ($125 000 CAD)	all	risk-based	Compulsory	Government

Sources: "International Banking Survey," *Economist*, 7 April 1990, p. 65; *Banker*, September 1991, p. 19, "International Banking Survey," *Economist* 27 April 1996, p. 18; **www.worldbank.org/research/interest/confs/upcoming/deposit_insurance/home.htm**, "Deposit Protection and Investor Compensation in Germany" Deutsche Bundesbank *Monthly Report*, July 2000, 29–46, **http://www.iadi.org/html/Default.aspx?MenuID=209** and J. Barth, G. Caprio, Jr., and D.E. Nolle (2004), "Comparative International Characteristics of Banking," Economic and Policy Analysis working paper 2004-1, Office of the Comptroller of the Currency, U.S. Treasury, January.

[a] The amounts in parentheses are Canadian-dollar equivalents calculated at January 2005 exchange rates. Figures are rounded to the nearest thousand.
[b] A financial institution can opt out if it does not accept retail deposits (i.e., of less than $150 000).

Insurance Corporation (CompCorp). Other proposals include plans to modernize the CDIC's expectations of how financial institutions should operate in a sound fashion (known as the Standards of Sound Business and Financial Practices). New practices were put in place in 2001.

Guaranteeing equal competition in the marketplace would mean insuring either all types of financial institutions or none at all. Alternatively, Nobel laureate James Tobin has suggested that only a nation's transactions balances—that is, its pure chequing account balances—be insured against losses; other bank liabilities, he says, should be backed by high-quality assets, such as Treasury bills or other government bonds.[30] A variant of this plan would provide deposit guarantees to accounts paying relatively low interest rates (for example, daily interest chequing accounts).

A simpler but obvious reform would be to let premiums on deposit insurance fully reflect the risks undertaken by the depository institutions. The only way to reduce the moral hazard problem is to assess premiums on the basis of the composition of an institution's balance sheet. Unfortunately, such a proposal presents several practical difficulties.[31] First, balance sheets show

30 James Tobin, "Financial Innovation and Deregulation in Perspective," *Bank of Japan Monetary and Economic Studies* (September 1985): 19–29.
31 The CDIC has had the power to charge risk-based premiums since 1987, but has only recently exercised it, in large part because of the difficulties discussed here. The Wyman Report, referred to previously, concluded that it was not possible to establish risk-related premiums. The report did, however, advocate co-insurance, whereby 90% of individual deposits up to $100 000 would be insured.

book values instead of market values, so an institution's true financial position is not always clear.[32] Second, it would be difficult to gain the necessary agreement across financial institutions about how risk levels and premiums should be related to each other. Third, as the U.S. savings and loan fiasco has shown, regulators would have to be prepared to act on their expectations of the implications of current bank behaviour. Otherwise, they would end up, as they often do now, reacting to events beyond even the government's control. Fourth, the cost of policing such a scheme would be very high. Regulators would have to update balance sheets constantly, estimating the market values of vastly different assets. And they could not simply average the default risk of assets in a portfolio, since what matters is the correlation of returns in a given portfolio. Moreover, obtaining a really useful picture would require regulators to consider other types of risk, such as inflation and interest rate risk, that are often not mentioned in the current debate. (Treating government bonds as riskless may be all right for making a point in a textbook, but it is hardly true of the real world.)[33]

Are there other routes to improving the system? Since the moral hazard problem is the greatest one, anything that raises the stakes for the owners of a financial institution in the event of a failure will reduce their temptation to manage their portfolios recklessly. One device would be to raise the capital requirement. In other words, if the proportion of equity to total assets were raised, failure would become more costly to the owners (see Chapter 11). Another would be to change the governance of the CDIC to make it more accountable to the institutions who pay the premiums and who are best able to assess risk. Moreover, it might be helpful to make membership in the CDIC voluntary.[34] Combined with a more independent organizational structure, such a reform might encourage better risk management by firms joining the CDIC, and it would be easy to identify those institutions that chose not to join.

The 1998 Task Force on Financial Reforms recommended that the responsibilities of the CDIC be more clearly differentiated from those of OSFI. This separation might be accomplished, for example, by transferring responsibility for determining what is sound banking practice to OSFI, which, after all, is mandated to supervise the financial industry. Other reforms that might be contemplated include requiring the CDIC to disclose its rating of member institutions or providing incentives for the private sector to report information that would allow depositors to form an opinion about the soundness of the institutions in which their deposits are held. Although the production of information can mitigate the adverse selection problem, it also raises the question of who will pay for the information. After all, if some depositors pay and act on the requisite information, others can free-ride by simply taking advantage of the information others have paid for. Even if the government were to release the information to all, many might feel uncomfortable with a public institution providing private information.

One difficulty with all reform proposals is that banks and near-banks are increasingly acting as brokers or intermediaries in transactions that appear only as off-balance-sheet items. Involvement in interest rate swaps, futures, and options, to name but a few examples, does not appear directly in their balance sheets, although these activities expose them to default risk.

All the previous suggestions have relied on the protection of deposits at face value. But what if deposits, instead of being protected in this fashion, were backed by the value of the assets of the deposit-taking institution? How would such a scheme work? Consider the development of chequable money market mutual funds (MMMF), first introduced in the United States and

---

32 Balance sheets' use of historical costs, although required by generally accepted accounting principles in most countries, creates problems that go beyond deposit insurance premiums. Reporting assets and liabilities at their historical cost, not the market values on which decision makers presumably act, can delay public detection of a risky or insolvent institution. Even regulators can be misled. Had different accounting rules been used, the insolvency of the Canadian Commercial Bank would have been evident much sooner than it was and US regulators would have known about the looming S&L scandal much earlier than they did.

33 For more details on this and related issues, written in an easy-to-understand fashion, see F.F. Cargill, and T. Mayer, "U.S. Deposit Insurance Reform," *Contemporary Policy Issue*s 10 (July 1992): 95–103.

34 Indeed, this proposal has found its way into the federal government's review of the financial sector. See 1997 *Review of Financial Sector Legislation: Proposals for Chang*e (Ottawa: Department of Finance, June 1996).

FINANCIAL FOCUS 16.1 — THE SAVINGS AN LOAN FIASCO IN THE UNITED STATES

U.S. banking failures arising out of the depression of the 1930s led to the introduction of competition-stifling banking reforms, most notably ceilings on interest rates placed on deposits and on the commercial loans of savings and loan (S&L) institutions, which are equivalent to Canadian trust companies.

The rise in market interest rates during the late 1970s and 1980s led to severe distortions in the U.S. financial system. The interest rate ceiling eventually was repealed, but it was too late for the S&Ls, which, at the end of the 1970s, found themselves with short-term deposits open to market interest rates and long-term loans that had been made at low interest rates.

By the early 1980s, most of the S&Ls became technically *insolvent*: Their liabilities exceeded their assets. As the crisis deepened, many became more and more inclined to invest in risky propositions, such as junk bonds, futures, and options, thereby compounding the problem facing the industry. Aided by the forbearance of regulators, who tended to react only after the problem was out of control, several S&Ls were emboldened to engage in fraudulent activities. Many simply collapsed.

These actions by the S&Ls perfectly illustrate the consequences of moral hazard. No one is sure of the total cost of bailing out the industry, but some estimates are as high as US$300 billion!

The banking crisis affected more than 1500 banks and led to some important reforms. For example, the FDIC is required to find the least costly solution to help wind down an insolvent bank. A postmortem of the S&L crisis concluded that the reforms dramatically reduced the effective protection to depositors as well as increasing market discipline. In other words, the moral hazard problem has been reduced by forcing large, uninsured depositors to pay attention to the financial operations of the banks they deal with.

Questions for Discussion

1. What does the S&L crisis say about the role of government in regulating the financial sector?
2. In what sense were the S&Ls caught with a severe mismatch between their assets and liabilities?

Source

U.S. Federal Deposit Insurance Corporation (FDIC), *History of the Eighties: Lessons for the Future* (Washington, D.C., 1997).

---

available in Canada. Deposits have a claim, in the form of shares, on the market value of the assets of the bank, instead of on their face value. As the value of the assets changes, so does the value of the shares. A fall in the value (price) of the shares, rather than causing a run on deposits, means a higher current yield (since the return produced by the assets is, at least for some time, fixed). This advantage attracts new depositors and thus prevents a loss of liquidity.

A much discussed reform proposal is one that would require banks to issue what is called junior or subordinated debt. Holders of this type of debt are the last to receive payment in the event of an insolvency. Suppose the government were to regulate the interest rate on such debt, capping it at a slight premium over, say, relatively riskless Treasury bills. Given the earlier discussion of the relationship between risk and return, we would expect investors to snap up this kind of debt only if the bank is operating at low risk. The capping of the rate on such debt would also have the advantage of preventing the holders from pressuring the bank to take on risky ventures, since they would not share in the possible gains. However, the subordinate debt holders do face the loss of their investment if the bank fails. Clearly then, such investors would have sufficient incentives to ensure that banks remain solvent.[35]

As you no doubt realize by now, the topic of deposit insurance is both interesting and controversial. Several proposals exist that address many of the problems with current arrangements. Indeed, the difficulties surrounding the question of whether there is too much deposit insurance have even led to the suggestion that banks be allowed to do as few things as possible with as little risk as possible, thereby effectively eliminating the need for deposit insurance. As attractive as this idea might sound to some, it is unlikely to receive serious consideration.

---

35 This proposal was suggested by Charles Calomiris of Columbia University. See "The Postmodern Bank Safety Net," available at **www.aei.org**.

Financial Stability
Forum
**www.fsforum.
org**

Although the chapter has examined individual countries' experiences with deposit insurance, there has been no comparative discussion of the experiences, advantages, and drawbacks of existing depositor protection schemes, and the possibility or feasibility of adopting common international practices. Discussions of these issues continue under the auspices of the Financial Stability Forum set up to ensure worldwide financial stability in the wake of the Asian crisis of 1997–98.

Of course, deposit insurance is but one aspect of the rules of the game involving the financial sector and the management of risk. As alluded to in several places in this chapter, outright government regulation is another device used to manage financial asset risk. It is to this topic that we turn our attention in the next chapter.

SUMMARY

- Insurance against losses in deposit-taking institutions is known as deposit insurance.

- Deposit insurance in Canada is run by the Canada Deposit Insurance Corporation, a Crown corporation.

- Deposit insurance is thought to be necessary because the failure of a bank or other depository institution can lead to fears that all other banks will fail, thus creating bank runs. Fear is contagious.

- Deposit insurance protects depositors up to a maximum of $100 000, but there are a number of ways to effectively increase coverage by several multiples.

- Although the CDIC is a federal agency, several provinces have their own depositor protection plans to cover provincially regulated financial institutions. Quebec has its own deposit insurance plan that mimics the CDIC's plan.

- All major industrial countries have depositor protection plans. They are, for the most part, similar to the Canadian plan. Differences exist in the degree of protection afforded by various plans. Also, in many countries, several plans are administered by the financial industry. Canada is one of the pioneers in the development of risk-based premiums.

- Deposit insurance is afflicted with two problems: moral hazard and adverse selection. Moral hazard refers to the fact that banks can take advantage of insurance to take more risks. Adverse selection arises because insurance may increase the probability of bank failure because depositors have less reason to monitor bank activities.

- Solutions to the moral hazard problem include deductibles and co-insurance. A deductible is a fixed cost borne by the depositor in case of a bank failure; co-insurance means that the depositor bears a fraction of the loss resulting from the closing of a failed bank.

- Solutions to the adverse selection problem include increasing the cost of a bank failure to large depositors, forcing them to monitor banking activities more closely; and fuller disclosure of regulators' evaluation of the soundness of individual banks' practices.

- Despite recent changes in the structure and organization of deposit insurance in Canada, including risk-based premiums and a promise of less forbearance, proposals continue to be made for improvements.

- Some advocate a much narrower base of coverage against depositor loss. However, financial innovations are partly accomplishing the same objective.

- Other ideas include amalgamation of various depositor and investor protection programs as a means of levelling the playing field among financial institutions whose differences are blurring.

IMPORTANT TERMS

adverse selection, 312

Canada Deposit Insurance Corporation
   (CDIC), 314

co-insurance, 312

deductible, 312

deposit insurance, 314

moral hazard, 312

PROBLEMS

1. Suppose a depositor has $100 000 in a savings account with a Canadian chartered bank. What is the loss to the depositor in the event the bank fails? What if $50 000 was in a joint account?

2. Now suppose that the CDIC is able to collect 80% of the value of the deposits in the failed bank considered in the previous question. What would the loss be to the depositor if the entire $100 000 was in a single savings account?

3. TRUE, FALSE, or UNCERTAIN: "Buyers would gladly pay $5000 for a good used car, but asymmetric information means that they may not be willing to pay more than $4000 for any used car." Explain.

4. TRUE, FALSE, or UNCERTAIN: Moral hazard is a problem before a transaction takes place, whereas adverse selection arises after a transaction has been completed.

DISCUSSION QUESTIONS

1. During the 1980s, what do you think drove deposit-taking institutions to take more risks? Explain.

2. Why did the CDIC or the government not discipline banks and near-banks more effectively in the wake of the failures during the 1980s?

3. Which do you think is the more important drawback to the current deposit insurance scheme: adverse selection or moral hazard? Explain your answer.

4. Assume you agree with the discussion about deposit insurance issues outlined in this chapter. Why haven't the politicians made appropriate changes? Explain your answer.

5. Why is the political motive for introducing deposit insurance possibly an important one?

6. Why has the Canadian Bankers Association often opposed the current structure of premiums?

7. What are some of the advantages and drawbacks of risk-based premiums? Explain.

8. Why has the independence of the CDIC from government interference possibly been an important policy issue?

9. List some of the rationales for deposit insurance.

ONLINE APPLICATIONS

Go to the CDIC's Web site at **www.cdic.ca**. Click on *Deposit Insurance Calculator*. Try different scenarios to see what depositor losses would be in the event of a bank failure. Next, click on *CDIC and You*, scroll down the page, and click on *Quiz on Deposit Insurance*. See how many questions you can answer correctly after studying the material in this chapter.

References can be found on **www.mcgrawhill.ca/college/siklos**

PART SIX

The Institutional Framework in the Canadian Context

Theories of Banking

LEARNING OBJECTIVES

After reading and studying this chapter, you should be able to

17.1 list and describe several modern theories of banking. These include

17.1 the theory of multiple expansion of deposits

17.2 the profit-maximizing theory of the banking firm

Explain some approaches to risk management. These include

17.3 gap analysis

17.4 duration analysis

17.5 explain the theory that focuses on the potential conflict between management and the banking firm's shareholders' predictions about bank behaviour

Earlier in this text we broadly described what banks do and the functions they fulfil in the financial system. In this chapter, we examine more formally the processes by which banks create assets and liabilities.

All modern theories of banking focus on the banks' role as intermediaries. As we have seen, the essence of intermediation is that some institutions have a comparative advantage in the processing of information. The core function of intermediation is to convert nonliquid liabilities into liquid assets, and banks can fulfil that "go-between" role by providing a service no other institution can.

To get to the essence of their deposit-creating and lending functions, we make a few simplifying assumptions. Also, although we briefly describe how deposits are created when transactions take place between Canada's chartered banks and its other banks, we leave the institutional details about the different types of banks for subsequent chapters and concentrate here on the theory of banking.

Unfortunately, there is no single theory of banking. As we will see, theories abound in this area and none has been embraced as the foundation for a unifying theory of banking. One branch of the literature stresses the loan-creation activities of banks. Accordingly, we begin this chapter with an analysis of the multiple expansion of deposits concept.

Another approach to the question of what banks do suggests that they behave like other profit-maximizing firms, and so we can rely on the view that forms the backbone of microeconomic theory. Thus, we consider here a version of the familiar theory of the banking firm.

Finally, an older tradition in the finance literature views banks in a different light altogether.

As a well-known article puts it:

> The concern with banks in macroeconomics centers on their role as portfolio managers, whereby they purchase securities from individuals and firms (and a loan is, after all, just a purchase of securities) which they then offer as portfolio holdings (deposits) to other individuals and firms.[1]

To illustrate this view of bank behaviour, we use a very simple expression of the portfolio approach, inspired by concepts developed in Chapter 13.

As should be clear from a reading of the previous chapters, banks today also are in the business of managing risks. This is a complex and evolving field. However, we present only simplified versions of two models of risk management that are widely used by financial institutions today. Finally, we look at the view of banks as organizations that are run by managers and directors but owned by shareholders. The preferences of the two groups can come into conflict. We briefly examine the implications of this view.

These approaches, it is worth pointing out, are complementary, not contradictory.

17.1 THE THEORY OF MULTIPLE EXPANSION OF DEPOSITS

Central to the understanding of any banking system is the notion of the multiple expansion of deposits, which is the process by which the system multiplies one dollar of reserves into many dollars of deposits, apparently creating money. As a well-known economist said years ago:

> The problem of the manner in which the banking system increases the total volume of the circulating medium, while at the same time the lending power of the individual banks is severely limited, has proved to be one of the most baffling for writers on banking.[2]

What puzzles students is the fact that although individual banks are restricted in the amount of deposits they can create, the banking system as a whole is able to expand deposits by a multiple. To see why this is the case, let us consider some simplified numerical examples. We'll start with a single bank (which can create a limited amount of deposits) and work up to a system.

The whole "secret" of deposit creation rests in public confidence. Only small children believe a bank keeps in its vaults every penny of every deposit it takes in. In fact, only a fractional reserve—a small percentage of total deposits—is kept to maintain liquidity and provide for depositors who want the use of some or all of their funds. The rest is used for money-making activities, of which the primary one is the making of loans.

BANK RESERVES IN CANADA

A bank's **reserve ratio**—the proportion of total deposits to be held in reserve—may be set by law or by prudence and custom. With the 1991 *Bank Act* (see Chapter 18) reserves are solely held for the sake of prudence. Legal restrictions establishing reserve ratios do not exist. As a result, chartered banks sharply reduced the amount of funds deposited at the Bank of Canada, essentially to meet requirements for clearing purposes. Nevertheless, banks will continue to hold reserves, and one way of understanding the process of deposit creation is via the analysis of a bank's balance sheet.[3]

A SINGLE BANK

Let's start with the simplest possible example. Suppose an individual, call her Ms. A, deposits $1000 to her demand account at the Little Bank. For the sake of illustration, let us assume that

---

1 E. Fama, "What's Different about Banks?" *Journal of Monetary Economics* 15 (January 1985): 29–40.

2 From L. Mints, *A History of Banking Theory*, as quoted in T.H. Humphrey, "The Theory of Multiple Expansion of Deposits: What It Is and Whence It Came," *Federal Reserve Bank of Richmond, Economic Review* (March/April 1987): 3–11, 3.

3 In Chapter 22 we consider a more complete example of the ways in which the Bank of Canada will ensure that the banking system maintains sufficient reserves.

the bank sets aside 5% of deposits as **reserves**. This figure may seem high but this is not the case, as we will see. To avoid confusion with cases in which the reserve requirement is mandated by law, we will refer to the 5% figure as a **target reserve**. Reserves above this level can still be referred to as excess reserves, but where the excess is relative to the level of reserves the banks *want* to hold as opposed to being *required* to hold.

What happens to the other $950? As long as it is simply sitting in the bank, it is an **excess reserve**—an amount of money that neither law nor prudence requires the bank to hold and that has an opportunity cost. So the bank wants to put that money to work in the form of a loan.

Suppose the Little Bank lends the $950 to Mr. B at 10% per year. This strategy will work nicely if the Little Bank is the only bank in the economy. Mr. B will use the funds to pay his creditors, who will make deposits to their own accounts, from which they will pay their bills, and so on. All the money will flow in and out of the Little Bank, creating the multiple expansion process we detail in the next subsection.

But suppose the Little Bank exists in a more realistic economy, one with five or six or dozens of competitors. If it lends Mr. B the $950, each of his creditors may patronize a different institution, and the funds may not flow back into the Little Bank. What will it use to pay Ms. A next month when she wants her $1000?

Unless Little Bank is a monopoly, most of that $950 is not really excess. To put the point another way, an individual bank that has competitors cannot safely lend (or otherwise tie up) any amount greater than the reserves it actually holds.

A BANKING SYSTEM

The situation for a whole banking system is more like that of a monopoly bank, especially if, as is usual, the system has a clearinghouse operation.[4]

A Simplified Balance Sheet

A simplified balance sheet will help to clarify our discussion of deposit expansion. Let's set one up (Table 17.1) for a system comprising two banks: the First Typical Canadian Bank (FTCB) and the Second Typical Canadian Bank (STCB). Both have the following assets and liabilities:

Assets	**Liabilities**
Cash, *CUR*, to meet daily withdrawal demand of depositors	Deposits, *DEP*
Target reserves (*RES*)	Advances from Bank of Canada (*ADV*)
Loans, *L*	Net worth (equity or capital)
Securities, *SEC* (bonds and other financial instruments)	
Physical assets (land and buildings)	

Notice that we are making a few simplifying assumptions. For example, on the liability side, where a variety of deposits exists, we consider only demand deposits. We relax this assumption later. We concentrate on the behaviour of the private sector—known as the *nonbank public*—ignoring other sources of deposit expansion.

To simplify matters still further, we also assume (1) that banks always aim to minimize their excess reserve (*ER*) holdings (so that these are only temporary), (2) that once a deposit is made into the banking system; there are no cash withdrawals while banks adjust to their new financial situation, and (3) that all banks have the same target reserve levels.

---

4 The Canadian clearinghouse, an automated interbank settlements system operated by the Canadian Payments Association, is described in Chapter 2.

Table 17.1   Multiple Deposit Expansion: The Basics

Initial deposit (in cash)

First Typical Canadian Bank (FTCB)		Second Typical Canadian Bank (STCB)	
Assets	Liabilities	Assets	Liabilities
NO CHANGE		+ $1000 *CUR*	+ $1000 *DEP*
		of which	
		$50 *RES*	
		$950 *ER*	
		$1000	

Cheque written on STCB

FTCB		STCB	
Assets	Liabilities	Assets	Liabilities
+ $1000 *CUR*	+ $1000 *DEP* ◄— − *$1000* CUR		− $1000 *DEP*
of which			
$50 *RES*			
$950 *ER*			
$1000			

New loans issued by FTCB

FTCB		STCB	
Assets	Liabilities	Assets	Liabilities
+ $950 *L* ◄—	+ $950 *DEP*	NO CHANGE	
	⋮	⋮	
+ $950 *CUR*	− $950 *DEP* ┐ + $950 *CUR*		+ $950 *DEP*
		of which	
		$47.50 *RES*	
		$902.50 *ER*	
		$950	

The creation of deposits via the multiplier process

Initial cash deposit	$1000	
New Loans: STCB	$ 950	= $1000 − (5% of $1000)
FTCB	$ 902.50	= $950 − (5% of $950)
⋮	$ 857.38	= $902.50 − (5% of $902.50)
	⋮	
Total Deposit Expansion	$1000 + $950 + $902.50 + … = $20 000	

The Effect of a Cash Deposit

Now suppose that Ms. A makes her $1000 deposit into the STCB. She makes it in cash (that is, currency). What is the effect on the economy's money supply? You can follow the answer through on Table 17.1.

Recall that M1, the narrow definition of the money supply, consists of currency circulating outside banks, *CUR*, and chartered bank demand deposits, *DEP*.[5] The transaction *initially* has no effect on the money supply since it represents simply a reallocation from currency to deposits. In algebraic terms, since

$$M1 = CUR + DEP$$

the initial effect on the money supply, as measured by the change in it, $\Delta M1$, can be written

$$\Delta M1 = -\Delta CUR + \Delta DEP$$
$$= -\$1000 + \$1000 = \$0$$

What is the effect on the entire banking system? Ms. A's $1000 cash deposit requires, initially at least, that the cash reserves of the STCB rise by $1000. To meet its target reserves on deposits, the bank allocates $50—5% of $1000—to these reserves, while the remainder ($1000 − $50 = $950) becomes excess reserves in the sense described earlier.

Suppose now that Ms. A writes a cheque for $1000 to her landlord, Mr. B, who deposits it in his account at the FTCB. If we ignore any time delay for cheque clearing, the first effect of this transaction is to eliminate the cash increase at the STCB. Its financial situation returns to where it was prior to the original deposit. The FTCB now, however, experiences a rise of $1000 in deposits, which, as before, signals a rise of $50 in target reserves with the remainder, $950, representing excess reserves.

So long as there are no cash withdrawals, the banking system still has some excess reserves. Since these reserves incur an opportunity cost, the FTCB seeks to use them to make a commercial loan or purchase securities. Suppose the bank loans the $950 to Mr. C, who uses it to pay a debt to Miss D. She deposits the proceeds, again in the form of a cheque, into her account at the STCB. The balance sheet of the FTCB first shows a rise in loans outstanding of $950 and then a withdrawal in the same amount, thereby eliminating all its excess reserves. Overall, the FTCB still has the original deposit increase of $1000, necessitating a rise in target reserves of $50, but it is fully loaned up, meaning that it no longer has any excess reserves.

Since Mr. C used his loan to pay Miss D, a depositor at the STCB, that bank now experiences a deposit increase of $950. It must add $47.50 (5% of $950) to its target reserves: The remainder ($950 − $47.50 = $902.50) now represents excess reserves. So far, the original $1000 deposit at the STCB has spawned an additional $1852.50 ($950 + $902.50) in deposits at both banks.

The fundamentals of multiple deposit expansion should now be clear. The desire to eliminate excess reserves creates an opportunity for banks to expand deposits through the acquisition of assets in the form of loans. (We leave it as an exercise to determine whether the same result would be obtained if a bank chose to acquire securities instead of making new loans.)

The Algebra of Deposit Expansion

Recall that we left the STCB with excess reserves. If it chooses to make further loans to the public, the deposit expansion process will continue. How long? The bottom panel of Table 17.1 shows the answer. It is easiest to reach it algebraically. (For convenience, the argument—and assumptions—are summarized in Table 17.2.)

---

5 In what follows, notations in capital letters refer to actual dollar amounts of the variable in question. Lowercase letters are used to denote fractions of some aggregate.

Table 17.2	The Creation of Deposits in Algebraic Form

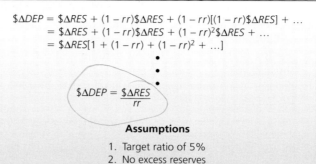

$$\$\Delta DEP = \$\Delta RES + (1 - rr)\$\Delta RES + (1 - rr)[(1 - rr)\$\Delta RES] + \dots$$
$$= \$\Delta RES + (1 - rr)\$\Delta RES + (1 - rr)^2\$\Delta RES + \dots$$
$$= \$\Delta RES[1 + (1 - rr) + (1 - rr)^2 + \dots]$$

$$\$\Delta DEP = \frac{\$\Delta RES}{rr}$$

Assumptions

1. Target ratio of 5%
2. No excess reserves
3. No currency drain

Let's derive the equation. We know from our discussion above that target reserves, *RES,* are a constant fraction, *rr,* of deposits, *DEP.* Therefore, we can write

$$RES = rr \cdot DEP \qquad (17.1)$$

where *rr* is the reserve ratio. Since we want to compute the total change in deposits, given an initial cash deposit of some amount, and since the targeted reserve ratio is assumed to be fixed, equation (17.1) becomes

$$\Delta RES = rr \cdot \Delta DEP \qquad (17.2)$$

where ΔRES represents the change in target reserves and ΔDEP represents the change in deposits. Returning to the numerical example in Table 17.1, we see that, initially, the cash deposit of $1000 is equivalent to the change in target reserves. Therefore,

$$\$1000 = 5\% \cdot \Delta DEP$$

from which we can conclude, using equation (17.2), that

$$\Delta DEP = \frac{1}{rr} \Delta RES \rightarrow \Delta DEP = \frac{\$1000}{5\%} = \$20\ 000 \qquad (17.3)$$

Equation (17.3) shows that the initial rise of deposits and reserves of $1000 is multiplied 20 times (= 1/0.05) to satisfy the requirement that there be no excess reserves, other than for the targeted amount, in the banking system. It comes as no surprise then that the term $1/rr$ is referred to as the **deposit multiplier**. Here,

$$\frac{1}{rr} = \frac{1}{0.05} = 20 \qquad (17.4)$$

What is the effect on the money supply? Recall that initially

$$\Delta M1 = -\Delta CUR + \Delta DEP$$
$$= -\$1000 + \$1000 = \$0$$

Once we consider the effect of the multiple deposit expansion, however, we see that the final impact on the money supply is

$$\Delta M1 = -\$1000 + \$20\ 000 = +\$19\ 000$$

where $-\$1000$ represents the original fall in the amount of currency in circulation, and $+\$20\ 000$ is the total expansion in deposits. Clearly, then, the behaviour of the money supply is inextricably tied to the behaviour of banks.[6]

---

6 We develop more precise behavioural relationships between the two in Chapter 22.

Two of the assumptions made in deriving equation (17.3) require further discussion. To the extent that either or both banks decide to hold some excess reserves, the deposit multiplier will be reduced. Since total reserves, TR, are simply the sum of target and excess reserves, we can write

$$TR = RES + ER \qquad\qquad (17.5)$$

where ER = excess over target reserves. Moreover, since by equation (17.1) we can express target reserves as a function of deposits, equation (18.5) becomes

$$TR = rr \cdot DEP + ER \qquad\qquad (17.6)$$

If we assume that banks want to hold no excess reserves, equation (17.5) is equivalent to equation (17.1). However, banks may want to hold some excess reserves. How much do they want to hold? The question is difficult, and the answer almost certainly varies from bank to bank. Different banks have different needs. For many, seasonal cash needs dominate their decisions on excess reserves. For others, it is conditions particular to the region in which they are located. We can, however, formulate a simple hypothesis based on observation of how excess reserves tend to fluctuate in the banking system as a whole. Assume that excess reserves depend on the nominal interest rate, the reasoning being that banks that have a targeted level of reserves are reluctant, given the opportunity costs,[7] to add to them. In other words, excess reserves would be negatively related to the opportunity cost of holding money. We can summarize this argument algebraically by rewriting equation (17.6) as

$$TR = rr \cdot DEP + ER(R) \qquad\qquad (17.7)$$

Equation (17.7) differs from equation (17.6) in making excess reserves a function of the interest rate. Dividing both sides of equation (17.7) by DEP, we obtain

$$\frac{TR}{DEP} = \frac{rr \cdot DEP}{DEP} + \frac{ER(R)}{DEP}$$

which can be further simplified as

$$tr = rr + er(R) \qquad\qquad (17.8)$$

where tr is the total reserve ratio—that is, total reserves, TR, as a proportion of deposits, DEP. Note that in the numerical example outlined in Table 17.1, $er(R)$ was assumed to be zero. In that case,

$$tr = rr$$

Therefore, if we allow for excess reserves, the change in deposits becomes

$$\Delta DEP = \frac{1}{rr + er(R)} (\Delta RES) \qquad\qquad (17.9)$$

where the term $1/[rr + er(R)]$ is the deposit multiplier. The only difference between equation (17.9) and (17.3) is the addition of the $er(R)$ term in the denominator, which reflects the fact that if banks choose to hold excess reserves, they cannot expand deposits as much as they could if they chose to hold no excess at all. Algebraically, since $er(R)$ is positive,

$$\frac{1}{rr} > \frac{1}{rr + er(R)}$$

That is, $1/rr$ is larger than the deposit multiplier alone when there are positive excess reserves.

---

7 Before the introduction of the current reserve management system, all required reserves were subject to an opportunity cost. Under the new system, only cash on hand incurs an opportunity cost because balances at the Bank of Canada earn interest if they are positive (in the case of a negative balance there is a penalty interest rate to be paid). Again, see Chapters 4 and 22.

A SYSTEM WITHOUT REQUIRED RESERVES

So far we have assumed that banks target a fraction of deposits as reserves. Although this is certainly sensible, it was pointed out that this fraction might be close to zero. In fact, banks do keep a nontrivial fraction of some of their deposits at the Bank of Canada and in the form of notes and coins, although their levels have fallen since the passage of the 1991 *Bank Act* and the transition to zero required reserves. There is a seasonal component in reserves, which rise not surprisingly, during December (also see Figure 2.2 in Chapter 2).

To deal with a system of new required reserves, we could simply assume that all reserves are, in effect, a function of the need to maintain some minimum amount to satisfy regular cash needs such as those arising out of the use of ABMs (automated banking machines) plus an adjustment for the calendar to deal with seasonal effects.

This would mean that we could rewrite equation (17.9) as follows:

$$\Delta DEP = [1/(k + seas_t)]\, \Delta RES$$

where $k =$ some minimum desired reserve-ratio level, and $seas_t$ fluctuates according to the calendar to capture seasonal effects. However, notice that the principles involved in deriving and using equation (17.9) are unaffected by the use of the equation.

THE EFFECT OF A CURRENCY DRAIN

A *currency drain*, also called a *cash drain*, means a cash withdrawal from the banking system. If we simply reverse the analysis of Table 17.1 and equation (17.9), we see that a currency drain implies a multiple contraction of deposits. Every bank experiences some currency drain every day when some depositors demand part or all of their funds in cash. Indeed, some individual banks end up with a net drain for a few days, even in the most expansionary monetary system.

The entire banking system can also experience a cash drain, perhaps for a considerable period. Such a contraction of deposits can have a variety of causes. One is a change in the public's desire to hold currency.[8] Public policies, such as actions by the Bank of Canada on its own account or as the federal government's banker, can also influence the quantity of cash and the reserves of the banking system.

Continuing with our earlier numerical example (see Table 17.2), suppose that the public holds a constant fraction of deposits in the form of cash. Therefore, we define

$$cur = CUR/DEP$$

Earlier, we saw that with a target reserve ratio of 5%, the resulting multiplier was 20 ($= 1/rr$). If *cur* is 5%, the multiplier, or equation (17.4), becomes

$$1/(rr + cur) = 1(0.05 + 0.05) = 10 \qquad \textbf{(17.4A)}$$

A currency drain then has the effect of reducing the multiplier, since cash that the banking system would ordinarily use to create new deposits is withdrawn, reducing the size of the original multiplier.

THE EFFECT OF A CHANGE IN THE COMPOSITION OF DEPOSITS

A limitation of the simplified balance sheet presented in Table 17.1 is that it lumps together different types of deposits. In particular, the distinction between demand and term deposits is entirely ignored. This drawback is easily remedied. Consider Table 17.3 in which the liability side of the FTCB balance sheet is modified to show two types of deposits: demand deposits, DD, and time or fixed-term deposits, TD. The sudden withdrawal of funds from a time deposit usually in-

---

8 As we'll see in Chapter 22, it is relatively straightforward to analyze the public's behaviour in this regard.

Table 17.3	Deposit Expansion when Deposit Composition Changes

First Typical Canadian Bank
Initial change from time of demand deposit

| No Change | $+\$1000\ DD$ |
| | $-\$1000\ TD$ |

Impact on reserves

$RES_d\ +\ \$40\ (4\%\ of\ +1000)$	No Change
$RES_t\ -\ \$10\ (1\%\ of\ -1000)$	
net\ \ \ \ $+\ \$30$	

Impact on assets

| $RES\ +\$30$ | No Change |
| $SEC\ -\$30$ | |

volves a penalty of sorts.[9] As a result, the likelihood of sudden withdrawal is lower for time deposits than for demand deposits. Consequently, the portion of reserves targeted against the possibility of withdrawals from fixed-term deposits will also be much smaller than for demand deposits.

Table 17.3 assumes that this fraction is 1%, while the fraction of deposits held as reserves against demand deposits is now assumed to be 4%, so the total reserve ratio is still 5%.

Also suppose that a depositor of the First Typical Canadian Bank transfers a matured time deposit into her chequing account at the same bank. For simplicity, we assume no currency drain and no leakage to other banks. Initially, the FTCB experiences no changes in total deposits, since the transaction simply represents a transfer from one type of deposit to another (see the first panel of Table 17.3). However, as a result of the transfer, the bank's overall reserve requirements do change. The reserves for demand deposits (RES_d) rise by \$40—4% of $+\$1000$—and the reserves for time deposits fall by \$10—1% of \$1000. In net terms, the FTCB requires $\$40 - \$10 = \$30$ of additional reserves. Consequently, it must change its portfolio to satisfy the new reserve requirement. One solution—there are others, which are left as an exercise—is to sell some of its holdings of securities, thereby reallocating its assets, leaving liabilities unchanged. (Of course, the sale of a security will have further effects of the kind considered previously.)

TRANSFER OF DEPOSITS TO A NEAR-BANK

The near-banks, such as trust companies, do hold reserves against deposits, but they were never legally bound by specific reserve requirements.[10] In any event, there is also no reason to believe that every bank's cash management technique will be identical, which leads to potential differences in actual reserves against different types of deposits. Moreover, deposits in the near-banks are not counted as part of the monetary aggregates M1 and M2.[11] Thus, if an individual transfers funds from, say, a demand deposit in the FTCB to a time deposit in a trust company, the chartered banks will experience a currency drain, necessitating the calling in of loans or the sale of securities. M1 and M2 will also be affected. Broader monetary aggregates, such as M2+, do include deposits in near-banks and so reflect any shifts in deposits between them and the chartered banks.[12]

---

9 It may be implicit, as when interest income that would otherwise be earned is lost, or explicit, as when there is a monetary penalty for withdrawal if the term of the deposit was specified in advance.

10 Different regulations for different parts of the banking system are not restricted to Canada. See, for example, Chapter 25.

11 We could consider other monetary aggregates but the essentials of the analysis to follow would be unaffected.

12 As near-banks become more like chartered banks, it is conceivable that the rather artificial distinctions between M2 and M2+ will vanish. The existing distinctions are largely a matter of statistical expediency.

Table 17.4 illustrates two scenarios involving transactions between a chartered bank and a near-bank. For the purposes of illustration, we assume that both institutions hold the same reserves against time deposits and keep excess reserves to zero.

In the first case, the transfer of a demand deposit out of the chartered bank contracts those deposits according to the deposit multiplier, and the near-banks are able to expand their deposits, also by a multiple. If the transfer is made into a time deposit at a near-bank then, given the arguments outlined in Table 17.4, the shift means an overall expansion of deposits in the bank and near-bank sectors taken together. As far as the monetary aggregates are concerned, however, the direction of movement depends on which definition is used. M1 and M2 fall. The M2+ measure, in contrast, rises.

Two considerations should be kept in mind in assessing the effects of transactions between chartered banks and near-banks. First, most near-banks hold deposits at chartered banks.[13] Thus, in holding reserves against the new time deposit, the near-bank may choose to increase its deposits. If it does so, the drain of deposits from the chartered bank would be smaller than previously argued. Second, reserves held against time deposits need not be the same in the chartered banking and near-banking sectors. Any difference can influence the size of changes in the money supply.

In the second scenario in Table 17.4, an individual switches a time deposit from a chartered bank to a near-bank (perhaps because the latter offers terms that the depositor perceives as more attractive). The chartered banks experience a multiple contraction of deposits. The opposite holds for near-banks, which can now engage in a multiple expansion of deposits. The net effect on narrow monetary aggregates, such as M1 and M2, is negative. The impact on a broader measure of the money supply is a function of the reserve ratio for time deposits in the two segments of the banking sector. Whether the near-banks decide to raise their deposits in the chartered banks will also influence the size of the change in the various measures of the money supply.

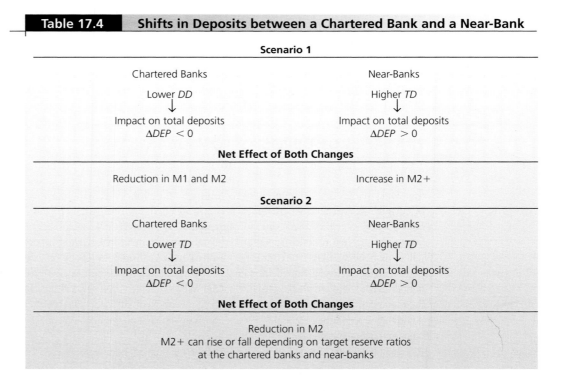

Table 17.4	Shifts in Deposits between a Chartered Bank and a Near-Bank

Scenario 1

Chartered Banks	Near-Banks
Lower *DD*	Higher *TD*
↓	↓
Impact on total deposits	Impact on total deposits
$\Delta DEP < 0$	$\Delta DEP > 0$

Net Effect of Both Changes

Reduction in M1 and M2	Increase in M2+

Scenario 2

Chartered Banks	Near-Banks
Lower *TD*	Higher *TD*
↓	↓
Impact on total deposits	Impact on total deposits
$\Delta DEP < 0$	$\Delta DEP > 0$

Net Effect of Both Changes

Reduction in M2
M2+ can rise or fall depending on target reserve ratios
at the chartered banks and near-banks

---

13 These deposits form part of Canada's large and active interbank market.

17.2 THE BANK AS A FIRM

The deposit multiplier leaves out some important considerations, such as the degree of competition in the industry and the fact that the ability and willingness of a market to absorb, say, additional loans depends in part on prevailing interest rates. This section remedies these omissions by outlining a simple model of the financial firm.

This approach requires a bit of thought. When we defined what financial insititutions do (Chapter 3), we faced the problem of putting it in terms of the conventional way in which economists view firms: that is, of having inputs and a physically definable output. The *intermediation* function is the one that distinguishes financial firms from others. Yet many observers of the industry associate banks primarily with their deposit-taking function. Indeed, it is convenient to view banks as *depository firms*—that is, firms that produce deposits.[14] Such an approach is convenient because it allows us to analyze banks as if they were like any other firm, guided, as the economist assumes, by the principle of profit maximizing—that is, they attempt to reach the most profitable level of output by keeping costs per unit at the lowest level possible.

As was just pointed out, the model to be outlined below appears to leave out some of the details of the transformation that takes place from deposit taking to loan making. In essence, lenders delegate the costs of monitoring the creditworthiness of borrowers to the banking firm. This delegation benefits lenders and society as a whole but, of course, there are also potential costs, especially if the bank fails and depositors lose their funds. All these aspects of the growing complexity of providing intermediation services are difficult to model in a straightforward fashion. Nevertheless, it is convenient and not altogether unrealistic to assume that the spread between borrowing and lending rates is a key determinant of banking activity (see, for example, Chapter 11). This position is the one that we will adopt in the following section.

THE MODEL

Let us set up a model, assuming the depository firm's "output" consists of deposits which are a function of several determinants such that

$$DEP = DEP(R_{DEP}, R_a) \qquad (17.10)$$

where

R_{DEP} = deposit interest rate
R_a = yield on alternative financial instruments
DEP = deposits

In other words, the variables influencing the size of deposits are the real interest rate paid on them and the yield available on alternative financial instruments in the economy. There could be other determinants such as service charges, location, income, and wealth, but these are omitted to keep the model as simple as possible. In what follows, we also ignore the effect of inflation. The cost of supplying deposits can be viewed as consisting of two elements, one explicit and the other implicit. The explicit component is measured by the rate paid on deposits, R_{DEP}, and the implicit component reflects operation costs—salaries, maintenance of physical assets, and so on. Since more deposits may signal the need to hire more staff or expand banking operations, we can assume that the implicit costs are also a function of deposits. Therefore, to simplify the discussion we assume that costs are essentially captured by deposit costs, which are a function of deposits. In other words, we write

$$R_{DEP}(DEP) \qquad (17.11)$$

---

14 Alternatively, we could model that banking firm as one that "produces" loans, but the essence of the model we are developing would remain unchanged.

where

$$DEP \uparrow \rightarrow R_{DEP} \downarrow$$

Equation (17.11) is nothing other than the rising marginal cost rule. Thus, as the bank seeks more deposits, it raises the rate paid on deposits in order to attract the additional depositors. But these same deposit costs must rise at an increasing rate to attract additional deposits. We assume, for the sake of exposition, that the firm offers only one type of deposit.

Similarly, although several alternative assets exist, it seems preferable to let R_a represent some financial asset that acts as a substitute for deposits. In this setup, the banking firm books a certain volume of deposits (in an amount to be specified below), which are transformed, via the process of intermediation, into loans that are used by borrowers to generate assets whose return is R_a. To keep things as simple as possible, assume that the rate charged on loans is R_a. Clearly, this assumption is not entirely realistic. For example, borrowers potentially can reinvest their loans in ventures that can earn more than R_a, or returns below R_a. It is simply convenient to assume that loan rates and R_a are the same. You might well ask: If there are opportunities to earn R_a, why can't individuals simply take direct advantage of them? There are several reasons. First, individuals may find it too costly to look for the best investment opportunities. Second, individuals may be constrained by liquidity and not have the financial wherewithal to take advantage of existing investment opportunities. Third, as noted earlier, depositors delegate monitoring and risk-taking costs via the intermediation process. For all these reasons, it makes sense that $R_{DEP} < R_a$, that is, the interest rate on deposits is below the interest rate on loan interest-earning assets. Recall from Chapter 11 that $R_a - R_{DEP}$ is simply an interest rate spread and that it is, typically, a positive number.

Now the average yield on assets likely depends on the amount of assets purchased, which, in turn, depends on the volume of deposits used to finance this purchase. Also, we know from previous discussions that some banks obtain lower yields than others because the Bank of Canada auctions off Treasury bills from the highest to the lowest price. Similarly, we can reasonably assume that all firms seek out the highest-yielding assets, and thus they purchase the better-yielding ones first and the lower-yielding ones only as necessary. Consequently, it seems reasonable to hypothesize that

$$R_a(DEP) \tag{17.12}$$

where

$$DEP \uparrow \rightarrow R_a \downarrow$$

Equation (17.12) encapsulates both the positive relationship between deposits and asset yields as well as the diminishing marginal revenue aspect of the function.

The profit function of the firm is then simply

$$\text{Profit} = \text{Revenues} - \text{Costs}$$

or

$$\text{Profit} = R_a(DEP) \cdot DEP - R_{DEP}(DEP) \cdot DEP \tag{17.13}$$

Equation (17.13) describes the fact that the banking firm earns revenues of $(R_a \cdot DEP)$—that is, an average yield or $R_a\%$ multiplied by the volume of outstanding deposits. It faces costs of $(R_{DEP} \cdot DEP)$—the deposit interest rate multiplied by the volume of deposits—as well as the other costs of operating the firm.[15]

---

15 Again, there are no doubt separate costs to managing deposits and loans but, to minimize notation, $R_{DEP} \cdot DEP$ can be thought of as capturing both.

Figure 17.1	Profit Maximization of the Banking Firm

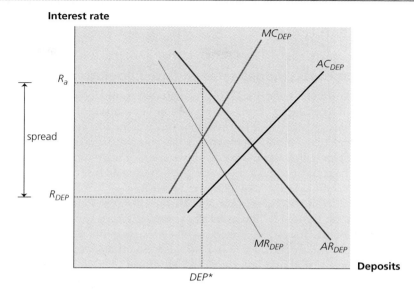

The banking firm faces falling average revenues, AR_{DEP}, and, consequently, diminishing marginal revenues, MR_{DEP}. Since total costs are a function of deposits, average costs, AC_{DEP}, rise with the volume of deposits. Therefore, marginal costs, MC_{DEP}, also rise with deposits. The optimum volume of deposits is DEP^*, the point that yields the profit-maximizing solution. The difference $(R_a - R_{DEP})$ is the spread between average asset earnings and average costs.

Note: The functional form has been dropped here to save space and because both R_a and R_{DEP} are functions of deposits.

Figure 17.1 illustrates the profit-maximization problem facing the banking firm. Its output, measured on the horizontal axis, is deposits. The vertical axis measures the various yields it faces. The curve labelled AR_{DEP} represents average revenues, which, as we saw earlier, fall with increases in volume of deposits. Consequently, marginal revenues, labelled MR_{DEP}, also fall. Note that the MR_{DEP} curve is below the AR_{DEP} curve (because marginal increases in the volume of deposits yield smaller and smaller revenue increments). On the cost side, the curve AC_{DEP} represents average costs and MC_{DEP} summarizes the marginal costs. The MC_{DEP} curve lies above the AC_{DEP} curve (because additional deposits increase the costs of providing them faster as more deposits are accepted).[16]

Now recall how we find the profit-maximizing level of output for a firm. So long as marginal revenues are greater than marginal costs, profits rise (because additions to total revenues are larger than additions to total costs). They will cease to rise when marginal revenues are equal to marginal costs. After that point, as is clear in Figure 17.1, any additional deposits will add more to costs than to revenues (that is, $MC_{DEP} > MR_{DEP}$). Therefore, profits reach their maximum at the point at which the revenue from an additional dollar of deposits is exactly offset by the cost of providing that additional dollar of deposits. This profit-maximizing condition can be written in equation form as

$$MR_{DEP} = MC_{DEP} \qquad (17.14)$$

16 In a perfectly competitive environment, the MC curve would be horizontal because if one bank tried to lower the interest rate offered on deposits, it would receive none. We are therefore assuming that the typical bank portrayed in this analysis has some market power. Consequently, it must raise the interest rate to attract more deposits or lower the interest rate to attract more loans. One obvious source of market power is that intermediation is a service that only banks specialize in.

According to Figure 17.1, the condition summarized in equation (17.14) yields deposits of DEP^*. With that volume of deposits, the banking firm earns an average asset yield of R_a through the loans it makes and incurs average costs of R_{DEP}. The spread between the two reflects the average profit per dollar of deposits.

Application of the Model: Interest Rate Regulation

The model illustrated by Figure 17.1 can be used to consider a variety of situations in the banking industry. For example, if we wish to explore the impact of a cost-saving technological improvement, we need only shift the marginal and average cost curves to the right.

Another change for consideration is a loosening of regulations, permitting banks to compete in an area in which they have previously been forbidden to do so.

The average and marginal revenue curves presumably shift to the right because enhanced market opportunities lead to higher average revenues.

The model can also be used to describe the effects of some distortions caused by government regulations. Figure 17.2 illustrates a hypothetical case in which, say, a restriction of some kind on the types of activities a bank can engage in effectively limits the interest rate that can be paid on deposits. In the absence if any impediments on a bank's activities, the bank would attract DEP^* in deposits, resulting in an interest rate spread of $R_a^* R_{DEP}^*$. This situation essentially is depicted in Figure 17.1. Now, suppose that a maximum of $R'_{DEP} R'_{DEP}$ can be paid due to a re-

| **Figure 17.2** | **The Impact of Government Regulations on the Market for Deposits** |

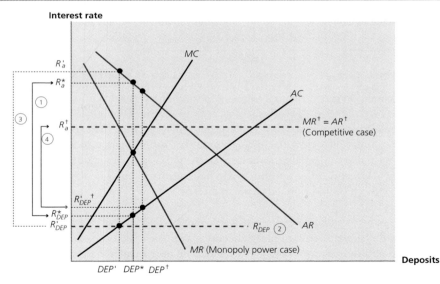

Initially the profit-maximizing level of deposits is DEP^*, as in Figure 17.1. With regulation effectively limiting deposit rates to R_{DEP}, fewer deposits are booked at banks. As a result, fewer asset purchases can be made, so average asset revenues $R_a(DEP)$ rise. The result is a larger spread between asset returns and average costs. Notice that the spread rises by more than the difference between the profit-maximizing deposit rate and the ceiling. $MR^\dagger = MC^\dagger$ illustrates the case where the banking firm operates in a perfectly competitive industry. This scenario produces the smallest spread of all.

① Spread with no government regulation: $R_{DEP}^* R_a^*$
② Government regulation effectively limits payment of interest on deposits to R'_{DEP}
③ Spread with government regulation: $R'_{DEP} R'_a$
④ Spread in a competitive market $R_{DEP}^\dagger R_a^\dagger$

striction that limits the opportunities to pay higher returns on deposits as conditions warrant. Since the deposit rate is relatively less attractive to depositors (R'$_{DEP}$ is less than R*$_{DEP}$), the volume of deposits is lower. At this reduced volume, the banking firm now generates average revenues of R_a', which is higher than the profit-maximizing rate. Because there are fewer deposits, fewer assets are purchased. As a result, the spread rises (i.e., $R_a' R_{DEP}' > R_a^* R_{DEP}^*$). Since less intermediation is available, profits are maximized by increasing the spread between borrowing and lending rates. Again, a look back at the example of a spread shown in Chapter 11 will show that, on average, these have fallen over the years as financial markets have become more competitive.

The Role of Competition

Indeed, we can use the theory of the firm framework to discuss the role of competition in the financial industry. Imagine an average revenue curve that is perfectly flat (as illustrated in Figure 17.2 by the line labelled $MR\dagger = AR\dagger$). According to this scenario, which is the one faced by the perfectly competitive firm, the average and marginal revenue curves coincide. Each additional dollar of deposits always yields the same additional revenue because each firm is so small in relation to the entire industry that when additional deposits are turned into assets, they have only a trivial impact on asset returns. Consequently, the perfectly competitive firm can treat average and marginal revenues as constant. The profit-maximizing solution is now to set $MR\dagger_{DEP} = MC_{DEP}$, which yields a deposit volume of $DEP\dagger$ and average asset returns of $R_a^\dagger$.

The consequence of perfect competition is to reduce the spread between average asset returns and the average deposit rate (to $R_a^\dagger R\dagger_{DEP}$). Therefore, the slope or elasticity of the demand for deposits can be used as a gauge of the degree of competition in the banking industry.

17.3 GAP ANALYSIS

Although the preceding analysis leads to much insight about the economic forces influencing the banking industry, it omits consideration of uncertainty or term to maturity, so we are still unable to measure banking performance adequately. What approach can we use?

We can safely assume that risk aversion leads banks, like individuals, to seek to reduce portfolio risk for a given portfolio return. They could use the kind of portfolio analysis (matching debts and assets) that we examined earlier (see Chapter 13), but given the volume of debts and assets involved, it is doubtful that banks are willing to perform the necessary risk–return calculations. Fortunately, a relatively simple alternative exists called gap analysis.

Essentially, **gap analysis** proceeds by subdividing assets and liabilities into components that are rate sensitive—that is, influenced by interest rate changes—and components that are not. Then the gap is calculated as

$$GAP = IRSA - IRSL \tag{17.15}$$

where

$IRSA$ = interest-rate-sensitive assets
$IRSL$ = interest-rate-sensitive liabilities

Assets that are sensitive to interest rates include variable-rate loans and T-bills, among other items. Liabilities in the same category are daily interest rate accounts.

Fixed-rate assets (such as long-term government bonds) and liabilities (such as long-term loans) count for little here.

Table 17.5 gives the breakdown for the First Typical Canadian Bank and the calculation of equation (17.15). The positive gap of $20 million means that an increase in interest rates of, say, 3% would increase the bank's revenues to 0.03 × $20M = $600 000. A positive gap may be a

ECONOMICS FOCUS 17.1 — CAPPING CREDIT CARD INTEREST RATES

Nowhere is the impact of interest rate regulations more dramatically revealed than in the debate about capping interest rates on credit cards. Both Canadian and U.S. politicians occasionally talk about forcing banks to reduce or cap the interest rates charged on credit card balances. So far, however, governments have generally avoided legislating interest rates on this kind of debt, preferring to resort to moral suasion to nudge interest rates lower.

Borrowers often fail to realize that credit card debt is unsecured. Also, since credit card purchases are increasingly replacing cash transactions, they provide convenience, which is a valuable commodity. The combination of these two factors—not a lack of competition in the credit card industry—explains the spread between credit card interest rates and other interest rates.

There are also a couple of additional reasons why ceilings on credit card interest rates could be catastrophic. First, credit card securitization is a large market. Card issuers package the amounts receivable from credit cards to back or finance the issue of bonds. The threat of a cap has the effect of raising the risk of this kind of debt. Second, the

public appears to be ignorant about alternative ways to finance debt, and just plain lazy in paying off credit card balances. Moreover, those most financially strapped—and thus most at risk of defaulting—resort to this type of debt finance so that high credit card rates simply reflect the risks of default and the costs of not obtaining financial information.

Questions for Discussion

1. Are there good reasons for banks to demand relatively higher interest rates for credit card balances?
2. Is it "rational" for some consumers to borrow via their credit cards?

Sources

"Catastrophic Cap," *Economist*, 23 (November 1991): 81.

"Many Keep on Paying High Rates on Cards Through Bad Planning," *Wall Street Journal* (26 December 1991): A1.

"Solving the Credit Card Mystery," *Wall Street Journal* (26 December 1991): A12.

reflection of a bank's belief that interest rates will rise since its revenue (and, presumably, profit) picture will improve.

Unfortunately, any simple approach to measuring bank performance always has a catch. Recall that increases in interest rates adversely affect the market value or price of assets such as bonds. Since market values are not reflected in balance sheets, gap analysis ignores them. Yet a 3% rise in interest rates can substantially reduce the value of the fixed-rate assets. Indeed, depending on the term to maturity of the long-term assets and whether the bonds need to be sold on the market, a 3% rise in interest rates can reduce the fixed-rate component of assets sufficiently to make net worth negative, thereby bankrupting the banking firm.

As a result, several banks evaluate a measure of the gap, called *incremental gap*. This version of equation (17.15) is a function of the term to maturity of the assets and liabilities. For example, one can evaluate the gap for assets and liabilities that mature in three years or less, and then for a term of three to five years, and so on. Increasingly, banks are making it easier to determine the maturity structure of their balance sheet and will often provide incremental gap measures.

Table 17.5   An Illustration of Gap Analysis

First Typical Canadian Bank			
Assets		**Liabilities**	
Rate-sensitive	$70M	Rate-sensitive	$50M
Fixed-rate	$30M	Fixed-rate	$40M
		Net worth	$10M

Rate-sensitive assets – Rate-sensitive liabilities = gap
$70M   – $50M   = $20M

Another drawback of the gap measure is that the focus is on net interest income, whereas shareholders will undoubtedly value other aspects of a bank's performance, as we shall see.

Despite this drawback, gap analysis is frequently used by banks in managing interest rate risk.

17.4 DURATION ANALYSIS

A different approach to evaluating interest rate risk, and one that nowadays most banks' annual reports present, is to explicitly consider the length of time assets and liabilities of a bank yield a certain stream of income or interest expense. The first step (**duration analysis**) involves calculating the so-called duration of a financial instrument, which essentially can be defined as a weighted average of the maturities of the payment stream generated by the assets or liabilities in question. This, of course, means that we have to resort to the present value concept first encountered in Chapter 5.

There it was shown that the present value of a stream of income (i.e., cash flow) earning R% per year is

$$P = \$X_1/(1 + R) + \$X_2/(1 + R)^2 + \dots + \$X_n/(1 + R)^n \qquad (17.16)$$

where $\$X_1$, $\$X_2$, …, $\$X_n$ is the cash flow received annually over n years. Suppose that we now weight the cash flow according to the number of years in the future it is expected to be received. Why? In part because the investor may not be indifferent to cash flows received next year versus ten years in the future. Alternatively, some investments may produce a cash flow immediately, while others will only begin to generate revenues many years into the future. Consequently, we rewrite (17.16) by first dividing both sides by P, so that we obtain

$$1 = [\$X_1/(1 + R)]/P + [\$X_2/(1 + R)^2]/P + \dots + [\$X_n/(1 + R)^n]/P \qquad (17.17)$$

Equation (17.17) calculated the present value of annual cash flows as a percentage of the present value of the entire stream of income. It is clear that the left-hand side must add up to one since each year's cash flow is now expressed as a fraction of the total cash flow. Now, weight each year's cash flow by the number of years before it is received. If we do so, then (17.17) becomes

$$dur = 1 \cdot [\$X_1/(1 + R)]/P + 2 \cdot [\$X_2/(1 + R)^2]/P + \dots + n \cdot [\$X_n/(1 + R)^n]/P \qquad (17.18)$$

where _dur_ is called the duration of an asset. Consider a simple numerical application of the duration concept. Suppose an asset expects to generate $250 in the first year and $375 in the second year. If the return on the asset is 5%, the present value of the cash flow is

$$P = \$250/1.05 + \$375/(1.05)^2 = \$238.10 + \$340.14 = \$578.24$$

The asset's duration is then

$$dur = 1 \cdot \$238.10/\$578.24 + 2 \cdot \$340.14/\$578.24 = 1 \cdot 0.4118 + 2 \cdot 0.5882 = 1.59$$

or slightly more than a year and a half. Put differently, the average waiting time until receiving the asset's present value is 1.59 years. The same principle can be used to evaluate the duration of a flow of disbursements or some other type of liability.

Note that in equation (17.16), it is assumed that the interest rate is constant. Depending on how large n is, that is, the number of years until maturity, this assumption may or may not be realistic. Banks, and their shareholders, may be equally interested in how the present value of a project is influenced by a change in interest rates and duration. It can be shown (we will skip the details here) that present value change due to an interest rate change is approximately equal to its duration. So we can write

$$\Delta P/P \approx - dur \cdot \Delta R \qquad (17.19)$$

where $\Delta P/P$ is the percentage change in the present value of an asset and ΔR is the change in the interest rate.[17] Continuing with the preceding numerical example, suppose the interest rate used in the previous present value calculations rises from 5% to 6%. Therefore, $\Delta R = 6 - 5 = 1$, and the present value of the asset then becomes

$$P = \$250/(1.06) + \$375/(1.06)^2 = \$235.85 + \$337.75 = \$569.60$$

In terms of equation (17.19) we obtain

$$\Delta P/P = (\$569.60 - \$578.24)/\$578.24 \approx -1 \bullet [(.....)/\$578.24]$$

The previous result simply says that, as the interest rate rises, the present value falls, just as we saw in Chapter 5. We can also evaluate the impact of the duration measure on a banking firm's balance sheet as follows. Recall that a firm's net worth is the difference between its assets and its liabilities, that is,

$$NW = A - L$$

Therefore, changes in net worth (see Chapter 9), are simply[18]

$$\Delta NW = \Delta A - \Delta L = (\Delta A/A)A - (\Delta L/L)L$$

Now, if we define dur_A and dur_L as the duration of assets and liabilities, respectively, then the previous expression can be rewritten as

$$\Delta NW = - dur_A[\Delta R/(1 + R)]A + dur_L(\Delta L/L)L$$

Or, finally,[19]

$$\Delta NW = - [\Delta R/(1 + R)](dur_A A - dur_L L) \qquad \textbf{(17.20)}$$

We can then define the gap, measured in terms of duration, as

$$durGAP = dur_A(A/L) - dur_L \qquad \textbf{(17.21)}$$

Notice that (17.21) says that, when $A=L$, $durGAP$ is simply the difference between asset and liability duration. Of course, net worth, that is, $A-L$, is usually different from zero. If $durGAP$ is positive then asset values change more than the value of liabilities.

Let's summarize what equation (17.21) predicts. First, the larger the duration gap, the greater is the exposure to interest rate risk. This can most easily be seen by noting that $durGAP$ rises if dur_A rises but none of the other variables rises. This means that there is a growing mismatch between assets and liabilities that can be a source of greater risk. Notice also that if A/L rises the exposure of net worth to risk also rises since, as will be recalled, $NW = A - L$.

Duration gap can be an effective way of determining the interest rate risk a bank is exposed to. Yet, as the preceding discussion also suggests, calculating duration gap is much more complicated than the simple gap measure outlined previously. Moreover, just because an interest rate changes does not mean that all interest rates throughout the term structure also change by the same amount (see Chapter 7). Yet, this is implicitly assumed in the duration gap calculation.

---

17 The symbol $\approx$ means approximately equal. Actually, the right hand side is $-dur \, \Delta R/(1 + R)$, but we will skip the exact expression for now, since at low interest rate levels this portion of the expression is very small.

18 Make changes on both sides of the equation defining NW. Next, multiply and divide each term on the right-hand side of the equation, respectively, by A/A and L/L.

19 Equation (17.20) is found by using equation (17.19), where $\Delta P/P = -dur \bullet (\Delta R/(1+R))$. Notice here the '=' replaces the '$\approx$' in (17.19) for convenience. Next, P is essentially replaced by NW or $A-L$ and dur by $dur_A - dur_L$ to obtain the equation shown.

17.5 THE PRINCIPAL–AGENT MODEL

The approaches considered in this chapter focus, directly or indirectly, on the bank's bottom line, that is, on the management of its balance sheet.

However, in the area of industrial organization, much research has been done on the relationship between managers and CEOs (chief executive officers) and their shareholders or debtholders. In this framework, CEOs are viewed as the agents while the shareholders (and possibly other debtholders) are viewed as the principals. This type of analysis is also clearly applicable to bank behaviour. The resulting issues have been given the name **principal–agent problem**.

The two groups may, however, be in conflict. We first saw this in Chapter 11 in the discussion of whether it makes any difference for a firm to borrow via equity issues or through the selling of bonds. The difficulty is that the agent may, at times, be more concerned with his or her own fortunes than with those of the owners. These concerns have led to much discussion about the "optimal" design of a contract to foster outcomes that satisfy both agents and principals (indeed, as we will see in Chapter 21, this has affected how some central bank governors are appointed). The design of such contracts also involves issues of attitudes toward risk. Thus, for example, if the CEO is risk averse but the shareholders are risk neutral, there will be conflict, since shareholders will want to maximize, say, dividends, regardless of risk, whereas the CEO will trade off risk versus return in a manner previously described in Chapter 13. This means that to understand the principal–agent problem, we have to make assumptions about the utility function of these two groups.

To illustrate some of the issues involved, consider the information in Table 17.6. The table gives the probability that the bank's CEO will generate profits of 5 or 15 depending on the amount of effort expended (which might be a combination of hours worked and skills for the job). If effort equals 1, the expected profit will be $3/4(5) + 1/4(15) = 7.5$; under effort equals 2, the expected profit is $1/4(5) + 3/4(15) = 12.5$. Clearly, shareholders will prefer the latter outcome. But how to achieve this if the salary of the CEO is fixed? Perhaps by providing the CEO with extra perks such as a generous expense account. Alternatively, a contract could specify a small salary if profits turn out to be less than expected and a bonus tied to the level of profits if they end up higher than, say, 7.5—the expected profit when effort equals 1. Not surprisingly, many companies have shown interest in tying CEOs' salaries to company performance.

At a fundamental level, the problems discussed above arise because it is not always possible or feasible for the principal to monitor the agent constantly. In addition, it is also possible that although shareholders take a long-term view of the firm's activities and prospects, the managers may take a short-term view. This is another source of conflict between agent and principal that can produce a less than optimal outcome for the firm. These, and the other problems referred to above, are manifestations of the problem of asymmetric information whereby the managers possess more information about the market the firm operates in than the shareholders do.

Table 17.6	A Numerical Example of the Principal–Agent Model	
	Profit	
Effort	5	15
1	3/4	1/4
2	1/4	3/4

Note: The above table gives the level of profit earned by a bank as a function of the level of effort produced by the CEO. Each of the four possible outcomes has a probability attached to it.

SUMMARY

- Banks perform a unique service in the financial sector. They are intermediaries that transform illiquid liabilities into liquid assets.

- There is no unique explanation of the ways in which banks accomplish the intermediation function. Accordingly, the chapter surveys a variety of models of bank behaviour.

- In this chapter, we examine the mechanics of deposit and loan creation in the banking system.

- One way of understanding what banks do is to consider the theory of multiple expansion of deposits. Because only a fraction of the funds deposited at banks needs to be kept immediately available (called targeted reserve ratio), banks can create additional deposits by some multiplier. The theory predicts that the deposit multiplier is $1/rr$, where rr is the targeted reserve ratio.

- The size of the deposit multiplier is ultimately a function of several variables such as the fraction of certain deposits held as reserves, seasonal influences, and the general level of interest rates.

- An alternative view of what banks do assumes that the banking firm maximizes profits. In doing so, it takes deposits and issues loans until it reaches the point at which marginal cost equals the marginal revenue of an additional dollar of deposits.

- The profit-maximization model can be used to explain the spread between loan rates and deposit rates.

- This model can also be useful in analyzing how the spread is influenced by government regulation, technological change, and the degree of competition in the industry.

- Banks have to manage assets and liabilities simultaneously. A simple way of determining whether interest rate changes will enhance or reduce the bank's revenues is to calculate the gap, the difference between interest-rate-sensitive assets ($IRSA$) and interest-rate-sensitive liabilities ($IRSL$) or $GAP = IRSA - IRSL$.

- Since cash flows and disbursements occur over time, we can make an adjustment to the usual present value calculations by evaluating duration, a weighted average of the present value of a cash flow. Duration can also be used to calculate a duration-adjusted gap called the duration gap. Duration gap is measured as $dur_A (A/L) - dur_L$, where A/L is the share of assets to liabilities, and dur_A and dur_B represent the duration of assets and liabilities (measured in years), respectively. Dur itself is the weighted (by years 1 to n) present value (a function of the interest rate R) of a stream of income ($\$X$) divided by the price ($P$) of the asset or liability, that is, $1 \cdot [\$X_1/(1 + R)]/P + \ldots + n \cdot [\$X_n/(1 + R)^n]/P$.

- Conflict can arise between the managers who run the bank and the shareholders who own the bank. This conflict gives rise to the principal–agent problem. Therefore, the way in which the managers are rewarded for their effort can have an important impact on the profitability of the firm.

IMPORTANT TERMS

deposit multiplier, 330
duration analysis, 341
excess reserves, 327
gap analysis, 339

principal–agent problem, 343
reserve ratio, 326
reserves, 327
target reserves, 327

PROBLEMS

1. At one time, some economists argued that banks should hold 100% reserves against their deposits. How would the deposit multiplier process work then?

2. If the target reserves on deposits is set to zero, the deposit multiplier is infinitely high. Is this statement true, false, or uncertain? Explain your answer.

3. Assume a reserve requirement of 10%. If deposits fall throughout the entire banking system by $1000 million and, thus, systemwide primary reserves decline by $100 million, necessitating loans of $900 million to be called in, will the deposit contraction process be completed? Use a balance sheet for your answer.

4. Suppose that in the example illustrated (Table 17.1), the Second Typical Canadian Bank decides not to lend out the extra $950 in reserves. How much deposit creation will take place in the banking system?

5. Show the impact of a cost-saving technological improvement on the banking firm model of Figure 17.1.

6. Suppose there are two types of deposits. Using Figure 17.1, describe the process by which the banking firm would select the profit-maximizing volume of deposits.

7. Suppose a bank's assets and liabilities have been reclassified into assets and liabilities that are rate sensitive and those that are not. The data are as follows:

Assets		Liabilities	
Rate-sensitive	$400M	Rate-sensitive	$200M
Fixed-rate	$200M	Fixed-rate	$400M

Evaluate the gap for this bank. What is the effect on total revenues of a 2% fall in interest rates?

8. Suppose that in the example illustrated in Table 17.1, the STCB chooses to purchase securities instead of making loans. How much deposit creation will take place in the banking system?

9. Suppose that in the example considered in Table 17.3, the FTCB decides to call in loans instead of selling securities. Trace the impact on deposits for the banking system as a whole.

10. Suppose that in the example considered in Table 17.3, the transfer is from demand deposits to time deposits. Trace the impact on the deposits of the banking system.

11. Suppose that in the first scenario considered in Table 17.4, the near-bank decreases its time deposits at the chartered banks. What would happen to M1? M2? M2+? Explain your answers.

12. Suppose that in the second scenario in Table 17.4, the near-banks keep reserves (against the rise in their time deposits outstanding) in the form of demand deposits at the chartered banks. What happens to M1? to M2? Explain your answers.

13. Suppose that financial instruments generate the following stream of income: $1000 in the first year, $1500 in the second year, and $2000 in the third year. Assuming that market interest rates are 6%, calculate the duration. What would happen to the market value of these instruments if the market interest rate were to rise to 9%?

14. Assume that a bank has assets of $100 million with duration of 15, and liabilities of $95 million with a duration of 9. Calculate the duration gap.

15. Assume that a bank has assets of $75 million with duration of 6 and liabilities of $65 million with a duration of 6. What is the duration gap? What would happen to net worth if market interest rates rose by 2%? How would the bank reduce interest rate risk in the event of an interest rate increase?

16. Show, using a figure such as Figure 17.1, that the interest rate charged to a good customer (i.e., low risk of default) would differ from one charged a bad customer (i.e., high risk of default).

17. Compare, using the framework developed in Figure 17.1, the spread for a bank that happens to have more "dishonest" customers than another.

18. Suppose a bank expects a cash flow of $100 a year over an eight-year period. Using an interest rate of 9%, calculate present value of the cash flow and its duration. Interpret duration in words.

19. True, false, or uncertain: "The higher the interest rate for a project of a given maturity, the lower the duration." Explain.

20. The principal and interest on a $1000 loan are to be repaid in 20 years. The principal and interest on another $1000 loan are to be repaid as follows: $900 in the first year and $100 in year 20. Given this information, which loan effectively has the shorter maturity and why? What is the duration of both loans?

21. Asset duration is 2.88, liability duration is 1.59, assets are $1000, liabilities are $920. What is the duration gap? How do you interpret the result?

DISCUSSION QUESTIONS

1. Perfect matching of assets and debts will result in a zero gap. In what sense is this statement true? Explain.

2. If a bank expects interest rates to fall, will it prefer a positive or a negative gap? Do you need to qualify your answer?

3. Does the growth of ABMs (automatic banking machines) increase or decrease the need for banks to keep cash reserves on hand?

4. Explain how intermediation implies benefits in terms of lower risks and higher liquidity but at the expense of delegation costs.

5. Does the theory of multiple expansion of deposits bring out the intermediation function of the banking firm? Explain.

6. Is it likely that different banks will have different target reserves? Why?

7. Explain why marginal costs for the banking firm must be rising while marginal revenues must fall. Also, why is average revenue above marginal revenue while marginal costs are above average costs? Use Figure 17.1 for your answer.

CANSIM QUESTIONS

Go to the CASIM II Web site. Download "Notes and coins outside the Bank of Canada" (V37173), and "deposits of members of the Canadian Payments Association" (V36650). Calculate the ratio of the sum of these two items as a percentage of personal savings deposits at chartered banks (V36814). This ratio gives an approximate indication of the reserve ratio discussed in this chapter. Plot the relevant data over a two-year period and explain the behaviour of this series in light of the discussion in this chapter.

References can be found on **www.mcgrawhill.ca/college/siklos**

Chartered Banks: History and Performance

LEARNING OBJECTIVES

After reading and studying this chapter, you should be able to

18.1 explain free banking and legal restrictions as they relate to the role of the banking sector and its interaction with the government

18.2 describe how banking developed from commercial banking and how and why banks obtain charters in Canada

18.3 identify the major aspects of the *Bank Act* and how the Act governs and restricts the behaviour of banks

18.4 list and describe the key issues facing the chartered banks today

18.4 determine the prospects and forces that will influence chartered banks in the future

18.5 explain the financial performance of chartered banks in Canada in terms of asset–liability management, size, and profitability

Having broadly outlined various analytical approaches to understanding bank behaviour and performance, we can turn to a description of the Canadian banking system.

This subject is a large and fascinating one. We begin this chapter with an examination of the chartered banks. (We'll turn to other depository institutions, as well as the rest of the financial system, in a separate chapter.) We review the **Bank Act** and its revisions over the years and reflect on the process of financial innovation and its influence on chartered banks. Finally, we describe the actual performance of chartered banks over the past few decades, paying particular attention to the way regulation and globalization have shaped their asset–liability management.

We will examine separately how regulatory practices have shaped and continue to shape bank behaviour in Canada (see Chapter 20). Therefore, what follows is a largely descriptive discussion of the history and performance of chartered banks over the decades.

18.1 THE EVOLUTION OF COMMERCIAL BANKING

When Canadians say "bank," they are usually referring to a **chartered bank**, which is a specific kind of private banking firm, federally chartered and regulated, that accepts deposits and makes loans.

The Canadian chartered banks can be called commercial banks, which is the term used in most countries to refer to privately owned institutions in the business of borrowing funds by the issue of short-term deposits or bank notes and of making short-term, self-liquidating loans to finance firms' inventories. (In the strict sense, a *self-liquidating loan* is one expected to generate funds for its own repayment.) Although custom as well as the inflation and deregulation of the 1970s and 1980s has fundamentally altered the way the chartered banks do business, they are, for the most part, still recognized by their commercial lending function.

Thus, our history of the chartered banks can be clarified by some discussion of the evolution of the way people think about how commercial banking should work.

FREE BANKING

We are used to thinking that social welfare demands that the banking industry be regulated to some extent.[1] The initial financial development of Canada was influenced by this view and by the cautious approach to banking taken in contemporary England. But it was also much influenced by the free banking experiments of Scotland and the United States in the first half of the nineteenth century. As the phrase suggests, **free banking** consists of a financial system that is largely unregulated and that can be entered easily without, for example, obtaining a charter or meeting huge capital requirements. Given the current trends toward financial deregulation around the world, it is not surprising that the study of previous experiences with minimal state regulation in financial affairs has blossomed in recent years. The basic philosophical tenet of economic activity unfettered by regulation is that individuals or groups of individuals will tend, perhaps in an evolutionary fashion, to seek out institutional arrangements that minimize the costs of doing business. Competition does not produce financial instability (say, from banks' reckless behaviour to obtain and hold on to customers), as critics contend; rather, it fosters stability. A lender of last resort, such as a central bank, is unnecessary. Competition leads to an economy with many banks, none of which monopolize the financial system. Thus, for example, Scotland had 19 banks by 1844 (after which free entry was no longer allowed). The four largest supplied almost half the notes in circulation.

Despite some controversy about the degree to which Scottish banks were actually unregulated (there were restrictions on the denominations of notes that private banks could issue, and some barriers to entry), the overall evidence on the success of free banks appears positive.

> The [Scottish] banking system made rapid strides in both stability and efficiency. Freedom to issue notes ensured healthy competition and adequate banking services wherever they were in demand. The regular notes exchanges made the banks watchdogs of one another and prevented any bank from getting seriously out of line with the general development of the economy. The notes exchanges were forerunners, in fact, of modern clearing houses. Scotland did not altogether avoid bank failures, but its record with respect to stability was much better than those of most countries in similar stages of development.[2]

The small geographical size of Scotland may also have played a role, as well as the proximity of the Bank of England, which could have, in principle, acted as a lender of last resort.

LEGAL RESTRICTIONS

A different perspective on the evolution of banks is suggested by those proponents of the *legal restrictions view*. They claim that regulation has shaped our current financial institutions and specifically that only regulation forces the public to hold noninterest-bearing government debt (that is, currency). In a laissez-faire or free banking world, banks as intermediaries would, for example, offer interest-earning currency in small denominations suitable for transaction purposes. (It will come as no surprise that not everyone is so sanguine about the possibility of interest-earning money.)

---

1 One reason is fear that the failure of one bank will become contagious, leading to additional failures. As we will see in Chapter 25, such *bank runs* have been common in the United States throughout that country's financial history.
2 R. Cameron, *Banking in the Early Stages of Industrialization* (New York: Oxford University Press, 1967):170. The United States's experience with free banking was apparently not so successful. See G. Gorton, "Banking Theory and Free Banking History," *Journal of Monetary Economics* 16 (1985): 267–76.

18.2 DEVELOPMENT OF COMMERCIAL BANKING IN CANADA

We think of banks as institutions that accept deposits and make loans. In the eighteenth and early nineteenth centuries, however, an equally important function was issuing bank notes. Provided these notes could be easily converted into *specie* (not always true, as some found to their sorrow), they were "as good as gold" and far more convenient for transactions. But a government does not want its people (still less, its merchants, traders, and developers) exposed to the dangers of "money" that may suddenly become worthless.[3] So many countries began to regulate the issue of bank notes.

Another contemporary convention was the requirement that any joint-stock operation (what we would call a limited liability company or a corporation) obtain a charter from the appropriate legislature. Banking charters especially were not easy to obtain, particularly in the farflung colonies of Great Britain, which was developing a tradition of careful, conservative banking.

In 1792 and again in 1807 and 1808, groups of Montreal merchants formed banking ventures that failed because they could not obtain permission to issue notes. In 1817, another group applied for a charter and meanwhile opened its doors as the Bank of Montreal. The application, caught in political battles and bureaucratic delay, was not granted until 1822. Meanwhile the Bank of New Brunswick and the Bank of Upper Canada were granted charters in 1820 and 1821, respectively.

All these charters essentially authorized a bank organization to

- issue notes.
- lend for commercial purposes and incur an indebtedness up to a stipulated amount.
- open branches (usually).[4]
- report to the government on its financial activities periodically.

This conservative, regulated pattern, based on a British model,[5] set the standard for the Canadian banking system, one quite different from that already under way in the United States.[6]

More Canadian banks were chartered during the next quarter century, all in growing urban areas. Although the country went through hard economic times in 1837–38 and again in 1847–50, few of these banks failed, perhaps because they were so few (some had near-monopolies in their areas).

Because bank charters were usually granted to men with the "right" sociopolitical ties, objections from populists were inevitable. They pleaded for free—unchartered—banking to establish small banks under local control with local funds, to ease the introduction of banking facilities in areas of smaller population, and to expand the effective market for government securities (which were becoming an important source of financing). The populists got their way in Upper Canada in 1850, when the legislature introduced a free banking statute, modelled on banking laws in place in New York State. This free banking was not, however, entirely unregulated. There were, for example, rules specifying the minimum start-up capital as well as a requirement that notes be redeemable in specie on demand. And charters were still available (the U.S. states that adopted free banking laws simultaneously abolished chartering). Moreover, banks had emergency access to funds in markets in London and New York.

---

3 A healthy amount of self-interest was also involved since, by monopolizing the note issue, governments also generate revenue for themselves (called seigniorage, as we saw in Chapter 2).

4 New Brunswick specifically forbade branches, and Upper Canada authorized them. Lower Canada made no explicit provision either way, but given the absence of restrictions and subsequent history, we may assume they were permitted.

5 It had also been the model for the First and the Second Banks of the United States in 1792 and 1816, respectively. But the individualistic Americans distrusted "big money." Each bank was successful, but the U.S. Congress would renew neither charter.

6 Yet, the adoption of a nationwide branch banking system was inspired by the writings of Alexander Hamilton, the first Secretary of the Treasury of the United States. See R.M. Breckinridge, *The History of Banking in Canada* (Washington, D.C.: United States Government Printing Office, 1910): 7–8. This volume was published as part of the U.S. National Monetary Commission's report.

Free banking was not much of a success in Canada. Only five new banks were founded under the *Free Banking Act*; two failed and the others converted to legislative charters, which permitted branches and the issuing of bank notes. Since mortgages and personal loans were prohibited throughout this whole early period, banking was largely limited to commercial lending activities. By the 1860s, however, an important and a peculiarly Canadian provision had widened the scope of banking activities. The banks were permitted to lend against goods still in the possession of the borrower. In other words, the collateral could be a bill of lading or a warehouse receipt—often for agricultural goods[7]—an arrangement that does not meet the strict definition of a self-liquidating loan. This famous rule, known as Section 88 or the "pledge section" was introduced in 1859. It gave the banks an important role in Canadian agriculture and mineral resource development. But the fact that the collateral had to be available when the loan was granted (as opposed to some expectation that it would be available sometime in the future) severely restricted the growth of economic activity in Canada.

18.3 TRACING THE EVOLUTION OF BANKING REGULATION: THE *BANK ACT*

About the same time that commercial banking and other financial services were spreading throughout the infant Canada, government was beginning to intervene in the emerging financial system more effectively and on a broader scale than in earlier periods. In Canada, perhaps the most important regulation of banks has taken the form of the federal *Bank Acts* throughout the years. Through them we can trace the development of banking since Confederation.

THE FIRST *BANK ACT*

The *Constitution Act, 1867* granted the newly formed federal government of Canada monopoly powers in all areas of banking and currency issue. Shortly thereafter Parliament enacted the *Bank Act* of 1871, the first of a series of statutes that would regulate the activities of all chartered banks.

Perhaps the most important break from the past was the gradual introduction of a state monopoly on the issue of currency. Initially, the government monopolized the issue of $1 and $2 notes, called Dominion notes. Private bank notes, although not legal tender, could be redeemed for specie or Dominion notes. (Private bank notes remained popular. For example, between 1873 and 1913, they represented approximately 95% of all notes and demand and notice deposits held at chartered banks.) One possible reason for monopolizing the low-denomination note issue was to protect the least sophisticated individuals from the effects of a bank failure. Assuming the least sophisticated (and likely the poorest) individuals held small denomination notes, a government monopoly in the issue of such notes would, in effect, represent a state guarantee that these notes could be redeemed for goods and services.

THE *BANK ACT* OVER THE YEARS

The first *Bank Act* came into effect in 1871 (as noted above), and the legislation was to be revised every ten years. Table 18.1 summarizes the Act's history by listing the years in which revisions were enacted and some of the most important characteristics of each. It is, of course, possible to discuss only some of the principal provisions of the legislation enacted over the past 130 years or so.

Since there is considerable information in Table 18.1, bold characters highlight important milestones in the history of *Bank Act* legislation. Although the choice of important *Bank Acts* is somewhat arbitrary, they do highlight instances in which the legislation reflected the need for major structural reforms in the banking sector.

---

7 Only a select group of agricultural commodities, such as grains, qualified initially.

Information about financial legislation can be found at the Department of Finance's Web site **www.fin.gc.ca**

We can spot two overriding or summarizing themes: (1) widening of the scope of chartered banking operations, and (2) concern over bank safety. An example of the increasing scope was the frequent broadening of the "pledge section." The types of commodities for use as collateral were redefined with the introduction of every *Bank Act* until after World War II, when restrictions were essentially lifted and banks allowed to stipulate their own collateral requirements.

The concern for bank safety was first met in 1891 with the creation of a Bank Circulation Redemption Fund to guard against the loss of funds when a note issue became valueless because a bank had failed. Further bank safety enforcement provisions over the years included the extension of auditing of bank activities, culminating in the creation of government supervision of the banking system, and the introduction of deposit insurance.[8]

In addition, many regulations were altered or dropped over the years because they proved unnecessary or inconsistent with the prevailing financial environment. For example, initially, all bank directors had to be British subjects. This restriction was later relaxed to apply only to a majority of directors and subsequently, it was dropped altogether.

The degree to which *Bank Act* revisions represented fundamental changes in the regulations governing chartered banks has varied considerably over time. The first two sets of regulatory changes were fairly minor. The first major overhaul of the financial system took place in 1891 with the introduction of more stringent start-up capital requirements and more extensive supervision over private note issue. During the first half of the twentieth century, four important events shaped revisions of the *Bank Act*: the crisis of 1907, the Great Depression, the creation of the Bank of Canada, and the push for global markets. Of course, the two world wars also played roles in the timing of regulatory reforms.

THE CRISIS OF 1907

The crisis of 1907 originated, like many Canadian recessions, in the United States. Several bank failures there triggered bank runs. Part of the problem may have been that the relative importance of the agricultural sector in the activity of the U.S. economy and the banks' heavy loans to farmers led to seasonal interest rate fluctuations that corresponded with seasonality in the demand for money. Similar difficulties faced Western Canadian farmers, and a very poor crop in 1907 exacerbated the situation. The Canadian government stepped in to facilitate the provision of credit. Thereafter, the role of government in providing credit and in influencing the portfolios of chartered banks became increasingly important.

The need to finance the war and the resulting disruption in the international payments flow led to the *Finance Act*, 1914, and effectively made the government the lender of the last resort, by providing access to Dominion notes, until the Bank of Canada was formed in 1935. This change also meant that Canada was effectively no longer under the gold standard. The *Finance Act* also heralded the introduction of a monetary market of sorts: The government advanced notes against its own securities without any constraint on expansion.

THE 1920s AND 1930s

The failure of the Home Bank (1923), which a royal commission blamed on the misconduct of several officers, led to more stringent oversight of the chartered banks. And the government's role as lender of last resort was reinforced when it advanced grants to the Home's creditors.

This increasing regulation may have proved its value in the 1930s. The Great Depression brought a tremendous contraction to the U.S. banking system, but Canadian banks experienced no failures or runs during that period. Some analysts think that Canada's salvation was the stability provided by a banking system with few institutions and an extensive branch framework. An

---

8 Deposit insurance is discussed separately in Chapter 16.

Table 18.1	**The Bank Act: A Chronology**

Enacted	Principal Characteristics
1871	• **Definition of a bank** • **Decennial revision process** • Minimum denomination $4
1881	• Scope of banking operations widened to increase commercial borrowing opportunities • Provisions to enhance security of the financial system
1891	• Increased start-up capital (an entry barrier) • Bank Circulation Redemption Fund introduced • Notes to circulate at par
1901	• Increase in the number of products against which commercial concerns could borrow • Canadian Bankers' Association given oversight powers over members
1914	• **Provision for bank audits** • Provision for loans to be made in anticipation of sales (easing financial distress of farmers) • *Separate Finance Act*: **government lender of last resort**
1924	• Changes in reporting financial transactions • Continuance of the *Finance Act*, 1914 • Tightening of requirements for creation of banks (following the failure of the Home Bank)
1935	• **Severe limits on private note issue in anticipation of the Bank of Canada** • **Reserve requirements to be held with the Bank of Canada** • Permitted collateral for commercial loans expanded yet again
1945	• Bank financial statements to be made public • Ban on further issue or reissue of private bank notes • Creation of the Industrial Development Bank (separate act)
1954	• **Permission for banks to offer mortgages issued** under the *National Housing Act* • Legal reserve ratio raised; control by the Bank of Canada • Establishment of a money market • Issuances of Bank of Canada advances
1967	• **Deposit insurance introduced** • **Removal of interest rate ceiling** • **Banks free to enter mortgage-lending field** • Secondary reserve requirement introduced
1981	• **Subsidiaries of foreign banks permitted charters in Canada** (*Schedule II*) • Changes in reserve requirements • Conventional and residential mortgages capped at 10% of Canadian dollar deposits • Banks permitted entry to new fields: financial leasing and data-processing services • **Creation of the Canadian Payments Association**
1980s (interim measures)	• Increase in the limit on domestic assets of foreign banks (to 16% of industrywide assets) • Creation of position of superintendent of financial institutions • Approval for banks to acquire discount brokerage firms
1991	• **Comprehensive banking law** • **Permission for chartered banks to own trust companies** (but they continue to be barred from selling life insurance) • **Maintenance of rule that chartered banks must be widely held** • Trust companies permitted to offer commercial loans • **Chartered bank reserve requirements to be phased out** • Real estate holdings permitted for as much as 70% of capital
1998 (interim measure)	• Proposed bank mergers denied
1999	• New legislation dealing with foreign branches in Canada
2001	• **Bill C-8 to Amend the Bank Act and Establish a Financial Consumer Agency of Canada (Royal Assent 14 June 2001, entry into force 24 October 2001)** • Monitor public commitments made by financial institutions designed to protect the interests of consumers • New Schedule III banks allowed to operate in Canada with fewer branching restrictions • Bring legislation in line with WTO rulings (supersedes NAFTA rulings) • Significantly ease branching and other restrictions on business carried out in Canada • Define rules for mergers and acquisitions but requires ministerial approval

Go to
**http://www.cba.ca
/en/default.asp** and
search for Bank
Milestones
for an interactive
guide to changes in
the Canadian bank-
ing sector since
1867.

Sources: A. Power, and D.K. Varma, *The Touche Ross Guide to Financial Reporting for Canadian Banks* (Toronto: CCH Canadian Ltd., 1984); *Bank Act: Orders and Regulations with Guidelines, Interpretation Bulletins and Other Regulatory Documents*, 3d ed. (Don Mills, Ont.: Richard de Boo Publishers, 1989); *The Canadian Bank Act 1980* (Price Waterhouse Canada); J.W. O'Brien, and G. Lermer, *Canadian Money and Banking*, 2d ed. (Toronto: McGraw-Hill, 1969); A.B. Jamieson, *Chartered Banking in Canada* (Toronto: Ryerson Press, 1953), "Restructuring the Canadian Financial Industry," *Bank of Canada Review* (Winter 1992–93): 21–45; Department of Finance, "Foreign Branch Banking Legislation Comes into Force," *News Release* 99-060, June 1999, available at **www.fin.gc.ca**.

alternative view suggests that an effective government bailout saved a banking system that had become essentially insolvent. In any event, government involvement in the workings of the financial system increased and culminated in the creation of a central bank, the Bank of Canada.

THE MODERN PERIOD

The end of World War II heralded a period of strong economic growth, and banks lived in a world of relative calm. It was shattered by the oil price shocks of the 1970s. Consequent inflation necessitated the introduction of new financial products; the prospect of financial innovations was encouraged by the uncertainty and volatility of interest rates during the 1970s, which made it difficult for banks to manage their assets and liabilities in a profitable manner.

In general, financial legislation after the 1970s was also meant to liberalize the regulations governing chartered bank behaviour. In a break with the past, Canada, like most governments around the world, began to *deregulate* in many areas—that is, to reduce its regulation of business activities, including approval for new investments and types of products. For the chartered banks, deregulation has meant gradual removal of impediments to the type of products offered and to restrictions on the kinds of firms eligible to apply for a charter. Thus, chartered banks were allowed to enter the residential mortgage-lending field, to engage in financial leasing, and to provide data-processing services, among other financial services. By 1981, subsidiaries of foreign banks could obtain a bank charter; domestic Canadian banks became Schedule A (now called *Schedule I*) banks and foreign subsidiaries Schedule B (now *Schedule II* and *Schedule III*) banks. Permission for chartered banks to acquire brokerage firms led to a buying spree during the late 1980s and early 1990s. Thus, for example, the Bank of Montreal purchased Nesbitt Thomson in 1987 and Burns Fry in 1994, the Bank of Nova Scotia purchased McLeod, Young, Weir in 1988, and the Canadian Imperial Bank of Commerce bought Wood Gundy. During the same year the Royal Bank acquired Dominion Securities. Finally, in 1993, the Toronto-Dominion Bank purchased Marathon Brokerage.

The number of chartered banks had grown to 66 by January 1991. The number now stands at 70.[9] Restrictions remain on the overall size of the foreign segment of the chartered banking system, but they have not, so far, proven to be a constraint on the growth of foreign banks in Canada. Moreover, the government has taken steps to end the separation of commercial lending from securities underwriting. (The same steps were taken with new legislation that took effect in the United States at the end of 1999; other nations' financial systems have no such separation of financing functions.)

THE *BANK ACT* OF 1991

So rapid was the process of financial innovation and deregulation that the *Bank Act* of 1981 was outdated before it was passed. As a result, existing legislation, which did not provide for contingencies or activities outside the legislation, were forbidden territory (the legal term is *ultra vires*). For this reason, several stopgap reform measures (see Table 18.1) were introduced during the 1980s, and the *Bank Act* of 1991,[10] written in coordination with some other new financial legislation, offered many changes. Pressure also came from a number of provincial initiatives. For example, Quebec permitted financial institutions under its jurisdiction to offer a complete range of financial services as well as commercial–financial links.[11] Previously, we also saw how the federal and Ontario governments agreed to lift restrictions on ownership of securities dealers. Thus,

The list of banks in Canada can be found at **www.cba.ca**

---

9 Nineteen of these are domestic Schedule I banks (for example, Royal, Bank of Montreal, TD, CIBC, Bank of Nova Scotia, Canadian Western Bank, Laurentian, National), twenty-nine foreign bank subsidiaries, or Schedule II banks (for example, ING Bank, HSBC), and twenty-two foreign bank branches (for example, Citibank, Deutsche Bank) now referred to as Schedule III banks.

10 The Senate passed the new *Bank Act* on 13 December 1991. The statutes were proclaimed in June 1992.

11 See *Reform of Financial Institutions in Quebec: Objectives, Guiding Principles and Action Plan* (Government of Quebec: Associate Minister for Finance and Privatization, October 1987).

the need for a major overhaul of the financial sector became evident to all interested parties. One of the consequences of globalization is that the new *Bank Act* permits an institution to engage in any financial activity unless it is specifically prohibited from doing so in the new Act.

The current regulatory environment favours the creation of equal or near-equal competition throughout the financial sector and thus the virtual elimination of the *four pillars approach* to financial institutions (see Chapter 3). Therefore, instead of legislating for one branch of the financial system in isolation from the others, the new Act introduces a comprehensive set of reforms for all types of financial institutions, especially chartered banks, trust companies, and insurance companies.

For example, the 1991 *Bank Act* phased out required reserves,[12] levelling some terms of competition between near-banks, which never had had to meet the requirements, and chartered banks, which had. This change does not mean that banks do not hold reserves. Rather, banks were required to average, at a minimum, zero reserves over some specified period of time. However, since both the Bank of Canada and other central banks commonly refer to this as a state of zero-reserve requirement, we will follow their wording.

Although reserve requirements have long been a cornerstone of bank regulation, they no longer seemed necessary for ensuring the safety of the financial system. The ease with which liquidity is available has considerably reduced the need for idle cash to be held as reserves, and the Bank of Canada possesses more effective means of controlling the amount of liquidity in the economy. Moreover, other countries, including Switzerland, have eliminated reserve requirements with no sign that their financial systems have become more unstable. Finally, the banking system itself has become more efficient, reducing the need for holding cash reserves. All financial institutions are now permitted to offer a much wider range of financial services within each branch, such as portfolio management and investment advice. Other services, such as trust services, can be "networked," that is, offered via subsidiaries or related institutions.

Another example of the Act's levelling of competition is the provision that allows chartered banks to pursue real estate development previously engaged in by trust and insurance companies. To get around previous restrictions on owning or erecting buildings not for their own use, several of Canada's largest chartered banks had created wholly owned realty subsidiaries. This brought banks into conflict with other private developers, who borrowed from the same banks, and thus raised the question of the fairness of a market in which the lenders were competing with potential borrowers for the same contracts. Even as the legislation was being debated during 1991, several chartered banks began to purchase trust companies. Thus, in 1993 the Royal Bank acquired Royal Trust. In 1991 the Laurentian Bank purchased Standard Trust and in 1992 it purchased General Trust and Guardian Trust. During the same year, the Canadian Imperial Bank of Commerce purchased Morgan Trust, and the Toronto-Dominion Bank acquired Central Guarantee Trust and, later, Canada Trust. Moreover, a number of insurance companies already own trust companies, and further takeovers are imminent.

Perhaps one of the greatest difficulties facing the legislators when revising the *Bank Act* was the ownership rules, because Schedule I banks were required to be widely held, whereas trust and mortgage loan companies were closely held institutions. The 1991 *Bank Act* produced a complex compromise. Essentially, trust, mortgage loan, and insurance companies would continue to be closely held. These institutions now came under the Schedule II designation. However, federal institutions with capital of $750 million or more were required to have at least 35% of shares widely held within five years.[13]

One major source of division left in the financial industry concerns whether banks should be permitted to sell insurance directly. The chartered banks argue that the current *Bank Act* limits consumer choice, and that nonbanking institutions have been able to encroach on the traditional lending

---

12 Implementation of the phase-out began in November 1991 and was completed before the July 1994 deadline. See "The Evolution of Routine Bank of Canada Advances to Direct Clearers," *Bank of Canada Review* (October 1992): 3–22.

13 For more details on these and other changes, see "Restructuring the Canadian Financial Industry," *Bank of Canada Review* (Winter 1992–93): 21–46.

function of the chartered banks.[14] The insurance industry counters that allowing banks to sell insurance directly will lead to the effective disappearance of an independent insurance industry. They point to trusts and investment dealers who have been largely taken over by the chartered banks.[15] Obviously, the insurance industry has not disappeared (see the next chapter).

THE *BANK ACT* OF 2001

At the end of June 1999, the minister of finance outlined a "framework" that, after consultations, provides a basis for the next *Bank Act*.[16] The proposed framework had the following objectives:

1. Provide all financial institutions with "flexibility" to enter new lines of business subject, however, to some constraints. In particular, chartered banks will continue to be barred from automobile leasing and the sale of life insurance at the retail level, and ownership limitations will persist.

2. Lighten "whenever possible" the regulatory burden on all institutions.

3. Increase consumer protection via the creation of a new agency to ensure financial institutions comply with government-mandated protection policies.

4. Improve the monitoring of financial institutions' policies toward lending to small and medium-sized businesses.

The vision outlined by the minster of finance was intended to enhance competitiveness. For example, trust companies would be permitted to diversify their balance sheets through access to investment vehicles they were previously prevented from using. Credit unions would be allowed to form national alliances or networks, presumably to take advantage of economies of scale. Access to the CPA would be available to life insurers and, at last, attempts were made to ease the costs of entry into the financial sector. Finally, banks would be able to form holding companies, as in the United States and the United Kingdom, permitting them to offer nontraditional banking services and permit separation into regulated and nonregulated companies.

Read more about the GATS on the World Trade Organization's Web site
www.wto.org

As with all proposals, the devil is in the details. Interestingly, there was little recognition in the proposals about global pressures for reform. In 1999, the WTO General Agreement on Trade in Services (GATS) came into force, and Canada is a participant. The GATS intends to liberalize cross-border transactions by breaking down the barriers that, for example, discriminate between domestic and foreign banks. Canada took a step in this direction with legislation enacted in December 1999 (see Table 18.1). One of the responses to globalization has been consolidation in the financial sector worldwide, but, as we have seen, the government is reluctant to allow big domestic banks to merge with other large domestic banks. Yet, it is precisely such pressures that some analysts deem vital to the growth of the largest banks, as noted earlier. Moreover, the proposals struck some observers as attempts to patch up existing problems or assuage lobbying interests. As more than one analyst has pointed out, however, the ideal financial legislation is one that provides equality of opportunity, not equality of outcome.[17]

The thorny issue of ownership remains. Plans are to create a three-tier regime with large, medium-sized, and small banks. Banks with equity of less than $1 billion will be deemed to be small in size and, therefore, not subject to ownership restrictions. Medium-sized banks (equity of $1 to $5 billion) will also be permitted to be closely held, but subject to a significant portion of widely held shares (35%). The top tier of banks (over $5 billion in equity) must be widely held, but the 10% rule will be relaxed considerably (to 20%).

---

14 Canadian Bankers' Association News, Press Release of 16 November 1995. In the 1996 Budget Speech, Finance Minister Paul Martin confirmed that banks will not be permitted to sell insurance directly.

15 Banks point out that the insurance industry fears competition in what they feel is an inefficient industry.

16 See Department of Finance, "Reforming Canada's Financial Services Sector: A Framework for the Future," 25 June 1999, available at **www.fin.gc/finserv/docs/finservrept_e.pdf**.

17 E.H. Neave, and F. Milne, "Revising Canada's Financial Regulation: Analysis and Recommendations," C.D. Howe Institute Commentary, 1998.

Learn about the
reforms at
**www.fin.gc.ca/
access/fininste.
html**

Related to the ownership question is the contentious issue of mergers. Although the finance minister retains final say about mergers in the new legislation, a merger review process is now in place. For institutions with more than $5 billion in equity, a formal review will take place, with public input. The Competition Bureau, the Office of the Superintendent of Financial Institutions, and the House Committee on Finance will provide advice and make recommendations to the finance minister. Banks wanting to merge will now have to submit a Public Interest Impact Assessment (PIIA). The PIIA must contain an explanation of the rationale for the merger. It must also outline the costs in the form of branch closures and the impact on the level of service offered to the public. Moreover, the PIIA must explain how the merged bank will fare in terms of international competitiveness, as well as the impact the merger will have on the financial industry as a whole.

At long last, after many years of study and volumes of proposals, the finance minister tabled a Bill in June 2000 to reform Canada's financial services sector. The details of the legislation, almost one thousand pages long, are intended to be a comprehensive bill linking all the various existing pieces of legislation covering financial sector market participants. There are now three types of banks. Schedule I banks are essentially the large, domestically owned chartered banks; Schedule II banks are foreign bank subsidiaries operating in Canada; Schedule III banks are branches of foreign institutions that have been authorized to do banking in Canada and, therefore, receive permission to branch directly into Canada (see footnote 9 for examples of banks under each one of these headings). Schedule II banks are also members of the CDIC (see Chapter 16).

The *Bank Act* of 2001 is part of a single bill that governs the behaviour not only of traditional banks but of other financial institutions, most notably insurance companies. In addition, following the U.S. lead (see Chapter 25), bank holding companies will be permitted. This change will enable financial institutions to operate a variety of independent subsidiaries in all areas of finance. The blending of banks and insurance companies especially will continue and intensify in coming years as the latter are being turned into stock companies (see next chapter).

The new legislation also provides enhanced consumer protection, via the creation of the Financial Consumer Agency of Canada, and requires that financial institutions provide a minimal set of banking services at an "affordable" cost and provide extensive details and advance notice about branch closures. In addition, a Canadian Financial Services Ombudsman (CFSO) is to hear complaints from consumers and small businesses about their relationships with financial institutions. All banks and federally legislated financial institutions will be required to join the CFSO.

The final piece of legislation was given Royal Assent in June 2001. It is no longer just a Bank Act, but now covers virtually the entire financial services sector by merging several older pieces of legislation.

18.4 THE CHANGING BUSINESS OF BANKING

INNOVATION

The pace of change in the worldwide economy continues unabated, impinging on the financial system. Political and economic developments, from the crumbling of the Iron Curtain to the Canada–U.S. Free Trade Agreement (FTA) and the North American Free Trade Agreement (NAFTA), have had a lasting impact on the Canadian financial sector. Several recently introduced innovations also seem likely to have a substantial impact in the years to come.

A theme common to many *Bank Act* revisions has been the desire to adapt regulations to existing and future financial innovations. Regulations that cause financial institutions to invest resources into areas either unlegislated or unforeseen in the existing legislation have also encouraged innovations. An example is provided by *automated banking machines* (ABMs). They spread across the country at a remarkable pace, quickly becoming the method of choice for many individuals' transactions with a bank. Yet banking legislation did not foresee various associated problems (such as liability in the event of theft or fraud). Consequently, the legal system had to create precedents governing ABMs and their use. Table 18.2 provides some aggregate statistics that show the tremendous growth of ABMs in Canada. The data in the table are a bit misleading because the apparent falling off of the number of bank ABMs fails to capture a trend that began in the late 1990s. By the end of 2003 there were actually more than 42 000 ABMs in Canada, but only 39% were owned by banks, the rest being operated by private concerns. You may have seen the emergence of the ubiquitous "white box" that dispenses cash only (at a fee, of course) but is not owned by the banks.

Not all types of innovation are so well received at first. The *debit card* is essentially a means of settling transactions without cash or cheque via an electronic transfer of funds from, say, the purchaser's bank account to the merchant's bank account. Although such cards offer major advantages including lower transactions costs for the banking industry (less paper and fewer human operations are required to transfer funds between bank accounts) and increased security for bank customers (the risk of loss of cash is lowered), the public was slow at first to accept them, despite banks heralding them as the arrival of yet another revolution in the financial industry.

Visit Interac's
Web site at
www.interac.org

Debit cards, however, have since become the most popular method of payment in Canada. No doubt the formation of Interac, an association permitting shared payment through ABMs and point-of-sale terminals (POS), has greatly enhanced the appeal of debit cards. As popular as debit cards are, one should not ignore the tremendous growth and popularity of Internet and telephone banking. In 2000, it is estimated that there were almost six million customers using Internet banking, having grown almost eightfold since 1999. It has overtaken telephone banking, at least in terms of the number of transactions, with approximately 190 million transactions completed over the Internet in 2003, versus 90 million transactions completed over the phone.[18]

The above developments suggest that the business of banking is changing. No longer are chartered banks simply deposit-taking and commercial lending institutions. Instead, the banks are full-service financial institutions. As a consequence, chartered banks are increasingly relying on fee-based services, while interest expenses are declining in importance.[19]

New instruments and tools continue to be offered as banks promise the cashless society. Cards now exist that take the place of money altogether. Such cards, occasionally referred to as "smart" cards, work very much like phone cards currently in use in Canada with one notable exception, namely that once all the "money" on a card is used up, it can be "recharged" at a local bank (for a fee, of course).

But with innovations come concerns about security and confidentiality of funds stored in effect "electronically," prompting concerns among regulators about how to deal with new forms of theft.

Perhaps even more revolutionary is e-money, or the transfer of funds over the Internet. This method bypasses completely the conventional deposit-taking institutions, unless they begin to provide

Table 18.2	Number of Bank ABMs in Canada		
	Year	Number	Percentage bank-owned
	1995	13 261	76
	1996	13 911	75
	1997	14 484	75
	1998	15 481	65
	1999	16 626	62
	2000	17 174	54
	2001	16 806	47
	2002	16 546	41
	2003	16 624	39
	2004	16 160	35

Source: Canadian Bankers' Association Research and Data Service, *Canadian Bank Facts* (various annual editions), and Interac Association.

Note: The data are at Oct. 31 of each year. "Number" refers to bank-owned machines.

18 Data were obtained from **www.cba.ca.**
19 See "Competition, Competitiveness, and the Public Interest," Background Paper #1 Task Force on the Future of the Canadian Financial Sector, September 1998, available at **www.fin.gc.ca/toce/1999/finserv_e.html**.

ECONOMICS FOCUS 18.1 — CHARTERED BANKS AND FREE TRADE

In October 1987 the Canadian and U.S. governments completed the Canada–U.S. Free Trade Agreement (FTA), and during the summer of 1992, the governments of Canada, the United States, and Mexico reached agreement on a similar treaty called the North American Free Trade Agreement (NAFTA). The primary objective of free trade is the eventual elimination of trade barriers and access for each country to the others' markets with a minimum of government interference.

The passage of these pieces of legislation has not led to a rush to buy banks in either Mexico or the United States, although the Bank of Montreal, for example, has been acquiring interests in both U.S. and Mexican banks. The peso crisis of the early 1990s (see Chapter 8) and the savings and loan debacle of the 1980s (see Chapter 25) did not help make the U.S. or Mexican banks terribly attractive to Canadian banks. It is interesting, however, to see what the agreement specifies for financial institutions. (The NAFTA provisions for the financial sector are similar.)

- U.S. bank subsidiaries in Canada are exempt from the 16% ceiling on assets of foreign banks as a percentage of total domestic chartered bank assets.
- Canada drops its restrictions on U.S. firms' purchases of stock in federally regulated insurance and trust companies.
- U.S. firms seeking entry into Canadian financial markets are treated like Canadian applicants in the review process.
- Banks are permitted to underwrite and deal in debt securities fully backed by the federal government or the provinces.

Although the U.S. financial system is more fractionalized and regulated in some respects than the Canadian, the FTA ensures that any new federal regulations will apply to Canadian banks operating in the United States and vice versa. It is important to note, however, that provincial and state regulations of the financial sector are unaffected. Therefore, considerable limitation to U.S. access is still possible, though the U.S. federal government, in the wake of the savings and loan scandal, is taking a more active role than previously in regulating the entire financial system.

Questions for Discussion

1. Is free trade in financial services as important as free trade in goods? Can such trade be regulated properly or prevented?
2. Even if there is free trade, what type of economic and noneconomic considerations would make Canadian chartered banks hesitate to buy U.S. or Mexican banks, or to start a bank in either country?

Wells Fargo
wellsfargo.com

a network or some framework to help facilitate financial transactions for their clients. Indeed, all banks have a presence on the World Wide Web. The overall implication is that the branch of the future is more likely to involve a PC screen at home than a line in front of a teller's window.[20]

These developments suggest the potential for "virtual banks," that is, banks with an electronic presence but no physical presence in Canada, such as ING Direct. Indeed, Wells Fargo, one of the largest U.S. banks, began to offer commercial loans and other banking services to Canadian customers. Clearly, this type of activity was not contemplated by the *Bank Act*. After considerable discussion, the government passed into law in 1999 an amendment to the *Bank Act*. Essentially, "virtual banks" are permitted to set up shop in Canada, but are limited to accepting deposits over $150 000 while their lending activities are exclusively at the wholesale level.[21]

OTHER ISSUES

Other issues that *Bank Acts* and other Canadian financial legislation have attempted to address over the years include a variety of economic and social concerns. Two recurring points are market concentration and regional concerns.

---

20 One study that confirms what has been stated elsewhere in this text, namely that regulators will avoid the chance to implement much-needed reforms (i.e., the regulator as lagging indicator of institutional change), is J.L. Evans, "Technical Change and the Regulation of Financial Services," in L. Mints and J. Pesando, *Issues in the Reform of the Canadian Financial Services Industry* (Toronto: C.D. Howe Institute, 1996), and W. Dobson, *Prisoners of the Past in a Fast-Forward World: Canada's Policy Framework for the Financial Services Sector* (Toronto: C.D. Howe Institute, 1999).

21 See Department of Finance, "Foreign Branch Banking Legislation Comes into Force," *News Release* 99–060 (28 June 1999), available at **www.fin.gc.ca**.

MARKET CONCENTRATION, MERGERS, AND ACQUISITIONS

A concern sometimes expressed about the Canadian financial system is its apparently high **market concentration** (the extent to which a small number of firms in an industry account for a large proportion of its output, employment, profits, and/or assets). As shown in Table 18.3, roughly three-quarters of the core activities of banks, that is, deposit-taking, mortgage lending, and consumer loans, were conducted through chartered banks. This figure may indicate an increase in the competition or economic efficiency of the financial system over time.

Nevertheless, the Canadian banking system is clearly dominated by a few large banks, so we can understand the popular belief that they collude in some fashion to generate monopoly profits. Yet, there is little evidence that collusion or monopoly profits are a facet of the performance of the Canadian banking system. Moreover, chartered banks do not seem to be less competitive than trust or mortgage loan companies, despite different ownership rules.

Nevertheless, the anticompetitiveness of banks is a view that continues to be aired with regular frequency. Part of the problem is that banks seem to have focused on scale as being important to remain competitive with other leading banks of the world, whereas bank profits have recently been sustained via economies of scope such as through the growth of ABMs, and telephone and Internet banking. Critics also focus on the drop in the number of branches, though it is clear that the "bricks and mortar" view of banking is outmoded.[22] Finally, critics of the present position of banks regarding consolidation focus on worries about providing a monopoly to a few banks.[23] As we shall see below, economists have long ago shown that the number of firms (or banks in the present case) in a market or an industry is less important than what is called contestability (see below). Put another way, technology may give an edge to some firms today, but that

Read about Canada's competitiveness in the financial sector at **www.weforum. org**

Table 18.3	Principal Activities of Financial Institutions, 2004		
Personal deposits	**Dollar Value** (in millions $CDN)	**Percentage share**	**Cansim II**
Chartered Banks	401 644	72.5	v36814
Trust Companies	10 444	1.9	v37060
Credit Unions	140 899	25.4	v122590
Life Insurance Companies	984	0.2	v37020
Total	553 971		
Residential mortgages	**Dollar Value** (in millions $CDN)	**Percentage share**	**Cansim II**
Chartered Banks	367 536	78.8	v36724
Trust Companies	6 964	1.5	v37050
Credit Unions	77 538	16.7	v122577
Life Insurance Companies	4 245	3.1	v30710
Total	466 283		
Consumer loans	**Dollar Value** (in millions $CDN)	**Percentage share**	**Cansim II**
Chartered Banks	186 017	87.9	v36717
Trust Companies	245	0.1	v37052
Credit Unions	20 678	9.7	v122575
Life Insurance Companies	4 665	2.2	v37013
Total	211 605		

Source: Bank of Canada, *Banking and Financial Statistics*, calculated from Tables C1, C2, and D1, D2, and D4.

---

22 For an interesting account on this question see J. Clemens, M.T. Low, F. Mihlar, with J.L. Francis, "The Rational Consolidation of Banking in Canada, *Fraser Institute Critical Issues Bulletin* 1998.

23 One of the classic references is H. Demsetz, "Why Regulate Utilities?" *Journal of Law and Economics* 11: 55–65.

is no guarantee that the same firms will maintain that same edge in the marketplace tomorrow. Perhaps in part for this reason, growth in spending by banks on technology has been strong.[24] The growth of electronic forms of banking, or virtual banking, as in the widely publicized entry of Wells Fargo, a U.S.-based bank, and GE Capital Corp., among other such entrants, can easily erode the ability of the few remaining banks to raise prices.

Remember that although depository institutions have different ownership structures, a fact that may have an influence on the industry's competitiveness, they also aim to satisfy different segments of the financial market. For example, the chartered banks are heavily involved in international banking, which is highly competitive, whereas the other depository institutions are not. Moreover, the ability of chartered banks since the 1970s to compete in the market for residential mortgages has increased competition in an industry in which trust companies were historically dominant.

Nevertheless, some concern has been raised that Canadian banks, in general, may be less competitive than they ought to be because ownership restrictions and financial barriers to starting up banks imply an absence of contestability. Contestability refers to the likely success of potential competitors entering a particular industry. In the present context, this means that banks are barred from acquiring other banks, and therefore this places a limit on the size of Canadian institutions. Canadian banks are well behind in size, at least by comparison to banks around the world.[25] None of the Canadian chartered banks ranks in the top 50 in terms of size. But there is another reason why contestability is important. If banks need not worry about the threat of a takeover, they may be less efficient than possible. It should be noted, however, that links between mergers and acquisitions and efficiency are not clear-cut and the topic is the subject of some controversy.

There are a number of other ways to measure how competitive a particular market is. Some studies have looked at bank profits (see the end of this chapter), others have looked at the reaction of banks to changes in costs, while still others have examined how bank stocks react to regulatory changes. Another commonly used measure of competitiveness, as suggested by the analysis in Chapters 11 and 17, is to examine the spread between borrowing and lending rates. According to the World Economic Forum, the spread between borrowing and lending rates in Canada is among the lowest in the G-7. All in all, and despite the methodological difficulties involved in evaluating the state of competition in a market, Canadian banks appear to be operating in a fairly competitive market.[26]

In recent years, the focus has moved away from the question of barriers to entry to the question of how much consolidation is consistent with a competitive environment. The issue came to a head when, in 1998, the Royal Bank and the Bank of Montreal announced plans to merge. In April, the CIBC and the TD Bank announced similar merger plans. The plans were announced despite ongoing activities of the federal government, which was involved in a mid-term review of the 1991 *Bank Act*. Following an analysis by the Competition Bureau and the Office of the Superintendent of Financial Institutions, the minister of finance rejected the bank merger proposals in a press release at the end of 1998.[27] Although the rejection was based on purely economic grounds, there were more than a few hints that the ultimate decision had distinct political overtones. Nevertheless, the decision to block the mergers was based on the following criteria:

1. Mergers would lead to an "unacceptable" increase in market concentration.

---

24 According to the Canadian Bankers' Association's "Fast Stats," the amount spent on technology rose from $2.45 billion in 1997 to $3.90 billion in 2003.

25 Based on the rankings reported annually in the magazine *The Banker*.

26 See L. Boothe, "Competition and Profitability in the Financial Services Industry," in *Issues in the Reform of the Canadian Financial Services Industry,* edited by J. Mintz and J. Pesando (Toronto: C.D. Howe Institute, 1996), W. Dobson, *Prisoners of the Past in a Fast-Forward World: Canada's Policy Framework for the Financial Services Sector* (Toronto: C.D. Howe Institute, 1999), and *Task Force on the Future of the Canadian Financial Services Sector* (MacKay Task Force), September 1999.

27 See Department of Finance, "Minister of Finance Announces Decision on Bank Merger Proposals," *News Release* (December 1998): 98–123, available at **www.fin.gc.ca**.

2.   Mergers would produce a "significant reduction of competition."

3.   Mergers would affect the federal government's ability to "address future potential concerns."

As noted earlier, the banks argued that financial sector consolidation was a worldwide trend, most notably in the United States, and equated the need for maintaining efficiency, and presumably bank profitability, in the global financial world with the need to increase size. As the CEO of the CIBC wrote, following the rejection of the merger proposals, "a merger would have been in the best long-term interests of Canadians and shareholders...."[28] Regardless of the pros and cons of mergers, the MacKay Task Force pointed out the need for a process by which merger proposals can be addressed, and the minister of finance agreed. When the minister of finance released a paper outlining a framework for a revision to the *Bank Act* in June 1999, the report stated that mergers would be permitted, but the process appears to be highly politicized and costly.[29]

Consolidation continues apace as this is written, but the banks appear to be taking the path of least resistance by widening the scope of their operations as opposed to making outright mergers amongst themselves. This is clearly evident from the TD-Canada Trust merger; the merger between National Bank and the Altamira Investment Sevices (a mutual fund) in mid-2002 is a later example of such a trend. The impact of these developments is particularly evident in the portion of the trust industry that operates independently of the banking sector, as we shall see in the following chapter. As we shall see in Chapter 20, we are still waiting for the federal government to reveals its plans for bank mergers.

REGIONAL CONCERNS

Several *Bank Acts* over the years have reflected the peculiarly Canadian attempt to maintain strong centralized institutions and regional interests. The industry's desire to concentrate financial centres in Montreal and Toronto became quite evident by the 1920s, as institutions either moved to the centre of the country or merged with stronger banks whose activities were centred there.

Although this centralized development of the financial system may be said to be efficient in an aggregate sense, that view has not been shared by some of the regions, most notably the West and the Atlantic Provinces. Indeed, early Canadian financial history is full of cases in which the outlying regions felt wronged by the financial centres of central Canada. Although many changes in the *Bank Act* have been intended to mitigate some of the credit difficulties faced by producers in the West and in Atlantic Canada, the perception that the centre has too much influence has persisted. Certainly a cursory examination of the distribution of the assets of chartered banks by region reinforces such an impression. For example, in 2004, the Atlantic Provinces (Newfoundland, Nova Scotia, Prince Edward Island, and New Brunswick) had 3.0% of chartered banks' total assets but 7% of Canada's labour force. Of total assets, 10.0% were located in Quebec; 38.8% in Ontario; 10.3% in the Prairie Provinces (Manitoba, Saskatchewan, and Alberta); and 9.8% in British Columbia. The labour force proportions were, respectively, 23.4%, 39.4%, 17.2%, and 13.9% (numbers may not add to 100% because of rounding).[30] Of course, chartered banks are not the only deposit-taking institutions, so these figures may be somewhat biased. Credit unions and caisses populaires are, for example, important financial institutions in the Prairies and Quebec, but chartered banks tend to be the only national institutions.

---

28 C. Baillie, "TD Says Merger Decision Disappointing," *Canada News Wire,* December 1998, available at **www.newswire.ca**.

29 A merger would require review by several agencies and the House of Commons, public hearings, and be subject to a possible rejection by the minister of finance, who would retain final say on the matter. See Department of Finance, "Reforming Canada's Financial Services Sector—A Framework for the Future," June 1999, available at **www.fin.gc/finserv/docs/finservrept_e.pdf**.

30 Percentages calculated from data in *Bank of Canada Review*, Tables C5, H5, and H6. The percentages do not add up to 100 because a substantial proportion of assets cannot be readily assigned to a particular region.

POINT–COUNTERPOINT 18.1

CONSOLIDATION IN THE BANKING SECTOR: IS IT BAD?

One of the most important developments in financial systems worldwide is the wave of mergers and acquisitions (M&A) in the banking industry. M&A have received considerable attention economywide but, in part because of the *externalities phenomenon* mentioned in this chapter, they raise a number of concerns about their desirability. Compared to other countries, M&A activity in the Canadian banking sector has been stunted, largely because of the federal government's concerns over competition, as well as public perceptions that mega-banks would result in higher interest rates and poorer banking services. The 1998 MacKay report on the financial services sector made a point of noting that the large Canadian commercial banks have a poor reputation with the public for the quality of their services. Yet, at the same time, an international survey of banking systems suggests that we are "over-banked." Each bank office in Canada covers 1857 inhabitants, whereas in the United States the figure is 22 772. Moreover, only the United States, Germany, and Japan have more financial institutions than Canada does. Of course, opponents of mergers—and there are many—can also point to other statistics to make their point. Comparative figures for most industrial countries suggest a great deal of asset concentration in Canada.

Research in the area of bank consolidation is at an early stage, and the existing evidence has tended to rely almost exclusively on U.S. data. We are only now beginning to see studies for other countries, but the pressure on Canadian banks to consolidate is powerful. So, is consolidation of the Canadian banking sector good, or, as the minister of finance claimed in 1999 in rejecting the merger plans of the Royal Bank–Bank of Montreal and TD–CIBC, would consolidation concentrate financial assets in Canada too much? For example, the Competition Bureau reported on the bank merger proposals, stating that it would be "concerned" that a merger would restrict competition exclusively if the post-merger share of the merged entity exceeded 35% of the market, or if the post-merger share of the four largest firms in the market exceeded 65%. The table on the next page considers the pros and cons of increased bank consolidation.

This Chapter also explores the controversy over the recent merger proposals made by some of the largest banks in Canada, and why the government turned down their applications.

Questions for Discussion

1. What is meant by an optimally efficient scale? Why might it be difficult to measure?
2. How would you define a "market" for a bank? Does the Competition Bureau's definition appear straightforward to you?

The oil boom in the 1980s in Western Canada only reinforced the desire of Westerners for their own share of financial or banking power. The first expression of this desire to shift the balance of banking power to the Western part of the country came at the Western Economics Opportunities Conference in July 1973. This ultimately led to the formation of several Western banks, including the Canadian Commercial Bank (CCB) in July 1975, and the Northland Bank, in December 1975. Unfortunately, the banking practices of these newly formed banks in Western Canada led to some of the most spectacular banking failures in Canadian financial history. These practices also spawned a royal commission to investigate the causes of the failures and to make some recommendations.[31]

Both banks were based in Western Canada and both aimed to attune their operations to the financial needs of Westerners, although the CCB also had visions of becoming a large national

---

31 W.Z. Estey, *Report of the Inquiry into the Collapse of the CCB and Northland Bank* (Ottawa: Minister of Supply and Services, August 1986).

POINT	COUNTERPOINT
• Economies of scale and scope require large institutions.[1] • Larger institutions are less likely to fail, reducing the impact of a financial crisis. • Large institutions may be able to deliver more shareholder value than smaller ones. • Financial transactions are proving to be more complex, necessitating large institutions to reduce their risks and ensure they are successfully completed. • Bank consolidation can be an efficient vehicle to eliminate excess capacity in the financial sector. • Deregulation is a spur to consolidation. • Consolidation in the banking sector does not lead to monopoly pricing (i.e., higher interest rates on loans or fees). • Consolidation is difficult to measure and evaluate. Technological change makes it difficult even for large banks to develop excessive market power.	• Considerable uncertainty exists about estimates of the optimally efficient scale of a bank. • Larger institutions are more likely to be considered "too big to fail," increasing the risk of a large bailout. • Corporate control and management may be more difficult in larger institutions, leading to poor decision making. • Complexity may require specialization in carrying out transactions not necessarily under one roof, but through outsourcing or correspondent banking. • Market mechanisms may be just as efficient in eliminating excess capacity. • Deregulation may enhance entry into the financial system and thereby enhance competition. This is called contestability. • Consolidation has been shown in some markets to lead to higher fees and interest rates, especially on small business loans. • Consolidation can restrict consumer choice and lead to less service, lower deposit rates, and higher loan rates. • Enhanced efficiency can also lead to higher profits. • Consolidation leads to excessive profits.

[1] Economies of scale and scope were defined earlier (see Chapter 2).

Sources

J. Allen, Y. Ziu, "Efficiency and Economies of Scale of Large Canadian Banks," Bank of Canada working paper 2005–13.

A.N. Berger, R.S. Demsetz, and P.E. Strahan, "The Consolidation of the Financial Services Industry: Causes, Consequences, and Implications for the Future," *Journal of Banking and Finance* 23 (February 1999).

Competition Bureau of Canada, "The Merger Enforcement Guidelines as Applied to a Bank Merger," 14 December 1998.

W. Dobson, "Prisoners of the Past in a Fast-Forward World: Canada's Policy Framework for the Financial Services Sector," C.D. Howe Commentary, December 1999.

bank, headquartered in Western Canada.[32] The Northland Bank was, by contrast, a regional bank. It seemed doomed from the start, as evidenced by the lack of banking experience of its CEO and the high turnover rate of its senior staff.

The Northland Bank and the CCB each had a tendency to make bad loans, in part by lending large sums of money to relatively few borrowers and in part by excessively concentrating loans and other investments in a narrow geographical area, thereby avoiding some of the obvious benefits of diversification. Moreover, loans were often backed by the resource sectors or real estate at a time when expectations were for rising prices (and thus a rising ability to repay loans in the future) in all major sectors of Western Canada's economy. The CCB also expanded into the growing California economy,[33] which was also experiencing a real estate boom of unprecedented proportions.

When the loans they had made turned out to be bad, both banks sought to avoid failure by refusing to recognize, in an accounting sense, the nonperformance of the outstanding loans.[34]

---

32 The CCB was a national bank, but on a small scale to begin with. It later expanded into Eastern Canada and California.
33 By purchasing a minority interest in Westland Bank, a bank heavily involved in the California real estate market.

Moreover, by capitalizing—in effect, raising the size of loans outstanding—and accruing uncollected interest payments—pretending that the interest will be received at some time—both banks gave misleading pictures of their financial positions. Although these accounting devices are common responses to good loans that later turn out to be bad loans, provisions are usually made to write off bad loans over time, as many chartered banks did during the 1980s when their foreign loans turned sour. Neither the CCB nor the Northland Bank made these provisions.

Despite advances by the Bank of Canada and several failed attempts by the inspector general of banks[35] to merge both banks with the National Bank, among others, both banks were liquidated in 1985, leaving the Canada Deposit Insurance Corporation with huge losses (see Chapter 16).

As the Estey Commission report makes clear, it was the *Bank Act* and the lax supervisory role of the then–inspector general of banks that allowed the situation to get out of hand. Proper supervision would not have permitted either bank to capitalize and accrue interest for as long as it did, and the public would have been warned about the banks' risky portfolio practices. Moreover, proper supervision would have prevented the Bank of Canada from having to bail out—unsuccessfully as it turned out—a failing bank due to its mismanagement. Finally, proper supervision of banking practices would have permitted the responsible agency to step in and take over a mismanaged institution before the financial situation became unsustainable. Thus, the Northland Bank and CCB failures are as much a story of regionalism in banking as they are about inadequate regulations and supervision in the financial industry.

Regional concerns can never be far from the minds of legislators in Canada, and these have in part shaped the structure of the financial system. The reliance on a branch banking system and the long-standing use of the pledge section in the *Bank Act* are examples of the importance given regional concerns. The tension between regional and national concerns will, however, continue to shape and influence chartered bank policy.

LENDING TO SMALL AND MEDIUM-SIZED BUSINESSES

During the elections that led to the return of the Liberals in late 1993, one of the campaign issues dealt with the belief that chartered banks deliberately avoid loans to small and medium-sized businesses. Even before the elections, changes were made to the *Small Business Loans Act* to encourage banks to increase their lending to these types of businesses. Banks have often viewed small businesses as far riskier loan candidates than large corporations. Moreover, transaction costs in monitoring and managing loans to small businesses are likely to be higher than for a loan to some large conglomerate. Since the last recession, however, banks have apparently had a change of heart because they see small and medium-sized businesses as having relatively greater potential for growth.[36] Moreover, the Bank of Canada (in *Banking and Financial Statistics*, Table C7) now publishes data giving the number of loans to various sectors of the economy, which certainly means that banks are more aware of the significance of such loans from a public policy perspective.

Nevertheless, a report to the Task Force on the Future of Financial Services in Canada reaffirmed the view that the small and medium-sized business segment of the market receives sub-par service, in comparison with small to medium-sized business abroad, especially in the United States.[37]

---

34 As Estey's report makes clear, Alberta's recession during the early 1980s played a secondary role in influencing the financial health of both banks.

35 The name of this office was subsequently changed to the Office of the Superintendent of Financial Institutions.

36 S. Thorn, "Banks Renew Interest in Small Businesses," *The Globe and Mail* (23 November 1993): C5.

37 See McKinsey and Co., "The Changing Landscape for Canadian Financial Services: New Forces, New Competitors, New Choices," research report prepared for the Task Force on the Future of the Canadian Financial Services Sector, September 1998, exhibit 2–24.

18.5 THE PERFORMANCE OF CHARTERED BANKS

The CBA is the principal association for Canadian banks **www.cba.ca**

How have the Canadian chartered banks performed over the years—say, since the end of World War II? Here we examine the composition and management of their portfolios (using the approach whose theory we considered in the last chapter) as well as their size and profits.

ASSET AND LIABILITY COMPOSITION

We begin with an overall examination of asset–liability management since the end of World War II. Tables 18.4 and 18.5 show the major asset and liability components of chartered bank balance sheets as percentages of total assets or liabilities at selected intervals.

We can see some unmistakable trends caused largely by two factors: government regulation and the dramatic rise in interest rates since the late 1970s, followed by their decline in the 1990s.

On the asset side (Table 18.4), notice that reserves have been falling steadily and are now close to zero. This decline is a direct consequence of various relaxations in reserve requirements.

Overall holdings of Government of Canada bonds have also fallen substantially over the years, and the relative popularity of long- and short-term bonds was reversed in favour of the latter. Part of the explanation for these portfolio shifts was the substantial indebtedness of the Canadian government occasioned by the need to finance World War II. As the war debt matured during the late 1950s, the government first converted it into long-term debt and then switched its borrowing requirement toward the short-term end of the market. The relative desirability of short-term debt was heightened during the great inflation of the 1970s and early 1980s and the increased default risk of the 1980s. The high (real) interest rate policy of the early 1990s and the recession early during that decade reversed the trend as banks once again held more government securities.

Chartered banks have also become increasingly less important holders of provincial and municipal securities. One reason is again the effects of inflation. Another is the tremendous growth in the number of financial system participants, especially foreigners, who have increasingly been inclined to hold debt issued in Canada.

Banks, in recent years, have turned to holding more corporate securities, as strong economic growth coupled with reduced default rates have combined to make their yields more attractive. In addition, the end of deficit spending at both the federal and provincial levels has also effectively reduced the supply of government-backed securities (see Chapter 4).

Table 18.4	Principal Assets of Chartered Banks					
	1950	**1960**	**1970**	**1980**	**1990**	**2004**
Treasury bills	1.5%	13.3%	6.6%	3.0%	3.1%	1.8%
Foreign assets	9.6%	18.4%	33.8%	44.7%	36.9%	34.2%
General loans	28.2%	34.1%	38.9%	37.9%	34.5%	21.5%
Long-term government securities	23.2%	6.8%	5.6%	0.5%	0.6%	1.4%
Short-term government securities	8.3%	7.4%	4.8%	0.4%	0.3%	2.1%
Other securities	19.6%	6.8%	2.4%	3.1%	3.5%	7.7%
Reserves	9.6%	6.7%	4.2%	2.9%	1.0%	0.2%
Residential mortgages	0.0%	6.6%	3.6%	7.5%	20.1%	19.3%

Sources: Bank of Canada Banking and Financial Statistics; Historical Statistics of Canada, 2d ed., No. CS11–516E (Ottawa: Minister of Supply and Services, 1983). The data for 2004 are for November. Reserves represent Bank of Canada deposits, notes, and coins. Other securities are provincial, municipal, and corporate securities. Short-term government securities mature in three years or under. General loans represent loans to persons and businesses. May not add up to 100% due to rounding.

Table 18.5	Principal Liabilities of Chartered Banks					
	1950	**1960**	**1970**	**1980**	**1990**	**2004**
Advances	0.0%	0.0%	0.0%	0.0%	0.0%	0.0%
Demand deposits	33.4%	27.3%	16.4%	6.2%	4.4%	7.0%
Shareholders' equity	4.0%	6.3%	3.7%	2.7%	3.5%	4.3%
Foreign liabilities	9.7%	16.9%	31.3%	45.3%	39.3%	35.1%
Notice deposits	4.4%	3.7%	10.3%	13.7%	12.7%	13.3%
Personal savings deposits	48.5%	45.8%	38.4%	32.1%	40.1%	21.0%

Sources: Bank of Canada Banking and Financial Statistics; Historical Statistics of Canada, 2d ed., No. CS11–516E (Ottawa: Minister of Supply and Services, 1983). See sources for Table 18.4. Totals may not add up to 100% due to rounding and/or omitted items.

An interesting illustration of the impact of financial regulation is the rise in the share of residential mortgages held by chartered banks. Recall that the severe restrictions on their mortgage lending began to be lifted with the 1967 *Bank Act*. The relatively attractive returns on mortgage lending during the 1980s no doubt spurred the shift toward residential mortgages.

Finally, general loans, primarily of the commercial variety, continue to be one of the largest domestic asset of chartered banks. Despite the deregulation of the 1970s and 1980s, chartered banks can still properly be labelled commercial banks. This name suggests that, so far at least, chartered banks have retained a comparative advantage in the commercial lending market.

The liability side of the balance sheet (Table 18.5) has also had some noticeable changes. First, advances from the Bank of Canada, have tended to be negligible.[38]

It is also clear that financial innovations have made their mark. The removal of the deposit rate ceiling and the introduction of a variety of types of deposits have reduced the spread between rates on deposits and rates on a variety of alternative financial assets. Thus, the share of demand deposits plummeted, while the share of notice deposits rose until lower (nominal) interest rates in the 1990s made bank deposits generally unattractive.

The globalization of the financial system has contributed to a growing reliance on the foreign sector for funds. Indeed, foreign currency liabilities has been the largest liability item since the 1980s.

Finally, the share of equity has remained more or less stable over the years. It did, however, average slightly lower during the 1980s and 1990s than in the 1950s or 1960s, a reflection of the increase in leverage in chartered banks.

ASSET AND LIABILITY MANAGEMENT

Table 18.6 shows in detail the balance sheet of all chartered banks. The essentials are summarized at the bottom of the table. A substantial proportion of assets and liabilities are fairly liquid and rate sensitive.

A third of assets are in foreign currencies. Almost half of Canadian dollar liabilities are classified as fixed term (though, thanks to financial innovations, these need not all be at a fixed rate of interest). By contrast, almost 75% of assets (typically loans) are of the less liquid variety. Again, some of these may be of the fixed or floating variety (for example, as in the case of mortgages). About two-thirds of the liabilities are fixed term; a similarly large percentage are in the form of long-term loans.

Overall, Table 18.5 tells us that chartered bank assets and liabilities are fairly well matched. The gap appears to be largely positive. However, as we saw in the previous chapter, the sign of the

---

[38] See Chapter 4, which does reveal that Bank of Canada advances rose during the 1980s as a result of the wave of failures discussed earlier.

Table 18.6	The Balance Sheet of Chartered Banks (November 2004, millions of dollars)

Assets		Liabilities	
Liquid			
Notes and coins	3 567	Personal savings deposits[9]	401 644
Deposits at the Bank of Canada	130	Nonpersonal and notice deposits	249 381
Treasury bills[1]	29 592	Demand deposits[10]	125 587
Government of Canada bonds[2]	64 800		
Short-term assets[3]	32 760		
Total liquid assets	130 849	Total deposit	776 612
Less Liquid			
Personal loans[4]	186 017	Government of Canada	2 615
Government	2 366	Bankers' acceptances	36 854
Businesses[5]	201 027	Subordinated debt	22 081
Nonresidents[6]	21 316	Foreign currency	131 202
Mortgages[7]	385 485		
Securities[8]	127 413		
Total less liquid assets	923 624	Total liabilities[11]	1 245 817
Total Canadian dollar assets	1 248 138		
Net foreign currency assets[12]	–12 397		

Summary
(as a percentage of total assets or liabilities)

Liquid assets	10.4	Personal deposits	32.2
Less liquid assets	74.0	Nonpersonal + other deposits	30.1
		Foreign currency	10.5
Total assets	84.4	Total liabilities	72.8

Source: *Bank of Canada Banking and Financial Statistics*, Tables C1 and C2.

Notes:
1 Amortized value.
2 All maturities.
3 Call and short loans, short-term paper, and other.
4 Personal loans, credit cards, lines of credit, and other.
5 Reverse repos, business loans, and leasing receivables.
6 Reverse repos and business loans.
7 Residential and nonresidential.
8 Provincial, municipal, and corporate.
9 Chequable, nonchequable, fixed term.
10 Less private sector float.
11 Not all items shown, so total does not add up.
12 Total foreign currency assets are 656 455. This represents 34% of total Canadian and foreign currency assets.

gap depends on the precise maturity structure of assets and liabilities. We can obtain a better idea of the size of the gap by examining Table 18.7, which reports the gap for the Royal Bank of Canada at the end of its 2003 financial year. Given the prominence of foreign currency assets and liabilities, as well as the rapid changes in the exchange rate in the last few years (see Chapter 8), it is not surprising that the gap is evaluated according to the currency denomination of the balance sheet item. Recall that a positive gap is a signal that a bank anticipates a rise in interest rates, and the opposite holds for a negative gap. The negative figures for terms of three months or less suggest the Royal was anticipating a fall in interest rates toward the end of 2003 and toward the middle of 2004. However, the balance sheet figures suggest a short-term rise in interest rates during the first half of 2004 and beyond. In the event, interest rates did rise until late in the Fall of 2004, when the Bank of Canada took a pause in predicting future interest rate rises. Note also how the gaps for off-balance-sheet items tend to offset on-balance-sheet items for some short-term maturities, a clear illustration of how banks have used derivatives to partly insulate themselves against interest rate risk. The longer-term gap figures put the bank at an advantage if rates rise over a year into the future or longer.

It is worth emphasizing again some of the difficulties we face in analyzing bank behaviour by relying on balance sheet figures. First, classifying assets according to the degree of risk embodied in them is not always straightforward. The liquidity of the instruments is much more obvious. Second, balance sheets do not reflect items such as swaps, futures, and options; this omission can impart a strong bias to gap calculations. For this reason, the Royal Bank also publishes the gap in its off-balance-sheet items. These are also given in Table 18.7.

SIZE

So far our description has focused only on the chartered banks in aggregate. It is also of some interest to consider how large some of these institutions are in relation to their industry as a whole. This information is useful in assessing how competitive the banking industry is and where the banks are regionally based, as well as how large the Canadian banks are in relation to some of the many foreign banks that now operate in Canada.

Table 18.8 lists some of the largest chartered banks (measured in terms of asset size). The largest six are Schedule I banks. Before 1980, no foreign-based bank was chartered in Canada; in only two decades, many grew to be among the largest banks in the country but none has yet made it into the top five.

Especially interesting is the growth of U.S.-based banks in Canada. Most chartered banks, Schedule I or Schedule II, continue to have their headquarters in Toronto or Montreal, although because of the restructuring of bank organization in recent years, it is unclear whether this translates into a reinforcing of the concentration of financial decisions in the centre of the country.

PROFITS

Our description of the chartered banks has concentrated on the structure and size of balance sheets, which represent the stock of assets and liabilities that banks enjoy. But banks also accumulate wealth for their shareholders by earning profits. Indeed, few items in the financial news catch the public's attention as much as reports on bank profits.

A common misperception is that bank profits always rise with increases in interest rates. In fact, making precise statements about the relationship between interest rates and profits is difficult because estimates are based on the book values published by the banks, instead of the more informative market values. Gap analysis teaches us that profits are a function of the manage-

Table 18.7	Gap Analysis, Royal Bank of Canada (31 October 2003, millions of dollars)				
			Term to Maturity		
	Immediate	**≤ 3 months**	**4–6 months**	**7–12 months**	**1–5 years**
Canadian dollar	(24 709)	(7433)	(1860)	4025	37 851
Foreign currency	(26 898)	(2186)	(794)	763	11 109
Gap	(53 902)	9885	3879	2657	35 982
Off-balance-sheet gap	(51 607)	9619	2654	4788	48 960
() means negative					

Source: Royal Bank of Canada 2003 Annual Report **www.rbc.com/investorrelations/pdf/ar_2003_e.pdf**

Table 18.8	Canada's Largest Chartered Banks, 2004			
Assets (billions)	Head Office	Name	Schedule	Web address
429	Toronto	Royal Bank	I	www.royalbank.com
311	Toronto	Toronto-Dominion	I	www.tdcanadatrust.com
279	Toronto	Nova Scotia	I	www.scotiabank.com
279	Toronto	CIBC	I	www.cibc.com
265	Toronto	Bank of Montreal	I	www.bmo.com
89	Montreal	National Bank	I	www.nbc.ca

Sources: "One Thousand," *The Globe and Mail Report on Business*, July/August, available from **www.globeandmail.com**, and Canadian Bankers' Association, *Bank Facts*, available from **www.cba.ca**. Reprinted with permission from The Globe and Mail.

Note: Asset figures are rounded to the nearest billion.

ment of assets and liabilities jointly. Thus, if a bank is able to lock in assets at relatively high interest rates and then borrow at lower rates, profits will rise. In other words, precisely because the gap can be negative, bank profits tend to be related to interest rate changes inversely, not positively as many people believe.

A cross-country comparison of equity returns (ROE) reveals no empirical connection between size (as measured by bank capital) and profitability. In addition, cost efficiencies and diverse income sources are the driving forces behind the relatively high profitability of Canadian banks. Indeed, Canadian banks were ranked among the top three most profitable in the industrial world in a survey of 16 countries.[39] Others have argued that the desire to merge is driven by the need to maintain cost economies in a market that is experiencing excess capacity.[40] This need can only be addressed via a reduction in the size of the branch network, and this is a politically sensitive option in the Canadian context. A separate study concludes that efficiency gains have largely been tapped.[41]

SUMMARY

- Commercial banking has evolved over the centuries from free banking to the current system with extensive government involvement in the financial sector.

- This chapter surveys the history and performance of the chartered banks in Canada.

- Intermediation can be thought of as the process of facilitating the process of turning liabilities (such as deposits) into assets (such as loans). An important financial intermediary in Canada is the chartered banks, which are private depository institutions that are federally chartered and regulated.

- Chartered banks are also called commercial banks because they have concentrated their expertise on loans for commercial purposes.

- Chartered banking in Canada began shortly after Confederation in 1867, when the federal government began to regulate the financial system.

- The centrepiece of financial legislation is the *Bank Act*, which used to be revised approximately every ten years. Nowadays financial legislation is revised as necessary.

- The first *Bank Act* was proclaimed in 1871; the latest *Bank Act* became law in 2001.

39 See R.T. Smith, "Money in the Bank: Comparing Bank Profits in Canada and Abroad," C.D. Howe Commentary, 1999.
40 G.F. Matthewson, and N.C. Quigley, "Reforming the *Bank Act*: Regulation, Public Policy and the Market," C.D. Howe Commentary, 1998.
41 McKinsey and Co., "The Changing Landscape for Canadian Financial Services: New Forces, New Competitors, New Choices," research report prepared by the Task Force on the Future of the Canadian Financial Sector, September 1998, exhibit 2–52.

- Table 18.1 provides a chronology of *Bank Acts* throughout Canada's history and the main features of each *Bank Act*.

- The most important forces facing modern banking today are innovation, technological change, and consolidation. They are making possible the creation of virtual banks and the reduction in the volume, cost, and time in completing financial transactions. These same forces are also pushing for the creation of even larger banks to take advantage of scale economies.

- Other issues continue to affect the commercial banking sector in Canada today, in-

cluding whether large banks should be permitted to merge, the types of financial activities they should be restricted from becoming engaged in, and their attitudes toward lending to small and medium-sized businesses.

- Asset and liability management at the chartered banks has changed significantly over the past few decades because of large swings in interest rates, innovations, and globalization in financial markets. Nevertheless, banks remain very profitable institutions.

IMPORTANT TERMS

Bank Act, 347
chartered bank, 347

free banking, 348
market concentration, 359

PROBLEMS

1. Is it feasible to pay interest on currency? Why or why not?

2. That residential mortgage lending interest rates might be higher in Atlantic Canada than elsewhere in the country proves that banks show a bias against Eastern Canadian borrowers. True or false? Explain your answer.

3. The Estey Commission revealed how capitalization of interest can mislead shareholders into thinking a bank is financially healthy when it is not. Use a simplified balance sheet to illustrate why this might be the case. What other accounting practice considered in this text might also mislead shareholders about the true state of a bank's financial health. Why? (Hint: See Chapter 11.)

4. Try to estimate the gap for all chartered banks based on the data in Table 18.6. Rely on the simplest definition of the gap (equation 17.15). How comparable are the results with those of the Royal Bank of Canada (Table 18.7)?

5. Why do the gap data in Table 18.7 suggest that the Royal Bank forecasts the future course of interest rates in attempting to maximize profits?

6. If the on-balance-sheet gap suggests that short-term rates are expected to rise, describe how derivatives can be used to offset the rise.

DISCUSSION QUESTIONS

1. Based on the evidence in this chapter, is it your impression that financial regulations anticipate changes in the banking industry or vice versa? Why? Why not?

2. One argument against free banking is that the cost of monitoring all the various notes

from individual banks would be too large. What does this statement mean?

3. Creating barriers to entry through regulation is an anti-competitive practice and one that induces wasteful activity. What does this statement mean?

4. Do you think it is appropriate to compare the share of chartered bank assets by region with the share of the labour force by region? If so, why? If not, why not?

5. What do you think of the argument that governments need to regulate banks to prevent money from becoming worthless?

6. "Governments are slow in adapting to financial innovations." Give an example from the history of chartered banking.

7. Why have the FTA and NAFTA not been a boon to Canadian chartered banks?

8. Does it make economic sense to make it extremely difficult for large banks to merge? Explain.

9. Do the data in Table 18.3 suggest that chartered banks have excessive market power? Explain.

10. Does it make sense to revise financial services legislation as problems or issues come up or at regular intervals?

11. The *Bank Act* sets limits on what chartered banks can do. Would it not be easier if the government instead let banks do what they like, so long as they meet certain standards to safeguard the safety of financial system?

ONLINE APPLICATIONS

1. Go to the C.D. Howe Web site at **www.cd-howe.org**. Click on *Publications* and then on Publication by Year, and look for the study of bank profitability by R. Todd Smith (1999). Discuss the various ways of measuring the efficiency, size, and profitability of banks, and assess whether Smith's results are convincing, in light of the material in this chapter and Chapter 17.

2. Go to the Web site of one of the banks listed in Table 18.8 (except for the Royal Bank). Download the latest Annual Report and find the notes to the table that present information about the gap. Compare the gap for your chosen bank with the data in Table 18.7. What do you conclude?

3. Go to the Department of Finance's Web site at **www.fin.gc.ca**. Click on *Publications* and choose *1999 Publications*. Next, scroll down until you find the document *Reforming Canada's Financial Services Sector: A Framework for the Future*, 25 June 1999. Discuss the pros and cons of the proposed policy regarding mergers, as well the recommendation regarding the creation of three tiers of banks in terms of capital size.

CANSIM QUESTIONS

Go to the Web sites listed in Table 18.8. Download the Annual Reports for the last couple of years and find the "Net Income" (profits in economics parlance) for as many years in the past as you can. Next, download series V39078 (Bank Rate) from the CANSIM databank. Examine the relationship between profits and interest rates. What do the results suggest?

References can be found on www.mcgrawhill.ca/college/siklos

Other Depository Institutions

LEARNING OBJECTIVES

After reading and studying this chapter, you should be able to

19.1 list some other depository institutions besides chartered banks and describe the key aspects of their operations such as their size

19.2 explain the role of trust and mortgage loan companies in Canada and their importance in the financial system today

19.3 explain the role of credit unions in Canada, their history, and their importance in the financial system today

19.4 understand some of the key features of the remaining types of deposit-taking institutions

19.5 describe the roles of nondeposit-taking institutions and how they fit into the overall financial system

19.6 identify the key activities of financial and leasing corporations

19.7 explain the activities of investment dealers

19.8 obtain a general overview of government financial institutions

19.9 get a general understanding of the insurance industry

19.10 discuss the environment in which investment and pension funds operate and the various types of institutions and instruments they provide

19.11 outline the essentials of the pension fund industry, both private and public

Although Canada's financial institutions are increasingly alike, there continue to be good reasons to distinguish among types of depository institutions. The country's depository institutions that are not chartered banks long satisfied a particular set of financial needs of the Canadian public, and they continue to do so. These institutions have traditionally been referred to as near-banks because, although they appeared to offer many of the same services as the chartered banks, they were legally prevented from using the term "bank." The 1991 *Bank Act* removed this prohibition, as well as some restrictions on their activities. But tradition dies hard. Even if the barriers of the four-pillar financial system are no longer as effective as they once were, it will be some time before depository institutions become largely indistinguishable from each other. In any event, it is useful, for historical reasons alone, to examine these types of institutions separately.

Consequently, this chapter provides an overview of the history and activities of three types of depository institutions: trust and mortgage loan companies; credit unions (called caisses populaires in Quebec);[1] and a few other smaller depository institutions. The remainder of the chapter is rounded out by considering nondepository financial institutions.

19.1 THE SIZE OF THE NEAR-BANK SECTOR

During the 1980s, other depository institutions began to take away market share from the chartered banks. But with the passage of the 1991 *Bank Act*, chartered banks began to buy up existing trust companies. In the space of four years, the size of depository institutions, other than chartered banks, began to decrease substantially from previous levels due to the restructuring of the financial industry in Canada. For example, if we combine the assets of chartered banks with those of trust, mortgage loan companies, and credit unions, then the share of total assets controlled by chartered banks stood at approximately 91% by the end of 2004. By comparison, the same figure was 66.2% in 1989.

19.2 TRUST AND MORTGAGE LOAN COMPANIES

A **trust company** is a depository institution that may also offer services as a corporate trustee. In other words, it has two distinct roles:

1. An intermediation function, by channelling deposits and making loans, primarily in the form of mortgages.

2. A fiduciary (trusteeship) function, by providing **estates, trusts, and agencies** (**ETA**) business— that is, by administering assets it does not own.

A **mortgage loan company** (**MLC**) also accepts deposits and makes mortgage loans, thus providing intermediation services. As we will see, there are several types of MLCs today, and some are owned by chartered banks.

Trust companies and mortgage loan companies arose as separate kinds of institutions. But because they both play such an important role in the mortgage market and because the most recent data on the financial sector lump them together, it seems convenient to treat both of them here under one heading.

Another similarity is that both the federal and the provincial governments regulate these institutions. Most are federally regulated, especially since the *Bank Act* of 1991 (see the previous chapter) eased the distinctions between chartered banks and other depository institutions.

At the provincial level, Ontario, Quebec, Alberta, and British Columbia regulate the trusts in their jurisdictions, whereas Saskatchewan, Manitoba, and the Atlantic Provinces have chosen to delegate supervision to the federal superintendent of financial institutions. Many trust companies, must, however, answer to more than one regulator. The Canadian Constitution assigns property and civil rights to the provinces. Thus the fiduciary component of trust companies' business is subject to provincial legislation, even if the institution is federally incorporated. This overlap has led to duplication with the resulting inefficiencies, since regulation is a costly activity.

THE HISTORY OF TRUST COMPANIES

The first trust company in the country was the Trust and Loan Company of Canada, formed in 1843 in Kingston, Ontario. Chartered banks were not allowed to act as trustees, so a number of

---

1 Unless otherwise noted, we use "credit unions" to refer to credit unions and caisses populaires.

these separate institutions were created in the second half of the nineteenth century. Early in the twentieth century, trust companies were authorized to accept deposits but not to issue cheques. They became true financial intermediaries in the 1920s when they started to borrow in their own names and engage in the process of asset transformation as opposed to acting purely as financial agents.

Today the ETA function continues to be the most important component of trust companies, although their role as depository institutions has grown rapidly. As part of the ETA function, trust companies sponsor mutual funds of various kinds, act as trustee for various corporate bonds and stocks, serve as agents for real estate agencies, and perform the function of investment managers. A currently important area is their role as trustees for the pooled pension funds of large employers and unions.

Mortgages are also an important source of profit, and the *Bank Act* of 1991 opened new business possibilities by permitting trust companies to make commercial loans. This change is especially important since similar ownership restrictions on trusts as are imposed on banks were also put in place in the last few years (see Chapter 18). It will be increasingly difficult to distinguish the trusts from the chartered banks.

As we saw in the previous chapter, most trusts are now wholly owned subsidiaries of the chartered banks. As a result, by 1999 there was only one large trust company, namely Canada Trust (CT), and several smaller ones, but the trust sector that is not subsidiary to some chartered bank is becoming smaller still. On 10 January 2000 the board of Canada Trust accepted an offer by the TD Bank to buy all its outstanding shares. Following regulatory approval in March 2000, CT Financial became a wholly owned subsidiary of a chartered bank. Desjardins Trust, based in Quebec, is now one of the largest trusts in Canada, and is not directly affiliated with a chartered bank.

THE HISTORY OF MORTGAGE LOAN COMPANIES

Historically, mortgage loan companies preceded trust companies. Chartered banks were long precluded from offering residential mortgages, and MLCs were founded to meet the need. The first were patterned after the building societies that still exist in the United Kingdom; they were known as terminating societies because an individual joined one only to borrow enough to purchase land or a house; once the loan was repaid (in instalments), association with the society was terminated.

The activities of MLCs expanded after 1874, when they were allowed to raise funds by issuing debentures. By increasing the amount of funds they had available for lending, MLCs could increase their activities beyond the narrow geographical limits of building societies. They ceased to be terminating societies and became permanent societies.

Today there are three different types of MLCs.

1. Some are simply deposit-taking mortgage companies, operating under either the federal *Loan Companies Act* or similar provincial legislation.[2] Assets are limited to deposits and certain debt instruments such as debentures. Liabilities must primarily be invested in mortgages.

2. Since 1973, federally regulated MLCs have been permitted to create mortgage investment companies (MICs). MICs do not take deposits, but rather allow investors to enjoy the benefits of portfolio diversification through investment in mortgages, bonds, and equities.[3] In addition, MLCs can raise funds through the sale of shares as well as debentures with a term of fewer

---

2 This statement is actually a simplification. To avoid having to give too many details here, they are called savings certificate, investment certificate, or investment contract companies. These institutions, which operate under provincial regulation, differ from other MLCs not in their investment practices but in the nature of the savings investments they offer.

3 Primarily mortgages because of legal restrictions in the *Loan Companies Act*. But permission to invest in equities confers some tax benefits that conventional MLCs do not enjoy.

than five years. (The latter are insured by the Canada Deposit Insurance Corporation.) There are also MLCs under provincial jurisdiction; they are similar to federally regulated ones except they raise funds primarily by issuing guaranteed investment certificates.

3.   Institutions known as **real estate investment trusts** (**REITs**) exist primarily to finance mortgages. They differ from real estate developers in that they operate via a *declaration of trust*; that is, shares are issued and shareholders receive all net income in the form of annual dividends, which has tax advantages for them. Anyone affiliated with an REIT is limited to channelling funds solely through the trust, which can hire an agent or adviser to offer advice about how to invest its funds.

ASSETS AND LIABILITIES

Table 19.1 traces the recent development of trusts' and MLCs' principal assets and liabilities. Mortgages continue to dominate assets, a reflection of these institutions' traditional roles. Despite the chartered banks' entry into residential mortgage lending in the late 1960s, the trusts and MLCs still provide many of the mortgages in Canada. Perhaps the most noticeable item is the sharp reduction in the size of trusts and mortgage loan companies not owned by chartered banks. This is especially the case when the size of mortgages (asset) and deposits (liability) in 2004 relative to 1990 is considered. This dramatically captures the impact of chartered bank purchases of trusts in the 1990s.

On the liability side, term deposits, many in the form called *guaranteed investment certificates* (GICs), dominate the balance sheet. Savings deposits, principally of the chequing variety, make up significantly less of the total, and their share has fallen dramatically owing to financial innovations and the 1967 elimination of deposit ceilings, which fostered greater competition. Although the asset and liability composition of trusts affiliated with chartered banks is very similar to that of the independent trust sector, the total assets of the latter group of institutions is now considerably smaller.

We discussed in Chapter 16 (on deposit insurance) how a wave of failures (especially in Ontario) affected trusts in the late 1980s and into the early 1990s. The effect is not immediately apparent from Table 19.1, in part because many of the failures were due to illegal behaviour on the part of unscrupulous individuals.

Table 19.2 provides a summary of the balance sheet position of trust and mortgage loan companies that are not chartered bank subsidiaries. A comparison with earlier editions of this textbook will make it abundantly clear how much independent trusts have shrunk in the Canadian financial marketplace.[4]

19.3 CREDIT UNIONS AND CAISSES POPULAIRES

A **credit union** is a depository institution that emphasizes saving and lending at a local level. Its shareholders are its own depositors and borrowers.[5] It is established as a nonprofit organization, and these institutions are provincially regulated.[6]

Credit unions grew because small investors and savers had little access to the financial system. The fact that Canada's early banks, like those of almost all contemporary economies, concentrated

---

4 In the first edition of this textbook (1994), total assets of trusts for 1989 was $125 909 million. In the second edition (1997) total assets for 1995 fell to $77 519 million. In the third edition (2001) total assets for 1999 shrank to $58 338 million. These figures make it clear how quickly independent trusts have disappeared.

5 Some credit unions do not limit borrowing to members.

6 The tax benefits of nonprofit status have eroded since 1972, when credit unions became liable for corporate taxes. Nevertheless, their members still reap some tax advantages; for example, they pay no income tax on the earnings distributed to them as rebates.

| Table 19.1 | Trust and Mortgage Loan Companies: Asset and Liability Composition, 1990 and 2004 |

	Percentage of Total Assets 1990	Percentage of Total Assets 2004	2004 Assets as a Percentage of 1990 Assets
Mortgage	53.2	56.9	9.7
Term deposits	6.0	5.8	87.0
Long-term bonds	2.8	8.7	28.1
Short-term instruments	6.2	8.7	12.7
	Percentage of Total Liabilities 1990	**Percentage of Total Liabilities 2004**	**2004 Liabilities as a Percentage of 1990 Liabilities**
Term deposits	70.5	72.6	9.4
Share equity	5.0	8.4	15.5
Savings deposits	19.6	12.7	5.9

Source: *Bank of Canada Banking and Financial Statistics,* Table D1. The figures for 2004 are for the third quarter and apply only to those trust companies not affiliated with the chartered banks. Sum of shares is less than 100% as not all asset or liability shares were calculated. Mortgages are for both residential and nonresidential types.

Note: The "deposits" shown as assets are the funds that trusts and MLCs have placed with other institutions. The "deposits" shown as liabilities are, of course, funds held for clients.

The "movement Desjardins"
www.desjardins. com/en/index.jsp

on commercial banking spawned the development of "people's banks" whereby individuals and small businesses with modest means formed community-based financial institutions. This cooperative movement was especially prevalent in Germany, Great Britain, Italy, and the Scandinavian countries, among others, where it continues to be important. Cooperative institutions were also part of the early development of the financial system in the United States, where they became today's savings and loan associations (S&Ls), credit unions, and mutual savings banks.

Perhaps the best known of the cooperative banks in Canada are the **caisses populaires** of Quebec. Alphonse Desjardins, inspired by the cooperative movements in Europe and the inability of farmers and individuals to obtain credit, founded the first in 1900 in Levis, Quebec. The movement spread throughout the province, with individual caisses operating more or less as separate units but united under the leadership of Desjardins. By the 1920s, regional associations were formed, and, following the Great Depression, all the regional unions were brought together in a federation known today as the Confederation des caisses populaires et d'economie Desjardins, or more simply, the Caisses populaires Desjardins.

The credit union movement also became a feature elsewhere in Canada. It started in the French-speaking communities of New Brunswick, Ontario, and Manitoba, but in the 1930s, it spread to the Maritimes (the Antigonish movement) and then to the Prairies. In both Eastern and Western Canada, credit unions tended to serve rural communities, differing somewhat from the institutions of the Desjardins movement, many of which were based on urban parishes. The credit unions outside Quebec also often had relatively more flexible lending policies, like those of the U.S. movement, which had inspired their development.

A common feature in the development of all credit unions in Canada has been the formation of regional unions or *centrals* to facilitate cheque-clearing[7] and to act as lenders of last resort. Thus, centrals could confer some of the advantages of the vast branch networks established by the chartered banks, but centrals being creatures of individual credit unions, power could emanate from the grassroots, not from the centre.

---

7 With the formation of the Canadian Payments Association (CPA) in 1980, local credit unions gained access to the nationwide cheque-clearing system on an equal basis with other deposit-taking institutions. Nevertheless, most have opted to rely on the CPA via the network of national centrals.

Table 19.2	Balance Sheet Position of Trust and Morgage Loan Companies		
September 2004			
Assets (Millions)		**Liabilities (Millions)**	
Cash, items in transit and term deposits[1]	369	Savings deposits[7]	1557
Short-term paper (Treasury bills, bankers' acceptances, other)[2]	963	Term deposits[8]	8 887
Long-term bonds (federal, provincial, corporate)[3]	1069	Share equity[9]	1027
Residential mortgages[4]	6 964		
Personal loans[5]	245		
Total[6]	12 248	Total	12 248

Sources: All data from Table D1 in Bank of Canada, *Banking and Financial Statistics.* All data are also available from CANSIM II database, Table 176–0028; the series numbers are shown below.

Notes: Items shown do not add to total since not all balance sheet items are shown. Only the major items are listed.
1 V37038 + V37057 + V37040 + V37041
2 V37042 + V37044
3 V37046 + V37047 + V37048
4 V37050
5 V37052
6 V37055
7 V37035
8 V37064
9 V37073

Although credit unions are spread across Canada, they are more important in some regions than in others. For example, roughly 40% of savings deposited at credit unions outside Quebec are booked in British Columbia, and 12% in Saskatchewan, whereas the same figure is only 19% in Ontario. Moreover, although 30% of credit unions are based in Ontario, 19% are located in Saskatchewan and another 12% in Alberta. Although credit unions thrive in Quebec (aggregate savings deposits are at almost the same level as combined savings deposits in the rest of Canada), the credit union industry appears to be showing signs of decline. For example, there were 566 credit unions at the end of the third quarter of 2004, down from 676 as recently as 2001Q3. The same trend is noticeable in the number of credit union locations. On the other hand, the number of Canadians affiliated with credit unions has remained stable over the last few years at 4.65 million.

Today there are provincial central credit unions regulated by provincial legislation. Since 1973, they have been authorized to accept deposits, make loans, and act as agents for their locals—powers much in line with those enjoyed by trust companies. Moreover, the CDIC can act as a lender of last resort to the provincial centrals.

These are also quasi-national bodies—in particular the Credit Union Central of Canada (CUCC) and the Caisses populaires Desjardins in Quebec—which, among other things, enable the transfer of funds from one provincial central to another. For example, the CUCC attempts to ensure sufficient liquidity in the financial system and lobbies the federal government on behalf of its members. The new financial services sector legislation (see Chapter 18) would remove any remaining regulatory barriers to the formation of a single national entity. This legislation would permit credit unions outside Quebec to emulate the development of the Desjardins movement more formally.

The Credit Union Central of Canada **www.cucentral. ca/index.htm**

ASSETS AND LIABILITIES

Table 19.3 traces the recent development of the principal assets and liabilities of local credit unions. Cash loans to members and mortgages form the vast majority of assets. But in line with the credit union philosophy of conservative financial management, cash and demand deposits, primarily with centrals, also represent a significant proportion of total assets.

| Table 19.3 | Local Credit Unions: Asset and Liability Composition, 1990 and 2004 |

	1990 Percentage of Assets	2004 Percentage of Assets	Cansim II Numbers
Cash & Demand Deposits	8.2	3.5	V122572+V122580
Loans	15.1	12.7	V122575
Mortgages	44.2	47.5	V122577
	1990 Percentage of Liabilities	**2004 Percentage of Liabilities**	**Cansim II Numbers**
Deposits	87.1	86.4	V122590
Equity	6.1	7.3	V122595+V122596

Source: Bank of Canada, Banking and Financial Statistics, Table D2.

Note: The "deposits" shown as assets are the funds that credit unions have placed with other institutions. The "deposits" shown as liabilities are, of course, funds held for clients.

The distribution of liabilities is instructive. Members' equity, originally a basic source of the funds credit unions raised, is now a small fraction of total liabilities. Deposits, primarily of the savings or term kind, are the principal source of funds. This development is explained by the fact that local credit unions are no longer institutions whose membership is narrowly defined along parish, occupational, or geographical lines and that they have begun to resemble other deposit-taking financial institutions.

The financial structure of these institutions is clearly simpler than that of, say, chartered banks. Thus, deposits account for more than 80% of funds raised, and assets are primarily in the form of mortgages and cash loans. In this respect, the asset composition of local credit unions has not changed much since 1985.

Credit unions have quietly evolved as financial supermarkets, offering a wide variety of services from personal loans, mortgages, and cheque-clearing, to insurance and travel-related services. This entity is precisely the type of financial institution that the other deposit-taking institutions seek to become.

Table 19.4 summarizes the balance sheet position of credit unions. Unlike independent trusts, credit unions have grown steadily in size over the years.[8]

19.4 OTHER DEPOSIT-TAKING INSTITUTIONS

Although the *Constitution Act, 1867* gave the federal government jurisdiction over the country's whole financial system, its primary interest historically was commercial-type banks. As we have seen, however, other types of depository institutions arose as the public need for them grew. Some were trust companies, mortgage loan companies, and cooperatives. Others were savings banks, a type of deposit-taking institution present in most parts of the world (usually called a thrift in the United States) that specializes in holding individuals' savings, usually in time deposits, and making loans to households.

---

8 Once again it is interesting to consider the growth of the credit union sector over the years. In the first edition of this textbook (1994) the total assets for 1989 were reported as $16.77 million. In the second edition (1997), the same figure stood at $98.5 million. By the time the third edition was published (2001), total assets had risen to almost $120 million.

Table 19.4	Balance Sheet Position of Credit Unions		
	2004 Quarter 3		
Assets (Millions)		**Liabilities (Millions)**	
Cash, demand, and term deposits[1]	14 382	Deposits[7]	140 899
Short- and long-term bonds[2]	6 798	Loans[8]	1 699
Shares in credit union centrals[3]	686	Members' equity[9]	11 966
Personal and nonpersonal loans[4]	42 748		
Residential and nonresidential mortgages[5]	89 722		
Total[6]	163 171	Total	163 171

Sources: Data from Table D2, Bank of Canada *Banking and Financial Statistics*. Data are also available from CAMSIM II database, Table 176–0026. CANSIM II series numbers shown below.

Notes: Columns do not add to totals due to items not shown. Only major balance sheet items are shown.
1 V122572 + V122580 + V122581
2 V122582 + V122583 + V122584 + V122585 + V122586 + V122587
3 V122573
4 V122575 + V122576
5 V122577 + V122578
6 V122571
7 V122590
8 V122589
9 V122595 + V122596

Alberta Treasury
branches
www.atb.com

Because Canadian savings banks originated at local or regional levels, most of them became provincially regulated institutions. A couple of exceptions are the Quebec savings banks and provincial government savings offices.

Indeed, a variety of provincial governments have, over the years, offered banking services, particularly in remote or rural areas. Currently, the only significant deposits are at the Province of Ontario Savings Offices and the Alberta Treasury Branches. Although these institutions mostly act as savings banks, they do make loans to small businesses and to farmers, although a relatively large share of their funds naturally are invested in provincial securities.

For many years, the federal government did supervise some banks under the *Quebec Savings Bank Act*, which was originally quite restrictive, barring these savings banks from engaging in commercial lending and limiting their operations first to a single branch (except in Montreal) and later to branches only in Quebec. The Act expired in 1991 and was not renewed because it was no longer needed. Since 1969, the only institution falling under it had been the Montreal City and District Savings Bank, which, in 1987, became a Schedule II chartered bank operating under the name of the Laurentian Group.

19.5 OTHER FINANCIAL INSTITUTIONS

As a group, deposit-taking institutions are the largest financial intermediaries in Canada. However, a variety of other intermediaries—leasing and consumer finance companies, investment dealers, government financial institutions, insurance companies, mutual funds, and pension funds—also play an important role in the country's financial system.

In a sense, each kind of institution fulfils an intermediation function *in addition* to at least one specialized function. For example, insurance companies protect policyholders against unexpected and generally unwanted events, but they often couple insurance with ways for individuals to save for retirement or to leave bequests. Mutual funds and pension plans take advantage of the efficiencies inherent in the pooling of funds by many contributors. Some combinations of services are precluded by government regulation. Deposit-taking institutions are barred from selling insurance, for example; banks are prevented from leasing cars, an area of specialization of some financial corporations. Government financial institutions, however, fill financing gaps in certain areas of the economy where the private sector is thought to have failed or where banks or other financial institutions would find it unprofitable to operate.

With the deregulation of the financial sector, banks and near-banks continue to be relatively larger, at least as measured by asset size.

19.6 FINANCIAL AND LEASING CORPORATIONS

Firms in the finance company segment of the financial industry are essentially involved in the creation of debt with the funds used for purchasing specific goods and services at the corporate, wholesale, or retail levels. Credit is secured by mortgages or current and anticipated income or sales, and by the sale of debentures.

TYPES OF INSTITUTIONS

Four major categories of institutions come under this heading.

GMAC: An example of a leasing company
www.gmacfs.com

1. Acceptance or sales finance companies make loans to consumers via retailers. For example, a car dealer takes a signed contract to buy an automobile to the finance company, which "accepts" it by purchasing the contract (for its face value plus a discount factor). The acceptance company is then the lienholder and collects regular payments. Not surprisingly, acceptance companies that finance the sale of automobiles are generally the largest in terms of asset size.

   Many acceptance companies are wholly owned subsidiaries of the manufacturers of products ranging from automobiles to dishwashers to computers. Having a basically captive market for financing seems like a good opportunity for large corporations, which have shown great interest in acting as intermediaries. But they have met with mixed success, especially during the 1980s when the predilection of such finance arms for making real estate loans led to considerable losses for some. This diversification did not enhance returns, primarily because it was done in areas in which these firms had little or no expertise. However, the leasing industry has successfully fended off attempts by the chartered banks to obtain permission to enter the auto-leasing market, thus preserving considerable market power in this area.

   Acceptance companies may also finance inventories.

2. Consumer loan companies make cash advances to individuals for the purchase of goods and services and for debt consolidation. Since the chartered banks and near-banks have become increasingly competitive in the personal loans market, the consumer loan companies' market has shrunk and has become concentrated on low-income customers, who are often high-risk borrowers.

3. **Financial leasing corporations** engage in leasing equipment, primarily to firms that can then enjoy the benefits of the items without some of the risks of ownership. Leases are of two kinds. A *full-out financing lease* covers the anticipated life of the asset. The payments cover the cost of the equipment (perhaps at the wholesale level) as well as a margin for the lessor's costs of operation and a profit. But the lessee has acquired a debt without the costs of having to obtain the funds first and then negotiate a price for purchase. Alternatively, an *operating lease* does not cover the anticipated life of the asset, but the lessee typically has the option, at the end of the lease, of purchasing the asset at a price stated by the lessor at the time the contract is signed. If the lessee fails to purchase the asset, it can, of course, be leased (or sold) to someone else.

4. Business financing institutions serve primarily as an alternative to banks in their traditional commercial lending activities. Business financiers may also engage in other activities, such as the financing of inventories, *factoring* (the selling or discounting of accounts receivable to a specialist, who undertakes to collect the amounts owing), the financing of exports and of specific types of construction, and the provisions of working capital (the excess of current assets over current liabilities).

They may also be involved in bridge financing—that is, supplying funds until longer-term financing arrangements can be worked out.

In the past, merchant banks were included under the heading of business financiers but, since the 1980 *Bank Act*, many of them have become Schedule II banks. **Merchant banks**, in addition to arranging regular business loans, deal in *venture loans* (that is, loans to high-risk enterprises) and advise and assist clients who are seeking mergers or acquisitions. Venerable institutions such as J.P. Morgan and Rothchild's are called merchant banks. These types of institutions have grown quickly in an attempt to capitalize on the financing needs of rapidly growing emerging markets in Asia, Latin and South America, and Eastern Europe. Another stimulus for growth has been the relative decrease in the role of banks in business financing.[9] Large corporations with an international outlook need the financial services of institutions that can offer a complex set of financial arrangements, not simply borrow or lend money.

J.P. Morgan
www.jpmorgan.com

ASSETS AND LIABILITIES

Table 19.5 gives a snapshot of the principal balance sheet items for sales finance and consumer loans companies in 2000 and 2004. On the asset side, sales finance and consumer loan companies have clearly focused their efforts on personal loans and leasing, where current regulations offer some protection from competition. Nevertheless, business credit, as a percentage of total assets, has not changed dramatically over the years.

Turning to liabilities, we note the shift toward holding more long-term liabilities and away from short-term debt, a clear reaction to the low and stable interest rates of the late 1990s. Perhaps in parallel with these developments, leverage ratios also have risen over the past decade or so.[10]

19.7 INVESTMENT DEALERS

Investment dealers primarily *underwrite* securities, which involves purchasing newly issued debt from government or corporations and then reselling it in the secondary market. A select few, called *primary market dealers*, have privileged access to credit (from the chartered banks via day-to-day loans or the Bank of Canada via special purchase and resale agreements if needed) and are designed to purchase federal government securities.[11]

---

9 As a rough indicator, business loans made by chartered banks represented just over 17% of Canadian dollar assets at the end of 1995. By the end of 2004, this percentage had fallen to about 12%. This percentage has remained steady for the last few years.

10 It should also be added that, as a result of the changes that have taken place in the industry over the past few years, it is becoming difficult to give a good historical picture of the evolution of this segment of the financial sector. Statistics Canada now defines this sector as consisting of both public and private institutions that engage "…in extending credit or lending funds raised by credit-market borrowing (e.g., by issuing commercial paper and other debt instruments) and by borrowing from other financial intermediaries." (*Notes to the Bank of Canada Banking and Financial Statistics*, January 2005, p. 25.)

11 See Chapter 4 for a discussion of this procedure, which essentially originated in the 1950s when the government wanted to ensure the presence of a ready market to absorb its debt. *The Bank of Canada Review* publishes the list of primary dealers in every issue.

Table 19.5	Asset and Liability Composition of Sales Finance and Consumer Loan Companies, 2000, 2004		
Assets	**Percentage of Assets 2000**	**Percentage of Assets 2004**	**Cansim II numbers**
Personal Credit	18.7	21.0	V1404827
Business Credit	17.5	13.3	V1404828
Leasing contracts	13.0	17.2	V1404829
Liabilities	**Percentage of Liabilities 2000**	**Percentage of Liabilities 2004**	
Long-term debt	27.7	16.1	V1404834
Short-term debt	36.2	40.8	V1404835

Source: Data is adapted from the Statistics Canada CANSIM database **http://cansim2.statcan.ca.>**, Series V1404827, V1404828, V1404829, V1404834 and V1404835. Sum of shares is less than 100% as not all asset or liability shares were calculated. Short-term debt includes bankers' acceptances and other short-term paper.

Ontario Securities
Commission
**www.osc.gov.
on.ca**

Until a few years ago, Canadian investment dealers were independent institutions. When 1989 changes to federal banking regulations permitted banks to own brokerage houses, however, most investment dealers became wholly owned subsidiaries of banks. Others are subsidiaries of large foreign firms. Indeed, examination of the top six investment dealers in Canada reveals that all are wholly owned subsidiaries of chartered banks.[12]

Unlike many other areas of the Canadian financial system, investment dealers are regulated by provincial bodies, usually called securities commissions, and the rules differ considerably across provinces. Nevertheless, to guarantee access to the Toronto Stock Exchange, most adopt rules set by the Ontario Securities Commission (OSC). In effect, these rules have become a quasi-national standard for securities dealers. Ongoing attempts to form a national body to regulate underwriting activities created a stir in the industry and continue to be rejected by several provincial bodies. We will discuss some of the proposed alternatives in Chapter 20, as well as the pros and cons of a single national regulator versus some model that would permit continued significant provincial involvement.

Unlike dealers, brokers act as agents for investors, that is, they are purely "go-betweens." All investment brokers are members of the *Investment Dealers Association* (*IDA*), an industry association that provides self-regulation. Investment brokers' assets represent a relatively small fraction of the total financial sector.

19.8 GOVERNMENT FINANCIAL INSTITUTIONS

The federal and provincial governments have for many years made credit available to the private sector directly or indirectly through Crown corporations. The list of these institutions is exceedingly long, but a few of the better known ones are worth mentioning.[13]

The *Canada Mortgage and Housing Corporation* (*CMHC*), the third largest financial services company in Canada, assists specific types of residential construction, such as housing for individuals and families with low income. It also insures private mortgages issued by banks to individuals unable to meet a minimum down payment, thus protecting those institutions against the default risk. The *Business Development Bank* is a lender of last resort for firms unable to obtain financing through conventional means; most are interested in raising funds for fairly new, high-

12 See *The Globe and Mail*, "Top 1000," July 2005, available at **www.globeinvestor.com/series/top1000/**.
13 Not included in this list are the Bank of Canada and the Canada Deposit Insurance Corporation, which provide implicit and explicit subsidies and other guarantees. These institutions are so important in their own right that they receive separate treatment in this book; see Chapters 16, 22, and 23.

CMHC
**www.cmhc-
schl.gc.ca**

Business Development
Bank
www.bdc.ca

Export Development
Corporation
www.edc.ca

risk ventures. The *Export Development Corporation*, the eighth largest financial services company in Canada, provides financing to foreign concerns for the purchase of Canadian exports. This assistance to Canadian producers mitigates some of the risk, such as credit risk, that cannot be eliminated through, say, bankers' acceptances because banks are unwilling to absorb the high level of risk involved in a particular transaction. *Farm Credit Canada* is a government financing arm meant to assist the agricultural sector. It provides the long-term credit required to finance, for example, the machinery and equipment used in farming.

Finally, the government's financial intervention is also significant in its programs to facilitate regional economic expansion, its various incentives to reduce unemployment in regions where it is chronically high, and its bewildering array of other schemes whose objective is to "equalize" opportunities across provinces and regions.

19.9 INSURANCE COMPANIES

The Canadian Life
and Health Insurance
Association
www.clhia.ca

Insurance is a contract to pay a premium in return for which the insurer provides financial compensation if a specified event occurs. In effect, the insurance company pools the risk of many policyholders. If the group is large enough, actuaries can predict the incidence of most kinds of losses (but not the individuals to whom they will happen); thus, premiums can be calculated so that they total, on average, enough to pay claims, cover administrative costs, and give the company a profit.

In Canada, regulations originating in the last century have produced an industry that specializes in insurance. The industry retains its oligopoly status over the sale of insurance to the public.[14] The industry may even expand. The latest *Bank Act* did away with many of the strict provisions that stipulate the activities insurers can engage in. Insurance companies are able to acquire deposit-taking institutions and so offer more banking services. Banks are also permitted to buy insurance companies (but not to sell insurance in their branches). Manulife Financial was the first insurer to directly purchase a bank. Manulife Bank of Canada was formed in 1992 with the merger of three small regional trust companies.

KINDS OF ISSUERS

Insurance firms can be either joint stock companies, owned by shareholders, or mutual companies, owned by their policyholders. Most (about 95%) are incorporated and regulated federally, though a few are provincially regulated.[15]

It should also be noted that government-owned corporations are major providers of property and casualty insurance in British Columbia, Quebec, Manitoba, and Saskatchewan. The most important development in the industry came into force in 1999 when the federal government passed legislation permitting **demutualization**. Demutualization permits the conversion of mutual companies into joint-stock companies. Since the legislation became law in 1999, most of the large life insurers have elected to demutualize.

Canada has three kinds of insurance companies, divided by the type of insurance they write: life; property and casualty; and accident and sickness.[16] Any firm that offers life insurance must maintain for it a **segregated fund**—that is, accounts separate from those for the rest of its activities.

---

14 There are a few exceptions. Insurance has long been sold by credit unions, which qualify as "fraternal benefit societies," and chartered banks sell specific forms of insurance (health, car rental) through their credit card operations. Companies also work via the banks to provide life insurance coverage for mortgage loans.

15 The regulations described here are federal. Provincial regulations are similar, though companies incorporated in Quebec are less restricted in investments and ownership.

16 Two or three kinds may, however, be wholly owned by a single holding company.

Some property and casualty firms offer **reinsurance**. In a kind of secondary market, they assume a share of the insurer's liability in return for a share of the premiums. Risk is shifted. (Liability for payment to the policyholder who suffers a loss remains, however, with the insurer, not the reinsurer.)

Insurance companies may not take deposits or make many kinds of loans. But they have found mechanisms that enable them to offer equivalent services. Commercial loans are allowed if they are secured by property; personal loans are possible if backed by the cash value of a life insurance policy. And by selling annuities, payments from which are deferred into the future against periodic deposits, insurance companies effectively play the role of intermediaries.

Compcorp
www.compcorp.ca

Canada's insurance companies may not, however, participate in the Canada Deposit Insurance Corporation. Instead, they have set up their own contingency fund against defaults on policies. The Canadian Life and Health Compensation Corporation (Compcorp); guarantees, within certain limits paralleling the coverage provided by the CDIC for deposit insurance (see Chapter 16), life insurance companies, accident and sickness policies, and annuity contracts.

Unlike the United States, where insurance activities are relatively unregulated, no insurance company in Canada failed between 1875 and 1990 (despite some near disasters during the nineteenth and early twentieth centuries). In 1991 two insurance companies, the Cooperants Mutual Life Insurance Society (which switched from federal to provincial jurisdiction in the 1980s) and the Sovereign Life Insurance Company (based in Calgary), failed. The most prominent failure in Canada, however, occurred when Confederation Life (Confed) collapsed in 1994. Like many financial institutions, Confed had invested heavily in real estate. When the real estate market collapsed following the recession of 1991–92, Confed's capital was insufficient to cover anticipated losses. Confed's capital–asset ratio (actually called the minimum continuing capital and surplus ratio by the Office of the Superintendent of Financial Institutions, which oversees the financial industry) looked acceptable, although it was below the industry average at the time. In reality, Confed's capital was grossly insufficient to meet its obligations.[17] In 1998, several years after the Confed collapse, an agreement was reached that permitted policyholders to recover 100% of their investment.

Attempts to merge with Great-West Life, one of the largest insurance companies (see Table 19.5) failed precisely because Great-West had concluded that Confed's balance sheet was worse than presented to regulators, ratings agencies, and policyholders. Confed, a 123-year-old company, failed in August 1994, at which time federal regulators seized control of the company.[18]

A trend in Canada since the 1990s has been the incursion of insurance companies from other countries, mainly from Europe. Foreign insurance companies are separately regulated by the federal government. They must, among other things, keep sufficient assets in the country to match their Canadian liabilities.

TYPES OF INSURANCE CONTRACTS

Much of the insurance sold today is **term insurance**. The insurer contracts to cover a risk (death, fire, accident, and so on) for a set period. Premiums are collected from policyholders and claims are paid to the relatively few who experience the event.

Life insurance companies also offer two other types of contracts. One is permanent insurance, which combines life insurance with savings; if a policyholder has not died by a specified age (often 65), he or she receives a lump-sum payment.[19] The premiums are partly actuarially based;

---

17 Look back at Chapter 11 to see the difficulty with conventional accounting measures of the capital–asset ratio.
18 For a description of the sequence of events that led to Confed's collapse, see R. McQueen, "The Story Behind the Death of a Giant," *Financial Post* (14 September 1994): 10–11.
19 These policies, also called whole life policies, are still available, but are much less popular than they were in the past.

the excess is the savings.[20] By contrast, term insurance premiums are actuarially based and so these premiums rise with age.

Another kind of contract is an **annuity**, which provides a stream of payments, usually on retirement, to an individual or his or her beneficiaries. A variety of such schemes exists. One of the best known is the **registered retirement income fund** (**RRIF**), a version of which promises a rising payment schedule until age 90. The premium is often paid as a lump sum, usually a rollover from a registered retirement savings plan (RRSP).[21]

ASSETS AND LIABILITIES

Because the payouts are long term in nature, life insurers' assets are largely invested in bonds and mortgage loans, although the fraction of assets invested in equities has risen substantially in recent years to take advantage of the bull market for stocks. In addition, life insurance companies have moved aggressively into wealth management and away from traditional life insurance products.

As a result, assets and liabilities are well matched for life insurers. The same is true for property and casualty insurers, except that their investments and claims are primarily short term.

SIZE

Table 19.6 provides a list of some of the largest insurance companies in Canada by revenues generated. Despite the recent proliferation of foreign insurance companies, Canadian firms lead the industry.

19.10 INVESTMENT FUNDS AND COMPANIES

One of the ways in which intermediaries improve the efficiency of the financial system is through the pooling of funds, thus diversifying risks to a greater extent than is possible for the typical individual investor. This is, in essence, what investment funds (**mutual funds**) and **investment companies** do.[22] They exist for the sole purpose of purchasing securities of other firms, financial

Table 19.6	The Largest Insurance Companies in Canada, end of 2004		
(A) Life Insurance		**(B) Property and Casualty Insurance**	
Company	Revenues ($billions)	Company	Revenues ($billions)
Manulife	27.2	Fairfax Fin. Holdings	7.5
Great-West Life Co.	21.8	Co-operators Group	6.0
Sun Life Assurance	21.8	Ins. Corp. of B.C.	3.9
Industrial Alliance	3.7	ING Canada	3.8
Desjardins Life	2.8	E-L Financial	1.9
		Soc. de l'assurance automobile	0.9

Source: "One Thousand," *The Globe and Mail, Report on Business,* July, August 2005. Figures are for December 2004. Reprinted with permission from The Globe and Mail.

---

20 A type of whole life policy in which the premiums were paid for a fixed term, called "vanishing premiums," was introduced in the 1980s, but, in some cases, the premium did not vanish. This led to court cases in the United States, which prevented insurance companies (in Canada too) from extracting premiums beyond the specified term.

21 RRSPs are discussed later in the chapter, with pensions. On reaching age 69, holders of RRSPs must collapse these funds, paying the deferred tax or transferring them to an approved annuity scheme. Life insurance companies can themselves accept RRSP deposits.

22 Technically the two differ. Investment funds are what are usually called mutual funds. Investment companies are legally defined as principally engaged in holding securities issued by other companies. Some investment companies are called holding companies because they have a controlling interest in one or more corporations. For our purposes here, we can ignore the difference.

or not. Participants own shares or "units" whose value is proportional to the value of the total pool of funds.

Anyone can set up investment funds, and they are not closely regulated. Some are established as trusts by other financial institutions (subsidiaries of banks and trust companies, for example). Others are separate companies, chartered provincially or federally. Many banks have entered the mutual funds market, and, as we briefly describe below, a large variety of investment funds exists.

KINDS OF INVESTMENT FUNDS

The Investment Funds Institute of Canada is an industry association for open-end funds
www.ific.ca/eng/home/index.asp

For simplicity, investment funds can be categorized in two ways. One is according to how they are set up, which affects how they are sold. *Closed-end funds* have a fixed number of shares that cannot be redeemed on demand. After the original issue is sold, the shares are traded on the secondary market.[23] Alternatively, an investment fund can be an *open-end* mutual fund, which means there are no restrictions on the issue of shares to new subscribers, and shares can be redeemed on demand at net asset value (the market value of all the fund's assets less any liabilities, divided by the number of shares).

The other way of classifying mutual funds is by the type or types of investments they make. A few are unspecialized. Many, termed equity funds, invest principally in common shares; some choose to concentrate on a particular sector of the economy, such as energy or pharmaceutical companies. Bond funds allocate their resources to the purchase of government securities or corporate bonds. Mortgage funds invest in financial instruments, usually bonds, used to finance mortgage lending. Money market funds invest in short-term bonds, such as Treasury bills and commercial paper.

The popularity of mutual funds suggests that we should explore some of the reasons for their success. As financial wealth rises, investors look to take advantage of the benefits of diversification. As we have seen, mutual funds can provide this as well as economies of scale and scope, especially to individual investors. The growing importance of having to plan for retirement in an aging population also plays a role in the growth of mutual funds. Nevertheless, the particular appeal of *no-load* funds, where investors pay no up-front brokerage fees (unlike load funds for which they do), raises the question of whether these perform better than other types of funds or better than if the investor were to construct a portfolio by himself or herself. One worry is that, in the absence of easy access to fees paid to fund managers, investors in no-load funds may in fact be worse off than under any alternative because the monitoring fees may be considerably higher than either with load funds or with the management of one's own portfolio.

Mutual funds have been in the news in recent years because some have questioned their performance; as well, regulators became concerned by some of their trading practices. At the core of recent discussions has been an issue known as market timing. Investors expect that the value of their mutual funds will be essentially the value of stocks (and bonds or other investments) divided by the number of fund shares. However, there is nothing preventing a particular fund, or its manager, from setting the price at some arbitrary moment of the day (or night). The problem is that once the value of the funds is set, say at 4 p.m. each day, the announced price instantaneously becomes stale. Since shares are traded 24 hours a day all over the world it can become extremely complex to determine the correct value of a fund. As a result, some funds have resorted to relying on the fact that if markets in North America rise one day then it is likely that shares in Asia will increase in price the following day. Therefore, an investor could buy shares of a fund that includes Asian stocks at the 4 p.m. deadline and sell them the next day, pocketing the increase in the value of the fund without informing the investor. Market timing, therefore, is an attempt to

---

23 One use of such shares is to acquire control of other corporations, in which case the fund becomes a kind of *holding company* (a firm that owns a controlling interest in the shares of one or more other corporations and thus has the right to supervise its management).

profit from the difference in timing between the close in one market and the opening of another market elsewhere in the world. This is simply another form of arbitrage, a concept we encountered in Chapter 8.[24] An academic from Stanford made the headlines in 2002 and 2003 by estimating that this kind of arbitraging activity could earn between 35% to 70% annually.[25] A recent report by the Ontario Securities Commission suggests that the effects do not appear excessively large, but the added scrutiny has lead to a financial settlement for investors.[26] Some have pointed out that if regulators go after all mutual funds, the resulting increased compliance costs will cause some funds to cease to exist, producing negative implications for competition. In addition, it is not always the case that when prices rise in one region of the world they must necessarily increase elsewhere the next day. In other words, market timing is a form of forecasting what prices might be in the future elsewhere, and this brings risks as well as rewards. Nevertheless, it is clear that the industry has been less than transparent, resulting in a loss of credibility. Hence, if compliance costs rise, the industry may have only itself to blame. As for the anticompetitive effects of increased scrutiny of the mutual fund industry: There are options other than mutual funds—especially in view of the questions raised about their relative performance.[27]

19.11 PENSION FUNDS

Facilitating the reallocation of consumption over time is an important function of financial intermediation. The premier devices for doing so are **pension funds**, which are arrangements for accumulating a portion of a worker's income tax-free until retirement and then paying out periodic benefits. We'll discuss private and public plans, which work quite differently. We'll also look quickly at registered retirement savings plans, which are not truly pension plans but share some of their characteristics.

PRIVATE PENSION PLANS

Private pension plans are pension plans established by private employers (or in some cases, by unions), regulated by the provincial governments. They are also registered with the federal government so that participants can obtain deferral of income tax on contributions until they are paid out as pensions.

Private pension plans exist in great variety. A plan may be *contributory* or *noncontributory* (the employer does or does not match the employee's contributions); voluntary or compulsory (the employee may or may not choose whether to join the plan); *trusteed* or *insured* (managed by a trust company or a committee of trustees, the contributors, or by an insurance company).[28]

Plans also vary according to when members are entitled to draw retirement benefits, and what sort of death benefits accrue to the survivors of a planholder who dies before retirement.[29]

Most important, private pension plans differ on the basis of which benefits are earned. In a *defined-benefit plan*, a policyholder who retires is guaranteed a specific benefit. It may be calculated

---

24 An illustration of this phenomenon is clearly laid out in a letter by the Investment Company Institute (a lobbying group for the Mutual Fund Industry in the U.S.) that can be found at: **www.sec.gov/divisions/investment/guidance/tyle043001.htm**.

25 See E. Zitzewitz, "How Widespread is Latetrading in Mutual Funds?" *American Economic Review Papers and Proceedings* (May 2005).

26 See "Report on Mutual Fund Trading Practices Problem," Ontario Securities Commission, March 2005.

27 There is insufficient space here to go into the relevant details. Some key references are, however, in the bibliography of this chapter.

28 Insured pension plans are, in effect, group annuities. Although common, they tend to be used for relatively small groups. The large pension plans usually are trusteed.

29 A frequent provision is that survivors are entitled to the benefit's *commuted value*, which is the present value of the implicit income stream.

in a variety of ways (perhaps x dollars a month or y% of the individual's average earnings over some period) and it may be indexed for inflation, but the amount is known. Since actuaries can predict with some accuracy the number of policyholders who will be collecting benefits at a given time in the future, they can say whether such a plan is fully funded (its current assets equal the present value of expected benefits).[30] For example, suppose a worker contributes $1000 a year for 20 years. If the annual return is expected to be 8% per year, the value of the accumulated savings would be $45 762 after 20 years.[31] If the defined benefit plan pays less than $45 762, the plan is underfunded.

In a *defined-contribution plan* (also called a money-purchase plan), benefits are not known. They vary according to the amount of accumulated contributions and the return on the fund's investments.

What private pension plans have in common is provincial regulation. They are also registered with the federal government, however, so that income tax on contributions is deferred until they are paid out as pensions.

Are defined-benefit plans superior to defined-contribution plans? In the former, employers assume the risk since they (or their trustees) must make investment decisions and make up shortfalls to fully fund the plan. But, as we know, risk and return are positively related to each other. Therefore, although employees may think it advantageous to have someone else bear the risk, they may be doing so at the expense of receiving lower return and, consequently, fewer funds at retirement age.[32]

Canada Pension Plan
www.cpp-rpc.gc.ca/indexe.html
Canada Pension Plan Investment Board
www.cppib.ca/index_en.html

PUBLIC PENSION PLANS

A public pension plan is one operated by a government. The largest are the Canada Pension Plan (CPP) and Quebec Pension Plan (QPP), which, since 1966, have provided retirement benefits to all members of the Canadian labour force between the ages of 18 and 65 (or 70 depending on circumstances). Membership in the funds is mandatory. Contributions are a fixed percentage of earnings, to a maximum, and are matched by the government.

Until recently, CPP contributions were invested in provincial nonmarketable government bonds, but benefits were paid out of general revenues. The QPP operates in similar fashion, except that the accumulated funds are managed separately by the *Caisse de Dépôt et Placement*, which acts like an ordinary (but huge) pension fund.

In 1999, after several consultations with provincial governments, the CPP obtained the authority to invest in equities. In addition, the CPP is now managed at arm's length from government by an investment board (called the CPP Investment Board). The aging of the labour force during the past decade or so has resulted in benefits' exceeding the value of the accumulated contributions. The federal government has used several increases in contributions levels and the switch to market investing to prevent the CPP fund from being extinguished sometime during the early part of the twenty-first century. The QPP shows fewer signs of running out of its accumulated funds, but it still seeks to operate on a pay-as-you-go basis.

---

30 Some provinces require that private pension plans be fully funded. This requirement arose because some companies were accused of deliberately diverting funds from pension plans, which, in some cases, led to serious underfunding problems.

31 The future value of such an annuity can be calculated in one of two ways: (1) $1000(1.08) + $1000(1.08)^2 + \ldots + $1000(1.08)^{20}$, where the last term is the value of $1000 in 20 years and the first term is the value of $1000 contributed in year 20 (remember from Chapter 5 that interest is earned at the *end* of a period, here a year); (2) application of the formula for the future value of an annuity of $1000 a year for 20 years, namely $[(1.08)^{20} - 1]/0.08$, which would yield the same answer.

32 The problem here, known as *moral hazard*, is perhaps best illustrated with the management of public funds. Instead of investing them at market rates, the government simply borrows what it needs for benefits at an interest rate it sets itself! To the extent that the public sector never has to worry about the government running out of money, no particularly serious problem is created. But if a private sector company behaves in essentially the same way—for example, by appropriating "surplus" pension funds—the outcome is usually not to the benefit of the employees.

Table 19.7 shows the value of holdings of the CPP Investment Board as of the end of 2004. In 2001, the board began to invest in private equities,[33] though these represent only 5% of total holdings. Of the public equities, 65% are Canadian, with the remainder divided roughly equally between U.S. and non-North American holdings.

The unsustainability of the previous system came to a head in 1996 when the finance minister announced the phasing out of the current system and introduction of a new system, tentatively called Seniors Benefits, which would pay out tax-free pensions to seniors on a sliding scale, depending on their income. Under this plan, which would have replaced the current Canada Pension Plan and Old Age Security systems, "wealthy" seniors, that is, those who earn more than $52 000 (or a couple who earn more than $78 000) would no longer receive any benefits. There are still many skeptics who argue that the current plan, despite the phasing in of a sharp increase in contributions over the past few years, continues to be underfunded. Nevertheless, it is unlikely these problems will surface until at least 2015.

Canada has a variety of public pension plans in addition to the CPP and QPP. Many public groups and Crown corporations—from the British Columbia Civil Service to Ontario Hydro—have plans for their employees. They generally resemble private plans, but the money flows through a public agency.

REGISTERED RETIREMENT SAVINGS PLANS (RRSPs)

Many working Canadians are not covered by an employer's pension scheme, and others foresee that the retirement benefits from such a scheme will not be sufficient in their declining years. These people can place a certain amount of income in special trust accounts called **registered retirement savings plans** (**RRSPs**). As with pension plan contributions, no tax is assessed on this income or on its yield as long as it remains in the tax-sheltered account. When the individual is between ages 65 and 69, he or she must collapse the RRSP; if the proceeds are used to buy an annuity or RRIF, however, tax is due on the benefits only as they are paid out. Despite the tax-shelter status of RRSPs, only a third of the labour force makes contributions annually. Nevertheless, almost two-thirds of the labour force has some type of pension plan (RRSPs or registered pension plan).

Although there are regulations on the investments the trustees of an RRSP can make, no special form of intermediation is involved. Indeed, RRSPs are offered by banks, trust companies, life

Table 19.7	**The Major Holdings of the Canada Pension Plan Investment Board and the Canada Pension Plan**
Holdings	**December 31, 2004 (billions)**
Cash	0.4
Public equities	40.5
Private equities	2.5
Government Bonds	6.4
Total CPP Investment Board	**50.6**
Canada Pension Plan	
Cash	4.3
Government bonds	22.3
Total CPP assets	**26.6**
CPP Investment Board as % of total CPP assets	65.5

Note: Totals may not add up due to rounding and omission of smaller items. Data are from **www.cppib.ca/invest/holdings/index.html**.

---

33 "Private market investments consist of equity in general partners that manage private equity funds, buyout and venture capital funds, real estate and infrastructure projects, and energy and natural resource assets." From **http://www.cppib.ca/index_en.html**.

insurance companies, brokers, and mutual funds. Financial intermediaries compete hard for the funds because the market for RRSPs (as for RRIFs) is huge—worth several billion dollars annually. These tax-deferment plans tend to be the saving vehicle of choice.

In recent years, the strong performance of U.S. and international stock markets brought considerable attention to the rule limiting investment in foreign assets. According to this rule, the foreign content limit of RRSPs was limited; exceeding the amount triggered a tax penalty. Critics argue that such limits force "home bias" in investment, thus preventing those who wish to save for their retirement from enjoying higher returns occasionally available outside Canada. Moreover, the development of derivatives considerably weakened the restriction imposed by the rule (the process by which this is accomplished is left as an exercise). The rule was eliminated in 2005, but it is doubtful that the "home-bias" problem will be significantly affected in the coming years because returns elsewhere in the world no longer seem as attractive as they once were.

SUMMARY

- This chapter surveys Canada's various depository institutions other than the chartered banks.

- The trust companies and the credit unions are the principal firms under the heading of "other depository institutions."

- The relative importance of other depository institutions has decreased considerably in recent years, because of the combination of reforms introduced with the 1991 *Bank Act* and the general trend toward consolidation in the financial sector.

- The primary business of trusts is the estate, trust, and agency (ETA) functions. Trusts, along with mortgage loan companies (MLCs), are also defined by their important function as mortgage lenders.

- Credit unions and caisses populaires emerged as local alternatives to savings and borrowing institutions, since access to chartered banks was severely restricted several decades ago.

- The credit union movement remains important in certain regions of the country, such as Western Canada and Quebec.

- Credit unions formed centrals to try to take advantage of scale and scope economies not possible at the level of individual credit unions.

- These other depository institutions have tended to specialize in mortgages and other loans to households. They are trying to branch out into other activities as the differences between them and the chartered banks diminish.

- This chapter also surveys financial institutions whose functions differ from those of deposit-taking institutions.

- These other financial institutions perform some intermediation functions but they also allow consumers to either shift risk or shift income from the present to the future.

- Leasing companies offer a specialized form of lending for the purpose of purchasing physical assets for the most part.

- Investment dealers underwrite securities. These dealers act as brokers rather than as intermediaries since they do not create new assets. Instead, they facilitate the transfer of funds from lenders to borrowers.

- Insurance companies allow individuals to reduce the costs of unforeseen events. But because these companies also accept deposits for the purposes of deferring current income, they also perform an intermediation function.

- Investment companies and funds invest a variety of assets, fractions of which can be purchased by individuals who are therefore able to cheaply acquire a diversified portfolio.

- Pension funds allow individuals to reallocate their income thus also facilitating the maintenance of consumption over a lifetime. Many funds are privately run but a government-run or public pension plan also has an important place in Canada.

IMPORTANT TERMS

annuity, 385

caisses populaires, 376

credit union, 375

demutualization, 383

estate, trust, and agency (ETA) business, 373

financial leasing corporations, 380

insurance, 383

investment companies, 385

investment dealers, 381

merchant bank, 381

mortgage loan company (MLC), 373

mutual funds, 385

pension funds, 387

real estate investment trusts (REITs), 375

registered retirement income fund (RRIF), 385

registered retirement savings plan (RRSP), 389

reinsurance, 384

segregated fund, 383

term insurance, 384

trust company, 373

PROBLEMS

1. Examine Tables 19.2 and 19.4. Based on the information provided, does it appear that assets and liabilities are well matched? Why or why not? Does it appear that leverage is high relative to conventional banks? (Hint: Look at the data in Chapter 11.)

2. The table below shows the evolution between 1990 and 1999 of the short-term and long-term debt of sales, finance, and consumer loan companies. Given the behaviour of short- and long-term interest rates during the same period (also shown below), did these institutions act in such a way as to minimize their debt costs? Discuss your answer.

	1990	1991	1992	1993	1994	1995	1996	1997	1998	1999
Treasury bill rate	11.51	7.43	7.01	3.87	7.04	5.54	2.85	3.99	4.66	4.62
Long-term government bond rate	10.34	8.32	7.86	6.57	9.07	7.11	6.37	5.61	4.89	5.43
Short-term debt (millions of dollars)	9 196	7 310	6 738	6 208	8 498	8 888	10 565	16 710	18 804	18 224
Long-term debt (millions of dollars)	9 376	9 723	8 952	8 873	9 474	11 115	11 409	16 825	23 414	23 081

Source: Bank of Canada Review, various issues, Table A2 and D3.

3. Do investment fund managers as a whole respond to risk–return considerations and suffer any consequences as outlined in this text? The following table shows the dollar holdings of three important assets as well as total assets held by investment dealers during 1999. Discuss how the financial events of 1999 may be reflected in the balance sheet changes. (Recall that the stock market boomed during that year.)

Assets	1998–99 (thousands of dollars)		
	First Quarter 1998	First Quarter 1999	Second Quarter 1999
Preferred and common shares	86 901	107 630	109 649
Bankers' acceptances	23 425	28 399	29 622
Canada Treasury bills	35 862	34 894	34 674
Total assets	271 784	320 370	325 908

4. A life insurance company operates an investment fund. The following table shows the hypothetical accumulated value of a single deposit of $10 000 at various years as a function

of three different interest rate levels. The figures assume that an "acquisition fee" has been deducted to cover administration expenses. Calculate the dollar and percentage amount of the acquisition fee. Would you expect that fee to vary according to the size of the deposit?

End of Year	5%	10%	12½%
5	$12 154	$ 15 345	$ 17 164
10	15 516	24 708	30 928
15	19 802	39 786	55 740
20	25 270	64 084	100 441
30	41 167	166 201	326 165
40	67 056	431 093	1 059 741

5. The following table gives the 1-year, 5-year, and 10-year average return on a variety of assets, which are indexed according to their risk characteristics (specifically, default risk and income risk). Plot the risk–return combinations for the three periods separately. Are the results consistent with the analysis in the text? If so, why? If not, why not? Does the risk index make sense?

Asset	Risk Index	1-year	5-years	10-years
Savings account	1	6.21	6.68	7.66
Five-year term deposit	2	10.00	7.84	11.85
Five-year GIC	2	11.25	10.01	13.19
Canada Savings Bond	0	10.87	9.69	11.03
Three-month Treasury bill	0	10.97	10.71	11.24
TSE300 at close	3	11.58	6.20	10.04
S&P 500	3	26.73	10.89	12.81
Equity funds	5	31.66	15.26	15.95
Balanced funds	3	24.39	10.56	15.53
Consumer Price Index	—	5.66	4.75	5.09

Source: The Globe and Mail, 17 October 1991, p. C2.

6. Why has the fixing of caps on RRSPs in nominal terms meant an effective reduction in the tax advantage provided by this kind of tax shelter?

DISCUSSION QUESTIONS

1. Why do you think legislation barred chartered banks from engaging in estate, trust, and agency business?

2. Explain why, historically, credit unions were created and why they may have played a relatively larger role in some areas of the country than in others.

3. Apart from banking-type services, what other important functions are filled by trust companies?

4. What economies of scale and scope can credit union centrals exploit? Explain.

5. The Canadian population is aging. Why does this put more pressure on the CPP and QPP? Does this also affect private pensions? Explain.

6. What kind of specialized service do finance and leasing companies perform that banks do not?

7. Why did banks find it natural to take over much of the investment dealer industry?

8. What kind of gaps are filled by government-run or -backed financial institutions?

9. Why are mutual funds so popular? Why do some feel they are a "rip off"?

10. Is there a link between the growth in the importance of leasing among sales and finance companies and the restriction preventing banks from entering auto leasing?

11. Why did so many insurance companies want to demutualize? What are the benefits?

12. What motivated the federal and provincial governments to radically change how the CPP invests its funds? Explain.

13. Discuss some of the issues surrounding the market timing phenomenon. Do you think it is possible to outlaw this practice? Is this a legitimate form of arbitrage?

ONLINE APPLICATIONS

1. Go to the CUCC's Web site at **www.cucentral.ca**. Click on *Financial data*. Next, choose *Financial Statements* (any year) and scroll down to *interest rate sensitivity*. Interpret the figures in terms of the text's earlier analysis of asset–liability management principles.

2. Repeat question 1, except choose *Deposit Insurance* from the CUCC's home page. Try to construct a table outlining the essential features of each province's deposit-protection program. Next, compare the deposit insurance scheme across provinces, as well as against the CDIC's program (see Chapter 16).

3. Go to the Insurance Compensation Board's Web site at **www.compcorp.ca**. Click an item under *Coverage by Product*. Compare coverage with that provided by deposit insurance (see Chapter 16) and list the similarities and differences.

CANSIM QUESTIONS

Go to the CANSIM Web site and download Canadian population data (V1). Collect data for two years of your choice but make sure they are at least ten years apart. Construct a histogram or a bar chart measuring total population on the vertical axis and population by major age groups (i.e., 0–4 years, 5–9 years, 10–14 years, and so on). Confirm that the Canadian population is indeed aging. How important a factor was this in prompting reforms to the CPP system?

References can be found on **www.mcgrawhill.ca/college/siklos**

CHAPTER 20

Managing Risk: Regulation of the Financial System

LEARNING OBJECTIVES

After reading and studying this chapter, you should be able to

20.1 identify the key elements influencing the regulation of the financial system

20.2 list and describe the dilemmas facing policymakers and regulators today

20.3 identify the three dominant themes of regulation today and why there is no one classification that fits all sizes

It is natural to think of risks as being uniquely determined by the marketplace. The preceding three chapters certainly give the impression that free markets in the movement of funds dominate today. Although this is largely true, we have yet to discuss systematically one important player in the financial system, namely the role of government as regulator. For well over a century governments at the federal and provincial levels have imposed rules, regulations, and oversight mechanisms on the financial sector. Are these actions a result of public pressure, or are there more basic forces that naturally lead governments to, in a sense, manage some of the risks created by the financial sector?

Part of the desire to regulate the financial industry stems from historical developments, particularly over the past 20 years. We'll look at whether special circumstances highlighted the role of government in recent history.

Finally, if we accept that some form of government involvement is necessary, how should regulation proceed? In other words, does regulation come in specific forms and, if so, what are some of the dilemmas facing governments in dealing with financial sector reform and regulation?

As you will see, this chapter raises many questions. In addition, the chapter brings together several issues discussed throughout the text. Nevertheless, the focus here is on the forces leading to the regulation of the financial system, the goals of those forces, and the problems and choices facing governments in this area.

20.1 GUIDING PRINCIPLES OF GOVERNMENT REGULATION

Government regulation exists to fill a gap apparently left by the market. As we have already seen (for example, in Chapter 3), the financial industry is unique in our economy if only because, historically, when one bank fails, many others follow. Therefore, the **contagion** effect of bank failures is thought to be much stronger in the financial industry than in other industries. For example, in Canada, several trust companies failed within a very short time in the early 1990s, in part because of the severe recession that hit a part of the country, and also in part because of drawbacks with the existing regulatory framework (also Chapter 16). The U.S. financial system, perhaps more than most, has experienced the devastating impact of waves of bank failures, first during the Great Depression of the 1930s, and then again in the late 1980s, when the saving and loan industry virtually collapsed.[1]

Market failure occurs for other reasons as well as those mentioned above, such as dishonesty and attempts to rig financial markets or transactions, leading to demands by the public that governments protect citizens from such abuses. Finally, the public may expect the financial industry to reach more lofty social goals that may or may not conflict with the profit-earning goal of managers and shareholders.

We can therefore summarize the guiding principles of government regulation as follows:

- Ensuring the safety of the financial system, through what are often referred to as the **prudential requirements** of regulation. This goal can be satisfied in several ways, such as through the provision of deposit insurance, or via disclosure rules to mitigate the asymmetric information problem that pervades many financial transactions (see Chapter 3).[2] Indeed, deposit insurance is important enough that we devote an entire chapter to its function and operation in Canada and elsewhere (see Chapter 16).

- Promoting efficiency. Rules that assist financial institutions in providing services for the least cost or in the most effective manner possible can, in theory at least, be profitable to shareholders and beneficial to consumers.

- Ensuring competition. Regulation can be used to ease entry of potential competitors when they perceive either a profitable opportunity or one that has not yet been exploited by current market participants. Alternatively, competition can also help ensure that services are provided most efficiently to the consumer of financial services.

- Promoting social goals. Although financial sector participants are private institutions run for the benefit of shareholders and managers, a larger national interest may exist that regulators want to promote. For example, regulators may feel the need to ensure that asset ownership is primarily in domestic hands, or that consumers in sparsely populated regions have access to a minimum of financial services.

It is clear that some of the guiding principles or goals of financial regulation can occasionally come into conflict with each other, and financial history is replete with examples that reinforce this point.

20.2 WINDS OF CHANGE: LEVELLING THE PLAYING FIELD

Regulation of the financial sector has, in many ways, been a cyclical phenomenon. In the nineteenth century, the era of free banking, governments in Canada were happy to allow banks to be largely self-regulated. Thereafter, government involvement grew as banks, which were largely in existence to satisfy purely commercial needs, exhibited a desire to branch out into different areas of finance. Simultaneously, a growing population and the growing desire by the public to hold financial assets or to engage in activities linked to finance provided opportunities for new institutions, leading policymakers to extend their regulatory mandate.

---

1 There is a large literature which attempts to identify the determinants of crises and whether there are early warning signs. Weak economic performance in the months leading up to a banking crisis as well as weak law enforcement and a poor regulatory framework are the leading indicators of a crisis. Some of the literature with detailed data and case studies is listed at **www.mcgrawhill.ca/college/siklos**.

2 Recall from Chapter 3 that asymmetric information arises when the two parties to a financial transaction do not have the same information to base their decision on.

However, if we focus on the past two decades of Canadian financial history, we see that the winds of change have been particularly strong. Table 20.1 is a highly selective chronology of key events that have had a major impact on the role and influence of government regulation in the financial sector. We can, in addition, highlight the driving forces behind the Canadian financial system. These forces have converged, with one dominant objective in mind, namely, to level the playing field among financial institutions in Canada. Why? Primarily the reason is that, until recently, the regulation of the Canadian financial system has been a patchwork that constrained the different players in different ways. By the 1980s, many analysts became convinced that these regulations added up to an inefficient and possibly uncompetitive environment that was increasingly out of step with international developments. In a sense, Canadian regulators have come full circle. Regulation, as we will see, is now thought of as ensuring that a minimum of prudential controls are imposed on financial institutions. Previously, regulations attempted to control virtually every aspect of the operations of financial institutions.

What are the major forces leading to a levelling of the playing field in the financial sector? The most important of these forces include the following:

- Technological change. Many analysts have identified improvements in computing technology as the principal driving force behind the financial system in recent years. The development of Internet banking, dramatic improvements in payments technology (for example, debit cards), and the scale economies created by the tremendous increase in computing power and the concomitant reduction in computing costs have all combined to change the financial landscape. At the same time, however, technology has also ushered in a new era of competition in the provision of financial services. No longer are traditional banks the sole source of finance, nor are they as vital as they previously were in the provision of retail-level financial transactions. Although the resulting opportunities have no doubt delivered many benefits, they have complicated considerably the problems faced by regulators, as we will see.

- Globalization and consolidation. Although the internationalization of financial markets, referred to as globalization, is not an entirely new phenomenon, it has experienced a tremendous resurgence over the past two decades thanks to worldwide efforts to deregulate financial markets. The growing consolidation in the financial industry is itself related both to renewed globalization and to technological developments. Globalization has raised the bar necessary to

Table 20.1	**A Selective Chronology of Change in the Canadian Financial Sector**
Year	**Event**
1985	First in a series of chartered bank failures
1987	Mid-term regulatory reforms to the existing *Bank Act*
1990–93	Series of failures of trusts, especially in Ontario (failures elsewhere in the country predate this wave)
1990s	• Consolidation and acquisition in the Canadian banking system accelerate • Financial innovations accelerate • Attempts to regulate payments and banks on a global scale accelerate
1998	• Merger plans of four large Canadian banks turned down by the minister of finance • *Report on the Future of the Financial Services Sector* released
1999	• Demutualization of insurance companies begins • Major deregulatory effort in the United States approved
2000–01	Comprehensive revision of the *Bank Act* in Canada
2006?	New guideliness for bank mergers

Note: The above list is selective and serves simply to illustrate some of the key events directly influencing the form of financial regulation in Canada. Chapters 19, 20, 21, and 23 offer details on these and other events of note in the evolution of the financial sector.

compete on an international scale. In the case of technology, lower costs have made it easier to attract entrants into the financial industry. However, the growing complexity of financial transactions and the attendant risks involved (for example, as in the case of derivative products, discussed in Chapter 15) have also contributed to improving the level at which today's financial services can be provided efficiently. Despite the publicity given to notions of globalization, it may surprise many that, when it comes to the financial sector, globalization and consolidation lags far behind other sectors or industries in the economy. For example, one study[3] reports that in Europe, which one would have thought would be ripe for consolidation, almost two-thirds of firms chose a host nation bank over a home nation bank to conduct much of their financial business. Politics, taxes, and culture, among other factors, continue to represent significant barriers in the area of finance.

- Improved payments and settlements systems. As recently as ten years ago, central banks in industrial economies were instrumental in helping the banking system clear payments and settle both large and small financial transactions. In addition, payments systems differed substantially across countries. Today, payments and settlements are essentially conducted in real time (see, for example, Chapters 4 and 15), with little or no intervention by central banks. Moreover, techniques to settle payments are converging across countries in an attempt to minimize the systemic risks that existed with older settlement systems. Clearly, technology, combined with a renewed desire to reduce direct government intervention in the financial system, has altered the role of regulation.

- Frequency of regulatory reform. As we saw in Chapter 18, the centrepiece of financial legislation in Canada is the *Bank Act*. Originally, the Act was to be revised every ten years. The pace of change would force different governments either to delay or avoid needed reforms. However, by the 1990s, the outcry from domestic financial institutions became too loud to ignore. In addition, the pressures of global competition led to a series of interim measures as well as a move to effectively revise the *Bank Act* at least every five years. Indeed, it is no exaggeration to say that today the *Bank Act* is a work in progress. New developments, typically unforeseen by all the parties involved, including financial market participants, are forcing more frequent changes in the legislation governing the financial industry. However, there remains one constant, namely that financial sector legislation is still a lagging indicator of changes taking place in the financial sector. A good example concerns regulations about the circumstances under which bank mergers will be permitted. The federal government has been promising new regulations since shortly after the last *Bank Act* came into law. However, as this is written, banks are still waiting for the promised rules.

- Jurisdictional issues. Largely as a result of history, regulatory jurisdiction has been divided among federal and provincial governments. The widespread view in the nineteenth century was that finance mattered only to the commercial sector. By the early part of the twentieth century, however, the growing needs to finance noncommercial enterprises, together with the proliferation of alternatives to finance from commercial banks, revealed a chasm between the federal and provincial governments in their respective responsibilities to regulate financial institutions. It was only in the early 1990s that the rift between levels of government over regulatory authority began to diminish. However, significant problems remain. For example, securities regulation is a provincial matter, again by custom, not through any constitutional prerogative. Recent attempts to create a national agency have failed, and Canada is clearly out of step in this area. Typically, in other countries, securities regulations apply at the national level.

- Demographics. It has been widely reported in the press that the population is aging, with major consequences for the provision of financial services. The intermediation service offered by the conventional banking institution (see Chapter 18), which consists of transforming illiquid assets

---

3 A. N. Berger, Q. Dai, S. Ongena, and D.C. Smith, "To What Extent Will the Banking Industry be Globalized? A Study of Bank Nationality and Reach in 20 European Nations," *International Finance Discussion Papers*, No. 725, May 2002.

into liquid assets, the phenomenon some refer to as the "transmutation of assets," is less important to a population that is accumulating large amounts of financial wealth. As a result, wealth management is becoming a dominant financial service, as the tremendous growth of mutual funds and pension funds attests. Banks, for example, are rapidly changing their business emphasis to be in line with these demographic changes but, in doing so, are creating new challenges for regulators, who must now increasingly focus their attention on the disclosure requirements of mutual funds, for example, and adapt to the changing prudential requirements raised by these changes.

- Corporate governance. The sometimes close connection between industry and financial markets, as highlighted by the series of scandals that began in 2001 with the Enron and WorldCom cases and continued through 2002 with more revelations of fraud, corruption, and shady dealings that hid accurate financial information from the public, led policymakers to revise their views about corporate governance. Indeed, as this is written there are powerful forces pushing for reforms that include new oversight bodies to ensure that accurate financial information is provided to the public, jail sentences for CEOs who fail to adequately report company earnings, and truly arm's length board members independent of the senior executive to provide meaningful outside input and ensure corporate accountability. Since the Enron and WorldCom affairs are not really a new phenomenon[4] it remains to be seen how meaningful the reform movement will be.[5]

Keeping abreast of changes in the regulation of the financial system
www.fin.gc.ca/ access/finiste.html

IS ASYMMETRIC INFORMATION A THING OF THE PAST?

Many industry observers claim that the intermediation function is a special characteristic of banking. However, in an Internet era, it is reasonable to ask whether other types of institutions can take advantage of the resulting reduction in information and participation costs in financial transactions. The short answer is yes. However, although information is clearly plentiful and inexpensive software to evaluate risks, for example, is widely available, the complexity of financial transactions has also increased. Moreover, expert advice is still needed to properly evaluate and assess risks in financial transactions and, more importantly, to bear such risks. Hence, it is not clear whether asymmetric information is entirely a thing of the past. It may simply be that the location and nature of the problem have been affected by technological improvements.

Nevertheless, since technology has increased the participation of nontraditional institutions in the provision of finance, important implications arise for the regulation of the financial system. For example, the regulation of institutions is likely to produce different results than a form that aims to regulate the functions of an institution.

DOES ONE SIZE FIT ALL?

The forces of globalization and consolidation led to attempts to streamline the regulatory function and to a reconsideration of whether a single piece of legislation is capable of summarizing the regulatory needs of vastly different institutions that have in common only the fact that they are involved in some aspect of finance. These considerations led to changes in the so-called regulatory framework. For example, Canada was one of the first industrialized nations to combine the

---

4 See R. Smith, "Enron's Rise and Fall Mirrors Collapse of Middle West Utilities 70 Years Ago," *Wall Street Journal Online*, 4 February 2002, available at **online.wsj.com**.

5 These reforms have proved controversial, especially in the U.S. Indeed, many firms have voluntarily delisted their stock from U.S. exchanges to avoid the provisions of what is called the Sarbanes-Oxley Act of 2002 (for additional information, see **www.sarbanes-oxley.com**; a summary of the regulations can be found at **www.aicpa.org/info/sarbanes_oxley_ summary.htm**). In Canada, the 2003 budget also brought in changes to improve the enforcement of financial regulations nationwide and to strengthen corporate governance rules, as well as changes in the criminal code to increase penalties for individuals who violate financial laws.

insurance and deposit-taking regulatory agencies under one roof, namely under the Office of the Superintendent of Financial Institutions (or OSFI; see Chapter 16). Nevertheless, some aspects of prudential regulation still reside at the provincial level, though the situation is much improved relative to a decade ago.

At the international level, attempts have been made to carry out a convergence in banking and financial regulations, spearheaded by the Bank for International Settlements (BIS, see Chapter 26). It has been pointed out that Canada is the only country with multiple regulators, and that this situation increasingly will hamper businesses' ability to raise capital. The Canadian Bankers Association (CBA) released a report in the summer of 2003[6] in which they pleaded for reforms in this area. Essentially two proposals have been put forward:

- A national regulator, but one in which the provinces and territories would play a role. Jurisdiction would essentially be turned over to the federal government;

- Maintain the current system but harmonize legislation across the country, thereby permitting each regulator to issue a "passport" providing a stamp of approval valid across the entire country.

The CBA favours the national regulator approach and points out that frustrations over the inefficiencies inherent in regional regulation of securities issuance eventually led the U.S. and Australia to adopt a national solution. Then-Finance Minister John Manley appointed a "wise-persons" committee which also reported its findings at the end of 2003, calling for a national regulator.[7] The only region of the world in which the passport approach is in use is the European Union. However, the CBA contends that the "cultural" differences within the EU are not replicated in Canada. Hence, a national solution is the only sensible one. Not everyone is in favour of the national approach, especially the province of Quebec (although the Ontario government does support the national regulator concept). Hence, although a uniform standard for approving the issue of securities is deemed desirable, it is not obvious that this is best enforced through a single regulator. Instead, why not have the federal government act as coordinator of national rules, while letting the provinces effectively issue the necessary "passport"?[8]

The internationalization and centralization of regulatory activities is not without costs. First, although Canada is a G-7 member, the size of its financial sector is small in international terms. Consequently, it may not have as much influence as it might like in global reform efforts. Second, international pressures to reform the regulatory framework may conflict with domestic goals, at least as enunciated by governments in office. Thus, for example, when the finance minister denied the merger plans of four large Canadian chartered banks (see Chapter 18 for details), his action was interpreted as largely stemming from domestic political influences. This decision appears to fly in the face of the wave of consolidation worldwide of large and small financial institutions. Third, centralization of regulatory activities may do wonders for reducing the overlap among governments and existing regulators, but it may also make the resulting regulators less responsive to the various constituencies, with sometimes conflicting objectives vying for their attention. For example, when the U.S. Federal Reserve attempted to increase considerably its supervisory powers in the wake of the savings and loan fiasco (see Chapter 25), the U.S. Congress blocked the move on the grounds that too much centralization of the supervisory function would weaken the division of powers among existing agencies, a notion that has always been anathema in U.S. political thought. In a similar vein, some have blamed the Japanese Ministry of Finance, which, until recently, not only oversaw banks but also the central bank (the Bank of Japan), for failing to come

---

6 "Proposals for an Efficient and Effective Securities Regulatory System in Canada," *Canadian Bankers Association*, June 2003.

7 See **www.wise-averties.ca/main_en.html**.

8 Chant J., "A Passport Solution," *National Post* (22 July 2003): FP11. The provinces have their own views on the securities regulation issue. More information is available at **www.securitiescanada.org**.

to grips with the implications of the massive insolvency of the Japanese banking system the country is still coping with. The oversight of the powerful Finance Ministry was simply insufficient, with the consequence that necessary decisions and the proper supervision of the financial system were woefully inadequate.

It would seem, therefore, that one size does not fit all in the regulatory context.

CANADA'S POSITION

It is useful, before discussing the various general forms of government regulation, to briefly step back and consider some of the salient restrictions facing banks in Canada in which regulation is a determining factor. As we have seen, banks in Canada still occupy a key position in the Canadian financial system (see Chapters 3 and 18). Consequently, the manner in which regulation affects banks is likely to be an important barometer of the state of current and expected future regulatory activity. Tables 20.2 and 20.3 summarize the main points.

Table 20.2 illustrates areas of bank regulation in Canada that are at variance with developments in selected other countries in four vital areas. For example, bank holding companies are widely used in the United States, the United Kingdom, Australia, and Germany, to name but four countries where this institutional form is permitted. Originally created in the United States

Table 20.2	Ownership Rules and Restrictions: A Selective Cross-Country Comparison

Bank holding companies permitted?	
Yes	**No**
Australia	
Germany	
United Kingdom	
United States	
Canada (limited and permitted only since 2002)	

Universal banking permitted?	
Unrestricted	**Restricted**
Germany	Canada
New Zealand	
United Kingdom	
United States	

Competition from foreign banks?	
Significant	**Small (15% or less)**
Australia	Canada
New Zealand	
United Kingdom	
United States	

Banking industry concentration?	
Low	**High**
Germany	Canada
United Kingdom	
United States	

Table 20.3	Existing Regulatory Barriers Facing Banks in Canada and in the United States	
Form of Regulation	**Status in Canada**	**Status in the United States**
Interest rate regulation	None	None
Restriction on type of financial activities	Some	None
Restrictions on entry	Some	Few
Restrictions on ownership	Some	None
Restrictions on international financial transactions/movements of funds	None	None

to avoid regulatory restrictions on the opening of branches across state lines (see Chapter 25), bank holding companies are now seen as a useful device to permit common ownership of distinct companies engaged in a wide variety of financial transactions. Bank holding companies are now permitted under the latest version of the *Bank Act* (see Chapter 18), though there are a number of thresholds that must be exceeded before one can create them.

A second area of global regulatory differences concerns the ability of nonfinancial firms to own financial institutions. The worry among regulators in Canada and elsewhere has always been that the nonfinancial firm might use the deposits of a bank it owns as a direct source of finance, thereby putting the bank potentially at risk of failure. Such restrictions are largely disappearing among many, but not all, of the major industrial countries.[9]

A third salient characteristic of Canadian bank regulations concerns restrictions on foreign ownership. As we saw in Chapter 18, this concern has come in different forms in Canada's history. Suffice it to say that the degree of market penetration by foreign banks is considerably higher in several other countries, with no apparent detrimental effect on domestic finance.

Finally, concerns have been expressed about the degree to which deposits, for example, are concentrated among the five largest banks in Canada. In contrast, it has been argued, a more competitive environment has meant significantly lower concentration levels in several other countries. This issue is controversial, not only because analysts disagree with the importance attached to such measures as indicators of competitiveness, but also because the high concentration of deposits has also been accompanied, some would argue, by a more stable banking system less prone to crises or failures.

Table 20.3 highlights, in comparison with the United States, some of the areas in which reforms introduced in 1999 have changed the regulatory and competitive frameworks significantly, and in which policymakers will have to make important regulatory decisions. In particular, restrictions on the range of activities in which banks are permitted to engage, restrictions on entry (whether from domestic or foreign sources), and restrictions on ownership are three areas that present dilemmas for policymakers as they struggle to follow the guiding principles of regulation outlined earlier.

20.3 FORMS OF REGULATION

Governments face three different regulatory options with, of course, different consequences for the financial system. As will become apparent, the existing regulatory framework in Canada is essentially a mixture of the three. This situation is perhaps inevitable, since financial transactions are becoming more complex, increasingly involve cross-border transactions, and since, based on the historical record, the regulatory framework generally lags behind developments in the financial sector.

---

9 A recent analysis of the pros (mostly) of permitting mergers between banks and insurance companies is S. Stewart, "A Case for Allowing Bank-Insurance Mergers: Shareholder Value," *The Globe and Mail* (15 September 2003): B1, B5.

SELF-REGULATION

It should be immediately obvious to anyone reading the text that not every aspect of a bank's operations can be regulated, nor is it desirable or efficient to do so in a market economy. After all, the market is a dispassionate regulator of sorts through entry to and exit from an industry, as well as through competition. In addition, however, financial institutions find it in their best interests to regulate themselves. For example, ethical considerations exist between customers and firms in the same industry that could be resolved through self-regulation. There are also incentives to practise good conduct vis-à-vis the public more generally that can only be achieved if member institutions police themselves to some extent. Generally, this policing is accomplished via associations among member institutions. One such association with a long history in Canada is the Canadian Bankers' Association, but similar associations exist in other segments of the financial sector, as noted elsewhere in this textbook.

Canadian Bankers'
Association
www.cba.ca

Finally, modern corporations generally do not allow all decisions to be made by one individual. Rather, a board exists not so much to oversee the day-to-day operations of a financial institution as to ensure that conflicts between management and shareholders are minimized (the possible consequences of such conflicts are explored in the next chapter), and to allow a broader perspective to influence the decision-making process. Indeed, some analysts have suggested that, in the Canadian context, weaknesses in **corporate governance** practices are responsible for many of the failures in the financial sector in Canada in the 1980s and 1990s. Clearly, it is conceivable that some regulation aimed at strengthening the role of boards and providing them with better information to make timely decisions is one avenue open to future reform. Alternatively, several models of corporate governance are already in place, many with proven track records so that self-regulation remains a viable option.

Nevertheless, self-regulation can only go as far in a modern financial system as the overriding principle of prudential regulation allows, and concerns over competitiveness naturally lead to some formal type of intervention. We now consider the major forms in which such regulation can be implemented.

INSTITUTIONAL REGULATION

In the days when banks overwhelmingly dominated the financial scene in Canada and the vast majority of loans were of a commercial nature, it was evident that regulating the activities of institutions was appropriate. Hence, **institutional regulation** was developed. Indeed, it was in large part because of these kinds of considerations that banking-type activities were so narrowly defined in Canada (also see Chapter 18).

As the Canadian economy expanded rapidly during the twentieth century, new specialized institutions emerged because of the practice of institutional regulation. As a result, trust companies emerged to fill the estate, trust, and agency functions (also known as the fiduciary function), insurance companies emerged to fill a gap in the protection of individuals and firms against unforeseen events, and investment dealers emerged to handle the securities underwriting function. As the separation of functions became more ingrained in the structure of the Canadian financial system, the outcome was the so-called four pillars concept discussed previously (see, for example, Chapter 1).

Regulators certainly had good reasons in the past century to build firewalls between these specialist institutions and then separately regulate them. The general lack of financial sophistication among the public until fairly recently, the fear of creating overly large and unresponsive financial institutions, and the experience of the Great Depression generally soured policymakers on the notion that financial institutions should have unfettered access to every area of finance.

By the 1960s, however, the growth in world trade, and the growth in financial wealth alongside it, together with the easing of restrictions on the movement of capital, led to a change of heart among regulators. The market was beginning to reassert itself and promised some measure of discipline for the behaviour of financial institutions. In addition, since financial transactions were becoming more prominent worldwide, regulated financial institutions were finding ways around existing regulations, either by expanding abroad, or by shifting activities elsewhere to avoid domestic regulations.

Explore the Royal Bank Web site at **www.royalbank. com**, Canadian Tire Acceptance Ltd. at **www.ctal.com**, and GE Capital at **www.ge.com**

Almost simultaneously, the patchwork of legislation in Canada aimed at regulating activities of financial industry participants was permitting the blurring of activities. This blurring was facilitated by attempts by some participants to avoid federal legislation through the cover of often more lax provincial regulations. Of course, such developments also came at a cost. Compliance costs escalated and conflicts between federal and provincial jurisdictions also imposed additional costs on industry participants. However, as noted earlier, technological innovations permitted existing financial institutions to broaden their financial product offerings while allowing the opportunity for nonfinancial firms to begin offering financial services.

All of these forces suggest that the institutional form of regulation was becoming outdated. Nevertheless, the latest *Bank Act*, although a step in the right direction in treating institutions alike that more or less fulfil the same functions in the financial sector, remains a document rooted firmly in the institutional regulation era.

FUNCTIONAL REGULATION

Banks today are complex institutions subdivided into several components that specialize in certain areas of finance. Thus, one group may deal with mutual funds, another with the brokerage end of the business, still another with insurance needs, while the conventional bank branch carries out the deposit-taking and loan-making functions and may act as the front door to other divisions of the organization. The banking arm may be further subdivided into wholesale and retail banking divisions. The Royal Bank, for example, is one such institution, but all the major chartered banks (see Chapter 19) are now structured along similar lines. Similarly, nonbank institutions may also have separate divisions. One division produces the goods and services the firm is traditionally known for, while another may be a capital group that provides large-scale finance or perhaps insurance or credit card products. Two notable examples include Canadian Tire Acceptance Ltd. and GE Capital.

The upshot is that institutions are no longer necessarily recognizable by their traditional roles. It is therefore potentially inefficient, not to say costly, to attempt to regulate institutions rather than the various functions a particular institution fulfils. Although the above developments are fairly recent, there is a long list of reports and analyses stretching back to the late 1960s that advocate **functional regulation**. Most recently, the MacKay Report on the Future of the Financial Services Sector made the same point, and there are indications that governments have heeded the call to take a new approach to the regulation of the banking system. Under functional regulation, regulations would seek to ensure that the following three aims be met by each function:

- safety and soundness in business practices
- market conduct conducive to competition
- protection of consumers' interests

Additional regulations may be required, if deemed socially beneficial, to ensure that adequate safeguards exist to prevent, for example, one division from unduly financing itself from another division that may be a poor financial performer. Similarly, regulations to protect the consumer may require clear disclosure rules to prevent the tied sale of financial products from another division of the same institution to an unwitting customer. This practice is called **self-dealing**. Indeed, there is a good possibility that a separate consumer watchdog will perform some of these tasks alongside the Office of Superintendent of Financial Institutions (OSFI) in the coming years. As noted previously, a change in focus toward the functional approach would also legitimize the use of bank holding companies as a means of facilitating the regulatory process.

SUMMARY

- Regulation is aimed at ensuring that financial institutions satisfy a series of guiding principles deemed beneficial to society.

- The guiding principles of financial regulation are prudential requirements, the promotion of efficiency, the encouragement of competition, and the promotion of social goals.

- The regulatory efforts in Canada over the past 20 years have been aimed at creating a level playing field among the increasingly diverse group of institutions providing financial services.

- Forces leading to a level playing field include improvements in technology, globalization and consolidation, improvements in payments and settlements systems, an increase in the frequency of regulatory reforms, the resolution of some jurisdictional issues, and demographic changes in Canadian society.

- Asymmetric information, one of the raisons d'être of banks, has changed but has not disappeared entirely. Information costs may be lower, but financial transactions are becoming more complex.

- Globalization and consolidation may be leading to a convergence in regulations across countries, but domestic influences on financial regulations will remain in the years to come.

- Important differences in regulatory frameworks exist across countries. They are summarized in Tables 20.2 and 20.3.

- There are three major forms of regulation: self-regulation, institutional regulation, and functional regulation.

- All three forms are currently practised in Canada. Historically, however, institutional regulation has dominated the Canadian scene.

- Technology has led to a preference for functional regulation as traditional banking firms become increasingly complex financial institutions; nontraditional firms are also entering the financial arena.

IMPORTANT TERMS

contagion, **394**
corporate governance, **402**
functional regulation, **403**

institutional regulation, **402**
prudential requirements, **395**
self-dealing, **403**

DISCUSSION QUESTIONS

1. What are the guiding principles of government regulation? Can you list them in order of importance? What guided your ranking?

2. Why is the contagion effect in the banking industry a more serious problem than in other industries? What are the implications of this phenomenon?

3. Explain how the guiding principles of government regulation can conflict with each other. Can you give an example from recent Canadian financial history to illustrate your point?

4. Does the fact that regulation is a lagging indicator of financial evolution pose a problem for achieving the goals of regulation? Why?

5. What are the main forces behind levelling the playing field among financial institutions? Are some of these forces more important than others in your opinion? Why?

6. "Asymmetric information is a thing of the past." Evaluate this statement and its implications for the banking industry.

7. What are some of the key areas of difference between the regulatory framework in Canada and elsewhere? Are some of the differences more important than others? Why?

8. What are the principal forms of government regulation? Briefly define them.

9. What has been the dominant form of regulation in Canada, in a historical sense? Why?

10. Analysts prefer the functional form of regulation. What changes in the financial system led them to this conclusion?

ONLINE APPLICATION

Go to **http://www.wise-averties.ca/ main_en.html** and download the wise persons committee review of the structure of securities regulation in Canada.

1. What are the committee's principal recommendations?

2. What are the pros and cons of the single regulator model?

3. What is the "passport solution" to regulating securities underwriting?

4. Would the passport model be more politically acceptable? Is it likely to be a better model in economic and regulatory terms?

References can be found on **www.mcgrawhill.ca/college/siklos**

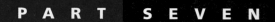

Central Banking and Monetary Policy

The Role of Monetary Policy

LEARNING OBJECTIVES

After reading and studying this chapter, you should be able to

21.1 define monetarism and main competing theories of monetary thought

21.2 explain what the Phillips curve represents

21.2 describe the role played by inflation expectations and how they are measured

21.3 determine why there is inconsistency in optimal monetary policy

21.4 explain the roles played by quantity theory and the real bills doctrine in understanding the influence of monetary policy and what they predict

21.5 list the channels of the monetary transmission mechanism, and discuss what we can learn from them and why they are varied

21.6 determine whether monetary policy contributes to economic growth

This textbook has considered how the monetary authorities and the financial system as a whole interact with each other, as well as how they influence key macroeconomic variables such as interest rates. However, the discussion so far has been relatively silent about differing views economists have about the role of money and financial markets more generally in influencing overall economic performance, that is, macroeconomic outcomes. These considerations influence recommendations made about policies that are eventually implemented, so it is important to have some understanding about policy debates.

Some exposure to these questions is also vital if you are to understand the comments of elected public officials or central bankers, for, as Milton Friedman put it almost 40 years ago,

> "In years when thing are going well,…monetary policy is an exceedingly potent instrument and…the favorable course of events is largely the result of the skillful handling of this delicate instrument by the monetary authority. In years of depression, on the other hand,…monetary policy is but one of many tools of economic policy,…its power is highly limited, and…it was only the skillful handling of such limited powers as were available that averted disaster." (Friedman 1962, p. 233)

Friedman's somewhat cynical view is prompted by the belief held by most economists that policymakers of all stripes are motivated by self-interest and portray their performance in the best possible light. The material in this chapter will help you begin to see through the pronouncements of policymakers.

You should think of this chapter as a bridge to the study of macroeconomics. Typically, courses in macroeconomics develop models that allow for the study of business cycles and economic growth. The present chapter is intended to whet your appetite for the study of such models, without developing them in great detail, and to outline some of the major practical policy questions that have been or are currently being debated by academics, business leaders, and policymakers. You will gain some understanding of how the discussion fits into the broader picture of the role of monetary policy in the overall economy. The next two chapters consider the problem of conducting monetary policy as seen through the institution of the central bank, arguably the most important financial entity in any modern economy.

WHY ECONOMISTS DISAGREE

Disagreements among economists sometimes arise because of differences in focus. Some prefer to concentrate on long-run problems; others are more interested in short-run problems. Alternatively, some concern themselves with how best to measure some economic variable, whereas others are more interested in exploring conditions under which they can evaluate the economic effects of certain government policies. In many cases, however, debates persist because no single ideology prevails. Perhaps the best-known and most publicized of these arguments is about whether the monetary sector influences the real sector of an economy. The debate has ebbed and flowed since the late eighteenth century.

The school of thought most associated with these views is called *monetarism*,[1] and we devote a portion of this chapter to discussing its essentials. There is, however, some good news on the monetary policy front.[2] Disagreements among economists remain, but they have narrowed considerably in recent years as far as views about, for example, the desirability of low inflation and the design of monetary policies needed to guarantee such an outcome. We explore these questions in further detail in the next two chapters.

21.1 MONETARISM AND COMPETITIVE THEORIES

As the science of economics developed in the late eighteenth and the nineteenth century, its leading practitioneers—Adam Smith, David Ricardo, John Stuart Mill, Jean-Baptiste Say, and many others—worked out a self-correcting model of a free-market economy. The laws of supply and demand would produce a vigorous and growing economy with full employment so long as government did not fetter the mechanisms with regulations or income redistributions. Changes in the money supply directly influence prices (and nothing else).

This **classical economics** predominated until the 1930s, when it was superseded by the school founded by John Maynard Keynes. His major work, *The General Theory of Employment, Interest and Money*, was published in 1936 and was much influenced by the experience of the Great Depression. He and his followers believed that equilibrium in the economy might involve considerable unemployment. To avoid that outcome, they said, the government should use regulation and fiscal policy (including deficit spending). Money was not very important.[3]

For a time, it seemed that **Keynesianism** would rule forever. By the mid-1950s, howver, there arose in the United States an increasingly influential group of economists who would eventually be responsible for a renaissance in the study of the importance of money. These monetarists would turn the debate in their favour, especially after the 1970s, when the Keynesians failed to account for some of the ills troubling the economy, such as persistent and rising inflation.

---

1 The success of monetarism has not been unchallenged. For example, there has been a resurgence of classical view of the economy and the role of money. A recent approach, called *real business cycle* analysis, begins by showing that money does not matter in determining real business cycles. Instead, monetary policy is believed to react to real factors operating in the economy. Space precludes any discussion of these theories here; interested students need to consult a fairly advanced macroeconomics textbook. For example, see D. Romer, *Advanced Macroeconomics:* Second Edition (New York: McGraw-Hill, 2001), Chapter 4.

2 There is considerable agreement that a sustainable fiscal policy is desirable, but we do not pursue this question any further.

3 Indeed in the early stages of the Keynesian era, the *General Theory* was often portrayed as saying that money did not matter at all. As Allan Meltzer, a leading economist in this field, contends, this gross exaggeration arose in part because Keynes seemed preoccupied with policy issues, such as high unemployment, so monetary problems appeared at least to take a back seat.

FLASHBACK 21.1

SHORT-RUN VERSUS LONG-RUN FLUCTUATIONS IN ECONOMIC ACTIVITY

As the chapter points out, disagreements over the role of monetary policy revolve around its impact on economic activity. Since real GDP is the usual proxy for economic activity, it is the measure on which the concept of the business cycle is based (Chapter 6 discusses measurement problems associated with the real GDP measure). Taken literally the business cycle captures the rather irregular movements in economic activity. Although it is a rather old-fashioned view, students of business cycles think of economic activity as consisting of a trend, a business cycle, a seasonal cycle, and an irregular cycle. The notion of a cycle captures the idea that economic activity moves up and down over time. But exactly what are we referring to, real GDP or the rate of growth in real GDP? Both measures are used throughout this text and both are useful. Let us ignore both the seasonal (we discussed seasonal influences on the money supply in Chapter 2) and irregular cycles. Irregular cycles are simply unpredictable movements in real GDP once we have found the trend, business cycle, and seasonal components of movements in real GDP. A stylized version of real GDP is shown below.

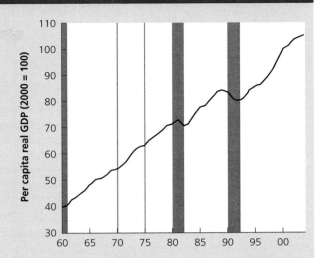

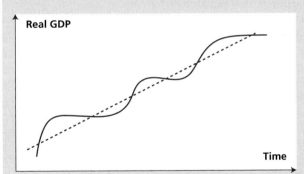

The solid line shows movements in a hypothetical measure of real GDP over time. There is a general upward movement in real GDP that is called the trend. The fluctuations up and down represent the business cycle component. We can summarize the trend aspect of real GDP movements by drawing a dashed line through actual real GDP. Notice that, as a consequence, actual real GDP occasionally will rise above the hypothetical trend while, at other times, it is below trend. If the trend represents the influence of growing population, improvements in economic capacity or productivity, then whenever actual real GDP rises above trend the economy is expanding in relative terms.

Controlling for the effect of a growing population is relatively easy since we can simply divide real GDP by population size. However, evaluating the effects of improvements in productivity (such as the impact of computer or Internet technology) is much more difficult since it can take several years to see their effects. Indeed, during the 1990s, many policymakers in the U.S., including Alan Greenspan, chairman of the Federal Reserve Board, believed that strong economic growth was being driven by such technological changes and that a golden era of growth had arrived. The recession of 2000 changed minds quickly.

Returning to the above figure, when actual real GDP is below trend, the economy is contracting or in recession. Now the trend in real GDP is a straight line. Why? Simply because it is the easiest way of summarizing the impact of economic phenomena, such as technological change, that require a long time to take effect. Therefore, it is the short-run fluctuations that require the involvement of monetary policy, and that is where the controversy begins. As you might imagine, there is considerable interest in measuring business cycle movements. Moreover, there are more sophisticated ways of measuring the trend component of business cycle activity. Finally, the hypothesized real GDP measure in the above figure makes it seem easy to differentiate recessions from expansions. If one examines actual real GDP for Canada, as shown above, it is sometimes more difficult to distinguish an expansion from a recession. In Canada, Statistics Canada occasionally will report on whether the Canadian economy is in an expansion or in a recession. In the United States, the National Bureau of Economic Research is viewed as being responsible for deciding whether the U.S. economy is in an expansion or in a recession.

Dates for expansions and contractions are 1960-61, 1970, 1975, 1981–82, 1990-1992. More precise dating can be found in Cross (1996). Data are from International Monetary Fund, *International Financial Statistics* CD-ROM. Per capita real GDP is real GDP (2000=100) divided by population.

Additional sources:
Cross, P. "Alternative Measures of Business Cycles in Canada: 1947-1992," *Canadian Economic Observer* (February 1996).

Frank, R.H., B.S. Bernanke, L. Osberg, M.L. Cross, and B.K. MacLean, *Principles of Macroeconomics*, First Canadian Edition (Toronto: McGraw-Hill Ryerson Ltd), Chapter 12.
National Bureau of Economic Research, *Business Cycle Expansions and Contractions*
http://www.nber.org/cycles.html/

Policymakers in the United Kingdom, the United States, Canada, and elsewhere began to adopt what they believed to be a monetarist stance.

What, then, is **monetarism**? The question itself has spawned considerable literature. To our minds, the following are the essential, defining tenets.

1. In the long run, money is neutral.

2. The price level and inflation are monetary phenomena.

3. Business cycle movements are caused by monetary policy.

At its root monetarism is based on empirical observation, most notably of U.S. economic performance over long periods of time. It is not at all clear that there are many theoretical differences between Friedman's view and those originally set out by Keynes.[4] By contrast, as we shall see below, monetarism was succeeded in popularity by the *new classical economics*, which emphasized theoretical differences with Friedman's monetarist views, but broadly agrees with the essential tenets of monetarism outlined above. The main theoretical differences have to do with the new classicists' belief that individuals successfully optimize when making economic decisions, in much the same way that we have used the optimization principle throughout the text. Another fundamental principle of new classical economics is that all individuals care about economic variables or magnitudes expressed in real terms. Again, the text has often referred to the importance of looking at the behaviour of real magnitudes instead of just nominal ones, in understanding how financial markets and the economy function.[5]

Despite the fact that most central banks have abandoned monetary targets, the most notable exception being the European Central Bank, it may be a little premature to write off monetarism completely as a theory that has passed its prime. There are indications that in Canada and the U.S., broad measures of the money supply may still have predictive content for future inflation. Moreover, in 1999, the Bank of Canada held a conference to discuss the role of money in Canada's transmission process.[6]

For most of the rest of this chapter we'll consider and discuss these propositions.

---

[4] As you have no doubt already noticed, entire texts have been written seeking to interpret the various economic philosophies developed during the twentieth century. Some were cited earlier. Two other texts worthy of note are D. Laidler, *Fabricating the Keynesian Revolution* (Cambridge: Cambridge University Press 1999), and D. Laidler, *The Golden Age of the Quantity Theory* (Princeton, N.J.: Princeton University Press, 1991).

[5] For more details on these history of thought issues that we cannot devote more space to here, see, for example, K.D. Hoover, *The New Classical Macroeconomics* (Oxford: Basil Blackwell, 1988), and P.J. Miller (ed.), *The Rational Expectations Revolution* (Cambridge, Mass.: Cambridge University Press, 1994).

[6] *Money, Monetary Policy, and Transmission Mechanisms*, Proceedings of a conference held by the Bank of Canada, November 1999, available at **www.bankofcanada.ca/en/conference/con99/con99.htm**. Also, see J. Attah-Mensah, "Recent Developments in the Monetary Aggregates and Their Implications," *Bank of Canada Review*, Spring 2000, and D. Laidler, "Passive Money, Active Money, and Monetary Policy," Bank of Canada Review, Summer 1999. A defence of the European Central Bank's strategy to monitor money supply developments is contained in, for example, "Issues Related to Monetary Policy Rules," *Monthly Bulletin*, European Central Bank (October 2001): 37–50.

21.2 THE NEUTRALITY OF MONEY

When monetarists speak of the **neutrality of money**, they mean that monetary policy cannot affect the unemployment rate or the price level in the long run. Let's explore that concept and its implications. A **Phillips curve** plots the usually inverse relationship between inflation and unemployment. There appears to be a tradeoff between the two. Thus, society can obtain lower inflation only by accepting higher unemployment (or lower output), and vice versa. Clearly, to the extent that monetary policy can influence prices, money cannot be neutral. This understanding was the strict Keynesian view of the world until the 1960s and could be used to justify, for example, state intervention to help an economy out of a slump. Keynesians are often referred to as interventionists: They favour policies aimed at fine-tuning the economy to achieve a presumably socially desirable goal such as low unemployment.

A Web site devoted to a basic explanation of the Phillips curve **www.j-bradford-delong.net/multimedia/PCurve1.html**

The monetarist view, by contrast, is that choosing a particular combination of inflation and unemployment creates forces that defeat the policymakers' attempt to reach a particular unemployment rate. For example, higher inflation eventually brings about changes in individuals' expectations of inflation. We know, however, from the Fisher effect that any effect on the real interest rate will be temporary. Since only changes in the real interest rate can have real economic effects once the new equilibrium is attained, a monetary policy aimed at permanently lowering unemployment cannot have any lasting economic effects. In other words, unemployment can deviate only for a short time from its long-run value, which is primarily affected by technological change and policies that favour or discourage labour-force mobility from one region or occupation to another. Thus the Keynesian trade-off disappears in the long run (the Phillips curve becomes vertical),[7] though it may exist in the short run.

EXPECTATIONS OF INFLATION IN THE SHORT RUN

How long is the short run? The answer depends on your view of how individuals form their expectations of future prices (that is, their *expectations of inflation*).

Adaptive Expectations

Monetarists of several generations, including Irving Fisher, claim that the effects of monetary policy occur with lags that are long and variable and, therefore, uncertain. This result hinges critically on the **adaptive expectations hypothesis**, the theory that people form their expectations of inflation by extrapolating from ("adapting to") the past behaviour of prices and continually revising their forecasts on the basis of their previous errors.

Although the idea that people learn from their past mistakes is intuitively appealing, it is suspect. Why? In a world in which inflation was more or less stable, we would surely expect individuals eventually to learn enough from their past mistakes to avoid making them in the future. But, as we have seen, inflation tends to rise or fall persistently. Suppose it rises over a considerable period. Then, an individual who uses a forecast mechanism that looks only at the past will never catch up to actual inflation rates. Similarly, in an era of falling inflation, individuals will persistently overestimate actual inflation.

An Algebraic Interpretation of Adaptive Expectations

An adaptive expectations model can be defined as follows:

$$\hat{P}_t = \hat{P}_{t-1} + b(P_{t-1} - \hat{P}_{t-1})$$ **(21.1)**

---

7 Indeed, in his 1977 Nobel lecture, Milton Friedman proposed that the inflation and unemployment rates could be *positively* related to each other—that the Phillips curve could actually be upward sloping. Friedman explained this possibility as arising from the fact that as inflation goes up, so does its volatility. Since greater volatility implies more uncertainty, one result is less efficiency in the economy as a whole, which translates into a higher unemployment rate. The likelihood of this situation occurring has been greatly reduced by the past few years of relatively low inflation, but that was certainly not the case in the late 1970s, when Friedman prepared his lecture.

where

$\hat{P}_t$ = the forecast for the price level at time t (today)

$\hat{P}_{t-1}$ = the forecast for the price level at time $t-1$ (last period)

P_{t-1} = the actual value of the price level at time $t-1$

$P_{t-1} - \hat{P}_{t-1}$ = the last period's forecast error

Equation (21.1) says simply that the current forecast of the price level (that is, at time t) is based on last period's or yesterday's forecast of the same price level, plus an adjustment factor that recognizes the error made in that previous forecast. The extent to which past mistakes are important in adapting the forecast is summarized in the coefficient b. If $b = 0$, the current forecast is unaffected by past forecast errors. Therefore, equation (21.1) becomes

$$\hat{P}_t = \hat{P}_{t-1} \tag{21.2}$$

The current forecast is the same as last period's forecast; in other words the individual's expectations remain unchanged.

At the other extreme, if $b = 1$, equation (21.1) becomes

$$\hat{P}_t = \hat{P}_{t-1} + P_{t-1} - \hat{P}_{t-1} \text{ or } \hat{P}_t = P_{t-1} \tag{21.3}$$

The current forecast is equivalent to the last period's actual value for the price level. (This forecast is often referred to as "naive" because it suggests that the individual believes that the immediate past will simply be repeated.)

In reality, people expect the value of b to lie somewhere between 0 and 1. Suppose that $b = 0.5$ and that an individual's expectations for the year 2006 were correct. Then,

$$P_{2006} = \hat{P}_{2006} = 100$$

where 100 refers to the value of, say, the consumer price index for that year. Using these 2006 values, we applied equation (21.1) for four more years. Table 21.1 shows the results. Notice how badly

Table 21.1	A Numerical Example of Adaptive Expectations		
			Forecast Error
	P_t	$\hat{P}_t$	$(P_{t-1} - \hat{P}_{t-1})$
2006	100	100	0
2007	110	100	10
2008	115	105	10
2009	125	110	15
2010	140	117.5	22.5

Initially, the forecast is correct: $P_{2006} = \hat{P}_{2006} = 100$. Subsequently, equation (21.1) is applied. For example,

$$\hat{P}_{2007} = \hat{P}_{2006} + 0.5\,(P_{2006} - \hat{P}_{2006})$$
$$= 100 + 0.5\,(100 - 100)$$
$$= 100$$
$$\hat{P}_{2008} = \hat{P}_{2007} + 0.5\,(P_{2007} - \hat{P}_{2007})$$
$$= 100 + 0.5(110 - 100)$$
$$= 100 + 0.5(10)$$
$$= 105$$

ECONOMICS FOCUS 21.1   THE CHANGING PHILIPS CURVE

The 1960s—the heyday of the Phillips curve—does produce a downward-sloping best-fit line, but the inflation–unemployment combinations for the 1970s and 1980s show no obvious trade-off. During the 1970s, inflation hovered around unemployment rates of 5% to 8.5%, indicating why the natural rate hypothesis emerged to replace the Phillips curve.

Since the 1980s, however, we have seen inflation rates falling considerably from double-digit levels to around 2%, with the unemployment rate fluctuating between 6.8 and 12%. The clockwise movement in the unemployment rate relative to inflation is suggestive of a shifting Phillips curve around an unemployment rate of 9 to 9.5%. However, such high rates of unemployment led researchers to ask how this could happen. The result was Blanchard and Summers's hysteresis theory of unemployment. According to this view, countries with a substantial unionized labour force experience persistent unemployment because the "insiders"—the unionized workers—negotiate wages that can keep the "outsiders" out of work for long periods.

Comparing the 1960s with the period since, we can imagine a short-run Phillips curve shifting up and then down as expected inflation is higher or lower. Milton Friedman suggested, however, that the Phillips curve might be positively sloped. Notice that inflation was more variable in the 1970s than during the 1960s. Since more variability means more uncertainty, Friedman reasoned that inflation variability might also have an independent and positive influence on inflation.

Questions for Discussion

1. This box alludes to the possibility of a positively sloping Phillips curve relationship. Can you explain how this is possible? (Hint: Think of the risk–return relationship described in Chapter 13; recall footnote 7 of this chapter.) Draw the appropriate diagram and explain your result.
2. Does it appear that the slope of the Phillips curve has changed between the 1960s and the 1980s and since? What are the implications for the conduct of monetary policy?

Sources

O.J. Blanchard, and L.H. Summers, "Hysteresis and the European Unemployment Problem," in *NBER Macroeconomics Annual* 1986, edited by S. Fischer (Cambridge, Mass.: The MIT Press, 1986): 15–78.

M. Friedman, "Nobel Lecture: Inflation and Unemployment," *Journal of Political Economy* 85 (June 1977): 451–72.

A.W. Phillips, "The Relation between Unemployment and the Rate of Change of Money Wage Rates in the United Kingdom, 1861–1957," *Economica* 25 (1958): 283–99.

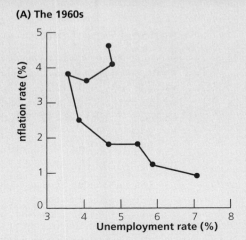

(A) The 1960s

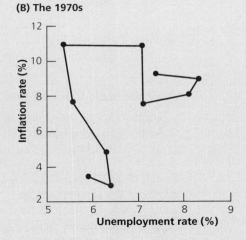

(B) The 1970s

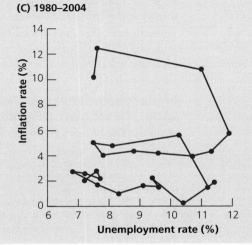

(C) 1980–2004

the adaptive expectations framework performed. The forecast errors rise over time, rather than fall as we would expect if individuals were learning from the history of the price level. The reason is simple: Mistakes of the past keep being repeated.

Rational Expectations

Given that the adaptive expectations hypothesis involves individuals' being prone to overestimating or underestimating inflation, it is not surprising that monetarists believe in long and variable lags for the effects of monetary policy. It is also not surprising that economists long sought to model the way individuals actually form expectations rather than resort to some mechanical, "black box" approach that ignores the tools of economic analysis. Monetarist ideas can be recast by substantially changing the understanding of how individuals form expectations.

The basic tenet of the **rational expectations hypothesis**, which has revolutionized economic analysis, was advanced as early as 1961 by John Muth. Specifically, he suggested that

> expectations, since they are informed predictions of future events, are essentially the same as the predictions of the relevant economic theory…The hypothesis asserts three things: (i) information is scarce, and the economic system does not generally waste it; (ii) the way expectations are formed depends specifically on the structure of the relevant system describing the economy; (iii) a "public prediction"…will have no substantial effect on the operation of the economic system (unless it is based on inside information).[8]

In other words, when individuals make a forecast, they have, in effect, some economic model in mind, and any errors in that forecast are irrelevant to future forecasts. Only the current structure of the economy is relevant in generating price-level forecasts.[9]

An Algebraic Interpretation of Rational Expectations

A simple example will illustrate the idea of rational expectations. Suppose that the public believes the price level is determined by the past behaviour of the money supply. Specifically, let

$$P_t = aM_{t-1} + v_t \qquad \qquad \textbf{(21.4)}$$

so that the current price level is a fraction, a, of the last period's money supply, M_{t-1}, plus some unpredictable component, v_t.

Further, suppose that, on average, the unpredictable component is zero. In other words, prices are proportional to the money supply, again on average. It is reasonable then to suppose that a plausible forecast of the price level at time t, namely $\hat{P}_t$, is also proportional to last period's money supply, so we can write

$$\hat{P}_t = aM_{t-1} \qquad \qquad \textbf{(21.5)}$$

What then is the average forecast error? It is simply

$$P_t - \hat{P}_t = aM_{t-1} - aM_{t-1} = 0 \qquad \qquad \textbf{(21.6)}$$

In other words, forecasts are, on average, correct, since forecast errors are expected to be zero on average. Therefore, in contrast to the adaptive expectations approach, the rational expectations hypothesis does not permit individuals to make systematic forecast errors.

---

8 J. Muth, "Rational Expectations and the Theory of Price Movements," *Econometrica* 29 (1961): 315–25.

9 If the structure of the economy changes, so does the model or the nature of the relationship in an existing model. This idea implies that the large-scale models of the economy that were popular in the 1960s are inadequate as tools for the analysis of policies because they ignore changes in economic structure. This is the central idea of the *Lucas critique*, which has had far-reaching implications in the economics profession. Indeed, Robert Lucas of the University of Chicago was awarded the Nobel Prize for his work in this area. However, the topic is beyond the scope of this text.

WHAT DOES IT ALL MEAN?

The implications of rational expectations for the neutrality of money, therefore, centre on the speed with which the Phillips curve trade-off disappears. The reason that lags are long and variable in the monetarist view stems largely from the assumption of adaptive expectations. With rational expectations, there is no trade-off worth considering.[10] The public knows the structure of the economy and cannot, therefore, be systematically fooled by policymakers if the policymakers follow some fixed rule for money supply growth. But is the solution that simple? Unfortunately, no, as we will see in the following section.[11]

To recap, adaptive expectations imply that the public can be easily fooled, especially if monetary policies change. By contrast, if we take literally the predictions of rational expectations, it becomes almost impossible to fool the public. Although these two mechanisms that economists use to characterize how expectations are formed are useful, the reality is probably a mixture of elements from the adaptive and rational expectations models. Indeed, Thomas Sargent[12] argues that just a couple of decades ago even policymakers knew considerably less about how the economy functions than we do today. So, if policymakers were themselves more prone to making mistakes or were finding it difficult to know whether their policies were having the desired effect on inflation, then it is highly unlikely that the general public would do better. In other words, it is probably the case that the public's ability to form expectations of the future has evolved over time. The resulting mix of elements from the adaptive model and the rational expectations model produces, of course, a more complex approach to dealing with how individuals form expectations. In what follows, however, we will not pursue these complications.

One final point. Notice that the neutrality of money issue revolves around whether monetary policy has *real* effects on unemployment or output. No one disputes the impact of monetary policy on nominal variables such as *nominal* output.

21.3   RULES VERSUS DISCRETION IN THE CONDUCT OF MONETARY POLICY

This Web site has various information and links about NAIRU pages **stern.nyu.edu/ ~nroubini/NAIRU. HTM**

The implication of the foregoing ideas is striking. Since monetary policy cannot have long-lasting real effects on the economy, it is better for the authorities to follow a rule—such as the simple one of fixing the money supply so that $P_t = aM_{t-1}$, which was assumed in equation (21.4)—rather than discretion in formulating and implementing monetary policy. But will the authorities do any such thing? And will the "rule" they choose be a useful one? Let's further explore what we have discovered about monetary policy.

THE POLITICAL TEMPTATION TO STIMULATE THE ECONOMY

Few economists consider monetary fluctuations neutral, *at least in the short run*. The reason is, in large part, errors in forecasting the future—that is, expectational errors.[13] If we assume, however,

---

10 If there are no systematic forecast errors, $(P_t - \hat{P}_t)$—that is, v_t—is uncorrelated through time. Unfortunately, this is not the case. For this reason, the Phillips curve theory assuming rational expectations has had a distinctly mixed reaction.

11 The foregoing analysis does not consider the implications that arise when it is assumed that workers negotiate labour contracts that last anywhere from, say, two to four years. This implies that changes in prices and wages are staggered over time depending on what the labour contract stipulates wage changes will be over the life of the agreement. Since it is quite likely that individuals (and union leaders) will make mistakes in forecasting inflation (either favourable or unfavourable), this permits monetary policy to have real effects because some groups in society willingly gamble on future price and wage developments based on expectations formed today. There is insufficient space to consider the details of the arguments. These can be quite involved. Interested students can consult D. Romer, *Advanced Macroeconomics*, Second Edition (New York: McGraw-Hill, 2001), Chapter 6.

12 T.J. Sargent, *The Conquest of American Inflation* (Princeton, N.J.: Princeton University Press, 1999).

13 The sources of these errors are undoubtedly varied. Individuals may confuse price changes of the commodities they happen to buy with changes in the overall consumer price index. Workers sign contracts that commit them to wage increases before they know actual price increases. Alternatively, since there are costs to changing prices (called "menu" costs) this too will imply lags in the adjustment of prices. A detailed discussion of these issues is impossible here.

ECONOMICS FOCUS 21.2   A SIMPLE MACROECONOMIC MODEL: THE AD/AS MODEL

Although the material covered in this chapter does not require that we fully develop a model of the economy, many of the concepts and predictions outlined below derive from a macroeconomic model that is part and parcel of some introductory and most intermediate macroeconomic textbooks. Known as the AD/AS model, which stands for aggregate demand/aggregate supply, it can be used to explain how monetary policy (among other policies such as fiscal policy) drives inflation. At its simplest level, it is essentially the macroeconomic equivalent of the supply and demand model used earlier to explain the determination of bond prices or interest rates (see, for example, Chapter 6). Simply put, a rise in the money supply in real terms (what we called real balances in Chapter 12) raises aggregate demand, other things equal. What might prompt such a rise (or a fall) in real balances? Since the real money supply is money supply divided by the price level (again refer back to Chapter 12 for a refresher), one factor would be a rise in the money supply. We considered just such a scenario in Chapter 6. The flowchart below illustrates the links just described:

$$M \uparrow, \bar{P} \Rightarrow \frac{M}{P} \uparrow \Rightarrow Y \uparrow$$

M is the money supply, P is the price level, assumed to be constant (this explains the bar over P), M/P are real balances, and Y is aggregate demand (real GDP). Similarly, if prices increase, then real balances fall, leading to a fall in aggregate demand. Again, a flowchart summarizes the relevant relationships:

$$\bar{M}, P \uparrow \Rightarrow \frac{M}{P} \downarrow \Rightarrow Y \downarrow$$

Now it is the money supply that is held constant while prices rise, leading to a fall in real balances and, consequently, a reduction in aggregate demand.

Finally, we know that rising prices mean that inflation (the symbol for inflation, π, was introduced in Chapter 5) is present in the economy (and falling prices signify deflation). Therefore, rising prices, or inflation, are associated with lower aggregate demand. This relationship is summarized in the diagram below:

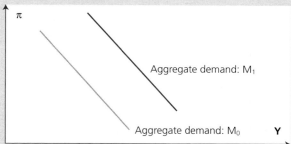

FIGURE 21.2A Aggregate Demand Curves

The diagram illustrates the negative relationship between inflation and real GDP. It also shows that if monetary policy is expansionary because the money supply increases (or an increase in money growth takes place; again see Chapter 6), then there is more inflation at each and every level of Y.

Now we can turn to aggregate supply in the economy. It seems reasonable to assume that, in the short run at least, producers will respond to rising prices (that is, inflation) by increasing the amount of output supplied, thereby giving rise to an upward-sloping aggregate supply curve. Again this parallels the story told earlier in terms of the links between price and the quantity of financial assets supplied in the marketplace. In the long run, however, producers see no benefit in supplying more output, since the prices they receive for their products are offset by the prices they pay to produce them (in the form of higher wages and prices for inputs into production). The figure below illustrates.

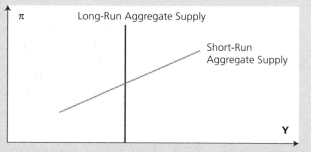

FIGURE 21.2B Short-Run and Long-Run Aggregate Supply Curves

As we shall see in the text below, it is precisely the relationship between output and inflation that gave rise to one of the most important relationships in economics, known as the Phillips curve. Equilibrium is then the intersection between aggregate demand and aggregate supply. The implications for inflation, however, will differ as between the short run and the long run. Again, a diagram illustrates.

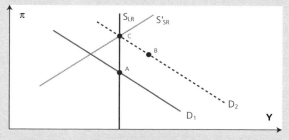

FIGURE 21.2C Short- and Long-Run Equilibria

Initially, the economy is in macroeconomic equilibrium at point A, which is at the intersection of aggregate demand (D$_1$), the short-run aggregate supply curve (S$_{SR}$), and the long-run aggregate supply curve (S$_{LR}$). A rise in the money supply shifts the aggregate demand curve to the right to D$_2$, which implies that, in the short run, inflation and output both rise. However, if money has no long-run effects, as suggested by the monetarists, then inflation eventually rises and aggregate output reverts back to its original value. This takes place at point C, where there is a new intersection between the aggregate demand curve and the short-run and long-run aggregate supply curves.

Students will notice that explanations of the impact of monetary policy are expressed in terms of either output or the unemployment rate. Does it make a difference? Since, as noted earlier, economists are preoccupied with the impact of monetary policy on the business cycle, it is natural to use real GDP as the point of reference. Policymakers and the media, however, might express more concern over developments in the labour market, as reflected in the behaviour of the unemployment rate. Fortunately, according to what is called Okun's law, there appears to be a straightforward link between movements in aggregate output (Y) and the unemployment rate (u). Okun's law is a rule of thumb which predicts that a 1% increase in the unemployment rate (over and above the natural rate, a concept described in the text below) results in a 2% decrease in Y relative to its trend (see **Flashback** in this chapter).

Sources

Frank, R.H., B.S. Bernanke, L. Osberg, M.L. Cross, and B.K. MacLean, *Principles of Macroeconomics,* First Canadian Edition (Toronto: McGraw-Hill Ryerson Ltd).

R. Dornbusch, S. Fischer, R. Startz, F.J. Atkins, G.R. Sparks, *Macroeconomics,* Sixth Canadian Edition (Toronto: McGraw-Hill Ryerson Ltd, 2002).

Questions for Discussion

1. The first flowchart links a rise in real balances to a rise in aggregate demand. The discussion assumes "other things are equal." What must be assumed to remain constant for this relationship to hold? (Hint: See Chapter 12).

2. Can you explain why Okun's law is a reasonable depiction of the link between output and the unemployment rate?

that expectations are rational—that individuals do not systematically make mistakes in forecasting the future course of the economy—then monetary policy cannot systematically influence unemployment or output.

The logic of the previous paragraph can be summarized in a single proposition: Inflation and unemployment have a short-run trade-off, but no long-run trade-off. Figure 21.1 graphically displays this concept. The long-run Phillips curve is vertical, embodying the idea that the economy tends toward u^*, the economy's **natural rate of unemployment**, which is the unemployment rate that would be obtained if expectational errors disappeared.[14] (The phrase "natural rate of unemployment" is unfortunate, implying that some fraction of the work force is eternally condemned to being out of work. An alternative phrase, the **nonaccelerating inflation rate of unemployment [NAIRU]**, is perhaps both more tactful and more adequately descriptive of u^*.)

Two NAIRU positions are displayed in Figure 21.1. If inflation is π_1 and expected inflation is π_1^e, the economy settles at point A. Monetary policy may cause deviations from A along the short-run Phillips curve, but all that can be gained from a policy aimed at reducing the unemployment rate is both higher actual and expected inflation, such as point B. Why? As the unemployment rate falls, the resulting rising demand for goods and services pushes inflation up. One way to stimulate aggregate demand is via an increase in the money supply (See the **FLASHBACK** in this chapter and Chapter 6). Since, according to the discussion of expected inflation, rising inflation will eventually influence expected inflation, the result is that the expected inflation line will also shift upward. Eventually, when actual and expected inflation are once again the same, the economy will settle at point B, that is, when $\pi_2 = \pi_2^e$.

The path from A to B need not, of course, either be smooth or occur quickly, and the diagram is only suggestive of the route taken to a higher inflation rate.

The problem, however, is that if politicians are tempted to deliver lower unemployment, believing that their re-election prospects are thereby enhanced, they will do so. Hence, even if society believes that zero inflation is desirable (such as at point C in Figure 21.1), the politicians will

---

14 "Natural" unemployment should not be confused with structural unemployment, which arises because of normal frictions in the labour market, such as changes in the demographic characteristics of the population.

have a bias toward positive inflation, since it is the only way, in the short run at least, to reduce the unemployment rate. Thus, economic policies will tend to deliver some inflation. [15]

The situation can be reversed in the case of a government intent on reducing inflation, say from π_1 to π_3 in Figure 21.1. Unless expectations of inflation adjust very quickly, the disinflation will come at the cost of a higher unemployment rate until the economy settles at point D. The size of the resulting "short-term" gain is a function of whether society believes in the motives and policies of the government, what economists refer to as the **credibility** of policies.

THE TIME-INCONSISTENCY PROBLEM

The problem just stated has been labelled the **time-inconsistency problem of monetary policy**.[16] The phrase captures the notion that policymakers have an incentive to deviate from their promise if individuals commit themselves to act as if the announcement were to be believed. It is partly for this reason that the question of policymakers' credibility in making economic promises has proven important in economic analysis of late.[17] In a sense, policymakers are continually playing monetary policy games with the public that produce the positive bias in inflation.

| **Figure 21.1** | **Phillips Curves in the Short Run and the Long Run** |

Inflation rate, actual and expected

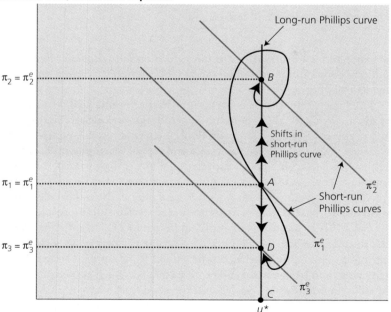

The vertical Phillips curve reflects the neutrality of monetary policy in the long run; there is no inflation–unemployment trade-off. The downward-sloping curves describe a short-run trade-off between the same two variables. Each time there is a change in the expected rate of inflation, the trade-off curve shifts. The time-inconsistency problem arises because, even though society prefers point C, policymakers generate a result such as A or even B as they continually attempt to exploit the short-run trade-off.

---

15 This raises the issue of the autonomy of the monetary authorities, which is discussed in Chapter 23.

16 The 2004 Nobel prize in Economics went to the originators of the concept, Edward Prescott from the U.S. and Finn Kydland from Norway. See the citation at **http://nobelprize.org/**.

17 It might be argued that policymakers with a reputation for promising and delivering low inflation may be relatively successful at avoiding the time-inconsistency problem. Unfortunately, even these policymakers have a distinct bias toward positive inflation, at least according to the theory.

ECONOMICS FOCUS 21.3   WHAT IS NAIRU?

Clearly, the concept of the natural rate of unemployment is central to the idea that there is no long-run trade-off between inflation and unemployment. Although economists argue that some unemployment will always exist, simply because there are constantly frictions in the labour market—people voluntarily enter and leave the labour force for professional and personal reasons—estimating NAIRU has proven to be one of the most vexing topics in macroeconomics.

Typically, NAIRU is estimated as the unemployment rate consistent with a nonaccelerating inflation rate in the Phillips curve relationship. In equation form, this means

$$\Delta\pi_t = c - bu_t + e_t \qquad [a]$$

where $\Delta\pi$ is the change in inflation, u is the unemployment rate, and e is a term that captures all possible influences on the change in inflation, other than the unemployment rate. The coefficient b measures the sensitivity of changes in inflation to the unemployment rate, while c is a constant. Using annual Canadian data from 1980 to 2004, we can obtain a measure of NAIRU by estimating the above equation and asking what the unemployment rate is if $\Delta\pi$ is zero. The result is an estimate of 8.5%.

The assumption that NAIRU has been constant since 1980 is a rather strong one, so we might want to apply the above equation over several shorter periods to obtain a changing estimate of NAIRU. It turns out, however, that doing so creates some implausibly large estimates of NAIRU. The reason is that NAIRU is supposed to represent a long-run measure, while some of the estimates we obtain range anywhere from 8% to 12%. These estimates are also rather large.

Another approach to estimating NAIRU consists of smoothing out the year-to-year variations in unemployment over time to capture the evolving trends in the unemployment rate, as shown in the figure below. Given the wide variety of NAIRU estimates, there is, not surprisingly, debate and uncertainty about what NAIRU actually is, as one symposium on the subject makes clear.

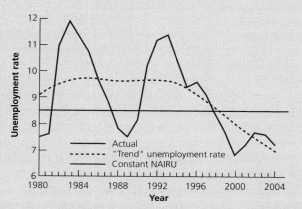

Source: Symposium, "The Natural Rate of Unemployment," *Journal of Economic Perspectives* 11 (Winter 1997) and author's calculations.

Questions for Discussion

1. Based on equation [a] what is NAIRU? If $c = 2\%$ and $b = 0.5$, what then is NAIRU?
2. If you were to produce several estimates of NAIRU based on the figure above, what might these look like? Discuss any major events that influenced your calculations.

The time-inconsistency problem certainly sounds like a reasonable depiction of the facts, perhaps requiring a healthy dose of cynicism about government officials. How realistic is the theory? As we shall see in Chapter 23, independent central banks are able to withstand pressure from politicians to inflate. It may be different for central banks not autonomous of government control. Alan Blinder,[18] former vice-chair of the Board of Governors of the U.S. Federal Reserve System, and a well-known academic prior to and following his stint at the Board, does not buy the time-inconsistency story. He argues that central bankers never think in terms of trying to "fool" the public and are keenly aware of the difficult balance between policies that affect inflation and unemployment or output in the short run. However, because inflation is easier to measure and forecast—though not without difficulty as we saw in Chapter 6—knowing how current output growth or unemployment stands vis-á-vis the potential or natural rate is a much more difficult task. Perhaps in part for that reason, central bankers sound as if all they care about is inflation, when they most likely care about the state of the real economy as well.

---

18 See A. Blinder, *Central Banking in Theory and Practice* (Cambridge, Mass.: The MIT Press, 1999).

An Algebraic Interpretation of the Credibility Problem

The foregoing result can be demonstrated more formally. Suppose a government wants to reach zero inflation, but also desires an unemployment rate of less than u^*. Recall that u^* is the unemployment rate that keeps inflation stable at some level. As depicted in Figure 21.1, it can reduce unemployment only so long as $\pi > \pi^e$—that is, so long as actual inflation is greater than expected inflation—because then a short-run Phillips curve is relevant.

In other words, the short-run Phillips curve can be described by the following equation

$$\pi = \pi^e - \alpha(u - u^*) \tag{21.7}$$

so that, as in Figure 21.1, where u is less than u^*, π is greater than π^e. The coefficient α then simply describes the negatively sloped short-run Phillips curve.

To the extent that the government achieves such an outcome, it benefits politically and its loss is reduced. But since the public dislikes inflation, there is also a political price to be paid for the relatively high inflation rate. We can summarize these two effects by writing a *loss function* as follows:

$$L = \frac{1}{2}\,(\pi - \pi^e)^2 + \frac{\beta}{2}\,(u^* - u)^2 \tag{21.8}$$

The terms in brackets are squared to emphasize, in the case of inflation, the difference between a 1% miss in π relative to π^e versus a 5% unexpected inflation. The latter is a rather large dose of unexpected inflation, and by squaring $(\pi - \pi^e)$, we give such errors a correspondingly larger weight than if unexpected inflation is small. The loss function gets its name from the fact that the economy suffers whenever inflation and unemployment depart from their equilibrium values.

Similarly, the second term in equation (21.8) describes the political gain of an unemployment rate lower than u^*. The coefficient β describes the importance policymakers attach to the unemployment objective, while $\frac{1}{2}$ describes the weight placed on the inflation objective.[19] As in the case of inflation, we want to make a distinction between small and large deviations from NAIRU, and this is again accomplished by squaring the second term in the equation.[20] Equation (21.8) makes it clear, therefore, that unexpectedly high inflation $[(\pi - \pi^e) > 0]$ is politically costly, as is an unemployment rate that is higher than the NAIRU $[(u^* - u) < 0]$. Widespread agreement exists among academics and public officials that something like equation (21.8) describes the loss function of monetary policy.

Although the government wants, presumably, to minimize L, there are two cases to consider. The government can commit to delivering an inflation rate of $\pi = \pi^e$ at all times. An inflation target that is fully credible might deliver this type of result.[21]

But what if the government did not want to commit to a particular inflation rate and, instead, set policy after it determined the public's expected inflation rate? This situation implies that the policymakers minimize equation (21.8), given the relationship summarized in equation (21.7). The details of the derivation are left as an exercise for those who are interested, but the bottom line is that, as we might expect, when there is no commitment, if the government chooses an inflation rate that is higher than expected, the public will catch on and revise expectations of inflation upward, thereby defeating the original aims of the policy. Society ends up with more inflation than is desirable when such "games" are played.

---

19 Why? If $\beta = 0$, then only inflation matters. If $\beta > 0$, then a mix of unexpected inflation and deviations from the NAIRU affect policymakers' losses.

20 Note that no time subscript is added. By assuming that this year's trade-off can be treated independently of next year's trade-off, we can analyze the problem, abstracting from the time element. Clearly, this assumption is unrealistic, but its absence would add considerably to the mathematical difficulty of the analysis.

21 If an inflation target is fully credible, then private sector forecasts will tend to be the same as the stated inflation target.

TOWARDS A NEW TRADE-OFF

The 1990s signalled a renewed interest in rules for the conduct of monetary policy. One such rule, since named Taylor's rule (see Chapter 23 for more details), links interest rate developments with the behaviour of inflation and the real economy, summarized by real GDP relative to some trend. We can write the rule simply as

$$R_t = g_\pi \, \pi^{gap} + g_y y^{gap} \tag{21.9}$$

where π^{gap} is the difference between actual inflation and some desired or numerical target for inflation, and y^{gap} is the difference between actual and some potential level of real GDP. The latter variable can be thought of as the flip side of the difference between $u^* - u$ that appears in equation (21.8). Because of difficulties in measuring the NAIRU[22] many economists prefer working with the output gap (as y^{gap} is referred to) than with the unemployment rate. For our purposes, however, the differences are not essential.

Find out more about monetary policy rules at **www.stanford. edu/~johntayl/ PolRulLink.htm**

Given equation (21.9), we immediately see that if R_t changes frequently, or is very volatile, this is a reflection of the volatility of the two right-hand side variables. We also notice from equation (21.8) that if both inflation and GDP (or unemployment) are very volatile, the loss will also be larger. Consequently, Taylor[23] advocates a rule that results in a trade-off between the variability of inflation and the *variability* of the output gap.[24] Figure 21.2 illustrates a few such potential trade-offs. Much like the indifference curve analysis described in Chapter 10 or the portfolio selection analysis of Chapter 13, policymakers choose a point on the output gap–inflation frontier. Clearly, frontier A is preferred over frontier B, since combinations of inflation and output volatility are smaller anywhere along frontier A. However, once a frontier is chosen, the actual point selected on the frontier depends on the preferences of the central bank and/or the government. Hence, the point labeled SIT would describe a "strict" inflation-targeting central bank willing to accept high rates of output volatility. By contrast, a central bank that chooses the point SOT (strict output targeting) would forego stability in inflation in order to get low variability in the output gap. Finally, the point FIT (flexible inflation targeting) describes most central banks in the industrial world today. The chosen point reflects concern for *both* inflation and output gaps.

THE BASE DRIFT PROBLEM

Presumably, the simpler the rule for the conduct of monetary policy, the easier for the public to forecast the future course of the price level. The difficulty is in establishing a rule that guarantees commitment. Otherwise no rule will produce zero or even low inflation.

During the 1980s, many governments announced their plans for money supply growth to build their credibility as inflation fighters. Unfortunately, the way in which they have actually implemented their monetary policy has made it even more difficult to forecast future prices.

As we have seen, money supply control stems from the monetary base. Knowing control is not perfect, the monetary authorities stipulate a target range of money growth rates. So far so good;

---

22 One should not, however, minimize the difficulties in measuring the output gap. Indeed, disagreements over how to measure the output gap exist, and there exist several techniques to estimate the values for y^{gap}. See, for example, C. Dupasquier, A. Guay, and P. St-Amant, "A Comparison of Alternative Methodologies for Estimating Potential Output and the Output Gap," Bank of Canada working paper 97-5.

23 This idea is developed in J.B. Taylor, "The Inflation-Output Variability Trade-Off Revisited," in J.C. Fuhrer (ed.), *Goals, Guidelines, and Constraints Facing Monetary Policymakers* (Boston: Federal Reserve Bank of Boston, 1994). John Taylor was under-secretary (International Affairs) of the U.S. Treasury. A general description of the trade-off is also contained in L.E.O. Svensson, "Independent Review of the Operations of Monetary Policy in New Zealand: Report to the Minister of Finance," February 2001, available at **www.rbnz.govt.nz/monpol/review/Indrevopmonpol.pdf**.

24 The technical details are beyond the scope of this text. However, a definition is that the optimal rule is one that minimizes a weighted sum of the variance of the inflation and output gaps.

Figure 21.2 **The New Trade-Off: Inflation versus Output Gap Variability**

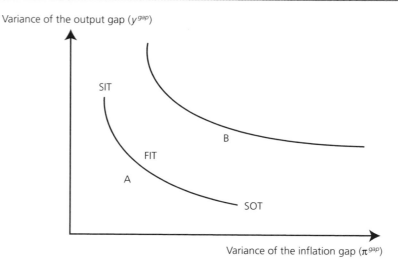

The figure expresses the trade-off derived from monetary policy rules as summarized in equation (21.9) combined with a loss function of the type shown in equation (21.8). Increases in inflation volatility or in the volatility of the output gap increase losses to policymakers. Consequently, the frontier labelled *A* is preferred over frontier *B*. However, once a frontier is chosen, the point on the frontier is dependent on the preferences of policymakers. A strict inflation-targeting central bank will choose point *SIT*, a strict output-targeting central bank will select point *SOT*, and the flexible inflation-targeting central bank will pick a point such as *FIT*.

individuals can presumably measure the performance of the monetary authorities by examining the difference between actual and targeted growth rates. But if the target is revised every so often in terms of actual performance, rather than the previously announced target, then the target is allowed to drift over time. What happens is the **base drift** problem, which has considerable consequences for forecasting the behaviour of the monetary authorities.

For example, suppose that the government announces a policy of targeting the level of the money supply so as to achieve a 3% growth rate per year.[25] Starting from a level of 100, the money supply target would be $100(1.03) = 103$ for the end of the first year, $100(1.03)(1.03) = 106.1$ for the end of the second year, and so on (see the first column of Table 21.2). Suppose the money supply actually grows at a 4% annual rate, the target growth rate is kept constant, but the base used to calculate the target money supply level is revised by using the actual value. In other words, the base is allowed to drift. For example, instead of a target money supply of 106.1 in the second year, the revised target is $104(1.03) = 107.1$ (see column 4 of Table 21.2). As the final column in the table shows, the difference between the revised target and the original target can grow over time. Hence, a new type of uncertainty is introduced in predicting the money supply and presumably the price level, thereby making monetary policy even more difficult to decipher.

Not surprisingly then, most countries abandoned formal money growth targets by the early 1990s. Two notable exceptions to this rule are Germany, which stuck by its money growth targets despite embarrassing misses, and the European Central Bank, which also has a money growth target.

---

25 In actuality, the growth rate would be given as a cone-shaped range, rather than a specified point. The essence of the argument is not affected by our simplification.

Table 21.2	A Moving Target: Base Drift			
Year	Target	Actual	Revised Target	Revised Less Original Target
1	103.0	104.0	—	—
2	106.1	108.2	107.1	1.0
3	109.3	112.5	111.4	2.1
4	112.6	117.0	115.9	3.3
5	116.0	121.7	120.5	4.5

The money supply is originally 100 and is targeted for a 3% growth rate. Then for year 1, the target is 100(1.03) = 103, and for year 5, the target is $100(1.03)^5 = 116$. (Note that compounding is permitted.) Suppose, however, that the money supply actually grows by 4% per year. The result produces the "actual" column. Rather than continuing with the original target, the authorities announce revised targets, reflecting 3% growth based on actual estimates of the previous year. For example, in year 2, the revised target is 104(1.03) = 107.1, and so on.

21.4 TWO THEORIES OF MONEY

Much of the preceding discussion has centred around the view that the key to inflation lies in the conduct of monetary policy. What is the presumed connection between the two? We address two theories in this section.

The 1990s saw growing interest in adopting inflation targets (also see Chapter 23). This policy is perceived as being more transparent to the public than money growth targets and more likely to produce macroeconomic outcomes that are desirable from society's standpoint. An alternative commitment mechanism is to provide sufficient autonomy to the central bank to short-circuit the temptation by governments to inflate the economy.

Perhaps the most venerable theory linking monetary policy and the price level is the equilibrium relationship summarized in the *quantity theory of money*. As we will see below, the attraction of the money supply as a target is enhanced by the stability in the relationship between money and nominal GDP. In other words, if velocity—a concept discussed in Chapter 12—is stable, then money growth can provide a useful forecast of future inflation. The question of which measure of the money supply policymakers should monitor remains (see Chapter 3). Its central feature— a tenet central to monetarist thought—is that "inflation is always and everywhere a monetary phenomenon."[26] By contrast, the *real bills doctrine* takes exception to the strict monetarist view of inflation but sees a connection between inflation and printing money to cover government debt. We briefly explore both views.[27]

THE QUANTITY THEORY

Although the quantity theory has evolved through several versions, it is perhaps best known in its current form as the relationship between the nominal quantity of money in circulation and the nominal income it generates. More formally, a given money stock, *M*, in equilibrium explains a fraction of nominal aggregate income, *Y*, so we can write

$$M = k \cdot Y \qquad (21.10)$$

As we know, *Y* can also be written as the product of the price level and real income (more precisely, income in constant dollars), *Py*. Equation (21.10) thus becomes

---

26 M. Desai, *Testing Monetarism* (London: Frances Pinter, 1981), Chapter 1.

27 Space does not permit an analysis of the origins and development of either theory. See, however, M. Friedman, "Quantity Theory of Money," in the *New Palgrave: Money*, edited by J. Satwell, M. Milgate, and P. Newman (New York: W.W. Norton, 1989): 1–40; and T.J. Sargent, *Rational Expectations and Inflation* (New York: Harper & Row, 1986), Chapter 1.

$$M = k \cdot Py \tag{21.11}$$

where k is the fraction stipulating that the money stock is proportional to income. In particular, this fraction captures the fact that a given money stock will circulate or turn over several times during a given period—most often, one year—to generate a given level of nominal income. In other words, if we rewrite equation (21.11) as

$$M\frac{1}{k} = Py \tag{21.12}$$

then $(1/k)$ represents the *velocity of circulation*: A given money stock multiplied by its velocity will produce a certain level of income in a given period. For example, if the money stock is $5 billion and each dollar generates $2 worth of spending—which is income to someone—so that velocity is 2, then the quantity theory predicts that nominal income will be $10 billion, which is simply $5 billion × 2. Letting V represent velocity, we can finally write the quantity theory equation:

$$MV = Py \tag{21.13}$$

Moving from equation (21.13) to a theory of the price level is now but a short step. First, assume that velocity is constant.[28] Next, by invoking the natural rate of unemployment hypothesis examined earlier, we can also take the level of output as given.

Now let us copy equation (21.13), placing a bar over the variables we have just assumed to be constants:

$$M\bar{V} = P\bar{y} \tag{21.14}$$

With V and y fixed, fluctuations in P can be explained only by changes in M. It is in this sense that inflation is a monetary phenomenon.

Despite proponents' controversies about how to measure money and about whether monetary changes cause price changes, the quantity theory has endured as a theory of the price level for at least two reasons. First, because quantity theorists have, for the most part, not taken a firm stand about what constitutes money, the theory has proved fairly flexible, even as financial innovations have forced changes in the monetary measures used to proxy M over time.[29] Second, the theory has generally been a reliable tool for predicting the price level over the business cycle. This is not to say that there have been no episodes in which the quantity theory has failed. Indeed, as we will see below, it was its perceived lack of generality that stimulated the search for an alternative view of price level determination.

THE MODERN REAL BILLS DOCTRINE

The 1980s saw a re-emergence in a new form of an old idea called the real bills doctrine. In essence, the doctrine argues that the value of money and therefore its purchasing power can be explained by the value of the assets that back it.

Suppose we consider a nation's central bank like any other financial intermediary. It possesses assets and has liabilities and thus engages in leverage. Its liabilities are, however, "money" and are backed by assets purchased via money. Therefore, if the quantity of money is increased and assets, such as Treasury bills or other forms of government debt, are received in exchange for the money printed, there is no reason to expect this increase in the quantity of money to be inflationary. After all, the central bank's assets rise by the same amount as its liabilities. Or do they? If

---

28 Since only long-run factors influence it. Alternatively, we can simply assume that velocity is a random walk, so that it is essentially an unpredictable element. We have seen several examples in this book of time series that have this property (such as stock prices).

29 Because the quantity theory explains how GDP is determined, the GDP deflator is a more appropriate proxy for P than consumer prices.

FINANCIAL FOCUS 21.1

P*—THE HOLY GRAIL OF INFLATION FORECASTS?

If the velocity of circulation, V, is relatively stable, we can write the quantity theory as

$$P^* = \frac{(M \times V^*)}{Y^*}$$

If V^* and Y^* are the long-run values for V and Y and, therefore, stable, then the long-run value of P, denoted by P^* and called P-star, will be determined by the money supply, M.

Hence, if the actual prices are lower than P^*, they will rise until P^* is attained. Therefore, the "price gap," that is, the difference between P and P^*, should be a good indicator of inflation. Hallman, Porter, and Small, using U.S. data, and Gerlach and Svensson, using European data, find considerable evidence in favour of the P^* model.

To take a numerical example, suppose that V is 1.432, potential GNP is $418 134 million and M1 is $252 872 million. Then P^* is

$$P^* = \frac{(252\ 872 \times 1.432)}{418\ 134} = 0.87$$

Thus, if the actual price level was 1, the fact that P^* was less than P would mean that the price level would be predicted to fall. The opposite would hold when P^* was greater than P, which would signal inflation.

The figures at the right show what actual and potential output for Canada look like since the 1960s as well as the CPI versus P^* based on the money stock measure M1+ The effect of the recessions of the early 1980s and 1990s is quite evident, since actual GDP is below its potential value. In the same vein, we see that the CPI was persistently above P^* in the early 1980s, precisely when inflation began to fall sharply (in 1983 CPI inflation was 5.7%; by 1985 it had fallen to 3.9%). The reverse takes place in the late 1980s when actual inflation jumped to 5.0% in 1989 from 4.0% the year before. Since the 1990s the CPI has been consistently below P^*, which means rising inflation. Indeed, according to our calculations, the gap between P and P^* has widened, yet there was no sign of rising inflation toward the end of the 1990s.

Given the crucial nature of the assumptions of a stable velocity and an output level that oscillates around its potential level, it is not surprising that critics such as Christiano and Pechemino and Rasche have focused on this issue as a potentially weak element in the theory.

Questions for Discussion

1. What is P^* and why might it be a useful inflation forecasting tool?
2. What do you think is meant by the comment "the P^* model lacks microfoundations"?

Sources

L.J. Christiano, "P^*: Not the Inflation Forecaster's Holy Grail," *Federal Reserve Bank of Minneapolis, Quarterly Review* 13 (Fall 1989): 3–18.

S. Gerlach, and L.E.O. Svensson, "Money and Inflation in the Euro Area: A Case for Monetary Indicators?" *Bank for International Settlements* (July 1999).

J. Hallman, R. Porter, and D. Small, "Is the Price Level Tied to the M2 Monetary Aggregate in the Long Run?" *American Economic Review* 81 (September 1991).

R.A. Pechemino, and R.H. Rasche, "P^* Type Models: Evaluation and Forecasts," NBER Working Paper no. 3406 (August 1990).

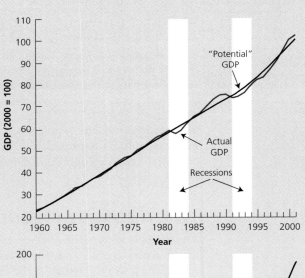

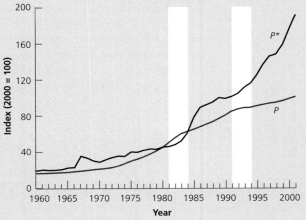

a central bank is called on to purchase increasing quantities of government debt that cannot be financed either through future issues or through taxation, the value of these assets will presumably fall. Consequently, the value of money will fall, which is to say that the price level will rise. But so long as money is backed by assets that have value, there is no need to link a particular money stock with a particular price level.[30] Unless individuals perceive that the government's debt will eventually be financed by printing increasing quantities of money, there is no need for money supply changes to create price level changes.

This view is the essence of a rejuvenated version of the real bills doctrine—a view that is strikingly different from the quantity theory. Indeed, it has been termed "an example of some unpleasant monetarist arithmetic."

When would the public fear printing money as a way of financing government debt? The example that comes most readily to mind is the case of a deficit running out of control.

A simple way of writing the government's deficit is

$$\Delta B_t = G_t - T_t \tag{21.15}$$

where
$$\Delta B_t = \text{change in government bonds outstanding at time } t$$
$$G_t = \text{government spending at time } t$$
$$T_t = \text{tax revenue at time } t$$

Equation (21.15) stipulates that if government expenditures exceed tax revenues, the resulting deficit will be financed through the sale of bonds. The transaction could be with the public. But if the deficit becomes "too large," the public may be unwilling to purchase these bonds in sufficient quantities to finance it. Then the government can instruct the central bank to issue enough money to meet the financing needs. On the central bank's balance sheet, the result will appear as

$$\Delta B_t = \Delta M_t \tag{21.16}$$

where ΔB_t is an addition to its assets, and ΔM_t, which represents the change in the money supply, is an addition to its liabilities. In the extreme, the market will value ΔB_t at zero. Such a valuation can take place only through inflation, since the value of money is measured by its purchasing power.

TWO THEORIES OF MONEY: CONCLUSION[31]

The stimulus for exploring the real bills doctrine was the empirical observation that during many historical periods, the money supply has grown rapidly without any corresponding increase in prices. To the extent that the version of the real bills doctrine that we have considered is more general than the quantity theory, because it can explain both high and low inflation episodes, it represents an improvement over the latter. However, to the extent that the episodes in which the quantity theory appears not to work well are the exception rather than the rule,[32] it will remain a prominent explanation of price level movements.

---

30 A quantity theory framework offers another way in which current money supply increases need not translate immediately into price level changes: Money supply changes can take time to influence prices. This is the essence of the idea of important "long and variable lags in the effect of monetary policy," expounded by Milton Friedman.

31 A more formal discussion of the difference between the quantity theory and the real bills doctrine is available in an appendix available on the text's Web site at **www.mcgrawhill.ca/college/siklos**.

32 We say "appears" because proponents of the quantity theory argue that episodes in which $g < \rho$ are rare. They also argue that the connection between money and prices will be weaker if we allow velocity to change over time.

21.5 WHAT TRANSMISSION MECHANISM?[33]

Having discussed at some length the likelihood that monetary policy does influence output or un-employment in the short run, it is worth pausing to ask exactly how this might take place. This explanation involves a discussion of the **transmission mechanism** of monetary policy, a topic in vogue during the 1960s and 1970s and lately revived as central banks and governments focus on combining low inflation with healthy economic growth.[34]

The current debate centres around four different "channels" through which monetary pol-icy might work. Obviously, researchers have generated empirical results favourable to all four points of view, which means that there is a grain of truth to each hypothesis or, to put it differ-ently, none of the explanations summarized below has been able to dominate the others.

The four views of the transmission mechanism are as follows:

1. The interest rate channel

2. The exchange rate channel

3. The impact of asset prices more generally

4. The credit channel

The interest rate channel is simply the liquidity effect first encountered in Chapter 6. Less money in the economy drives up interest rates, because there is less liquidity, and therefore has a negative impact on output. The exchange rate channel adds another element to the interest rate channel, namely that the exchange rate will *appreciate* because a higher domestic interest rate at-tracts capital inflows, which will *reduce* exports and increase imports, thus lowering output. The other asset prices channel argues that a lower money supply will make stocks *less* attractive to hold and, via the impact that lower stock prices have on Tobin's *q*, will lead to lower investment spending and thus to lower economywide output. Finally, the credit channel emphasizes the role of financial intermediaries in the transmission mechanism. According to this scenario, a lower money supply implies fewer bank deposits and fewer loans, via the multiplier process, which combined will translate into lower investment spending as well as lower output.

One way to arrive at this outcome is via the sale of government securities (i.e., an increase in the demand for loanable funds). This view focuses on the liabilities of the banking system since the policy amounts to the public holding less cash and fewer securities.

It is, therefore, important that bank loans and securities not be good substitutes. After all, if they were, banks could respond to a restrictive monetary policy by liquidating their securities holdings and leaving their loan portfolio unchanged. In addition, the Bank of Canada must be able to influence banks' lending policies. Otherwise, the banks could thwart any attempt to restrict bank loans.

One reason that empirical studies are unable to deliver decisive evidence for one of the above hypotheses is that, although the end result of monetary policy actions are the same in all cases, the intermediate steps need not be mutually exclusive. Thus, for example, hypotheses 3 and 4 both conclude that output falls because investment falls.[35]

---

33 This section relies on a large number of concepts and definitions covered throughout this text.

34 We will examine the transmission mechanism in Canada leading from a change in the overnight rate to changes in infla-tion. See Figure 22.6.

35 A recent survey of the literature and the empirical evidence can be found in C. Bean, J. Larsen, and K. Nikolov, "Financial Frictions and the Monetary Transmission Mechanism: Theory, Evidence and Policy Implications," working paper no. 113, European Central Bank, January 2002.

21.6 MONEY, FINANCIAL DEVELOPMENT, AND GROWTH

This is a Web site devoted to the issues surrounding the causes and consequences of economic growth
www.worldbank. org/
Follow the links from Economic Research to Research to Programs and then *Macroeconomics and Growth.*

The quantity theory tells us that inflation is purely a monetary phenomenon. Nevertheless, we also know that, in the short run at least, inflation, and thus money growth, have some influence on output. As economies around the world began to slow down in the 1980s and into the 1990s, economists began to turn their attention to the problem of what determines economic growth. Much of the attention centred on the role of technical innovations and how well a country is endowed with natural resources,[36] but there was general agreement that inflation was a detriment to economic growth. Yet, some also argued that the drive to zero inflation was extreme. After all, according to the Fisher hypothesis, if inflation is zero, then real interest rates will be positive. By contrast, with some inflation, real interest rates can be negative (as we saw in Chapter 5), which could spur economic growth.[37] This argument does not seem very convincing in light of our discussion, early in this text, about the costs of inflation. After all, even a little inflation, say 2% a year over 20 years still implies an almost 50% rise in the price level, which is hardly conducive to efficiency.[38] Figure 21.3 shows very clearly the connection between inflation and economic growth. Before the oil shock of 1973–74, that is, in a period of relatively low inflation, there is a definite positive relationship between economic performance and inflation. Turning to the post-oil shock period, the

---

Figure 21.3   **Inflation and Economic Growth in the G-7**

(A) Pre–Oil Shock

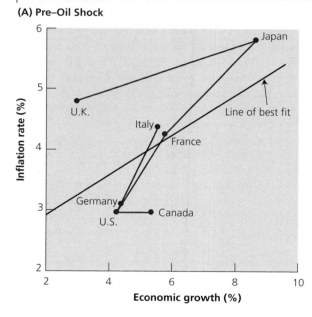

(B) 1975–2004

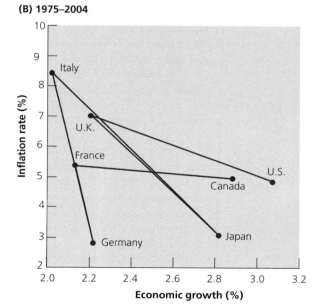

Source: International Financial Statistics CD-ROM.

Note: Inflation is the percentage change in the consumer price index. Output growth is the percentage change in real GDP. Simple averages were calculated for each country for the periods indicated.

---

36 See C.I. Jones, *Introduction to Economic Growth*, Second Edition (New York: W.W. Norton and Co., 2001).
37 This is known as the "Summers" effect, named after an economist at Harvard University who was U.S. Secretary of the Treasury during the Clinton presidency.
38 For the argument that zero inflation is, in some sense, "optimal," see J. Konieczny, "The Optimal Rate of Inflation: Competing Theories and Their Relevance to Canada," in *Economic Behaviour and Policy Choice Under Price Stability* (Ottawa, Ont.: Bank of Canada, 1993).

ECONOMICS FOCUS 21.4   POST HOC ERGO PROPTER HOC?

"Post hoc ergo propter hoc" (Latin for "After the fact so because of the fact") is the name given to a common flaw in logic: Because B follows A, B is caused by A. The phrase was used in a famous 1970 article by the Nobel Laureate James Tobin to argue that just because monetary policy actions (as measured by changes in the money supply) precede changes in prices or real income does not mean that monetary policy is necessarily the cause of these price or income changes.

The fallacy is surprisingly common. For example, Friedman and Schwartz argue persuasively that monetary policy caused the Great Depression of the 1930s in the United States. But a closer reading of their work suggests instead that other factors, such as bank failures, created an economic downturn, which was then magnified by the inappropriate response of the U.S. central bank, the Federal Reserve. Monetary policy did not cause the Great Depression; it only enhanced and prolonged its effects.

Another example comes from the monetarist argument that monetary policy is the prime determinant of nominal income, to the exclusion of fiscal policy. This notion was translated into a model (called the St. Louis model because it was developed by researchers at the U.S. Federal Reserve Bank of St. Louis). Essentially, the model assumes that nominal income is caused by past observations of some money supply measure and of some measure of fiscal policy, such as government spending. The theory behind the model in part stems from the view of money as a "cause" of changes in real income. The empirical evidence is overwhelmingly favourable to the view that past observations of the money supply explain nominal income movements but past fiscal policy effects have no influence whatsoever on the same variable. Thus, money matters and fiscal policy does not. There is, however, an important flaw in the St. Louis analysis. It assumes that current nominal income could not cause either future monetary policy or fiscal policy. Raj and Siklos demonstrate, however, that although monetary policy causes nominal income, the same variable influences

future and perhaps expected fiscal policy. In other words, policymakers react to the joint effects of inflation and real income changes by modifying future fiscal policy.

Although it is true that the role of money has been downgraded in recent years, it is making a comeback of sorts. As noted in the text, years of financial innovations have distorted the role of money in the transmission mechanism, so much so that the quarterly projection model (QPM), used by the Bank of Canada to formulate projections for the Canadian economy, does not explicitly include a monetary aggregate. Money plays a passive role in this type of analysis. But if the various channels through which monetary policy operates are correct, money should be viewed as playing a rather active role instead. David Laidler makes the point to argue that monetary aggregates should not be entirely left on the sidelines.

Questions for Discussion
1. Why is knowledge of the direction of causality between money and the business cycle considered important?
2. Use a flowchart to explain how monetary and fiscal policy might be related to each other and to economic activity more generally. Does the transmission mechanism matter?

Sources
M. Friedman, and A.J. Schwartz, *A Monetary History of the United States* (Princeton: Princeton University Press, 1963).
D. Laidler, "The Quantity of Money and Monetary Policy," Bank of Canada Working Paper 99–5 (April 1999).
B. Raj, and P.L. Siklos, "The Role of Fiscal Policy in the St. Louis Model: An Evaluation and Some New Evidence," *Journal of Applied Econometrics* 1 (July 1986): 287–94.
J. Tobin, "Money and Income: Post Hoc Ergo Propter Hoc?" *Quarterly Journal of Economics* 84 (May 1970): 301–17.

outcomes are quite different. This period is one of relatively high inflation and stagnant economic growth. It is experiences such as these that led policymakers to advocate that central banks focus on inflation as the goal of monetary policy. It is too early to tell, however, whether a return to low and stable inflation during the 1990s will augur the high growth rates achieved during the 1960s.[39] Early indications are that the answer is no.

The connection between inflation and economic growth implicit in Figure 21.3 ignores, of course, other factors that could also influence growth.[40] Nevertheless, the fact remains that the link between inflation and economic growth is not a clear one.

---

[39] Also recall that the 1960s were a period of relatively stable exchange rates, an important consideration in explaining economic performance.

[40] The relationship between inflation and growth appears also to be sensitive to the choice of countries sampled, as others have found. It is beyond our scope, however, to consider the issue in any greater detail.

Beyond the question of the potential role of monetary policy in influencing economic growth is the question of whether the development of the financial system as a whole contributes to economic development. After all, the works of the great economists such as Schumpeter and Bagehot, in the nineteenth century and at the beginning of the twentieth century, emphasized how banks, in particular, can spur economic growth by providing the necessary liquidity to fund productive investment. Indeed, there is considerable evidence[41] that stock market liquidity—measured by the volume and value of trading relative to the size of the economy—and banking development—evaluated as the fraction of bank loans to the private sector as a percentage of GDP—are both positively related to overall economic growth. Hence, we can conclude this chapter as we began this text, namely by repeating the idea that the existence, functions, and development of the financial system in Canada, and elsewhere, spur overall economic growth. There are, therefore, excellent micro-and macroeconomic reasons to study and understand the economic role of financial intermediaries.

SUMMARY

- The debate about the importance of money centres on how important money supply changes are in explaining business cycle fluctuations.

- Monetarists place the money supply at the centre of their models because they believe inflation is entirely a monetary phenomenon. In the short run, monetary policy can influence real economic activity, but in the long run, money is neutral. The basis of monetarists' views is the Quantity Theory of money summarized by the expression

$$M\overline{V} = P\overline{y}$$

where M is the money supply, V is the velocity of circulation which is constant in the short-run, P is the price level, and y is output, also constant in the short-run.

- Understanding the role of money in the economy requires that we model the formation of inflationary expectations. Expectations may be understood as adaptive—individuals learn from their past mistakes—or rational—individuals use their forecasts of inflation on an economic model that can change over time.
  —The adaptive expectations hypothesis is summarized by the expression

$$\hat{P}_t = \hat{P}_{t-1} + b(P_{t-1} - \hat{P}_{t-1}),$$

where $\hat{P}_t$ is the price level forecast at time t, and $P_{t-1} - \hat{P}_{t-1}$ is the forecast error made in the previous period (time $t-1$). Individuals therefore use last period's forecast and add a correction factor for the forecast error made in the previous period.
  —In the case of rational expectations, the forecast for the price level at time t is based on some economic model. For example,

$$\hat{P}_t = aM_{t-1}$$

indicates that last period's money supply (M) determines this period's forecast for the price level.

- Analyzing the role of money can be facilitated by looking at a Phillips curve, which summarizes the relationship between the monetary side of an economy—and thus, inflation—and the real side, as measured by unemployment. The equation for the short-run Phillips curve is written

$$\pi = \pi^e - \alpha (u - u^*)$$

where inflation (π) is determined by expected inflation (π^e) less an adjustment for the degree of slack in the economy assumed to be a function of the difference between the unemployment rate (u) relative to some desired level for the unemployment rate (u^*).

---

41 See, for example, R. Levine, "Financial Development and Economic Growth: Views and Agenda," *Journal of Economic Literature* 35 (June 1997): 687–726, and R. Levine, and S. Zervos, "Stock Markets, Banks, and Economic Growth," *American Economic Review* 88 (June 1998): 537–58.

The impact of economywide slack on inflation is affected by the size of the coefficient α.

- In the short run there is a negative relationship between inflation and unemployment; in the long run the Phillips curve is vertical.

- Because monetary policy is so important, economists debate whether policymakers should be allowed discretion in conducting monetary policy or rather should be tied to fixed rules known to the public.

- If policymakers are willing to commit themselves to a particular inflation rate, then the central bank should be able to deliver the inflation the public expects; otherwise there will be more inflation than is socially desirable.

- Not everyone agrees that money supply changes automatically lead to proportionate changes in the price level (as in the quantity theory of money). One theory, called the real bills doctrine, concentrates on the role of government deficits and the point at which they can become inflationary.

- The channels through which monetary policy affects economic activity are varied, but they ultimately involve the financial system.

- Monetary policy can contribute to economic growth and inflation, but it is the development of the financial system that has a critical role to play in overall economic performance.

IMPORTANT TERMS

adaptive expectations hypothesis, 411
base drift, 422
classical economics, 408
credibility, 418
Keynesianism, 408
monetarism, 410
natural rate of unemployment, 417
neutrality of money, 411

nonaccelerating inflation rate of
  unemployment (NAIRU), 417
Phillips curve, 411
rational expectations hypothesis, 414
time-inconsistency problem of monetary
  policy, 418
transmission mechanism, 427

PROBLEMS

1. One reason given for the existence of a short-run Phillips curve is the presence of wage contracts. Explain how labour contracts permit the existence of a short-run inflation–unemployment trade-off. (Hint: Think of a link between wages and prices.)

2. In constructing Table 21.1, we assumed an adjustment coefficient of 0.5. Reproduce the table assuming an adjustment coefficient of 0.2 and of 0.9. Which coefficient produces the fastest adjustment of expectations? In what sense is the adjustment coefficient a "black box"?

3. In constructing Table 21.2, we assumed that actual money growth was 4% per year. Suppose instead that actual money growth was

Year	Actual Money Growth
1	4%
2	1%
3	–2%
4	6%
5	3%

Calculate the actual money stock levels, revised target levels, and the difference between the revised and original target values. What conclusions do you draw?

4. The figures on the next page give the annual unemployment and inflation rates for France, the United Kingdom, and Canada. Plot a Phillips curve for each country for 1985–97. Discuss the results in light of the issues considered in this chapter. Also compare the results to the Canadian experience over the same period. (Hint: This was a period of falling inflation rates, so think of the impact of this development on inflationary expectations.)

Year	United Kingdom Unemployment %	United Kingdom Inflation %	France Unemployment %	France Inflation %	Canada Unemployment %	Canada Inflation %
1985	11.20	6.07	10.20	5.83	10.50	3.95
1986	11.80	3.43	10.40	2.54	9.60	4.17
1987	10.60	4.45	10.50	3.29	8.90	4.36
1988	8.40	4.91	10.00	2.70	7.80	4.02
1989	6.30	7.80	9.40	3.50	7.50	4.99
1990	5.90	9.48	8.90	3.38	8.10	4.76
1991	8.10	5.85	9.40	3.22	10.40	5.62
1992	9.90	3.73	10.10	2.37	11.20	1.51
1993	10.40	1.56	11.10	2.11	11.20	1.84
1994	9.40	2.48	12.40	1.66	10.40	1.90
1995	8.30	3.41	11.60	1.78	9.55	2.17
1996	7.54	2.45	12.10	2.01	9.70	1.58
1997	5.70	3.13	12.30	1.20	9.22	1.62

Source: International Financial Statistics CD-ROM (Washington, D.C.: International Monetary Fund).

5. Describe, in flowchart form, the four transmission mechanisms described in this chapter.

6. Would the analysis of the rational expectations model change if the price level forecast were a function of a variable other than last period's money supply (for example, last period's interest rate or exchange rate)? Explain.

7. Is it possible for individuals to make persistent forecast errors under rational expectations? How would this case be represented in terms of equation (21.4)?

8. If α in equation (21.7) increases, what happens to the inflation–unemployment trade-off? Would policymakers be more or less likely to exploit the trade-off under these circumstances? Explain.

9. Minimize equation (21.8) under both the commitment and no commitment cases.

10. Equation (21.8) describes a loss function for policymakers. Explain intuitively, and with the help of the following numerical values, why its setup makes economic sense. Assume that $\pi^e = 3\%$, $\pi = 5\%$ versus 7%. Let $u^* = 7\%$ and $u = 6\%$ versus 4%, respectively.

11. Figure 21.3(B) shows average inflation and economic growth in the G-7 countries since 1975. The table below gives the averages since 1990. Try to draw the relationship between these two variables and determine whether growth rates have risen or fallen as average inflation rates in the G-7 have fallen. Comment on the result.

Country	Percentage Economic growth	Percentage Inflation
Canada	2.56	2.28
France	1.74	1.89
Germany	2.36	2.05
Italy	1.42	3.60
Japan	1.58	0.63
U.K.	2.17	3.29
U.S.	2.93	2.85

DISCUSSION QUESTIONS

1. Evaluate the statement: "Countercyclical monetary policy is still effective if money is neutral in the long run."

2. Evaluate the statement: "The stability of velocity is important for the monetarist philosophy."

3. What is monetarism?

4. What is meant by the term "neutrality of money"?

5. What is the difference between adaptive and rational expectations?

6. Is there a connection between the "shape" of the Phillips curve over time and economists' ideas about the trade-offs between inflation and unemployment?

7. Describe the time-inconsistency problem.

8. What is the base drift problem and why did it lead most central banks to abandon monetary targeting?

9. What are the two theories of money?

10. Why is commitment in monetary policy considered important?

ONLINE APPLICATION

1. Go to the OECD Web site at **www.oecd.org**. Go to *statistics*. Next choose *labour* followed by *prices*. You will obtain recent data on prices, inflation, and unemployment in OECD economies. Choose the G-7 countries (see Figure 21.3 for the list) and choose a sample consisting of at least 10 years of data.

    (a) Does it appear that there is some kind of trade-off between inflation and un-employment? Is it more apparent in some countries than in others?

    (b) Has inflation fallen in the G-7 countries only? Does it appear that the disinflation is common across several countries? If so, do the unemployment costs appear to be common as well?

References can be found on **www.mcgrawhill.ca/college/siklos**

CHAPTER 22

The Bank of Canada and the Tools of Monetary Policy

LEARNING OBJECTIVES

After reading and studying this chapter, you should be able to

22.1 explain why central banks were created

22.2 list the functions of the Bank of Canada and describe how it began

22.2 determine whether political motives led to the creation of the Bank of Canada

22.2 describe the milestones and important characters in the history of the Bank of Canada and monetary policy

22.2 explain how inflation targeting works

22.3 list the most important tools through which the Bank of Canada influences financial markets

22.3 describe what prompted the emergence of some of the newer tools at the Bank's disposal

22.4 explain the transmission mechanism of monetary policy

By the early twentieth century most Western industrialized countries had adopted a banking system headed by a central bank entirely owned by the state. Thus was abandoned the notion of free banking; the state gradually exercised complete control over the issue of currency, and following World War II, central banks were called on to control monetary policy and eventually to ensure price stability. These new roles were in line with an increasingly popular way of understanding economies: *monetarism*, which emphasizes the relationship between the money supply and inflation.[1]

Along the way, however, other schools of thought came and went and came back again, such as Keynesianism, the rational expectations revolution, new classical economics, the real business cycle approach, to name but a few of the monikers in the history of economic thought. Chapter 21 reviewed many of the central ideas behind the various schools of thought.

This chapter explores the workings of the Bank of Canada. We begin with a discussion of its origins and provide a sketch of the history of monetary policy since its formation. In recent years, the Bank of Canada has been at the forefront of a movement to adopt inflation targets. We examine the nature of the policy in some detail.

The second part of the chapter is devoted to the tools of monetary policy that central banks have available, focusing on the way they are used by the Bank of Canada. We also consider some

---

1 This statement should not be taken as a definition of monetarism. We examined a definition in Chapter 21.

of the other functions of Canada's central bank (serving as a lender of last resort, acting as banker for the federal government, and managing the government's foreign exchange reserves).

Chapter 23 examines the instruments and targets of monetary policy in more detail as well as the issue of central bank independence from the political authorities. Chapter 21 considered the possible links among monetary policy, the price level, and output.

22.1 THE FOUNDING OF CENTRAL BANKS

See the "Old Lady" cartoon at the Bank of England's Web site **www.bankof england.co.uk/links /setframe.html** click on About the Bank

Many countries established central banks decades, even centuries, earlier than Canada (see Table 22.1).

In many cases, the primary reason was the need for a *lender of last resort*. Modern central banks were created as lenders of last resort. Nevertheless, as Table 22.1 shows, several central banks also came into being to finance the needs of war or to help manage a financial crisis. Recall that under a fractional reserve system, banks maintain only a small percentage of their deposits in the form of reserves. If one bank experiences a run, it will likely find itself short of cash. Worse, the run can easily spread to other banks.[2] Such runs may be averted by the action of a lender of last resort—a strong bank ready to meet other banks' liquidity needs. Thus, the emergence of central banking was a natural evolution of the financial industry. Indeed, in countries such as England, central banks were created from existing private banks that had solid reputations for managing their finances and the financial needs and gold reserves of the government. The "Old Lady of Threadneedle Street," as she is known, was naturally called on to aid in resolving liquidity crises. Such a role was strengthened if the central bank issued its own, well-received notes. Indeed, the momentum for establishing central banks was probably increased by the realization that they enabled governments to monopolize the issue of currency and thus extract additional revenues for themselves in the form of *seigniorage*.

Central banks have, of course, evolved. The lender of last resort, although still a core function of a typical central bank, is no longer what we tend to think of when discussing monetary authorities. Indeed, the new European Central Bank (see Chapter 26) is not formally permitted to act as a lender of last resort. Instead, the focus of central banks has, in recent years, shifted toward exchange rate policies, international financial cooperation, the maintenance of price stability, and bank–government relations.

Visit the central banks of the world **www.bis.org/ cbanks.htm**

Table 22.1	Year When Selected Central Banks Were Established	
Country	**Year Established**	**Reason**
Belgium	1850	Banking crisis
Canada	1934	Lender of last resort
France	1800	Manage public debt
Germany	1876	Unification
Italy	1893	Unification
Japan	1882	Modernization of financial system
Sweden	1668	Finance war
Switzerland	1907	Eliminate private note issue
United Kingdom	1694	Finance war
United States	1913	Lender of last resort

Source: P.L.Siklos, *The Changing Face of Central Banking* (Cambridge: Cambridge University Press, 2002).

---

2 As we saw in Chapters 16 (also see Chapter 25), such an outcome was not unusual in the United States, at least before World War II.

■ 22.2 THE BANK OF CANADA

ORIGINS

The Bank of Canada was created in 1934.[3] Did it emerge because of some inherent weaknesses of the Canadian banking system? Or was its creation a purely political phenomenon?

Two historic events of the 1930s were influential in the formation of the Bank of Canada. The first was the Great Depression. The simultaneous contraction of the money supply (instead of the expansion that would have been necessary for the economy to expand) was viewed as a failure of the existing arrangements for monetary policy. The second event was the effective end of the gold standard, which, as we have seen, had prevented excessive monetary expansion and, therefore, inflation. Yet, unlike the United States and many other countries that had central banks and still experienced the Depression, Canada saw no bank failures during the 1930s. Neither did Canada experience explosive inflation between December 1928, when the country withdrew from the gold standard, and the opening of the Bank of Canada. Indeed, if anything, the main problem facing central banks and, hence, part of the impetus for the spread of central banking throughout the world, was the fear of deflation.[4]

So perhaps the impetus was largely political. One factor was simply the uneasiness of hard times combined with Canadian regionalism. The MacMillan Commission, a royal commission struck in 1933 to investigate the possibility of establishing a central bank in Canada, returned a favourable, though narrow, majority report after conducting hearings nationwide. As two economic historians have noted:

The Bank of Canada
**www.bankof
canada.ca**

> Domestically, in an environment where traditional trust in the beneficial nature of the market system was eroding and a spirit of nationalism was rising, political pressure was mounting to halt the deflation which was frequently blamed on the concentrated banking industry.[5]

Deflation was especially hurting farmers, who blamed the banks for creating it and colluding to close branches in Western Canada. Simultaneously, populist sentiment was rising in the West.

Other political forces also led to the creation of the Bank of Canada. One was the need for Canada to coordinate its increasingly international economic policies with those of other countries. In particular, unlike the United States and Britain, Canada had no central bank that could be used to manage monetary policy, including the exchange rate. Indeed, paralleling the introduction of the Bank of Canada was the creation of the Exchange Fund Account in 1935, to "aid in the control and protection of the external position of the Canadian monetary unit."[6] Without a central bank, Canada lacked an effective institution for accomplishing the necessary tasks. Another factor was Canada's evolution toward becoming a fully sovereign state after World War I. Establishing a central bank was simply another manifestation of its growing independence from Britain. Thus, when the *Bank of Canada Act* was passed by Parliament in 1934, it was probably enacted more for political reasons than for economic ones.

The Bank, which officially started operations in March 1935, was initially a private institution with stock issued—no one directly linked to a chartered bank could own any of it—and dividends paid out to shareholders up to a stated maximum; any additional profits were to accrue to the federal government. After the election of a Liberal government in 1936, however, the Bank was completely nationalized, and by 1938 the government had acquired all of the shares.

---

3 Royal Assent was received on 3 July 1935.
4 See R.C.K. Burdekin and P.L. Siklos, *Deflation* (Cambridge: Cambridge University Press 2004).
5 M.D. Bordo, and A. Redish, "Why Did the Bank of Canada Emerge in 1935?" *Journal of Economic History* 47 (June 1987): 415.
6 Statutes of Canada 1935.

HISTORY

Entire volumes have been written about the Bank of Canada and its performance,[7] and the record of its monetary policy has been mentioned in various places throughout this text. Here we outline only some of the most salient features of its history.

Pre-War Era

The earliest days of the Bank of Canada were marked by its working to smooth seasonal variation in interest rates and to make a market for government debt.

Its greatest early contribution lay in its role as a provider and regulator of cash in the economy. In the mid-1930s, Canada was still a rural-based economy, experiencing considerable seasonal fluctuation in the demand for currency and thus in interest rates. A perceived advantage of creating a central monetary authority was that it could manage the money supply in such a way as to smooth out seasonal variation in interest rates. The Bank was successful in this effort. Ever since, it has been the money supply that has experienced seasonality in its movements.[8]

When the Bank of Canada began operations at the end of the Great Depression, it was under political pressure to somehow use monetary policy to manage the economy in the face of worldwide confusion. Thus, it is not surprising that its stated objectives were on a grand scale nor that it did not meet all of them. It did, however, quickly create a market for government debt instruments (particularly, but not only T-bills). This development was vital, given the contemporary world's trend toward great involvement (that is, greater spending) by government in the economy. This active market would prove especially useful during the war years, when government deficit spending soared.

Another important feature of early Bank of Canada history was its fairly frequent reliance on moral suasion. This tendency was not surprising, given the highly concentrated nature of the Canadian banking system during the 1930s. After all, in 1935, when the Bank opened its doors to the public, the country had only 10 chartered banks.

Early Postwar Period

The early part of the postwar period was marked by high government debt, the need to reintermediate the Canadian economy following wartime controls, and the great demands for reconstruction and industrialization. Still in vogue was the Keynesian prescription of government spending to ensure high employment, which translated into a policy of "cheap money"—that is, relatively low interest rates. Indeed, interest rates were artificially low, since they were essentially pegged at the government's behest.[9]

In 1953, following the Korean War, the Bank of Canada faced its first major recession. It responded, exactly as it should have, by easing monetary policy and assisting the financing of government deficits.

---

7 A partial list includes E.P. Neufeld, *Bank of Canada Operations and Policy* (Toronto: University of Toronto Press, 1958); R.A. Shearer, J.F. Chant, and D.E. Bond, *The Economics of the Canadian Financial System: Theory, Policy and Institutions*, 3d ed. (Scarborough, Ont.: Prentice-Hall, 1995), especially Chapters 12 and 24; T.J. Courchene, *Monetarism and Controls: The Inflation Fighters* (Toronto: C.D. Howe Institute, 1976); T.J. Courchene, *No Place to Stand?* (Toronto: C.D. Howe Institute, 1983); P.W. Howitt, *Monetary Policy in Transition: A Study of Bank of Canada Policy, 1982–1985* (Toronto: C.D. Howe Research Institute, 1986); T.J. Courchene, *Money, Inflation, and the Bank of Canada: An Analysis of Monetary Gradualism, 1975–1980* (Montreal: C.D. Howe Institute, 1981); G.S. Watts, *The Bank of Canada Origins and Early History*, edited by T.K. Rymes (Ottawa: Carleton University Press, 1993); and P. Howitt, *Monetary Policy in Transition: A Study of Bank of Canada Policy, 1982–85* (Toronto: C.D. Howe Institute, 1986).

8 Recall from Chapter 2 that seasonality is an issue only for narrow aggregates, such as M1; broader monetary aggregates display little seasonality.

9 Because the Bank was still supporting the war debt. We have already seen the distortions in the financial system that are created when interest rates are pegged at some value inconsistent with market equilibrium. A similar policy was in place in the United States at the time.

The Coyne Affair

The latter 1950s were marked by controversies on topics that perhaps sound less familiar today: high interest rates, particularly in a time of recession; the Canadian–U.S. exchange rate; and the control of inflation.

During 1955 and 1956, the economy was booming, and the dangers of inflation lurked. The Bank of Canada encouraged the development of the money market [often using it itself for open market operations (OMOs)] and generally followed a restrictive monetary policy. But market interest rates were rising, and in late 1956, after raising the Bank Rate several times, the Bank allowed it to float by tying its movement to the T-bill rate, a significant policy change.

By the end of the 1950s, the economy had softened, unemployment was high, the exchange rate was fairly high,[10] and interest rates were climbing, creating, among other things, a considerable differential with those current in the United States and other world capital markets. The Bank also had to find large amounts for government financing (a new phenomenon for it in peacetime—in 1956, for example, monetary policy had been assisted by a large government surplus). And it faced the approaching maturity of the wartime Victory Bonds. Partly as an anti-inflation measure, the debt was rolled over into long-term bonds. One consequence of this action was a sharp increase in the average maturity of government debt (from approximately 8 years to 15 years); another was the necessity of a temporary expansionary policy, but it was soon reversed. The Bank of Canada again began to restrict the money supply. The policy worked in that little inflation occurred. But interest rates were driven up, the difficulties of exporters increased, U.S. capital poured into the country—and unemployment soared. The culmination of these events was one of Canada's best-known policy conflicts between the Bank and the government: the **Coyne affair**.[11]

James Coyne, who had become only the second governor of the Bank of Canada in 1955, believed strongly that the Bank needed to be rather interventionist, in particular to control inflation and the growth of credit in the economy.[12] The Governor's *Annual Reports* make fascinating reading, and Coyne's confidence in his abilities and certainty that his stewardship of the Bank was the correct one are unmistakable. For example, the 1958 *Annual Report* states that "…the central bank must continue to emphasise its major and essential role of regulating the rate of change in overall monetary supply in such manner as is consistent with and, so far as monetary action can, will contribute to, sound and sustained economic growth under stable prices." (page 9) His policy of high interest rates at a time of rising unemployment produced severe tension with the federal government of the day, which was led by John Diefenbaker, and with the minister of finance, Donald Fleming. Inflation rates were rising and since Canadians and their governments were used to relatively low interest rates, it came as a bit of a shock that the Bank suggested the need for a tightening of monetary policy by raising interest rates. Many policymakers did not see the link between nominal interest rates and inflation (students of the Great Depression will be familiar with this argument). They simply assumed that higher nominal interest rates automatically translate into tighter monetary policy. However, you will recall that, in Chapter 5, we saw that the ease or tightness of policy is dictated by the level of the real interest rate. Adding fuel to the fire was Coyne's penchant for making speeches, a now widely accepted practice among central bankers, and

---

10 Canada was then on a floating exchange rate regime, having left the Bretton Woods Agreement in 1950. It would return to that fixed-rate system from 1962 to 1970.

11 It is easy to forget that the U.S. economy was experiencing similar difficulties. Indeed, the U.S. Federal Reserve had only recently re-established its autonomy from government, and there were serious conflicts between the Fed and the Congress on the one hand, and between the Fed and the Administration on the other. A major difference between the U.S. and Canadian cases is that central bank autonomy was not established in Canada. For a recent description of U.S. monetary history at the time, see R. Bremner, *Chairman of the Fed William McChesney Martin Jr., and the Creation of the Modern American Financial System* (New Haven, CT: Yale University Press, 2004).

12 Coyne's many other ideas included requiring chartered banks to hold secondary reserves and bringing the banking system into more conformity with the U.K. and U.S. models to permit more long-term lending to consumers (to finance housing purchases, for example). And it was Coyne who initiated the floating bank rate and oversaw the conversion of the Victory Bonds.

criticizing the (Conservative) federal government's fiscal policy. It became apparent that the government was unclear about its authority over the central bank. Fleming stated publicly that the government cannot influence its central bank. Yet, the original *Bank of Canada Act* gave the finance minister ultimate responsibility over any disagreement between the governor and the board. By 1960, politicians, bankers, and even the academic community were complaining that the Bank appeared obsessed with the control of inflation at the expense of everything else.

> It has its eye firmly fixed on the moral wickedness of the slightest changes of inflation and is unmoved by the patent facts of growing unemployment and stagnating national income.[13]

The controversy reached a climax in mid-1961, although the battle was fought out not on its true grounds—the independence of the Bank—but on the details of Coyne's pension. When the board of the Bank asked Coyne to resign, he refused. As a result, the government introduced a motion in Parliament declaring an expansionary fiscal policy and a vacancy in the post of governor. The Commons passed the bill, but the opposition-controlled Senate defeated it. Following another public display in which Coyne attacked the government, he did resign, and the motion was passed. You can hear the CBC's report on the resignation of Coyne by going to www.archives.cbc.ca/500f.asp?id=1-173-1599-11085.

Not surprisingly, the Coyne affair produced a revision in the government–Bank of Canada relationship. Louis Raminsky, the incoming governor, agreed that the government has the ultimate responsibility for monetary policy. But he insisted that any disagreement between the government and the Bank must be followed by a written directive from the minister of finance requiring the Bank to change its policy to conform with the government's wishes. He also stated that should a disagreement of this kind take place, he would implement the government's wishes and immediately thereafter resign his post. This relationship continues to this day, although no directive has ever been issued.[14]

The 1960s to the 1990s: Searching for an Anchor for Monetary Policy

The 1962–70 period was a time of fixed exchange rates. Many of the Bank's activities were concerned with maintaining the Canadian dollar at US92.5¢. Both the economy and inflation were less important problems.

This relatively peaceful period came to an end with the oil price shocks of the 1970s. The resulting *stagflation*—the unusual combination of a stagnating economy and high inflation—led to the abandonment of the Keynesian prescription and stimulated renewed interest in money control as advocated by monetarists.[15] This culminated in the 1975 Saskatoon Monetary Manifesto in which the governor of the Bank of Canada, Gerald Bouey, announced that the Bank would practise **monetary targeting**—work to hold the growth of the money supply to an explicit range—rather than interest rate control.[16] In particular, the governor stated:

> Whatever else may need to be done to bring inflation under control, it is absolutely essential to keep the rate of monetary expansion within reasonable limits. Any programme that did not include this policy would be doomed to failure. There is no way of preserving its value if money is created on an excessive scale.[17]

Termed the Strategy Gradualism (since the object was to reduce over time target growth rates in M1 from an initial range of 10% to 15% per annum), the policy encountered the diffi-

---

13 H. Scott Gordon, *The Economists versus the Bank of Canada* (Toronto: The Ryerson Press, 1961): 15.

14 Indeed, some people theorize that the system reduces overt argument between the Bank and the government. Disagreement might force the issuance of a directive, which no minister of finance wants to do. See T.K. Rymes, "On the Coyne–Rasminsky Directive and Responsibility for Monetary Policy in Canada," in *Varieties of Monetary Reforms: Lessons and Experiences on the Road to Monetary Union*, edited by P.L. Siklos (Boston: Kluwer Academic Publishers, 1994): 351–66.

15 Monetarism was described in Chapter 21.

16 The economic implications of this choice are considered in Chapter 26.

17 T.J. Courchene, *Monetarism and Controls: The Inflation Fighters* (Montreal: C.D. Howe Institute, 1976): 25.

culties inherent in monetary control. Suffice it to say that, partly as a result of the second oil price shock of 1979, it was deemed a failure, since inflation once again began to rise toward double-digit levels. Perhaps more important, the policy led to considerably more volatile interest rates and thus magnified the problem of interest rate risk. Some critics suggested that the policy was too gradual;[18] others that the Bank should not have focused on the M1 aggregate.[19]

The recession of 1981–82 led to the next phase of monetary policy. The Bank of Canada would tolerate or even encourage high interest rates if they were necessary to stem inflation. This policy resulted from a growing focus on the primary role of the central bank as a guarantor of price stability. Indeed, as the 1990s began, proposals appeared to enshrine the goal of price stability into the *Bank of Canada Act*.

The ongoing recession of 1991–93 did not alter this view. In fact, John Crow, the previous governor, stated that the current, excessively broad mandate of the Bank of Canada "muddies the accountability of the institution."[20] It appears surprising that the governor would ask that the central bank be more accountable; traditionally, central banks seem to prefer that their actions and motives be secret. But the lesson learned from the stagflation of the 1970s is that high inflation and cheap money eventually create the need for a correction of some kind, which tends to produce large economic costs in the form of lost output and high unemployment rates. Nevertheless, it is also important to point out that monetary policy can do no more than assist economic activity. Economic growth or the lack thereof requires policies other than purely monetary ones, especially if monetary policy is viewed as being neutral in the long run.[21]

Indeed, the events of the early 1990s produced considerable controversy among academics and analysts, reminiscent of the debate in the early 1960s over the Coyne affair, over whether the severe recession was deliberately engineered by the Bank of Canada. In a presidential address to the Canadian Economics Association, Pierre Fortin laid the blame squarely on the policy of inflation targeting. He then called the early 1990s in Canada the era of the "Great Canadian Slump."[22]

Ultimately, however, Canada has a small, open economy, so external forces not under the Bank of Canada's control are likely to be important influences on the Canadian economy.[23] Moreover, the clear lesson from the Coyne affair is that the government, led at the time by the Conservative Prime Minister Brian Mulroney and Finance Minister Michael Wilson, having accepted the policy of inflation targeting, got precisely the monetary policy it wanted. To lay the blame entirely on the Bank's shoulders is giving the Bank far more influence and authority than it can possibly have.

Inflation Targeting and the Current Objective of Monetary Policy

Not long after John Crow became governor of the Bank of Canada in 1987, he laid out a specific agenda for disinflation. The first statement to this effect was made during the Hanson Lecture at the University of Alberta in January 1988. In the course of this lecture, Crow argued that "monetary policy should be conducted so as to achieve a pace of monetary expansion that promotes price stability in the value of money. This means pursuing a policy aimed at achieving and maintaining stable prices."[24] But it was not until February 1991, just one month after the GST was in-

---

18 It is interesting to note that the United States also eventually abandoned a money control rule, even though its policy was anything but gradual. Unexpected changes in the relationship between money, income, and prices also doomed the money targeting experiment.

19 Our earlier discussion of money multipliers could certainly lead to the conclusion that, had the Bank focused on M2, it might have acceded to the wishes of those who favoured greater monetary restraint.

20 "Bank of Canada Not a One-Man Show: Crow," *Financial Post* (17 January 1992): 5.

21 We examined the question of monetary neutrality in Chapter 21.

22 See P. Fortin, "The Great Canadian Slump," *Canadian Journal of Economics* 29 (1996): 761–87.

23 See C. Freedman, and T. Macklem, "A Comment on the Great Canadian Slump," *Canadian Journal of Economics* 31 (August 1998): 646–65.

24 J.W. Crow, "The Work of Monetary Policy," *Bank of Canada Review* (February 1988): 4.

troduced, that the federal government sealed its approval of the **inflation-targeting** approach when the then-Finance Minister Michael Wilson, in presenting his budget, announced numerical inflation targets.[25] Thus, after New Zealand, Canada became the second country in the world to adopt inflation targets. The initial three targets were as follows:

1. 3% inflation by December 1992

2. 2% by December 1995

3. Price stability defined as less than 2% by the second half of the 1990s[26]

During the federal election campaign in the fall of 1993, there was much discussion about whether the incoming Liberal government, which was about to replace the Conservatives, would share the same commitment to low inflation. Governor Crow was not reappointed for a second term but was replaced, as had been the custom at the Bank, by his senior deputy-governor, Gordon Thiessen.[27] The target bands were first extended to the end of 1998, again to the end of 2001, and were renewed again in May 2001, shortly after the present governor, David Dodge, took office upon the retirement of Gordon Thiessen. Since 1998, the inflation targets were redefined as consisting of a range of 1 to 3% inflation with the midpoint of 2% regarded as the most desirable outcome. A decision about the specific meaning of the term "price stability" has been deferred ever since. The current inflation targets are to remain in place at least until 2006. Therefore, the current regime puts in place a five-year horizon, an extension in length relative to the earlier three-year inflation target agreement.

Although the Bank of Canada has made it clear that the target was in terms of overall CPI, exceptions or adjustments were to be made for some changes in food and energy prices. As a result, the Bank's operational target is in terms of core CPI, which is total CPI minus the effects of some of the most volatile components of the CPI.[28] Significantly, however, inflation-targeting central banks usually stress that only the immediate effects of shocks to inflation would be accommodated; second-round effects, such as those that might affect wages, were not to be validated by monetary policy. The operational guidelines were clarified in the most recent inflation targets agreement when core inflation—a measure of the underlying trend in inflation—officially became the operational guide to monetary policy. Figure 22.1 shows the evolution of the CPI since 1991, as well as the target band and its midpoints. It is immediately clear that inflation in the CPI and CPI excluding the most volatile components of food and energy prices and the effect of indirect taxes, also referred to as "core inflation," display quite different behaviour. As is clear from Figure 22.1, core inflation is less volatile, so there is a smaller chance that the Bank will mistake any rise in inflation as a signal to raise interest rates.

Another major development in the area of monetary policy was the drive to increase the Bank's accountability and transparency of its operation. As noted earlier, central banks have often been surrounded by a certain aura of mystery because they kept their operations and objectives relatively sheltered from public scrutiny. In 1995, however, the Bank of Canada released its first *Monetary Policy Report*,[29] a semiannual document created to enhance the Bank's ability to communicate publicly its

---

25 For a description of this period in the history of the Bank of Canada, see D.E.W. Laidler and W.B.P. Robson, *The Great Canadian Disinflation: The Economics and Politics of Monetary Policy in Canada, 1988–93* (Toronto: C.D. Howe Institute, 1993).

26 See "Targets for Reducing Inflation: Further Operational and Measurement Considerations," *Bank of Canada Review* (September 1991): 3–23.

27 The tradition would be broken with the appointment of the current governor of the Bank, David Dodge, who came from government, but outside the Bank.

28 "A variant of the CPI that excludes the eight components with the most volatile prices—which account for 16 percent of the CPI basket—(fruit, vegetables, gasoline, fuel oil, natural gas, mortgage interest, intercity transportation, and tobacco products) as well as the effect of changes in indirect taxes on the remaining components. (Prior to May 2001, the Bank of Canada used the CPI excluding food, energy, and the effect of changes in indirect taxes as its measure of core CPI.)" Taken from **http://www.bankofcanada.ca/en/graphs/notes-1-target.htm**.

29 See Bank of Canada, *Monetary Policy Report* (May 1995).

Figure 22.1	Canada's Inflation Target

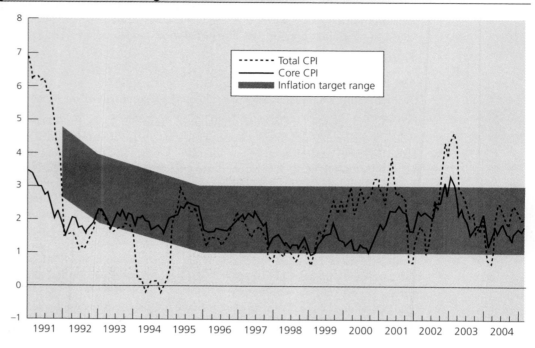

The vertical axis represents the percentage change, on an annual basis, of the CPI and the CPI excluding food, energy, and indirect taxes. The dots inside the target band represent the midpoint of the band.

Source: **http://www.bankofcanada.ca/en/inflation/index.htm**

operations and objectives. Indeed, the inaugural issue stressed that greater accountability implied meeting the following criteria:

1. A clear policy objective,...

2. A medium-term perspective (given the long lags for the full impact of monetary policy actions on the economy),...

3. Recognition that monetary policy works through both the interest rate and the exchange rate.

In 2002, the Bank adopted fixed dates for announcing changes in the Bank rate and announced it would also provide a public statement justifying its decision, whether rates changed or not. Beginning May 2001, the Bank was also required to devote particular attention to any breaches of the inflation target ranges shown in Figure 22.1, and the measures to be taken to return inflation within the agreed-upon inflation objectives.

A major impetus for greater openness in monetary policy was the belief that central banks might be pursuing something other than price stability.

"By setting out a clear objective, and with the commitment of the government, the Bank hoped that future public assessments of monetary policy performance would focus more clearly on its record of achieving price stability."[30]

Satisfying 1 to 3 from the first *Monetary Policy Report* required a policy that aimed for price stability, as currently defined by the inflation-control targets. Assisting the development of a new

---

30 G. Thiessen, "The Canadian Experience with Targets for Inflation," The Gibson Lecture, *Bank of Canada Review* (Winter 1998–99): 89–107.

effective mandate was the *Manley Report*,[31] which was virtually ignored, no doubt because of an imminent election as well as the heat emanating from the Constitutional debate. The Report called for a clearer mandate for the Bank, with price stability as the overall objective, as well as greater accountability. Otherwise, the committee that prepared the report did not go very far in suggesting any major redesign of the governance of the Bank.[32]

Was the Bank of Canada ahead of its time in committing itself to price stability? Not exactly. Figure 22.2 illustrates why central banks, governments, and academics came to the conclusion that something had to be done, because inflation could be harmful to economic growth. Average inflation and economic growth, together with the volatility of inflation and output growth, were negatively related to each other throughout the 1980s, especially among the countries that eventually adopted inflation targets. The first country to take major steps in using inflation targets to achieve disinflation was New Zealand, which announced the first in a series of Policy Target Agreements in 1990. The New Zealand example has served as a model, and as Table 22.2 shows, several countries have followed suit. Unlike New Zealand, however, most countries' inflation targets are agreements between the central bank and the government and do not represent statutory requirements. However, these targets have been successfully met in most cases, although this took place in a period of recession and weak aggregate demand. A test of sorts came during the second half of 2001 when the threat of a recession loomed large in North America, followed by the terrorist attacks on the U.S. in September. These events threatened the onset of deflation. The Bank of Canada was quick to point out that an inflation target means deflation is to be avoided as much as too much inflation.

As discussed in the accompanying Point–Counterpoint focus box, inflation targeting is just the latest in a series of monetary policy rules or regimes that were adopted, and subsequently

---

| **Figure 22.2** | **The Rationale for Inflation Targeting** |

(A) Inflation and Real GDP Growth in Selected Inflation-Targeting Countries

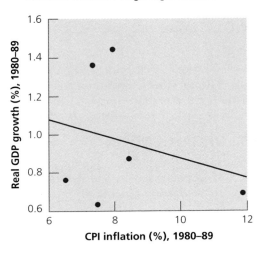

(B) Volatility of Real GDP Growth and Inflation in Inflation-Targeting Countries

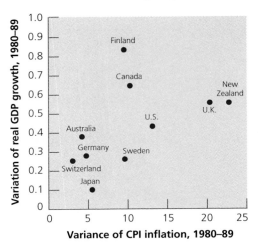

Inflation in the CPI is averaged over the sample shown. Inflation-targeting countries are Australia, Canada, Finland, New Zealand, Sweden, and the United Kingdom. Noninflation-targeting countries are the United States, Germany, Japan, and Switzerland.

Source: *International Financial Statistics* CD-ROM (Washington, D.C.: International Monetary Fund).

---

31 See First Report of the Sub-Committee on the Bank of Canada/Eighth Report of the Standing Committee on Finance "The Mandate and Governance of the Bank of Canada" (February 1992).

32 See D.E.W. Laidler, *How Shall We Govern the Governor?* (Toronto: C.D. Howe Institute, 1991).

Table 22.2   Inflation Objectives and Targets in a Selection of Countries

Country (Month/year introduced)	Price Index	Annual Target Band or Range	Defined Horizon for Objective?	Exceptions or Caveats
Australia (01/1993)	CPI	Average of 2%–3% "over the cycle"	No	Mortgage interest, government controlled prices, and energy
Canada (02/1991)	CPI	1%–3% since 1995	Yes	Indirect taxes, volatile components of food and energy prices
New Zealand (03/1990)	CPI	1%–3%, on average over the medium term	Yes, updated periodically	Commodity prices, indirect taxes, significant government policy changes that affect prices
Sweden (01/1993)	CPI	1%–3% since 1995	No	Indirect taxes and subsidies
United Kingdom (10/1992)	Retail Price Index	2½% since June 1997	No	Mortgage interest payments
European Union* (01/1999)	HICP**	Close to but below 2%	Medium term	None
Switzerland (01/2001)	CPI	Below 2%	No	Short-run fluctuations in energy prices, and imports
Norway (03/2001)	CPI	Around 2.5%	No	Changes in interest rates, excise duties, and extraordinary temporary disturbances
Iceland (03/2001)	CPI	Around 2.5% with a band of ± 1.5%	Yes	Unspecified, except that notice will be taken of trends in the underlying rate of inflation

*Consists of the 12 members of the European Monetary Union (see Chapter 26).
** Harmonized index of consumer prices.

Sources: Adapted from P.L. Siklos, "Inflation Target Design: Changing Inflation Performance and Persistence in Industrial Countries," *Review of the Federal Reserve Bank of St. Louis* 81 (March/April 1999): 47–58; "The Stability-Oriented Monetary Policy Strategy of the Eurosystem," European Central Bank *Monthly Bulletin* (January 1999): 39–50; P.L. Siklos, *The Changing Face of Central Banking* (Cambridge: Cambridge University Press, 2002).

dropped, in the "Unending Search for Monetary Salvation."[33] This much should be clear from a reading of the Bank of Canada's history: whether inflation targets represent the last word in the search for such policies remains to be seen. Only time will tell.[34]

RESPONSIBILITIES AND ORGANIZATION

Broadly speaking, the Bank of Canada is responsible for the conduct of Canada's monetary policy and for facilitating the growth of economic activity and the attainment of low levels of unemployment. Indeed, the preamble to the **Bank of Canada Act** specifies the following objectives:

> To regulate credit and currency in the best interests of the economic life of the nation, to control and protect the external value of the national monetary unit and to mitigate by its influence fluctuations in the general level of production, trade, prices, and unemployment, so far as may be possible within the scope of monetary action, and generally to promote the economic and financial welfare of the Dominion.

---

33 This is the title of the article by S. Fischer, which appears in the 1995 issue of *Macroeconomics Annual*, edited by B.S. Bernanke, and J.J. Rotemberg (Cambridge, Mass.: The MIT Press, 1995): 275–86.

34 In fact, price level or inflation targeting is not as new as it might appear. Sweden adopted such a policy for a time during the 1930s. See L. Jonung, "Knut Wicksell's Norm of Price Stabilization and Swedish Monetary Policy in the 1930s," *Journal of Monetary Policy* 5 (October 1979): 459–96.

ECONOMICS FOCUS 22.1 HONEY, I TANKED THE MARKET

Central bankers have often been accused of avoiding accountability in their attempts to maintain a favourable public image. In other words, central bankers have a predisposition for "cheap talk." More revealing is the comment by Fed chair Alan Greenspan: "I spend a substantial amount of time endeavoring to fend off questions and worry terribly that I might end up being too clear" (Wessel 1996). Greenspan is even more famous for the effect of his "irrational exuberance" remark, which led to a sharp fall in world stock markets.

By contrast, the Bank of Canada introduced in 1995 a *Monetary Policy Report* aimed at promoting and explaining how it goes about conducting monetary policy in a manner consistent with its inflation targets.

Central bankers must also worry about how and what they say in public for fear that markets will misinterpret their words and overreact. Take the example of Laurence Meyer, appointed in 1996 to the U.S. Federal Reserve Board (he has since left that post). In a speech in April 1997, he tried to explain the Fed's decision to raise interest rates in March, while avoiding giving hints about possible future interest rate moves. He even released an advance version of the text and had staff at the Fed check for possible ambiguities in the speech. Despite these precautions, within hours of his speech to the Forecasters' Club in New York, wire-services announced: "Fed Gov Meyer Signals More U.S. Interest Rate Increases Likely." An earlier speech of his in January 1997 also sent tremors through the market,

prompting Meyer's wife to say: "Well, you finally did it. You tanked the market."

With so much at stake when interest rates change, the words of a central banker mean a lot and, desperate for any clues about what the future portends, the media will put whatever spin it can on the utterances from a central banker to get attention. The same is true in Canada, with speeches by the governor regularly featured in the headlines of most newspapers (they are also reprinted in the *Bank of Canada Review* as well as on the Bank of Canada's Web site at **www.bankofcanada.ca**).

Questions for Discussion

1. What do you think is meant by the term "cheap talk"? Can it be a useful "tool" of monetary policy?
2. Is it right for financial markets and the public to hang on every word uttered by central bankers? What dangers might this pose?

Sources

D.B. Sicilia, and J.L. Cruikshank, *The Greenspan Effect* (New York: McGraw-Hill, 2000).

D. Wessel, "Fed Governor Tries Not to Move Markets," *Wall Street Journal* interactive edition, 25 April 1997.

——— "Greenspan Prepares Talk to Congress," *Wall Street Journal* interactive edition, 17 July 1996.

Meyer, L.H. *A Term at the Fed: An Insider's View* (New York: Harper Business, 2004).

In addition to those sonorous long-term goals, the Bank must also meet a number of shorter-term objectives. In its day-to-day operations, its functions include

1. Conducting open market operations.

2. Controlling monetary policy through interest rate control and monetary base management.

3. Acting as the federal government's fiscal agent.

4. Acting as a lender of last resort.

5. Conducting a number of other operations, such as foreign reserves management.

Since we have already considered in earlier chapters how central bank operations can influence interest rates, we do not further examine this issue here. Rather we concentrate on the impact of the Bank's operations on its balance sheet. A condensed version of that sheet appears in Table 22.3.

Notice that the table reveals that in 2004 almost two-thirds of the Bank's assets consisted of government debt of various types and maturities and over 90% of its liabilities were in notes in circulation. Although the percentages have fluctuated somewhat over the years, these two items have accounted for the lion's share of assets and liabilities. The rising share of notes in circulation in the Bank of Canada's total liabilities, in great measure, is a result of the diminished role played by reserves of the banking system, which were phased out in 1994.

The *Bank of Canada Act* (section 8) formally places responsibility for the conduct of monetary policy on the governor, who is directly responsible to the minister of finance. Under the current organizational structure, the federal government appoints 12 directors, with the governor and the senior deputy-governor (and the deputy minister of finance, ex-officio), who make up the board of directors and select the governor, subject to government approval. The Bank of Canada (section 10) requires that the directors come from diversified occupations; it does not mandate regional representation but, by custom, Quebec and Ontario always have two representatives and the other provinces have one each (the territories have no representatives). Monetary policy is made not by the board but by the governor and his senior advisers, who form the governing council. The *Monetary Policy Report*, the series of semiannual reports on monetary policy since 1995, increased to a quarterly frequency in 2000 and identified the members of the council by name.

22.3 THE TOOLS OF MONETARY POLICY

Canada's is a small, open economy. As a result, interest rate changes and exchange rate movements are the key indicators of the stance of monetary policy.[35] Not surprisingly then, the tools at the disposal of the Bank of Canada reflect the needs of domestic finance as well as those of external influences. However, just as the financial system has evolved rapidly over time, so have the tools and their uses. We begin with the primary tool of monetary policy today, the operating band for the overnight rate. It is also useful to examine tools that are used less frequently, such as open market operations, or even that have ostensibly been abandoned, such as reserve requirements, for at least two reasons. First, they are still in widespread usage in other countries, most notably the United States and the European Union. Second, they represent essential elements in the understanding of the evolution of monetary policy implementation in Canada.

THE OVERNIGHT MARKET

The overnight market has existed in Canada since the 1950s as a means of providing short-term liquidity to the money market. Thus, for example, chartered banks introduced day loans to help finance investment dealers' inventories of government of Canada securities. Eventually, the collateral that could be used for such financing was broadened considerably. By the early 1970s,

Table 22.3	A Condensed Balance Sheet of the Bank of Canada (Year Ending 2004, in Millions of Dollars)		
Assets		**Liabilities**	
Government of Canada direct and guaranteed securities		Notes in circulation	44 241
		Deposits	
Treasury bills	13 629	Government of Canada	1 063
Government bonds maturing in		Chartered banks	382
≤ 3 years	9 154	Other Canadian Payments	119
> 3 years	20 408	Association members	
Bank of Canada advances[a]	500	Foreign central banks & others	383
Other investments	2.6	Foreign currency liabilities	384
Foreign currency deposits	513	Other liabilities	130
Other assets	2 895	Total	46 731
Total	46 731		

Source: Bank of Canada Annual Report 2004. Figures are rounded to the nearest dollar.

[a] To members of the Canadian Payments Association.

---

35 Indeed, as we shall see in Chapter 23, the Bank of Canada pioneered a concept called the Monetary Conditions Index, to summarize the ways in which these two variables are indicative of the ease or tightness of monetary policy.

interbank deposits were created as a means of ensuring that financing was available for the banks to meet their reserve requirements (discussed later in this chapter). Subsequently, financial innovations of the kind discussed earlier in this text (see, for example, Chapter 4) created other means of short-term financing in the form of repos and foreign exchange swaps (also discussed later in this chapter). The Bank of Canada has, as we have seen, facilitated and encouraged the development of instruments to ensure the necessary liquidity in the financial system.

The fast pace of financial transactions meant that the weekly setting of the Bank Rate (discussed below) was an inadequate device for the Bank of Canada to signal its desired interest rate stance. Consequently, in April 1994, the Bank of Canada formalized its role in the overnight market by adopting an **operating band** for the overnight rate. Figure 22.3 illustrates how the band operates and, as we shall see, the overnight market operates hand in hand with the existing zero reserve requirement regime and the **Large Value Transfer System** (**LVTS**; also see Chapter 4).

Much of the activity in the overnight market takes place in the morning hours when participants—primarily deposit-taking institutions—evaluate their liquidity needs. For the most part, the Bank has aimed at ensuring that settlement balances are zero, that is, the daily cash requirements of members of the Canadian Payments Association (CPA) offset each other in the aggregate.[36] The Bank of Canada can control these settlement balances because final settlement of all payments among CPA members is conducted through their accounts at the Bank.

Returning to Figure 22.3, we see that the operating band is defined as the spread between the bank rate and the deposit rate. The former is the rate charged on overdrafts at the Bank; the latter is the rate paid to clearers that have net positive settlement balances. In addition, the Bank announces a target rate to signal to markets the location of the operating band.

| Figure 22.3 | The Bank of Canada's Overnight Rate Operating Band |

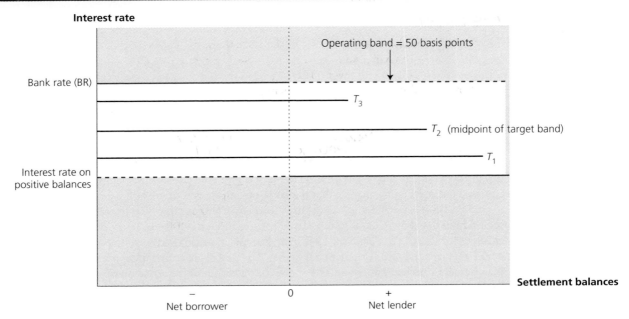

The operating band for the overnight rate is the difference between the bank rate and interest paid on positive balances. The spread between the two is 50 basis points. The lines T_1, T_2, and T_3, are hypothetical targets the Royal Bank of Canada might have for the overnight rate. Since 1999, the target has been the midpoint of the operating band (i.e., T_2).

---

36 On 24 September 1999, the Bank announced a positive target of $200 million, with higher targets if necessary. Previously, the Bank aimed for a zero target.

POINT–COUNTERPOINT 22.1

INFLATION TARGETING: THE HOLY GRAIL OF MONETARY POLICY?

The twentieth century was marked by the adoption of several types of monetary regimes. Ostensibly, the objective was to ensure a combination of stable prices with consistent economic growth. Unfortunately, most of the regimes adopted were eventually abandoned. Dissatisfaction arose for a variety of economic and noneconomic reasons.

The gold standard, for example, arguably represented a failed attempt by Great Britain to restore the financial hegemony it had had before World War I. The Bretton Woods system of pegged exchange rates (see Chapter 26), largely the creation of U.S. policymakers, was abandoned in the 1970s when U.S. inflation policy became intolerably at variance with inflation in Germany, most notably. The European exchange rate mechanism suffered a major setback in 1992 when Germany's expansionary policies were too far apart from the contraction underway in the rest of Europe. Canada, the country with perhaps the most experience with a floating exchange rate, also adopted fixed exchange rates periodically when suitable or politically necessary. The 1970s and 1980s were marked by attempts to adopt monetary targeting in several industrial countries in light of the apparent triumph of a form of monetarism in vogue at the time. Procedural and technical problems led to the abandonment of these types of regime by the mid-1980s in most of the countries that had adopted them (see Chapters 6 and 21, for example).

Although several adherents continue to use fixed-exchange-rate-type regimes (see Chapter 8) there is, on balance, a slight preference for floating regimes. Together with the growing recognition that central banks are responsible solely for monetary policy and not for economic performance more generally,[1] a need arose for some kind of "anchor" or gauge of monetary policy performance. This idea was not entirely new. For example, former Bank of Canada Governor Louis Rasminsky pointed out to a House of Commons committee in 1966 that Canada had enjoyed good economic growth in a period of stable prices.

It is in such an environment that inflation targeting emerged as the preferred choice. It permitted central banks to rely on an indicator of monetary policy widely understood and followed by the public. Moreover, inflation targeting explicitly recognized that domestic economic conditions are dependent on a combination of domestic and external factors, namely interest rates and exchange rates. However, as noted earlier, countries that have adopted inflation targets have not yet been put to a serious test.[2] Can it be that inflation targets are the holy grail of monetary policy?

As this is written, inflation targeting has now outlived all of the monetary regimes tried since World War II.

In the first years following the introduction of the operating band, the Bank of Canada announced targets anywhere within the operating band. A target rate at the midpoint of the band, namely T_2 in Figure 22.3, signals that the present band will be maintained. A target near the top of the band, such as T_3, is an indication of a probable rise in the operating band whereas, of course, a target set at T_1 suggests that the Bank of Canada is contemplating a lower operating band.

On 4 February 1999, the bank shifted to an environment in which the target would always be the midpoint of the target range when it fully introduced the real-time electronic settlement mechanism called the LVTS. Before the LVTS, the manipulation of government deposits was an important device that ensured zero settlement balances.[37] The role of government deposits as a tool of liquidity management has changed. Figure 22.4 shows the behaviour of the actual overnight rate, the operating band, and the target rate since 1994. It is immediately clear that the Bank has frequently used this device to signal ease or tightness in monetary policy.

The LVTS operates each business day from 8 A.M. to 6 P.M. and permits clearers to achieve settlement balances of zero (or as targeted by the Bank of Canada) on a real-time basis. Overdrafts

---

37 Prior to the introduction of the LVTS the Bank of Canada relied on the "drawdown and redeposit" technique. The Bank of Canada continues to neutralize the net effect of government transactions in the banking system via the twice-daily auction of government balances to LVTS participants. In 2001, the Bank announced that it would discontinue the second round except under extraordinary circumstances.

POINT	Counterpoint
• Inflation targets are transparent and widely understood by the public. • Inflation targets have been more successful than other monetary policy regimes. • Inflation targets make it clear that there is no trade-off between inflation and real variables such as economic growth and unemployment. • Inflation targets are more credible than money supply or exchange rate targets. • Inflation targets preserve domestic purchasing power, an important indicator of a nation's standard of living. • Inflation targets allow for sufficient flexibility for independent monetary policy actions while accounting for international influences on domestic markets.	• Central banks do not always target the overall CPI, which can be confusing. • Low and stable inflation has been experienced by both inflation- and noninflation-targeting countries, so it is not clear how much credit should be given to the adoption of the targets themselves. • Many still believe that there is, at least in the short run, some kind of relationship between inflation and economic growth or unemployment. • Inflation targets are credible so long as inflation is within the stated bands. Otherwise inflation targets need not be more credible than other types of monetary policy regimes. • Inflation targets mean that central banks can ignore a variety of economic problems such as high domestic interest rates, current account deficits, and exchange rate volatility. • Inflation targets are set too low. A little inflation is a good thing.

Questions for Discussion

1. Why is there a potential problem with the definition of inflation in inflation-targeting countries?

2. Should central banks be responsible for more than just inflation? Does inflation targeting mean that the central bank cares about nothing else?

1 Fiscal policy and productivity are two other contributors to economic growth.
2 With the possible exception of New Zealand, where the targets were breached for a brief period in 1994 and then again in 1998. See, for example, P.L. Siklos, "Charting a Future for the Bank of Canada: Inflation Targets and the Balance Between Autonomy and Accountability," in *Where We Go From Here,* edited by D.E.W. Laidler (Toronto, Ont.: C.D. Howe Institute, 1997): 101–84.

for LVTS participants are charged at the bank rate, while surpluses earn an interest rate at the lower limit of the operating band. Balances are determined at the end of the day. A pre-settlement trading period (notionally from 6:00 to 6:30 p.m. each business day) is also in force to permit clearers to achieve their desired settlement balances conditional on the operating band in place. The 50-basis-point spread that defines the operating band is considered sufficiently large for clearers to adjust their settlement cash position rather than to rely on Bank of Canada financing. Paper-based items such as cheques will still require clearing on a overnight basis using the **Automated Clearing Settlement System (ACSS)**. Negative balances in the ACSS are charged at the bank rate plus 1.5%, while surplus balances earn the deposit rate less 1.5% (see Figure 22.3).

ADVANCES

As we would expect from a lender of last resort, central banks lend directly to banks. In Canada, the means used are called Bank of Canada advances. The interest rate is the bank rate.

Until March 1980, the Bank of Canada set the bank rate independently, and so it signalled the direction the Bank wanted interest rates to take. Since then the bank rate has floated with the Treasury bill rate, losing much of its significance as a distinct tool of monetary policy. Recognizing this, the Bank began in 1996 to tie the bank rate to changes in the overnight rate, as discussed earlier. Even over a year, Bank of Canada advances do not normally total huge sums. The overall increase

| **Figure 22.4** | **The Overnight Rate in Canada, 1994–2004** |

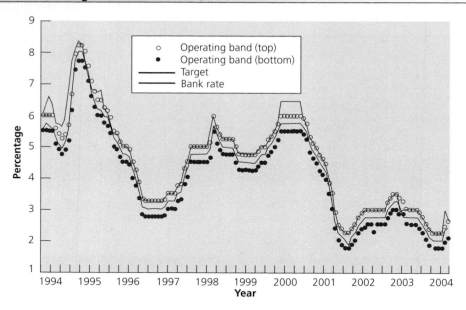

The target and the bank rate are the same after 1996. Before that period, the target was set by the Bank of Canada somewhere within the existing operating band. The operating band became the primary tool of monetary policy in April 1994 when operating bands were introduced.

Source: Bank of Canada Banking and Financial Statistics, and CANSIM, the bank rate (V39078), high operating band (V39077), low operating band (V39076), target rate (V39079).

in the mid-1980s is partly explained by changes in the cheque-clearing process following the *Bank Act* of 1980, which increased the number of institutions eligible for financial help from the Bank of Canada. The sharp rise in advances in 1985 resulted largely from the collapse of the Canadian Commercial Bank.

BUYBACKS

Central banks possess a variety of other instruments to influence the reserves of the banking system. One such tool is the special purchase and resale agreement (SPRA) described in general terms in Chapter 4.

As we have seen, the SPRA was introduced in 1985 to alleviate temporary shortages of liquidity that would otherwise push the overnight rate above the ceiling of the operating band. Conversely, the Bank of Canada engages in a Sales and Repurchase Agreement or SRA when it wants to prevent the overnight rate from falling below the bottom of the operating band depicted in Figure 22.3. Table 22.4 provides a simplified numerical example. As with several examples to come, we will illustrate the process by which the effects of Bank of Canada policies impact the financial system by using a simplified version of a balance sheet for each of the players involved in the various transactions to be considered. This means considering the effects of changes in the assets and liabilities of the institutions concerned.

Generally, the idea behind an SPRA is for the Bank of Canada to offer to buy a security, such as Treasury bills or other short-term Government of Canada bonds, and sell them back, normally the next business day.

Suppose then that a CPA clearer calls in a loan of $100 million from an investment dealer. Initially, the investment dealer's liabilities fall by $100 million, as does the amount of loans outstanding at the CPA clearer (step 1). Since this implies less liquidity in the system, the result would, other things equal, be higher overnight rates. If the Bank of Canada deems this to be an undesirable outcome, it can simply buy $100 million worth of government securities from the investment dealers' inventory in exchange for $100 million in cash, with an agreement to reverse the transaction the following day (step 2). The resulting injection of liquidity could be deposited at the Bank of Canada and show up in the books of the CPA clearer (step 3).[38] An SRA would, of course, operate in reverse.

FOREIGN EXCHANGE TRANSACTIONS AND INTERVENTION

One of the functions of the Bank of Canada is to manage the country's foreign exchange reserves, which it holds in what is called the **Exchange Fund Account** (**EFA**). By managing this account (under the authority of the Ministry of Finance), the Bank of Canada can influence the reserves of the banking system and thus finance the temporary cash requirements of the government without having to resort to, say, a new bond issue. Table 22.5 illustrates the result of what is called a **foreign exchange swap**. The Bank of Canada reduces the EFA by $100 million through the sale of foreign exchange and uses the proceeds to increase government deposits. It can redeposit the proceeds with the chartered banks, which then experience a rise in reserves, with consequences that should be clear by now. Of course, these swaps are temporary; the drawing down of foreign reserves is accomplished by a futures contract to replenish EFA at some future date.[39]

A different kind of swap was introduced in 1991. Rather than swap foreign exchange with the EFA, the Bank of Canada began to swap foreign currencies for Canadian currency. In this kind of arrangement, foreign currencies are sold to buy Canadian dollars; at a future date, the transaction is reversed, with the foreign currencies being bought back for Canadian dollars. The government uses these swaps, which are short term, to obtain Canadian dollars without having to

Table 22.4	Illustrating the SPRA

Step 1: A CPA clearer calls in a loan of $100 million from an investment dealer.

A	CPA Clearer	L	A	Inv. Dealer	L
Call Loan	− 100			Call Loan	− 100

Step 2: To prevent the reduction in liquidity from step 1, the Bank of Canada offers an SPRA to the investment dealer, who uses government securities as collateral.

A	Bank of Canada	L	A	Inv. Dealer	L
Govt Sec.	+ 100			SPRA	+ 100

Step 3: The CPA clearer can then potentially increase deposits at the Bank of Canada.

A	CPA Clearer	L	A	Bank of Canada	L
Deposit at Bank of Canada	+ 100			Deposit by CPA clearer	+ 100

---

38 Since there is now a positive change in settlement balances at the Bank of Canada and, assuming that a zero balance is desired, the Bank uses the LVTS to ensure that no net change in cash occurs.

39 If the central bank's objective is simply to effect a portfolio reallocation, it can use an open market operation to sterilize or neutralize the impact of a foreign exchange transaction immediately, rather than in the future. Go back to Chapter 8 to study how sterilization works.

borrow in the domestic market. The costs of such swaps depend on the relative interest rates in the different currencies, as well as the relationship between spot and forward exchange rates.

As is clear from the above example, intervention of some kind in the foreign exchange market can influence interest rates and the spread between U.S. and Canadian interest rates. Therefore, such intervention can, in principle, be employed to affect the exchange rate (go back again to Chapter 8 for a discussion of the connection between interest rates and exchange rates). Several volumes have been written about whether central banks can have a permanent effect on the exchange rate, and the general consensus is that such intervention is ineffective or, at best, effective for only a short period of time.[40]

The Bank of Canada has repeatedly stated that its intervention has the sole objective of maintaining "orderly markets," meaning that foreign exchange intervention is useful only as a means of mitigating the volatility of exchange rates.[41] Moreover, in line with its philosophy of permitting markets to dictate the value of the Canadian dollar, the Bank of Canada has not intervened often in the past few years.[42]

Table 22.5   A Foreign Exchange Swap

Initial Situation
Bank of Canada

Assets		Liabilities	
Foreign currency assets	+100[a]	Deposits Government of Canada	+100
↑ From the Exchange Fund Account			

After Redeposit
Bank of Canada

Assets		Liabilities	
No change		Deposits Government of Canada	−100
		Chartered banks	+100

Chartered Banks

Assets		Liabilities	
Reserves At Bank of Canada	+100	Deposits Government of Canada	+100

a This actually comes under the heading "Other Investments" but the meaning is clearer with the above definitions. The amount shown is the Canadian-dollar equivalent at the spot rate.

---

40 See, for example, K.M. Dominguez, and J.A. Frankel, *Does Foreign Exchange Intervention Work?* (Washington, D.C.: Institute for International Economics, 1993) and J.O. Grabbe, *International Financial Markets*, 3d ed. (New York: Prentice-Hall, 1996), Chapter 21.

41 See, for example, J. Murray, M. Zelmer, and D. McManus, "The Effect of Intervention on Canadian Dollar Volatility," in *Exchange Rates and Monetary Policy*, Proceedings of a Conference held by the Bank of Canada, October 1996 (Ottawa, Ont.: Bank of Canada, 1997): 311–60.

42 Beginning in July 1999, the Bank of Canada announced on its Web site its foreign exchange intervention practices. For a more recent analysis of the role of foreign exchange intervention, openness, and the role of inflation targeting, see J. Rogers, and P.L. Siklos, "Foreign Exchange Market Intervention in Two Small Open Economies: The Canadian and Australian Experience," *Journal of International Money and Finance* (2003).

OPEN MARKET OPERATIONS AND BANKING RESERVES

The buying and selling of government securities in the open market has direct effects on interest rates, as we have discovered. Thus, these *open market operations* (*OMO*) of the Bank of Canada can be seen as a method of intervention in the market for loanable funds. The objective is to influence interest rates in ways compatible with its overall monetary policies. Although Bank of Canada intervention in the domestic securities market is mainly through the SPRAs and SRAs discussed previously, it is worthwhile examining OMOs since, historically at least, they were the intervention method of choice.

Most OMOs tend to rely on the sale of Treasury bills, although the SPRA and SRA can be considered as other means to conduct OMO. To influence the demand for loanable funds, the Bank must decide whether to add more T-bills to its portfolio (buy more than those that mature during the week) or let the portfolio go down (sell more bills than those that mature).

The simplified balance sheet in Table 22.6 illustrates. Suppose the Bank of Canada decides to purchase from the chartered banks $100 million more T-bills than those that are maturing that week. Its assets rise by that amount. If the chartered banks are the institutions that simultaneously decide to reduce their holdings of T-bills,[43] the net effect of the OMO is to raise their reserve deposits by $100 million. It is equivalent to a portfolio reallocation away from T-bills toward more reserves. Note, however, that the effect on the chartered banks is entirely on their assets. Their liabilities are unaffected because the entire amount of the increase is initially in *excess reserves*.[44] As discussed in Chapter 17, excess reserves can generate a multiple expansion of bank

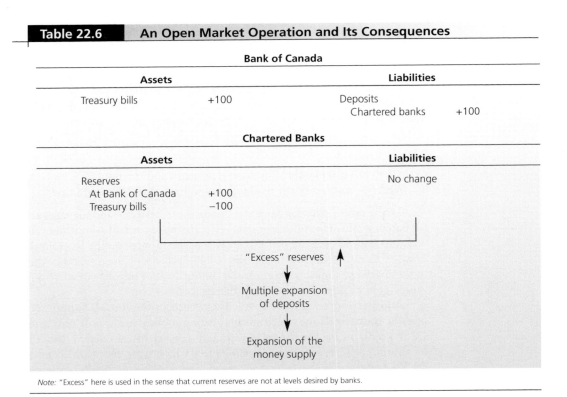

Table 22.6	An Open Market Operation and Its Consequences

Bank of Canada

Assets		Liabilities	
Treasury bills	+100	Deposits	
		Chartered banks	+100

Chartered Banks

Assets		Liabilities	
Reserves		No change	
At Bank of Canada	+100		
Treasury bills	−100		

"Excess" reserves

Multiple expansion of deposits

Expansion of the money supply

Note: "Excess" here is used in the sense that current reserves are not at levels desired by banks.

---

43 The transaction could have involved investment dealers. We choose the banks for our example because the effect of an OMO on their excess reserves is immediate and drives the money supply.

44 Excess to its originally desired position, since reserve requirements have been phased out.

deposits and thus the money supply. (We return to this point a little later when we formally model the money supply process.)

The OMO is a powerful tool because its effect on excess reserves is immediate. Several central banks continue to rely on this practice. One difficulty with OMOs is that they are apparently costly to undertake and, with capital mobility nearly perfect, central banks can use other tools to influence interest rates more effectively.

OTHER TOOLS

Moral Suasion

Central banks sometimes resort to **moral suasion**—making suggestions, in private or in public, to influence people or institutions. The Bank of Canada may, for example, ask the system's banks to cooperate in observing some ceiling on interest rates[45] or in easing credit allocation voluntarily. A harsher view of what moral suasion stands for was made by Thomas Courchene: "Moral suasion …gives the Bank of Canada the freedom to revise the *Bank Act* between decennial revisions."[46]

Although the Bank of Canada has often resorted to moral suasion in the past, it has probably been practised more extensively by the governments of the day. (Consider the recurring parliamentary discussions about the interest rates charged on credit card debt.) Moreover, deregulation and globalization are probably making moral suasion a rather ineffective tool of monetary policy. It is presumably easier to use, the smaller the number of banks and the more closed the financial system is to international influences.

Base Control

By far the largest liability item in the Bank of Canada's balance sheet is notes in circulation. A distant second are deposits of the chartered banks and other members of the Canadian Payments Association, which represent the reserves of the banking system. Together they account for over 90% of all of the Bank's liabilities (see Table 22.3). Recall that the sum of these two items is known as the *monetary base,* or *high-powered money.* So we can write

$$CUR + RES = \text{Monetary Base} \tag{22.1}$$

where
CUR = currency (held by chartered banks and the public)
RES = reserves of the banking system held at the Bank of Canada

To the extent that the Bank of Canada issues currency and manages and supervises the need for banks to maintain sufficient reserves, it has **base control**—control over the monetary base— and thus control over the size and growth of the money supply. Its control is by no means total, however. It cannot dictate the currency requirements of the public nor the size of the variations in the chartered banks' reserves. And it cannot control transfers to and from various classes of deposits, even though these moves influence cash reserves.

Another source of uncontrollable growth in the money supply stems from the process of **debt monetization**, which means issuing money to support government spending. As we are all keenly aware, the federal government persistently ran deficits for years. The primary form of finance has been through the sale of bonds to the public and to foreigners, but the Bank of Canada always has the option of purchasing the bonds outright from the government, simply issuing a quantity of notes sufficient to complete the transaction. Table 22.7 illustrates.

---

45 For example, in establishing the Winnipeg Agreement, in effect from 1972 to 1975, the Bank of Canada asked the banks to hold a ceiling on interest rates on term deposits.

46 T.J. Courchene, *Money, Inflation, and the Bank of Canada: An Analysis of Canadian Monetary Policy from 1970 to Early 1975* (Montreal: C.D. Howe Institute, 1976): 124–7.

Table 22.7	Monetizing the Debt and the Possible Consequences

Bank of Canada

Assets	Liabilities
Government securities +100	Bank of Canada notes +100

↓

Chartered Banks

Assets	Liabilities
Reserves At Bank of Canada +100	Deposits Government of Canada +100

↓

Multiple expansion of deposits
Multiple expansion of the money supply

Suppose the federal government issues $100 million of government bonds, all of which are purchased by the Bank of Canada, which then issues $100 million in notes. If the government wishes, it may deposit the proceeds at chartered banks, which now experience a sudden rise in reserves. And an increase in reserves has the potential to lead to a multiple expansion of deposits and of the money supply, with consequences for inflation, as we know all too well.

Remember, however, that the Bank of Canada can offset any imminent rise in the money supply through a variety of means, as we have seen. In any event, debt monetization has represented only a minor source of Canadian government finance, except during the war years.

The Base and the Money Multiplier

In Chapter 17, we outlined a simple money multiplier process. We can demonstrate more formally the links between central bank actions and the money supply. In doing so, we assume that the monetary aggregate of interest is M1, the narrow definition of the money supply.[47]

Recall the definition of the M1 money supply: the currency in circulation plus demand deposits. In equation form, we write

$$M1 = CUR + DEP \qquad (22.2)$$

where DEP = demand deposits (at chartered banks) and CUR is as previously defined.

The public determines the currency component of M1, and the banking sector creates demand deposits. Clearly, it makes a great deal of difference how the public chooses the proportions of currency and deposits because, as we have seen, currency injections or withdrawals from banks have multiplicative effects on the money supply. For this reason, economists have long been interested in the currency–deposit ratio, cr, which is

$$cr = \frac{CUR}{DEP} \qquad (22.3)$$

Strictly speaking, the public determines cr, so it cannot be directly controlled by central bank actions. But for the moment, let us take cr as given.

---

47 This simplification is sufficient to illustrate the relevant issues and problems, even though the Bank of Canada itself prefers to monitor broader aggregates, such as M2+.

We have already seen a link between M1 and central bank actions in equation (22.1). For convenience, we repeat it:

$$Base = CUR + RES$$

where

Base = the monetary base, or high-powered money
RES = target reserves of the banking system

Now we express M1 and Base in terms of *DEP* with the help of some simple algebra. Dividing both sides of equation (22.2) by *DEP* yields

$$\frac{M1}{DEP} = \frac{CUR}{DEP} + \frac{DEP}{DEP} = cr + 1 \tag{22.4}$$

Similarly, for high-powered money, dividing by *DEP* gives us

$$\frac{Base}{DEP} = \frac{CUR}{DEP} + \frac{RES}{DEP} = cr + rr \tag{22.5}$$

where $rr = RES/DEP$ represents the reserve ratio discussed previously. Then we rewrite equations (22.4) and (22.5) as

$$M1 = (cr + 1)DEP$$
$$Base = (cr + rr)DEP$$

Finally, if we evaluate

$$\frac{M1}{Base} = \frac{(cr + 1)}{(cr + rr)} \tag{22.6}$$

we obtain an expression for the proportion by which M1 exceeds Base.

Equation (22.6) is the expression for the **money multiplier**. It is fundamentally determined by two variables: *cr* and *rr*. The latter is currently set by the banking sector.

Why is *cr* potentially an important variable? Consider the example of an open market operation. When the Bank of Canada purchases bonds from chartered banks, the proceeds create excess reserves that set in motion the money multiplier process. Thus, holding *R* constant, *rr* rises, which produces the increase in the money supply that an OMO policy is supposed to produce, and, in the process, reduces *cr*. But suppose that the public is satisfied with the level of *cr* attained prior to the open market operation. If it shifts funds from deposits to currency to restore *cr* to its original and presumably "optimal" level, then the money multiplier is affected. Thus, we must not assume that the central bank policies that influence the reserves of the banking system are independent of the behaviour of the public. (Unfortunately, this fact makes it even more difficult to gauge the significance of high-powered money changes on the money supply.)

Reserve Requirements

The manipulation of reserve requirements is a tool available to the central banks in several countries. Reserve requirements were phased out in Canada by July 1994.

Canada's financial history was marked by the imposition of two types of reserve requirements. Primary reserves, consisting essentially of cash, were used to protect depositors from the possibility of liquidity shortages at chartered banks that might precipitate a run on the banks. These reserves typically represented about 10% of demand deposits. Generally, banks were required to meet their reserve requirements over a two-week period.

In the 1960s, the Bank of Canada obtained the authority to impose secondary reserve requirements. This reserve required chartered banks to hold certain highly liquid assets, such as Treasury bills and loans to investment dealers.

Both types of reserves have since been phased out. The motivating factors are easy to see. First, primary reserves represent a tax on the chartered banks alone in the form of forgone interest on what came to be considered excessive liquidity requirements in an age of electronic transfers and overnight funds. Second, primary and secondary reserve requirements represented a form of regulated portfolio allocation. Chartered banks were not completely free to manage their asset portfolios to obtain the best possible returns. Third, as alluded to above, the reserve requirement system discriminated against chartered banks since other financial institutions (e.g., credit unions) did not have to meet similar requirements. Finally, lags in calculations and the resulting uncertainty in assessing how much liquidity was available became inconsistent with the tremendous speed with which funds moved between financial institutions. An arrangement less prone to systemic risk was required.

Other countries that have moved away from the imposition of cash ratios have different rules. Switzerland, for example, outlaws overdrafts, requiring that clearing banks ensure a positive balance with the Swiss National Bank before transactions can be completed. In addition, Switzerland, as well as Australia, require banks to keep some liquid assets for precautionary purposes. In Sweden, alternatively, a bank whose clearings normally result in a negative balance with the central bank may be required by the latter to borrow to meet cash reserve needs. U.K. banks have not been required to hold reserves against deposits since 1971, but neither can they borrow directly from the Bank of England. Instead, money market dealers are used as a source of cash reserve financing. The United States and the European Union still impose reserve requirements, but they are relatively small.

22.4 THE TRANSMISSION MECHANISM

By now it should be clear that the two main factors influencing the economy as a whole, and inflation in particular, are interest rate and exchange rate changes. Since the Bank can influence the level of the exchange rate for a very short period at best (days if not simply hours) there remains only the interest rate as the core instrument of monetary policy. Figure 22.5 is taken from the Bank of Canada's Web site (the address is visible) and illustrates how interest rates and exchange rates combine to affect the inflation rate. Notice that "financial markets" are at the beginning of a long chain of events, referred to as the **transmission mechanism**, leading to price changes ,and that these can take roughly up to 24 months. Therefore, whenever the Bank of Canada (or the U.S. Federal Reserve) changes interest rates, it's with a view to influencing price level developments more than a year from now. In a sense, we have come full circle, by filling in most of the blanks concerning the place of markets, institutions, and individuals (via their expectations of future asset prices) in the transmission mechanism outlined back in Chapter 1 (see Figure 1.4). The transmission mechanism is therefore a representation of how long it takes for the full impact of monetary policy, as summarized by an interest rate change, on inflation in particular, and economic activity more generally. Figure 22.6, also from the Bank of Canada's Web site, shows this clearly for the case of an interest rate increase. Obviously, the arrows are reversed for a decrease in the overnight rate.

| Figure 22.5 | The Transmission Mechanism in Canada |

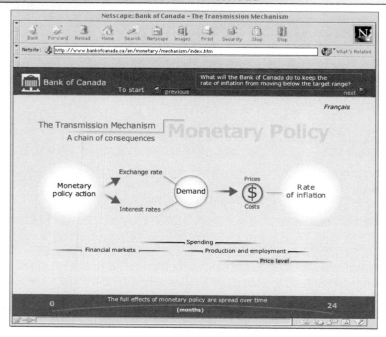

This is the transmission mechanism as depicted by the Bank of Canada on its Web site. Compare it with the transmission mechanism concept first introduced in Chapter 1 (see Figure 1.4).

Source: Reproduced with permission from the Bank of Canada.

| Figure 22.6 | The Overnight Rate and the Transmission Mechanism |

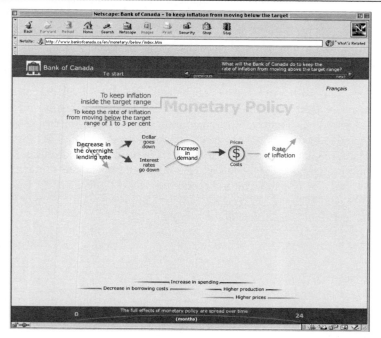

The transmission mechanism operates primarily through a change in the overnight rate, as discussed in this chapter.

ECONOMICS FOCUS 22.1

IMPLEMENTING MONETARY POLICY AND THE REAL-TIME DATA PROBLEM

The discussion of the transmission mechanism makes it appear that monetary policy is simply a matter of knowing when pressure on prices requires interest rates to rise. In practice, however, central banks also need to consider how quickly to change interest rates and by how much. As the various public pronouncements of central bankers such as Alan Greenspan of the U.S. Federal Reserve, or David Dodge of the Bank of Canada, make clear, there is much art in the conduct of monetary policy. More will be said about this point in the next chapter. As is also clear from a reading of this text, central banks rely on a host of models to help them decide whether or not to change interest rates or implement some other policy change. All these models require data of the kind that we have seen in a large number of figures and tables in this text. Indeed, the Bank of Canada is among a growing number of central banks that regularly publishes a list of the key monetary policy variables. This enables the public to get a glimpse of some of the vital economic data that central bankers use to determine their interest rate decisions (in the Bank of Canada's case go to **http://www.bankofcanada.ca/en/graphs/a1-table.htm**).

Unfortunately, as we have also seen (Chapter 6), macroeconomic data are revised on a regular basis for a variety of reasons, including improvements in the measurement of economic activity or changes in views about what consumers buy. This raises an additional problem for a central bank concerned with inflation control because when decisions are made, the data are often subject to revision later. This can mean that a decision to raise or lower interest rates can, in hindsight, prove to have been the wrong policy after all. Orphanides (2001) made this point by essentially reconstructing the data that members of the FOMC in the U.S. Federal Reserve (see Chapter 25) would have had at their disposal when monetary policy decisions were made. The problem is particularly acute for aggregate output measures, such as real GDP. Why? First, as we saw, the data are often subject to significant revisions over time, sometimes several years after the first data were made public. Second, as Figures 22.5 and 22.6 make clear, the Bank of Canada reacts to the prospect of higher inflation only when demand rises faster than the economy's capacity to produce. However, this requires another estimate, namely of overall economic capacity, and economists cannot agree on which measure is best. As a result, several measures of capacity output exist. How important are these considerations? The figure below, using data from Cayen and van Norden (2005) illustrates what real GDP less

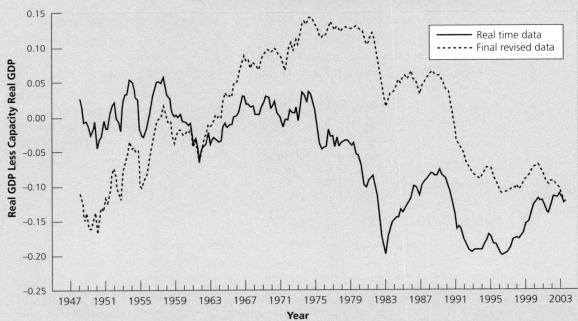

Real Time versus Final Data for Real GDP: Canada

Data are from J.-P. Cayen and S. Van Norden, "La fiabilite des estimations de l'ecart de production au Canada," working paper 2002–10. The broken line is the final revised data; the solid line is the real-time data. A linear trend was used to estimate capacity real GDP.

capacity real GDP for Canada looks like since 1947. A positive value indicates excess demand and, consequently, rising inflation. Obviously, a negative value suggests falling inflation, since the economy experiences excess capacity. Notice that the real-time data indicated relatively little excess demand during the 1970s precisely when inflation eventually soared (go back to Chapters 1 or 5 to see a plot of inflation during this period). By contrast, the final revised data showed sizable excess demand during this period. Clearly, policymakers were being seriously misled for several years. The other noticeable aspect of the figure below is the sharp and persistent differences between real-time and final data. No wonder central banks are cautious when discussing their economic outlook

Questions for Discussion

1. Do you think the real-time data problem is as severe for prices as for output? Explain.
2. Do you think that some other technique for measuring the economy's capacity output could narrow the gap between real-time and final revised data? Explain.

Sources

Cayen, J-P, and S. Van Norden, "The Reliability of Canadian Output Gap Estimates," *North American Journal of Economics and Finance*, 2005.

Orphanides, A., "Monetary Policy Rules Based on Real-Time Data," *American Economic Review* 91(4): 964–985.

SUMMARY

- Canada's central bank is called the Bank of Canada. It was founded in the 1930s, much later than the founding date of central banks in many other countries.

- The Bank of Canada is responsible for the management of the country's monetary policy; it is also the banker for the banking system and for the federal government.

- The history of monetary policy in Canada is marked by several phases during which the country fixed its exchange rate, then floated it, and later adopted monetary targets.

- Dissatisfaction with earlier regimes led the Bank of Canada to pioneer inflation targeting as its objective.

- The Bank of Canada has a vast array of tools to influence financial markets. The most important present-day tool is to target the overnight rate. It does so by stipulating an operating band of 50 basis points around the overnight rate.

- In conjunction with the overnight market, payments are cleared through the LVTS, a real-time settlement system.

- This chapter considers a number of other Bank of Canada transactions such as open market operations, foreign exchange swaps, buybacks, and monetizing the debt.

- Some of these tools such as open market operations are no longer used as frequently as in the past, although foreign exchange transactions can, at times, be important.

- The Bank of Canada might intervene in the foreign exchange market to reduce the volatility of the exchange rate.

- Other tools that have been abandoned in Canada, but are still used elsewhere, include moral suasion, monetary base control, and the imposition of reserve requirements.

IMPORTANT TERMS

Automated Clearing Settlement System (ACSS), 449
Bank of Canada Act, 444
base control, 454
Coyne affair, 438
debt monetization, 454
Exchange Fund Account (EFA), 451
foreign exchange swap, 451

inflation targets, 441
Large Value Transfer System (LVTS), 447
monetary targeting, 439
money multiplier, 456
moral suasion, 454
operating band, 447
transmission mechanism, 457

PROBLEMS

1. Using balance sheet accounts for the Bank of Canada and the chartered banks, illustrate an open market sale of $100 million to the chartered banks. What happens to the monetary base?

2. Why might a commercial bank borrow from another commercial bank, at a relatively high rate, instead of from the Bank of Canada at the bank rate?

3. Using balance sheet accounts for the Bank of Canada and the chartered banks, illustrate the effect of a transfer of $50 million from government deposits at the Bank of Canada to government deposits at the chartered banks. What happens to the monetary base?

4. What kind of policy action by the Bank of Canada would sterilize the foreign exchange swap considered in Table 22.5?

5. What will happen to M1 if

   (a) cr increases?

   (b) k decreases?

   (c) rr increases?

   (d) R decreases?

   (Assume that when one variable changes, all the others are held constant.) Explain your answers.

6. Suppose chartered banks borrow $100 million from the Bank of Canada. As a result, excess reserves are reduced by the same amount. What happens to M1? Explain your answer.

7. Explain how the monetary base is affected by each one of the following economic events and how the Bank of Canada can offset them:

   (a) Income tax payments received by April 30

   (b) Holiday shopping in December

   (c) A postal strike

8. True, false, or uncertain: Whenever the government incurs a deficit, it requires the Bank of Canada to print the necessary notes. Explain your answer.

9. Illustrate a scenario whereby the Bank of Canada uses an SRA instead of an SPRA as in Table 22.4 (use the same balance sheet account definitions as in the table).

10. True, false, or uncertain. "SPRAs are used by the Bank of Canada when it wants the overnight rate to rise." Explain.

11. According to the definition of inflation targeting in Canada, the Bank operates on the basis of core inflation as opposed to inflation in total CPI. Does this make good economic sense? Does it also present some problems for the Bank of Canada? Explain.

12. Suppose that the Bank of Canada, with the agreement of the government, wants to intervene in foreign exchange markets to raise the value of the Canadian dollar relative to the U.S. dollar (i.e., effect an appreciation of the Canadian dollar). Would the Bank purchase or sell foreign exchange? Illustrate the impact of such a policy using the balance sheet items as in Table 22.5.

13. Provide an example under which the Bank of Canada would want to engage in a foreign exchange swap of the kind illustrated in Table 22.5.

14. The various arrows in Figure 22.6 linking changes in the overnight rate to the value of the dollar are left unexplained. Use economic analysis to fill in the details.

15. Explain the direction of change in the link between the exchange rate and interest rates and demand in Figure 22.5, relying on the economic analysis developed in this text. Finally, make the link between demand and inflation, again using one of the theories discussed earlier in the text.

DISCUSSION QUESTIONS

1. Rank the functions of the Bank of Canada in the order of their importance. Explain why you have chosen this ranking.

2. Why can moral suasion be useful, under certain circumstances, in the conduct of monetary policy? What are some of the difficulties in relying on moral suasion in the present banking environment? Explain your answer.

3. Why was the Coyne affair a defining moment in the history of the Bank of Canada?

4. What are inflation targets and why does inflation targeting represent an important policy change?

5. In what sense were the origins of the Bank of Canada largely political?

6. Why are OMOs less useful than they were, say, 30 years ago?

7. Many central banks abandoned monetary targeting during the 1980s. Why do you think this is the case?

8. Why do you think inflation targets are defined in terms of a band instead of a single point?

9. What is the organizational structure of the Bank of Canada? Who sets monetary policy at the Bank?

10. Explain how the Bank of Canada sets a target for the overnight rate.

11. How does the LVTS system ensure that there are zero settlement balances at the end of each day? (Hint: You may want to go back to Chapter 4 and review the relevant material found there.)

12. Why do shifts in the operating band for the overnight rate signal a change in the stance of monetary policy?

13. Are all deflations bad? Can you think of a good deflation? Explain.

ONLINE APPLICATION

1. Go to the Bank of Canada's Web site at **www.bankofcanada.ca**. Download the latest *Monetary Policy Report* and read it. Does it explain the conduct of monetary policy in a clear fashion? Is it transparent what the Bank does and why it makes its decisions?

2. If you have access to the IMF's International Financial Statistics data set (it is available online to subscribers at the CHASS Web site at the University of Toronto at **data center2.chass.utoronto.ca**, try to replicate Figure 22.2. You will need to download consumer prices (annualized percentage change), and real GDP (1990 = 100). Next, you will need to calculate the percentage change in this variable [$X(t) - X(t - 1)/X(t - 1)$, where X is real GDP].

Download the series back to 1980 at either the monthly or quarterly frequencies. In addition to replicating Figure 22.2, compute the means and standard deviations for inflation- and noninflation-targeting countries for 1980 to 2001. Are the results different? Now calculate the same statistics for the inflation-targeting countries since the targets were introduced in each country (see Table 22.2). Are the results different? What do the various results say about the success of inflation targets?

3. Go to the Reserve Bank of New Zealand's Web site and download their monetary policy game at **http://www.rbnz.govt.nz/education/0116902.html**. Be sure to read the "readme.pdf" file prior to starting the game. See if you can generate a liquidity trap, that

is, a deflation in New Zealand. What are some of the drawbacks of this "game"?

4. The Swiss National Bank has essentially the same monetary policy game. Go to **http://www.snb.ch/e/geldpolitik/text-mopos.html**, download the game, and see if you can create conditions of hyperinflation this time around.

 ## CANSIM QUESTION

Go to the CANSIM Web site. Download the following series since 1960, at the annual frequency. Assets: Treasury bills (V36653), three years or fewer government bonds (V36655), three years or more (V36654 less V36655), and foreign currency deposits (V36661). Liabilities: Notes in circulation (V36672), deposits by members of the Canadian Payments Association (V36678 plus V36676; previously the chartered banks). Plot these principal assets and liabilities. Have there been any significant changes in the composition of assets and liabilities at the Bank of Canada since 1960? What might be some reasons for this? The discussion in some earlier chapters (for example, Chapters 1, 18, and 20) might be useful.

References can be found on www.mcgrawhill.ca/college/siklos

The Art of Central Banking: Targets, Instruments, and Autonomy[1]

LEARNING OBJECTIVES

After reading and studying this chapter, you should be able to

23.1 explain the distinction between economic variables that are instruments of monetary policy and those that are targets of monetary policy

23.2 describe why monetary policy involves choosing either to control an interest rate or to control the money supply, but not both

23.2 explain how the Monetary Conditions Index works and what it measures

23.3 analyze why political influences arising from elections or partisan political factors, or from the legal relationships between a central bank and the government, are important

23.3 determine why central banks might follow rules in setting interest rates

Since central banks are generally responsible for matters of monetary policy, their actions influence or are influenced by movements in interest rates, monetary aggregates, and exchange rates. We have already described various empirical features and theories relative to these three variables, ignoring the special rules of the central bank. Having described such an institution in the previous chapter, it now seems appropriate to discuss the place of the central monetary authority in the financial system.

In doing so, we focus on principles applicable to all (or most) industrialized countries. We might have chosen otherwise. The art of central banking is sometimes considered to be specific to the particular financial institutions of an economy and thus to vary greatly from country to country. However, globalization and increasing agreement that central banks should be independent of the fiscal authorities have reduced differences among financial systems. As a result, this chapter concentrates on general principles.

We might ask if central banking is indeed an art. As we will see in this chapter, central banking today is in practice a mix of art and science. This science is helpful to understanding what central banks do, but there is indeed quite a lot of art in knowing when to take action.[2]

---

1 This chapter title is taken in part from a book by R.G. Hawtrey. In that book, Hawtrey describes the various links between central bank actions and economic activity in general, as well as the design of central bank institutions. See R.G. Hawtrey, *The Art of Central Banking*, 2d ed. (New York: Kelley, 1970).

2 To quote Alan Blinder, former vice-chair of the U.S. Federal Reserve and professor of economics at Princeton University: "Having looked at monetary policy from both sides now, I can testify that central banking in practice is as much art as science. Nonetheless, while practicing this art, I have always found the science quite useful." See A. Blinder, *Central Banking in Theory and Practice* (Cambridge, Mass.: The MIT Press, 1999): 17.

We begin with a discussion of the targets and instruments of monetary policy. The instruments are the variables that can be influenced directly by central bank action, and they are well known. Somewhat more controversy exists about the targets of monetary policy, especially as the role of central banks has evolved over the past decade or so.[3] Should a central bank try to reach its goals by affecting the money supply or by controlling interest rates?[4]

Next, we consider the advantages and the disadvantages of monetary control and of interest rate control. Even if neither approach is inherently superior, perhaps one is easier to follow or has fewer harmful side effects.

The chapter concludes by considering central bank independence. What does independence mean? What are the economic consequences of ignoring it? What is the evidence of the relationship between central bank independence and economic performance?

23.1   TARGETS AND INSTRUMENTS OF MONETARY POLICY

All monetary authorities face problems choosing and meeting final goals. We can illustrate the inherent difficulties with the help of a diagram such as the one in Figure 23.1. Central banks possess **operating instruments**—tools with which they can do their work, such as manipulating the monetary base, changing the overnight rate, conducting open market operations (OMOs), and so on.[5] Changes in these operating instruments more or less directly influence **intermediate targets**, which are usually some measure of the money supply or some key interest rate (one that is related to most other interest rates in the economy). In countries that target inflation, such as Canada, the intermediate target might be the current forecast of inflation.[6] Hence, an intermediate target is best thought of as a variable that provides useful information about final goals.

The point of central bank action is not only what actually happens to these intermediate targets (the size of the money supply, for example, is not very interesting per se), but also (and just as important) the performance in the economy of various **ultimate goals**, such as inflation, unemployment, and exchange rates, individually or in some combination.

The difficulty of achieving some final target in this two-stage process is partly posed by the uncontrollables of monetary policy. For example, the influence of operating instruments on intermediate targets is largely determined by the size and stability of the money multipliers. But which money multiplier should be selected from among the long list of candidates? The issue is no different from the question of which monetary aggregate is the best indicator of the money multiplier over time, and choosing M1 or M2+ leads to a dramatically different picture. Moreover, how stable is the money multiplier chosen? If it is predictable, the monetary authorities will have a fairly good idea of the link between the operating instrument and the intermediate target. Otherwise their actions will have a significant measure of uncertainty.

---

3 For those interested in the details of this evolutionary process, see P.L. Siklos *The Changing Face of Central Banking: Evolutionary Trends Since World War II* (Cambridge: Cambridge University Press, 2002).

4 An observant student might ask: What about controlling the exchange rate? In Chapter 8 we entertained the possibility that policymakers might want to fix the exchange rate. Nevertheless, a growing number of countries have found that having an independent monetary policy requires a floating-type exchange rate regime. In essence then, there is no need to discuss central bank policy under a pegged exchange rate since that policy is dictated by the central bank in the country to which the exchange rate is pegged. Moreover, Canada has the distinction of having employed a floating rate longer than any other industrial country. Therefore, we do not explicitly consider the exchange rate, although, as we shall see later in this chapter, it can still play an important role in the conduct of monetary policy.

5 These tools are discussed in Chapter 22 and elsewhere, so we do no more than list them here.

6 This point is made by Lars Svensson, "Inflation Forecast Targeting: Implementing and Monitoring Inflation Targets," *European Economic Review* 41(6): 1111–46. Such a policy can be dangerous. Why? Simply because forecasters might then always project inflation to be equal to the announced inflation target, thereby providing no useful information to policymakers. See B. Bernanke, and M. Woodford, "Inflation Forecasts and Monetary Policy," *Journal of Money, Credit and Banking* 29 (4): 653–84.

Even if intermediate targeting is well within the reach of central banks, the questions remain of specifying the final target and of predicting its course. Thus, the two problems that plague the relationship between operating instruments and intermediate targets also remain. The behaviour of the velocity of circulation can, for example, sever the link between a monetary aggregate and inflation. And, unless monetary policies as practised by the central bank are believed by the public—that is, unless they are credible—the final target may not be attained.

Another question is whether a central bank should be committed to a single target, such as **price stability**, or seek to achieve multiple objectives, such as a combination of inflation, unemployment, and economic growth. The difficulty with specifying multiple final targets is that they often conflict with one another. For example, inflation and unemployment targets may not be compatible goals (see Chapter 21). Add to this the complications that arise because of the relationship between exchange rates and interest rates, and an optimal policy mix becomes more difficult still to attain.

Finally, policymakers' goals may conflict with those of the central bank or with those of the public. Someone has to decide for which group in society the policy mix should be optimal.

23.2 MONETARY VERSUS INTEREST RATE CONTROL: A SIMPLE CHARACTERIZATION

Despite the room for error, central banks do take action in financial markets. We can use a simplified supply–demand diagram to explore the consequences for interest rate stability of a policy

Figure 23.1   Instruments and Targets of Monetary Policy

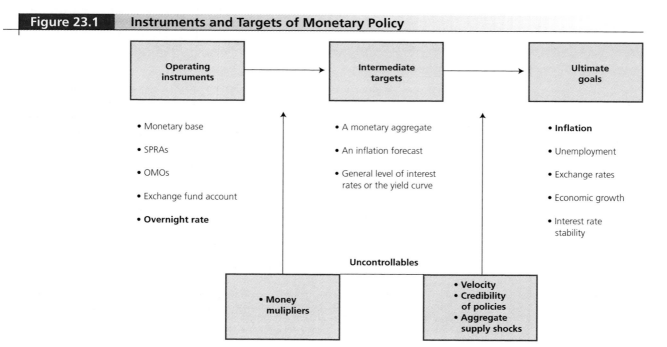

The lists here are by no means exhaustive. Ultimate goals, for example, might also include stability in financial markets and full employment. In bold characters are the chosen operating instrument and ultimate goal of monetary policy in Canada.

ECONOMICS FOCUS 23.1   OUT OF CONTROL?

Most central banks have a long-term objective (sometimes vaguely stated) of promoting economic growth and achieving price stability (low or zero inflation). Meeting the latter goal can impart an inflationary spin to an economy. Moreover, some analysts suggest that recent changes in the financial systems have undercut the efficacy of some of the central banks' tools. Deregulation—the removal of capital controls, interest rate ceilings, and credit-rationing, to name but a few examples—may have reduced central banks' ability to influence the growth of credit, with the loss of control meaning higher inflation in the future. An OECD study suggested that central banks now need to practise interest rate "overkill" to achieve credit control. (In other words, interest rates have to rise by a larger percentage and for a longer period than in the past to achieve a reduction in credit demand. In economic terms, this translates into a lower interest elasticity of credit demand with respect to that interest rate.) All this is a reaction to the belief that bond and foreign exchange markets drive monetary policy rather than the other way around. The reaction of Mexico's government in the wake of the 1994 devaluation of the peso, and pleas by presidents of such countries as Argentina and Peru to foreign investors not to take their billions out of their economies are examples of this phenomenon.

Ironically, when the Eurodollar market experienced meteoric growth during the 1960s and 1970s, similar concerns were expressed. The U.S. Federal Reserve had no direct control over this market. The worry then was, what would happen if all Eurodollars were repatriated to the United States? Clearly, the resulting expansion in credit would be tremendously inflationary. The fears proved unfounded; today most Eurodollars remain offshore to finance trade and other financial needs abroad. Nevertheless, there is always the potential for financial innovations to reduce the efficacy of domestic central banks' control over monetary policy.

A further reason for the concern expressed about the ability of the regulators and the monetary authorities to control the financial system stems from the plethora of scandals that have plagued financial markets over the past few years. The Japanese brokerage scandal, in which large firms were compensated for losses incurred at the hands of brokerage firms, the fraudulent activities of the Bank of Credit and Commerce International (BCCI), and the attempt by Solomon Brothers to corner the market for U.S. securities, to name but three examples, suggest to some that financial practices can no longer be effectively regulated. Even the *Wall Street Journal* says, "Regulation is a lagging indicator" (28 August 1991); that is, financial innovations that overcome some existing regulatory obstacles occur at a far faster rate than does the ability to legislate their uses.

The Asian crisis in 1997 also led to fears of a global financial meltdown that fortunately did not take place. Each of the foregoing examples raises the issue of the pitfalls that central bankers, in particular, face in dealing with day-to-day events and how they might affect the marketplace and the economy as a whole versus their responsibility for the maintenance of price stability (and perhaps adequate economic growth). The latter is a longer-term objective that requires some patience. Hence, the danger always exists that policymakers can develop "tunnel vision," thereby overreacting to what appear to be random events with little lasting impact on the overall objectives of monetary policy. As a result, whereas central banks during the 1980s were not specifically mandated to consider financial stability of the financial system as a separate goal of monetary policy, by the 1990s, at least half of the central banks in industrial countries were directed to concern themselves with the maintenance of a stable financial system.

Questions for Discussion

1. If interest rate overkill is practised, does the policy have wider implications for inflation or economic growth?
2. Would the shift in funds toward stock markets also lead to central banks practising a form of overkill in setting interest rates?

Sources

"The Bank of Canada and the Money Market," *Bank of Canada Review* (May 1989): 17–33.

"Out of Greenspan's Hand," *Economist* (27 October 1990): 81.

D. Sanger, "Do Financial Markets Now Make Policy?" *New York Times* (19 November 1995): 3.

P.L. Siklos, "Pitfalls and Opportunities for the Conduct of Monetary Policy in a World of High Frequency Data," in *Information in Financial Asset Prices*, Proceedings of a conference held by the Bank of Canada (Ottawa, Ont.: Bank of Canada, 1999): 331–69.

for which the intermediate target is **monetary control**—controlling the money supply—versus one that aims at **interest rate control**. This is, of course, a significant simplification of the problems apparent from Figure 23.1,[7] but it will clearly illustrate the dilemmas and difficulties faced by central banks in conducting monetary policy.

We start with a familiar framework. Figure 23.2(A) shows various representations of the demand for money, which we first encountered in Chapter 6. Recall that this demand is positively related to the price level, P, and to real income, y, and negatively to the nominal interest rate, R. The vertical axis in Figure 23.2(A) reproduces the functional relationship between these variables and the demand for money that was derived earlier in the book. The black downward-sloping line shows one such demand for money curve drawn for a particular level of real income, nominal interest rate, and the price level. Because of changes in other unpredictable factors, the curve shifts over time. Suppose these unpredictable factors, which we'll summarize by the term u, influence money demand in a fashion that is random but averages to zero.

Figure 23.2(B) shows the money supply function, which we also encountered in Chapter 6. Once again the functional relationship that drives the quantity of money supplied is also shown on the vertical axis of Figure 23.2(B). The quantity of money supplied is positively related to the nominal interest rate. But, as we saw in Chapter 22, the money supply is influenced by other factors that are not under the direct control of the monetary authorities: the currency–deposit

---

Figure 23.2   Instrument Control: The Basic Relationships

(A) Demand for Money

$$M_t^d = P_t \cdot f(y_t, R_t) + u_t$$

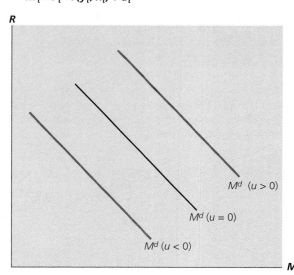

(B) Money Supply

$$M_t^s = l(R_t) \cdot \text{Base}_t + v_t$$

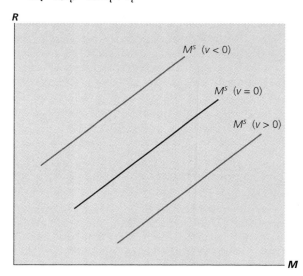

The demand for money curve is downward sloping but shifts randomly over time because of u, whose mean is zero. The black line in panel (A) is the demand curve when u is at its mean of zero; the grey lines are the demand curves when u is less than or greater than zero. The supply of money curve in panel (B) shifts randomly with v because the monetary authorities do not exercise perfect control over the money supply. v also may be negative or positive but its mean is zero. (For more on the demand for money curve, see Chapters 6 and 11; for more on the supply of money curve, see Chapters 6 and 22.)

---

7 We do not, for example, consider other possible final targets. Neither do we discuss the choice of an appropriate monetary aggregate nor which operating instruments are used. What follows is a restatement of sorts of the classic analysis by Poole. See W. Poole, "Optimal Choice of Monetary Policy Instrument in a Simple Stochastic Macro Model," *Quarterly Journal of Economics* 84 (May 1970): 197–216.

ratio and the reserves of the banking system. Here we lump together the effects of these un-controllables in the term v. Once again, we assume that although v shifts the money supply function in an unpredictable fashion, it averages zero.

MONEY SUPPLY CONTROL

Let us now consider the implications of monetary and interest rate control, starting with the former. We stressed in the last chapter that money supply cannot be perfectly controlled through manipulations of high-powered money. The basics are outlined in Figure 23.3(A).

Suppose for the time being that, on average, the money demand function is at $\overline{M}_0^d$. Consequently, we ignore the short-run unpredictability in money demand. If money supply is controlled within the M_{max}^S and M_{min}^S range, then interest rates will fluctuate between R_{min} and R_{max}. Note, however, that if money demand is steeper, as in $\overline{M}_1^d$, interest rates become poten-tially more volatile as the range $[R'_{max}, R_{min}]$ is larger than $[R_{max}, R_{min}]$. If the central bank wants to limit interest rate volatility then, in principle, it could tighten the range of values taken by the money supply (proving this result is left to you as an exercise). As we already know, tightening the range is easier said than done and, despite the fact that the European Central Bank for one has a **money supply growth target**, this approach has lost its appeal among many academics.[8]

Figure 23.3   Money Supply Targeting

(A) Money Supply Targetting When the Slope of the Money Supply Changes

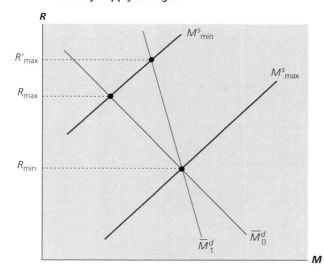

(B) Money Supply Targeting and Money Demand Uncertainty

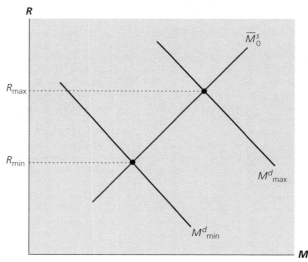

Panel (A) illustrates how changing the slope of the money demand function affects the variability of interest rates for a given range of money supply values. Interest rate volatility is greater the more inelastic (i.e., the steeper) is money demand. In panel (B), interest rate variability is caused by uncertainty about the position of the money demand function.

---

8 See B. Bernanke, and F.S. Mishkin, "Central Bank Behavior and the Strategy of Monetary Policy: Observations from Six Industrial Countries," *NBER Macroeconomics Annual* 1992 (Cambridge, Mass.: The MIT Press, 1992): 183–227, and L.E.O. Svensson, "Monetary Policy Issues for the Eurosystem," Carnegie–Rochester Conference Series on Public Policy, 51 (1) (1999): 79–136. Laidler cautions that policymakers ignore information in money supply data at their peril, although dif-ferent monetary aggregates send different messages about the future course of inflation and economic growth. See D.E.W. Laidler, "Passive Money, Active Money, and Monetary Policy," *Bank of Canada Review* (Summer 1999): 15–25, and P.L. Siklos, and A.G. Barton, "Monetary Aggregates as Indicators of Economic Activity in Canada: Empirical Evidence," *Canadian Journal of Economics* (February 2001): 1–17.

Now consider the case shown in panel (B) of Figure 23.3. Suppose that, on average, the money supply curve is at $\overline{M}_0^S$, but the central bank must cope with an uncertain money demand that ranges from $M^d{}_{min}$ to $M^d{}_{max}$. Even if the monetary authorities stay the course, interest rates will range between R_{max} and R_{min}. The more uncertain is money demand (i.e., the larger is u), the more volatile interest rates will be (this, too, is left as an exercise).

If interest rate uncertainty is considered inherently undesirable because it creates uncertainty about the consistency of monetary policy actions or makes it more difficult for investors to make decisions, then a cautious central bank might be inclined to implement a policy in which interest rates are controlled or at least change slowly over time.

INTEREST RATE PEGGING

Check out the role of money growth targets at the European Central Bank
www.ecb.int

Suppose that instead of trying to control the money supply, a central bank decided to peg interest rates. In the extreme, it might simply decree that the interest rate be set at R^* in Figure 23.4. Equilibrium money supply values would range between M_{min} and M_{max}. More realistically (because no central bank completely controls the money supply), it might allow interest rates to fluctuate freely within a band, denoted as in the figure as R_{min} to R_{max}. Then the equilibrium money supply values would range between M_0 and M_1. Notice that the effect of pegging the interest rate is to render the money supply curve perfectly elastic.[9] The reason is that a central bank that is pegging interest rates has undertaken to supply quantities of money sufficient to ensure that the interest rate stays within the designated bands. Indeed, the Bank of Canada officially an-

| Figure 23.4 | **Interest Rate Pegging** |

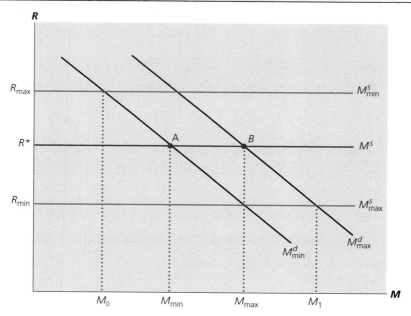

If the central bank pegs the interest rate at R^*, the equilibrium money supply will fluctuate between M_{min} and M_{max}, consistent with equilibrium points A and B. In other words, the money supply function becomes perfectly elastic. Alternatively, the central bank may intervene only if there are indications that the interest rate will rise above R_{max} or fall below R_{min}. The variation of the equilibrium money supply is held to M_0 and M_1.

---

9 Except within the interest rate target zone, if such a zone exists.

nounces a target band for overnight interest rates, one of its main tools of monetary policy (see Chapter 4).

CONTROLLING THE MONEY SUPPLY OR INTEREST RATES?

Which of the two control techniques is superior? Is it preferable to minimize fluctuations in the money supply over time, or would the Bank be better off pegging interest rates?

As we have seen, two problems face policymakers. One is the relative sizes of u and v, that is, the disturbances to the money demand and money supply functions. It is therefore important for central banks to forecast these disturbances. The second is the uncertainty about the slope of the money demand and supply curves, which complicates matters further.[10] Whether the interest rate is pegged at R^*, or is allowed to fluctuate between R_{min} and R_{max}, Figure 23.4 shows that the money supply becomes volatile. Considerable evidence exists that central banks prefer interest rate stability over money supply stability, for reasons already discussed. As a result, the interest rates they directly control change slowly and gradually.[11] Figure 23.5 shows the operating band for the overnight rate. The actual overnight rate, as we have seen earlier (Chapters 4 and 22), always fluctuates within the band. Since this instrument was introduced, we have seen a sharp rise in the target interest rate in late 1994 and early in 1995, as fears of resurgent inflation in the United States pushed the Fed funds rate sharply higher around the same time. Notice that the overnight rates fell back slowly, reaching early 1994 levels more than a year later. As inflation fears subsided, interest rates continued to fall until the Asian crisis hit the world economy. The crisis had a strong impact on the U.S.–Canadian dollar exchange rate, and therefore Canadian interest rates, throughout the summer

| Figure 23.5 | The Overnight Rate Band in Canada |

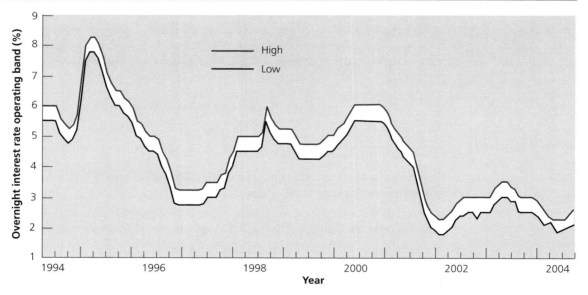

Source: Adapted from Statistics Canada, CANSIM II database, series V39076 (Low) and V39077 (High).

---

10 Indeed, in another classic article, Brainard shows that central bank forecasting exercises no longer produce the "optimal" outcome when policymakers are unsure about the slopes of these functions. See W. Brainard, "Uncertainty and the Effectiveness of Policy," *American Economic Review* 57 (May 1967): 411–25.

11 This is known as the interest rate "smoothing" principle. See M. Goodfriend, "Interest Rates and the Conduct of Monetary Policy," *Carnegie-Rochester Conference Series on Public Policy* 34 (1991): 7–30, and C.A.E. Goodhart, "Central Bankers and Uncertainty," *Bank of England Quarterly Bulletin* 39 (February 1999): 102–14.

of 1998.[12] After the crisis, interest rates came down only slowly as inflation fears reappeared, in the face of strong economic growth in both the United States and Canada, as the world economy overcame the Asian flu.

Finally, the meltdown of the stock market in 2000–2001, resulting from fears that technology stocks were overvalued, the imminent arrival, or so it was thought, of a severe recession, as well as the repercussions of the events of 9/11, led to a sharp fall in 2001. As this is written, the bias has once again turned toward rising future short-term rates since fears of a persistent slowdown eased considerably in early 2002.

The discussion so far has focused on using the interest rate or the money supply as the instruments of monetary policy. What about the exchange rate? Recall that in Canada's postwar monetary history, the exchange rate has been allowed to float more or less freely. Hence, the exchange rate is not an instrument of policy. Does this mean that the exchange rate does not matter? Clearly not, for Canada's is a small, open economy, and external influences loom large on the domestic economy. However, we saw as early as in Chapter 8 that in a floating exchange rate system this determines the evolution of the relationship between Canadian and foreign, most notably, U.S. interest rates. Consequently, the Bank of Canada and financial markets are keenly interested in the link between domestic interest rates, the exchange rate, and what this means for the state of monetary policy. We consider below a simple indicator of that relationship, but one that can be fraught with problems if misused.

WHY SMOOTH INTEREST RATES?

Figure 23.5 makes clear that interest rates change slowly, and that central banks do not react immediately to every blip in inflation or exchange rates. Thus, for example, during the fall of 2004, the Bank of Canada predicted strong economic growth for 2005. However, as the exchange rate began to appreciate very rapidly, the Bank began to have second thoughts about the impact on Canadian businesses highly dependent on exports to the U.S. Therefore, although the Bank at first expected to raise its target for the overnight interest rate, it changed course once new data showed their initial views were too optimistic. "Recent data suggest that Canada's economic growth in the fourth quarter of 2004 was marginally weaker than previously expected, owing partly to a somewhat more pronounced adjustment to the past appreciation of the Canadian dollar."[13] This quote suggests a couple of things. First, the exchange rate does matter, even though the Bank does not attempt to control its course. We explore the implications of this view below. The second implication is that central banks are cautious when changing interest rates.[14] Why? Economists point to a number of factors that explain this kind of behaviour:

1. Forecasts are uncertain and subject to change. Therefore, central banks have to be cautious about their outlook for the economy.

2. Central bankers worry about their reputation. If they increase interest rates quickly and then reverse course, the public might think they are not terribly competent.

3. Frequent interest rate changes can be costly for banks, businesses, and the public, since they require a variety of adjustments, from portfolio reallocation, to the setting of different lending and borrowing rates, to the costs of operating a business.

---

12 Notice also that interest rate developments in 1998 are broadly consistent with the view that the Bank of Canada does not target the exchange rate (details are left as an exercise), though it might use foreign exchange intervention to dampen exchange rate volatility, that is, by "leaning against the wind." Indeed, Bank of Canada researchers reached the same conclusion by analyzing a longer period of data. See J. Murray, M. Zelmer, and D. McManus, "The Effect of Intervention on Canadian Dollar Volatility," in *Exchange Rates and Monetary Policy*, proceedings of a conference held by the Bank of Canada (Ottawa, Ont.: Bank of Canada, 1996): 311–61.

13 From **http://www.bankofcanada.ca/en/fixed-dates/2005/rate_25015.htm**

14 Many have recently written about the interest rate-smoothing phenomenon. See, for example, B. Sack and V. Wieland "Interest Rate Smoothing and Optimal Monetary Policy: A Review of Recent Empirical Evidence," *Journal of Economics and Business* 52: 205-28.

4. As long as a central bank is credible, it can change expectations of future inflation by simply threatening to change interest rates without actually doing so. The result should show up in the term spread (as discussed in Chapter 7).

Not everyone agrees with this assessment. Some argue that plots such as Figure 23.5 are an illusion stemming in part from looking at data over long periods such as a quarter or even a year.[15] Still another study argues that, once we control for the fact that central bank decisions today affect the economy, and inflation in particular, several months in the future, it appears that there is interest rate smoothing when an inflation-targeting central bank acts aggressively to ensure that inflation remains within the stipulated target.[16] Nevertheless, the evidence seems to suggest that central banks do smooth interest rates, and some central bankers have admitted so explicitly.[17]

The Bank of Canada's MCI **www.bankof canada.ca/en/ backgrounders/ bg-p3.html**

THE MONETARY CONDITIONS INDEX

Trying to divine what a central bank does preoccupies economists and financial market participants. Any piece of financial or economic news that might affect the interest-rate-setting behaviour of the central bank is the subject of intense scrutiny and analysis. This is particularly true in the United States, where the regular meetings of the Federal Reserve Open Market Committee (FOMC) have the media guessing about the direction of interest rates. Of course, given our economic and financial ties to the United States, the Bank of Canada is not immune to Fed moves.

Canada's is a small open economy, and so interest rate movements may not always clearly signal the present stance of monetary policy. In part for this reason, the Bank of Canada has developed what it calls the **Monetary Conditions Index** (**MCI**). The MCI is best thought of as a judicious combination of interest rate movements and exchange rate movements.[18] The actual formula used by the Bank of Canada is

$$MCI = (R_t - 7.90) + (100/3) [\log C6 - \log (91.33)]$$

where R is the 90-day yield on commercial paper, C6 is the Canadian dollar index against its major trading partners (U.S., E.M.U. countries, Japan, U.K., Switzerland, and Sweden), 7.90% is the corporate paper rate in January 1987, and 91.33 is the exchange rate against the C6 in the same month. As can be seen from the definition, the MCI is a combination of interest rate movements relative to some benchmark (7.90%), as well as exchange rate movements, again relative to some benchmark (91.33). The objective of the equation is to ask whether, relative to these benchmarks (these were chosen because the index takes on a value of zero in January 1987), monetary policy is tighter or looser. An interest rate rise or a depreciation of the currency anticipates higher future inflation. Therefore, a higher MCI signals tighter monetary policy. Recall from Chapter 8 that the two variables are linked to each other via the interest rate and purchasing power parity theories. In the current setup, interest rate movements account for approximately two-thirds of movements

15 G. Rudebusch "Term Structure Evidence on Interest Rate Smoothing and Monetary Policy Inertia," *Journal of Monetary Economics* 49: 1161-87.

16 C. Goodhart "The Monetary Policy Committee's Reaction Function: An Exercise in Estimation," *Berkeley Electronic Press* (forthcoming 2005).

17 W.B. English, W.R. Nelson, and B. Sack "Interpreting the Significance of the Lagged Interest Rate in Estimated Monetary Policy Rules," *Contributions to Macroeconomics* 3(1), 2003, article 5; B. Sack "Does the Fed Act Gradually? A VAR Analysis," *Journal of Monetary Economics* 46 (August 1998): 229-56. Ben Bernanke, a former governor of the U.S. Federal Reserve, explains why central banks change interest rates gradually in "Gradualism," remarks at an economics luncheon cosponsored by the Federal Reserve Bank of San Francisco and the University of Washington, 20 May 2004, available from **www.federalreserve.gov**.

18 For more details about the MCI, see C. Freedman, "The Role of Monetary Conditions and the Monetary Conditions Index in the Conduct of Policy," *Bank of Canada Review* (Autumn 1995): 53–60, and C. Freedman, "The Use of Indicators and of the Monetary Conditions Index in Canada," in *Frameworks for Monetary Stability: Policy Issues and Country Experiences,* edited by T.J.T. Baliño and C. Cottarelli (Washington, D.C.: International Monetary Fund, 1994).

in the MCI. By following movements in the MCI, the Bank attempts to create monetary conditions that follow as closely as possible a path consistent with its inflation target objective.

The Canadian dollar depreciated strongly against the U.S. dollar beginning in the summer of 1998, and there was a great deal of confusion about whether the Bank of Canada was content with MCI levels, which were dropping, prompting the Bank to raise interest rates. In doing so, the Bank appeared to contradict its own stated policy of not trying to "...maintain a precise MCI level by adjusting interest rates in response to every exchange rate wiggle."[19]

Other central banks, such as New Zealand's Reserve Bank, have also used an MCI to assist in evaluating what the appropriate stance of monetary policy should be. The IMF too has used the MCI in describing the stance of monetary policy in selected countries. Despite the usefulness of the MCI (the Bank of Canada continues to publish the index) as a tool to understand the connection between interest rate and exchange rate changes, it has fallen out of favour because markets can easily become confused about the importance a central bank places on exchange rate changes versus changes in interest rates.[20] An inflation-targeting central bank must allow the exchange rate to float freely, as we saw earlier (for example, as in Chapter 22), and so cannot be seen as playing interest rate changes against changes in the exchange rate. In any event, most observers agree that central banks are incapable of influencing the level of the exchange rate, except temporarily, although they have far more influence on interest rate levels.

23.3 CENTRAL BANK AUTONOMY AND INFLATION

If it is one of the central bank's responsibilities to achieve some final target such as price stability, it must be permitted to do so without political interference. However, we can never entirely omit a role for politicians. After all, their electoral fortunes will be influenced by prevailing economic conditions, which are at least partly the fruit of the central bank's actions, and politicians directly control the tools of fiscal policy, which also influence the economy. In this section, we look at each of these temptations to interfere with the central bank. Finally, we consider the evidence on **central bank autonomy**, or **independence**, and inflation control (also see the discussion of Bank of Canada history in the previous chapter).

The price of autonomy, however, is greater accountability and transparency. This means that, since central bankers are not elected, they must ultimately be held accountable for their actions to the government and the public. In part for this reason, central banks have provided more information about what they are doing and how they expect to act in future, including the provision of information about their outlook. Therefore, we also briefly discuss the concepts of transparency and accountability.

THE POLITICAL BUSINESS CYCLE

An only slightly cynical view of the inherent tension between a government and a central bank is that it produces cycles in economic activity that can be linked to election dates. This **political business cycle** argument presumes that politicians can and ultimately will attempt to manipulate economic aggregates, such as inflation, unemployment, and economic growth.

The United States, where elections are held on a regular schedule, provided the early testing ground for this theory. Critics objected that politicians could not possibly fool voters all of the time, and the political business cycle concept fell out of favour in economic circles for a time. Alternatively, if political parties are ideologically motivated, economic cycles may reflect partisan preferences over

---

19 Bank of Canada, *Monetary Policy Report* (May 1995): 14.
20 For an explanation of some of the dangers of relying on an MCI-type measure, see P.L. Siklos, "Is the MCI a Useful Signal of Monetary Conditions? An Empirical Investigation," *International Finance* 3 (November 2000).

time; for example, "conservative" governments may gear their policies so as to achieve a relatively low rate of inflation, whereas their "liberal" counterparts may prefer to focus on reducing unemployment. In addition, the timing of elections in many countries, including Canada, is uncertain. Governments in such countries may try to avoid losing a vote by selecting an election date prior to any anticipated recession.

Much of the work on political business cycles assumes that governments tend to resort to monetary policy to generate outcomes favourable to re-election. The reason is that, unlike fiscal policies, whose implementation can involve considerable delays (legislative, among others), monetary policies can be put in place fairly quickly. But this view presumes that government directly controls monetary policy—in other words, that central banks have no possibility of independent action. Thus, say proponents of political business cycles, if a central bank is pursuing a policy of price stability in the midst of a recession and an election looms, that bank will likely have to abandon its action at the behest of its political masters.

Is there empirical evidence favouring the political business cycle theory? The very nature of the argument makes it difficult to prove, in part because it is not so easy for politicians to manipulate monetary policy at will.

Consider four aggregates that might be influenced by political considerations: the unemployment rate, interest rates, the exchange rate, and economic growth. Unemployment in Canada has tended to fall just before an election. By contrast, interest rates rose before at least half the elections. More often than not, the exchange rate also rose (meaning a more expensive U.S. dollar in Canadian terms).[21] Finally, average real GDP growth has tended to peak before an election (though the timing has been variable). Thus, there is, at least superficially, some evidence that economic cycles are influenced by electoral events.[22]

COMPATIBLE FISCAL POLICY

Even if the political business cycle is not operating, and a country otherwise wants its central bank to be independent, the institution can be severely hampered if its monetary policy is inconsistent with the government's **fiscal policy** (that is, its use of its taxing and spending powers). Thus, fiscal policy can result in inflation even if monetary policy is geared to prevent it. The conflict between the two sets of policies is one reason economies show a distinct bias toward some inflation. (We explored this point and other issues in the debate about the importance of money in Chapter 21.)

THE RECORD ON INFLATION CONTROL

Clearly, a central bank in a democracy cannot be entirely independent of the political system since the voters invest ultimate responsibility for economic performance in their elected officials. Moreover, the well-known tendency of central banks to shroud their actions in secrecy (a feature that is disappearing), and the complexities of understanding what the future holds for the economy as a whole, make it even more difficult to ascertain what they actually do and how much their actions differ from those of the political authorities.[23] Yet, it is now generally recognized that maintaining accountability is simplified by permitting central banks to focus on the goal of price

---

21 Canada was on a fixed exchange rate regime during the 1963, 1965, and 1968 elections. Some argue that the use of monetary policy to achieve political ends is more likely under flexible exchange rates than under fixed exchange rates.

22 One might also wonder: Since central banks are more independent, could they create their own political business cycle? After all, some argue that the first President Bush lost the election because of Alan Greenspan, the chair of the U.S. Federal Reserve. Available international evidence suggests that central banks cannot be blamed for such cycles. See E. Leertouwer, and P. Maier, "Who Creates Political Business Cycles? (Should Central Banks Be Blamed?)," *European Journal of Political Economy* 17 (September 2001): 445–63.

23 Indeed the "bureaucratic theory" of central bank actions argues that the Bank of Canada acts in its own self-interest as opposed to pursuing some economic objectives.

stability, rather than by selecting some other variable from the available "menu" (see Figure 23.1).[24] This development is most vividly reflected in the growing number of countries that have adopted inflation targets (see Chapter 22). Futhermore, a positive byproduct of price stability is increased stability in economic performance, with all its attendant benefits for unemployment rates.

There is increasing recognition that countries with low inflation tend to outperform other countries in terms of economic growth. Perhaps for this reason, many countries are now trying to stabilize prices. Figure 23.6 shows the evolution of inflation rates in seven countries over 40 years. In the early 1970s, their inflation rates diverged considerably. But stagflation taught even politicians to dislike inflation, and by the 1980s the rates were beginning to converge.

All this evidence on the desirability of price stability led policymakers in the 1990s to favour making it the primary goal of central banks and enshrining some form of autonomy for these institutions to counter the political temptation to inflate the economy before an election. Germany, Austria, Switzerland, and, more recently, New Zealand, Canada, the United Kingdom, Japan, and a few other countries (see Chapter 22), now mandate that their central banks maintain some form of price stability.[25] A legislated goal of price stability is also mandated for the newly established European Central Bank of the European Union (see Chapter 26).

EVALUATING CENTRAL BANK INDEPENDENCE

How convincing is the evidence linking, in particular, inflation and the degree to which a central bank is autonomous or independent? First, there is the problem of defining what is meant by

| Figure 23.6 | Inflation Rates over Time in Selected Industrialized Countries |

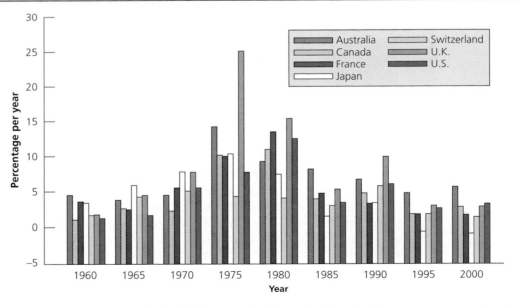

Source: International Financial Statistics CD-ROM (Washington: International Monetary Fund). Data refer to the year-over-year percentage change in each country's consumer price index at five-year intervals.

---

24 The governor of the New Zealand central bank must achieve precise price stability objectives or face the possibility of dismissal.

25 Many economic studies find that a central bank's statutory independence is of considerable importance in determining its inflation performance. Yet, the record of countries where such independence exists suggests otherwise in several instances. For an alternative view, see D.R. Johnson, and P.L. Siklos, "Political and Economic Determinants of Interest Rate Behaviour: International Evidence," *Economic Inquiry* (October 1996), for empirical evidence that suggests that statutory independence, although important, is not a sufficient condition for achieving low inflation.

independence. It surely does not mean that a central bank can do whatever it pleases. Rather, the term independence, or autonomy, refers to whether a central bank has instrument versus goal independence.[26] That is, can the central bank choose the instruments of monetary policy freely? Or are the goals of monetary policy specifically mandated? In countries such as New Zealand, there is no goal independence because the central bank is mandated to achieve a specific inflation target. By contrast, there is instrument independence because the Reserve Bank of New Zealand can use whatever means it has at its disposal to achieve the stated inflation target. In Canada's case, the inflation targets are not mandated by legislation but rather by mutual agreement between the finance minister and the governor of the Bank of Canada. As we have seen, however, the Bank of Canada's mandate is currently very broad, so it has both goal independence and instrument independence. But, since the Bank has been operating under an inflation targeting regime since 1990, goal independence no longer effectively exists.

How is independence measured? Economists have generally adopted two approaches. One, very popular of late, is to rank central banks according to some interpretation of their statutes.[27] One such exercise divides central bank laws into the following categories (the list that follows is a partial one).

1. *Monetary policy formulation.* Here the object is to determine who decides the formulation of monetary policy: the central bank or the government.

2. *Conflict resolution.* Here the issue is how disagreements between the government and the central bank are resolved. Does the governor have to resign? As we have seen in the Canadian case, this proved to be an important question in connection with the Coyne affair.

3. *Central bank objectives.* How precisely defined are the objectives of the central bank? In other words, how much goal independence is there?

4. *Term of office.* For how long is the governor appointed? Does the term coincide with or overlap the term of the politicians who head the government?

5. *Limitations on lending to government.* How difficult is it to borrow from the central bank, that is, to effectively monetize the debt (see Chapter 26)?

Table 23.1 shows four such rankings. Four of the five rankings use information about central bank legislation applicable during the 1980s or earlier. Siklos updates Cukierman's ranking for the 1990s. It is immediately clear that Switzerland and the United States generally lead the pack and, as Figure 23.6 also reveals, these same two countries often have the lowest inflation rates. However, there are two major criticisms levelled at this approach. First, how is it that the same piece of legislation leads to such different rankings? A good example is the Bank of Japan. Its inflation performance is among the best, but it ranks near the bottom in three of the four rankings and near the top in only one. Why? Because, in legal terms the Bank of Japan was, until 1997, subservient to the Finance Ministry. What made it effectively independent was the autonomy of the Finance Ministry from the rest of government. A second problem is that legislation governing central banks changes very infrequently. Thus, for example, both the Bank of Japan and the Banque de France became statutorily much more autonomous toward the end of the 1990s, and this is not reflected in the rankings. On the other hand, developments in New Zealand have catapulted New Zealand from near the bottom of the earlier rankings to near the top, while the newly created European Central Bank leads the pack. Another objection is that it may be more important for a central bank to have a clear mandate to keep inflation under control via an inflation target than to provide autonomy in the statutes of the central bank. By contrast, as is clear from Figure 23.6, inflation performance over the last 30 years has changed dramatically. One reason is

---

26 See S. Fisher, "Modern Central Banking," in *The Future of Central Banking*, edited by F. Capie, C. Goodhart, S. Fischer, and N. Schnadt (Cambridge: Cambridge University Press, 1994).
27 See A. Cukierman, *Central Bank Strategy, Credibility and Independence* (Cambridge, Mass.: The MIT Press, 1992).

Table 23.1	**Qualitative Rankings of Central Bank Independence**

Cukierman (1980s)	Grilli et al. (1980s)	Burdekin and Willett (1980s)	Parkin (1980s)	Siklos (1990s)
Switzerland	Germany	Germany	Germany	European Central Bank
Germany	Switzerland	Switzerland	Switzerland	New Zealand
Austria	United States	Austria	United States	Switzerland
United States	The Netherlands	United States	Japan	Germany
Denmark	Canada	Canada	Denmark	Austria
Canada	Italy	The Netherlands	Canada	United Kingdom
The Netherlands	Austria	United Kingdom	The Netherlands	United States
Ireland	Denmark	Australia	United Kingdom	Denmark
Luxembourg	Ireland	France	France	Sweden
Iceland	Australia	New Zealand	Sweden	Canada
Britain	New Zealand	Sweden	Italy	Netherlands
Australia	France	Italy	Belgium	Ireland
France	United Kingdom	Belgium	Australia	Japan
Sweden	Belgium	Japan	New Zealand	Australia
Finland	Japan	Denmark	Austria	France
New Zealand	Sweden	Ireland	Ireland	Finland
Italy	Norway	Norway	Norway	Italy

Source: A. Cukierman, *Central Bank Strategy, Credibility, and Independence* (Cambridge, Mass.: The MIT Press, 1992), Table 19.4; V. Grilli, D. Masciandaro, and G. Tabellini "Political and Monetary Institutions and Public Financial Policies in Industrial Countries," *Economic Policy* (October 1991): 342–92; R.C.K. Burdekin, and T.D. Willett, "Central Bank Reform: The Federal Reserve in International Perspective," *Public Budgeting and Financial Management* (1991): 619–50; M. Parkin, "Domestic Monetary Institutions and Deficits," in *Deficits*, edited by M.G. Porter (Clayton, Australia: Monash University, 1986): 24–39; P.L. Siklos, *The Changing Face of Central Banking* (Cambridge: Cambridge University Press, 2002), Table 2.7.

Learn more about central banks in industrial countries at **www.wlu.ca/ ~wwwsbe/faculty/ psiklos/central banks.htm**

the exchange rate regime. As we have seen (in Chapter 8), a country's inflation rate is dependent on whether the exchange rate is fixed or not. The reason, therefore, that inflation rates were comparable in the 1960s was that exchange rates were more or less tied to the U.S. dollar. After the oil shock of 1973–74, exchange rates became flexible and inflation rates began to differ considerably between countries. Although exchange rates remained flexible into the 1990s, more and more central banks began to view inflation as an evil, and all began to aim for lower inflation, which explains the convergence of inflation rates in the early 1990s.

Another objection to the rankings tabulated in Table 23.1 is that they assume a causal relationship between the degree of statutory independence and inflation performance. Instead, it may be more plausible to argue that if the public and the financial sector are simply opposed to inflation, the central bank will deliver low inflation, regardless of the statutes spelling out its objectives. Otherwise, how could we explain the record of low inflation in the United States and in Germany, where price stability is understood to be the objective of the respective countries' central banks, even though neither institution is mandated to achieve a numerical inflation objective?

CENTRAL BANK ACCOUNTABILITY AND TRANSPARENCY

Accountability in monetary policy goes hand in hand with greater transparency. A central bank that is required to achieve an inflation objective is expected, or may be required, to account for its actions once the government has set the objective, preferably with the agreement of the monetary authority. Some have suggested that, as in New Zealand, the employment contract of the head of the central bank should include a performance clause tied to inflation performance (see **Economics Focus 23.2 – A Contract for Central Bankers?**). One worry with such a proposal is that a central bank governor might want to keep inflation low regardless of the economic consequences. In the extreme, inflation might stay low even though there was an economic depression. In practice, of course, this would not likely happen, since the political pressure to take account of real economic activity would be too great for any central banker—even one with an inflation performance clause—to ignore. Transparency, therefore, helps the central bank build credibility. As the governor of the Bank of Canada publicly stated, the trust that is acquired through greater transparency "can be thought of as a kind of social capital—a shared asset that benefits everyone, including the central bank."[28]

Transparency and accountability are often seen as complementing each other. One problem is that there is no consensus yet on the precise meaning of both terms. Theoretical approaches and implications of accountability and transparency in central banking also are varied. For example, Siklos (2002) defines accountability to include the precision with which the goals of monetary policy are outlined.[29] Transparency, on the other hand, is determined by the quantity, type, and clarity of information provided to the public. In other words, "transparency plays the part of self-imposed commitment: by disclosing the basis of the policy decisions, the central bank enables the general public to assess their adequacy."[30] Table 23.2 provides a chronology of changes in accountability and transparency at the Bank of Canada since 1991.

The definition of price stability has attracted relatively more controversy in academic circles. The literature has reached a broad consensus: Price stability does not mean zero inflation (see **Economics Focus 23.3 – Why Zero Inflation?**). Instead, a 1-3% inflation range is believed to be approximately consistent with price stability. One aspect of the controversy concerns whether inflation defined on the basis of core inflation enhances transparency. Monitoring core inflation requires that the central bank draw attention to the distinction between aggregate demand and supply shocks (see Chapter 21). The reason is that not all shocks require an interest rate response or need threaten a breach in the inflation target. For example, an oil price increase is bound to be inflationary. However, unless businesses use this as an excuse to permanently increase prices and, thus, inflation, the central bank will accommodate the immediate effect of these shocks, but will not permit inflation expectations to increase permanently. However, this distinction may be lost on the public who may not much care for such subtleties, instead equating loss of purchasing power with movements in the overall CPI (often referred to as headline CPI). Indeed, labour contracts, either explicitly or implicitly, are negotiated with future changes in CPI in mind, not core inflation. So long as core and CPI inflation move closely together it is not clear that inflation targets in terms of core inflation improve transparency. If, however, the two inflation measures diverged from each other, this would complicate the communications problem facing the central bank.[31]

REACTION FUNCTIONS AND MONETARY POLICY RULES

Check out information about central bank statutes, objectives, and other pertinent information
www.bis.org/ cbanks.htm

A second approach to the analysis of central bank behaviour consists of estimating what are called *reaction functions*. These are basically equations that are supposed to model what central banks actually do. To take a simple example, let's assume that the central bank conducts policy by changing the interest rate. One way we can distinguish between central banks then is to examine how they might react to inflation, unemployment, or electoral pressures. A central bank that cares only about inflation would attach a zero coefficient to increases in unemployment. By contrast, a central bank could choose to respond only to unemployment changes and not at all to inflation. Of course, an intermediate case occurs when the central bank responds to both inflation and unemployment changes. In addition, a politically motivated central bank would also respond to political pressure in the form of elections and partisan changes in government (i.e., from Liberal to Conservative). Finally, a central bank such as the Bank of Canada can ill afford to conduct an

28 Dodge, D. "Trust, Transparency, and Financial Markets," Remarks of the governor of the Bank of Canada to the Greater Halifax Partnership, 11 June 2002, available at **www.bankofcanada.ca/en/speeches/**.

29 Siklos, P.L. *The Changing Face of Central Banking: Evolutionary Trends Since World War II* (Cambridge: Cambridge University Press, 2002).

30 Deutsche Bundesbank, "Monetary Policy Transparency," *Monthly Report* 52 (March 2000): 15-30.

31 See Laidler, D.E.W., and Aba, S. "It's Time to Ignore Core Inflation," *C.D. Howe Institute Backgrounder* 45, November 2000. The authors raise doubts about the focus on core inflation in the Bank of Canada objectives. It is interesting to note that at least one *Monetary Policy Report* (Bank of Canada 2003 April) devotes considerable space to explaining why core and headline inflation have diverged from each other roughly since 2000.

Table 23.2	Changes in the Bank of Canada's Accountability and Transparency, 1988-2004: A Chronology
Dates	**Nature of Change/Announcement**
January 8, 1988	Governor Crow's Hanson Memorial Lecture advocating the goal of price stability
February 6, 1991	Announcement of inflation control targets in the federal government's budget speech (2-4% range in the CPI by the end of 1992, 1.5-3.5% by mid-1994 (revised to 1-3% in December 1993, renewed in 1995 (3 years), 1998 (3 years), and 2001 (6 years).
May 3, 1995 (first)	Monetary Policy (inflation) Reports since 1995. Beginning in 2000, quarterly updates were issued.
April 15, 1994	Band and target for overnight interest rates
October 28, 1996	Midpoint of band targeted by the Bank
April 12, 1995	New foreign exchange market intervention guidelines announced
July 1998	Foreign exchange market interventions to be announced on the Web site
September 19, 2000	Fixed dates for announcing changes to the Bank rate
May 17, 2001	Renewal of 1-3% inflation target for 5 years. Clarification of core inflation as the operational guide for monetary policy.
2003	Indicators of capacity and inflation pressure in Canada
2004	Published business outlook survey

Sources: Adapted from P. Siklos "Assessing the Impact of Changes in Transparency and Accountability at the Bank of Canada," *Canadian Public Policy* XXIX (September 2003): 279-99, and updated from various Bank of Canada publications.

exclusively "made in Canada" interest rate policy (look back at the Mexican peso case considered in Chapter 8 to see why). Therefore, domestic interest rate changes will also be influenced by foreign interest rate developments. A simple way to summarize the above relationships is with the help of the following equation:

$$\Delta R_t = a_0 + a_1 \Delta U_{t-1} + a_2 \Delta \pi_{t-1} + a_3 POL_t + a_4 \Delta R_{t-1}^{US} \qquad (23.1)$$

Equation (23.1) says that a change in the interest rate (say the Treasury bill rate) is a function of the previous experience with unemployment, measured as a change in the unemployment rate from last period (usually a month because unemployment data are released on a monthly basis), last period's inflation rate, a "political variable" (for example, whether there was an election or a change in government that month), and whether there was a change in interest rates in the United States. The relative importance of each consideration is evaluated by estimating the size of the coefficients a_0 to a_4. This approach to measuring what central banks do comes to a different conclusion than the approach that focuses on the legislative mandate of a central bank. In particular, it appears that central banks are more alike than they appear based on measures of statutory independence. Certainly, a look at the inflation performance of several countries reveals this as a definite possibility (see Figure 23.6). Furthermore, central banks behave quite differently according to whether exchange rates are pegged or not.[32]

The fact that central banks in the industrial world either have statutory independence or effectively operate autonomously from government has rekindled the possibility that central banks should operate according to some rule. A rule is, to quote the prominent monetary economist Allan Meltzer, "nothing more than a systematic decision process that uses information in

---

32 See D.R. Johnson, and P.L. Siklos, "Political and Economic Determinants of Central Bank Behaviour: Are Central Banks Different?" *Economic Inquiry* (October 1996).

ECONOMICS FOCUS 23.2 — A CONTRACT FOR CENTRAL BANKERS?

It was pointed out in this chapter and the previous one that governments have been searching for ways to ensure low inflation performance and to avoid the temptations of using the central bank to exploit the short-run Phillips curve. One solution that has received considerable attention among economists is to have the central bank governor's contract tied to inflation performance. The New Zealand case comes to mind, of course, since the central bank's budget is nominally fixed, and the governor can be dismissed if inflation exceeds the agreed upper portion of the target band. Yet, it seems impractical to follow up on such a suggestion if only because, even in the private sector, contracts tied strictly to performance alone are extremely rare. Nevertheless, it is interesting to consider why such contracts might help solve the time-inconsistency problem discussed in this chapter. Consider a model of the economy described by the following equations:

$$U = U_n + (\pi - \pi^e) \qquad [a]$$
$$W^{SOC} = (U_n - U) - b\pi \qquad [b]$$
$$W^{CB} = sal + (U_n - [U + k])^2 - b\pi^2 \qquad [c]$$

Equation [a] describes the natural rate hypothesis in terms of inflation. Thus, if inflation is higher than expected then, other things being equal, actual unemployment is lower than the natural rate. Equation [b] is society's welfare function (soc). Again, any inflation reduces social welfare. Finally, equation [c] is the welfare function of the central bank (CB), which is partly a function of the salary of the governor (sal). Notice that the central bank can tolerate a different level of unemployment than society (by an amount k assumed to be constant). The solution to the problem of maximizing welfare, when k cannot be zero, is the following (we leave the details as an exercise)

$$\pi = k/b \text{ and } U = U_n$$

which is simply the inflation bias result that was derived earlier (see equation [23.8]). Suppose, however, that to avoid the inflation bias, the governor of the central bank signs a performance contract that looks like the following:

$$sal = sal_0 - \lambda\pi \qquad [d]$$

where sal_0 is a base salary and λ is some fraction of inflation performance that reduces the governor's salary. The maximization problem in this case reduces to (again leaving the problem as an exercise)

$$\pi = (k - \lambda)/b, \ U = U_n \qquad [e]$$

Notice from equation [e] that as long as λ is greater than zero, inflation with a performance contract will be *lower* than without a contract, and the unemployment rate will not be the same. This fact is the essence of the proposal that central bank governors should sign performance contracts.

Questions for Discussion

1. What is a performance contract for a central banker meant to accomplish? Why is such a thing perhaps impractical?
2. Does the belief in a short-run Phillips curve play a role in arguing against a contract for central bankers?

Sources

C. Waller, "Performance Contracts for Central Bankers," *Review of the Federal Reserve Bank of Saint Louis* 77 (Sept/Oct 1995): 3–14.

C. Walsh, "Recent Central Bank Reforms and the Role of Price Stability as the Sole Objective of Monetary Policy," *NBER Macroeconomics Annual* 1995 (Cambridge, Mass.: The MIT Press, 1995): 237–52.

a consistent and predictable manner."[33] The idea is not a new one, since Nobel Laureate Milton Friedman advocated a fixed money growth rule to ensure stable inflation.

The latest incarnation of monetary policy rules proposes that central banks set interest rates according to the following equation:

$$R_t = \bar{\pi} + 0.5\,(\bar{\pi} - \pi^*) + 0.5\,(y_t - \bar{y}_t) + \bar{\rho} \qquad (23.2)$$

where $\bar{\pi}$ is the average inflation rate, π^* is a target for inflation (formal or informal), and $(y_t - \bar{y}_t)$ is the output gap, that is, the percentage difference between actual and potential real GDP. The coefficient 0.5 indicates that for a one unit (or percent) increase in desired or targeted inflation or the output gap, the central bank should respond by increasing the interest rate by 0.5%.

---

33 Allan H. Meltzer, "Commentary: The Role of Judgment and Discretion in the Conduct of Monetary Policy," in *Changing Capital Markets: Implications for Monetary Policy*, Federal Reserve Bank of Kansas City (1993): 223.

ECONOMICS FOCUS 23.3   WHY ZERO INFLATION?

In 1988, the then–new governor of the Bank of Canada, John Crow, proposed that the Bank's goal be zero inflation. "Monetary policy should be conducted as to achieve a pace of monetary expansion that promotes stability in the value of money. This means pursuing a policy aimed at achieving and maintaining stable prices," he said (*Bank of Canada Review* [February 1988]: 4).

The policy of zero inflation raised considerable comment both in the press and among academics. What are the benefits of zero inflation? Some academics contend that the certainty of future price level stability would be beneficial to the economy. Others argue that the biases in the measurement of prices (see Chapter 6) preclude zero inflation as a practical target. For Canada, estimates suggest that actual CPI inflation overstates the "true" inflation rate by a maximum of 0.5%. One recent estimate for the U.S. economy suggests the net benefits of a zero inflation environment are positive. Much of the debate centred not on whether zero inflation was desirable, but whether it was feasible. Lucas explained that regional diversity would make the zero inflation goal difficult to achieve in Canada. Moreover, he pointed out that the Bank of Canada has little credibility in reaching its stated goal. Johnson pointed out that there were fundamental inconsistencies between the federal government's fiscal policy, with its distinct bias toward inflation, and the Bank of Canada's professed desire to eliminate inflation entirely. So much debate was sparked by the Bank of Canada's objective that the C.D. Howe Institute sponsored two conferences and several volumes summarizing the various views on the subject, as did the Bank of Canada.

By the time former Finance Minister Michael Wilson brought down his budget in February 1991, however, the government had formally abandoned any pretence of wanting zero inflation, announcing objectives of 3% by the end of 1992 and 2% by 1995 in the core rate of inflation.

The core rate of inflation measures the rate of change in the consumer price index, excluding food and energy costs. One argument for this omission in evaluating the severity of inflation is that food and energy prices are significantly determined by aggregate supply considerations, which are determined by events such as bad weather, wars, or the oil price policies of OPEC (Organization of Petroleum Exporting Countries). Such costs cannot be influenced directly by the government's fiscal and monetary policies, which act on the aggregate demand side of the economy. The Bank of Canada argues, however, that the omission

is due to "the volatile nature of food and energy prices" (*Bank of Canada Review* [September 1991]: 3). Yet, it also says that "since 1979 they (food and energy prices) have exhibited no pronounced tendency to rise or fall on a sustained basis relative to prices of other goods and services" (*Bank of Canada Review* [September 1991]: 4).

Until the economy recovered from the recession, there was considerable controversy over the costs of reducing inflation. Some analysts, such as Pierre Fortin, argued that the Bank of Canada's "obsession" with low inflation triggered a sharp recession in the early 1990s. However, other analysts pointed out a number of flaws in Fortin's analysis.

Questions for Discussion

1. Should the Bank of Canada aim for zero or low inflation?
2. Does fiscal policy play a role in the inflation process?

Sources

Bank of Canada, *Price Stability, Inflation Targets and Monetary Policy*, Proceedings of a Conference held by the Bank of Canada (Ottawa, Ont.: Bank of Canada, 1997).

J.W. Crow, "The Work of Canadian Monetary Policy," *Bank of Canada Review* (February 1988): 3–17.

M. Feldstein, "The Costs and Benefits of Going from Low Inflation to Price Stability" NBER Working Paper 5469 (February 1996).

P. Fortin, "The Great Canadian Slump," *Canadian Journal of Economics* 29 (November 1996): 761–87.

C. Freedman, and T. Macklem, "A Comment on the Great Canadian Slump," *Canadian Journal of Economics* 31 (August 1998): 646–65.

D.R. Johnson, "An Evaluation of the Bank of Canada's Zero Inflation Target: Do Michael Wilson and John Crow Agree?" *Canadian Public Policy* 16 (December 1990): 308–25.

J. Konieczny, "The Optional Rate of Inflation: Competing Theories and Their Relevance to Canada," in *Economic Behaviour Policy Choice under Price Stability* (Ottawa: Bank of Canada, 1993): 1–40.

D.E.W. Laidler, *Where We Go From Here: Inflation Targets in Canada's Monetary Policy Regime* (Toronto: C.D. Howe Institute, 1997).

R.G. Lipsey, *Zero Inflation: The Goal of Price Stability* (Toronto: C.D. Howe Institute, 1990).

R.F. Lucas, "A Zero Inflation Target," *Canadian Public Policy* 15 (March 1990): 84–93.

Notice, therefore, that equation (23.2) assigns equal weight to the inflation and output GDP gaps, reflecting the belief that a central bank ought to be concerned not only about inflation but about the performance of the real economy as well. Finally, ρ is the average real interest rate.

Although the research so far on the viability of rules such as the one introduced in equation (23.2)—also known as Taylor's rule[34]—is promising, more research is needed. Why? Notice that Taylor's rule leaves out a role for monetary aggregates, or its desire to smooth interest rate fluctuations[35] and other pieces of information that might be relevant to an open economy such as Canada's.[36] Also, there is no way of directly observing the actual weights assigned to inflation or to the output gap by central bankers, nor does there appear to be any consensus on what they should be.

Figure 23.7 illustrates how Taylor's rule might operate in the Canadian context. We see that although policy was not as tight in the early 1980s, as Taylor's rule recommends, there is a long period, from about 1982 o 1996, when actual policy was almost always too tight, again relative to Taylor's rule. Nevertheless, the two curves agree fairly closely with each other, suggesting that such a rule might be a promising avenue for implementing monetary policy in the future.

Indeed, one might imagine equation (23.2) as being used to determine how much weight a particular central bank might place on inflation developments to the exclusion of all else. Lars Svensson, a well-known economist who studies central banks and how they practise policy, has pointed out that, in his opinion, and contrary to the views of some, no central bank cares only about

| **Figure 23.7** | **Taylor's Rule for Canada** |

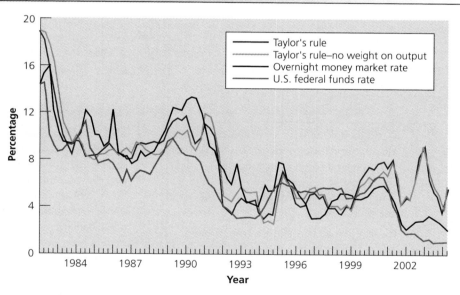

Taylor's rule is found by applying equation (23.2) when R is the overnight market interest rate, π is the four-quarter moving average of CPI inflation, π^* is 2%, as assumed by Taylor, and ρ is 3.5% (which is the assumption made about the real interest rate; see Chapter 5). The variable $(y_t - \bar{y}_t)$ is found by taking the percentage difference between the log of Canada's real GDP and an estimate of the trend of the log of the same series.

Source: Adapted from Statistics Canada, CANSIM II database **www.cansim2.statcan.ca/cgi-win/CNSMCGI.EXE**, series V1992067 (real GDP 1999$), V122514 [overnight money market rate (7 days)], V122150 (U.S. Federal funds rate), and V18702611 (CPI, 1992=100).

34 See J.B. Taylor, "Discretion versus Rules in Practice," *Carnegie-Rochester Conference on Public Policy* (December 1993): 1267–86.

35 As noted earlier, this practice may be central to how central banks actually conduct monetary policy. See S. Collins and P.L. Siklos, "Optimal Monetary Policy Rules and Inflation Targets: Are Australia, Canada, and New Zealand Different from the U.S?," *Open Economies Review*, 15 (October 2004): 347–62.

36 A less well-known version of equation (26.2), where the left-hand side is the growth rate of the monetary base (see Chapter 2), also exists and is called McCallum's rule.

inflation. In other words, no central bank practises "strict inflation targeting."[37] Such central banks, called "inflation nutters" by one of the deputy-governors of the Bank of England,[38] simply cannot describe how any monetary authority actually makes interest rate decisions. Interestingly, if one compares predictions from the Taylor rule where $(y_t - \bar{y}_t) = 0$ against the version shown in equation (23.2), there is little difference between them, suggesting that central banks don't really care about economic activity generally. However, this is misleading for two reasons. First, as discussed earlier, central banks change interest rates slowly and this is not captured in equation (23.2). Although there are many reasons for this kind of behaviour, one is that central banks do not want to rush to judgment about the impact of their decisions on overall economic growth. Second, it is easy to discuss in theory the concept of the output gap. However, in practice, it is very difficult to measure output. We saw this in Chapter 6 (**Economics Focus 6.2 Measuring Real GDP**). In addition, it is unclear how to measure potential GDP. Lastly, even if economists could agree on how to measure $(y_t - \bar{y}_t)$, the fact is that the required data come in slowly and are subject to several revisions. Therefore, since central banks have to make decisions in real time, there may be perfectly good reasons to underemphasize the output gap term, while underlining the fact that it is an important consideration in making decisions about what the stance of monetary policy ought to be at any given moment.[39] Instead, it is likely that central banks in the industrial world practise a form of "flexible inflation targeting," a policy that recognizes that a central bank that is democratically accountable to its citizens must also be sensitive to overall economic performance, not just the rate of inflation.

Finally, Figure 23.7 also shows the evolution of the U.S. Fed funds rate to illustrate the fact that, although U.S. and Canadian interest rates broadly move together, the relationship is not a lock-step one. We can thank the system of floating exchange rates for that.

SUMMARY

- Central banking is an art because it requires the manipulation of instruments to achieve multiple and sometimes conflicting targets, and because it requires central bankers to fend off interference from politicians and the public.

- Central banks can choose from a menu of instruments, such as open market operations, SPRAs, and the manipulation of the bank rate. The aim is to achieve an intermediate target, such as steady interest rates, that is closely related to some final target, such as low inflation and unemployment.

- This chapter presents a simple model according to which the central bank must choose manipulation of either a monetary aggregate or an interest rate as its instrument. The one that is not the tool becomes the intermediate target. The better instrument depends on whether the central bank prefers interest rate variability over money supply variability.

- Central banks today prefer an interest rate instrument because they tend to prefer interest rate stability over stability in the growth of some monetary aggregate.

---

37 L.E.O. Svensson, "Inflation Targeting in an Open Economy: Strict or Flexible Inflation Targeting," Public lecture held at the Victoria University of Wellington, New Zealand, *Victoria Economic Commentaries*, 15(1) (March 1998).

38 M. King, "Changes in UK Monetary Policy: Rules, Discretion in Practice," *Journal of Monetary Economics* 39 (June 1999): 81–97.

39 As a result, what appear to have been bad monetary policy decisions turn out to have been based on faulty GDP data. Hence, central banks have been stressing the need to focus on other indicators that give a relatively more reliable assessment of GDP performance, while remaining keenly aware of the importance of real economic performance in setting interest rates. See A. Orphanides and S. van Norden "The Unreliability of Output-Gap Estimates in Real Time," *Review of Economics and Statistics* 84 (November 2002): 569-83; and A. Orphanides. "Monetary Policy Rules Based on Real Time Data," *American Economic Review* 91 (September 2001): 964-85.

- In Canada, the interest rate on overnight loans is the principal instrument of monetary policy.

- An alternative way of interpreting the study of monetary policy in an open economy such as Canada's is to monitor the Monetary Conditions Index (MCI). The MCI is a weighted average of interest rates and exchange rates.

- A rise in the MCI signals tighter monetary policy, while a fall means looser monetary policy. A problem of interpretation arises with the MCI because it is an index. Therefore, tightness or looseness of policy is relative to the chosen base period, which may or may not always be appropriate.

- Many economists believe that key goals of monetary policy, such as inflation, output, unemployment, or the exchange rate, are subject to political influence and result in political business cycles.

- A topic of considerable interest and importance is how much independent action a central bank should be permitted. There appears to be a connection between inflation, economic performance, and the degree to which a central bank is statutorily independent.

- Attempts to evaluate central bank independence follow two distinct lines: Some believe there is a connection between inflation and the statutory relationship between a central bank and government; others examine how key economic variables such as inflation and unemployment interact with interest rate developments. The latter approach is called the reaction function approach.

- Although central banks around the world have become more independent, they have obtained their additional responsibilities by becoming more accountable to government and to the public, as well as more transparent about their operations.

- Central banks nowadays seem to follow a rule of sorts in setting interest rates known as Taylor's rule.

- Taylor's rule suggests that central banks respond to inflation and output developments and try to keep real interest rates more or less constant.

- The lessons from applying Taylor's rule are as follows: good monetary policy means that real interest rates will rise temporarily to dampen inflation expectations; bad monetary policy means allowing the real interest rates to fall when inflation rises.

IMPORTANT TERMS

PROBLEMS

1. Assume that the money supply curve is perfectly inelastic and subject to complete control by the central bank. Draw the appropriate liquidity preference diagram. Would interest rate stability disappear? What about money supply instability? Why?

2. True, false, or uncertain: The more elastic the demand for money, the greater the variability of equilibrium money supply fluctuations when interest rate pegging is in effect. Illustrate, using a liquidity preference diagram, and explain your answer.

3. Figure 23.4 illustrates a case in which interest rate control is the best instrument. Use a similar diagram to illustrate a case in which the best instrument is one that relies on money supply control.

4. Suppose the Bank of Canada wants to minimize interest rate variability. What is the best instrument of monetary policy? Illustrate, using a diagram, and explain.

5. Using Figure 23.3(A), show how tighter money supply control reduces interest rate variability.

6. Using Figure 23.3(B), show how greater money demand uncertainty increases interest rate variability.

7. Explain, using interest rate parity arguments, why interest rate developments shown in Figure 23.4 are consistent with the Bank of Canada not targeting the exchange rate.

8. Explain how a rise in the MCI signals tighter monetary policy.

9. What would Taylor's rule look like if:

    (a) the central bank did not care about the output gap

    (b) the central bank did not care about inflation

10. Suppose desired inflation is 2%, average inflation is 4%, and the real interest rate is 3%. Using equation (23.2), what is the interest rate when the output gap is +2%? −2%?

11. In the above question, suppose that the interest rate is 6% when the output gap is −2% and 8% when the output gap is +2%. What is the central bank's desired inflation rate in each case?

12. Draw a diagram with the interest rate on the vertical axis and inflation on the horizontal axis. Use a curve to illustrate the following cases:

    (a) a central bank that is neutral with respect to the real interest rate

    (b) a central bank that is aggressively raising interest rates in the face of higher inflation

    (c) a central bank that responds softly to an increase in inflation in terms of its interest-rate-setting behaviour

DISCUSSION QUESTIONS

1. Give an example and explain why there may be conflict between

    (a) intermediate targets

    (b) final targets

2. Do you think that the financial innovations of the past decade have made monetary policy more or less controllable by the Bank of Canada? Explain your answer. (Hint: See Chapter 4.)

3. What are the disadvantages of having a central bank satisfy multiple final targets? To whom are they disadvantages? Could these disadvantages be advantages to others? Explain your answer.

4. Discuss the pros and cons of achieving monetary stability and interest rate stability.

5. Why do you think politicians would rely less on monetary policy under fixed exchange rates than under flexible exchange rates? (Hint: See Chapter 8.)

6. What is meant by the term *central bank autonomy*?

7. Is the connection between inflation in the countries depicted in Figure 23.6 and the rankings in Table 23.1 a close one? Why or why not?

8. What is the difference between goal independence and instrument independence?

9. Why have several countries come to conclude that central banks should target inflation?

10. Central banks have come to fear a loss of control over monetary policy in recent years. Why?

11. Why might using an inflation forecast as an intermediate target be inappropriate? Explain.

12. Why do central bankers find it difficult to change interest rates frequently? Explain.

13. Explain how the public's or financial markets' attitudes toward inflation might limit the central bank's ability to generate inflation. What might be the source of their dislike of inflation?

14. Explain why granting more central bank autonomy gives rise to a demand for greater accountability and transparency from the central bank.

15. Would you agree that the developments listed in Table 23.2 are consistent with the Bank of Canada becoming more accountable and transparent? Give an example of each and explain how the objectives of greater accountability and transparency are met.

ONLINE APPLICATION

Go to the Bank of Canada's Web site at **www.bankofcanada.ca/en**. Click on *Research and Publications*, and then on *General Publications*. Find the *Weekly Financial Statistics* and find the data for the MCI. Interpret the movements in the MCI. What does the Bank of Canada have to say about the behaviour of this index? Check out earlier editions (prior to 2004) of the *Monetary Policy Report* and examine the Bank's discussion about MCI movements.

CANSIM QUESTION

1. Go to the CANSIM Web site and download the data series listed in Figure 23.7. Try to recreate the figure using the assumptions listed in the caption to the figure. Remember that to calculate the output gap, you need to take the logarithm of real GDP. For trend real GDP, assume that it grows 3.5% per year from the fourth quarter of 1979. What if trend real GDP grows at 2.5%?

2. Go to the CANSIM Web site and download the following series: the seasonally adjusted unemployment rate (V2062856), the Bank Rate (V39078), and the U.S.–Canadian dollar exchange rate (V37426). Download the data at the quarterly frequency, using data averaged over the quarter. Next, obtain election dates from the Elections Canada Web site **http://www.elections.ca/home.asp?textonly=false**. Plot the series and indicate the election dates and whether a Liberal or a Conservative won the election. Is an electoral cycle apparent? Is a partisan cycle apparent?

References can be found on **www.mcgrawhill.ca/college/siklos**

International Banking and Financial Institutions

International Banking

LEARNING OBJECTIVES

After reading and studying this chapter, you should be able to

24.1 describe how international banking activities and their regulations have evolved

24.2 discuss the history and evolution of the Eurocurrency market and analyze how its presence affects a typical bank's balance sheet

24.3 describe the essentials of international banking regulations

24.4 list the major developments in the area of risk, especially international debt crises

24.5 identify the essentials of how country risk is determined

We cannot study the financial system of our own country in isolation from the financial activities of the rest of the world. It is essential to know about the financial systems of other major countries, about globalized financial markets and the kinds of problems that arise there, and about some of the international finance institutions at work in the world (some of this material is dealt with in Chapter 26).

International banking can mean two things. It can refer to Canadian banks operating abroad or to foreign banks operating in Canada. Since regulations and risk considerations are influenced by the location where the banking is conducted, both forms of international banking are interesting subjects.

In this chapter, we examine a variety of topics: the growth of international banking and financial centres; the Eurodollar market; the international debt crisis and the growing importance of country risk; and attempts to create a global system of financial regulations.

This disparate information will provide a good background for the following chapters in this part, which discuss the U.S. financial system and several institutional approaches to international financial cooperation.

24.1 INTERNATIONAL BANKS AND FINANCIAL CENTRES

International trade has grown tremendously, especially since the end of World War II. Because traded goods and services must be paid for, there is a need for facilities and institutions that can handle international transactions. They are also needed to handle capital flows, which have exploded as *capital controls* (barriers to international capital investments) have been removed worldwide.

To the extent that banks[1] have international sections, operate offices in other countries, or have branches or subsidiaries outside their home country, they can be considered international banks. The internationalization of the world's banking sector is considerable.

Table 24.1 lists the 10 largest banks in the world. U.S. and Japanese banks dominate. Only a few years ago, Japanese banks dominated the rankings to a far greater extent.[2] However, the severe recession of the 1980s, the development of more stringent capital requirement rules (see Chapter 11 and later in this chapter), together with the wave of consolidation in U.S. banking combined to reduce the relative size of Japanese banks. Much international banking—international lending and borrowing, interbanking operations, and foreign currency transactions—is conducted in **international financial centres**, cities that have become convergence points for such activity. Such centres possess advantages such as geographical location, an expert labour force to draw on, and a stable political and economic environment. One study also suggests that banking centres persist or are successful the lower the inflation rate is in that country, the more financially developed it is, and the fewer the restrictions on reserve requirements.[3] Government encouragement is also now a consideration. Nevertheless, the forces of globalization appear to be strong enough that in a small cross-section of advanced industrial countries (including Canada) there is no apparent evidence of a "home field advantage" when it comes to banking.[4]

London, New York, and Tokyo are the prime international banking centres: London because it has long been a centre for the gold market and because it is where the Euromarket was born; New York because it is the financial capital of the United States, the dominant economic power since the end of World War II. Recently, they have been challenged by Frankfurt, the banking centre of a reunified country at the heart of a united Europe.[5] Zurich is also important because of Swiss expertise in banking matters. Much lending also originates in London, which continues to retain its status as the world's largest banking centre.

Some of the growth of the other centres has been at the expense of New York and London. New (and in some cases very small) countries have also been entering the game, in large part be-

Keep track of the world's largest banks at **www.thebanker. com**

Table 24.1   The World's Largest Banks, 2004

Rank[a]	Name	Country
1	Citigroup	United States
2	Credit Agricole	France
3	HSBC Holdings	United Kingdom
4	Bank of America	United States
5	J.P. Morgan-Chase	United States
6	Mizuho Fin. Group	Japan
7	Mitsubishi Tokyo Financial Group	Japan
8	Royal Bank of Scotland	United Kingdom
9	Sumitomo Mitsui Financial Group	Japan
10	BNP Paribas	France

Source: *The Banker* (July 2004).

[a] According to Tier One Capital (defined in Chapter 11). Ranking is based on capital in billions of U.S. dollars.

---

1 Unless otherwise stated, we deal in this chapter with banks, not with other financial institutions with an international dimension, such as those that assist export financing or are creatures of international government actions (for example, the International Monetary Fund and the International Bank for Reconstruction and Development, which are described in Chapter 26). For Canada, this approach means focusing on the chartered banks, since the trust companies generally do not operate abroad.

2 For example, in a previous edition of this textbook, the top six banks in 1995 were all Japanese.

3 See J. Eaton, "Cross-Border Banking," in Blejer et al. (Eds), *Financial Factors in Economic Stabilization and Growth* (Cambridge: Cambridge University Press, 1996): 140–174.

4 See A.N. Berger, R. Deyong, H. Genay, and G.F. Udell, "Globalization of Financial Institutions: Evidence from Cross-Border Banking Performance," *Brookings-Wharton Papers on Financial Services* (2000): 23–125.

5 And a city in which the cost of living is relatively low.

cause U.S. financial regulations have not kept pace with international financial developments. Thus, several hundred banks have offices in the Cayman Islands, where there are no taxes, no reserve requirements, no waiting periods before corporations can issue bonds, and where secrecy provisions exist, which, like those of Switzerland, protect clients from indirect supervision of their activities by other countries.

The IMF (see Chapter 26) too has begun to pay more attention to the activities of these institutions since they may impact domestic and international financial stability, and because of the money laundering questions that have come to the fore since the September 11, 2001 terrorist attacks in the U.S.[6]

It comes as no surprise that many governments give cities preferential treatment[7] for organizing **offshore banking centres** (also referred to as international financial centres)—international banking facilities that cater to nonresidents. Indeed, countries such as the Cayman Islands, Luxembourg, Hong Kong, and the Bahamas are perhaps best known as tax and regulatory havens for banks.

Canadian chartered banks have long had an international presence. By the late nineteenth century, they had operations in various cities in the United States, Great Britain, and the Caribbean. In addition, Canadian banks have a wide network of correspondent arrangements in countries or cities where they have no other official representation. (A *correspondent bank* handles another bank's affairs in a jurisdiction where the latter has no legal standing.) And since the proclamation of the 1980 *Bank Act*, various foreign banks have opened chartered banks in Canada.

We have already discussed (Chapter 8) the fact that prices in different countries can be understood only with the help of the concept of the exchange rate. Here we consider how international transactions have given rise to new types of financial instruments and the risks associated with their usage.

The growth of international banking has been facilitated by deregulation, which has permitted capital to flow freely across countries.

For a list of some important OBCs and their characteristics go to **www.imf.org/ external/ns/ cs.aspx?id=55**

24.2 THE EUROCURRENCY MARKET

Eurocurrencies are an excellent example of the way international banking has been innovative in meeting the explosive growth of international transactions and avoiding the domestic banking regulations of many countries.

SOME HISTORY

The word *Eurocurrency* is a generic term, denoting a financial instrument deposited or traded in a currency other than the domestic currency of the country in which the transaction takes place. As noted in Chapter 4, a common synonym is *Eurodollar*, a term that goes back to the origin of the market shortly after World War II.[8] World trade was resuming, but the Cold War was setting in. The countries of the Soviet bloc, fearing that the United States would seize their dollars or otherwise make them worthless, deposited their U.S. dollars in London. It quickly became apparent that these deposits, which were not subject to legal restrictions or reserve

---

6 For more information see **www.imf.org/external/np/mae/oshore/2000/eng/back.htm**.

7 In the 1980s, Canada was tempted to develop an international banking centre. It was originally intended to be located in Montreal, but political considerations led to Toronto and Vancouver being awarded rights to develop such centres, too. Although Montreal has fared well in persuading a variety of institutions to open international financial centres—59 were established in Montreal as of the beginning of 2000—it is unlikely that Montreal will achieve the scale of London or New York.

8 The practice of borrowing and lending in the foreign-denominated currency did exist earlier in the century, but it was considered a temporary device to, say, help local businesses build their international trading activities.

Daily interest rate information is published by the *Financial Times* of London at **www.ft.com**

requirements, were a ready source of the world's foremost currency. The initial growth of Eurodollars was great, and it was then much assisted by special taxes introduced in the United States during the 1960s. First, in 1963, U.S. purchases of foreign securities were taxed. Next, the tax was extended in 1965 to loans made by U.S. banks and foreign financial institutions to foreign borrowers. Finally, a quota-type system was instituted in 1965 to control bank loans to multinational corporations. Not surprisingly, all these moves gave financial institutions a great incentive to operate outside the United States but to continue to transact in U.S. funds. The number and size of Eurodollars exploded. Similar foreign deposits soon emerged in many of the major currencies, with the most prominent being Euromarks, Euroswiss francs, Europounds, and, more recently, Euroyen.

The number of Euro-type financial instruments has declined. The introduction of the euro in 1999 fixed exchange rates irrevocably among the 12 countries that now form the European Monetary Union (EMU) (see Chapter 26). Although the individual currencies continued to circulate until 2002, interest rates were already quoted in euros.

The main centre for Euromarket trading continues to be London (there is also significant activity in New York and Tokyo), and the basic interest rate is the **London interbank offer rate** (**LIBOR**), which is the interest rate large commercial banks charge each other for loans in the United Kingdom. Departures from it are a function of the riskiness and liquidity of the instrument in question. Because of the uncertainty associated with whether the host country will act as a lender of last resort in Eurocurrencies, the rates tend to be slightly higher than for instruments issued domestically by a particular bank.

Actually, many different LIBORs exist depending on the currency and the maturity of the instrument in question. Rates are published daily in the *Financial Times* of London. LIBOR is generally the term used to refer to the interest rate on Eurocurrencies regardless of whether or not the market in question is in London.

THE CREATION OF EUROCURRENCY

The size of the Euromarket, although exceedingly difficult to estimate with precision, is believed to exceed several trillion dollars U.S. Its existence enhances worldwide liquidity.

To see how a unit of Eurocurrency is created, consider the T-accounts in Table 24.2. Suppose the client of a Canadian bank transfers $100 million from its branch in Halifax to a Eurobank (which could be a subsidiary of the Canadian chartered bank or some unaffiliated institution). The liabilities of the Canadian bank are not altered; it records a drop of $100 million in Canadian-dollar deposits, but a $100 million rise in its Eurodeposits. If the same reserves hold against both types of deposits, there will be no repercussions in the Canadian financial system. But the Eurobank has experienced an increase of $100 million in Canadian currency, which is now available to be loaned out to borrowers interested in obtaining Canadian dollars. Moreover, since no country im-

| Table 24.2 | The Creation of Eurocurrency: A Simplified Example |

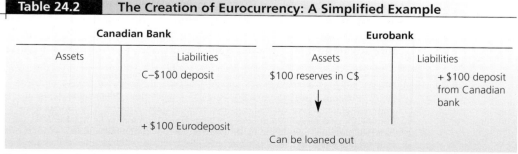

The client of a Canadian chartered bank transfers $100 million from an account in Canada to a Eurobank. The liabilities of the Canadian bank are unaffected, but $100 million in Euro-Canadian dollars has now been created.

poses reserve requirements on Eurocurrency deposits, the Eurobank is free to create additional deposits through *multiple expansion* (see Chapter 17).

International banking and Eurocurrency issues are covered at **www.euromoney. com**

IS IT SAFE?

Despite the liquidity Eurocurrencies have introduced to worldwide financial markets, they are not without danger, at least in theory. All those units of currency that exist abroad have the potential to be returned if foreigners who hold them decide to exchange them for their home currency or some other preferred currency. Just imagine what billions of U.S. dollars returned to the United States would do to the U.S. inflation rate! Canada could face a similar problem. So far, such worries have proven to be unfounded, since trading in different currencies is vital to international trade and finance.

24.3 INTERNATIONAL BANKING REGULATIONS

As the growth of the Eurocurrencies suggests, borrowing and lending, which used to be primarily domestic matters, have become more international in nature. Unfortunately, international banking offers not only great benefits, but also the possibility of great losses and scandal. And, unlike other economic endeavours, banking is regulated solely at the domestic level. The only international supervision comes from the voluntary participation of mostly industrial countries in the Bank for International Settlements' capital adequacy standards (see Chapters 11 and 26). However, no international set of rules exists with sanctions (from government bodies) that apply to all international banks.

At the centre of this difficulty is a problem called **national treatment**, which means that an organization (or individual) is subject to the laws of whatever country it is in. A bank branch or subsidiary located in, say, Canada, is regulated under Canadian law, although the parent is regulated by the laws of the home country. Similarly, a Canadian bank abroad must obey the banking laws that prevail in the country in which it operates. This system has enabled banks to exploit weaknesses in the regulations of a foreign country and to play the laws of one country against another. Thus, a bank can avoid national supervision in the United States by registering so that it is regulated by one or several states instead of by the Federal Reserve System. (But manipulation of regulatory structures has also enabled the banks to open up new markets, as in the development of the Eurocurrencies.)

Another problem is what we might call the structural changes in the financial industry since the 1970s. Thirty years ago, international lending was the almost exclusive preserve of banks, in part because domestic laws protected and favoured them. Today, myriad international agencies and investment bankers act as agents or intermediaries, forming syndicates that arrange international loans. Combined with the removal of capital controls in all Western industrialized countries by the end of the 1980s, the concept of an international money market permits the transfer of surplus funds from a country with surplus funds to one with a deficit. The banks no longer possess comparative advantage, natural or regulatory, over other financial market participants.

However, the wave of deregulation that swept the financial world over the last two decades of the twentieth century created problems because it was neither coordinated nor consistent across jurisdictions. For example, although restrictions on financial services practically disappeared in Britain and were substantially reduced in Canada during the 1980s, change lagged considerably in Japan and especially in the United States. Moreover, the world still has more than one model of a banking system. There is the **universal banking model**, in which underwriting is not a barrier to lending activities, unlike the model used in Canada and, until 1999, in the United States in which it is presumed that a bank holding an equity interest in firms to which it is making loans signals a conflict of interest. Some countries, even some federal countries, have

FINANCIAL FOCUS 24.1 — THE BANK OF CROOKS AND CRIMINALS INTERNATIONAL

The Bank of Credit and Commerce International (BCCI) did business in seven countries. Although supervisory agencies in at least a half dozen countries suspected fraud, there was little indication of its international scale until July 1991. One of the reasons for the delay in coordinated international legal action against BCCI was the absence of effective international supervision.

Considerable evidence now exists that a combination of bad management and fraud originated in BCCI's home base in Abu Dhabi. Illegal activities ranged from manipulating accounts to covering losses in stock trading to acting as a conduit for illegal payments by intelligence agencies such as the U.S. Central Intelligence Agency.

BCCI is not the first bank to exploit regulatory gaps arising out of the national treatment principle. In the 1980s the Vatican's banker, Banco Ambrosiano, was charged with fraud and illegal activities.

In every banking scandal of international scale, the common element has been the absence of international enforcement mechanisms and regulatory inconsistencies across countries. Thus, when BCCI engaged in an activity that one country found distasteful, little could be done because each country jealously guards its national sovereignty over financial regulatory matters.

Thus, for example, the Bank of England apparently refused to give crucial information to U.S. regulators.

Questions for Discussion
1. What are potential difficulties in developing global rules for bank behaviour?
2. Did it make a difference in the BCCI case that its home base was not in one of the industrial countries?

Sources
Lord Justice Bingham, *Inquiry into the Supervision of the Bank of Credit and Commerce International* (Her Majesty's Stationery Office, 1992).

J. Kerry, and H. Brown (Senators), "The BCCI Affair," available at **www.fas.org/irp/congress/1992_rpt/bcci/index.html**.

R. Thomson, *Apocalypse Roulette* (London: MacMillan, 1998).

---

a unitary system in which all financial institutions are regulated by a single jurisdiction; other countries have a **dual banking system** in which two jurisdictions have authority over the banking system. A variety of other differences in banking regulations create even more discrepancies.

Not surprisingly, many interested parties have proposed international regulation of banking. But that prospect raises almost as many questions as answers. Who would provide deposit insurance against a failure involving an international bank? Indeed, who would dispose of the assets of a failed international bank? Who would ensure that the goal of competition in the financial markets was achieved? Finally, given the variety of ways in which banks are regulated in different countries, how would an international harmonization take place?

The G-20 Web site
**www.g20.org
index.htm**

Nevertheless, there are signs of attempts at a form of convergence in international banking regulations. The trend is toward the universal banking model, as the recent U.S. reforms suggest (see the next chapter). An interesting development in this respect comes from the New Zealand experience. Much of the banking sector there is in foreign hands, with Australian ownership especially high. The governor of the Reserve Bank of New Zealand has recently suggested that, as a consequence, it is vital that a high degree of harmonization in banking rules and supervision between Australia and New Zealand be created.[9] Since such discussions are dependent on the cooperation of Australian authorities, one can perhaps understand, in spite of the apparent advantages that Australian banks have brought to the New Zealand economy, why authorities in Canada and elsewhere might be reluctant to permit large-scale foreign bank ownership in Canada. At the banking level, efforts are being spearheaded by the Bank for International Settlements (see Chapters 11 and 26); at the macroeconomic level, attempts at limiting the economic damage resulting from widespread bank failures are being led in part by the International Monetary Fund (Chapter 24). In 1999,

---

9 See A. Bollard "Enhancing our Trans-Tasman Banking Policy Harmonization," 23 March 2005, speech delivered to the Australasian Institute of Banking and Finance, available at **http://www.rbnz.govt.nz/speeches/1522447.html**.

the finance ministers of the G-7 created the G-20, a group of finance ministers and central bank governors from 19 countries, to promote international financial stability. Then-finance minister of Canada, Paul Martin, was selected as its first chair.[10]

The Asian crisis of 1997–98 revealed that banks in countries most vulnerable to weakly regulated banking systems have not, for the most part, adhered to the standards of the BIS, nor are their operations as transparent as those in, say, Canada. Moreover, businesses and banks in the local economies had little incentive to manage risks because it was usually assumed that Asian governments would back any claims, a clear expression of the moral hazard problem discussed in Chapter 16. Making the situation worse was the fact that almost two-thirds of the loans were short-term (a year or less). U.S. and Canadian banks escaped relatively unscathed since only about 5% and 13.1% of capital in the form of claims on Asian clients were booked in U.S. or Canadian banks, respectively.[11]

Beyond regulatory and supervisory issues is the role of tradition and culture in banking and financial services. Thus, in Europe for example, bank lending is more common than in North America, where corporate bonds and other forms of nonbank lending activities have developed far more quickly. Nevertheless, this is changing as technology forces convergence of banking functions across the globe and enhances the opportunities for alternative providers of financial products. Consequently, the philosophy that banks are a source of one-stop shopping is rapidly disappearing, leading traditional banks, including ones in Canada, to branch out into different fields in an attempt to keep up with financial market developments.

Another force for change is the perception that a "home field advantage" of sorts exists in banking: Domestic banks are relatively more efficient at home than are their foreign bank competitors. As noted earlier, recent evidence, however, suggests that the advantage is disappearing. One potential benefit of globalization is the provision of more efficient financial services worldwide. But this serves only to underscore the importance of international financial regulations.

24.4 THE INTERNATIONAL DEBT CRISIS

The consequences of unregulated banking activities on international lending can be disastrous for entire nations. One example is the international debt crisis. It has been going on since the early 1980s, when several countries could not afford to repay the interest or principal or both on their foreign debt obligations.[12] The best-known cases were in Central and South America, though loans made to several other countries also became "nonperforming."

The international debt crisis had its origins in the oil price shocks of the 1970s.[13] Countries that were net importers of oil had to either reduce citizens' standards of living or maintain aggregate via the accumulation of debt. The dramatic rise in foreign debt was assisted, at first, by low real interest rates. Indeed, we have already seen in Chapter 5, that *ex post* real interest rates were sometimes negative! No wonder banks like to lend to developing countries. First, as the saying goes, countries never go bankrupt. Second, there was the prospect of economic growth, which, combined with low interest rates, meant favourable conditions for borrowing. Few developing countries avoided

---

10 The G-20 consists of: Argentina, Australia, Brazil, Canada, France, Germany, India, Indonesia, Italy, Japan, Mexico, China, Russia, Saudi Arabia, South Africa, South Korea, Turkey, United Kingdom, the United States, and the European Union. The current chair is the finance minister from China. In 2006, Australia will take the chair.

11 See Basel Committee on Banking Supervision, "Supervisory Lessons to be Drawn from the Asian Crisis," working paper no. 2, June 1999 (Basel: Switzerland).

12 The international debt crisis is not a new phenomenon. Indeed, the current crisis has striking parallels with experiences during the nineteenth century and the first half of the twentieth century. Moreover, the concept of a grandiose plan to rescue overindebted countries (see below) is not new. (Indeed, some of the international institutions we examine in Chapter 24 were created to manage global debt problems of the past.) Many of these plans, like those of today, experienced relatively few successes.

13 Indeed, the true origins may have been in the inflation of the late 1960s. The monetary expansion that preceded that inflation meant that a considerable amount of liquidity was available for international lending by Western banks.

the attractive temptation of debt. Even oil-exporting countries, such as Mexico, were not entirely spared, particularly those that wished to raise their standards of living quickly. Despite the bonanza of increasing revenues from oil exports, the costs of raising the standard of living eventually led to the accumulation of foreign debt. The situation worsened when oil prices began to fall sharply in the latter part of the 1980s; these countries were now saddled with high debt and lowered revenues from their oil exports.

Some people believe that the banks of the Western industrialized world pushed the Third World nations at this time, encouraging them to take on foreign debt.[14] Others think they were simply behaving in a normal, profit-seeking manner.

Certainly the banks of the West either ignored or did not foresee the potential credit risk in loans to developing nations. Few warnings were sounded, even when real interest rates began to rise sharply in the industrialized world as these countries, including Canada, pursued a high interest rate policy designed to eliminate inflation. Thus, the crisis erupted suddenly in 1980 and 1981. The high real interest rates of the time were simply too great to be financed by developing countries' economic growth. Hence, countries such as Argentina, Bolivia, Brazil, Mexico, the Philippines, and Turkey, among others, could not maintain their payments.

By the mid-1980s, some had negotiated with the banks and international agencies for debt-rescheduling arrangements, which often included stringent conditions for revamping their economies.

One result of the crisis was that Western banks began swapping the debt of one country for that of another. Bankers differed in their perceptions of the likelihood of payment, so, for example, a bank with Mexican debt on its books would trade with a bank that held Chilean debt. By the mid-1980s, a secondary market for developing countries' debt existed. Interestingly, the creation of this market permitted a country to back its own debt at a substantial discount.[15]

That prices for debt in secondary markets began to rise quickly by early 1990 was in part a measure of how substantially lower interest rates and the worldwide economic boom of the 1980s helped countries service their debt.[16]

Fears of another international debt crisis emerged during the winter of 1994 when the Mexican peso devaluation led to massive outflows of capital from that country (see Chapter 8). An international consortium of central banks was formed and international cooperation among several governments, including Canada, attempted to prevent another crisis from taking place in 1995.

During the remainder of the 1990s, as financial liberalization continued unabated, capital flowed in vast amounts to Asian economies where relatively higher yields and lower risk were promised. This flow was accomplished through a combination of pegged exchange rates and an environment in which default was unlikely because of the belief that governments would bail out banks and businesses that might fail. When the crisis erupted in 1997, no amount of foreign exchange intervention could sustain the pegged exchange rate. Therefore, exchange rates collapsed in the crisis countries of Korea, Indonesia, Malaysia, the Philippines, and Thailand.

---

14 Certainly, even countries that had previously defaulted on loans were able to borrow fairly easily during the 1970s and 1980s. This granting of credit may not, however, have been greediness or myopia on the part of bankers, but rather a recognition of the fact that the likelihood of defaulting on a loan is determined primarily by current creditworthiness, not past behaviour. Moreover, it appears that previously defaulting countries could borrow only at relatively high rates. See S. Osler, "Have Commercial Banks Ignored History?" *American Economic Review* 83 (June 1993): 608–20.

15 By the end of 1990, prices in the secondary market for debt ranged from 10% to 70% of face value. It appears that the size of the discount is a negative function of the size of the debt outstanding and that this is a byproduct of deposit insurance and its attendant problems. See S. Osler, and H. Huizinga, "Bank Finance, Capital and Secondary Market Discounts on Developing Country Debt," NBER Working Paper 3961 (January 1992).

16 Some people think a rising price in secondary markets signals the economic prospects of the country in question. Unfortunately, research suggests that this may not be the case. Instead, it may be that some banks benefit at the expense of others when secondary market prices change. On this and related issues, see the articles in the *Journal of Economic Perspectives* (Winter 1990).

ECONOMICS FOCUS 24.1   ARE CRISES CONTAGIOUS?

Various financial crises during the 1990s, such as the Russian and Asian financial crises, appear to have spread on a global scale. For example, although some believe that the Asian crisis of 1997-1998 began in Thailand, an economically small country, its effects were felt in even the largest economies such as the United States and even Canada. This suggests that financial crises can spread across borders. Whether increased economic interdependence across the world over the past two decades is to blame is unclear since, as this text has pointed out on a number of occasions, globalization is not an entirely new phenomenon. Like economic activity, globalization has known cycles. Moreover, we also studied, in Chapter 8, how economic shocks can spread across countries when their exchange rates are fixed or pegged. This explains, in part, why Thailand's crisis spread first throughout much of Asia before worrying policymakers elsewhere. Another example, which we consider in more detail in Chapter 26, is the exchange rate crisis in Europe in 1992. These examples illustrate the role of policy or macroeconomic factors; not to be forgotten is the possibility of the spread of financial crises facilitated by the globalization in banking (see **Economics Focus 24.2 – What Causes International Financial Crises?**), a microeconomic phenomenon.

As a result of these developments, economists have become keenly interested in measuring contagion effects. Essentially, this amounts to asking whether an economic "flu" in one country can spread to other countries, just like the human variety of flu (and the policies necessary to "immunize" against such flus). Not surprisingly, it is difficult to separate cause from effect because correlation—the concept discussed in Chapter 13—does not imply causation. Moreover, studies of individual episodes, although they identify a few obvious common factors, such as bad economic policies (for example, high inflation, large deficits, and government debt), have come up with a large number of potential factors that can enhance or stop the spread of a financial crisis beyond one country's borders. Although a significant amount of research continues to be devoted to the topic, there will likely be more to come since the profession has not yet reached anything like a consensus.

Questions for Discussion
1. How would you define *contagion*?
2. To what extent can globalization as opposed to other factors enhance the likelihood of contagion effects?

Sources

Forbes, Kristin J., and Rigobon, Roberto, "No Contagion, Only Interdependence: Measuring Stock Market Comovements," *Journal of Finance*, 57 (5) (October 2002): 2223-61.

Fratzscher, Marcel, "On Currency Crises and Contagion," *International Journal of Finance and Economics*, 8 (2) (April 2003): 109-29.

Hartmann, P., Straetmans, S., and de Vries, C.G., "Asset Market Linkages in Crisis Periods," *Review of Economics and Statistics*, 86 (1) (February 2004): 313-26.

Kaminsky, Graciela L., Reinhart, Carmen M., and Vegh, Carlos, A., "The Unholy Trinity of Financial Contagion," *Journal of Economic Perspectives*, 17 (4) (Fall 2003): 51-74.

Karolyi, G. Andrew, "Does International Financial Contagion Really Exist?" *International Finance*, 6 (2) (Summer 2003): 179-99.

Moser, Thomas, "What Is International Financial Contagion?" *International Finance*, 6 (2) (Summer 2003): 157-78.

Pericoli, Marcello, and Sbracia, Massimo, "A Primer on Financial Contagion," *Journal of Economic Surveys*, 17 (4) (September 2003): 571-608.

Rigobon, Roberto, "On the Measurement of the International Propagation of Shocks: Is the Transmission Stable?" *Journal of International Economics*, 61 (2) (December 2003): 261-83.

Tai, Chu-Sheng, "Can Bank Be a Source of Contagion during the 1997 Asian Crisis?" *Journal of Banking and Finance*, 28 (2) Special Issue (Feb.2004): 399-421.

Keep up with news about financial crises and the international financial systems at **www.stern.nyu. edu/globalmacro**

HOW A DEBT CRISIS CAN AFFECT A BANK

So far we have concentrated on the impact of a debt crisis on borrowing countries. But most of the lenders were the commercial banks of industrialized countries, and they too faced disaster; several Canadian banks were, at one time, exposed to significant losses from loans to developing countries.

The impact of a default on a loan made to a country is similar to the impact of a loan default by an individual or private institution, and indeed is similar to the impact of any loss experienced by a bank (perhaps because of rising interest rates or a fall in real estate values). Table 24.3

| Table 24.3 | How a Debt Crisis Can Affect a Bank | | |

Before a Debt Crisis

Assets		Liabilities	
Loans	$1000	Deposits	$800
		Capital	$200

Default on $200 in Loans: One-Half Written Off

Assets		Liabilities	
Loans	$900	Deposits	$800
		Capital	$100

Default on $200 in Loans: Entire Amount Written Off

Assets		Liabilities	
Loans	$800	Deposits	$800
		Capital	$ 0

sets out an example, using T-accounts. The opening balance sheet shows a Canadian bank with $1000 in loans and $200 in capital. (Remember that banks are required to show only the book value of their assets and liabilities.) Suppose that $200 of the loans are to some developing country that suddenly announces it will default on both principal and interest payments. A not-uncommon step at this point is for the bank to write off, say, half the loan (on the assumption that payments will resume someday in the future). This approach leaves $100 in capital, thereby wiping out half the shareholders' equity. Alternatively, if the loan is expected never to be repaid, then the entire amount should be written off, thereby wiping out shareholders' equity entirely.

These scenarios may reflect the reality of the situation, but banks, thanks to the way they are regulated, can simply pretend nothing is wrong by, for example, listing the defaulting loan as "nonperforming," but nevertheless reporting assets and shareholders' equity as they were before. Of course, if the loan is indeed never repaid, the bank faces eventual insolvency since it cannot continue to pay shareholders' dividends or even its depositors when its capital is nonexistent.

No wonder then that the industrialized world's financial system was threatened with collapse in the early 1980s when the international debt crisis reached its peak.

The Asian crisis raised fears once again of another international meltdown as Japanese banks, in particular, became highly exposed to loans made to several neighbouring Asian economies and could not, or chose not, to protect themselves against the inherent liquidity and foreign exchange risks in such loans.

APPROACHES TO THE DEBT CRISIS

Get the latest Brady bond prices and yields **www.bradynet. com/index.html**

In March 1990, the *Brady Plan*, a plan to solve the international debt crisis named after Nicholas Brady, Secretary of the U.S. Treasury at the time, proposed a buyback of debt from secondary markets as a way of alleviating the debt burden for some countries. Mexico, Costa Rica, Chile, the Philippines, Venezuela, Bolivia, and Uruguay were some of the countries that took advantage of this scheme. Such a scheme, however, gives rise to a potential moral hazard problem. A secondary market that sells debt at a considerable discount may create an incentive for a country to become heavily indebted, default, and buy back its debt relatively cheaply. Fear of this situation has led many governments to impose strict and far-reaching economic reforms on the overly indebted countries.[17] (This insistence was the essence of the *Baker Plan*, named after James Baker, Brady's predecessor in the U.S. Treasury Department. The same point was an integral part of the Brady Plan.) Although the Brady scheme has proven to be a successful way for highly indebted countries to restructure their debt, Ecuador defaulted on its Brady bonds in 1999.

Two other solutions to the debt crisis have received some attention. One is the idea of converting debt into equity in developing countries' institutions. Although some examples of these **debt–equity swaps** exist, they have not proven attractive to banks because they involve both selling debt at a substantial discount and investing in regions or firms that are undesirable from a bank's perspective.

Another approach is **debt forgiveness**, which means effectively cancelling part of a country's indebtedness. Canada, among other countries, has implemented such a policy in a few circumstances, most recently in the aftermath of the tsunami that affected several countries in Asia at the end of 2004. The difficulty is that unless governments bail out the banks involved, writing off worthless assets affects the banks' capital–asset ratios. In addition, the moral hazard problem is magnified; a country may indebt itself freely when it anticipates debt relief in the future.[18]

However imperfect these solutions, they do represent attempts to recover some of the debt. By contrast, default means no recovery of debts at all. Moreover, history offers precedents when even fairly modest debt relief has made both debtors and lenders better off eventually. Germany, for example, could not service its foreign debt after World War II. In hindsight, the fairly modest debt relief effort was successful.[19]

The international debt situation is of some interest to Canadians. Canada makes large loans to the Third World, and it also borrows extensively from other nations. By 1996, Canada had one of the highest debt–GDP ratios of any of the OECD countries.[20]

Subsequently, a combination of growing surpluses, part of which has been used to pay down the debt, and strong economic growth reversed the debt–GDP ratio. Similar developments began to take hold in other highly indebted industrial countries. Nevertheless, many countries still suffer from high debt loads. Typically, these countries, as before, are developing or less developed countries. Calls for debt forgiveness continue into the twenty-first century.

As the twentieth century ended, the number and severity of financial crises continued to mount worldwide. As this is written, Argentina has defaulted on her debts and the debt loads of some African countries continue to be unsustainable. Despite the call for debt forgiveness, industrialized countries especially are becoming more convinced that the resulting moral hazard problem is too great to ignore. Moreover, unlike previous decades, governments in emerging markets especially have become far more sophisticated in devising ways to borrow. This means that the number and types of creditors have mushroomed so that, in the event of a crisis or the threat of a default, resolution has become far more complex and costly. Not surprisingly then, capital flows

---

17 One of the problems with these efforts has been how to apply more or less common standards to reform packages imposed on the diverse countries involved. Experience suggests, however, that resolution to debt problems has to be addressed on a country-by-country basis.

18 Not surprisingly, perhaps, the extent to which some debts have been forgiven has raised the price of developing countries' debt in secondary markets.

19 Debt relief for Germany after World War II consisted of interest rate reductions on outstanding debts, a delay in the repayment of principal, and repayment in dollars of debts that had been denominated in gold.

20 Recent research suggests that debt–GDP ratios in highly indebted developing countries are not much different from those in industrialized countries. Why then is a debt crisis not perceived as existing for the latter group of countries? Perhaps it is the ability of countries such as Canada to easily generate the necessary revenues to prevent a debt crisis from occurring. Also, the fact that industrialized countries grow substantially faster than developing countries means that ability to pay is unlikely to be impaired in the long run. See P.E. Guidotti, and M.S. Kumar, "Domestic Public Debt of Externally Indebted Countries," International Monetary Fund Occasional Paper 80 (June 1991); and *1991 International Monetary Fund: Annual Report* (Washington, D.C.: International Monetary Fund, 1991): 42–3.

to emerging markets, in particular, have dropped substantially.[21] Consequently, international organizations such as the International Monetary Fund and various governments have been grappling with ways to alleviate problems that arise in the event of a debt crisis. Current proposals that are gaining wide support[22] include:

1. Eliminating the requirement that 100% of bondholders agree to a change in the financial terms of loans. The current system makes it too easy for a minority of creditors to prevent necessary restructuring of loans.

2. A clear statement at the time loans are made describing the process by which a restructuring should proceed, if this proves to be necessary.

3. A clause explaining the conditions under which the debtor would initiate restructuring.

Despite the obvious advantage of these proposals several problems remain. These include: ensuring that the clauses are consistent with relevant legislation in the creditor countries, ensuring that restructuring does not prevent access to future borrowing, and the protection of domestic creditors to a government indirectly affected by a debt crisis. Only time will tell how successful the IMF and governments will be at reducing the frequency and severity of crises.

24.5 ASSESSING COUNTRY RISK

For reasons that should be clear from the previous section, banks and other institutions invest resources in assessing not only the riskiness of a loan to a particular firm abroad, but also the inherent riskiness of the other country, which is called **country risk**. Countries have unique features and histories that influence their economic fortunes over time. Hence, investing in Canada implies different risks than investing in, say, Mexico.

Country risk has essentially two components: transfer risk, which is the possibility that a borrower may not be able to convert the currency in which the loan was made into the lender's currency; and sovereign risk, which is the possibility of the borrower's inability or unwillingness to repay principal or interest or both.

Assessing the level of country risk requires judicious assessment of social, political, historical, and economic factors. Perhaps the most common indicator is the **debt–service ratio**: the payments needed to service the country's foreign debt as a percentage of some average value of its exports. Recall that exports provide foreign exchange earnings and thus the ability to finance foreign debt. Even exports as a percentage of GDP can be used as a simple measure of ability to pay.

In addition to quantitative measures of risk, potential lenders also consider qualitative characteristics, such as political risks (often determined by whether governments are democratically elected and whether they are "left-wing" or "right-wing").[23] Some combination of these characteristics can be used to generate a composite index. *The Economist* (actually its Economist

The Economist
**www.economist.
com**

21 According to J. Taylor, "Sovereign Debt Restructuring: A U.S. Perspective," speech given at the International Institute of Economics Conference "Sovereign Debt Workouts: Hopes and Hazards," 2 April 2002, Washington D.C.

22 See A. Krueger, "New Approaches to Sovereign Debt Restructuring: An Update on Our Thinking," speech given at the Institute of International Economics Conference "Sovereign Debt Workouts: Hopes and Hazards," 1 April 2002.

23 Left-wing governments are sometimes referred to as "liberal," which means that they favour a relatively high degree of government intervention. By contrast, right-wing governments are often called "conservative" because they prefer little government intervention.

Intelligence Unit branch), for example, produces just such an index for more than 80 countries, published on a quarterly basis. Investors are keen on this type of information because it will influence the risk premium they demand on investments in particular countries.

Another popular indicator of country risk is the so-called EMBI (Emerging Markets Bonds Index). It attempts essentially to measure the return on a hypothetical portfolio of bonds from countries relative to the return on select U.S. securities. Hence, the larger the spread, the greater the risk associated with holding debt from the country in question. Figure 24.1 illustrates the behaviour of this index for Argentina. Argentina defaulted on its debt in 2001 following the collapse of its currency that was supposed to be rigidly tied to the U.S. dollar in a currency board arrangement (see Chapter 8 for a definition). The seeds of Argentina's crisis perhaps were actually sown as far back as 1999, or even earlier. As is clear from the figure, the EMBI index showed a jump even before the actual crisis took place, an indication of how this type of statistic can be useful to investors in gauging the risk associated with investments in so-called emerging markets.[24]

| Figure 24.1 | **EMBI for Argentina, 1998–2004** |

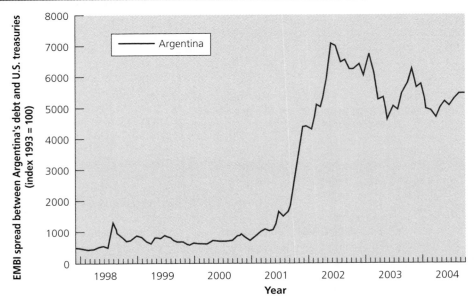

Source: J.P. Morgan, **http://www2.jpmorgan.com/MarketDataInd/EMBI/embi.html**

---

24 You will also recall that, in Chapter 7, we considered the role of the spread as an indicator of future inflation or economic performance. A good review of the relationship between Argentina and the IMF is contained in International Monetary Fund, "Argentina and the IMF, 1991-2001," A Report of the Independent Evaluation Office, 2004, available from **www.imf.org**.

ECONOMICS FOCUS 24.2 — WHAT CAUSES INTERNATIONAL FINANCIAL CRISES?

The IMF (studied in Chapter 26) recently reported that at least 130 countries have experienced a banking or financial crisis since the 1980s. The costs of such crises, typically the dollars needed to bail out failing financial institutions and restore financial stability to the affected economies, range from 3% to almost 25% of a country's GDP. The United States experienced the least costly crisis in these terms (see Chapter 25), whereas the financial collapses in Argentina and Chile, to give two examples, were among the largest recorded.

Economists are still arguing about the causes of some crises, especially the most recent Asian crisis. Generally, however, financial crises have two origins: a set of *macroeconomic* causes or *microeconomic* causes. Since the two types of causes can be related, these two categories are best thought of as a useful classification of the onset of a crisis.

Macroeconomic Causes

An inappropriate exchange rate, an abrupt end to inflation, and poor fiscal or monetary policies are all signs of an impending crisis. Unfortunately, crises can occur even when most of these conditions are not present. For example, in the Asian crisis, none of the countries concerned, except possibly Thailand, fits the profile of having a disequilibrium exchange rate with poor fiscal and monetary policies.

Microeconomic Causes

Problems at the level of financial institutions can occur because of poor banking strategies and operations, such as the inability to assess credit properly, the severe mismatching of assets and liabilities, or even fraud and corruption. Occasionally, a crisis is made worse by problems at the governmental or central bank levels. These problems include a failure to properly supervise banks or other financial institutions, inadequate accounting standards, rapid deregulation that encourages reckless financial behaviour, moral hazard, and a culture that does not encourage transparency in the reporting of financial operations.

Given the list of causes, it appears that it should have been possible to predict at least 10 causes of the last 5 crises! Yet, a closer look reveals that a large number of related factors explain the onset and severity of a crisis. In addition, there is often an idiosyncratic aspect to such crises. What about plans, such as the G-20 framework, to ensure that crises are not repeated? One influential analyst (Eichengreen, 1999) has stated that the rash of proposals in place are "politically unrealistic, technically infeasible, or unlikely to yield significant improvements in the way crises are prevented, anticipated or managed."

Questions for Discussion

1. Would you rank macroeconomic causes as more important than microeconomic ones, or vice versa?
2. Draw up a list of early warning indicators of a financial crisis. Do some factors stand out more in your mind than others?

Sources

M.D. Bordo, B. Eichengreen, D. Klingebiel, and M. Soledad Martinez Peria (2001) "Is the Crisis Problem Growing More Severe?" *Economic Policy* 32 (April 2001): 51–75.

B. Eichengreen, *Toward a New International Financial Architecture: A Practical Post-Asia Agenda* (Washington, D.C.: Institute for International Economics, 1999).

J. Furman, and J.E. Stiglitz, "Economic Crises: Evidence and Insights from East Asia," *Brookings Papers on Economic Activity* (February 1998): 1–135.

G.L. Kaminsky, and C.M. Reinhart, "The Twin Crises: The Causes of Banking and Balance of Payments Problems," *American Economic Review* 89 (June 1999): 473–500.

G.L. Kaminsky, S. Lizondo, and C.M. Reinhart, "Leading Indicators of Currency Crises," *International Monetary Fund Working Paper 97/79* (July 1997).

F.S. Mishkin, "Global Financial Instability: Frameworks, Events, Issues," *Journal of Economic Perspectives* 13 (Fall 1999): 3–20.

S. Radelet, and J. Sachs, "The East Asian Financial Crises: Diagnosis, Remedies, and Prospects," *Brookings Papers on Economic Activity* (January 1998): 1–74.

N. Roubini, "What Caused Asia's Economic Crisis and Its Global Contagion?" This is a vast Web site containing everything you ever wanted to know about financial crises, **www.stern.nyu.edu/globalmacro**.

SUMMARY

- This chapter considers a variety of different topics that come under the heading of international banking.

- Many of the transactions involving transfers of funds from one country to another are conducted via international financial centres. London is probably the biggest such centre.

- Other large international financial centres (IFCs) include New York and Frankfurt. Some IFCs are located on small islands and offer privacy and tax advantages to investors.

- The key Eurocurrency interest rate is called the London interbank offer rate (LIBOR).

- Eurocurrency markets avoid some of the regulations, such as reserve requirements, which permits not only more lending opportunities but also enhances the movement of capital across countries as well as facilitating international trade.

- A driving force in the international flow of funds is the Eurocurrency market. This market represents funds traded in a currency other than the one used in the country where the transaction takes place.

- The chapter describes two other issues of recent interest in the field of innternational banking: the international debt crisis, and the problem of the lack of uniform international banking regulations.

- At the centre of the problem of regulating banking activities is the fact that banks are subject to domestic laws first and foremost. This situation is known as national treatment.

- Most countries adhere either to the universal banking model or have a dual banking system. The main difference between the two approaches has to do with the types of activities in which banks are barred from engaging. Principally, these include the underwriting of securities and the selling of insurance. Universal banks are allowed to do both.

- The international debt crisis has both a macroeconomic and a microeconomic dimension. At the macroeconomic level, heavily indebted countries' ability to prosper is severely affected. At the level of individual banks, the debt crisis can easily make them effectively insolvent.

IMPORTANT TERMS

country risk, 500
debt–equity swaps, 499
debt forgiveness, 499
debt–service ratio, 500
dual banking system, 494
international financial centres, 490

London interbank offer rate (LIBOR), 492
national treatment, 493
offshore banking centres, 491
universal banking model, 493

PROBLEMS

1. Why do secondary debt markets have prices that always trade at a discount? Explain.

2. Explain why, in the absence of a government bailout, debt forgiveness has negative consequences for a bank's balance sheet.

3. In what sense is the prospect of a government bailout an example of a moral hazard problem (Hint: go back to Chapter 16 for the definition and an explanation of the concept).

4. Explain how the Eurocurrency transaction described in this chapter can have consequences for the Canadian money supply when the funds are transferred from demand deposits to foreign currency deposits.

5. Suppose that the transaction depicted in Table 24.3 is reversed. Are there any repercussions for the Canadian financial system? Explain.

6. In the example in Table 24.3 can you think of a situation where the bank in question would not have to write off any of the loans? If so, what are the potential implications for the financial system as a whole?

7. Continuing with the example in Table 24.3, suppose that the loan default is $300. What would happen to the bank's capital? Explain. Is there any way around the problem?

DISCUSSION QUESTIONS

1. How is an undervaluation of the Canadian dollar linked to the attractiveness of Euro-Canadian-dollar bonds from the foreign investor's perspective? Explain your answer.

2. Explain the moral hazard problem created when a country is able to repurchase its debt in a secondary market.

3. What caused the most recent international debt crisis? Explain your answer.

4. What are some of the determinants of successful international banking centres?

5. What are some of the key policy issues arising out of the operations of offshore banking facilities?

6. Is there a danger that Eurodollars will flood the U.S. financial system? Why or why not?

7. How would you rank, in terms of desirability, debt–equity swaps versus debt forgiveness as a means of dealing with the debt crisis? Explain.

8. What are some of the advantages and risks faced by banking systems with a large degree of foreign ownership? You might want to think about the case of New Zealand mentioned in this chapter.

ONLINE APPLICATION

1. Go to the G-20's Web site at **www.g20.org** and click in "communiques." Evaluate the 2004 Accord for Sustained Growth, found under G-20 Ministerial Communique, Berlin, 2004, in light of the issues covered in this chapter.

2. Go to the Web site that keeps track of international financial crises at **www.stern. nyu.edu/globalmacro**. Search for *Country risk* and select *Country risk analysis data* by Campbell Harvey.

(a) What is the difference between political risk, economic risk, and financial risk?

(b) Look at the summary analysis of country risk measures. Does the ranking (from riskiest country to invest in to the least risky country to invest in) surprise you? If so, why? If not, why not? What would your prior beliefs have been?

References can be found on **www.mcgrawhill.ca/college/siklos**

CHAPTER 25

The U.S. Financial System

LEARNING OBJECTIVES

After reading and studying this chapter, you should be able to

25.1 discuss why the financial systems of Canada and the United States differ

25.2 explain how the U.S. financial system of today can be traced to the history and tension between centralization and regionalism

25.3 describe how the U.S. financial system is structured and recent reforms that were legislated

25.4 determine how the U.S. central bank, the Federal Reserve, began, how it operates, and why it is autonomous

25.5 explore the principal tools of U.S. monetary policy

Although the growing volume and importance of international banking and the forces of globalization are encouraging similarities in financial behaviour and regulations around the world, each country retains certain idiosyncrasies in how its financial institutions are organized and regulated. Many are rooted in history. This chapter offers a glimpse of these differences by relating some basic facts about the U.S. financial system. Free trade and the fact that the United States is, by far, our dominant trading partner make it natural to consider its evolution and present structure in some detail. Moreover, in 1999, after many years of discussion and debate, the U.S. government finally passed its most comprehensive financial legislation since the Great Depression.

An advantage of studying experiences in other countries is that we can better understand how economic development and political considerations together have shaped their financial systems. We can also better appreciate how regulatory structures are influenced by the objectives and the financial needs of the public. Chapter 20 helps underscore these points.

Although these few pages cannot possibly do justice to the subject—entire texts are often devoted to a description of a single country's financial system—this chapter, plus the information throughout the textbook about how banks and other financial institutions are organized in the United States, should give you an appreciation of the similarities and differences between Canada and the United States.

25.1 HISTORICAL BACKGROUND

What distinguishes the U.S. financial system from that of many other countries is its dual (federal and state) control, which is reflected in the structure and organization of both its financial institutions and its central banking function.

The peculiar structure of the U.S. financial system is largely the result of political pressures familiar to Canadians: centralization versus regionalism. Soon after the United States was formed, opinion makers divided between those who wanted to see a strong federal system and those who favoured relatively strong states' rights.

The then-new constitution was ambiguous on whether the states or the federal government had jurisdiction over financial institutions.[1] Thus, even as the colonists moved westward and small local banks were established, Federalists staked their claim. Under their influence, the Congress chartered the First and the Second Bank of the United States (1791 and 1816, respectively) and endowed them with the exclusive right to open branches nationally. Neither lasted long, and both were political disasters—they were accused of redistributing credit to urban centres from rural areas (the United States was largely rural at the time) as well as lending exclusively to pro-Federalists.

The experience with the Bank of the United States, which effectively served as a quasi-central bank by providing "elastic" credit, was ill-suited to the ideology of the gold standard. As a result, it was not until 1913 that U.S. policymakers grudgingly accepted central banking. Once again, however, the tension between centralization and regionalism influenced the structure of the Federal Reserve system, at least until the Great Depression, when monetary policy actions became far more centralized.[2]

The result was the virtual abolition of nationwide banking. The states took over jurisdiction and each made its own rules. Some permitted only **unit banking**—no branches at all. Others allowed limited branching—say, within a designated locality or county. Still others eventually went so far as to permit branching throughout the state.

With the trend to small, local banks, it is not surprising that *free banking* became the rule in the nineteenth-century United States; anyone who could meet quite minimal requirements could open a bank. It is also not surprising that scandals and bank failures were frequent. Approximately one-third of the U.S. banking system was wiped out in the Great Depression.

One of the political responses to that tragedy was the introduction of deposit insurance (a U.S. invention), which also gave the federal government a way to extend its control over the banking system. To join the insurance scheme, which was a popular success, a bank had to meet stringent criteria for its assets and open its books and management techniques to inspection by federal examiners. Thus, the Federal Deposit Insurance Corporation (FDIC) helped to stabilize the system, although critics[3] believe the coverage is far too generous. Today deposits are insured up to US$100 000, but, as in Canada, a variety of devices can be used to raise the effective limit many times over.[4] Moreover, bank regulators and politicians have acted over the years on what is called the "too-big-to-fail" doctrine. If a large institution fails, all its depositors are reimbursed, even if their accounts exceeded the current limit on deposit insurance. Such a policy is unfair to small and conservative institutions; it can also encourage larger ones to be reckless, safe in the knowledge that the default risk to depositors is effectively zero. This situation is the moral hazard problem described in Chapter 16.

The FDIC's Web page
www.fdic.gov

25.2 U.S. FINANCIAL INTERMEDIARIES

Given the United States' legacy of state and federal jurisdictions in the area of banking, a *dual banking system* evolved. Among the depository institutions, in order of relative importance, are

---

1 In fact, although it specifies that the federal government has jurisdiction over "coin[ing] money and regulat[ing] its value," it makes no assignment of the regulation of banking.

2 Paralleling the creation of the Fed, which was meant to oversee commercial banks, was the Federal Home Loan Board System (FHLBS), intended to oversee the savings and loan banks.

3 See, for example, L. White, *The S&L Debacle* (New York: Oxford University Press, 1991).

4 One such device is to rely on brokered deposits. Money brokers take large sums of money and break them up into segments of $100 000. Thus, several million can be insured even though the spirit of deposit insurance was to offer protection up to $100 000 only.

1. *Commercial banks*, which, as their name implies, are primarily in the business of making commercial loans and taking chequable and savings deposits; especially since the early 1980s, mortgage lending has increasingly become a focus of activity. The commercial banks can be likened to Canadian chartered banks, but because of previous U.S. legal restrictions on branch banking, there are vastly more of them. Most are state chartered and largely state regulated.

2. **Savings and loan associations (S&Ls)**, which resemble Canadian mortgage loan companies, originally were largely restricted to mortgage lending.[5] With the post–World War II boom in housing, S&Ls grew rapidly. They experienced considerable difficulties during the 1970s and 1980s when market interest rates rose sharply, but the S&Ls faced a legal ceiling on the rate they could pay on deposits.

3. *Mutual savings banks*, which are similar to S&Ls except they are owned by their depositors.

4. *Credit unions*, which are like Canadian credit unions and organized along the same lines, such as by region or type of employment.

Unlike Canadian banks, U.S. banks must still meet reserve requirements. Since 1996, however, the system has been greatly simplified so that only demand deposits and a few other so-called transactions accounts, that is, accounts from which funds can be quickly transferred from one holder to another, require reserves. Nevertheless, the Fed retains the authority to impose reserve requirements on all types of deposits.

25.3 FINANCIAL REGULATORY PRACTICE: EVOLUTION AND ISSUES

We can argue that the variety of legal restrictions imposed on the U.S. banking system has made it a financial system which is innovative in some respects and laggard in others.

For example, the *Edge Act* of 1919 permitted the federal chartering of banks for the sole purpose of engaging in international banking. *Edge Act* corporations could take deposits from foreigners but not from U.S. residents. Since these situations are exempt from the severe restrictions on interstate banking, it is not surprising that *Edge Act* subsidiaries are a feature of most large U.S. banks today. In the 1980s, **international banking facilities** (**IBFs**) emerged. This device permitted banks to accept deposits from foreigners but not to be subject to interest rate limitations or reserve requirements.[6]

Another important reform was the *McFadden Act* of 1927, amended in 1933, which cleared up the legal status of branching and effectively barred it across state lines. Getting around this regulation has proven easy, however. A would-be financier simply sets up a bank holding company, which becomes the legal owner of separate banks in various states. Not being itself a bank, the holding company is not subject to the interstate banking restrictions. Legislation was passed to prevent further erosion of the *McFadden Act* and to limit these companies' potential to engage in nonbank activities, but a grandfather clause protected existing bank holding companies, and others quickly developed new variations to undermine the intent of the *McFadden Act*.[7] Moreover, the recent introduction of automated banking machines (ABMs) has led to the creation of networks, permitting a form of nationwide banking. The popularity of ABMs makes it unlikely that politicians will put a stop to such a use.

---

5 One difference between the U.S. and Canadian experiences is that, unlike Canada, U.S. governments fostered their development, because they were created as part of President Franklin Roosevelt's "New Deal" reforms meant to lift the country out of the Depression.

6 As such, IBFs have no separate identity, but represent a separate set of accounts at banks that have established these accounts. See "International Activities of US Banks and in US Banking Markets," *Federal Reserve Bulletin* (September 1999): 599–615.

7 For details, see M. Kohn, *Money, Banking, and Financial Markets* (Chicago: The Dryden Press, 1991), Chapter 8.

The Great Depression of the 1930s[8] eventually brought sweeping legislative changes to the U.S. financial industry. One, as we have seen, was the introduction of deposit insurance. Another (discussed in more detail later in this section) was a mandate to the Federal Reserve system, which acts as a central bank in the United States, to become more active in supervising banks and managing the nation's financial affairs.

A third set of 1930s' regulations actually originated in 1920s' scandals that involved the same person's owning and managing a commercial bank and an **investment bank** (the latter is much like a Canadian *investment dealer*, purchasing new issues of securities, and selling them in smaller parcels to investors). The investment branch of such an institution could, for example, sell debt with a high default risk to the commercial banking arm, thereby raising the risk to depositors. The uncovering of several such schemes prompted public outrage. The political result was passage of the ***Glass–Stegall Act*** of 1933, which prohibited commercial banks from selling or dealing in (that is, underwriting) corporate securities. The Act did not extend to government securities in part because they are considered default-risk free and in part because Congress sought to create the widest possible market for them. It also did not extend to the foreign operations of U.S. banks, a fact that many institutions have taken advantage of. This restriction did not exist in countries such as Germany and Japan, which have not experienced widespread banking failures.

The tremendous impact of the banking crisis during the Great Depression left the impression among many people, including legislators, that market competition in which one firm can undercut another could be ruinous for the banking sector. Consequently, the *Glass–Stegall Act* gave the Federal Reserve authority to regulate interest on bank accounts. The result was regulation Q, which placed a ceiling on deposit interest rates (but none on lending rates). At the time the regulation was put into effect, interest rates on Treasury bills were well below the ceiling, so no one was much upset. But during the 1970s, market rates rose substantially above what the banks could offer. Although the ceiling was gradually raised, it remained low enough to drive depositors to seek a better return elsewhere. The result was, for a time, considerable *disintermediation*. Banks, therefore, searched extensively for a way to avoid the restrictions of regulation Q. Some New England savings banks discovered a loophole allowing the payment of interest on chequable deposits. By calling a cheque a **negotiable order of withdrawal** (**NOW**), savings banks, which were barred from accepting demand deposits, could effectively offer chequable savings accounts. Since the deposit was a savings account, interest could be paid. But commercial banks could not offer similar accounts because they were prohibited from effecting what were technically third-party transfers of funds from savings. NOW accounts proved popular, and eventually legislation was passed permitting all depository institutions to offer them. Banks were also able to entice corporate accounts to return, avoiding the regulation Q restrictions, by, for example, offering *overnight bank repurchase agreements (repos)*.[9]

During the 1980s, the number of bank failures rose again, under the influence of high and rising interest rates, and the S&L scandal loomed. One response to this situation was the implementation of two major pieces of financial legislation. The first, the *Depository Institutions Deregulation and Monetary Control Act* of 1980, had three important objectives: (1) to phase out regulation Q, (2) to relax restrictions on the types of loans savings banks could offer, so they could tap the lucrative area of commercial lending and otherwise increase portfolio diversification, and (3) to impose uniform reserve requirements on all depository institutions and to allow them access to borrowing funds from the Federal Reserve system. Unlike Canada, however, reserve requirements persist in the United States and are not likely to be eliminated any time soon.

The 1982 *Depository Institutions Act* further relaxed the differences between commercial banks, savings banks, and other financial institutions. Thus, savings banks were permitted to

---

8 For a lively account of the economic and social consequences of the Great Depression in the United States, see J. Garraty, *The Great Depression* (New York: Harper & Row, 1987).
9 An alternative term for what Canadians call purchase and resale agreements (PRAs).

FINANCIAL FOCUS 25.1

THE GREAT DEPRESSION IN THE UNITED STATES AND CANADA: DID THE BANKING SYSTEM PLAY A ROLE?

It is now recognized that the Great Depression should be viewed as an international phenomenon with its roots in the gold standard. Eichengreen (1995), Temin (1989), and Bordo, Goldin, and White(1998) provide arguably the best recent accounts of the Great Depression. Comparing the U.S. and Canadian experiences is of considerable interest, not only because of the obvious close ties the two countries share, but also because of the differences in the respective financial systems that underscore the role played by the gold standard (also see **Economics Focus 8.1: Longing for the Gold Standard**). Despite the differences, there is one unmistakable similarity: Both countries experienced a Great Depression at roughly the same time and of comparable economic magnitude.

A general deflation in prices accompanied the Great Depression, but the lower prices raised real interest rates (see Chapter 5 and the Fisher equation). Prospective borrowers, if they feel that prices are expected to fall further, will also find credit becoming more expensive. In addition, loan default rates will be exacerbated if the deflation is unanticipated, scaring potential lenders away from making loans, thereby producing a credit "crunch," to use the modern term. The foregoing factors were the harbingers of a financial crisis that placed the banking system at the centre of the story of the Great Depression. Bernanke has documented how the Depression led to a massive failure of the credit allocation process.

There were two notable differences between the U.S. and Canadian financial systems during the Great Depression. First, until 1935, Canada had no central bank. Second, U.S. banking laws were aimed at preventing banks from forming oligopolies. The Canadian banking system permitted branch banking, whereas the U.S. system placed severe restrictions on this type of activity, effectively discouraging such behaviour. Bordo, Rockoff, and Redish report that, as a result, the Canadian banking system was more stable than the U.S. system. The number of bank offices fell substantially in both countries. Bank runs, whose social costs continue to be debated, figured prominently, but the Canadian experience was marked by a contraction in the size and reach of existing banks (from 18 in

1920 to 10 in 1929). Only one bank, the Home Bank, failed in 1923. Even if the U.S. banking system was more fragile than the Canadian one, we are still left with the startling conclusion that the much-touted stability of the Canadian financial system did not make the country immune to the severity of the Great Depression. Clearly, other forces must be at play, and research continues to find answers to this and other questions about the Great Depression's impact in Canada and the United States (Siklos, 2003).

Questions for Discussion

1. How might the Depression have made it relatively easier for Canadian banks, and more difficult for U.S. banks, to withstand the effect of a large reduction in liquidity?

2. Does the fact that the Great Depression was roughly as severe in the United States as it was in Canada suggest that the differences in the two banking systems were irrelevant?

Sources

B.S. Bernanke, "Non-Monetary Effects of the Financial Crisis in the Propogation of the Great Depression," *American Economic Review* 73 (March 1983): 257–76.

M.D. Bordo, C. Goldin, and E. White, *The Defining Moment: The Great Depression and the American Economy in the Twentieth Century* (Chicago: University of Chicago Press, 1998).

M.D. Bordo, H. Rockoff, and A. Redish, "The US Banking System from a Northern Exposure: Stability versus Efficiency," *Journal of Economic History* 54 (June 1994): 325–41.

B. Eichengreen, *Golden Fetters* (New York: Oxford University Press, 1995).

P.L. Siklos, "Understanding the Great Depression in the United States versus Canada," in *World Economy and National Economies in the Interwar Slump,* edited by T. Balderston (Basingstoke: The Macmillan Press, 2003), Chapter 3.

P. Temin, *Lessons from the Great Depression* (Cambridge: The MIT Press, 1989).

issue *money market accounts* (which operate like mutual funds but enable the depositor to redeem "shares" by writing cheques). The maximum for commercial loans as a percentage of a savings bank's total assets was also raised. Finally, the *Act* gave emergency powers to the deposit-insuring agencies to facilitate mergers between ailing or failing financial institutions and solvent ones.

The S&L debacle led to a major piece of legislation to provide funding to close down insolvent banks and also to strengthen the regulatory structure. The result was the *Financial Institution Reform, Recovery, and Enforcement Act* of 1989 (FIRREA). The **Office of Thrift Supervision** (**OTS**) was given enhanced responsibilites and the FDIC took over the deposit protection function for S&Ls previously handled by a separate agency. At the same time, a new agency, the Resolution Trust Corporation (RTC), take over responsibility for selling a wide variety of assets and winding down the operations of insolvent S&Ls. The RTC went out of business at the end of 1995.

In 1991, reforms to the FDIC, called the *FDIC Improvement Act*, limited the scope of deposit insurance in the case of brokered deposits and reduced the possibility of the invoking the "too-big-to-fail" doctrine by permitting earlier intervention by the FDIC in a bank suspected of being in financial difficulty.

Congress finally approved legislation in 1995 to deregulate the financial system to permit more widespread branch banking across states, as well as to relax some of the provisions of the *Glass–Stegall Act*.[10] Americans' deep desire to diffuse power as much as possible has resulted in an extremely complex web of regulatory agencies that defies easy categorization (see Table 25.2 on page 513) and protects their bureaucracies well.

In addition to state regulators, these three major regulators are the Treasury and its **Office of the Comptroller of the Currency** (**OCC**), the Office of Thrift Supervision (OTS), and the FDIC, which administers deposit insurance.

Both the OCC, established in 1863, and OTS, created in 1989, are bureaus of the U.S. Treasury. The OTS was created following the Savings and Loan crisis, and the fees it assesses on the institutions it regulates finance all its activities. We have briefly discussed the FDIC's activities elsewhere in this chapter and in Chapter 16. It should be added that, although the FDIC does not release its ratings on the safety and soundness of banks, it does provide a list of private institutions that compile and disseminate this kind of information for a fee.

Is the multiplicity of regulators a good thing? It is noteworthy that in countries such as Canada, there has been a tendency to limit the overlap of regulatory functions. The U.S. *Financial Services Act* of 1999 did not do away with multiple regulatory agencies. Why not? More regulators clearly imply overlapping responsibilities that create additional costs. More regulators also means that banks have an incentive to play one regulator against another. Overlapping responsibilities can also mean a slower response in the event of a crisis. However, several regulators provide a system of checks and balances. It is also possible that financial innovations are spurred when institutions seek to take advantage of differences in regulation across supervisory bodies. Finally, the bureaucracy of a sole regulator may be less responsive to needed reforms than in an environment where regulators must, in a sense, compete.

OCC
www.occ.treas.gov
OTS
www.ots.treas.gov
Treasury
www.treas.gov

THE *FINANCIAL SERVICES ACT* OF 1999

A more comprehensive bill to reform the banking sector was delayed for a time, in part because of a court case arguing what powers banks should have to sell insurance.[11]

The U.S. Congress finally brought about a comprehensive reform of legislation covering 50 years of previous Acts. The ***Financial Services Act of 1999*** (**FSA**), also known as the *Gramm–Leach–Bliley Act*, amends the *Banking Act* of 1933 (*Glass–Steagall Act*), as well as several other acts dating from the 1940s through the 1990s.

Among the highlights of the new legislation are the following:

- A bank holding company can now affiliate with any financial company (including insurance and securities companies).

---

10 Full implementation of what has been called the *Riegle–Neal Interstate Banking and Branching Efficiency Act* of 1994 has now taken place. See D.F. Amel, "Trends in the Structure of Federally Insured Depository Institutions 1984–1994," *Federal Reserve Bulletin* 82 (January 1996): 1–15.

11 This is also a hotly debated issue in Canada. In March 1996, the U.S. Supreme Court ruled that banks cannot be barred from selling insurance. See R. Wells, "High Court Rules Banks Can Sell Insurance," San Diego *Union-Tribune*, (27 March 1996): A17.

- Geographical restrictions on the sale of any financial product have been removed.

- Banks can underwrite any financial product, other than insurance underwriting or real estate development.

- Prudential and soundness requirements have increased. Banks must be well capitalized and well managed.[12]

- Limitations have been imposed on the total asset size of a subsidiary of a particular national bank.

- Commercial companies can no longer operate or own thrifts (after 4 May 1999).

- Restrictions on banks underwriting new insurance products were imposed after 1 January 1999.

- The collateral that small and rural banks can pledge to obtain liquidity from the Federal Home Loan Bank System (FHLBS) has been greatly expanded.

The new legislation considerably broadens the powers and instruments banks can engage in, though there are a couple of restrictions in the new legislation of interest to Canadians. First, limitations on the underwriting of insurance products parallel the position taken by Canadian legislators. Second, prohibiting commercial concerns from engaging in certain banking activities will limit the Wal-Marts or Canadian Tires of this world from entering the banking business.

CURRENT TRENDS

Even before the FSA was enacted, a series of reforms and other actions were taken by banks that changed the landscape of banking in the United States. One that is especially of interest to Canada is the tremendous consolidation of the banking sector. Figure 25.1 shows the significant drop in the number of banks, especially since the mid-1980s. Second, as a result of this

| Figure 25.1 | Number of U.S. Banks, 1984–2003 |

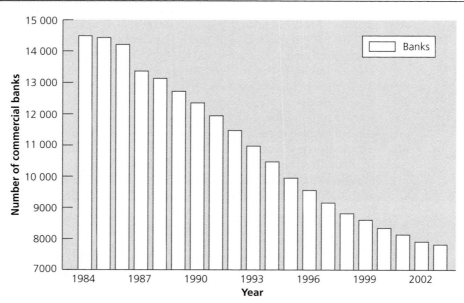

Source: FDIC, **www.fdic.gov**. Figures refer to the number of FDIC-insured commercial banks.

12 Unlike Canada, the U.S. continues to have mandatory reserve requirements. These have fallen continually over the years and have changed frequently. An annual review, together with historical information, is available at **www.federal reserve.gov/Releases/h3/hist/annualreview.htm.**

Table 25.1	The Ten Largest U.S. Banks, 2004
Name	**Total Assets (Millions of Dollars)**
Bank of America	706 888
J.P. Morgan	654 881
Citibank	648 243
Wachovia	368 871
Wells Fargo	364 698
Bank One	245 783
Fleet	213 732
US Bank	189 737
Suntrust	125 881
HSBC USA	110 305

Source: Board of Governors of the Federal Reserve System, **www.federalreserve.gov**.

consolidation, U.S. banks have once again become among the largest in the world. Table 25.1 lists the top 10 banks in the U.S. in 2004. Many of these banks represent the amalgamation of several smaller banks that were regionally based.

25.4 THE FEDERAL RESERVE SYSTEM

Board of Governors
of the Fed
**www.federal
reserve.gov**
You can find the
Web sites for individual Federal Reserve
Banks from the Fed's
Web site

The tension in the United States between federalists and advocates of states' rights, as well as the considerable influence of the rural and regional populations, delayed the founding of any central bank until the early part of the twentieth century, and then produced one unlike any other in the world. The **Federal Reserve** (**the Fed**), created by federal law in 1913, was not a single bank but a whole decentralized central banking system, comprising 12 banks, each the centre of a region and owned by its members. Membership was—and still is—voluntary. Each Federal Reserve Bank had sufficient autonomy to regulate the financial system in its own district. Each issued its own currency,[13] so interest rates and thus monetary policy were largely regionally determined. Nominally, a central agency in Washington, called the board of governors, coordinated national monetary and financial regulatory policies, but power was meant to come from below and not from above, consistent with a decentralized process.

Major reforms in the way the Fed operates occurred in the aftermath of the Great Depression. Henceforth, the seven-member board of governors would be responsible for determining the discount rate (that is, the rate at which the Fed lends to member banks), for setting reserve requirements (within limits), and for providing certain kinds of regulations. The board and the presidents of five Federal Reserve Banks form the **Federal Open Market Committee** (**FOMC**), which directs open market operations and, therefore, national monetary policy.[14] As a result, the current Federal Reserve system operates much like any other modern central bank, though vestiges of the decentralized structure persist. The FOMC holds eight regularly scheduled meetings a year, with additional meetings if the need arises (e.g., when there is a crisis such as September 11, 2001), to gauge the appropriateness of the current stance of monetary policy. Regional Feds and the board of governors provide economic information, analyses, and forecasts to the FOMC to assist in their decision making and deliberations.

The FOMC's statements are widely read around the world, and investors and other market participants pore over every word and utterance of the FOMC and, especially, its current chair, Alan Greenspan, for clues about the future course of interest rates or the Fed's thinking in general. A good example occurred on December 1996, when Alan Greenspan complained about

---

13 The front of old U.S. notes (the side on which appears a portrait of a past president) shows the name of the issuing Federal Reserve Bank on the left-hand side. However, new notes, which have begun to replace the old ones, no longer identify the Federal Reserve city. Most of the new notes are now in circulation.

14 The group always includes the president of the New York Fed, where open market operations are conducted. Note that since the board can always outvote the other members, ultimate control over monetary policy rests with that institution.

| Table 25.2 | U.S. Depository Institutions and Their Regulators: A Simplified Sketch |

Type of Bank	Chartering or Licensing Authority	Supervision	Insured By
National banks	OCC[a]	OCC[a]	FDIC
State banks	State	Federal Reserve	FDIC
Savings banks			
Federal	OTS[b]	OTS	FDIC
State	State	FDIC[c] & state	FDIC
Savings and loan			
Federal	OTS	OTS	FDIC
State	State	OTS & state	FDIC
Credit unions			
Federal	NCUAB[d]	[e]	NCUSIF[f]
State	State	State	NCUSIF

Sources: Federal Reserve *Annual Reports* (various years).

[a] Office of the Comptroller of the Currency, a division of the U.S. Department of the Treasury
[b] Office of Thrift Supervision
[c] Federal Deposit Insurance Corporation
[d] National Credit Union Association Board
[e] No NCUAB approval required to open a branch
[f] National Credit Union Share Insurance Funds or State Authorities

"irrational exuberance" in the stock market.[15] For a time, stock prices fell before resuming their upward course in the face of continued good economic news.

The Fed also operates the payments system, called **Fedwire**, and unlike the separate agency that runs the payments system in Canada, only depository institutions that are members of the Fed can participate in the Fedwire system. Although the membership consists of a large number of banks (see Figure 25.1), the top 50 account for around 80% of the total dollar value of transfers. Fedwire carries out transactions, and settlement is intraday, that is, in real time for all intents and purposes, for the following securities:

- U.S. Treasury bills
- securities in federal or federally sponsored agencies
- mortgage-backed securities and a select number of dollar-denominated debt issued by international agencies such as the World Bank[16]

Unlike many other central banks, however, the Fed is relatively independent of the government. Several reasons are usually cited. First, members of the board of governors are chosen for rotating 14-year terms that do not overlap those of the presidency.[17] Second, the Fed does not receive any appropriations from Congress; rather, it operates on the profits from its holdings of government securities and its loans to banks,[18] as well as the seigniorage earned from the issue of currency. Third, like many other central banks, the Fed conducts its operations in secrecy.

---

15 The necessity that the Fed, and heads of other central banks, speak about the behaviour of financial markets reflects the tension between the long-run goals a central bank is mandated to fulfil, such as price stability, versus the fear that one small event, originating in a financial market, could trigger a crisis of some kind. See P.L. Siklos, "Pitfalls and Opportunities for the Conduct of Monetary Policy in a World of High-Frequency Data," in *Information in Financial Asset Prices*, Proceedings of a conference held at the Bank of Canada, May 1998 (Ottawa: Bank of Canada, 1999): 331–69.

16 More details about Fedwire can be obtained at the Fed's Web site at **www.federalreserve.gov**.

17 The exception is the Federal Reserve chair, who is appointed for a four-year term that can coincide with that of the president. The rationale is that the U.S. president ought to be able to select (with the advice and consent of the Senate) the person who will head the Fed and with whom the administration must work.

18 The facility used to be limited to Fed members. Since 1982, however, it has been extended to all banks.

Table 25.3	Monetary Aggregates in the United States, 2004	
	Details	Billions of US$
M1	Currency outside Federal Reserve banks; demand deposits in commercial banks; travellers' cheques of nonbank issuers; NOW and ATS (automatic transfer service) accounts; less float	1343.7
M2	M1 *plus* savings deposits and small-denomination time deposits (less than $100 000); and retail money market mutual fund deposit accounts	6342.7
M3	M2 *plus* large-denomination time deposits and repos; term Eurodollars of U.S. residents held worldwide; balances in money market funds	9285.1

Source: Federal Reserve (Washington, D.C.: Board of Governors of the Federal Reserve): Table H6. Fuller definitions for these monetary aggregates can be found in the footnotes to the table. Data are seasonally adjusted.

Note: Data are for the end of October 2004.

Although Congress has recently forced it to announce in public the results of FOMC meetings (with a lag) as well as to testify twice a year before Congress on how monetary policy operates, such reforms have not adversely affected the Fed's independence.

U.S. monetary aggregates are defined in Table 25.3. As in Canada, financial innovations have reduced considerably the importance of M1, especially relative to M3. Perhaps the most important monetary policy tool is the **Federal funds rate** (**FFR**). Federal funds are entitlements to balances at the regional Fed banks. The FFR is roughly equivalent to the overnight rate in Canada. Virtually all depository institutions have access to these funds, which helps ensure the liquidity of the banking system.[19]

FEDERAL RESERVE OPERATIONS

The Federal Reserve was not originally created to actively intervene in the economy. The Great Depression changed all that. The structure of the Fed was centralized, and it was recognized that open market operations in particular represented an important instrument to control interest rates and therefore inflation. The advent of World War II effectively took away the interest rate instrument from the Fed and, consequently, some of its independence. The *Fed–Treasury Accord* of 1951 returned interest rate control to the Fed.[20] Until the early 1960s, however, the Fed relied mainly on the manipulation of reserves to implement monetary policy. The pace of financial innovations during the 1960s made it more difficult for the Fed to rely on money stock instruments of monetary policy, and so the interest rate instrument remained the principal tool of monetary policy. The ascent of monetarism (see Chapter 21) led to the formulation of explicit monetary targets during the 1970s in the United States and elsewhere. Part of the shift is also explained by the attempt by Congress to make the Fed more accountable to the public. The inflation and subsequent stagflation in the 1970s pointed to the need for a dramatic change. This change was accomplished by Paul Volcker, soon after his appointment by President Carter, who instituted a policy of strict monetary targeting. This policy led, in the United States and the rest of the industrialized world, to dramatic increases in both the level and volatility of interest rates, as we have already seen (for example, in Chapter 6). The Volcker experiment continued until approximately 1982; targeting reserves of the banking system as well as interest rate control have to this day served as instruments of monetary policy. Congress also intervened again in monetary policy affairs by requiring that the Fed chair periodically report to Congress in person as well as by way of a monetary policy report. This device has since been introduced in several other countries, including Canada.

19 For greater details on the operations of this market, see J.S.G. Wilson, *Money Markets: The International Perspective* (London: Routledge, 1993): 118–23.

20 A masterful account of the first decades of the Federal Reserve is A.H. Meltzer, *A History of the Federal Reserve* (Chicago: University of Chicago Press, 2003).

Historically, the Fed, like most other central banks, tended to raise or reduce interest rates *following* the appearance of economic evidence that such action was required. However, since Alan Greenspan became chair of the board of governors, he has made it clear on several occasions that the Fed must act in advance of what it believes the future course of the economy will be. This protection has resulted in a series of "pre-emptive strikes" against expected upsurges of inflation, followed by a gradual reduction in the Fed funds rate, as fears of higher future inflation among the FOMC members subsided. The mechanism used to ensure that the Fed provided a more transparent monetary policy, as well as to warn the public and financial markets that the Fed meant business, was the release of the minutes of the FOMC meetings. Meetings are usually scheduled for Tuesdays. These minutes were intended to announce whether the Fed tilted toward interest rate increases or reductions. Unfortunately, soon after the practice began, the Fed realized that its announcements could also confuse markets. In particular, market participants were unsure whether the Fed's bias in interest rate developments signalled an intention to change these rates or a possible change in rates. Moreover, the horizon the Fed had in mind was also left unclear. Even Alan Greenspan noted that the Fed's directive in August 1999 "was subject to differing interpretations."[21] Recognition of this problem has led to an attempt to ensure that the Fed's intentions are clear. Thus, for example, in the FOMC meeting of November 1999, the minutes state that "all the members supported raising the Committee's target for the federal funds rate by 25 basis points at this meeting." The minutes then go on to state that "any action might have to wait until the meeting in early February…[in the year 2000]" to contemplate further action.

In January 2000, the Fed announced that, shortly after each FOMC meeting, a statement would be issued announcing its "assessment of the risks in the foreseeable future to the attainment of its long-run goals of price stability and suitable economic growth."[22]

25.5   THE PRINCIPAL TOOLS OF MONETARY POLICY

OPEN MARKET OPERATIONS

The purchase or sale of U.S. government securities, principally Treasury bills, is one of the most important tools of monetary policy at the disposal of the Fed. As we have seen (for example, in Chapter 6), a purchase of bonds expands the money supply, whereas the sale of government bonds contracts the money supply. Occasionally, however, rather than deliberately attempting to influence the money supply, the Fed may act in a defensive manner, by using open market operations to prevent a change in the money supply that would otherwise take place because of events in financial markets. For example, if the Treasury sells securities that the Fed believes will have adverse effects on the money supply, the Fed can use open market operations to counteract such effects. Open market operations are conducted daily by the New York Federal Reserve Bank after consultation with the board of governors in Washington to determine the exact scale of operations. In addition, the New York Fed uses repos and reverse repos (see Chapter 4) as temporary devices in the conduct of monetary policy.

THE FED DISCOUNT RATE AND THE FED FUNDS RATE

The Federal Reserve also conducts monetary policy by making funds available to the banking system at its discount "window." The resulting loans are short-term (a few days at most) and are used by banks needing liquidity temporarily. The interest rate on such loans is the Fed discount rate—the subject of intense scrutiny by financial markets, since the FOMC sets it at its meetings. Supplementing the Fed's discount window is the U.S. version of the interbank overnight market

---

21 As quoted in R.W. Stevenson, "Fed Reconsiders Policy of Disclosing Tilt on Rates," *New York Times*, 8 October 1999.
22 See **www.federalreserve.gov**. An interesting account of the Greenspan years is contained in L.H. Meyer, *A Term at The Fed* (New York: Harper Collins, 2004).

FINANCIAL FOCUS 25.2

SEPTEMBER 11 AND THE GLOBAL FINANCIAL SYSTEM

The attacks on the World Trade Center in New York directly impacted one of the key financial marketplaces of the global financial system. Although the heads of central banks and financial institutions had gotten used to dealing with major financial crises with global repercussions, most recently the Asian financial crisis and the failure of the LCTM (Long-Term Credit Management) hedge fund, nothing approaching this magnitude had been experienced in living memory. As it happens, many of the world's top central bankers were away from their home offices on the day the terrorists struck New York. However, in a matter of days, finance ministers and central bankers agreed on a broad outline for action. First, there was a coordinated and significant reduction in key central bank lending rates, beginning with the Fed's decision to cut the Fed funds rate by 50 basis points on September 18. Almost simultaneously, the Fed and the European Central Bank made it abundantly clear to financial markets worldwide that liquidity would be available to private banks in abundant quantities and that existing regulations (such as collateral requirements) restricting certain types of loans to other financial institutions would not be enforced, at least until the crisis was over. Finally, the Fed reactivated a swap arrangement with the European Central Bank that would allow the ECB to make any loans to commercial banks in Europe in return for euros. These steps proved to be unnecessary, since liquidity was plentiful and the world's financial markets were able to easily weather the storm. Contingency plans already in place helped save the day.

Questions for discussion

1. Can you think of recent events with global implications that led central banks to have adequate contingency plans in place to help deal with a crisis such as September 11?

2. Did the extra steps to make liquidity available worldwide mean that the central banks wasted their time taking action in the wake of the terrorist attacks?

Source

G. Ip and J. VandeHei, "How Policy Makers Regrouped to Defend the Financial System," *Wall Street Journal*, 18 September 2001, available from **interactive.wsj.com/archive/retrieve.cgi?id=SB10 00760083847882520.djm**.

in Canada. The rate on such loans closely parallels the Fed's discount rate and is referred to as the Fed funds rate, a confusing term since the funds involved are not made available by the federal government or any other central authority. Instead, the funds are balances held by the banks in the Federal Reserve system. Because of the visibility and influence of the Fed's discount rate on liquidity in the financial system, not only in the U.S. but worldwide, it has become one of the most important tools of monetary policy. The global reach of the Fed's actions is intense, for example, as reactions to the attacks on September 11, 2001 (**Financial Focus 23.2: September 11 and the Global Financial System**) demonstrated.

SUMMARY

- The U.S. financial system differs in important respects from the Canadian system by virtue of its greater recognition of regional versus national interests, though this is changing.

- Until recently, branch banking was severely restricted in the United States.

- During the Great Depression, one-third of the banking system failed in the United States, whereas virtually no failures occurred in Canada.

- One of the most important reforms in the post-Depression era was the introduction of deposit insurance. This insurance is managed by the Federal Deposit Insurance Corporation (FDIC).

- Central banking did not effectively exist in the United States until 1913, when the Federal Reserve Board (Fed) was created.

- Early in the history of the Fed, decisions about monetary policy were decentralized. Following the Great Depression, power over the conduct of monetary policy was greatly centralized in Washington, with the board of governors of the Federal Reserve system.

- Commercial banks, savings and loan, mutual savings banks, and credit unions are the principal financial intermediaries in the United States.

- Banks in the United States must meet reserve requirements, unlike banks in Canada.

- Until recently, U.S. banks were prohibited from selling or dealing in corporate securities.

- U.S. banks face a multitude of regulators and supervisors. Although the overlapping responsibilities have been costly, they have also spurred financial innovations, many of which were later introduced into Canada.

- *The Financial Services Act* of 1999 represents the most comprehensive set of reforms to the U.S. banking system since the Great Depression. Many barriers, including ones affecting branch banking and underwriting have been removed. Others, such as barriers on the sale of insurance products, remain.

- Consolidation of the U.S. banking sectors is the dominant theme for the years to come, with a sharp downward trend in the number of banks and greater concentration among a few larger banks.

- The Federal Open Market Committee is the principal decision-making body of the Fed. It meets regularly and its decisions, as well as the comments of its chair, are watched and acted on around the world.

- Open market operations and the setting of the Fed funds rate (Fed funds) are the key instruments of U.S. monetary policy.

IMPORTANT TERMS

Federal funds rate (FFR), 514
Federal Open Market Committee (FOMC), 512
Federal Reserve (the Fed), 512
Fedwire, 513
Financial Services Act of 1999, 510
Glass–Stegall Act, 508
international banking facilities (IBFs), 507

investment bank, 508
negotiable order of withdrawal (NOW), 508
Office of the Comptroller of the Currency (OCC), 510
Office of Thrift Supervision (OTS), 510
savings and loan associations (S&Ls), 507
unit banking, 506

PROBLEMS

1. S&Ls borrow short term and lend long term. What is the problem with such a strategy when there is an unexpected increase in all interest rates? Why is it necessary that the increases be unexpected?

2. Explain, in terms of the Fisher effect of Chapter 5, how a pre-emptive strike against an upsurge of future inflation would lead to higher interest rates today.

3. In what sense can reserve requirements represent a tax on banks? Explain.

4. Suppose that the Fed engages in open market operations involving the sale of U.S. Treasury securities. Use the loanable funds framework of Chapter 6 to show what happens to the interest rate. Would Canadian interest rates be affected? Why or why not?

DISCUSSION QUESTIONS

1. The United States' financial system is often referred to as a dual banking system. Why?

2. Almost 70% of mortgages issued by the United States's S&Ls in 1984 had adjustable rates. By 1986, approximately 70% of mortgages had fixed rates. In retrospect, why did S&Ls wish they had issued fixed-rate mortgages in 1984 and adjustable-rate ones in 1986? Explain.

3. What arguments would you marshal for the policy that advocates the separation of commercial lending and securities-underwriting activities? Explain.

4. When the United States finally removed interest rate restrictions, its banks limited cheque-writing privileges on money market deposit accounts in particular. Why? Explain.

5. Outline the principal differences between the U.S. and Canadian banking systems considered in this text.

ONLINE APPLICATION

1. Go to the FDIC's Web site at **www.fdic.gov**. Click on *Industry Analysis*, then scroll down to *Bank Data and Statistics*, click on *Historical Statistics on Banking*, and then on *Banks and Thrift Failure Reports*. Find the total number of bank and thrift failures for 1980 to 1985. Contrast that number with the number of failures between 1995 and 1998. What might explain the large difference in the number of failures? Discuss.

2. Go to the St. Louis Fed's Web site at **www.stls.frb.org**. Click on *economic research*, then choose FRED II. Choose to download interest rates and the discount rate found under FRB rates. Next, under *consumer price index*, find the CPI for all urban consumers, seasonally adjusted. First, calculate the rate of inflation in the U.S. ($\{[CPI_t - CPI_{t-1}]/CPI_{t-1}\} \times 100$). Plot the discount rate and the Fed funds rate. They should move closely together since the Fed changes the discount rate while the Fed funds market responds to the setting of the Fed funds rate. Next, plot either the discount rate or the Fed funds rate against inflation. Does it appear from the plot that the Fed in recent years has been practising pre-emptive strikes against inflation, as opposed to waiting for actual inflation to change before acting?

References can be found on www.mcgrawhill.ca/college/siklos

CHAPTER 26

International Financial Institutions and Regulations

LEARNING OBJECTIVES

After reading and studying this chapter, you should be able to

26.1 explain why international financial institutions emerged

describe the origins, development, and current functions of international financial institutions:

26.2 Bank for International Settlements,

26.3 the Bretton Woods system

26.4 the International Monetary Fund,

26.5 the World Bank, and

26.6 the European Bank for Reconstruction and Development

26.7 explain how the European exchange rate mechanism works

26.8 understand the functioning of the European Monetary Union

Although serious international cooperation began after World War I, it produced few mechanisms in the financial sphere.[1] The need for international trade to rebuild war-ravaged economies after World War II did, however, lead to the creation of some international financial institutions, and facilitated the growth of international markets for foreign exchange and bonds. The collapse of the Soviet Union in the 1990s also led to demands for an institution to finance the reconstruction of the former centrally planned economies.

Of the monetary, trade, and development agencies that now exist, we examine three: the Bank for International Settlements, the International Monetary Fund, and the World Bank. We also consider the Bretton Woods system of fixed exchange rates, now abandoned but in place for almost a quarter century after World War II, and the European System of Central Banks, responsible for monetary policy in Europe.

26.1 FORCES CREATING INTERNATIONAL FINANCIAL INSTITUTIONS

Why was there a flurry of new international cooperative ventures after World War II? It has been suggested that problems inherent in the operations of the gold standard, the interwar propensity

---

1 The League of Nations was the first international agency to have some responsibilities over financial matters. However, because the United States never formally joined, it was not viewed as a particularly effective international financial agency. Central banks did cooperate at the time, somewhat informally and none too successfully. See Eichengreen (1992).

for countries to engage in beggar-thy-neighbour policies (one country attempts to artificially depreciate its currency to induce a favourable balance of payments outcome), and the destruction created by two world wars combined to foster a new mood of international cooperation. The resulting institutions (some of whose origins predate 1945) provided countries with rules of cooperation, financial resources that permitted the rules to be obeyed, and institutions that enabled the monitoring of the degree of international cooperation achieved.

Their success was not unqualified. Each of the institutions considered in this chapter failed in some sense to achieve its original lofty objectives. Yet all survived—in part because the costs of not cooperating usually seemed greater than the benefits of breaking the rules. When cooperation failed, it was because the relevant rules were not deemed credible. As noted at the beginning of this book, the notion of credibility is central to the understanding of all financial systems.

Indeed, it is the flexibility of existing arrangements that has led to the suggestion that there is a sort of cycle in countries' preferences for fixed versus flexible exchange rates. Thus, the 1970s and much of the 1980s were the heyday of flexible exchange rates; in the 1990s, a preference for fixed exchange rates has re-emerged in some quarters.[2]

The Asian financial crisis of the late 1990s, the burgeoning current account deficit in the U.S., and the pressures of a depreciating U.S. dollar and its impact on China's economic growth have all contributed to sour views against fixed exchange rates, at least among many academics. By contrast, membership into the Euro area requires a stable exchange rate. Hence, there is by no means universal agreement on which exchange rate regime is better, as Chapter 8 has already revealed.

26.2 THE BANK FOR INTERNATIONAL SETTLEMENTS

The war reparations imposed on Germany and the former Austro-Hungarian Empire after World War I had disastrous economic consequences for those countries and many others, such as the emergence of hyperinflations and the failure of several central banks. One response was the formation of the **Bank for International Settlements (BIS)** to serve and foster cooperation among central banks. Founded by the central banks of the United States, Great Britain, France, Germany, Italy, Belgium, and Japan in 1930, it expanded to 55 members as of 2004, including Canada. It is the world's oldest international financial institution.[3]

The BIS is owned by its shareholders,[4] primarily the central banks, and is run by a president and a board of directors that includes representatives of the central banks of the founding members and a few other countries, as well as representatives from finance, industry, and commerce appointed by the founding members.[5] At least one general meeting is held each year. Decisions are carried out by the general manager, currently Malcolm Knight, a Canadian and former deputy-governor of the Bank of Canada, and an administrative staff at headquarters in Basel, Switzerland.

Interestingly, the BIS uses the gold franc as its unit of account, originally linked to the Swiss franc's value in terms of gold, but now valued at US$1.94. Its balance sheets are reported in terms of the gold franc.[6]

---

2 The Group of 30, **www.group30.org**, is one prominent private institution that focuses on international financial issues and that has advocated a return to some form of fixed exchange rate.

3 The BIS was actually slated for extinction "at the earliest possible moment" [as quoted in R. Skidelsky, *John Maynard Keynes: Fighting for Britain 1937–1946* (London: Macmillan, 2000): 354] until Keynes intervened. Clearly, the moment has still not arrived.

4 In 2001, the BIS announced that all remaining privately held shares would be repurchased. A court case, brought about because some parties claimed additional amounts were due, finally was settled in 2003, and caused a delay in the final repurchase.

5 Collectively, these 10 countries, which include Canada, are known today as the Group of 10 or G-10 countries.

6 All other currencies held are converted into gold francs at the market exchange rate against the U.S. dollar.

In particular, the BIS serves as a forum where central banks can discuss and coordinate their respective monetary policies. It can also

- Buy and sell gold and foreign exchange.
- Make advances or borrow from its member central banks.
- Buy, sell, or discount bills such as Treasury bills or other marketable securities.
- Act as an agent or a correspondent for any central bank.
- Compile data relative to the performance of the international financial system.

Bank for
International
Settlements
www.bis.org

The borrowing and lending activities of the BIS are principally in the form of swaps against gold or foreign currencies.

The BIS played an important role during the debt crisis of the early 1980s when it granted credits to nonmember central banks, such as those of Mexico and Argentina, until these countries could make loan arrangements with other international agencies. The BIS also played a coordinating role in halting the Mexican peso crisis of 1994–95, and again during and following the terrorist attacks on September 11, 2001.

The BIS is also known in its capacity as a forum for international monetary cooperation. This function has become especially crucial at a time when interest rate differentials—for example, between the European Central Bank and the United States—have been a source of conflict about how monetary policies are being carried out by member countries. The collapse of the former Communist bloc and the need for those countries to develop central banks modelled on those in Canada and other Western industrialized countries also enabled the BIS to fulfil its role as an adviser to central banks and thus serve as a central bank for central banks.

The BIS is now best known as a forum for international banking supervision as a result of a 1974 decision by the G-10 to establish the Basel Committee on Banking Supervision. A key outcome of the committee's work is the BIS capital adequacy standards (see Chapter 11). In 1998, the BIS became home to the International Association of Insurance Supervisors, whose work parallels the Committee on Banking Supervision.

26.3 THE BRETTON WOODS SYSTEM

As the end of World War II came into sight, the victors were planning the postwar financial system. In July 1944, representatives of more than 40 nations met at the International Monetary and Financial Conference in Bretton Woods, New Hampshire. Led by U.S. and U.K. delegates,[7] they agreed that the financial structures of the post–World War I era had been largely a failure, that the mistakes of the past should not be repeated, and that the primary objective of the postwar order should be the creation of an international financial system that was multilateral and stable.

---

7 The two most influential figures at Bretton Woods were Harry Dexter White, of the United States, and John Maynard Keynes, of the United Kingdom. Keynes had also been a U.K. delegate to the Peace Conference of Versailles after World War I. When that group demanded harsh reparations from Germany, he resigned in protest, arguing that the European economies needed stabilization, not revenge, and he criticized the aftermath throughout the interwar years. See D.E. Moggridge, *Maynard Keynes: An Economist's Biography* (New York: Routledge, 1992) for a description of Keynes's role at the Bretton Woods Conference. Canadians also played an important role at the Bretton Woods Conference. See B. Muirhead, *Against the Odds* (Toronto: University of Toronto Press, 1999). White was accused of being a Soviet spy, and this explains, in part, why his name was relegated to second place behind Keynes. See J.M Boughton, "The Case Against Harry Dexter White: Still Not Proven," IMF working paper 00/49, August 2000, and "Why White, Not Keynes? Inventing the Post-War International Monetary System," International Monetary Fund working Paper No. 02/52, March 2002.

One of the ingredients of that stability would be freer trade than the world had ever known.[8] Another was a system of fixed exchange rates and **convertible** (tradeable) **currencies**.

To manage the new international order, the group, eventually working through the United Nations, created two institutions with an international membership (though dominated by the United States): the International Monetary Fund and the International Bank for Reconstruction and Development (also known as the World Bank). We will look more closely at these institutions after we consider the exchange rate system.

THE BRETTON WOODS ADJUSTABLE PEG EXCHANGE RATE SYSTEM

The architects of Bretton Woods wanted the advantages of the gold standard, but not at the cost of forcing all countries to pursue similar monetary policies. Thus, they fixed exchange rates but allowed them to fluctuate freely within a narrowly defined band. Moreover, they set up a mechanism to allow the fixed exchange rate to be adjusted in the event of need.

Therefore, each member of the IMF agreed to the following, which became known as the **Bretton Woods system** of *fixed exchange rates*:

1. Establish a *par value* for its currency and maintain the exchange rate within 1% of par.

2. Change that par value only on approval of the IMF, which the IMF would grant only if a member's balance of payments was in "fundamental disequilibrium."

In effect, the member nations pegged their exchange rates to the U.S. dollar.[9]

This par value system meant that IMF members had to fix the value of their currencies. Against what? The natural starting place was the price of gold.

As the dominant economic power of the immediate postwar era, the United States agreed to fix the price of gold at US$35 per ounce.[10] It could defend that price because it had a large supply of gold and of dollars. If the price went up it could release gold to the market, driving down its price. If the price went down, it could use its dollars to purchase gold and raise the price back to $35 an ounce.

The other countries then pegged their exchange rates to the U.S. dollar. If the rates were properly set and the price of gold held fixed, prices worldwide would be fixed. Thus, the architects envisaged there could be no sustained price level changes or inflation in the Bretton Woods system.

The system attempted to circumvent the automatic adjustment of the balance of payments. Recall that a loss of reserves stems from a balance of payments deficit and a rise of reserves from a balance of payments surplus. Now consider the following illustration.[11] Suppose a country pegs its exchange rate too low. Say the country is Canada, and the rate chosen is C$1 = US$1, although the market-clearing rate is closer to C$1.40 = US$1. With the overvalued Canadian dollar, there is soon excess demand for foreign exchange. To hold the rate fixed, the central bank must make its dollars more expensive by selling some of its reserves of gold or foreign currency. The system also works in the opposite direction. An exchange rate set higher than the market-clearing rate can be defended by purchasing reserves (usually U.S. dollars).

---

8 To this end, they created the *General Agreement on Tariffs and Trade* (*GATT*), an institution that continues to work to reduce trade barriers under the name of the World Trade Organization, **www.wto.org**. Many Bretton Woods participants also went on to help found other multilateral organizations, including what would become the Organisation for Economic Co-operation and Development (OECD) and the precursors of the European Community.

9 Doing so required that currencies be convertible. That is, someone wishing to buy Swedish kroner with U.S. dollars had to be able to do so. If there is no trading, currencies are not convertible. Some IMF members could not satisfy this condition until the late 1950s. As a consequence of World War II, many countries had no significant foreign exchange reserves or gold.

10 Since London was the centre of gold trading, it was the Bank of England that performed the transactions required to ensure that the fixed price was maintained.

11 For the background material necessary to understand this illustration, see Chapters 8 and 24.

But such transactions cannot go on forever. If the country is selling reserves, it will eventually run out of them. If it is buying foreign currency, it will eventually find the purchases strain its economy. Even more quickly, it will encounter the problems of changes in its money supply; enhanced by the multiplier effect, they can quickly mean inflation (from the increase in the money supply occasioned by selling reserves). Now a *sterilization* (offset) technique can be and often is used to prevent changes in the money supply resulting from foreign exchange transactions. If the central bank purchases foreign currency, it can sell an equivalent amount of domestic financial assets (say, bonds to the banks). The two transactions' effects on the money supply (which need not be simultaneous) offset each other, in theory at least. But sterilization in one direction cannot go on indefinitely either.

The creators of the system realized that its ideals could not be maintained at all times.[12] For this reason, they allowed some flexibility in exchange rate movements, they endowed the IMF with a pool of foreign reserves on which members could draw, they provided would-be borrowers with advice (accompanied by considerable moral suasion) on the management of their economies, and they provided a mechanism for changing par value if a country's balance of payments was in "fundamental disequilibrium."[13]

An illustration of some of the difficulties encountered by the Bretton Woods system early in its history comes from the actions taken by Canada in late 1950. The Canadian dollar's par was originally set at $1 and then devalued in 1949 to 90.9¢. Fearing that the currency was undervalued, the Bank of Canada decided in 1950 to abandon the fixed exchange rate system inherent in the Bretton Woods agreement and allow the dollar to float. Despite criticisms from the IMF, it continued to float until 1961, when it was pegged at 92.5¢ to the U.S. dollar. (Since that rate was not far from the one at which it was floating, it is not clear that the Canadian decision undermined the Bretton Woods arrangement.)

The system also had its share of successes, since there is strong evidence that economic growth was relatively high and inflation low throughout much of the Bretton Woods era.[14]

THE END OF THE BRETTON WOODS SYSTEM

Despite various crises and the inability of the IMF to enforce the Bretton Woods arrangements at all times (see Table 26.1), the 1950s and 1960s were decades of considerable price stability. But that was a period when a few international economic incidents provided major price shocks. Economics worldwide grew at a healthy rate, and the United States stood ready and able to sustain the system. That situation was coming to an end by the close of the 1960s. The Bretton Woods system did not survive much longer.

Two continuing, related problems with the system were its lack of a formal mechanism to generate exchange rate adjustments and countries' reluctance to change par values, even when it became clear that a major currency was out of line. Who would do the adjusting? When? By how much? The adjustment costs inherent in making a change provided an incentive for one country to wait until another moved.

By the end of the 1960s, the currencies of West Germany and Japan were clearly undervalued vis-à-vis the U.S. dollar. To describe the problem another way, the U.S. dollar was overvalued. The U.S. balance of payments deficit had grown tremendously, the supply of dollars outside the United States was many times larger than its gold reserves, and the demand for gold was soaring.

---

12 That the IMF survived is remarkable in view of the very strict rules it imposed on its members.

13 The term was never defined. It seems to have been used to mean chronic balance of payments deficits that could not be reversed without considerable inflation or deflation.

14 With the 60th anniversary of the IMF, celebrated in 2004, there has been renewed interest in the workings of the Bretton Woods system and in the suitability of limited exchange rate movements. See, for example, J.M. Boughton, "The IMF and the Force of History: Ten Events and Ten Ideas that Have Shaped the Institution," International Monetary Fund, working paper 04/72, May 2004. Also, see **http://jolis.worldbankimflib.org/Bwf/whatisbw.htm**.

For a time, Germany (and a few other countries) kept buying U.S. dollars—several billion within the space of days in spring 1971—to defend its par value. Then Germany finally allowed the Deutschmark to float. And, in August 1971, the United States announced it would no longer permit convertibility of its dollars to gold at $35 per ounce. Although the U.S. measure was announced as temporary, it effectively ended the Bretton Woods system of fixed exchange rates.

Although an attempt was made to patch up Bretton Woods in December 1971, through the *Smithsonian Agreement*—the price of gold would rise to $38 per ounce and exchange rates would be permitted to fluctuate in a wider band (2.25% instead of 1%)—by 1973 the major economic powers were on a de facto flexible exchange rate system that has persisted to this day.

Many people believe that the collapse of the Bretton Woods system was due to the unwillingness of Germany, Japan, and some of the other industrialized countries to defend the overvalued U.S. currency by continually absorbing excess supplies of dollars.[15]

An alternative view[16] is that because the Bretton Woods system effectively placed the world on a U.S.-dollar standard, the U.S. monetary policy dictated world inflation rates. According to this *monetarist* view (monetarism is defined more precisely in Chapter 21), if the U.S. money stock grew too quickly, the resulting inflation would be transmitted to the other countries in the fixed exchange rate system. Thus, the other countries in the system simply refused to support U.S. inflationary policies by 1970. In addition, the growing freedom of capital movements, as country after country dropped capital controls, meant growing pressures on exchange rates that central banks could not (or no longer wanted to) contain. The inevitable outcome of these pressures was to allow exchange rates to fluctuate freely.

Table 26.1	A Brief Chronology of IMF Crises until the End of the Bretton Woods Agreement
December 1945	Bretton Woods Agreement enters into force.
May 1947	France is the first country to draw funds from the IMF.
January 1948	Crises of the franc and subsequent ruling of France's ineligibility to use IMF resources.
September 1949	First major par value adjustment. Canada is among the participants as it devalues its currency.
February 1952	IMF inaugurates standby arrangement (a device to provide credit to member countries).
December 1958	Most Western European currencies achieve convertability.
November 1967	Severe balance of payments problems for the United Kingdom lead to a major devaluation of the pound (14.3% in terms of the dollar).
March 1968	$35/oz. price for gold no longer sustainable.
June 1968	France and the United Kingdom draw large amounts from the IMF (US$745 million and US$1.4 billion, respectively).
August 1969	France devalues the franc against gold (by reducing gold content of the franc).
September 1969	West Germany lets the Deutschmark float after pressure from persistent balance of payment surpluses. One month later the rate is fixed at a revalued rate.
May 1970	Canada lets the dollar float after several capital outflows to the United States.
August 1971	United States suspends the use of gold to settle international transactions. In effect, the announcement marked the end of the Bretton Woods Agreement.
December 1971	Smithsonian Agreement results in a realignment of currencies.

Source: M.G. de Vries, *The IMF in a Changing World: 1945–85* (Washington, D.C.: International Monetary Fund, 1986).

---

15 The fact that these countries felt strong enough to confront the United States may also be explained by the fading of U.S. hegemony in world economic affairs, particularly as the costs of the war in Vietnam were rising.

16 But not antithetical, as we will see below.

Long after the end of the Bretton Woods system, the major economic powers attempted to influence the value of the most important currencies. One such example was the so-called *Plaza Accord* of 22 September 1985 when the G-5 countries agreed to arrange to reduce the value of the U.S. dollar. The accord was largely unsuccessful, as was the *Louvre Accord* of 22 February 1987, when finance ministers of the G-3 attempted to target the U.S. dollar vis-à-vis the deutschmark and the yen. These targets were effectively abandoned after the stock market crash later the same year.

Ironically, the worlds' subsequent experience with floating—and volatile—exchange rates has proven to be an unsatisfactory one. Hence, many people would like to return to some sort of a regime with exchange rate stability. One manifestation of this desire is the European Monetary Union, which we discuss later in this chapter.

26.4 THE INTERNATIONAL MONETARY FUND

International
Monetary Fund
www.imf.org

The **International Monetary Fund (IMF)** was founded to promote international cooperation in economic matters, to provide a forum in which members could agree on a common code of conduct in their financial affairs, and to aid nations in solving balance of payments problems. This broad mandate means that one of its original purposes—the maintenance and enforcement of the Bretton Woods system of exchange rates—no longer exists. Indeed, some have argued the IMF should be dissolved since it cannot carry out its original mandate. However, it seems to have taken on a new role, along with the BIS, which was discussed earlier, of coordinating lending and borrowing functions, especially in crisis situations, and of helping emerging economies develop sound policies.

This help is accomplished via a policy of surveillance, whereby the IMF provides a comprehensive appraisal of a country's economic policies and the appropriateness of its exchange rate regime.[17]

ORGANIZATION AND STRUCTURE

Almost 200 countries are now members of the IMF. It is headed by a managing director (by custom, a European national), who chairs a board of governors that holds most of the organization's powers and usually meets once a year.

Each member's voting rights and borrowing rights are a function of its *quota*, a kind of subscription fee whose amount reflects relative economic position.[18]

The quotas provide the financial resources that the IMF can use to assist member countries with particular economic difficulties. A member can borrow quite easily against the first 25% of its quota, which is called the first *tranche*.[19] However, countries must demonstrate some commitment to overcoming balance of payments difficulties. Borrowing against additional tranches is progressively more difficult. In some circumstances, the IMF practises conditionality—that is, it denies access to its funds (and thus indirectly to international financial markets) until it is satisfied that the domestic monetary authorities are putting adequate adjustment policies in place.

---

17 Some of the information pertaining to the IMF's views of particular countries' policies is published in its Annual Report or the twice-yearly *World Economic Outlook*.

18 The quotas are denominated in special drawing rights (SDRs), an accounting unit devised by the IMF and explained later in this section. The quotas reflect the political influence of a country as well as its economic influence. An amusing illustration of the political influences on the size of quotas comes from R. Skidelsky [*John Maynard Keynes: Fighting for Britain 1937-1946* (London: Macmillan, 2000): 351], in relating the story of the Soviet representative who, when told that Soviet national income statistics did not justify the quota figure they asked for, "replied cheerfully that he would produce new statistics. He got his way." This may have been in part due to White's (see note 7) alleged sympathies with the Soviet regime.

19 From the French term for "slice."

This ability to impose stringent economic discipline on loan recipients gave the IMF a crucial—and some think successful—role during the international debt crisis of the early 1980s (see Chapter 24), and in managing the transition to a market economy in the former Socialist bloc countries.[20]

SDRs

One of the early difficulties the IMF faced was the shortage of gold and U.S. dollars in the world trading system. Many countries had political reasons for not liking the fact that the U.S. dollar was the dominant world currency, and many viewed the supply of gold as potentially unreliable, again for political reasons, because South Africa and the then–Soviet Union were two of the largest producers of gold.

Ironically, the importance of the U.S. dollar to the world economy meant that to supply a constant flow of reserves to the rest of the world, the United States would have to maintain a balance of payments deficit which, as we saw in Chapter 24, is not a desirable thing to do in the long run. Moreover, to do so would undermine the value of the U.S. dollar relative to gold, the other major reserve asset. So there was an inconsistency in the Bretton Woods system, called the *Triffin paradox*.

One response to this problem was the creation in 1969 of the **special drawing right (SDR)**, a new international reserve asset, to supplement existing world reserves of currency. The SDR was initially defined in terms of a gold content, but was redefined in 1974 as a weighted average of a basket of currencies; the weights are revised periodically.[21]

Although giving countries access to a new source of liquidity, such as the SDR, has distinct advantages, there is the danger that one country will overuse it at the expense of other countries. However, obtaining financial resources in SDRs is costly since borrowers are charged a competitive rate.[22] Therefore, even if a member borrows in SDRs for a prolonged period, it is not obvious that the borrower is benefiting at the expense of lenders (the other members of the IMF) unless the loan has a high default risk.

That the SDR has not become a more important international currency may, in part, be explained by the fact that since its introduction, financial markets in the Western industrialized countries have managed to create a host of new financial instruments that have effectively eliminated the worldwide shortage of liquidity of the earlier years of the IMF.

Nevertheless, SDRs have proven important to the developing nations, and it is they who have pushed hardest to increase the availability of this financial instrument.[23] The extent to which SDRs have provided additional financial resources is evidenced by the fact that developing countries continue to experience problems servicing their debt. By contrast, net-creditor countries rarely use any of their SDR allocations.[23] Clearly, the SDR can serve as an instrument of transfer of financial resources from the developed countries to the developing countries.

---

20 According to one first-hand account, the IMF generally attempted to reach a consensus with countries experiencing financial difficulties and not to impose ideologically motivated solutions. The fact that it played hardball on occasion may actually have had beneficial effects for some countries. For a markedly different view, which argues, among other things, that the focus on balance of payments problems is a far too narrow one, see J. Spraos, "IMF Conditionality: Ineffectual, Inefficient, and Mistargeted," *Essays in International Finance,* no. 166 (December 1986), Princeton University.

21 An intellectual antecedent of the SDR was a plan put forth by Keynes at the Bretton Woods Conference. Keynes wanted to create a new international currency unit called the "bancor." Its value would be fixed in terms of gold, and every country would then set the par value of its currency in terms of the bancor.

22 The rate charged on SDR loans is a weighted average of the yields on three-month Treasury bills in the United States, the United Kingdom, and France, the three-month interbank deposit rate in Germany, and the three-month CD rate in Japan.

23 See P. Norman, "Spanner in the Rolls-Royce Engine," *Financial Times* of London (4 October 1994): 17.

24 See W.L. Coats Jr., R.W. Furstenberg, and P. Isard, "The SDR System and the Issue of Resource Transfers," *Essays in International Finance,* no. 180 (December 1990), Princeton University.

Beyond the SDR facility, other mechanisms are available for countries in need of financial assistance. Stand-by arrangements, extended facilities, and enhanced structural adjustment facilities are all designed either for temporary balance of payments deficits, or for more fundamental economic problems requiring longer-term loans.

The need for alternative reserve currencies such as SDRs reflects an additional flaw in the Bretton Woods system, namely that the U.S. dollar, the reserve currency of choice, cannot be supplied in sufficient quantities to satisfy the needs of trade unless the U.S. perpetually runs a balance of payments deficit (also see Chapter 8). Moreover, as we saw, the Bretton Woods system relied on a fixed relation between the U.S. dollar and the price of gold. Clearly, this relationship cannot be maintained if the value of U.S. dollars used as reserves exceeds the country's gold reserves, as happened beginning around 1964. This flaw, referred to earlier as the *Triffin paradox,*[25] revealed not only the need for additional sources of liquidity, but also the unsustainability of the Bretton Woods system as originally designed.

FINANCIAL LIBERALIZATION

Since the mandate of the IMF includes facilitating and encouraging international cooperation in economic matters, this would seem to include efforts at reducing or eliminating barriers to trade and the liberalization of capital movements. There is little doubt that the 1980s saw a significant amount of capital liberalization worldwide.[26] Among the major developments have been the reduction or elimination of credit controls, the deregulation of interest rates, and the freer movement of capital globally. Indeed, there are some who blame the liberalization of capital markets for the onset of the Asian crisis, since it was apparently partly fuelled by "hot" money, that is, funds invested in short-term financial instruments that can be quickly sold and converted to other currencies. However, it is now becoming clear that, without a proper regulatory and supervisory structure, which was missing in most Asian countries prior to 1997, financial crises are more likely. As a result of these developments, the IMF, with the support of several industrial countries, has taken it upon itself to increase the surveillance of the financial market practices of emerging market economies. Another reason for the increased demands for information and caution at the IMF is the *moral hazard* (see Chapter 16) problem in international lending of the kind offered by institutions such as the IMF. If lending to countries facing some crisis does not lead to the creation of institutions to mitigate future crises there is a built-in incentive for future "bad" behaviour leading to the request for even more loans. Indeed, one of the lessons learned began to be applied in the case of Argentina in 2002, when the IMF refused to extend new funding, or provide the necessary "seal of approval" for other agencies or banks to lend to the country, until there were almost ironclad guarantees that the necessary institutional changes were in place to provide proper supervision, regulation, and sustainable fiscal policies.

THE FUTURE OF THE IMF

A great deal of attention has been focused on the IMF in recent years, especially in light of the Mexican crisis of 1994–95. Supporters of the IMF point to the fact that the original Articles of Agreement mandated the Fund's surveillance function. This role has been the primary one for the IMF in recent years. However, critics argue that the IMF acts to increase the role of "market discipline" imposed by private capital flows as the principal device to correct balance of payments disequilibria. Others believe that the IMF should act as an international country-rating agency. Still

---

25 Named after the Belgian economist who was a professor at Yale University.
26 See J. Williamson and M. Mahar, "A Survey of Financial Liberalization," Princeton Essays in International Finance, No. 211, 1999.

others believe that the IMF should become an international bankruptcy court.

It is clear that, with the adoption of flexible exchange rate regimes by most industrial countries, the original function of the IMF has all but become irrelevant, increasing the pressure on the IMF to reform. In addition, private capital flows have grown enormously, as has the membership of the IMF. All these factors have increased rather than reduced the financial demands on the IMF. Why? The Mexican crisis of 1994–95 presents an illustration. Mexico had a weak and inefficient banking system. Information available to market participants suggested that the government would maintain the peg, as it had for so long (see **Financial Focus 8.2**), even in the face of continued balance of payments difficulties. Finally, a large volume of short-term Mexican debt was denominated in U.S. dollars. Although this shielded investors from exchange rate risk, it did not offer protection from default risk (also see the discussion on the debt crisis in Chapter 22). Consequently, supporters argue that quick action by the IMF, in the face of capital market imperfections, can prevent a crisis affecting one country from influencing another, the so-called contagion effect. In this sense, a need exists for an international watchdog to prevent a global financial meltdown. Arguably, the IMF's role during the Asian crisis of 1997–98 represents an example in which the institution's intervention proved crucial, though not without the help of the major industrial economies, especially the United States. Lessons from the Bretton Woods experience live on, as the **Economics Focus 26.1: A Modern Version of an Old Problem? China versus the Rest of the World: Solving the Exchange Rate Riddle** reveals.

26.5 THE WORLD BANK

The IBRD
**www.worldbank.
org**

The **International Bank for Reconstruction and Development (IBRD)**, more often referred to as the **World Bank**, a United Nations affiliate, aids developing countries by

1. Assisting in reconstruction and development.

2. Promoting private foreign investment.

3. Making loans from its own funds and channelling aid from the developed countries.

4. Guaranteeing loans made to members.

5. Promoting the growth of international trade.

With more than 150 members, the World Bank is run by a president (by custom a U.S. citizen), who chairs a board of governors.

The World Bank was conceived at the Bretton Woods Conference as an institution to help finance the reconstruction of Europe after World War II. It began operations in 1946. Soon after, the advent of the United States' Marshall Plan[27] relegated the World's Bank role in Europe to a secondary one, so it sought to justify its existence through loans to developing countries.

The funds loaned out by the Bank are raised through members' subscriptions, through the retention of earnings on previous loans, and through the sale of bonds in international financial markets. The Bank also engages extensively in currency swaps. Because of the nature of the loans, their term is often for periods of 15 to 20 years. In addition, there is a grace period of up to five years should a member prove unable to repay the loan at maturity.

In the late 1970s, the Bank began to move away from loans aimed at specific reconstruction projects toward helping countries restructure their entire economies or some of their vital sectors.

---

27 In 1947, U.S. Secretary of State George Marshall, realizing that previous reconstruction plans had badly underestimated the need, offered a massive aid program to the countries of Europe, provided they worked together for economic recovery. Sixteen countries of Western Europe accepted, forming the Organisation for Economic Co-operation and Development, which set priorities for and administered what proved to be nearly $13 billion of assistance. Canada, which was experiencing severe balance of payments problems, also benefited, since the Americans agreed that Marshall Plan purchases could be made here as well as in the United States.

ECONOMICS FOCUS 26.1

A MODERN VERSION OF AN OLD PROBLEM? CHINA VERSUS THE REST OF THE WORLD: SOLVING THE EXCHANGE RATE RIDDLE

The problems inherent in the Bretton Woods system have not entirely disappeared. Many Asian economies kept their exchange rates fairly rigid throughout the early 1990s. The Asian crisis of 1997-98 forced some countries, such as Thailand, to permit more flexibility in exchange rate movements. Others, such as Hong Kong, Singapore, and especially China, continued to persevere with a more rigid exchange rate. China, in particular, has chosen de facto to fix its exchange rate against the U.S. dollar since 1995. Meanwhile, the time profile of inflation in China, shown below, reveals a rapid disinflation after 1995 followed by a two-year bout of deflation. Although some observers (e.g., Bernanke 2002) suggested that rapid productivity growth, that is, a supply side shock, might explain the deflation, Burdekin and Siklos (2004, 2005) and Siklos and Zhang (2005) conclude that traditional monetary policy was the main culprit. We already know from Chapter 8 that the connection between domestic and foreign inflation can work through the exchange rate. Therefore, when the exchange rate is fixed, domestic and foreign inflation rates should be equal, at least in equilibrium. Since the U.S. inflation rate was much lower in 1994 than in China, the adoption of the fixed exchange rate had the desired effect, as is clear from the figure below. Of course, the fact that the nominal exchange rate is fixed does not imply that the real exchange rate is fixed. Indeed, China's real ex-

change rate depreciated by 85% between 1984 and 1993 (Wang 2004). Not surprisingly, this has helped fuel tremendous economic growth, largely driven by spectacular export growth (Rumbaugh and Blancher 2004). Nevertheless, these developments have led many, especially in the U.S., to argue that the Chinese currency, the renminbi, is seriously undervalued, and that a revaluation or, better yet, a floating currency policy, should be adopted. There is little doubt that this view is prompted by the large current account deficit in the U.S. Nevertheless, as this is written, although Chinese policymakers are considering a currency revaluation, they have little reason to hurry, since the People's Bank of China, China's central bank, sits on an enormous stock of foreign exchange reserves built up through large current account surpluses. In this respect, the Chinese predicament differs from that of Germany or Canada during the heyday of the Bretton Woods era. The country seemingly can afford to postpone the inevitable for some time. However, by 2005, rising inflation and import costs, due to rising commodity prices from imports used as inputs into production, combined with the rapid depreciation of the U.S. dollar, became forces that cannot be ignored (Wood 2004). It would appear then that China's recent economic history suggests that the past can indeed repeat itself, albeit in new ways.

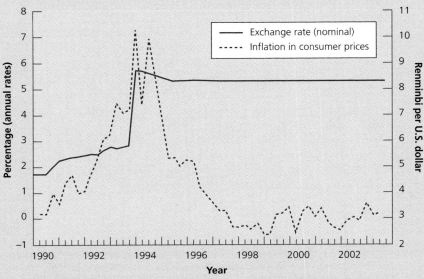

Source: Siklos, P.L., and Y. Zhang, "Inflation, Disinflation, and Deflation in China: Identifying the Shocks Driving Inflation," working paper, Wilfrid Laurier University, 2005.

Questions for Discussion

1. Why did the adoption of fixed exchange rates lead to such a buildup of foreign exchange rate reserves in China?
2. What are some of the historical lessons of the Bretton Woods system for the Chinese experience with fixed exchange rates?

Sources

Burdekin, R.C.K., and P.L. Siklos, "Evaluating Monetary Policy in China Since the 1990s: Estimates of Alternative Monetary Policy Rules," working paper, Wilfrid Laurier University, 2005.

Burdekin, R.C.K., and Siklos, P.L., "Fears of Deflation and the Role of Monetary Policy: Some Lessons and an Overview," in R.C.K. Burdekin and P.L. Siklos (Eds.) *Deflation: Current and Historical Perspectives* (Cambridge: Cambridge University Press, 2004): 1–27.

Rumbaugh, T., and N. Blancher, "International Trade and Challenges of WTO Accession," in *China's Growth and Integration into the World Economy: Prospects and Challenges*. E. Prasad (Ed.), International Monetary Fund Occasional Paper 232 (2004): 5-13.

Siklos, P.L., and Y. Zhang, "Inflation, Disinflation, and Deflation in China: Identifying the Shocks Driving Inflation," working paper, Wilfrid Laurier University, 2005.

Wang, T., "Exchange Rate Dynamics," in *China's Growth and Integration into the World Economy: Prospects and Challenges*. E. Prasad (Ed.), International Monetary Fund Occasional Paper 232 (2004): 21-28.

Wood, C., "Currency on a Collision Course," *Wall Street Journal Online*, 29 November 2005, **http://online.wsj.com/article/0,,SB11016819117248510 7,00.html**.

International Finance Corporation
www.ifc.org

Multilateral Investment Guarantee Agency (MIGA)
www.miga.org

For certain specialized purposes the World Bank acts through a number of affiliates. The *International Development Association* (*IDA*), for example, works for development in the poorest nations of the world, making very long-term loans that are often interest-free (though they carry some service charges). The *International Finance Corporation* (*IFC*) makes loans for the express purpose of aiding the growth of the private sector. The *Multilateral Investment Guarantee Agency* (*MIGA*) has as its mandate promoting foreign direct investment in developing countries. As the agency's name implies, it provides guarantees to investors against non-commercial risks, arising from currency inconvertibility or war and civil disturbance, to give but two examples. The MIGA also aims to improve investors' confidence that they will be protected against these risks.

Finally, the International Centre for the Settlement of Investment Disputes provides expertise for the conciliation and arbitration of investment disputes. This role is supposed to encourage foreign investment by creating a healthy atmosphere of mutual confidence between states and foreign investors.

The IMF and the World Bank are sister institutions, and they attempt to coordinate their work. The international debt crisis fostered more cooperation, since the World Bank began to require that a borrower meet certain conditions at the time a loan is made. Indeed, its conditionality often goes beyond any macroeconomic adjustments the IMF may require to policies that deregulate markets, thus promoting microeconomic efficiency, reducing or eliminating protectionism in trade, and promoting improvements and maintenance of a country's infrastructure (education, health, roads, and so on).

Many, including former chief economist of the World Bank and Nobel Prize recipient, Joseph Stiglitz of Columbia University, have criticized the World Banks' lending policies as outdated. Instead of a "one size fits all" approach, it has been suggested that the World Bank tailor its policies to the actual needs of borrower countries.[28]

---

[28] See J. Stiglitz, "The World Bank at the Millennium," *Economic Journal* 109 (November 1999), and C. Gilbert, A. Powell, and D. Vines, "Positioning the World Bank," *Economic Journal* 109 (November 1999). The attacks on the IMF by Stiglitz have often been of a personal nature. Ken Rogoff, the former chief economist of the IMF appointed in 2001, a former academic (at Harvard) and critic of the Fund, gave a stinging reply to Stiglitz's criticisms and personal attacks on former Fund personalities, in the form of an open letter. See **www.imf.org/external/np/vc/2002/070902a.htm**.

26.6 THE EUROPEAN BANK FOR RECONSTRUCTION AND DEVELOPMENT

The **European Bank for Reconstruction and Development** (**EBRD**) was set up in 1990 to help the former Communist countries of Europe to privatize public assets and make the transition to capitalism. In a sense, this institution to some extent supersedes the IMF and the World Bank as the international institution responsible for advising and implementing transitional policies in an important segment of emerging market economies. The EBRD's emphasis is on private sector restructuring and privatization. It will not bail out countries or institutions or fund balance of payments deficits. Funds to finance its operations are raised in international capital markets together with subscriptions. The largest subscribers are members of the European Union (almost 60% in 2002) followed by the United States (10%).

Although most transition economies have emerged from the "forced" recession or depression created by the transformation to a market economy and the introduction of democratic changes in the election of governments, the financial sector has, so far, proven to be the slowest to reform. Banks continue to be propped up by government subsidies in several transitional economies, and some of the central banks remain a significant source of credit for governments.

The EBRD is not the only multilateral finance agency. The Asian Development Bank (ADB) also makes loans and provides technical assistance in the Asia–Pacific region. The ADB raises funds from international capital markets and from contributions from member countries. Agricultural and rural sectors receive the most support. Indonesia, the People's Republic of China, Pakistan, and India are the largest recipients of aid.

The EBRD
www.ebrd.com,
The Asian
Development Bank
www.adb.org

26.7 THE EUROPEAN MONETARY SYSTEM

The **European Monetary System** (**EMS**) was an ambitious attempt to integrate the currencies of the European Community (EC). It fixed exchange rates but permitted them to fluctuate within a target zone. The chief advantage of the target zone system, also called the exchange rate mechanism (ERM), is its ability to prevent large swings in a country's current account when there are sharp swings in the nominal exchange rate. Illustrations that advocates of fixed rates point to in favouring fixed exchange rate systems are the impact of the large devaluation of the Mexican peso in early 1995, the devaluations in several Asian countries in 1997, and the sharp appreciation of the yen in 1992. In addition to the impact on the current account, there were large economic consequences for these countries as they all went into sharp recessions.[29] The ERM continues to exist—it's now called ERM II. The countries that opted out of the European Monetary Union (see below) adhere to its rules; it is expected that the so-called accession countries to the EU will also become members before qualifying for entry into the European Monetary Union.[30]

SOME HISTORY

Even before the collapse of the Bretton Woods system, six European countries—Belgium, France, West Germany, Italy, Luxembourg, and the Netherlands—signed the Treaty of Rome (1957), which led to the formation of the European Community (EC), and agreed to take steps to integrate their monetary policies (1968).

---

29 A strong proponent of fixed exchange rate type regimes is Williamson. See J. Williamson, *The Crawling Peg as an Exchange Rate Regime: Lessons from Chile, Colombia, and Israel* (Washington, D.C.: Institute for International Economics, 1996).
30 The accession countries are ones that have applied for membership into the European Union. They include Poland, Hungary, and the Czech Republic.

ECONOMICS FOCUS 26.2 — HOW COUNTRIES RESTRICT TRADE

There is virtually no limit to the devices countries may use to restrict trade. Here is a glossary of some of the principal means currently used.

Tariffs By imposing fees of various kinds, governments effectively raise the domestic price of foreign goods. In general, tariffs have fallen substantially since the end of World War II, thanks to the General Agreement on Tariffs and Trade (GATT), to various free trade agreements, and to the growth of the European Common Market.

Quotas, Bans, Voluntary Restraints Limits or outright prohibitions may be set on imports. All sorts of limits of these kinds exist for a variety of products ranging from shoes to cars.

"Buy Canadian" Government programs to exhort citizens to buy products made domestically (and often labelled as such).

Subsidies Government may help certain industries, thereby influencing their ability to export goods. Canadian examples range from the Export Development Corporation to outright tax breaks.

Rules and Regulations Products sold in a country must satisfy government-set criteria for emissions, quality, labelling, and so on. Countries can use such regulations to influence imports.

Price Fixing Goods are sometimes "dumped" in another country at an artificially low price.

Limits on Foreign Investment Governmental agencies are set up to review applications by foreigners who want to invest in the country. They can be a barrier to trade, especially if there are limits on how much of a local business can be owned by foreigners.

Piracy Governments that turn a blind eye to companies that produce copies of foreign goods without enforcing payment of, say, royalties also influence the balance of trade.

Questions for Discussion

1. Are there legitimate reasons for countries to restrict trade?
2. Does the advent of e-business limit the ability of barriers to trade to impede trade?

The plan was to set up a pool of reserves to help members maintain a fixed exchange rate and prevent speculative attacks against their currencies. By 1971, the political leadership of the EC member countries formally adopted a plan to achieve economic and monetary union within 10 years.

Almost immediately it was agreed that exchange rate fluctuations within the EC would be narrowed to a *band* (target range) smaller than the IMF allowed at the time.[31] This arrangement was called the "snake within the IMF tunnel."[32] In other words, the European system was a miniature version of the Bretton Woods arrangement.

The snake never functioned smoothly—West Germany and the Netherlands allowed their currencies to float temporarily—and was abandoned in 1973, when a devaluation of the U.S. dollar led the EC to float all of its currencies for a time. Nevertheless, EC members kept reaffirming their intention of achieving monetary and economic union.

In 1974, the second stage of the proposed union began with a pooling of EC members' foreign exchange reserves and gold, an increase in the EC's short-term credit facilities, and an agreement to intensify coordination of members' economic and monetary policies. Despite a variety of setbacks and delays, the EMS began to operate in March 1979.[33] The system's monetary unit would be called the **Ecu** (**European currency unit**),[34] and it represented a weighted basket of European currencies. Meanwhile it would serve as the numeraire (unit of account) for the exchange rate mechanism. The EMS also stipulated movements—2.25% (6% for Spain and the United Kingdom) in either direction of each other's currency values—and provided a mechanism to support economically the relatively less prosperous members of the EC.

---

31 Essentially, the rates were linked to the Deutschmark.

32 The United Kingdom, which was experiencing balance of payments difficulties, was excepted.

33 Initially, there were only six members—the original signators of the Treaty of Rome, but eventually they were joined by most EC members, including Italy and Ireland in 1978, Greece in 1981, and Spain and Portugal in 1986. The last holdout was the United Kingdom, which joined the EMS ERM in 1990, although it dropped out in September 1992 along with Italy. Meanwhile, even several nonmember countries, such as Sweden, in effect, adhered to the EMS system.

34 The "Ecu" was also the name of an ancient currency used in many countries, especially France, at various times over the centuries.

The EMS *realigned* (revalued) the currencies if the exchange rates could not be sustained within the zone, and despite the agreement to fix exchange rates rigorously, there were 27 re-alignments of the currency relationships between 1979 and 1983, and 12 more during the 1984–87 period.[35] After that, however, no further realignments were made until September 1992, when the United Kingdom and Italy left the EMS. Also, Ireland, Spain, and Portugal all devalued their currencies against the Deutschmark. In August 1993, the bands were widened to ±15% (except for the Netherlands).

This apparent stability in exchange rates between 1987 and 1992 puzzles economists, since the European countries showed considerable unwillingness to adhere to any of the fixed exchange rate regimes introduced in the past. Moreover, as is illustrated by the plot of the real effective exchange rates in Figure 26.1, several of the major currencies were incorrectly valued, at least in theory. Presumably, the longer a currency is overvalued or undervalued, the more likely a realignment. Why had none occurred prior to September 1992? Of the many possible explanations, a likely one is that the behaviour of EMS participants reflected a jockeying of positions before the **European Monetary Union** (**EMU**), a full **monetary union** within the EC.

THE TARGET ZONE SYSTEM IN ACTION

Consider Figure 26.2, which shows a hypothetical **target zone** for a currency. The exchange rate is allowed to fluctuate anywhere within the band defined by the lines *UB* and *LB*. The line in the middle is the *central parity* or the midpoint between *UB* and *LB* around which the exchange rate can fluctuate without necessarily producing an intervention in foreign exchange markets by central banks. The objective of the system is to narrow fluctuations in the exchange rate that might possibly enhance international trade. If a currency's exchange rate approaches either the top of the

| Figure 26.1 | Real Effective Exchange Rates in Five EMS Countries, 1980–1998 |

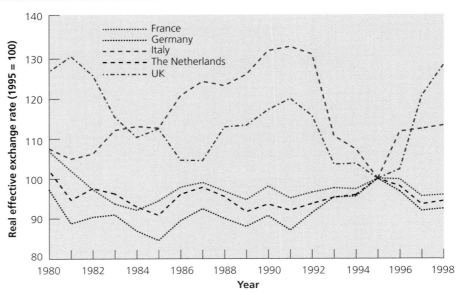

Source: International Financial Statistics CD-ROM (Washington, D.C.: International Monetary Fund). The real exchange rate measured is based on relative CPI calculations. Note that Italy and the U.K. left the EMS in September 1992. The U.K. joined the EMS only in October 1990. The EMS ceased to function as it was originally intended after September 1992. The countries considered all joined EMU on 1 January 1999.

---

35 See *European Economy*, no. 44 (October 1990): 42.

| Figure 26.2 | **The Target Zone Model: Hypothetical Illustration** |

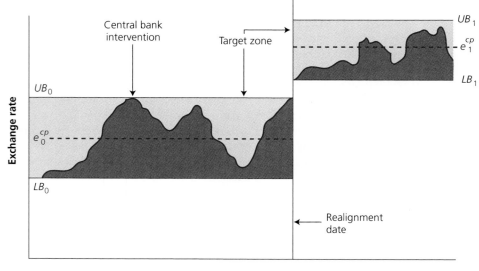

The vertical axis measures the hypothetical exchange rate level for a country. Time is measured on the horizontal axis. The lines *UB* and *LB* are the upper and lower bounds, respectively, of the target zone; e^{cp} is the central parity rate. The thick line inside the bands represents hypothetical fluctuations of the exchange rate. The vertical line illustrates the effect of a realignment. Here the exchange rate band shifts up to indicate a *devaluation* of the currency.

band or the bottom of the band, central banks are supposed to intervene to force the exchange rate to return within the band.[36]

But what happens if markets do not believe that central banks will defend the currency or view the economic policies of the participants as so divergent that the current parities are not credible? As the exchange rate approaches the upper or lower bound, central banks intervene in the foreign exchange market to change the course of the exchange rate. They do so in a variety of ways, such as buying or selling reserves of foreign exchange (say U.S. dollars in the Canadian context). In essence then central banks adjust their portfolio (see also Chapter 23).[37] What happens if this proves impossible? Then, as we have seen under the Bretton Woods period, sufficient pressure can be brought to bear, or reserves of foreign exchange can be exhausted, which would result in a **realignment**.[38] One such realignment is illustrated in Figure 26.2. In the EMS, unanimous consent of all participating members is required to change the central parity.

---

36 Under the Basle–Nyborg Accord of September 1987, central banks in the EMS can coordinate their activities to ensure the successful operation of the band.

37 Although there are continued calls to intervene in foreign exchange markets when the exchange rate is deemed un-favourable, much of the empirical evidence suggests that such interventions are largely ineffective. See, for example, H. Edison, "The Effectiveness of Central Bank Intervention: A Survey of the Post-1992 Literature," *Special Papers in International Economics*, No. 18 (Princeton, N.J.: Princeton University, 1993).

38 In the crisis of 1992 the then-president of the Bundesbank, Helmut Schlesinger, claimed that it had spent 92 billion DM to defend the British pound and the Italian lira. See *Financial Times* (4 October 1992): 1.

A simple way of testing the credibility of a target zone[39] is to use the theory of uncovered interest rate parity. From Chapter 8 we know, reproducing equation (8.9) below for convenience, that

$$R - R^f = (e^{exp} - e^s)/e^s \tag{26.1}$$

The equation states that the interest differential between two countries $(R - R^f)$ is equal to the expected depreciation of the exchange rate. If the right-hand side of equation (26.1) fluctuates within the defined bands, then the current central parities are credible; otherwise they are not. Figure 26.3 shows what the right-hand side of equation (26.1) looked like for the French franc until the crisis of 1992, which was a defining moment in the history of the EMS. It is immediately obvious that the target zone has often not been credible, necessitating frequent realignments.

| Figure 26.3 | Franc/Deutschmark Exchange Rates, 1979–92 |

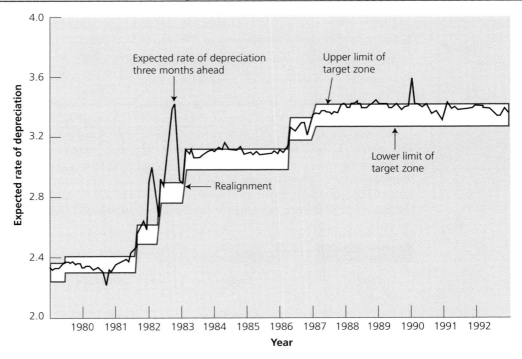

The vertical axis measures the right-hand side of equation (26.1), where e^{exp} is the three-month forward exchange rate for the French franc vis-à-vis the deutschmark. The bands are the horizontal lines that shift up (meaning a devaluation against the Deutschmark) every time a realignment takes place. The European Monetary System effectively collapsed in September 1992.

Source: P.L. Siklos, and R. Tarajos, "Fundamentals and Devaluation Expectations in Target Zones: Some New Evidence from the EMR," *Open Economies Review* 7 (January 1996): 33–59.

---

39 The target zone literature is large, with increasingly complex models developed because the simplest ones, such as the one described below, are unable to explain all exchange rate movements. For a literature review, see P.M. Garber, and L.E.O. Svensson, "The Operation and Collapse of Fixed Exchange Rate Regimes," in *Handbook of International Economics*, vol. III, edited by G. Grossman and K. Rogoff (Amsterdam: Elsevier Science, 1995): 1865–911. For more empirical evidence, see P.L. Siklos, and R. Tarajos, "Fundamentals and Devaluation Expectations in Target Zones: Some New Evidence from the ERM," *Open Economies Review* 7 (January 1996): 33–59.

26.8 EUROPEAN MONETARY UNION

In 1989, the EC issued the Delors Report, which laid out the ground rules leading up to EMU and the introduction of a single currency. A plan agreed to in December 1991 at Maastricht, the Netherlands, called for full EMU by 1999. At the end of 1995, leaders of the EU announced that the planned single currency would be called the **euro** and reaffirmed the launch date of 1 January 1999.

In the next phase of the transition, begun in 1992, which took four or five years, EC member countries were to achieve convergence in monetary and fiscal policies and thus, in effect, convergence in inflation rates. Essentially, the criteria are that member states are permitted

1. A maximum of 1.5 percentage points above the average of the three lowest national inflation rates.

2. A maximum of 2 percentage points above the average of the three lowest national long-term interest rates.

3. Budget deficits up to a maximum of 3% of GDP.

4. Accumulated public (government) debt of up to 60% of GDP.

5. Maintenance of stable exchange rates for at least two years.[40]

On 2 May 1998, the heads of state or governments in the European Union (EU) decided that 11 countries had fulfilled the conditions outlined above, although there was considerable controversy at the time about whether this was the case. Indeed, the German central bank, the Bundesbank, gave a rather critical assessment about whether the convergence criteria had been met by 1998, but concluded rather realistically that the "selection of the participants [in EMU] remains a political decision."[41] The participants in EMU are Belgium, Germany, Spain, France, Ireland, Italy, Luxembourg, the Netherlands, Austria, Portugal, and Finland. Greece was deemed not to have met the convergence criteria (although it finally did in 2000 and joined EMU in 2002), the U.K.

Table 26.2	Conversion Rates for the Euro, 1 January 1999	
Country	**Currency**	**Euro Rate**
Austria	Ash	13.760300
Belgium/Luxembourg	BFr/LFr	40.339900
Finland	FM	5.945730
France	FFr	6.559700
Germany	DM	1.955830
Ireland	I£	0.787564
Italy	L	1936.270000
Netherlands	Fl	2.203710
Portugal	Esc	200.482000
Spain	Pta	166.386000
Non-EMU Members		
Japan	¥	132.4554
Switzerland	SFr	1.6129
United Kingdom	£	0.7058
United States	$	1.1743

Source: **www.ecb.int/press/pr/date/1998/html/pr981231_2.en.html**

40 See European Monetary Institute, *Annual Report 1994* (April 1995), Frankfurt, Germany.
41 "Opinion of the Central Bank Council Concerning Convergence in the European Union in View of Stage Three of Economics and Monetary Union," *Deutsche Bundesbank Monthly Report* (April 1998): 39.

and Denmark obtained an opt-out clause in the Maastricht Treaty, while for the time being Sweden voluntarily stayed out of EMU.[42] In December 1998, the final irrevocable exchange rates between EMU participants were announced and are given in Table 26.2. Originally, the euro was set to about US$1.12 for each euro. By the middle of 2000, the euro had depreciated to below par with the U.S. dollar.

When full EMU commenced, every member's debt and currency became denominated in euros.

Paralleling these broad developments toward monetary union was the "single market program" ("1992," as it is almost universally called), which (in theory, but not practice) eliminated all intra-EC barriers by the end of 1992. The legislation is important for the market for financial services because it removes all exchange controls. This, in effect, means the removal of all barriers limiting the movement of capital within the EC.

What is the significance of such a move? Consider that just before the United Kingdom removed its exchange controls, the average or spread between the LIBOR and the rate on three-month bank loans was roughly 1.5 percentage points; within months, the spread was nearly zero! Thus, the removal of such regulations has a significant impact on a key variable we have been discussing throughout the text.

For banks in Europe, the 1992 legislation meant that any depository institution in one EC country was able to establish branches in any other member country. Each branch must, however, conform to local laws, an arrangement that can give rise to complications. For example, if a British bank establishes a subsidiary in France on the basis of its British banking licence, it must now meet the reporting requirements of two countries, which is clearly more costly than reporting to a single country. In addition, regulatory costs will increase because, should the bank or its subsidiary fail, both the British and the French authorities will have to coordinate their activities.

EMU implies the elimination of sovereignty in monetary matters for the EC member states. Precisely because of the loss of sovereignty in monetary affairs, some countries, most notably Germany, wanted to buy insurance against the possibility of a monetary policy that was too lenient. After all, before EMU, the German Bundesbank was the sole guarantor of price stability. Under EMU, Germany has only one vote among the 12 members of the euro area of the ECB. Therefore, to complement EMU, the heads of state of the EU adopted the Stability and Growth Pact in June 1997. Essentially, the Stability and Growth Pact (SGP) mandates financial penalties if deficits are excessive. Excessive deficits are ones that are larger than 3% of GDP unless there is a recession where real GDP growth falls by at least 2%. The actual mechanism leading to financial sanctions, however, is exceedingly complicated.[43] The Pact consists of regulations to ensure budget discipline among EMU members. Although the SGP continues to exist, it is unclear how seriously it is being treated by the member states. France, Germany, Ireland, Portugal, Italy, and Greece have all run into trouble in recent years over their excessive deficits or their accounting procedures, but sanctions have only been threatened. The EU has yet to collect fines from the states that have violated the provisions of the SGP.[44]

The **European Central Bank** (ECB) opened its doors in June 1998 in Frankfurt, Germany. Together with the national central banks that are EMU members, they form the **European System of Central Banks** (ESCB).

Prior to the opening of the ECB, the **European Monetary Institute** (EMI) opened its doors in Frankfurt, Germany, in January 1994. Its main task was to prepare the technical needs of a switch

---

42 Denmark, however, participates in ERM II (Exchange Rate Mechanism II). Their currencies fluctuate 15% and 2.25%, respectively, against the euro. See "Operational Features of the New European Exchange-Rate Mechanism," *Deutsche Bundesbank Monthly Report* (October 1998): 17–23.

43 A fairly detailed flowchart, which illustrates the complexity of the decision-making process leading to the imposition of penalties, is contained in "The Implementation of the Stability and Growth Pact," *European Central Bank Monthly Bulletin* (May 1999): 45–61.

44 The EU regularly issues a report card on the SGP. See **http://europa.eu.int/comm/economy-finance/about/activities/sgp/main_en.htm**.

to a single currency as well as to report to the EU on the progress toward convergence by individual member states. Consequently, the EMI had no responsibility for monetary policy. By the end of 1995 the member governments had approved a "changeover scenario" that focused on the need for the rigorous acceptance of the convergence criteria and that a legal basis be guaranteed so that all who use the euro can be safe in the knowledge that it is a means of payment. In addition, the goals of monetary policy in the euro and conversion of accounting standards were implemented in 1999. On 1 January 2002, the euro was successfully introduced and is now legal tender in 12 EU countries.

OBJECTIVES AND TASKS OF THE ESCB

The primary objective of the ECB and, by implication, the ESCB, is the maintenance of price stability. Price stability is defined as an inflation rate less than 2% in an Europe-wide index of consumer prices.[45] To achieve this objective, the ECB decided to give prominence to money growth as well as to a wide range of indicators such as wages, the exchange rate, the yield curve, and fiscal indicators.[46]

The principal decision-making body of the ECB is the governing council made up of the governors of the 12 euro-area national central banks. The executive board, consisting of six members chosen from the governing council, is responsible for the implementation of monetary policy. A general council, largely an advisory body, includes members from both euro-area and non-euro-area countries that are members of the European Union. The members of the executive board are appointed "by common accord of the Governments of the Member States" (article 11.2 of the ECB's constitution, available from **http://www.ecb.int/ecb/legal/pdf/en_protocol_18.pdf**).

The ESCB is responsible for defining and implementing monetary policy in the EMU. In addition, the ESCB conducts foreign exchange operations, holds and manages member states' foreign exchange reserves, and helps promote the Europe-wide payments system.[47]

The European
Central Bank
www.ecb.int

The primary monetary policy instruments consist of open market operations followed by a marginal lending facility that permits select financial market participants to borrow overnight from national central banks against eligible assets. Finally, banks in the EMU are required to hold reserves against short-term deposits.

In 2004, an historic enlargement took place. Ten new member states joined the European Union on May 1st—the Czech Republic, Estonia, Cyprus, Latvia, Lithuania, Hungary, Malta, Poland, Slovakia, and Slovenia. These countries must fulfill the Maastricht Treaty convergence requirements described earlier. By June 2004, Estonia, Lithuania, and Slovenia had entered into the ERM. In two years, assuming that their exchange rates do not experience "severe tensions," their admission into the euro area will be considered.

CURRENCY UNIONS

The study of the benefits and costs of two or more countries adopting a single currency, whether existing or an entirely new one, is an old one in economics. However, this issue has attracted growing interest since the successful launch of the European Monetary Union, and the awarding of the Nobel Prize in economics to Robert Mundell, who developed a theory of the ideal conditions for a currency union.

In a *currency union*, two or more jurisdictions share a single currency. The European Monetary Union is one such currency union. Canada has a currency union among its provinces, although some analysts question its efficiency.

---

45 The index is called the "harmonized index of consumer prices" (HICP).
46 See "The Stability-Oriented Monetary Policy Strategy of the Eurosystem," *European Central Bank Monthly Bulletin* (January 1999): 39–50.
47 Called TARGET (Trans-European Automated Real-Time Gross Settlement Express Transfer System). See *European Central Bank Monthly Bulletin* (March 1999): 39*–49*.

The interest in currency unions and how to organize them most efficiently has been heightened by the demise of the Soviet Union, and the breaking up of Czechoslovakia into the Czech and Slovak Republics. Although a currency union now exists by default, most of the successor states ended this arrangement. Nevertheless, the notion of a currency union organized along the same lines as the Bretton Wood arrangement does appeal to some.

The principal problem with the currency union in the former Soviet Union is the lack of credibility of the Russian-dominated central bank. Since inflation cannot be contained within parts of a currency union, many of the successor states claim that Russia is inflating its economy at the expense of the other republics. This is yet another example of the problem of externalities in financial systems. What do economists think are the essential ingredients of an "optimum currency area" (OCA)? Any such list would include the following:

1. *Labour mobility.* The freer the movement of labour, the fewer the regional disparities in unemployment rates.

2. *Capital mobility.* Capital should be mobile so that savings and investment can seek out the most profitable opportunities. Barriers to capital movements prevent this from happening.

3. *Openness and regional interdependence.* It makes sense to use the same currency if goods move freely between the regions and a significant portion of trade is done within a specific region.

4. *Industrial and portfolio diversification.* Economic shocks can be devastating to an economy, but these can be mitigated if there is sufficient diversification within the currency area. (We examined the benefits of diversification in Chapter 13.)

5. *Wage and price flexibility.* Because the exchange rate is fixed within a currency area, resources can only be allocated to their best uses if wages and prices are sufficiently flexible; otherwise the exchange rate has to perform this function.

Currency unions have attracted interest in Canada for another reason: In the summer of 1998, the Canadian dollar experienced a sharp fall in value against the U.S. dollar.[48] By 1999, the trickle of articles in the press on this issue became a flood as academics, spurred by a discussion in the federal Cabinet about closer economic ties with the United States, began publishing numerous works on the subject. The accompanying Point–Counterpoint box explores the pros and cons of a monetary union with the U.S. with a few additional considerations beyond the criteria for optimum currency areas (OCA) listed previously. Not surprisingly, the surge in the value of the Canadian dollar in 2005 put to rest talk of a common currency. Interestingly, earlier proponents of a currency union with the United States fell silent about why the conditions that should have led policymakers to drop the Canadian currency had suddenly vanished.

As we have noted, changes in inflation, interest rates, exchange rates, and economic activity are generated by shocks or disturbances such as a change in oil prices, a new objective for monetary or fiscal policy, a change in inflation expectations, or in consumer sentiment. Moreover, in an interdependent world, shocks originating in one country affect others, especially if they are in close proximity to each other and if there is considerable trading activity or openness, the conduit through which disturbances are transmitted becomes more prominent still.

It is important to note that, although a country entering into a monetary union eliminates all nominal exchange rate variability between the members of the monetary union, the variability of the real exchange rate is not eliminated. As we saw in Chapter 8, considerable real exchange rate variability exists in the Canadian dollar. Hence, much of the adjustment resulting from the adoption of the U.S. dollar would fall on domestic prices and wages. However, since the real exchange rate represents a combination of factors, variability might represent price level flexibility, in which case the United States and Canada would be good candidates for monetary union.

---

48 At the end of March 1998, the exchange rate against the U.S. dollar was $1.4163 Canadian. By the end of August the same year, the Canadian dollar had depreciated to C$1.5355.

POINT–COUNTERPOINT 26.1

SHOULD CANADA DROP ITS CURRENCY?

By the summer of 1998, voices opposed to Canada's flexible exchange rate regime became much more prominent. Courchene and Harris (1999) argue that flexible exchange rates in Canada have not acted as a shock absorber. Trade tends to be north–south (i.e., between Canada and the United States), instead of east–west (i.e., between provinces), and the trend globally is toward large regional trading blocks (e.g., in Europe), which favours the adoption of a common currency.

Murray (1999) and Laidler (1999) replied with equal force, pointing out several flaws in the Harris–Courchene view of the world. First, Canada and the United States are structured differently and face different economic shocks. For example, Canada is more dependent on commodities than is the United States. Second, if monetary sovereignty is lost, only fiscal policy is left, and the experience with discretion in fiscal policy has not been encouraging. Third, the Bretton Woods system of fixed exchange rates did not survive once the policies of Germany and the United States became poles apart. Fourth, little evidence exists that countries under a fixed exchange rate fare better economically than those that allow their exchange rates to float (Siklos, 1997). Finally, as the European example amply demonstrates, monetary unification implies a significant amount of political integration. Clearly, there is little indication that Canada and the United States would integrate their political institutions on the same scale as the Europeans.

Others who favour monetary union (Grubel, 1999) argue that the resort to a single currency within politically defined boundaries is artificial and not necessarily consistent with an economically efficient area. This result is clearly possible, but it is not immediately obvious that a single North American currency would protect us from "monetary misadventures." After all, the Europeans felt the need to supplement the Maastricht Treaty with the Stability and Growth Pact. If monetary union was all that was necessary, why the need for additional rules?

Currency unions are a hot topic elsewhere in the world too. The potential consequences of adopting the Australian dollar continue to be debated in New Zealand, and there have been suggestions that Latin and South American countries ought to form a currency union also. The Argentine crisis of 2001–02 also raised the eyebrows of many who once thought that its policy of more or less tying the value of its currency to that of the U.S. dollar made it a shining example of success, until incompetence, corruption, and an unsustainable fiscal policy led to the collapse of the regime and a return to a floating exchange rate.

The accompanying table (from Hochreiter-Korinek-Siklos, 2003), drawn from data around the time the debate over monetary union in Canada and elsewhere was heating up, shows that, despite differences in currency regimes between Australia, New Zealand, and Canada on the one hand, and the Eurozone on the other, the overall performance of these economies is not dissimilar. The table measures performance in terms of the requirements laid down in the Maastricht Treaty (see text). Clearly then, other factors must be considered.

Country	Year	Inflation (CPI)	Fiscal 1 (Deficit)*	Fiscal 2 (Debt)**	Interest Rate
Australia	1998	0.9	0.6	33.0	5.5
	1999	1.5	1.0	26.1	6.1
	2000	4.5	−0.2	26.6	6.3
New Zealand	1998	1.3	1.4	38.6	6.3
	1999	0.1	0.3	37.1	6.4
	2000	2.6	0.5	34.7	6.9
Canada	1998	0.9	0.5/1.0	116.2/64.9	4.89
	1999	1.7	1.6/0.8	111.6/61.0	6.18
	2000	2.7	3.2/1.8	104.9/51.8	5.35
Eurozone	1998	1.8 (0.7)	−2.2	76.9	4.8 (4.8)
	1999	1.3 (0.5)	−1.3	74.8	4.7 (4.8)
	2000	2.5 (1.6)	0.3	72.4	5.4 (5.4)

*First set of figures include provincial debt for Canada, second set of figures exclude provincial debt.
**Figures in parentheses are for euro area excluding Sweden, the U.K., and Denmark, which are part of the EU but have not adopted the euro.

Questions for Discussion

1. Of the five criteria for optimum currency areas, which would you say is most important in the Canadian context?

2. Notice that the discussion in the box says nothing about the exchange rate at which Canadians would exchange their currency for the U.S. dollar. Does this matter? What exchange rate would you select? Why?

Sources

Canadian Public Policy, "Special Issue: The EMU and the NAMU," 35 (March 1999): 285–332.

POINT	COUNTERPOINT
• No need to worry about converting Canadian for U.S. dollars at uncertain exchange rates. • Macroeconomic fundamentals do not explain exchange rate movements well. • Volatile exchange rates have a negative impact on economic performance. • Currency depreciations mean that Canadians may be less productive than Americans, negatively impacting our standard of living. • Trade is increasingly north–south rather than east–west, so it makes business sense to use a single currency. • Monetary policy would become more reliable since, historically, U.S. inflation and interest rates have been lower than those in Canada. • There would be more price competition since prices all over North America would be in terms of the common currency. • Closer economic integration might improve the transmission of technology and ideas across countries. • If labour mobility is permitted, wages in the United States and Canada will eventually be equalized. • Monetary union can provide an important impetus for financial market integration, as the euro-area experience demonstrates. Canada's financial markets are, however, already highly integrated with those in the U.S.	• Most foreign exchange transactions can be hedged and the transactions costs are not that large. • The Bank of Canada equation[1] suggests that a few fundamentals do a good job of explaining the U.S.–Canadian exchange rate. • The evidence is far from conclusive that exchange rate volatility and economic activity are closely correlated. • Why would firms no longer attempt to maximize profits? There is considerable evidence that Canada's productivity, and Ontario's in particular, is higher than the United States's productivity. • North–south trade has always been a feature of Canada–U.S. relations. It has remained a fact through different exchange rate regimes. Unless boundaries are redrawn, this is an irrelevant issue. • Past monetary experience is no guarantee of future good behaviour. We can easily cherry-pick periods of bad monetary conduct in the United States and good monetary conduct in Canada. • Prices for products reflect many factors, and it is unlikely that there would be more competition, especially since the advent of the Free Trade Agreement. • Unless a host of rules and regulations concerning the transfer of technology are changed, this is a highly unlikely outcome of monetary union. • It is doubtful that the United States would allow full labour mobility and, in any event, there is considerably less labour mobility within Canada than within the United States. • What exchange rate will be used at the time of monetary union?

1 The Bank of Canada equation models the real exchange rate as a function of commodity prices, the price of oil, and the U.S.–Canada interest rate differential. See Chapter 8 for an illustration.

T.J. Courchene, and R.G. Harris, "From Fixing to Monetary Union: Options for North American Currency Intergration," C.D. Howe Commentary, June 1999.

H.G. Grubel, "The Case of the Amero: The Economics and Politics of a North American Monetary Union," *Fraser Institute Critical Issues Bulletin*, September 1999.

D. Hargreaves, and J. McDermott, "Issues Relating to Optimal Currency Areas: Theory and Implications for New Zealand," *Reserve Bank of New Zealand Bulletin* 62 (September 1999): 16–29.

E. Hochreiter, A. Korinek, and P.L. Siklos, "The Potential Consequences of Alternative Exchange Rate Regimes: A Study of Three Candidate Regions," *International Journal of Economics and Finance* (2003).

L. Karlinger, "The Impact of Common Currencies on Financial Markets: A Literature Review and Evidence from the Euro Area," Bank of Canada working paper 2002–35, November 2002.

R. Lafrance, and P. St-Amant, "Optimal Currency Areas: A Review of the Recent Literature," Bank of Canada working paper 99–16, October 1999.

D.E.W. Laidler, "What Do the Fixers Want to Fix? The Debate about Canada's Exchange Rate Regime," C.D. Howe Commentary, December 1999.

R. Mundell, "The Case for the Euro I–II," *Wall Street Journal*, 24 and 25 March 1998.

———, "Making the Euro Work," *Wall Street Journal*, 30 April 1998.

J. Murray, "Why Canada Needs a Flexible Exchange Rate," Bank of Canada Working Paper 99–12, July 1999.

P.L. Siklos, "The Connection between Exchange Rate Regimes and Credibility: An International Perspective," in *Exchange Rates and Monetary Policy,* Proceedings of a Conference held at the Bank of Canada, October 1996 (Ottawa: Bank of Canada, 1997): 73–121.

An important consideration in the debate is whether the exchange rate acts as a "shock absorber," as proponents of Canada's flexible exchange rate regime contend. As we saw in Chapter 8, the relative purchasing power parity condition suggests that the exchange rate can absorb differences in inflation and interest rates. Existing empirical evidence is mixed, with some analysts suggesting that exchange rate movements act as a buffer against the potential negative effects of foreign shocks. Other evidence, however, points in a different direction.

SUMMARY

- This chapter surveys the institutions of and developments in the international monetary system.

- The principal organizations in the international financial system are the International Monetary Fund (IMF), the World Bank, and the Bank for International Settlements (BIS).

- The history of exchange rate arrangements in the post–World War II period can be divided into two parts. Exchange rates were largely fixed in the Bretton Woods period, which lasted until the early 1970s. Since then exchange rates have been flexible and generally market determined.

- The BIS was created after World War I to manage war reparation payments. Today, the BIS is a forum for central bankers. It also houses a committee to ensure that banks have adequate capital and has recently begun to house a similar institution for the supervision of insurance companies.

- The IMF's original role was to manage the pegged exchange rate regime after World War II, and to ensure that member countries did not fall into balance of payments difficulties. Today, the IMF acts as a surveillance mechanism to ensure countries implement "good" economic policies. It also has facilities to make loans to member countries.

- The World Bank is the IMF's sister institution. Originally mandated to help finance the reconstruction of a devastated Europe, it later became the leading international institution for long-term loans to developing countries.

- The European Bank for Reconstruction and Development is charged with providing financial assistance to countries in transition from a planned economy to a market economy.

- The European Monetary System was an attempt to fix exchange rates among its members.

- Exchange rates were permitted to fluctuate within a fairly broad band around what is called a central parity. Realignments were permitted under a variety of circumstances, such as large inflation differentials, and they occurred frequently.

- The EMS was meant as a stop along the road to monetary union. On 1 January 1999, 11 European Union countries were admitted into the European Monetary Union.

- The new pan-European currency is called the euro. Member countries' exchange rates were irrevocably fixed to the euro on 1 January 1999. Actual euro notes and coins were introduced in 2002 in the 12 countries of the European Union.

- The European Central Bank (ECB) is responsible for monetary policy throughout the EMU region. It is mandated to maintain price stability and uses a variety of financial indicators to ensure that its objective is met.

- The ECB is autonomous from member countries' governments.

IMPORTANT TERMS

Bank for International Settlements (BIS), 520

Bretton Woods system, 522

convertible currencies, 522

Ecu (European currency unit), 532

euro, 536

European Bank for Reconstruction and Development (EBRD), 531

European Central Bank (ECB), 537

European Monetary Institute (EMI), 537

European Monetary System (EMS), 531

European Monetary Union (EMU), 533

European System of Central Banks (ESCB), 537

International Bank for Reconstruction and Development (IBRD or World Bank), 528

International Monetary Fund (IMF), 525

monetary union, 533

realignment, 534

special drawing right (SDR), 526

target zone, 533

PROBLEMS

1. Explain why a nation in debt might prefer to borrow from a bank rather than from the IMF (other things being equal).

2. Explain why the currencies whose real, effective exchange rates are plotted in Figure 26.1 are over- or undervalued and why this creates pressures for a realignment of the currencies.

3. What is the Triffin paradox? Explain.

4. Explain how you could use equation (26.1) to predict the likelihood of an exchange rate realignment in the target zone exchange rate system.

5. The "excessive deficit procedure" in the Stability and Growth Pact is triggered whenever a member state exceeds the public deficit criterion, which is set at 3% of gross domestic product (GDP). France and Germany have exceeded this requirement for at least three years running. What does this outcome say about the SGP as a device to restrain the fiscal policy of the member states?

6. Explain in economic terms why the misalignment of real exchange rates shown in Figure 26.1 did not threaten the start of EMU.

DISCUSSION QUESTIONS

1. Explain how the establishment of the euro reduces transactions costs within the EC.

2. Explain how the creation of SDRs increases liquidity in the world financial system.

3. Why did central banks want to have an international body to coordinate some of their activities?

4. What are the principal functions of the BIS?

5. The Bretton Woods system collapsed in the early to mid-1970s. Why? What other major events not specifically mentioned in the text may also have indirectly contributed to the end of Bretton Woods?

6. What are the determinants of an optimum currency area (OCA)?

7. How does the target zone exchange rate system work and what can determine a realignment of the exchange rate within such a system?

8. What are the convergence criteria for the EMU and why are they important?

9. What is the principal purpose of the Stability and Growth Pact? What was the main reason for introducing it?

10. Discuss some of the advantages and disadvantages of the target zone system for exchange rates.

11. Why did European heads of state consider the convergence requirements to be important? Does the notion of convergence make economic sense?

12. Why did critics feel that the IMF lost its way in the world in the 1980s and 1990s?

ONLINE APPLICATION

1. Go to the IMF's Web site at **www.imf.org**. Click on *Publications*, then on *Browse by*: *Title*, then "A", then look for *Annual Reports 1999*. Download the Report (you will need the Adobe Acrobat Reader, available free at **www.adobe.com**). Read Chapter 2. It discusses attempts by the IMF and others to prevent the contagion of financial crises. Assess and discuss the IMF's arguments.

2. Go to the ECB's Web site at **www.ecb.int/ press/pr/date/1997/html/pr970715.en. html** and examine the currency symbol for the euro. Does it seem to you to accomplish the objectives of the designers? Next, click on *Statistics* and examine the daily nominal effective exchange rates of the euro (found by clicking on the left hand sidebar). Interpret the data.

3. Go to the World Bank's Web site at **www.worldbank.org**. Click on *Data and Statistics* and then on *Maps*. Examine the following macroindicators: GNP per capita and the labour force. Examine Canada's performance against other industrial and developing countries of your choice.

4. The EU decides on membership into the euro area based on "convergence reports." Go to **http://europa.eu.int/comm/econ omy_finance/about/activities/activities_ convergencereports_en.htm** and examine the commission's recommendation to admit Greece into the euro area in 2004. Now read the article in the *International Herald Tribune* on 24 September 2004 found at **http://www.iht.com/arti cles/2004/09/24/business/drachma.php**. What is your assessment of the EU's decision?

References can be found on www.mcgrawhill.ca/college/siklos

adaptive expectations hypothesis the theory that individuals adjust their forecast of inflation gradually, partly from learning from the mistakes (or forecast errors) of the past

adverse selection decision making that results from the incentive for some people to engage in a transaction that is undesirable to everyone else; the problem exists because of asymmetric information

annuity an instrument that converts a lump sum amount into annual instalments over a specified period

appreciation the increase in the value of one currency in terms of another

arbitrage pricing theory (APT) a model that suggests that there are several factors that can explain the links between market return and the return on a particular asset or portfolio of assets

asymmetric information when one party to a transaction has relatively more information than another

Automated Clearing Settlement System (ACSS) the system used in Canada to settle outstanding paper-based items (e.g., cheques) between financial institutions

balance of payments (BOP) a record of international transactions between countries

balance sheet an accounting format that describes the activities of a firm in financial terms

Bank Act federal legislation that regulates most deposit-taking and other financial institutions in Canada

Bank for International Settlements (BIS) acts as a central bank for central banks, originally created to coordinate German war reparations payments after World War I; the BIS is based in Basel, Switzerland

Bank of Canada the central bank of Canada, responsible for the conduct of monetary policy, it also acts as a banker for the federal government

Bank of Canada Act the piece of legislation that governs the operations, duties, and functions of the Bank of Canada

Bank of Canada advances loans made by the Bank of Canada to members of the Canadian Payments Association

bank rate the rate of interest charged by the Bank of Canada on loans made to members of the Canadian Payments Association; now tied to the overnight rate

bankers' acceptance a document that serves as a promise to pay where the bank has undertaken to guarantee payment when the debt is due

barter an exchange of commodities without money; transactions of this kind are inconvenient because of the problem of the "double coincidence of wants"

base control the means by which a central bank controls movements in the monetary base

base drift the upward revision of the base from which monetary growth targets are adjusted

basis the futures price less the spot price

basis point one-hundredth of one percentage point

bimetallism a monetary system based on the value of two precious metals, usually gold and silver

bond a debt instrument that promises to pay interest on a regular basis and to pay the principal at maturity

bond rating an evaluation by some agency of the risk of default by the issuer of a bond

Bretton Woods system the adjustable pegged exchange rate system negotiated at the end of World War II at Bretton Woods, New Hampshire; it ended in the early 1970s

brokers individuals who bring together a buyer and a seller and assist in the completion of a financial transaction between them

budget constraint the limits, usually dictated by income, within which consumers must decide how to allocate their consumption; it is steeper when p increases, flatter when p falls

caisses populaires cooperative, nonprofit, deposit-taking institutions that offer a large variety of services, including nonfinancial services, to individuals at the local or parish level; they operate in Quebec only

call option the right but not the obligation to buy an asset at a particular price during a stipulated period

Canada Deposit Insurance Corporation (CDIC) the agency in Canada that is responsible for the operation and supervision of the deposit insurance system

Canadian Payments Association the association responsible for cheque clearing for all financial institutions in Canada; membership is mandatory for all chartered banks and the Bank of Canada, but many near-banks are also members

capital account the part of the balance of payments that records net changes in domestic versus foreign holdings of financial assets

capital asset pricing model (CAPM) a simple relationship that links the return on a particular stock with the return on a portfolio made up of the entire market or some proxy

capital gain or loss the gain or loss incurred by an investor who sells a financial instrument at a price other than the purchase price; if the selling price is higher (lower) than the purchase price, the investor is said to make a capital gain (loss)

capital gain/loss return rate the profit or loss, in percentage, from a change in the price of a financial asset

capital market the market for financial instruments that mature in more than one year

capital mobility the ability to shift funds between countries easily; if there are no impediments at all and costs are minimal, capital is said to be perfectly mobile

capital ratio some measure of a firm's capital, such as shareholders' equity, divided by the assets of a firm

central bank the financial institution responsible for the conduct of a country's monetary policy; often, a central bank also acts as the banker for the central government

central bank autonomy or independence the degree to which the central bank of a country is able to work toward its objectives without intervention from politicians

certificates of deposit (CDs) a type of bank deposit that usually promises a fixed return on a large sum of money for a specified maturity; penalties may be imposed if the funds are withdrawn before maturity

chartered bank a bank that obtains a charter from the federal government and is federally regulated under the *Bank Act*

classical economics the body of economic theory that believes that a model of a competitive economy is appropriate and that market forces can be relied on to produce full employment

co-insurance a form of insurance where the insured is responsible for some of the losses covered by the insurance

consumption function a functional relationship that describes the economic variables, such as income and the interest rate, that determine consumption spending over time

consumption possibilities the opportunities available to consumers, with a given income, to consume goods and services today versus in the future

contagion refers to the idea that a financial crisis in one country or region is transmitted to other regions or countries

contractionary monetary policy the monetary policy aimed at reducing the level or growth rate of the money supply (the opposite of an expansionary monetary policy)

convertible currencies currencies that can be freely exchanged for one another

corporate governance the formal decision-making structure in a firm

corporate paper a form of corporate debt that typically matures in 90 days, but can mature in from 30 to 365 days

correlation statistic a statistical measure of the proportional strength of the linear relationship between two or more variables

cost-of-carry the costs associated with carrying an asset, such as financing, storage, and insurance costs

country risk the risk that a national government will default on its debt

coupon rate the stipulated return, typically on a bond, expressed as a percentage of the principal

covariance a statistical measure of the relationship between two or more returns across time or across states of the world

covered interest arbitrage the use of a forward foreign exchange contract to

hedge against foreign exchange risk as it affects the yield on foreign assets

Coyne affair the controversy of the late 1950s that ended with the resignation of James Coyne, governor of the Bank of Canada; originated with a monetary policy dispute between the federal government and the Bank of Canada

credibility a concept describing the extent to which announcements by government or central bank officials will be carried out as promised; credibility is considered to be a crucial ingredient in the successful implementation of monetary or fiscal policies

credit union a cooperative, non-profit, deposit-taking institution that offers a variety of services, including nonfinancial services, to individuals at a local level; credit unions operate in all provinces except Quebec

cross-rate the exchange rate between two currencies via a third currency

current account the part of the balance of payments that records the net change in exports and imports of goods and services

current and personal chequable accounts funds in accounts that can be removed without notice; these pay little or no interest

current yield the yield on a financial asset if it is sold in the current period

debt forgiveness a program to eliminate a debt liability as a write-off to the lender

debt monetization the issue of money by the central bank to support government spending

debt–equity swaps exchanges of debt issued via the bond market for an issue of shares

debt–service ratio the measure of a nation's ability to repay a debt; calculated as interest and principal over some period as a percentage of exports

deductible a fixed amount that is deducted from a loss claim against insurance

default risk the likelihood that a debtor will cease paying interest or principal or both

demand for money function the desire to hold some form of money; usually represented as a function of income and a proxy for the opportunity cost of holding money

demutualization the phenomenon in Canada whereby insurance companies become shareholder-owned corporations instead of being owned by the

policyholders

deposit insurance a form of insurance against losses from the failure of a financial institution

deposit multiplier the multiple by which deposits in the banking system can increase or decrease given an increase or a decrease in the banking system's cash reserves

deposit-taking institutions institutions that accept deposits and make loans

depreciation the decrease in the value of one currency in terms of another

deregulation the process by which legislation imposes fewer restrictions on the activities of an institution or industry

derivative products financial instruments derived from financial products bought and sold in the spot market; they include, for example, options and futures

devaluation an abitrary decrease in the value of a currency that had previously been fixed in value

diminishing marginal returns the principle that increases in input, other inputs held fixed, produce successively smaller increases in output

discounted bond a financial instrument that is sold at a price far below its face value

diversification the inclusion of more than one asset in a portfolio to reduce portfolio risk

dual banking system a financial system in which two classes of banks exist, each supervised and regulated by different levels of government or agencies

duration analysis similar to gap analysis, but assets and liabilities are arranged according to date of maturity

economic sectors the different groups that participate in the economy

Ecu (European currency unit) a weighted average of the currencies of the members of the exchange rate mechanism, which linked several European currencies; the Ecu was a candidate for the planned single European currency

efficient frontier those portfolios that provide the highest yield for any given level of risk

efficient markets hypothesis the theory that individuals make informed forecasts of the future based on all available information

equilibrium interest rate the market-clearing interest rate

equity premium puzzle describes the

empirical feature whereby stocks tend to outperform other financial assets in rate of return

estate, trust, and agency (ETA) business the primary function, also known as a fiduciary function, of trust companies; this function involves the management of funds left in trust by an estate or individuals where the trust company acts as an agent

euro the name of the European currency

Eurocurrency the market for deposits, loans, or bonds deposited or traded in a currency other than the one in which the instrument is bought or sold

European Bank for Reconstruction and Development (EBRD) the financial institution created to facilitate lending and other financial needs of the former centrally planned economies

European Central Bank (ECB) the central bank for the members of the European Monetary Union

European Monetary Institute (EMI) the precursor to the European Central Bank responsible for planning eventual monetary union in Europe

European Monetary System (EMS) the target zone exchange rate system that fixes exchange rates within a defined band; member countries agree to ensure, via central bank intervention, that the EMS target zone will be maintained

European Monetary Union (EMU) the plan, as contained in the Maastricht Treaty, to replace existing currencies of the members of the European Community with a single currency

European System of Central Banks (ESCB) the central banks in the individual countries making up the European Monetary Union

excess reserves reserves held by banks beyond required reserves; these required reserves were phased out in Canada

Exchange Fund Account (EFA) foreign exchange funds of the Canadian government; the EFA is managed by the Bank of Canada

exchange rate the price of one currency in terms of another

exercise (strike) price the price at which options are set

expansionary monetary policy a policy aimed at increasing the level or growth in the money supply

expectations hypothesis the theory that states that future interest rates can be forecasted by looking at the term structure because the return on a long-term bond is essentially the average return on short-term bonds over the same period

expectations of inflation a forecast of future inflation; the forecast can be extrapolated from past inflation alone, among many alternatives for generating such forecasts

expected return the weighted average of returns anticipated over time, where the weights are given by the probabilities of various states of the world

externalities phenomena whereby individual actions produce costs (or benefits) to other individuals over and above private costs and benefits

Federal funds rate (FFR) the interest rate on overnight loans of deposits at the U.S. Federal Reserve; also a barometer of interest rate levels more generally

Federal Open Market Committee (FOMC) the principal decision-making body of the U.S. Federal Reserve; it sets interest rates and is responsible for the implementation of monetary policy

Federal Reserve (the Fed) the U.S. central bank

Fedwire the system used by the U.S. Federal Reserve to allow member financial institutions to transfer funds electronically among themselves

financial assets that part of the national balance sheet that shows bank deposits, loans to various enterprises, and the public debt

financial flow accounts report how funds are used nationally in borrowing and lending activities

financial intermediaries institutions that channel funds between borrowers and lenders

financial leasing corporations companies that specialize in contracts to lease an asset over the anticipated term or life of the asset

***Financial Services Act* of 1999** the major piece of legislation reforming the U.S. banking and financial sectors

fiscal policy the policy by which a government resorts to expenditures or taxes to influence the economy as a whole

Fisher equation formula that states that the nominal interest rate is the sum of the real interest rate plus an expected inflation rate component

fixed exchange rate regime an exchange rate regime that pegs an exchange rate at a particular value

flexible exchange rate regime an exchange rate regime that allows the marketplace to determine the exchange rate independently; also called a floating system

flow measures measure flow of funds activity over time

flow of funds changes in asset and liability holdings during a given period

foreign exchange risk the risk that the exchange rate between one currency and another may fluctuate in a direction or to a degree unanticipated by investors dealing in assets denominated in a foreign currency

foreign exchange swap similar to an ordinary swap, except it involves the exchange of foreign currencies

forward contract a contract in which a seller undertakes to provide a buyer with an amount of an asset at some future date at a price agreed upon in advance

forward exchange rate the exchange rate on a contract to deliver foreign exchange at some future date at a price negotiated today

four pillars the term originally used to describe the specialized functions of the four different sectors of the Canadian financial system: chartered banks, trusts, insurance companies, and investment dealers; since the passage of the 1992 *Bank Act*, these divisions are no longer formally in place

free banking the doctrine that permits banks to issue their own currency and that suggests that there be a minimum of government regulation in the banking industry

functional regulation the philosophy that financial institutions should be regulated according to the type of activities they engage in

fundamentalist approach the position that states that the price of a stock is determined by fundamentals of a company's performance, such as the flow of anticipated dividends

futures contracts contracts to buy and sell an asset at a specified future date

gap analysis the subdividing of a bank's assets and liabilities into components that are rate sensitive and those that are not; the gap is the difference between the rate-sensitive assets and liabilities

Glass–Stegall Act a piece of U.S. legislation, passed in 1933, that prevented commercial banks from engaging in underwriting and dealing securities

globalization an expression for the growing integration of financial markets worldwide

gold standard a monetary system wherein the exchange rate is fixed to the price of gold

Gresham's Law the dictum that bad money drives out good; if two currencies exist in an economy, the one that is less valuable will tend to circulate, whereas the more valuable currency will be hoarded

hedge funds these represent a pooling of funds from wealthy investors and large institutional investors that use spot and derivative market instruments to reduce investment risk

hedging the process of using one transaction to offset the effect of another transaction, with the objective of reducing or eliminating risk entirely

holding period yield the return on a financial instrument during the period it is held, which is less than the period to maturity

hyperinflation inflation where prices rise faster than 50% per month

income risk the risk associated with fluctuations in income over time

income statement the statement that shows the difference between generated revenues and expenses incurred during a given period for an economic sector

inflation the rate of change in an aggregate price index such as the consumer price index (CPI)

inflation or deflation risk the risk stemming from the effect of inflation or deflation on real and nominal returns or assets

inflation targets several countries have redefined the objectives that their central banks have to meet in terms of a target for inflation; usually such targets are defined as ranges within which the rate of change in the CPI is expected to fluctuate

institutional regulation represents the set of rules and regulations that is aimed at institutions or firms

insurance contracts that protect individuals against unforeseen events that could have negative financial or physical consequences

interbank deposit bank funds deposited by one bank in another with which

the depositing bank usually does business

interest rate the price of renting money

interest rate control the intermediate target of a central bank policy to maintain interest rate stability

interest rate parity the condition that the differential between domestic and foreign interest rates reflects the forward premium or discount between currencies

interest rate pegging a policy of fixing an interest rate

interlisting of stocks stocks for a company listed on several stock exchanges at once

intermediaries institutions involved in the act of transforming assets and liabilities that results in the creation of new assets and liabilities; also institutions that borrow funds from savers and lend them to borrowers, and that provide financial services

intermediate targets economic variables that are only indirectly under the control of a policymaker, which the policymaker analyzes to determine whether a particular policy is having the anticipated effects on the economy as a whole

intermediation the function of transforming assets or liabilities into other assets or liabilities; this is the principal activity of most financial institutions

internal rate of return (IRR) the interest rate that equates an initial outlay with the present value of future net cash flows

International Bank for Reconstruction and Development (IBRD or World Bank) the financial institution created after World War II to facilitate lending and other financial needs of developing countries

international banking facilities (IBFs) U.S. banks that are permitted to accept deposits from nonresidents and that are not subject to reserve requirement rules

international financial centres typically large cities, such as London or New York, that, because of location or government subsidies, offer a variety of specialized financial services in close proximity to one another

International Monetary Fund (IMF) an international organization created after World War II to manage the international financial system

investment bank an intermediary that purchases new financial instruments

and sells them in smaller amounts to investors; also advises clients on mergers and acquisitions; also called a merchant bank

investment companies intermediaries that specialize in placing funds for their clients

investment dealers specialists who buy, sell, and advise in the securities market

Keynesianism theories associated with the work of John Maynard Keynes, including the belief that government action may be necessary when an economy is at less than full employment

Large Value Transfer System (LVTS) a system for influencing liquidity in the financial system introduced by the Bank of Canada in 1996 and used to affect the overnight rate that it targets

law of one price a law stating that, given certain assumptions, the domestic and foreign prices of a tradable good should be equal

lender of last resort usually, a central bank that can advance credit to a failing financial institution when no other sources of funds are available

letter of credit a draft authorizing funds when certain conditions have been met

leverage the activity of investing with borrowed funds

leverage ratio a measure of the debts of a firm divided by shareholders' equity

lifecycle hypothesis a theory stating that consumption spending is a function of an individual's age; thus, individuals accumulate wealth during their working years and consume their wealth following retirement, maintaining relatively stable consumption spending

liquidity the availability of funds to meet claims or the ease with which an asset can be sold

liquidity preference the desire to hold cash in preference to an alternative financial asset, such as a bond

liquidity premium the extra yield that must be paid to entice investors to hold long-term instead of short-term investments

liquidity risk the risk associated with a shortfall in the availability of funds

liquidity trap refers to the inability of additional injections of liquidity into the economy to reduce interest rates

loanable funds funds that are available to be borrowed for investment

London interbank offer rate (LIBOR) the rate of interest charged on bank funds in the London market to the "best" banks for a specified but short period

long position the purchase of an asset that is to be held until it matures or must be sold

M1 currency outside banks plus chartered banks' demand deposits net of the private sector float

M2 M1 plus nonpersonal notice deposits and personal savings deposits at chartered banks

M2+ M2 plus notice and term deposits at near-banks, generally, trust and mortgage loan companies

M3 M2 plus nonpersonal fixed-term deposits at chartered banks plus foreign currency deposits of residents booked in Canada

managed ("dirty") float regime a regime of flexible exchange rates in which the central bank intervenes occasionally to influence exchange rates; also called a "dirty" float

margin usually, a deposit placed as security against the purchase of an asset or used to ensure that a particular contract is fulfilled

marginal propensity to consume (MPC) a measure of the increase in consumption spending due to an increase in disposable income

market concentration the degree to which only a few firms account for most of the sales or output in a market; the more concentration, the less competitive a market is said to be

market risk the likelihood of changes in the future price of an asset

market segmentation the theory that markets for long-term and short-term assets are distinct; only the demand of and supply for funds in these markets determine relative interest rates between short-term and long-term assets

marked-to-market the settlement of an account done daily to reflect price changes at the close of trading each day

medium of exchange something that is generally acceptable in exchange for goods and services

medium or unit of account something that circulates and provides a standardized means of evaluating the relative price of goods and services

merchant bank an intermediary that purchases new financial instruments and sells them in smaller amounts to investors; also advises clients on mergers and aquisitions; also known as an investment bank

Modigliani–Miller (MM) theorem the theory stating that, under specific conditions, a firm will be indifferent between borrowing via bonds versus equity

monetarism theory that inflation can largely be explained by monetary policy; it's also critical of an activist monetary policy

Monetary Conditions Index (MCI) represents a linear combination of a short-term interest rate and an exchange rate; developed by the Bank of Canada to assess the ease or tightness of monetary policy

monetary control the intermediate target of a central bank policy to control the growth of some measure of the money supply

monetary policy the policy enacted by a government or a central bank that affects the money supply, interest rates, and the exchange rate

monetary targeting the attempt by central banks to control the growth of selected monetary aggregates

monetary union the act of choosing a new or existing common currency for a group of otherwise sovereign countries

monetization a situation in which the use of cash and cheques becomes increasingly common

money a commodity or device of some kind used to complete transactions in goods and services; a medium of exchange

money illusion the belief that nominal values are the same as real values; the individual does not understand that a price level change implies a change in the purchasing power of a given stock of money

money market the market for financial assets that mature in one year or less

money market mutual funds (MMMFs) funds that issue shares to holders backed by high-quality short-term assets; used by financial institutions as an alternative to ordinary bank accounts

money multiplier the multiple by which the money supply changes in response to a change in the monetary base

money supply (money stock) some measure of aggregate liquidity in the economy; includes definitions such as M1 and M2

money supply growth target a quantitative target for a measure of the money supply that is partially under the control of the central bank; generally, the target is a range

moral hazard the chance that an individual may have an incentive to act in such a way as to put that individual at greater risk; the individual perceives as beneficial a course of action deemed undesirable by another

moral suasion a technique used by a central bank to persuade financial institutions to change their behaviour voluntarily

mortgage loan company (MLC) financial institution that specializes in mortgage loans

mutual funds pools of funds from many sources all invested in a variety of assets, thereby permitting economies of scale, risk sharing, and risk reduction in investments

national balance sheet accounts set of balance sheets prepared for each group in the economy and for the economy as a whole

national treatment the fact that an organization in another country is subject to that country's laws; e.g., a branch of a Canadian bank in a foreign country is subject to that country's banking rules and regulations

natural rate of unemployment the rate of unemployment that arises because of normal frictions in the labour market and not because of monetary policy; it can also refer to the unemployment rate when inflation is zero; also called nonaccelerating inflation rate of unemployment (NAIRU)

negotiable order of withdrawal (NOW) a U.S. financial instrument created to circumvent a ceiling on interest rates (regulation Q); by calling a cheque a negotiable order of withdrawal, the account from which the funds are drawn is not legally called a chequing account, and so such an account can pay market interest rates

net worth (net wealth) total assets less total liabilities

neutrality of money the theory that a change in the money supply produces a proportional change in prices, leaving the real side of the economy unaffected

nominal income income measured in current dollars

nominal interest rate the total return on a financial asset including compensation for inflation

nonfinancial assets physical holdings of a sector, such as land or machinery

Office of the Comptroller of the Currency (OCC) the principal supervisory body in the U.S. financial system; a division of the U.S. Treasury

Office of Thrift Supervision (OTS) the agency that assumed supervisory functions over the savings and loan industry in 1989

offset transactions transactions in which the purchase of one asset is offset by the sale of another asset; two opposite positions are taken in the spot and futures markets

offshore banking centres financial centres that are also tax havens and that perhaps offer secrecy in financial dealings; also called international financial centres

open market operations the purchase or sale of government securities in the open market

operating band refers to the 50-basis-point (0.5%) spread between the rate paid on deposits held at the Bank of Canada and the interest rate on overdrafts at the Bank; the midpoint of the operating band is the Bank of Canada's target for the overnight market

operating instruments the policy tools used by a central bank, for example, to achieve specific monetary policy targets

opportunity cost the cost of something measured as the value of the next best available alternative; the cost of forgone actions

optimal cash management approach the attempt by an individual to minimize the costs of holding a given stock of cash

overnight rate band the range of interest rates charged on loans made overnight; large corporations use the overnight market to earn interest on funds that would otherwise be idle, and the Bank of Canada sets a target overnight rate to conduct monetary policy

over-the-counter (OTC) a secondary market for the sale of stocks held in an inventory that can be bought or sold at the prices offered by dealers

par value the value of a financial instrument, typically a bond, that is equivalent to its maturity value

pension funds devices to accumulate assets for retirement to which employees or employers or both can contribute; they usually offer tax-shelter benefits

permanent income hypothesis the theory that permanent income, that is, annual income based on expected lifetime earnings, determines actual consumption spending; since permanent income is stable, actual consumption spending is also stable

peso problem named after the Mexican peso, it describes a phenomenon in which the economic fundamentals predict a devaluation that almost never actually takes place

Phillips curve a function that relates the trade-off between inflation in consumer prices or wages and the rate of unemployment or output

political business cycle a cycle in which economic activity is linked to election dates as politicians resort to policies to ensure their re-election

portfolio a collection of financial assets

precautionary motive the demand for money that results from the desire to prepare for unforeseen expenditures

preferred habitat the particular term to maturity for which an investor has a distinct preference

present value the current value of a stream of future payments

price stability measured in terms of the consumer price index (CPI); there isn't a universally agreed-on definition of what constitutes price stability, but it is generally believed to be a rate of inflation in the CPI between 0% and 3%

primary market the market for newly issued financial instruments

principal–agent problem issues that arise when managers (agents) of a firm and the shareholders (principals) have conflicting objectives

production possibilities the opportunities available to a firm, with a given set of labour and capital, to produce today versus in the future

prudential requirements a set of rules and guidelines issued by government to which financial institutions must adhere in order to safeguard the deposits or investments of their clients

purchasing power the ability, usually of one unit of currency, to buy goods and services; can be measured as $1/P$,

where P is the price level measured, say, by the consumer price index

purchasing power parity (PPP) the situation that exists when the exchange rate between two currencies is such that the domestic purchasing power of those currencies is equivalent; two forms exist: absolute (in terms of price levels) and relative (in terms of inflation rates)

put option the right but not the obligation to sell an asset at a particular price during a stipulated period

quantity theory the theory that a direct relationship exists between the quantity of money in circulation and the price level: An increase in the quantity of money leads to a proportional increase in the price level; the relationship is summarized in the formula $MV = Py$, where M = stock money, V = velocity of circulation, P = price index, and y = measure of aggregate income

random walk in its simplest version, the notion that the best forecast of next period's value of an economic variable, such as stock prices, is its current value

rational expectations hypothesis the theory that market participants use economic information rationally; consequently, unexploited profitable opportunities do not occur in a persistent fashion

real balances a measure of the money stock divided by a price index; the purchasing power of a stock of money

real bills doctrine the view that any increase in the money supply should be fully backed (by tax revenue or bonds); otherwise money supply increases will be inflationary

real estate investment trusts (REITs) mortgage finance companies under the jurisdiction of an "adviser" or trust corporation

real exchange rate the exchange rate adjusted for changes in relative price levels in different countries

real income income measured in constant dollars; incorporates the effect of a loss of purchasing power due to inflation

real interest rate the return or yield on a financial asset excluding compensation for inflation

real return bonds Canadian government bonds that specify returns adjusted for inflation; used as a gauge for future inflation developments

realignment the act of changing the value of a fixed exchange rate

registered retirement income fund (RRIF) an annuity, pioneered by the insurance industry, to channel retirement funds that must be withdrawn from tax-sheltered instruments

registered retirement savings plans (RRSPs) tax shelters that permit taxpayers to accumulate savings toward their retirement

reinsurance insurance sold in the resale market

reserve ratio portion of total deposits held in reserve

reserves a portion of assets set aside by banks to provide for payments to be made, although reserves now generally serve as a means of enhancing depositor confidence; required reserves were phased out in 1994

revaluation an arbitrary increase in the value of a currency that had previously been fixed in value

Ricardian equivalence theory the theory, attributed mistakenly to the great, classical economist David Ricardo, that predicts that a tax cut will lead individuals to increase their savings to take account of the higher, future tax burden; also used to describe why there need not be a direct, positive relationship between interest rates and government deficit

risk the likelihood that an investment may prove to be unprofitable

risk averse the condition describing an individual who is willing to give up return to reduce risk

risk neutrality the situation in which an individual is concerned only with maximizing return irrespective of the level of risk

risk seeking the condition describing an individual who actually is willing to give up return to increase risk

savings and loan associations (S&Ls) the U.S. equivalent of Canadian mortgage loan companies or caisses populaires

savings deposits bank deposits that typically earn a rate of return and are highly liquid

secondary market the market for previously issued financial instruments

securitization describes the phenomenon whereby assets that are normally not liquid, such as mortgages, are made liquid by pooling them and reselling the combined amount as short-term assets; credit card debt as well as other types of assets normally illiquid are also securitized

segregated fund a portion of the insurance business that invests in mutual funds; these assets are kept separate from the rest of the insurance firm's activities; hence the term segregated

seigniorage the profit made from printing money

self-dealing the attempt to tie in the sale of a financial product with another from a different division of the same institution; customers may not be aware that this is taking place

short position the sale and delivery in the future of an asset, with the intent to buy it back at a lower price; often the seller does not own the asset but has borrowed it from a broker's inventory of assets

special drawing right (SDR) a unit of account created by the International Monetary Fund, it represents a weighted average of the exchange rates of a select group of industrialized countries

special purchase and resale agreement (SPRA) an agreement made by the Bank of Canada to purchase a financial instrument and resell it to the vendor at a different price sometime in the near future (usually overnight); to achieve certain goals, the Bank may sometimes reverse the procedure and sell securities one day and repurchase them the next

speculative motive the demand for money that results from the existence of the opportunity cost of holding money

speculator an individual who undertakes a transaction with a view to profit from a price change in the assets in question

spot market the market in which price and delivery of an asset are determined simultaneously; also called the cash market

spot rate the rate for immediate delivery of an asset, usually of a currency

spread the difference between borrowing and lending rates; also the difference between long-term and short-term interest rates

standard deviation of returns the square root of the variance of returns

sterilization the actions taken by a central bank typically to offset a potential change in the domestic money supply due to a foreign exchange transaction

stock exchanges markets where stock issues are traded

stock measures measure flow of funds activity at a particular moment in time

stock price indexes aggregate measures of the value of several stocks; examples include the Standard and Poor's (S&P) /TSX Composite and the Dow Jones Industrial Average

stocks shares of ownership that are sold by private corporations to raise funds

store of value the ability of money to command purchasing power in the future; considered one of the functions of money

swaps exchanges of interest payments between two debtors or exchanges of foreign exchange

System of National Accounts set of definitions that describe aggregate economic activity in Canada

systematic risk the risk associated with the fact that changes in the price of an asset change systematically with the prices of other assets

target reserves when required reserves were eliminated in Canada, the amount of reserves held became a function of cash management practices of individual banks necessary for daily operations

target zone an exchange rate system in which the exchange rate for the participating country is permitted to fluctuate within a specified range; the European Monetary System is the archetypical example of such an agreement

tax risk the risk that arises when there is a change in the tax system that affects the return of a financial instrument

term deposits bank deposits paying a market rate of return with limited liquidity

term insurance a type of insurance policy for a specified amount for a specified duration

term structure of interest rates the structure of interest rates on instruments that differ by term to maturity but are otherwise the same

time-inconsistency problem of monetary policy the theory that argues that policymakers' commitment to a given rate of inflation is not a credible one because policymakers always have an incentive to deviate from their promise and implement inflationary monetary policy

Tobin's *q* the market value of a firm's capital provided by the replacement cost of a firm's capital

transactions costs the costs, financial and nonfinancial, of completing some economic transaction; does not include the purchase price of the item in question

transactions motive the demand for money brought about by its use as a means of buying and selling goods and services

transmission mechanism the manner in which the monetary side of the economy can influence the real side of the economy

Treasury bills (T-bills) short-term financial instruments sold at a discount and issued by various levels of government

trust company a deposit-taking institution that also specializes in estate, trust, and agency business

TSX the name of the Toronto Stock Exchange

twin deficits describes the phenomenon of a deficit in the balance of payments that occurs simultaneously with a deficit in the government's budget.

The flip side is twin surpluses—a BOP surplus together with a government budget surplus

ultimate goals measures of overall economic performance, such as GDP growth, that are used to assess the impact or effectiveness of economic policies

underwriter an investment dealer who helps governments and corporations raise capital by buying new securities from an issuer at a discount and reselling them to investors

unit banking single-bank banking operations, as opposed to a banking operation with several branches

universal banking model a banking model in which there are no restrictions on the types of financial activities in which a bank can engage

utility maximization the principle in economics that consumers are assumed to attempt to reach the highest level of satisfaction that can be enjoyed in the consumption of goods and services, that is, the highest or maximum level of utility

value-at-risk (VaR) a set of techniques used to measure market risk; usually,

VaR measures the dollar exposure of a portfolio to changes in financial asset prices

variance of returns the weighted average of the squared deviations of asset prices or yields

velocity of circulation the turnover rate of money; usually measured as aggregate income (GDP) divided by a money stock measure

volatility a measure of the size of changes, for example, changes in the price of bonds

when-issued T-bill a Treasury bill that will be made available for purchase before it is actually issued; yields are viewed by some as a barometer of future interest rates

yield curve the curve of the yields to maturity of assets of different maturities; i.e., the yield curve describes the relationship between short- and long-term interest rates

yield to maturity the rate of return of a financial asset if it is held until maturity

| I N D E X |